1956

1956

John Saville, EP Thompson & *The Reasoner*

Edited by
Paul Flewers & John McIlroy

MERLIN PRESS

First published in 2016
by The Merlin Press Ltd
Central Books Building
Freshwater Road
London
RM8 1RX

www.merlinpress.co.uk

ISBN 978-0-85036-726-3

British Library Cataloguing in Publication Data is available from the British Library

Printed in the UK by Imprint Digital, Exeter

Contents

PREFACE

John Saville (1916-2009) and Edward Palmer Thompson (1924-1993) were two of Britain's finest socialist historians. The term is used advisedly: they worked in the Marxist tradition. Perry Anderson remarked of Thompson: 'Every major and nearly every minor work he has written concludes with an avowed and direct reflection on its lessons for socialists of his own time … Each of these texts has been in its own way a militant intervention in the present as well as a professional recovery of the past.'[1] The same might be said of much that Saville wrote: politics and history intertwine in his work. With other Marxist scholars of their generation they stand in contrast to contemporary 'historians of socialism' whose politics often have little in common with the radical left causes and figures their writings platonically celebrate.

Saville composed notable monographs, *1848: The British State and the Chartist Movement* and *The Politics of Continuity: British Foreign Policy and the Labour Government 1945-1946*, which addressed key moments in nineteenth- and twentieth-century labour history. These texts were only part of a sustained contribution contained in journal articles, edited collections and books. His interests ranged from discussions of primitive accumulation and limited liability to Owenism, Christian Socialism and judicial intervention in trade-union affairs. Saville's edited work, the ten volumes of the *Dictionary of Labour Biography*, the three volumes of *Essays in Labour History* and the *Socialist Register*, which he co-edited from 1964 to 1999, is central to his achievement as an historian, socialist intellectual and producer and promoter of working-class history. He was an activist who campaigned over CND, Vietnam, academic freedom and the 1984-85 miners' strike. Ralph Miliband observed: 'There are not many entries in the *Dictionary of Labour Biography* which record lives of greater dedication and integrity.'[2]

Edward Thompson enjoyed a worldwide reputation as the author of the ground-breaking and hugely influential *The Making of the English Working Class*. But he produced other work of enduring significance, notably his monumental biography of William Morris; the investigations undertaken with colleagues into the judiciary, crime and society in the eighteenth century, *Whigs and Hunters* and *Albion's Fatal Tree*; the essays on social history collected in *Customs in Commons*; and last, but not least, his posthumous volume on William Blake. For Eric Hobsbawm, Thompson was 'the only historian I knew who had not just talent, brilliance, erudition and the gift of writing but ... genius in the traditional sense of the word'.[3] Like Saville, Thompson was a lifelong activist and constant interrogator of the problems of the contemporary world. He is particularly remembered for his inspirational leadership of nuclear disarmament campaigns and for his pugnacious debunking of the cult of Althusserian philosophy that was unaccountably fashionable on the British left in the 1970s.

This book is about another aspect of their lives. It addresses the prominent part they played in the remarkable ferment which erupted during 1956 in the Communist Party of Great Britain (CPGB) of which they were both members. The catalyst was the denunciation of Stalin that Nikita Khrushchev presented in his 'Secret Speech' to the Twentieth Congress of the Communist Party of the Soviet Union. The crucial factor in driving and developing the crisis was the reaction of the party's leaders. They attempted to deal with what was for them an unexpected, decidedly unwelcome and increasingly awkward situation, by means of conservative, top-down management, employing flexibility over incidentals and firmness when their fundamental principles were questioned. Mistakes, even grave mistakes, the leadership conceded in a series of articles and statements, had been made in the Soviet Union during the Stalin era. But everything had been put right. The main task confronting the British party and the international Communist movement was to look boldly to the future rather than to rake over historical problems that were best forgotten.

Saville and Thompson were among the minority of CPGB members who were determined to discuss thoroughly the issues unveiled in Khrushchev's speech — and their implications. In March 1956, Thompson outlined his unease to *apparatchiks*, nationally and in Yorkshire, while Saville spoke critically at the important meeting of the CPGB Historians' Group held in early April. They were dissatisfied not merely with their leaders' statements on the matter, but also with the way in which the apparatus restricted discussion within the party press, impeded attempts to have the topic debated at a party conference, and attempted to divert concerns over Stalinism into the safer and hopefully controllable areas of party organisation and the party programme. Such were the feelings of Saville and Thompson at the leadership's obstructions, restrictions and prevarications that they took the bold step of publishing *The Reasoner*, a duplicated magazine which bore the rubric 'A Journal of Discussion'.

The first edition of *The Reasoner* was published in July 1956; the second appeared in September. The journal carried a wide range of material. It naturally concentrated upon the various issues that Khrushchev's 'Secret Speech' directly brought to light or less directly triggered off, not just within the CPGB but also within other Communist parties and the countries of the Soviet bloc. It featured material written by dissident British Communists, articles republished from the US left press, and commentaries from East Europe that had been specially translated for the magazine.

The publication of *The Reasoner* was as good as mutinous behaviour, and it gave the CPGB leadership a severe shock. Nothing like this had occurred for well over two decades. Although the party leaders were determined to prevent the insidious ideas of the magazine spreading amongst the membership, their statements demonstrated that they felt obliged to tread carefully and, in appearance, to be fairly magnanimous, at least by Stalinist standards, towards its editors. This uncharacteristically dexterous treatment of dissidence suggests that the party leaders were aware that too heavy-handed a response would almost certainly exacerbate an already delicate situation. All the same, a warning was given, and Saville and Thompson were ordered not to publish any further issues.

The hopes of party leaders that the ferment in the CPGB provoked by Khrushchev's 'Secret Speech' would die down and be safely diverted into a carefully-controlled discussion of the party's programme and internal regime were dashed during the latter half of the year when, also in response to Khrushchev's speech, unrest blew up within the Soviet bloc, particularly in Poland and Hungary. A breaking-point was reached between Saville and Thompson and the party leadership when the anti-Stalinist uprising in Hungary in late October was sharply suppressed by a Soviet military incursion. Saville and Thompson praised the revolt, and strongly condemned both Moscow's action and the support that the party's leaders gave to it. There could be no compromise now: in open disregard of the party leadership's instruction Saville and Thompson published the third and final edition of *The Reasoner* in November, and, sensing that the party was incapable of reforming itself, resigned their membership.

The text of all three issues of *The Reasoner* is reproduced in this book, together with a selection of articles and statements from party leaders and committees. The publishing of *The Reasoner* was by no means an obscure episode in the history of the left in Britain — indeed, it has been an almost unavoidable topic in accounts of the events of 1956. But while one or two articles from it have appeared in documentary compilations, the full contents of the magazine have not previously been republished. Also included in this collection is a delightful and insightful poem written by one of the magazine's contributors, Ronald Meek. It appeared in the second issue of a duplicated satirical sheet called *The Rhyming Reasoner*, and we are sure readers will find it as amusing as we did when we first read it.

An introductory essay provides readers with an account of the background to the events of 1956, locating what happened in the history of the party and the predicament of intellectuals in the 'Stalin–Zhdanov–Lysenko' era of British Communism. The book is rounded off by two essays from the editors. The existing literature says too little about Saville's and Thompson's stance on Stalinism before and after 1956.[4] Against that background, the first essay explores Saville's experience in the CPGB from 1934 and his attitude to Stalinism before and after 1956; the second examines Thompson's attempts to grapple with the meaning of Stalinism and the nature of Soviet society from the 1950s into the 1980s.

Paul Flewers has scanned and annotated the issues of *The Reasoner* and the selected documents. Minor errors and one piece of garbled prose have been corrected and the diacritics in Czech, Hungarian and Polish names that could not be produced on the typewriters of 1956 are now shown. Thanks to Kate Thompson, EP Thompson's daughter, and Richard Saville, John Saville's son, for their kind permission to publish the text of *The Reasoner*; and to Stephen Bird and Darren Treadwell of the Peoples' History Museum Manchester for their help over the years.

Paul Flewers and **John McIlroy**
July 2016

NOTES

1   Perry Anderson, *Arguments Within English Marxism* (Verso, London, 1980), p. 1.
2   Ralph Miliband, 'A Presentation', in David E Martin and David Rubinstein (eds), *Ideology and the Labour Movement: Essays Presented to John Saville* (Croom Helm, London, 1979), p. 30.
3   Eric Hobsbawm, *Interesting Times: A Twentieth-Century Life* (Allen Lane, London, 2002), p. 215.
4   The notable exception is Anderson, *Arguments Within English Marxism*, which is part of a wider polemic against Thompson's *The Poverty of Theory*.

CHRONOLOGY

1934	John Saville joins CPGB.
1935	Seventh Congress of Communist International endorses Popular Front strategy.
1936	Stalin Constitution introduced in Soviet Union. First Moscow Trial. Start of Spanish Civil War.
1937	Second Moscow Trial.
1938	Third Moscow Trial.
1939	End of Spanish Civil War. Hitler–Stalin Pact signed; Poland partitioned; start of Second World War. Communist International declares war to be imperialist on both sides.
1941	Soviet Union invaded by Nazi Germany; Communist International now backs Allied 'People's War'; Communist parties adopt policies of national unity and class collaboration.
1942	CPGB membership reaches its highest figure of 56,000. E P Thompson joins CPGB.
1943	Communist International dissolved.
1944	Stalin and Churchill agree the division of Eastern Europe at Yalta. E P Thompson's elder brother Frank, a CPGB member, executed whilst working with partisans in Bulgaria.
1945	General election in Britain: CPGB calls for new National Government; Labour victory; two CPGB MPs elected. CPGB continues class-collaborationist, anti-strike

policies into peacetime period.

Popular Front governments in power in most Eastern European countries; Communist parties win minority of votes but usually hold key ministerial posts.

1946	CPGB Historians' Group established. Churchill delivers 'Iron Curtain' speech at Fulton. Truman Doctrine announced, heralding Cold War.
1947	E P Thompson works on railway construction project in Yugoslavia; publication of *There Is a Spirit in Europe*, E P Thompson's commemoration of his brother Frank. Communist Information Bureau established; Western Communist parties adopt a more militant approach; Communist ministers expelled from French and Italian governments; Communist parties in Eastern Europe tighten their grip.
1948	Further tightening of Stalinist rule in Eastern Europe; Czechoslovakian Communist Party takes commanding position in government. Moscow moves against independently-minded Communist leaders: Tito excommunicated; Gomułka replaced by Bierut as First Secretary of Polish United Workers Party. Berlin Blockade. E P Thompson marries historian Dorothy Towers.
1949	Hungary declared a People's Republic. Show trial and execution of Rajk in Hungary and Kostov in Bulgaria. Formation of NATO. National government formed by Chinese Communist Party in Peking (Beijing).
1950	General election in Britain: narrow Labour victory; CPGB stands 100 candidates, both CPGB MPs lose their seats. Start of Korean War.
1951	James Klugmann's *From Trotsky to Tito* published by CPGB. Publication of first edition of CPGB programme *The*

	British Road to Socialism. General election in Britain: Conservative victory. Gomułka jailed.
1952	Show trial and execution of Slánský in Czechoslovakia. Poland declared a People's Republic. Nineteenth Congress of Communist Party of the Soviet Union; Malenkov delivers main report. Show trial of Soviet Jewish Anti-Fascist Committee; 'Doctor's Plot' against Stalin announced. Publication of second edition of *The British Road to Socialism.*
1953	Death of Stalin; de-Stalinisation commences; Malenkov and Khrushchev appear as main contenders for Soviet leadership; Beria tried and executed. End of Korean War. Strike wave in East Germany. Rákosi replaced by Nagy as Prime Minister of Hungary, remains General Secretary of Hungarian Communist Party.
1954	Gomułka released from jail.
1955	General election in Britain: Conservative victory. Malenkov sidelined by Khrushchev. Soviet rapprochement with Yugoslavia. Formation of Warsaw Pact. Nagy replaced by Rákosi as Prime Minister of Hungary. E P Thompson's *William Morris* published.
January 1956	CPGB declare socialism fully established in Soviet Union.
February 1956	Twentieth Congress of CPSU: Khrushchev denounces Stalin in his 'Secret Speech'. Discussion of consequences of Twentieth Congress starts in CPGB press. CPGB membership stands at 33,095.
March 1956	Western press publishes reports of Khrushchev's 'Secret Speech'. Twenty-Fourth Congress of the CPGB; closed session discusses 'Secret Speech'.

Discussion of consequences of Twentieth Congress continues in CPGB press; JR Campbell calls for its cessation.

Rákosi reluctantly rehabilitates Rajk, Bierut dies, replaced by Ochab as First Secretary of PUWP.

Intellectual debate about Stalin era and broader social issues starts in Poland and Hungary.

April 1956
Harry Pollitt assesses Twentieth Congress and role of Stalin.

Cominform dissolved.

May 1956
Pollitt resigns as CPGB General Secretary; John Gollan takes over; Pollitt becomes party Chairman.

Rajani Palme Dutt assesses Twentieth Congress and role of Stalin.

World News publishes John Saville's criticism of CPGB's handling of Khrushchev's 'Secret Speech'.

June 1956
Full text of Khrushchev's 'Secret Speech' published in West.

Dutt responds to his critics.

CPGB Political Committee statement on Khrushchev's 'Secret Speech'.

World News publishes E P Thompson's criticism of CPGB's political methods.

Strike wave in Hungary.

Uprising in Poznań, Poland, violently suppressed by state forces.

July 1956
Rákosi replaced on Soviet orders by Gerő as General Secretary of Hungarian Communist Party.

Publication of *The Reasoner*, no. 1.

August 1956
CPGB Yorkshire District Committee discusses *The Reasoner*.

CPGB Political Committee discusses *The Reasoner*.

September 1956
Publication of *The Reasoner*, no. 2.

CPGB Executive Committee demands Saville and Thompson stop publishing *The Reasoner*.

CPGB Executive Committee opens discussion on inner-party democracy and *The British Road to Socialism*.

October 1956	Nagy readmitted to Hungarian Communist Party; demonstrations in Budapest attacked by secret police; strikes and unrest in Hungary, workers' councils set up; Soviet armed forces enter Hungary; Nagy becomes Prime Minister; Soviet troops withdraw; Kádár becomes Communist Party's General Secretary. Reformers gain upper hand in PUWP; Ochab replaced by Gomułka as First Secretary; concessions obtained from Soviet government; attempts to rein in working-class discontent. *Daily Worker* backs Soviet incursion into Hungary and condemns uprising. British, French and Israeli forces attack Egypt; major anti-war protests in Britain.
November 1956	Hungary declares independence from Warsaw Pact; Soviet troops enter Hungary again; Nagy arrested; Kádár endorses Soviet invasion. *Daily Worker* endorses second Soviet incursion into Hungary. Publication of *The Reasoner*, no. 3. Saville and Thompson suspended from CPGB membership; both resign from CPGB.
December 1956	Repression continues in Hungary.
1957	Final suppression of unrest in Hungary. CPGB membership stands at 26,742, a reduction of 19 per cent from the previous year. Twenty-Fifth Congress of the CPGB — endorses party executive's line on Hungary, inner-party democracy and *The British Road to Socialism*. Wortley Conference brings together former CPGB members and other left-wingers, subsequently viewed as start of New Left. *New Reasoner* launched, including E P Thompson's key statement 'Socialist Humanism'. *Universities and Left Review* launched. Launch of Campaign for Nuclear Disarmament. Launch of Sputnik; 'anti-party' group of CPSU hardliners defeated; institutional reform of Soviet bureaucracy initiated.

	Mao launches 'Hundred Flowers' campaign encouraging criticism of regime, then closes it after four months.
1958	CPGB membership stands at 24,670, the lowest since 1941, but then revives modestly. Publication of third edition of *The British Road to Socialism*. Nagy tried for treason and executed. Launch of Great Leap Forward in China; start of Sino-Soviet tensions.
1959	E P Thompson's article 'The New Left' articulates movement's ethos. Final editions of *New Reasoner* and *Universities and Left Review* published. General election in Britain: Conservative victory. Socialist Labour League formed. Revolution in Cuba.
1960	*New Reasoner* and *Universities and Left Review* combine to form *New Left Review*. Publication of *Out of Apathy*, edited by E P Thompson, and including his essays 'At the Point of Decay', 'Revolution' and 'Outside the Whale'. Labour Party conference votes for unilateral nuclear disarmament and defeats calls to delete Clause IV of party constitution.
1961	E P Thompson's praises Raymond Williams' *The Long Revolution*. Twenty-Second CPSU Congress continues de-Stalinisation process. Berlin Wall built.
1962	Cuba Missile Crisis. Open breach between China and Soviet Union. E P Thompson departs from *New Left Review*.
1963	Publication of E P Thompson's *The Making of the English Working Class*.
1964	CPGB membership stands at 34,281, reaching its post-1956 peak, declining from then onwards.

Khrushchev deposed.
General election in Britain: Labour victory.
Publication of first annual *Socialist Register*, edited by
Ralph Miliband and John Saville.

JOHN McILROY

Communist Intellectuals and 1956: John Saville, Edward Thompson and *The Reasoner*

The seismic shock which convulsed British Communism in the wake of Nikita Khrushchev's revelations about Stalin at the Twentieth Congress of the Russian party (CPSU) in February 1956 can only be understood in relation to the history of the British party (CPGB) and, more specifically, its development since 1945. British Communism was rooted in the revolutionary aspirations of a minority of British workers. The forms it took, its changing politics, culture, organisation, and its resilience, were inextricably and decisively bound up with the policy of the CPSU and the Russian state. Had it not been for its members' identification with the Soviet Union and the political and material resources the Russians devoted to the CPGB, it is probable that by the early 1930s the party would have dwindled into permanent insignificance.

From 1934, Popular Front politics, derived from Soviet foreign policy, predicated on alignment with the British and French states to counter German aggression, anchored the party in British society. A turn to labour movement and cross-class alliances, 'anglicisation', the middle class and intellectuals, combined with trade-union recruitment to ensure modest growth. The Hitler–Stalin Pact, from 1941 uncritical support for the war effort to defend the Soviet Union, and from 1947 uncritical support for Stalin's Cold War affirmed the paramount importance of the connection with Russia.[1] Like all decisive moments preceding it, 1956, the crisis in the CPGB, the advent of the path-breaking journal *The Reasoner,* and the catapulting of John Saville and Edward Thompson to prominence, ultimately flowed from what was happening in the Soviet Union.[2]

Contemporary Communists acknowledged that their politics were determined by Soviet hegemony. The first issue of *The Reasoner* emphasised:

In practice, the interests of the British working class have been interpreted in such a way that we have identified them with the acceptance of the foreign policy of the Soviet Union and, at the same time, we have been indignant at accusations of blindly 'following Moscow'.[3]

In early 1957, Eric Hobsbawm remarked: 'We tell them that we do not give the USSR "uncritical support" but when they ask us when we disagreed with its policy, all we can point to is Nina Ponomareva's hats.'[4] Contemporary Communists were also conscious that Khrushchev's 'Secret Speech' ignited smouldering *matériel*: 'This is not an issue of sudden origin …'[5] One critic reflected: 'It would be quite wrong to date all of the concern and bewilderment from the Twentieth Congress. The waters had been accumulating behind the dam for many years. Khrushchev did not do much more than open the flood-gates.'[6]

This introductory essay examines the background to the crisis of British Communism in 1956. It traces the contours of Russian policy during the immediate postwar years and explains its impact on the politics and fortunes of the British party. It provides a commentary on the turmoil that enveloped the CPGB; the development of dissent on the part of many Communist intellectuals; the refusal of the leadership to address, let alone break with, the past; and the provenance and impact of *The Reasoner*. Confirming the significance of the forces of change, the essay stresses the enduring power of conservatism. The leadership and apparatus maintained the backing of the majority of members while intellectuals played diverse and sometimes conflicting roles. Khrushchev's 'Secret Speech' presented an unprecedented opportunity to re-evaluate and reorient British Communism. It was squandered and it never came again.

Situating 1956: From Stalin's Cold War to De-Stalinisation

Anglo-American imperialism's drive to world domination and hostility to the Soviet Union re-emerged as the war drew to a close, and 1947 witnessed the unravelling of what remained of the 'Grand Alliance'. Isolationism and Rooseveltian conciliation of Russia finally faded from White House agendas, and incompatible economic and geopolitical interests reasserted themselves. Controversy persists about Stalin's precise intentions.[7] Influenced by Russian nationalism, he possessed, as Gaddis notes, 'an imperial vision' and desire, as Zubok emphasises, to create a 'Socialist empire'. Security demanded expansion.[8] Ideological and nationalist motivations were in play. Stalin was determined to maintain and extend the considerable territorial gains in Eastern Europe that his partnership with Hitler had temporarily handed him. Further afield, he had no plans for the military conquest of Western Europe and was acutely aware of the priority of reconstructing the devastated Soviet economy. He remained ready to avail himself of relatively risk-free opportunities to extend the sway of Marxism-Leninism-Stalinism in the context of his prophecy of renewed capitalist crisis and inter-imperialist rivalry. Vyacheslav Molotov retrospectively reflected: 'Our ideology stands for offensive operations when possible, and if not, we wait.'[9] Appreciation of the balance of forces between the great powers ensured the emphasis in practical terms was on the waiting; there is no need to doubt the sincerity of periodic declarations of the importance of peaceful coexistence. On the whole, Stalin operated pragmatically and cautiously in reaction to events. He initially aspired, for example, to mould the East European states which the Red Army had occupied as mixed economies governed by Popular Front coalitions. The problems of micro-managing a complex and recalcitrant process and the pull that the world market exercised on subaltern capitalist economies combined with deteriorating relations with the West to provoke the shift to Sovietisation.

The hardening of US policy in tandem with the USSR's consolidation of control over Eastern Europe prompted through 1947 the Truman doctrine, promising support for subjugated nations; Marshall Aid, and its rejection by the Eastern bloc; creation of the Communist Information Bureau (Cominform); and the economic and social transformation imposed by the Stalinist state on the newly-acquired satellites.[10] Following its political compass, the CPGB deserted its immediate postwar politics which had reflected Stalin's earlier approach of collaboration with social democrats and 'progressives' in Eastern Europe. The party's pitch for continuation of a 'progressive' coalition which had morphed into critical support for the Labour government was laid aside, and British Communists turned towards waging Stalin's Cold War.[11]

The ideological foundations of the resonance that 'official Communism' had enjoyed between 1934 and 1945 rested on its ability to contrive a narrative which, occluding the meaning of democracy, liberty and workers' power, portrayed Stalinism as embodying all these things. Communism was conjured into the only hope of defeating Hitlerism; the liberal democracies were by their capitalist nature, which they shared with the dictators, appeasers; Russia, reinvented as a socialist society, was depicted as the bastion of anti-fascism and the guarantee of a free, democratic world. These ideas and their national correlative, pressure and concessions from Communists to engineer broad alliances to defend the Soviet Union and the laying aside of revolution, at least for the time being, exercised enduring influence on the CPGB. They had a profound, sometimes permanent impact on those intellectuals who joined it in the 1930s.[12] From 1947, imperialism, projected as having attained its highest stage in America's determination to exploit the world, replaced fascism in Soviet scenarios.[13] The CPGB operated on this perspective.

Its details were elaborated by Stalin's spokesman Andrei Zhdanov, and were adumbrated by the Cominform consisting of the CPSU, the ruling parties of Yugoslavia and Eastern Europe and the French and Italian Communists. The 'theory of two camps' was central. The imperialist camp, led by the US, had inherited aspects of fascism: it was bent on war against the Soviet Union and the eradication of socialism. The camp of progress was based on the Soviet Union and its foreign policy: its goals were national independence and democracy embodied in 'a lasting democratic peace'. Potential divisions within the reactionary camp could be exploited – the national Communist parties should win over 'progressive' sections of the bourgeoisie to the struggle for independence from American hegemony.[14]

The purpose behind these moves was limited: to exert leverage on Anglo-American imperialism to impel it to accept what Stalin saw as Russia's legitimate zone of influence in Eastern Europe and Germany; and to expand that role to secure purchase within the power structures of the liberal democracies in order to pressurise Western governments to adopt policies amenable to Moscow.[15] The Cominform's more militant line was not about the overthrow of capitalism, any more than the Popular Front had been. Stalin was willing to test the water, even take the offensive – witness the probes in Iran and Turkey in 1944-45, the blockade of Berlin in 1948 and the imprimatur for Kim Il Sung's invasion of South Korea in 1950. He was unwilling to risk world war. He retreated in the first two cases and prevailed upon Mao to play the leading role in Korea. There were reminders of the Third Period in the Cominform's virulent denunciation of imperialism, invocation of class struggle, incantation of the threat of a capitalist assault on the Soviet Union, and crude cultural leftism. Essentially, the new turn represented a variant of Popular Front politics. It centred on states and nations not classes, mothballed revolution in Europe and endeavoured to mobilise as broad a coalition as possible in the interests of Moscow's foreign policy. Its emblematic axes were the struggle against imperialism and the campaigns for cultural independence and world peace.[16] As Stalin observed: 'The current peace movement has the aim of drawing the popular masses into the struggle to preserve peace and avert a new world war. It does not therefore seek to overthrow capitalism and establish socialism; it limits itself to democratic aims.'[17]

Exhibiting what Thompson subsequently characterised as 'a servile attitude to the Soviet Union',[18] the CPGB endorsed Stalin's break with Tito and the Soviet identification of Tito with Trotsky and subversion of the 'progressive' camp. It registered no objection to the renewed repression in Russia. The purges and show trials in Albania, Bulgaria, Czechoslovakia, Hungary and Romania received King Street's seal of approval. The CPGB made no criticism of anti-Semitism or ethnic cleansing in the USSR. Neither leaders nor members of the British party publicly questioned the Gulag, the 'Doctors' Plot' or the suppression of the East German workers' rising in 1953. Everything was explained and justified by the threat of imperialist aggression, the consequent need for internal security and by resort to Stalin's development of Leninism: as progress towards socialism accelerates, bourgeois resistance intensifies. The Stalinist bible, *The History of the Communist Party of the Soviet Union (Bolsheviks) Short Course,* continued to be required reading for British Communists.[19] Stalin was lauded as an incomparable economist, path-breaking philosopher, cutting-edge scientist, iconic historian and pioneer of linguistics, as well as the greatest living political leader.[20] Even the *British Road to Socialism,* codifying the party's formal adoption of the national parliamentary path, was submitted for his approval.[21] After the dictator's demise the British party seamlessly accepted the authority of his successors and their turn to 'collective leadership'; shifts towards more meaningful 'peaceful coexistence'; reforms in the security services; releases from the Gulag; limited liberalisation in the satellites; the sidelining of the Cominform; the ending of the Korean War; and the rehabilitation of Tito. 'The thaw', with its limited de-Stalinisation, was an important staging post to 1956.[22]

Looking back, the editors of *The Reasoner* lamented the thoroughly unconvincing nature of the CPGB's postwar politics, the absence of any serious analysis of imperialism and the socialist alternative to it: '… we have increasingly substituted for the first, an oversimplified myth of the "two camps" and, for the second, utopian propaganda about the Soviet Union as the land of socialism – realised – the British people did not believe in or trust this central political message.'[23] The same verdict could be applied to the peace campaigns, largely restricted in day-to-day activity to the party's periphery and dominated by Stalinist policies. Nor did 'the masses' believe in or trust Russian directives refracted through the CPGB apparatus:

Relate every question affecting the masses to the issue of independence. Troops to Korea – it is MacArthur's orders. Two years' military service – it is an American demand. Rearmament – it is American orders. Attack on standards – it is US which insists.[24]

The British party acted on Zhdanov's injunctions against cultural contamination:

> ... this Congress calls on all Party organisations to develop the cultural
> struggle as part of the political struggle ... to increase activity against
> the Americanisation of Britain's cultural life, against reactionary film and
> debased literature and comics.[25]

The nationalism and patriotism of the Popular Front and the war continued.
'Britain and the Empire', the CPGB claimed, was 'to be sold piecemeal to
the American money-leaders.'[26] The impact was derisory. Party policy
interacted with the Cold War atmosphere, mild in comparison with the
US, to marginalise Communists. The Labour Party and many trade unions
introduced or strengthened bans and proscriptions. CPGB membership fell
from 42,123 in 1946 to 32,861 by 1955. The party lost its two MPs and
97 of its 100 candidates lost their deposits in the 1950 general election. Its
performance in the 1951 and 1955 contests confirmed the fall from grace
since 1945.[27]

From top to bottom, the CPGB was an orthodox Stalinist party. An
ageing, unimaginative leadership – General Secretary, Harry Pollitt; *Daily
Worker* editor, JR Campbell; vice-chair, Rajani Palme Dutt; the former MP,
Willie Gallacher; the industrial organiser, Peter Kerrigan – had internalised
Russian hegemony during the 1920s. Their ingrained Stalinist orthodoxy
and limited grasp of Marxism, combined with organisational ability and
inexhaustible stamina, was exemplified in Pollitt. His son remembered: 'His
own admiration for Stalin had always been unstinting and he excused his
faults – "crimes" was not a word he would accept – by speaking of the harsh
complexity of the times and/or the mistakes or deceits of subordinates.'[28]
Saluting 'our beloved leader and friend Joseph Stalin' on the occasion of
his seventieth birthday in 1949, Gallacher marvelled: 'Where is there such
another as this man Joseph Stalin?'[29] Younger leaders, such as the working-
class John Gollan and the middle-class George Matthews, were recalled as
'typical of Party bureaucrats in all parts of the communist world. Possibly
they were less bureaucratic than some, although they were very Stalinist.'[30]

There was, as Ronald Meek observed, accumulating discontent.[31] But it
was 'unfocussed, lacking in articulation ... expressed as often as not in jokes
and resistances'.[32] Organised opposition was negligible. Dissatisfaction
surfaced on a small scale around the 1945 congress which witnessed protests
against the continuation of the CPGB's wartime policy and demands for a
reassertion of class struggle as against the then current reformist tendencies;

and in 1947, in the Hertford, Welwyn Garden City and South-East London branches.[33] There were disputes over the conduct of the literary journals, *Our Time* and *Arena*, involving the poets Edgell Rickword and Randall Swingler.[34] In 1953, a small group in Glasgow, headed by the veteran Harry McShane, quit the party.[35] The break with Tito in 1948 provoked the secession of fellow-travellers from the British-Yugoslav Association, notably Konni Zilliacus, to form an alternative body and engendered individual disquiet. The dimensions of opposition were apparent at an aggregate of the party's London membership: Pollitt's denunciation of Tito was carried with 1000 for, two against and 20 abstentions.[36] One of the few members who did voice their misgivings about CPGB policy recalled the power of the myth of the USSR and the cult of Stalin:

> … we were completely blind to the realities of Stalin and the Soviet Union. We thought that if Stalin knew what was going on in the British CP he would be on our side … I remember Party meetings where speeches were littered with phrases like 'As Comrade Stalin has said' … During the later years of Stalin's life if his name was mentioned at a Party meeting we stood up in silent reverence.[37]

Situating 1956: Stalin's Intellectuals

The upheavals of 1956 had long passed into history when Edward Thompson invoked 'the tradition of *The Reasoner*' against his critics at a heated History Workshop conference in Oxford in December 1978. Thompson stressed the steadfastness and dedication to socialist principles of those who had initiated and sustained *The Reasoner*:

> All of the comrades associated with that tradition lived through the worst years of the ideological Cold War, and we were at the receiving end of it. When our own crisis came, in 1956 or thereabouts, not one person in that tradition … ran to *Encounter*, lamented that our God had failed, or called for the wholesale rejection of the Marxist tradition.[38]

In reality the problems and hostility Communist intellectuals encountered in Britain during the decade before 1956 paled in comparison with the predicament of their comrades in the Soviet camp. Yet Thompson and his counterparts displayed scant solidarity with Stalin's victims.[39] Information about the situation in Russia had increased from the second half of the 1930s; by the late 1940s more detail about the Gulag, the mass deportations, and the hounding of scholars, writers, artists and independent thinkers of all kinds was available throughout Western Europe.[40] CPGB intellectuals declined to speak for those who could not speak for themselves, and excoriated some who did as 'renegades'.[41]

Philosophers have pointed out that some people imagine utopias while others have to live in them. It was only gradually and with reluctance that the party intellectuals recognised that what they were supporting was 'but a new version of the inhuman reality against which, in declaring ourselves Socialists, we had rebelled'.[42] The novelist, Doris Lessing, a member of the CPGB writers' group in the years before 1956, reflected on the Communists, mainly intellectuals, she moved among:

> ... it was the most sensitive, compassionate, socially-concerned people who became Communists. (Among these were a very different kind of people, the power-lovers.) These decent, kind people supported the worst, the most brutal tyranny of our time with the possible exception of Communist China.[43]

Far from cultivating scepticism and pursuing the evidence, the search for truth often culminated in adoption of 'a religious state of mind identical with that of passionate religious True Believers'.[44] That state of mind all too often excluded from active human sympathy persecuted intellectuals, such as Anna Akhamatova and Mikhail Zoshchenko; the executed Jewish politicians and Yiddish writers and actors caught in the toils of Stalinist anti-Semitism; and, no less importantly, the countless victims eking out their miserable lives in the prison camps of Utopia.

In Britain, the often troubled relationship between intellectuals and Communism stretched back to the foundation of the party. Intellectuals lent credibility to the CPGB because of their status, expertise and assumed independence. Once recruited they were expected to subordinate these qualities to dogma and bureaucratic discipline.[45] This provoked the defection of the first generation. The conservative nature of Britain's intelligentsia ensured the party attracted only a handful of intellectuals in the 1920s and made few inroads into academic and cultural institutions. The '1917 generation', including William Mellor, J Walton Newbold, Morgan Phillips Price and Raymond Postgate, had largely decamped by 1924 in response to incipient Bolshevisation. This left Rajani Palme Dutt, Robin Page Arnot and, briefly, Andrew Rothstein in what was always a predominantly working-class leadership.[46] Others, notably Olive Budden, Emile and Eleanor Burns, Maurice Dobb, Clemens Palme Dutt, Walter Holmes, Allen Hutt and Dona Torr, performed pedagogic, research and journalistic roles and serviced party fronts. Like Stalin, Pollitt was suspicious of intellectuals and exhibited a strong preference for proletarian elements, as did party intellectuals themselves. As Stalinisation developed, Dutt was to be found catechising:

What is the work and role of Communists who belong to the bourgeois intellectual strata ...? Answer: *There is no special work and role of Communists from the bourgeois intellectual strata. There is only the work and role of all Communists ... he should forget that he is an intellectual* (except in moments of necessary self-criticism) *and remember only that he is a Communist and begin to act and work and believe as a Communist in all his activity, like any other Party member.*[47]

In the Popular Front years Moscow looked more kindly on traditional intellectuals than in the Third Period, and the CPGB tried hard to attract them. Pollitt told the party's 1935 congress: 'We must see in these students, intellectuals, authors, doctors, scientists and professors valuable allies who can be won for the working class.'[48] But the most prominent recruits, John Strachey, Cecil Day Lewis, Stephen Spender, and fellow travellers, such as Victor Gollancz and WH Auden, had defected by the end of the decade, and many more of 'the pink generation' subsequently peeled away. By the late 1940s, what the party termed 'intellectual and professional workers', were organised in groups – scientists, economists, historians, musicians, writers – under the jurisdiction of a cultural committee headed by Emile Burns.[49]

'Intellectual' was an umbrella term reflected in the heterogeneity of the CPGB contingent. Dutt and Burns were by now long established in the leadership, while Matthews was an up-and-coming man. Others, such as Maurice Cornforth, who helped edit *Soviet Weekly*, Douglas Garman, education officer in the late 1940s, and Dona Torr, worked for Lawrence and Wishart, the party publishing house. They performed a variety of educational, research, translation and writing assignments – as did James Klugmann, who edited *World News and Views* before succeeding Garman as education officer; Margot Heinemann, who replaced Klugmann at *World News and Views*; and Pat Sloan, who, like Brian Pearce and Rothstein, worked for the Society for Cultural Relations with the USSR. The only public intellectuals were the scientists JBS Haldane and JD Bernal.[50] Other activists were well known in their respective professions: Ivor Montagu in film; Rutland Boughton and Alan Bush, the composers; and Lessing. Prominent academics included the Cambridge economist, Dobb; the Oxford historian, Christopher Hill; the literary critic, Arnold Kettle; the scientist, Hyman Levy; and George Thomson, Professor of Greek at Birmingham University.

They were, without exception, apologists for Stalin and the USSR.

There were initiatives to encourage pedagogic engagement with workers through party classes, the Workers' Educational Association (WEA) and University Extramural programmes.[51] There was little attempt to transcend divisions between traditional intellectuals and the thinning ranks of autodidact worker-intellectuals and create the 'new intellectuals' prescribed by Gramsci. Traditional intellectuals were expected to act as exegetists, not theorists, to explain and justify party policy, not create it. The *locus classicus* in the early Cold War was Klugmann's adaptation of the Cominform tirade against Tito. Although his experience of Yugoslavia made him aware he was advocating a fictive case, Klugmann produced a book-length condemnation of Tito's turpitude.[52] Sacrifice of intellectual integrity was the lot of intellectuals who aspired to become 'professional revolutionaries' and ended up as servants of power.[53]

Beyond the cadre of functionaries, intellectuals were expected to ply their craft and utilise their professional expertise to further party influence in academic and cultural milieux, arenas dominated by the bourgeoisie and, after 1947, by anti-Communism.[54] The party encouraged them to get good jobs and achieve professional success. This could intensify pressures to conform and insulation and distance from socialist politics. If Dutt's formulation of the intellectual's role was simplistic and philistine, the pursuit of career progression had consequences in terms of social existence, consciousness and, in some cases, gradual estrangement from the CPGB.[55] Intellectuals rarely generated intra-party debate: '… political controversy within the British Communist Party has been barely discernible.'[56] Their social position and lack of direct involvement with working-class struggles emphasised difference and strengthened *ouvrièrism* in a predominantly working-class party which prioritised trade-union activity and increasingly defined it as a specialist sphere.[57] An activist argued:

> There has been a fairly steady drift of professional men and women out of the party and a falling-off of its influence in opinion-forming circles. An attitude to intellectuals has grown up which is oddly reminiscent of that of Wilhelm Weitling, the arch-proletarian 'professor eater' of the 1840s, towards Karl Marx and rarely does it meet with Marx's brisk retort that 'ignorance never did anyone any good'.[58]

There were differences of opinion and orientation between and within groups of CPGB members. But it is erroneous to assume a binary model which predicates a distinction between a Stalinist leadership, 'King Street', and a membership of 'honest socialists', relatively uncontaminated by Stalinism, less concerned with the party line or the Soviet Union; or what amounts to a federal model, where members who did not like the line simply did their own thing. Distinctions of role, gradations of political commitment, enthusiasm and activism, inequalities in knowledge and experience, ran through the CPGB. But we are discussing a disciplined *political party* and a bureaucratic centralist one at that. Whatever its imperfections in practice, leaders *and* members operated within the same political parameters; their politics, culture, and what they did, were shaped by Stalinism.[59] There was no meaningful attempt by members or leaders, workers or intellectuals, to question Stalin or to challenge party policy, still less to suggest alternatives to it, before Khrushchev gave the green light – a judgement which applies to those such as John Saville and Edward Thompson, who took up the cudgels against Stalinism in 1956.

The literature demonstrates that Communist intellectuals equated the Russian police state, coercive planning and brittle economic progress with socialism. They magnified advance and considered it permanent; they minimised repression and believed it was temporary. This was underpinned by uncritical appreciation of the anti-fascist struggles of the 1930s, Russia's wartime role, its contemporary resistance to imperialism and its fight for peace. The end, the Soviet Union's ability to move from socialism to communism, justified the means: forced labour, show trials and mass deportations, when they were acknowledged, were deemed necessary, but, on an historical scale, they were considered transient responses to imperialist encirclement and internal subversion. Bipolar vision ensured that one set of values was applied to condemn capitalist regimes, another to extenuate the rulers of Russia. Little credence was granted to revelations in the capitalist press in light of the role of the press lords and the crimes of capitalism. The balance of forces on the left meant there was no alternative to the Soviet Union and the CPGB; the attainment of communism tomorrow was worth the tribulations of today. Communists were on the side of 'the people' and would be vindicated by history.

Like their anti-Communist counterparts, CPGB intellectuals acted, to all intents and purposes, out of conviction. In similar fashion to the bourgeois ideology it disdained, Stalinism reflected aspects of reality. Capitalism *was* unjust, inefficient and predatory, America *was* anti-Communist, the Labour Party leadership *was* right-wing, the media *did* purvey ruling-class ideas. The Soviet Union *had* suffered sustained capitalist attrition and *was* fighting imperialism. Suitably elaborated and embellished, this provided a basis for identifying the interests of British workers with their enemy's enemy, glossing over the conflict between Soviet workers and their enemy, the ruling bureaucracy. In similar fashion to the bourgeois world view, Stalinist ideology mobilised maintenance mechanisms and interpretative filters which explained, challenged or evaded incompatible or uncomfortable evidence. The party, its press, meetings, activity and interaction with fellow Communists, provided insulation and mutual reassurance, although not on the scale of the larger French or Italian parties, from a hostile, uncomprehending world. Bourgeois intellectuals respected and admired their working-class leaders who epitomised what workers might become. They expressed pride in their party, felt a sense of belonging to an embattled, elect community, and developed a determination not to break ranks and join the renegades, symbolised by the confessional intellectuals Arthur Koestler and Ignazio Silone. Bureaucratic centralism which stifled dissent and democracy was equated with discipline, solidarity and unity in action. The urgency of day-to-day struggles and engagement with them acted as solace, justification and sometimes escape.[60]

Thompson depicted literary intellectuals, with few exceptions, as suppressing their personal inclinations over cultural questions. They were motivated by 'the classic self-abnegation of bourgeois guilt and self-mistrust in the face of "proletarian" truth'; lack of self-confidence in the face of the 'charisma' of leaders and officials; dread of 'apostasy'; belief in the cult of self-criticism; and the conviction that cultural issues were subordinate to the politics and practical initiatives of the party, with which, he implies, they did not disagree.[61] Others have detected an undercurrent of political anxiety in the immediate postwar years as the forward march of the CPGB was halted and party intellectuals encountered intensified antagonism in cultural milieux and the academy. The official history of the CPGB claims that worries, uneasiness and doubts about the party's politics were developing from 1948.[62] The excommunication and rehabilitation of Tito and Pollitt's lame explanation and repudiation of his earlier anathematisation certainly concentrated some minds.[63] A difficulty with this discourse of doubt is that it was assembled retrospectively and articulated only in the more favourable climate of 1956, when the Russians had validated misgivings. Nobody went public before the 'Secret Speech'. As Tom Kemp, an historian at Hull University who broke with the CPGB in 1957, remarked:

> It is all very well to say one had doubts – it is very easy to say so after the events ... But the main thing is that one operated a sort of self-censorship. One was very aware that seriously to raise differences was to come into conflict with the party leadership and its authority.[64]

Hobsbawm, who had visited the USSR with Hill in 1954-55, had more than doubts: he possessed 'strong suspicions' about the facts revealed 'amounting to moral certainty for years before Khrushchev spoke'.[65] Like his fellow intellectuals, he remained silent. Lysenkoism 'did not seriously affect him'. He did not believe 'the version of Soviet Party history' contained in the *Short Course*. He was not convinced by the Rajk trial in Hungary or the Czechoslovakian show trials. He was incredulous at the excommunication of Tito, and felt that Klugmann did not believe a word he wrote about it. Nonetheless: '... we stayed loyal to Moscow because the cause of world socialism could dispense with the support of a small if heroic and admired country, but not with that of Stalin's superpower.'[66] Saville recalled that he 'regretted' assorted Soviet decisions, was 'sceptical of the Soviet Union's arguments in their conflict with Tito' and was 'worried' by *From Trotsky to Tito*; but he suppressed his misgivings.[67] Recounting his loyalty to CPGB policy, Thompson remarked: 'That didn't mean that one didn't have many inner doubts and also wasn't guilty of many casuistries explaining away what one should have repudiated in the character of Stalinism.'[68] Eleanor and Michael Barratt Brown – he was an economist who worked for the WEA and subsequently in adult education at Sheffield University – remembered their adulation of Stalin and the Soviet Union and their silence about events in Eastern Europe. Suppression bred 'moral apathy'. Despite first-hand knowledge of Yugoslavia and awareness that the charges against Tito were fabricated and the show trials frame-ups, they kept their concerns 'for private discussion in our own home and did not raise them in the party out of a general desire to conform to the party line and out of fear of being accused of deviations'.[69]

Hill had lived in the Soviet Union for a year in the mid-1930s, authored a bizarre hagiography of Stalin, and pseudonymously published a book favourably comparing the USSR with Britain. He reflected after Hungary: 'We have been living in a world of illusions ... we have lived in a snug little world of our own invention. Some of us including myself have a grave responsibility for having hushed up some of the things that we knew.'[70] Lessing, who had also visited the Soviet Union, affirmed that Communists were capable of discovering the truth about what was happening from 'the plentiful evidence available'. However:

> ... if we had said what we thought in the only place available to us, the capitalist press, we would have been cast out of the Party and branded as traitors and inevitably isolated by bitterness and recrimination from a world movement in which we believed ... That is why we kept silent.[71]

The *Daily Worker* journalist Malcolm MacEwen, a graduate of Edinburgh University, former member of the party's Central Committee and a parliamentary candidate, was more specific and located his disillusion later:

> I can date the beginning of my disenchantment with Stalinism and the Soviet regime from 16 May 1955, the day on which Bulganin and Khrushchev stood on the tarmac at Belgrade airport and read their grovelling apology to the Yugoslav government and Communist Party ... The *Worker* had played a major part in spreading the lies about the Titoite conspiracy that had now been withdrawn ... I had to face up to the fact that all the trials based on the 'Titoite conspiracy' must have been frame-ups, and that we had made ourselves accomplices in the judicial murders of our own comrades.[72]

Discussing the leadership and its supporters, Levy, who had also visited Russia in the early 1950s, observed: 'Their socialist loyalty during the many years of socialist construction ... has become a conditioned habit of thought, a suppression of judgement and a danger to their integrity.'[73] The academic economist Ronald Meek hazarded that some Communists remained ignorant of the realities of Stalinism. Others, possibly the majority, continued to be loyal members, although they were aware of some of the facts, because they could see no meaningful alternative. A small minority knew most of the facts and protested while still maintaining that 'many of the errors and abuses and restrictions on liberty had their roots in certain objective conditions and foreseeing that they would begin to wither away when these conditions disappeared'.[74] The *Daily Worker* journalist Alison Macleod, whose notes taken at the time inform what is, perhaps, the best evocation of 1956, concluded:

> We knew about it and we did not care. We had, by an act of will, decided not to care. The rank-and-file comrades, stooges like myself, were deceived because we wanted to be ... how much respect ought I to have for myself? I could see that I had insisted on being lied to.[75]

The 'Secret Speech'

Nikita Khrushchev's speech delivered on 25 February 1956 to a closed session of the Twentieth Congress of the CPSU – the first since Stalin's death – detonated trauma across the Communist world.[76] News of the Russian leader's historic intervention appeared in the British press on Saturday 17 March 1956 and in the *Daily Worker* the following week. The next three months saw a gradual accretion of detail, culminating in the publication of a version of the speech in two newspapers in June.[77] A party organiser expressed the consternation among Communists:

> My generation had venerated Stalin as the man who triumphed against all odds to establish the world's first socialist state ... a worthy successor to Marx, Engels and Lenin. We had been brought up studying his *Foundations of Leninism, A Short History of the CPSU* and his shorter works. Every pronouncement he made was the subject of study ... but I had little doubt that the report was substantially true. This was the general feeling, although there were some comrades who did not believe it, or thought it was grossly exaggerated, reflecting a new power struggle. It caused intellectual turmoil among comrades and raised sharply a number of uncomfortable questions. How could it have happened? What had the CPSU been doing to allow it to happen? Where was democratic centralism? Did it mean that our estimate of Soviet society was wrong?[78]

Lifelong Communists were plunged into personal crisis. The aspiring young playwright Arnold Wesker, then a member of the Young Communist League, captured his mother's bleak bewilderment and existential angst:

> Leah, my mother ... does not know what has happened, what to say or feel or think. She is at once defensive and doubtful. She does not know who is right. To her the people who once criticised the party and were called traitors are still traitors, despite that the new attitude suggests that this is not the case ... If she admits that the party has been wrong, that Stalin committed grave offences, then she admits that she has been wrong. All the people she so mistrusted and hated she must now have second thoughts about, and this she cannot do ... You can admit the error of an idea but not the conduct of a whole life.[79]

The roots of the 'Secret Speech' lay in the problems debilitating the Soviet economy and political system: the stagnation in industry and agriculture; low labour productivity; and the dysfunctionality to economic and social progress of the terror which had become entrenched under Stalin. Khrushchev's purpose in reappraising the dictator was to pave the way for a more vigorous, but carefully calibrated, strategy of modernisation. He wanted to accelerate the course pursued since 1953, stimulate productivity through economic incentives, defuse workers' discontent, and elicit enhanced commitment through incremental increases in living standards, further refinement of the security organs and scaling back the Gulag. There was not the slightest intention of relaxing the bureaucracy's hold on power, diminishing its privileges or endangering the fundamentals of an economic and social order which had elevated Khrushchev and his fellow oligarchs, a system they identified with socialism. 'De-Stalinisation' was about improving that system, not transforming it. The 'Secret Speech' was about reining in Stalin's 'excesses' – not ditching Stalinism.[80]

Khrushchev's critique was devastating but circumscribed. He documented Lenin's criticisms of Stalin and his recommendation that the latter be removed as General Secretary. Starting with the murder of Kirov, he detailed the violations of 'socialist legality', the fictive charges and the confessions extracted by torture which characterised the trials of the Old Bolsheviks during 1935-38. He addressed the *Vozhd*'s purges of the party and the armed forces, his sustained refusal to countenance evidence that Hitler was preparing an invasion, and the autocrat's subsequent desertion of his post and costly military miscalculations. Exposing the postwar terror and ethnic cleansing, Khrushchev highlighted Stalin's disregard of collective leadership, his growing paranoia, brutality and self-glorification and its impact on party, economy and society.[81]

Apart from praising Stalin's role in 'the socialist construction of our country', Khrushchev was silent about the decade between 1924 and 1934, the years in which the Stalinist system was assembled and rooted in Russian society. The speech did not question the theory and practice of 'socialism in one country', the struggles against the Left Opposition, the United Opposition and the Bukharinist right; or the theory of social fascism and launching of 'Class Against Class' with its savage industrialisation and collectivisation, attendant famine and mass murder of the peasantry. There was nothing about the terror before 1935. Khrushchev focused on the last fifteen years of the Friend and Teacher of All Toilers, the Shining Sun of Humanity. He emphasised the elimination of party and state functionaries rather than the oppression of Russian workers. He ridiculed the despot's insistence that the terror was directed against remnants of the bourgeoisie. But he failed to account for his own and his fellow leaders' complicity in Stalin's crimes. What he revealed was the corruption of an individual. He did not consider the factors which had facilitated Stalin's power and its abuse. He did not question the social and economic basis on which Stalin and the CPSU rested or analyse the conditions prompting the emergence of a barbaric bureaucratic collectivism.[82]

The 'Secret Speech' was delivered against a background of manoeuvring for power among the former leader's acolytes. There were conflicting views on how far reform should run, different estimations of the risks of stimulating unrealistic expectations and fuelling unrest. Despite the absence of anything resembling a Marxist analysis, Khrushchev's pugnacious peroration had a powerful impact and unintended consequences. It contributed to a climate which turned instability into insurgency in Poland in June 1956, and into insurrection in Hungary during the autumn. The first was contained by means of changes in the Polish party's leadership and Russian restraint. But in Hungary, Imre Nagy's announcement of a multi-party democracy and withdrawal from the Warsaw Pact provoked Soviet intervention, Nagy's execution and the installation of the orthodox János Kádár regime. These events confirmed the risks in de-Stalinisation, and its limits.[83]

The shock of the revelations and their repercussions in the Soviet bloc produced a ferment in the European Communist parties – including the CPGB. It constituted an important opportunity, a chance to rethink the history and philosophy of 'official Communism' in relation to the ideas of Marx, Engels, Kautsky, Lenin, Trotsky and Bukharin as well as alternative streams of socialist thought. How had it happened? Was Stalinism inevitable? Were alternatives available? The possibility was there for Communists to re-examine how the phenomenon had developed, to go beyond Khrushchev to confront such questions as 'socialism in one country'; the strengthening of 'the dictatorship of the proletariat' as against 'the withering away of the state'; the growth of a parasitic bureaucracy which exploited and atomised the working class; the coercive extension of the Russian system across Eastern Europe; the identification of the development of the forces of production – not the development of workers' control of those forces, workers' power and workers' democracy – with progress towards human liberation; and the negative impact of the national Communist parties' mantra that the Soviet Union was a socialist society upon proletarian consciousness and workers' belief in the desirability of socialist transformation outside Russia. Some on the left were beginning painfully to understand that Stalinism reinforced bourgeois common-sense about revolution and made it harder to build an alternative to reformism. At the same time, ruling-class fears about the spread of Stalinism bred concessions to the working class and strengthened reformism. Khrushchev's revelations provided an opening which if fully utilised might at least begin to break this impasse. It was an unprecedented opportunity, but it was one which the leadership of the CPGB and many members had no intention of grasping. It was not only Khrushchev and Molotov but Thorez and Togliatti, Pollitt and Dutt, who had acted as willing accomplices – in each case supported by their own acolytes – in the making of Stalinism.

In line with their standing in the world Communist movement, Pollitt, Dutt and Matthews, the British delegates to the Twentieth Congress, had been excluded from the closed session. They had, however, been present when Khrushchev and Anastas Mikoyan denounced 'the cult of personality' at earlier meetings.[84] They knew the way the wind was blowing; but they were devoted to the memory and legacy of Stalin. Like their comrades in the CPGB leadership, they were unclear about how far Khrushchev wanted them to go, they had little inclination to stray beyond what he had made public and were reticent about going into the detail of what he had said. Pollitt, whose subsequent conduct suggested Khrushchev, not Stalin, was the problem, made no reference to the 'Secret Speech' in his initial reports on the congress in the *Daily Worker*. The first comments came from Matthews – but they were based on the open sessions. Stressing 'the incredible achievements of Soviet Communism', he noted 'an over-emphasis on the role of Stalin' and 'the cult of the individual'. But he underlined Stalin's 'great positive, services ... to the cause of socialism' and insisted that past errors had been corrected through a healthy reassertion of collective leadership in the Soviet Union.[85] Matthews set the tone of the leadership's initial response. There was no great cause for concern. 'Mistakes' had been made, but they had not undermined socialist advance in the Soviet Union and beyond.

The reaction of some members was different. Through March, sixty letters were published in the *Daily Worker,* raising questions about the personality cult, the CPGB's political reliance on the CPSU and party leaders' complacency. Even at this stage divisions were emerging: two-thirds of contributors were critical of Stalin, the Soviet Union and the CPGB leaders, the rest were pro-Stalin, illustrating his continued prestige in the party.[86] A *Daily Worker* journalist reflected that the Political Committee 'agreed to publication even of the most critical in the hope that the storm would blow itself out'.[87] As the Twenty-Fourth Congress of the CPGB, scheduled for 30 March, loomed, Campbell declared the discussion closed. Attempts to restore normality were overtaken by publication of details of the 'Secret Speech' in British newspapers on 17 March.[88] Nonetheless, most of the congress was taken up by discussion of the forward march of the USSR, the upsurge in colonial struggle, changes in the global balance of forces favouring the socialist bloc, and new opportunities for the party developing in the British labour movement.[89]

When the CPGB leaders first acquired authoritative knowledge of what Khrushchev had said remains unclear. Robert Service claimed in 1998 that the leaders of foreign parties were handed transcripts before they left Moscow. If this was so, Pollitt neglected to inform the membership. But

Service cites no evidence for his assertion. King Street did have to hand a six-page summary of the 'Secret Speech' compiled by Sam Russell, a party journalist, in Moscow. But censorship extended beyond self-censorship: it was not circulated to members and only a bowdlerised version was published in the *Daily Worker*. The stance of party leaders remained secretive and suppressive.[90] In a further attempt to defuse matters, they emulated the CPSU and organised a closed session of the congress to discuss the crisis. Pollitt, demonstrating less indignation than Khrushchev had, conceded mistakes had been made. But Stalin's contribution to socialist progress was tremendous, and the USSR was going from strength to strength.[91] One participant recalled: 'Pollitt made the most extraordinary statement (all too typical of his emotional approach to politics) that he respected revolutionaries who confessed to crimes they did not commit rather than "give in to the class enemy" ... '[92] The growing confidence of dissenters could be seen when Peter Fryer, another *Daily Worker* journalist, spoke from the floor, but 'the overwhelming majority of the active members of the British party were, however, still wholly concerned with domestic matters'.[93]

In an essay commemorating the twentieth anniversary of 1956, the veteran party loyalist Margot Heinemann ruminated:

> ... if our leaders had felt it possible to make at the time the kind of sharply critical statements the *Daily Worker* was reporting from Togliatti and the Italian CP ... some, though not all, of the later divisions might have been avoided and the way opened up for a new advance.[94]

This was wishful thinking. Pollitt:

> ... was incapable of abandoning the uncritical solidarity with the Soviet leadership on which he had built his political life and, like Khrushchev, he and his closest colleagues on the Political Committee still preferred secrecy to openness.[95]

Dutt was a theoretician in the sense that medieval schoolmen were theoreticians. He provoked one Communist intellectual to register the 'lasting conviction that he [Dutt] was not interested in truth, but used his intellect exclusively to justify and explicate the line of the movement, whatever it was'.[96] Campbell, whose son lived in Russia, 'must have known the truth for many years but his loyalty to the Soviet Union and the Political Committee overrode his conscience'.[97] Gollan and Matthews would only change, and then merely to a limited degree, when confronted by a new polycentric world.[98]

Pollitt's verdict on the 'Secret Speech' was published in *World News* on 21 April and 5 May 1956 (Document I). It would be wrong, he claimed, to minimise the damage Stalin had wrought – although, in comparison with Khrushchev, Pollitt was light on the details. However, the Soviet Union had been the victim of constant capitalist pressure, the threat from fascism which had materialised in 1941, and internal subversion. Stalin's abuses had 'occurred within the framework of a profound socialist advance and generally correct line of policy'. Pollitt praised Stalin's 'outstanding contribution to the building of socialism in the Soviet Union – the base for all the further advances of socialism in the world'. Mistakes and abuses thus remained secondary, and the Soviet Union remained healthy. 'Socialist legality' had been restored, while the 'great new vista opened out by the Twentieth Congress' promised 'an intellectual renaissance'. Pollitt corrected the CPGB's earlier position on Yugoslavia: *From Trotsky to Tito* was withdrawn from circulation. But it was wrong, he insisted, to dwell on the errors: '… all the basic Marxist principles have been proven correct.' It was time to turn the page.

The resolution of the CPGB's May Executive meeting, 'The Lessons of the Twentieth Congress of the CPSU' (*World News*, 19 May, Document II), assailed the critics:

> Some comrades have tended to concentrate on the weaknesses revealed at the Twentieth Congress, rather than to discuss these within the context of the great advances … It is quite wrong to refuse to face up to the errors and injustices … it is equally wrong to see nothing but the errors and abuses, to examine them out of the context of the tremendous total human advance. For if that is done there results a purely negative attitude, a lack of balance.

There were enough hostile forces attacking the USSR without British Communists amplifying the cacophony. The leadership regretted its own past mistakes 'made in good faith on the basis of false information' and promised a more critical attitude for the future – a specific concession was the appointment of a Commission on Party Democracy. The approach remained reactive and conservative. The apparatus simply followed the Russian lead, asserting a distinction between the unacceptable actions of Stalin and the integrity of the system he had done so much to forge and which continued to serve as the only model of socialism.

The message was repeated more uncompromisingly by Dutt in the May *Labour Monthly* (Document III). Amalgamating issues, such as East-West relations, the progress of the colonial struggle and Labour–Communist unity with the revelations in what he termed 'The Great Debate', he inquired: what were the basic questions? In a passage which alienated many Communists, Dutt explained:

> Not about Stalin. That there should be spots on any sun would only startle an inveterate Mithras-worshipper. Not about the now recognised abuses of the security organs in a period of heroic ordeal and achievement of the Soviet Union. To imagine that a great revolution can develop without a million cross-currents, hardships, injustices and excesses would be a delusion fit for ivory-tower dwellers in fairyland who have still to learn that the thorny path of human advance moves forward, not only through unexampled heroism, but also with accompanying baseness, with tears and blood. The Great Debate is about larger issues ... which were spotlighted by the Twentieth Congress ... First, the future of mankind in the nuclear age of East-West relations of peace and peaceful coexistence. Second, the future of the labour movement. Third, the future of the transition to socialism.

Dutt's Stalinist realism and political *machismo* constituted an exercise in displacement intended to reinfuse Communists with the hard-nosed mentality that 'You can't make an omelette without breaking eggs'; or as some Stalinists cynically put it: 'When you chop wood, the chips fly.' Rather than defusing criticism, his intervention intensified antagonism, necessitating a more emollient amplification in the June *Labour Monthly* (Document V). Dutt acknowledged that he had given the impression of discounting the gravity of Khrushchev's revelations and the shock they had engendered in Britain.[99] A review of Stalin's 'criminal misdeeds' had, he agreed, been indispensable to progress. But Dutt's undiminished admiration of his former leader shone through the darkness and at times overshadowed the recitation of his 'misdeeds'. Stalin had presided over the defeat of fascism, postwar reconstruction and 'the completion of the construction of socialism'. History would acknowledge the contribution of the Soviet people, but also 'the genius, unyielding courage, steadfastness and devotion to the revolution of Stalin'. Admittedly, virtues had turned into vices. But he was neither 'a tyrant' nor 'a dictator' to be compared with Bonaparte or Hitler. Dutt concluded:

> The evils that arose affected primarily the functioning of the apparatus, rather than the essence of the class power of the working people ...

Throughout this period, despite all the evils, the masses of the people were continuing to enjoy and exercise self-rule in running their affairs to a degree unknown in any capitalist democracy.

Here was the essence of the great illusion: Russia had been under Stalin, and it remained under Khrushchev, a socialist democracy; the economy was controlled and the country governed by workers. Recasting reality, Dutt suggested: '... the Twentieth Congress did not feel like the end of the world, not like "the god that failed" but like the sunrise breaking through the clouds and the dawn of a new day.'

In the spring of 1956, Khrushchev's exposé was receiving widespread publicity in the mainstream media and the British labour movement, while the CPGB leadership's lackadaisical response was attracting scathing criticism.[100] Pollitt was a major casualty of Stalin's fall from grace. At the end of April he suffered a haemorrhage which left him with impaired vision and prompted his resignation. He was replaced as Secretary by the lacklustre but crucially working-class and orthodox Gollan; the changing of the guard intensified the atmosphere of dislocation and sharpened the sense that the old order of Stalinist certainties was collapsing. By June, the text of the 'Secret Speech' was widely available. The version sent from Moscow to the Polish party had found its way into the hands of the US State Department – Khrushchev later claimed he leaked it to the CIA. It appeared in the *New York Times* and the London *Observer*. The *Manchester Guardian* published it as a pamphlet, as did the main American and British Trotskyist groups.[101]

On 21 June, the CPGB Political Committee issued a statement, 'Khrushchev's Report', complaining the party had still not received the official version from Moscow and remained dependent on 'enemy sources of information' (*World News*, 30 June, Document VIII). While repeating the Russian position, the statement took things further. It endorsed comments from the Italian and French parties and pronounced in commendable, although what would prove rhetorical, terms:

> ... it will be necessary to make a profound Marxist analysis of the causes of the degeneration of the functioning of Soviet democracy and party democracy, that it is not enough to attribute these developments solely to the character of one individual; and that a more adequate estimate of the role of Stalin both in its positive and negative aspects will be necessary.

The Reasoner and the Crisis of British Communism

It was at this stage with many Communist intellectuals 'facing the political equivalent of a nervous breakdown'[102] that John Saville, Edward Thompson and *The Reasoner* took a hand in events. Saville, forty years of age in 1956, was a lecturer in economic history at Hull University. He had been a member of the CPGB since 1934, was active at branch level and in the Historians' Group and had become aware of the significance of the revelations and their implications for the party by mid-March when he wrote to Pollitt expressing disquiet but pledging continuing loyalty. A milestone in Saville's – and other intellectuals' – development into oppositionists was the meeting of the Historians' Group held on 8 April 1956. Despite an address by Klugmann, who liaised with the group on behalf of the apparatus, resolutions were carried:

> … expressing profound dissatisfaction with the Twenty-Fourth Congress of the Br Party for its failure to discuss publicly the implications for the Br Party of the Twentieth Congress CPSU … and with the failure of the Party leadership to make a public statement of regret for the Br Party's past uncritical endorsement of all Soviet policies and views, the meeting calling upon it to make one as soon as possible, as well as to initiate the widest possible public discussion of all the problems involved for the Party in the present situation.[103]

This was essentially the basis on which *The Reasoner* would campaign. The significance of this meeting cannot be overestimated. It proved important in crystallising concerns, overcoming isolation and imparting a sense of collective dissidence. Saville subsequently contacted Ken Alexander, Ronald Meek and Christopher and Bridget Hill. By early April he was in touch with Edward and Dorothy Thompson. He had known the Thompsons since 1949 as a result of a shared interest in Chartism, although earlier contact had been slight and Edward played little part in the Historians' Group. Like Saville, the 32-year-old Thompson was a war veteran; he had joined the party in 1942, he was a member of the Yorkshire District Committee and a veteran of the party's peace campaigns. He worked as an adult education lecturer, specialising in literature but sometimes teaching history, in the Extramural Department at the University of Leeds, although many of his classes were in the Halifax area where he and Dorothy lived. Thompson recollected: 'I commenced to reason in my thirty-third year.'[104] In that spirit, he warmly welcomed Saville's initial letter. Thompson had already corresponded with Klugmann, criticising the leadership's inaction over the 'Secret Speech' and calling for a full debate within the party based on detailed examination of the CPGB's history and past errors.[105]

There was an instantaneous *rapport* between Thompson and Saville. Mutual appreciation set the scene for an intense and fruitful, if always argumentative and at times difficult, four-year partnership. They had a lot in common, although they were different in temperament and, as time would demonstrate, despite their shared enthusiasm for the Popular Front strain in their party's history, their approach to politics. Thompson was an individualist. Brimming with ideas, he was an inspiring writer and impassioned speaker who expressed himself powerfully, exuberantly, often polemically. Saville was also a frank and authoritative speaker, but with a more conciliatory manner, a team player and better organised. He exercised a calming influence and anchored what became between 1956 and 1959 a productive collaboration.[106] If Thompson had exhibited more signs of dissatisfaction, both had impeccable records of loyalty to the party. But they were incensed by the 'business as usual' attitude of the apparatus and were convinced that the moment had come to speak out. Their aim was to secure a proper exploration of the issues exposed by the 'Secret Speech'.[107] Their determination to do so was reinforced by the resolution of the party's National University Staffs Committee held in early May which argued that the problems engulfing the CPGB must be confronted.[108]

Saville's first intervention in the discussion, 'Problems of the Communist Party', appeared in *World News* on 19 May (Document IV) and introduced themes which would figure in the future. The CPGB, he argued, had demonstrated 'blind faith' in following the line of the CPSU and failed to convince the labour movement that socialism did not entail a police state and judicial murder. The British party had not so much defended the Soviet Union as countenanced its crimes, misdeeds and mistakes, and in his contributions Dutt had proved incapable of accepting this. The urgent need was for an honest, frank discussion of what had gone wrong in the past and how it could be rectified in the future. Many members were seriously questioning whether they should remain in the party because the majority of its leaders were in denial over the depth of the problems and were taking refuge in the need to prosecute the class struggle rather than 'wasting time on debate'. A second letter from Saville was spiked on the grounds that he had already had his 'crack of the whip'.[109]

It was difficult effectively to contest orthodoxy in the party press, although a number of critical contributions did get through, for example, Thompson's 'Winter Wheat in Omsk' (*World News*, 30 June, Document VI) and Derek Kartun, 'Ideas and Methods of Work' (*World News*, 14 July, Document IX).

Thompson's article demonstrated his inimitable style, polemical approach and moral indignation at what had happened and was still happening. The article suggested a similarity of outlook between Thompson and his new co-thinker Saville in its criticism of the Russian connection; but it went further in its comparison of Stalinist infallibility with 'Holy Church'; its invocation of the *moral* tradition of English socialism, from the Levellers, through the Chartists to William Morris and Tom Mann; and its insistence on the primacy of conscience, democracy and existing liberties.

Saville and Thompson had mulled over ideas for a discussion journal for party members, independent of leadership control, since early May. Thompson's unsuccessful attempt to muster support in the Yorkshire District, his unfruitful discussions with its organiser, Bert Ramelson, and correspondence with Klugmann, who played a straight bat, led him to believe it would be necessary to challenge the party leaders. Since the war they had 'been acting as High Priests interpreting and justifying the Holy Writ emanating from Stalin'.[110] The publication of a reply to 'Winter Wheat in Omsk' by Matthews, 'A Caricature of Our Party', in the same issue of *World News* (Document VII) and the magazine's refusal to permit Thompson a further response concentrated their minds. The die was cast. They had no desire to leave the party, although the possibility of expulsion was always in their minds. The first, 32-page mimeographed issue of *The Reasoner* was circulated in early July. The title derived generally from the conception of reason as the enemy of blind faith, more specifically from a distant predecessor of the same name edited by John Bone, a revolutionary bookseller and a former secretary of the London Corresponding Society. Bone, whose original *Reasoner* had ceased publication in 1808, was a fearless thinker and his paper combined support for the war against Napoleon with Jacobin demands. In adapting the appellation of what Thompson termed 'this honourably named periodical',[111] the editors of the new venture signalled their desire to re-establish continuity with earlier radical traditions based on intellectual independence and freedom of thought and their aspiration for a party and a socialism based on 'the exercise of free human reason'.

Saville and Thompson emphasised that their objective was a no-holds-barred discussion of Stalinist dogma and the CPGB's dogmatic practice with the quotation from Marx which appeared under the masthead: 'To leave error unrefuted, is to encourage intellectual immorality.' They went on to insist:

We take our stand as Marxists. Nothing in the events of the past months has shaken our conviction that the methods and outlook of historical materialism, developed by the work of Marx and Engels, provide the key to our theoretical advance and, therefore, to the understanding of these events themselves; although it should be said that much that has gone under the name of 'Marxism' or 'Marxism-Leninism' is itself in need of re-examination. History has provided a chance for this re-examination to take place; and for the scientific methods of Marxism to be reintegrated with the finest traditions of the human reason and spirit which we may best describe as humanism.[112]

It was imperative that Communists address the 'veritable crisis of theory' and 'the fear of ideas on the part of some members' and inquire anew: 'What is socialism?' As part of that project it was essential to remedy 'our general failure to apply a Marxist analysis to socialist countries and to the Soviet Union in particular. The absence of such an analysis is an admission of naivety or worse. This failure bred Utopianism and encouraged attitudes of religious faith …'[113]

One Communist later reflected:

To look at this paper after 40 years is to remember what hell it was to type stencils. If you made a mistake, you had to cover it with a substance resembling nail varnish. To place the stencil on the duplicator without crinkling it required neat fingers and a steady nerve. Then the duplication would go wrong, covering you with black ink. Only very determined people would use this method of putting across their views. The editors of *The Reasoner*, John Saville and E P Thompson, were not only determined but angry.[114]

The production and distribution of *The Reasoner*, it should be remembered, was entirely in the hands of Saville, Thompson, their families and a small number of local helpers. Thompson typed everything, then despatched the stencils by train from Halifax to Hull where the pages were run off on a requisitioned office duplicator. Each of the three issues occupied several weeks of work. The July issue of 350 copies quickly 'sold out' – most of them mailed free to friends, contacts and others they thought likely to be interested. Within weeks some 250 letters and many donations had been received, and a further 300 copies were duplicated. The only formal outlets were the Collets bookshops in London and Glasgow which were connected to the party – the Yorkshire shop refused to take copies. Interest spread –

by word of mouth and publicity in journals, notably *Tribune* and the *New Statesman*. Around 1000 copies of the second issue were produced and, by mid-November, 1500 copies of the final number had been circulated. Early supporters included Ken Alexander, a Sheffield University economist; the musician James Gibb; Bernard Stevens, the composer; and Randall Swingler, who helped from the outset; they were quickly followed by the art critic John Berger, Meek, Lessing, Levy, the *Daily Worker* journalist Malcolm MacEwen, and Saville's university contemporary Brian Pearce. *The Reasoner* attracted avid attention across the party and support from individuals and a few party units including the factory branch at Briggs' car plant in Dagenham.[115] *Daily Worker* journalists testified as to its impact in making their paper take the discussion more seriously.[116]

Bryan Palmer observed that the *New Reasoner* of the later 1950s is often referred to but rarely read.[117] That verdict is even more applicable to *The Reasoner*.[118] Reprinted here in its entirety, for the first time since 1956, its pages constitute a valuable and enduring contribution to the history of British Communism and the left more widely. They contain a compendium of contemporary criticism, a snapshot of what was wrong with the CPGB, and an example of the ability of some party members – however belatedly – to begin to anatomise its infirmities. Readers can study the accumulated concerns of members for themselves, starting with the editorials which Saville and Thompson provided and which stimulated and structured debate. The party, they argued, was neither autonomous nor democratic, neither critical nor creative – despite sincere socialists in its ranks. The 'Secret Speech' had brought embedded problems to the surface, but the leadership was not prepared to face them and the only hope for change lay in informed, reasoned debate among the members. Saville and Thompson saw their basic tasks as disentangling Marxism from the Stalinist canon of the CPSU and CPGB and transforming the theory and practice of British Communism.

For the first time in its history, the second-hand politics and *ersatz* democracy of the CPGB and the myth of the Soviet Union were subjected to a wide-ranging, sophisticated but accessible critique from within. For the first time in its history, intellectuals asserted their role inside the party as independent thinkers, as critics rather than technicians of power. More sombrely, as Russian tanks confronted Hungarian workers on the streets of Budapest, the narrative moved from insistence on transforming the CPGB to questioning whether that was possible. In the final issue of *The Reasoner*, published in the immediate aftermath of the invasion, Thompson scathingly dismissed the crucial political influence on British Communism as dehumanising people and replacing the complex realities of individuals and life with arid schema:

> Stalinism is socialist theory and practice which has lost the ingredient of humanity. The Stalinist mode of thought is not that of dialectical materialism but mechanical idealism … Stalinism is Leninism turned into stone … Stalinist analysis at its most degenerate becomes a scholastic exercise, the search for 'formulations', correct in relation to the text but not to life.[119]

This was distilled in the Hungarian events which banished Saville and Thompson's conviction that the party could be reformed from within. In a statement added at the last minute to the final number of the journal they wrote:

> The EC of the British Party must at once:
> 1) Dissociate itself publicly from the action of the Soviet Union in Hungary.
> 2) Demand the immediate withdrawal of Soviet troops …
> If these demands are not met we urge all those who like ourselves will dissociate themselves completely from the leadership of the British Communist Party, not to lose faith in socialism, and to find ways of keeping together. We promise our readers that we will consult with others about the early formation of a new Socialist journal.[120]

The editorials bound together an impressive if uneven range of contributions. Relatively short articles combined subjective experience with assessment of particular problems. A personal selection would include Thompson's contributions; the explorations of democratic centralism by Alexander, GDH Cole and 'PH'; Levy's discussion of dogma and unorthodoxy; John McLeish's testimony on the CPGB's degeneration; and Bob Davies' pioneering excavation of Stalinism in the 1930s. One aspect of *The Reasoner* which particularly exercised the leadership was the publication of the literature of other national parties. Dissent in the US party, accompanied by criticism of the Soviet Union, initially exceeded that in Britain, although it was ultimately unsuccessful, and *The Reasoner* carried excerpts from the US *Daily Worker* – its editorial on Rajk and a letter from the oppositionist Steve Nelson – as well as extracts from *Jewish Life* which exposed the history of anti-Semitism in the USSR.[121] With the help of the Leeds University academic Alfred Dressler, material was also published from the Polish party, as well as a first-hand account by Meek of developments there.

The CPGB leaders and members who supported them were far from pleased, particularly by the growing interest that the journal was attracting outside the party. The CPGB's bureaucratic centralist regime proscribed any expression of organised dissent. The last oppositional journal, the clandestine *Communist*, had appeared more than two decades earlier in 1932. It was swiftly suppressed and its promoters, the proto-Trotskyist Balham Group, promptly expelled.[122] Dutt had been licensed to publish *Labour Monthly* from 1921 as part of a long-term project in periphery-building – but Dutt was undisputedly orthodox.[123] Saville and Thompson, in contrast, were called to account within weeks of the first issue of *The Reasoner*. They were summoned to appear before the Yorkshire District Committee on 10 and 18 August and subsequently to a meeting of the Political Committee at King Street on 31 August, attended by Pollitt, Dutt, Campbell and Gollan.

Its editors denied that *The Reasoner* reflected a factional viewpoint. On the contrary, they claimed, it represented the 'general interests of the party' because the established press was not reflecting the concerns of the membership and was rationing publication of critical views. This was disingenuous. Saville and Thompson were criticising the leadership's politics as well as the party's philosophy and democracy. In their defence they asserted the need for 'free unfettered discussion' as an apparently permanent feature of a healthy Communist organisation: '… for democratic centralism to operate properly there must be free and open discussion.' This required a forum where discussion would not be controlled by the apparatus. Appealing to history, they cited the internal party fight conducted by Pollitt and Dutt from 1928 to bring existing party policy into line with the Third Period. The Political Committee avoided substantive issues and pointed out, with some justification, that according dissatisfied members rights to circulate their own publications and determine their content would undermine established mechanisms; collective democracy and the party would dissolve into a plethora of competing groups. There was, they noted, a network of *Reasoner* correspondents and at least one meeting had been convened. Saville and Thompson had every right to try to revise the rules at the next congress; until then, fairness demanded that they accept them. (See The Communist Party and *The Reasoner*: Documents, below.)

The Political Committee acted with calculated restraint and employed elements of repressive tolerance in order to convince members that *The Reasoner* was unnecessary, undisciplined and impermissible. However, its editors remained sceptical about the June promise to undertake 'a profound

Marxist analysis' of Soviet democracy and Stalin. As the documents disclose, events moved rapidly. Saville and Thompson refused to accept the decision of the Yorkshire District Committee that they cease publication and rejected similar instructions from the Political and Executive Committees. On 7 October, they informed Gollan, the new General Secretary, that in order to remove any impediment to the continuation of debate, the next number of the journal would be the last. When it appeared, in violation of further instructions to desist, the editors were suspended from membership for three months for refusal to carry out democratic decisions and conduct detrimental to the party. In the light of what had been a brief but intense learning curve, first-hand experience of the CPGB's intolerance of dissent and debate, even in times of turmoil, and, crucially, the leadership's support for Russian action in Hungary, they resigned from the party. They had spearheaded a breakthrough. Success, in the sense of theorising Stalinism and developing an alternative to it, remained to be achieved: it would prove elusive.

In its short life *The Reasoner* attracted strong support and publicised the critics' case throughout the party; it crystallised the opposition which had developed from February and intensified after Hungary. It helped break the ice and stimulate and organise discussion. It commenced – but far from completed – the addressing of Stalinism in Russia and its impact on British Communism. *The Reasoner* inspired solidarity. The Writers' Group, for example, expressed 'extreme dissatisfaction' with the Executive's attitude to the journal. The group elaborated a scheme, which was not required in the end, by which pairs of authors, Jack Lindsay, Hamish Henderson, Arnold Rattenbury, Montagu Slater, Swingler, Rickword, would act as editors – each duo being replaced by successors as suspensions and expulsions kicked in. Similar schemes were proposed by the historians and scientists.[124] However, support came from a minority. Party leaders could still rely on most members to back its decisions. Organising opposition in the CPGB remained what it had always been, an intractable task. Exiting on an individual basis, rather than collective, organised, purposive defection remained the conventional answer for those unwilling to remain in the party. In short the CPGB was irreformable.

Saville and Thompson reluctantly acknowledged this. The former recalled:

> … it was these meetings at King Street with the leading officials of the Communist Party that made me begin to recognise what I did not want to acknowledge, that we would never make a serious impact upon the

leadership and that the party hierarchy was imperishably bureaucratic. We were also becoming aware of the hostility that was growing against us among party members of longstanding … we recognised with both reluctance and dismay, the basic conservatism, not only of the leadership but of the rank and file.[125]

They had begun their journey with no intention of leaving the CPGB. The possibility was always there and events changed things. By October Saville was writing: '… it has become very clear that the leadership is Stalinist to a man and that it is going to be impossible to shift them.'[126]

Endgame: From the Demise of *The Reasoner* to the Special Congress

Coming hot on the heels of the 'Secret Speech', Hungary convinced Raphael Samuel, a 22-year-old member of the Historian's Group, a passionate Communist who came from a party family and was studying for a PhD at the London School of Economics, that this was indeed the position. After painful reflection, he decided he had no alternative to breaking with the party he had grown up in. Samuel remained in a minority. Years later he wrote about the hold Stalin exercised over the hearts and minds of British Communists in the early 1950s: 'The cult of Stalin, however astonishing it may appear – or shameful to those who at some point in their lives practised it – was very much of a piece with the central Communist imagination of its time.'[127] Stalin was imagined in a variety of ways by his followers around the world, and the CPGB version differed from the icon venerated in Russia or China:

> The English Stalin, although praised by Communists in hardly less extravagant terms, was an altogether more down-to-earth figure, corresponding in some way to our idealised conceptions of ourselves. He was a man of few words and simple tastes, personally modest and of an essentially practical intelligence. We admired him as a kind of Russian Churchill, for his combination of indomitable courage and earthy common sense … We thought of him as level-headed and unflappable; a man who went quietly about his work and kept his head in a storm. Above all he was a patient *teacher*, very much concerned with the problems of the ordinary Party member … [128]

It is, perhaps, unsurprising that even after Hungary many CPGB members proved reluctant to turn their backs on the past, to trade in the chimera of the selfless revolutionary nonpareil for the reality of the gifted but unscrupulous political fixer, tyrant and mass murderer, and to exorcise the vision of 'Uncle Joe' they had cherished for so long. Images of the avuncular genius were engraved on their consciousness and would take time to erase. If the intensity and durability of their attachments inoculated some against interrogation and reassessment of their intellectual and emotional convictions, others whose membership had been peripheral to their lives, or who had long been inactive and found membership of the CPGB a disadvantage or embarrassment, bailed out. Hungary also influenced some of the party's best-known trade unionists to move towards the exit. They included Les Cannon of the electricians' union; Jim Hammond, Bert Wynn and Alex Moffat of the mineworkers' union; George Smith and Brian Behan of the woodworkers; Dick Seabrook of the shop-workers; and John Horner and Jack Grahl of the Fire Brigades' Union.[129] Others voiced their complaints about the party and the Soviet Union but stayed loyal. This group included Arnold Kettle, who initially opposed the invasion of Hungary; the London University lecturer Jim Fyrth, who was critical of party democracy; and Hobsbawm. The latter signed a statement from CPGB intellectuals in the *New Statesman* which protested against the party Executive's 'uncritical support' for the Russian action in Hungary but included the caveat: 'Not all the signatories agree with everything in this letter.'[130] This followed his letter published in the *Daily Worker* which stated: 'While approving with a heavy heart of what is now happening in Hungary, we should also say frankly that we think the USSR should withdraw its troops from the country as soon as this is possible.'[131]

Other intellectuals, such as the Hills and MacEwen, were campaigning over internal democracy; Peter Fryer, whose reports from Budapest had been suppressed by Campbell who had sent him to report for the *Daily Worker*, was in the forefront of agitation over Hungary; while Levy kept the spotlight on anti-Semitism in the USSR.[132] The 67-year-old Scot, who had journeyed from the slums of Edinburgh to head the mathematics department at Imperial College London, led a CPGB delegation which flew to Russia in October 1956 to investigate the position of Jews. Levy had been a member of the party for over a quarter of a century. He had been prominent among those who had highlighted the plight of the Jews in Hitler's Germany – while proudly boasting that Stalin's Russia was the only country in which anti-Semitism was a crime against the state. In the winter of 1956 Levy was devastated at what he found:

Then came the discovery from private conversations by Comrade Levy with Jews that the years 1948-1952 were known among them as 'The Black Years', the period during which many Jews were dismissed from their posts. Jewish poets and workers were arrested and charged with treason and executed ... Those arrested and charged in secret were prominent political or cultural workers. Shortly after his arrest, the immediate relatives of the arrested man would be deported to some distant place ... Finally, the husband would be shot perhaps after torture to try to force him to confess or to incriminate others. In this way, practically the whole of the Jewish Anti-Fascist Committee was liquidated.[133]

It was a chilling snapshot of Stalinist normality after the war against fascism, the CPGB's myopia and self-delusion, and the sustained refusal to face reality on the part of its intellectuals. Levy was in despair: it speaks volumes for the hold the party still maintained over the newly-enlightened that with a summary of the report published in the CPGB press he remained a member.[134]

By January 1957, party leaders retained the active support or silent consent of most members, their reluctance to uproot embedded beliefs stiffened by the Anglo-French adventure in Suez and 'counter-revolutionary activity' in Hungary which reminded them of the real enemy – imperialism. What was involved was not simply the strength of traditional loyalties and the primacy of anti-imperialism. Equally important was the renewal of illusion embodied in the conviction that the Soviet Union was in the process of reforming itself. The leadership benefited from the notion of 'self-reform' and the emphasis it placed on optimism and the future; its configuration of the Twentieth Congress as drawing a line under the past which provided a prelude to new opportunities; the potential they discerned in Khrushchev's brand of de-Stalinisation; and the possibilities they believed that developments in Britain and the Third World were disclosing for extending Communism beyond the Soviet Union. Accepting this perspective, most of the rank and file took Hungary in their stride.[135] Party leaders were able to shepherd discussion away from fundamentals, the nature of Stalinism, what it meant and how it had occurred, and steer debate into safer channels, towards consideration of party policy and internal democracy. As early as August, Thompson's was the sole voice raised on the Yorkshire District Committee to challenge the suppression of The Reasoner. By December, the Executive's solidarity with the Russian invasion of Hungary – only Kettle and Max Morris opposed the resolution – had been endorsed by 240 party branches, with 69 against and 23 undecided.[136] The apparatus curbed the spread of opposition by refurbishing the myth of the Soviet Union and appealing to discipline and tradition, infused with workerism. As Saville remembered: '... anti-intellectualism within the Party was developing fast.'[137]

It was apparent from March 1956. A delegate to the CPGB congress referred to the danger of intellectuals disrupting the party. Pollitt was reported to have laid the ferment at their door.[138] There was an element of truth in this. That ultimately it was caricature was suggested by the number of workers who had quit the party by early 1957.[139] But intellectuals could always be found who were willing to scapegoat their dissenting comrades. Joan Simon claimed:

> ... there is a violent anti-Communist campaign going on and in such a situation, as Lenin often had to point out, intellectuals invariably have a tendency to lose their heads ... most intellectuals don't really know what class solidarity means, and so expressing their anger within the Party if it does not immediately meet their individual demands becomes almost an occupational disease at times of crisis.[140]

Kettle attacked 'the immodest parading of conscience and moral superiority which some of our middle-class intellectuals have gone in for'.[141] Andrew Rothstein compared the condition of the CPGB in 1957 with the position in the Russia of 1907 where workers had been 'bewildered and confused by groups of backboneless and spineless intellectuals who had turned in upon their own emotions and frustrations to rend the Party, instead of using their capabilities to rally themselves around it'.[142] When a number of intellectuals, Thompson among them, signed a critical letter published in the *New Statesman* and *Tribune*, they were censured. Matthews lamented:

> The Party leadership must accept its share of responsibility for not appreciating sufficiently that such comrades have special problems, are subjected to different influences from those that face comrades in the factories and need special help from the Party.[143]

Hungary confirmed the critics in their convictions.[144] But the opposition had never been unified and had always reflected different orientations. Saville and Thompson had resigned. Others, such as Hill, MacEwen and Henry Collins, believed something could still be salvaged within the party and focused on the Commission on Inner-Party Democracy, which met from September 1956 and the Special Twenty-Fifth Congress, scheduled for 19-22 April 1957. John Daniels, Fryer, Pearce and others were now working with the Trotskyists; they argued it was important to fight both inside and outside the CPGB while conceding that the defeat of the apparatus looked extremely unlikely. This approach was reflected in the establishment of Socialist Forums which brought together CPGB dissidents and others on the left. The movement received a fillip from the conference held at Wortley Hall, near Sheffield, which Saville and Thompson attended, on 27-28 April, just after the Special Conference. Some 25 CPGB members were involved, together with ex-members, independent socialists and Trotskyists, and a journal, *Forum,* was launched. It was a step towards the New Left.[145]

The commission was a procedural concession from a leadership intent on carrying the membership with it, while consigning the crisis to history without making political concessions. For their opponents, the commission and congress represented a last chance to make their case inside the CPGB. The commission constituted a cameo of the conflicting roles that intellectuals played in 1956 and confirmed the balance of forces inside the party. It included ten employees of the CPGB, notably Burns, Klugmann and the national organiser, Bill Lauchlan, as well as several regional organisers. Its secretary, Betty Reid, a university graduate who ran the Central Organising Department and the Security Committee, was a byword for orthodoxy which she enforced as the party's expert on Trotskyism. Its chair was the veteran *apparatchik* John Mahon, who 'did not see his role as leading an investigation; he saw it as securing the defeat of the "revisionists"'.[146] There were five rank-and-file members – Hill; MacEwen, who in the course of the inquiry resigned from his post as features editor of the *Daily Worker*; two teachers, Peter Cadogan, who subsequently joined the Trotskyists, and Joe Cheek; and the motor-worker shop steward Kevin Halpin. The commission was split from the start. The majority were determined to restrict discussion to institutional arrangements and the working of democratic centralism. Cadogan, Hill and MacEwen, supported by Halpin, wanted a wider investigation covering the Tito debacle, how the party press had regulated discussion of the 'Secret Speech' and how democratic centralism operated in the CPSU.[147]

The commission pitted apparatus intellectuals against dissident intellectuals. In a typical Stalinist exercise, the latter were represented but heavily outnumbered while the former did their duty and, on slender evidence, salved their consciences by expressing off-stage the routine doubts.[148] Halpin, Cheek and Harry Bourne, a regional organiser, supported the majority report with reservations. Cadogan – who Reid branded 'a traitor' for sending a letter to the *News Chronicle* condemning the invasion of Hungary, for which he was suspended from membership – Hill and

MacEwen produced their own document.[149] The majority endorsed the status quo. They rejected charges that the Political Committee, made up of full-time staff, *de facto* controlled the Executive Committee – which theoretically governed the party between congresses – and dominated the apparatus, partly by means of the recommended list of nominees for election to the Executive. The majority saw little wrong with the monolithic conception of the party, which it claimed emulated democracy in British trade unions, rather than stemming from changes in the CPSU in 1920-21. Problems lay not with the Russian military model, the invocation of 'iron discipline' and the subordination of democracy to centralism, but with the failure of members to make this brand of bureaucratic centralism work through insufficient interest and activity.[150]

The minority confirmed the unrealised potential of 1956 by rejecting the Stalinist model. They urged the lifting of the ban on factions and the abolition of the leadership slate for Executive elections. Extending party democracy, their report argued, was a necessary precondition for organic membership commitment to centralism and unity in action. The CPGB, it insisted, in a reproach to its history, had to be reformed as an autonomous party with its own programme and independent politics. Uncritical adherence to Russian policy:

> … identifies Communism in the minds of British people with the denial of personal freedom … Communism's greatest strength is, or should be, the truth. Without access to the truth Communists cannot take the right decisions … truth cannot be dissected into those parts which are helpful to our cause, and therefore publishable, and those parts which are harmful, and must therefore be suppressed. Truth has to be taken as a whole, and the more damaging truth may be, the more necessary it is to know it, if mistakes are to be put right, and injustices undone.[151]

That this eloquent rebuke to intellectuals who refused to live by the values to which they paid lip-service fell on deaf ears, was illustrated at the Special Congress. The intention was to end the turmoil on the leadership's terms, and the congress achieved closure on that basis. To read its reports and resolutions is to reread the leadership statements of 1956 reproduced in this book. Gollan's keynote speech gave precedence to the fight for peace; the economic situation in Britain; the failure of the Conservative government; and the need for unity with Labour. The General Secretary stressed again the achievements of Russian socialism, despite Stalin's abuses. He repeated:

It has been argued that Stalin's mistakes arose out of some inherent characteristics of the Soviet Socialist system. On the contrary, the system had steadily developed, and proved able to face its supreme test only because it was a people's system. Political power was in the hands of the people.[152]

The Political Resolution claimed:

... the terms 'Stalinism' and 'anti-Stalinism' have been spread by enemies of Communism and found echoes among some Communists. The mistakes made by Stalin ... must not be seen in isolation from the great services he rendered to the Socialist development and human advance of the Soviet people.[153]

There was no shedding of illusions in the workers' state and no back-pedalling over the crushing of the advance of the Hungarian people:

If counter-revolution had won, Hungary would have been a war-base in Central Europe, a Hungary on the way back to capitalism. If the Soviet government had not responded ... they would have failed in their class duty.[154]

As for their opponents, their 'revisionist ideas' had engendered a retreat from Marxism to social democracy:

It has been said that many of our best comrades have left the Party. We cannot agree. They are not our best comrades, otherwise they would not have left ... to abandon the Communist Party is to abandon Marxism.[155]

Mahon's report on party democracy rejected the minority report out of hand: it was impermissible to permit members '... to campaign for a minority viewpoint; to give individuals the right to publish their own material outside Party control; that branches should have the right to mandate their delegate to Congress ... Such proposals seek to elevate the individual above the collective, the minority above the majority ...'[156]

The Bourbons of British Stalinism did not yield an inch. Amendments were heavily defeated amidst acclamation of the virtues of democracy in the Soviet Union from Frank Haxell, General Secretary of the electricians' union, probably Britain's least democratic trade union. Michael Barratt Brown, Hill, Levy and the writer Alick West gave voice to aspects of the critique of

Stalinism developed since the 'Secret Speech'. They were opposed by Bush, Kettle and Rothstein, each of whom attacked their fellow intellectuals – despite Gollan's insistence that the CPGB was only opposed to those who succumbed to bourgeois ideology[157] – and equally stridently by union activists led by Reg Birch. His fellow shop stewards, Johnny McLoughlin – who argued that British Communists shared the responsibility for the injustices Communists had perpetrated in other countries – and Brian Behan – who having initially hesitated, now opposed the invasion of Hungary and called for a re-evaluation of how Stalinism had developed – carried the banner of dissent. When the dust settled, the leadership remained firmly in the saddle. The Minority Report of the Commission on Democracy was rejected by 472 votes to 23 with 15 abstentions.[158]

In the face of powerful arguments for renewal the party reaffirmed its past. In the longer term the Hammersmith Congress did not quite play out as 'the Congress of Re-Stalinisation' that the Trotskyists marshalled outside the hall by Fryer and Gerry Healy had predicted.[159] In a changing world the cement that had held the CPGB together continued to crumble: in little more than a decade the leadership would find itself disowning the Russian invasion of Czechoslovakia. More immediately, CPGB leaders who had enjoyed some success in identifying criticism with the intellectuals were unable to stave off a steep decline in membership which went beyond the intellectuals. It dropped by 27.7 per cent from 34,117 in June 1956 to 24,670 in February 1958. At that point 9447 members had quit the party.[160] There was subsequently some recovery. By 1964, the party had more members, 34,281, than it had at the beginning of 1956. Perhaps most importantly, 1956, the *New Reasoner* and the New Left did not succeed in creating a real, enduring alternative, in the shape of a small, anti-Stalinist, socialist party representing a plurality of opinion, internal democracy, a viable programme and a convincing strategy. That this remains an unfulfilled project seven decades on, illuminates the inability of the British left fully to absorb the lessons of 1956.

For the CPGB something had died and things would never be the same. After 1956, there was a loss of certainty, a flagging in confidence, an erosion of the earlier sense of superiority and mission. Its claim to exercise a monopoly on Marxism was seriously dented. It has been argued that the death of Stalin, the Berlin uprising, the rehabilitation of Tito, the 'Secret Speech' and the invasion of Hungary provoked 'a qualitative shift within the collective consciousness of the European intelligentsia in general' away from sympathy with Communism.[161] In Britain, where such support had always been shallow, the process arguably commenced in 1947. But it was vindicated by 1956 and illustrated in the emergence of the New Left: unlike the CPGB it gave intellectuals freedom to think, to innovate, and to begin to develop a pluralistic rather than a monolithic Marxism. The contradiction between the CPGB genus and the genuine intellectual was voiced by Gollan:

> Our Party intellectuals, whilst they fight for Marxist ideas within their own particular fields, can play a part of the greatest importance. What we have opposed, and will always oppose, is the introduction of petty-bourgeois ideas and practice into our Party theory and life.[162]

Thinking which diverged significantly from 'Marxism', as defined in Stalinist terms by the leaders of the CPSU and the CPGB, reflected the consciousness and interests of a hostile class and could not be tolerated.

The CPGB limped on into old age. The failure of its critics to deepen and extend the analysis sketched in *The Reasoner* into a root-and-branch rejection of Stalinism meant that the party, its ideas and the ideological baggage of thousands of former members continued to be a stumbling block to left-wing regroupment and the creation of a political alternative which was fully conscious of the debacle of British Communism and the dead-end it represented. Impressive if exaggerated economic statistics, the Sputniks, Yuri Gagarin and the Cosmonauts provided a brief respite for the flaking Soviet myth. By the 1970s Communist influence in the unions, often the result of work in earlier decades, was greater than ever before, the tight control over intellectuals was relaxed and recruitment recommenced. But the party was fissiparous, lacking in cohesion and leaking membership, which declined to 20,559 by the end of the decade. A degenerative gene which interacted with the toxic dependence on the Soviet Union was the CPGB's economism and adaptation to trade unionism. For a decade after 1956, the power of the Russian connection endured, and the funding of a depleted CPGB by the CPSU received a new lease of life.[163] After Czechoslovakia, the cult of the Soviet Union was still present but diminished. On the one hand, Eurocommunism burgeoned; on the other, identification of socialist progress with trade-union militancy intensified. Fragmentation set the stage for implosion. Fittingly, and in accordance with its history, the party's demise coincided with the disintegration of its guiding star, the Soviet Union.[164]

NOTES

Thanks to Paul Flewers for his comments on an earlier draft of this essay.

1   For discussion of the Russian connection and the literature, see, for example, John McIlroy and Alan Campbell, 'Histories of the British Communist Party: A User's Guide', *Labour History Review*, Volume 68, no. 1, 2003, pp. 33-59; John McIlroy and Alan Campbell, 'A Peripheral Vision: Communist Historiography in Britain', *American Communist History*, Volume 4, no. 2, 2005, pp. 125-57; John McIlroy, 'Restoring Stalinism to Communist History', *Critique: Journal of Socialist Theory*, Volume 41, no. 4, 2013, pp. 599-622.

2   The primacy of this relationship in understanding the CPGB is denied or evaded by certain writers, some of whom feel obliged to bolster a shaky case by caricaturing our interpretation. One historian claims that we argue that 'the leaders and members of the parties of the Comintern were little more than puppets dancing to Moscow's tune'; Communists, he states, 'were loyal to Moscow because they wished to be' (Neil Redfern, *Class or Nation: Communists, Imperialism and Two World Wars* (IB Tauris, London, 2005), p. 72). Nothing resembling Redfern's statement appears anywhere in the article he cites. Rather it observes: 'The Russians misdirected the anti-capitalism of British workers. But this was ultimately a matter of consent not coercion.' We specifically distanced ourselves from conceptions of '"automaticity" with British activists executing Russian instructions like robots' (McIlroy and Campbell, 'Histories', pp. 41, 48). An article published three years before Redfern's book rejected the idea that CPGB members were 'robots', 'slaves' or 'marionettes' of Moscow. It affirmed that their subordination 'was largely the product of a voluntary impulse on the part of British Communists. In the end, compliance stemmed from the beliefs and values of party members projected onto the Comintern and the USSR. It was freely chosen not coerced ...' (John McIlroy and Alan Campbell, '"Nina Ponomareva's Hats": The New Revisionism, the Communist International and the Communist Party of Great Britain, 1920-1930', *Labour/Le Travail*, no. 49, 2002, pp. 159, 167)

3   'Editorial: Taking Stock', *The Reasoner*, no. 1, July 1956, p. 5.

4   Eric Hobsbawm, 'Letters', *World News*, 26 January 1957. Nina Ponomareva, a Russian discus-thrower competing in the games at London's White City in 1956, was arrested for allegedly stealing five hats from C&A Modes in Oxford Street. The Soviet Union withdrew its team in protest at this 'provocation', but the *Daily Worker* regretted this response.

5   'Editorial: The Case for Socialism', *The Reasoner*, no. 2, September 1956, p. 4.

6   Ronald L Meek, 'What Should We Do About *The Reasoner*?', *The Reasoner*, no. 2, p. 8.

7   For discussion of the early Cold War see, for example, John Lewis Gaddis, *We Now Know: Rethinking Cold War History* (Oxford University Press, Oxford, 1997); Vladislav Zubok and Constantine Pleshakov, *Inside the Kremlin's Cold War: From Stalin to Khrushchev* (Harvard University Press, London, 1996); Geoffrey Roberts, *Stalin's Wars: From World War to Cold War* (Yale University Press, New Haven, 2006); Vladislav Zubok, *A Failed Empire: The Soviet Union in the Cold War: From Stalin to Gorbachev* (University of North Carolina Press, Chapel Hill, 2007); Melvyn P Leffler and Odd Arne Westad (eds), *The Cambridge History of the Cold War, Volume 1: Origins* (Cambridge University Press, Cambridge, 2010); Jonathan Haslam, *Russia's Cold War* (Yale University Press, New Haven, 2011); Robert Gellately, *Stalin's Curse: Battling for Communism in War and Cold War* (Oxford University Press, Oxford, 2013).

8   Gaddis, *We Now Know*, p. 28; Zubok, *Failed Empire*, pp. 19-20.

9   Quoted in Gaddis, *We Now Know*, p. 31. Gaddis emphasises 'Stalin's opportunism, his tendency to advance in situations where he thought he could do so without provoking

too strong a response' (p. 72). See generally Vladimir O Pechatov, 'The Soviet Union and the World 1944-1953', in Leffler and Westad, *Cambridge History*, pp. 67-89.

10   For Eastern Europe, see RC Raack, *Stalin's Drive to the West 1938-1945: The Origins of the Cold War* (Stanford University Press, Stanford, 1995); Norman Naimark, 'The Sovietisation of Eastern Europe 1944-1953', in Leffler and Westad, *Cambridge History*, pp. 175-97; Timothy Snyder, *Bloodlands: Europe Between Hitler and Stalin* (Basic Books, New York, 2010); Anne Applebaum, *Iron Curtain: The Crushing of Eastern Europe, 1944-1956* (Allen Lane, London, 2012).

11   Noreen Branson, *History of the Communist Party of Great Britain 1941-1951* (Lawrence and Wishart, London, 1997), pp. 156-59. Between Stalin's termination of the Comintern in 1943, aimed at cementing the Grand Alliance, and the launch of Cominform, liaison with national parties was exercised directly by the CPSU; see Mark Kramer, 'The Role of the CPSU International Department in Soviet Foreign Relations and National Security Policy', *Soviet Studies*, Volume 42, no. 3, 1990, pp. 429-46.

12   François Furet, *The Passing of an Illusion: The Idea of Communism in the Twentieth Century* (University of Chicago Press, London, 1999). For the impact of these ideas on the CPGB, see Jim Fyrth (ed), *Britain, Fascism and the Popular Front* (Lawrence and Wishart, London, 1985).

13   Furet, *Passing*, pp. 396-437.

14   G Procacci (ed), *The Cominform: Minutes of the Three Conferences 1947/1948/1949* (Feltrinelli, Milan, 1994). The CPGB was not invited to join. It was informed of policy via the French party and the Cominform journal, *For a Lasting Peace, For a People's Democracy*.

15   Haslam concludes, too definitively, that at the termination of hostilities: 'Stalin and his closest supporters had every intention of seeking domination over Europe ... Quite apart from the Marxist-Leninist impulse the belief was firmly fixed that Russians had a right to dominate the continent in light of the enormous blood sacrifice of war. It is a theme reiterated at unexpected moments in subsequent years.' (Haslam, *Russia's Cold War*, pp. 395-96) Elements of ambivalence and uncertainty were always present. A more persuasive interpretation is that in 1945 Stalin was determined to control Eastern and Central Europe while, as openings emerged, extending Russian influence and pressure in what he accepted was imperialism's sphere in Western Europe through coalition governments of the left, spearheaded by the French and Italian Communist Parties.

16   Procacci, *Cominform*, passim; Fernando Claudín, *The Communist Movement: From Comintern to Cominform* (Penguin, Harmondsworth, 1975), pp. 455-79, 576-97.

17   Quoted in Claudín, *Communist Movement*, p. 580.

18   E P Thompson, 'Reply to George Matthews', *The Reasoner*, no. 1, p. 15.

19   Thompson later reflected: '*The Short History of the CPSU (B)*, which was the fundamental "education" text of Communists from Stalingrad to Cardiff, from Calcutta to Marseilles, is a document of the very first historical importance – a gigantic historical fabrication for the induction of idealist and military mental habits.' (E P Thompson, 'Edgell Rickword', *Persons and Polemics* (Merlin, London, 1994), p. 241)

20   See, for example, Sam Aaronovitch, 'Stalin As an Economist', *World News and Views*, 10 December 1949; Maurice Cornforth, 'Stalin and Dialectical Materialism', *World News and Views*, 10 December 1949; JD Bernal, 'Stalin As a Scientist', *Modern Quarterly*, Volume 8, no. 3, Autumn 1953, pp. 133-43; Christopher Hill, 'Stalin and the Science of History', *Modern Quarterly*, Volume 8, no. 3, Autumn 1953, pp. 198-212.

21   George Matthews, 'Stalin's British Road', *Changes*, 23 September 1991. For short surveys see Henry Pelling, *The British Communist Party: A Historical Profile* (A and C Black, London, 1958), pp. 140-69; Willie Thompson, *The Good Old Cause: British Communism 1920-1991* (Pluto Press, London, 1992), pp. 76-99; James Eaden and David

Renton, *The Communist Party of Great Britain since 1920* (Palgrave, Basingstoke, 2002), pp. 108-17; Philip Deery, '"The Secret Battalion": Communism in Britain during the Cold War', *Contemporary British History*, Volume 13, 1999, pp. 1-28.

22   For 'the thaw' see Joshua Rubinstein, The Last Days of Stalin (Yale University Press, New Haven, 2016); Haslam, *Russia's Cold War*, pp. 133-63; and Robert Service, 'The Road to the Twentieth Party Congress: An Analysis of Events Surrounding the Central Committee Plenum of July 1953', *Soviet Studies*, Volume 33, no. 2, 1981, pp. 232-45. The CPGB mourned Stalin as 'the greatest working-class leader, genius and creative thinker that the world has ever known' (*Daily Worker*, 7 March 1953). Harry Pollitt eulogised: 'Stalin – loved as no other man in world history has ever been loved by working people … Stalin – who has written golden pages in world history whose lustre time can never efface … with tear-blinded eyes and a grief we have not the language at our command to describe, we swear that our Communist Party and our *Daily Worker*, will do all in our power to pick up that banner of national independence that Comrade Stalin spoke about … ' (*Daily Worker*, 6 March 1953)

23   'The Case for Socialism', *The Reasoner*, no. 2, p. 3.

24   Quoted, Pelling, *British Communist Party*, p. 14; Claudín, *Communist Movement*, pp. 576-80.

25   Quoted in Andy Croft, 'Authors Take Sides', in Geoff Andrews, Nina Fishman and Kevin Morgan (eds), *Opening the Books: Essays on the Social and Cultural History of the British Communist Party* (Pluto Press, London, 1995), p. 92.

26   *Daily Worker*, 12 September 1949.

27   Branson, *History*, pp. 206-08, 231; Steve Parsons, 'British McCarthyism and the Intellectuals', in Jim Fyrth (ed), *Labour's Promised Land: Culture and Society in Labour Britain 1945-51* (Lawrence and Wishart, London, 1995), pp. 224-46; Karen Potter, 'British McCarthyism', in Rhodri Jeffrey-Jones and Andrew Lownie (eds), *North American Spies: New Revisionist Essays* (Edinburgh University Press, Edinburgh, 1991).

28   Brian Pollitt, 'Voyage Round My Father', in Phil Cohen (ed), *Children of the Revolution* (Lawrence and Wishart, London, 1997), p. 113.

29   William Gallacher, 'Joseph Stalin', *Communist Review*, December 1949, pp. 739-44.

30   Eric Heffer, *Never a Yes Man* (Verso, London, 1991), p. 38; and see Edward Upward's novel, *The Rotten Elements* (Penguin, Harmondsworth, 1978).

31   Meek, 'What Should We Do …?', p. 8.

32   Thompson, 'Edgell Rickword', p. 240.

33   Heffer, *Yes Man*, pp. 33-39; Lawrence Parker, *The Kick Inside: Revolutionary Opposition in the CPGB, 1960-1991* (November Publishing, London, 2007). The *Daily Worker*, 26 November 1945, reported that dissenting resolutions 'were defeated by overwhelming majorities'.

34   Andy Croft (ed.), *A Weapon in the Struggle* (Pluto Press, London, 1998), pp. 152-53; Thompson, 'Edgell Rickword', pp. 232-38.

35   Harry McShane and Joan Smith, *Harry McShane: No Mean Fighter* (Pluto Press, London, 1978), pp. 242-51.

36   Branson, *History*, p. 196. The party archives contain letters questioning aspects of party policy, see, for example, Peoples' History Museum, Manchester, Communist Party Archive (CPA) CP/Cent/EC/02/02, Discussion on EC Report, 8 July 1950 – but no discernible changes in response.

37   Heffer, *Yes Man*, p. 38; Eric Heffer, 'Joseph Stalin', *Independent Magazine*, 30 December 1989. In the early 1950s, the Communist folksinger Ewan MacColl wrote the *Ballad of Joe Stalin*:
Joe Stalin was a mighty man and he made a mighty plan
He harnessed nature to the plough to work for the good of man
He's hammered out the future, the forgeman he has been

And he's made the worker's state the best the world has ever seen.
(Quoted in Raphael Samuel, *The Lost World of British Communism* (Verso, London, 1985), p. 136)

38　E P Thompson, 'The Politics of Theory', in Raphael Samuel (ed), *People's History and Socialist Theory* (Routledge and Kegan Paul, London, 1981), p. 402.

39　When Thompson inquired, 'Where was Althusser in 1956?', Perry Anderson retorted: 'Where was Thompson in 1952 (Doctors' Plot) or 1951 (Slánský Trial), for example?' See E P Thompson, *The Poverty of Theory* (Merlin, London, 1978), p. 324; Perry Anderson, *Arguments Within English Marxism* (Verso, London, 1980), p. 117.

40　Paul Flewers, *The New Civilisation? Understanding Stalin's Soviet Union 1929-1941* (Francis Boutle, London, 2008); Tony Judt, *Past Imperfect: French Intellectuals 1944-1956* (University of California Press, Berkeley, 1992), pp. 168-86.

41　The censorship of Soviet artists in the *Zhdanovshchina* which affected, among others, Anna Akhamatova, Mikhail Zoshchenko, Sergei Prokoviev and Dimitri Shostakovich, was defended by CPGB 'experts' such as John Lewis and Emile Burns, and criticised by British journals, notably *Horizon*. Some on the non-CPGB left tried to address the issues – see Raymond Williams, 'The Soviet Literary Controversy in Retrospect', *Politics and Letters*, Summer 1947, pp. 21-31. For a succinct summary of the purges and labour camps in Stalin's last years, see Moshe Lewin, *The Soviet Century* (Verso, London, 2005), pp. 99-141. For anti-Semitism, see Gennadi Kostyrchenko, *Out of the Red Shadows: Anti-Semitism in Stalin's Russia* (Prometheus Books, New York, 1995); Joshua Rubinstein, *Stalin's Great Pogrom* (Yale University Press. New Haven, 2001).

42　Ignazio Silone in Richard Crossman (ed), *The God That Failed: Six Studies in Communism* (Hamish Hamilton, London, 1950), p. 118.

43　Doris Lessing, *Walking in the Shade: Volume 2 of My Autobiography* (Harper Collins, London, 1997), p. 52.

44　Lessing, *Walking in the Shade*, pp. 53-54. Lessing cited Arthur Koestler's observation that most Communists were aware of what was occurring under Stalinism but had their personal 'secret explanation': the truth was being kept from 'Uncle Joe', rank-and-file Communists would eventually organise to remove a corrupt leadership, and so on.

45　In that light, Judt concluded that fellow-travellers whose perceived independence was not compromised by membership provided Communism's most valued assets (Judt, *Past Imperfect*, p. 118). Like other Communist parties, the CPGB adopted a broad definition of intellectuals – scholars of all kinds, scientists, artists, performers, teachers, members of the liberal professions. David Caute points up significant differences within this category between, for example, creators and disseminators of ideas: see David Caute, *Communism and the French Intellectuals* (Andre Deutsch, London, 1964), p. 12.

46　Perry Anderson, 'Components of the National Culture', *New Left Review*, no. 50, July-August 1968, pp. 3-57; Neal Wood, *Communism and the British Intellectuals* (Victor Gollancz, London, 1959), pp. 75-79.

47　R Palme Dutt, 'Intellectuals and Communism', *Communist Review*, September 1932, p. 425, emphasis in original. See generally Wood, *Communism and the British Intellectuals*; John McIlroy, 'The Establishment of Intellectual Orthodoxy and the Stalinisation of British Communism 1928-1933', *Past and Present*, no. 192, 2006, pp. 187-226; Steve Parsons, *Communism in the Professions: The Organisation of the British Communist Party Among Professional Workers, 1933-1956* (unpublished PhD thesis, University of Warwick, 1990). Taking account of the differences between France and Britain and their respective Communist parties, there is useful material in Caute, *Communism and the French Intellectuals*; and Judt, *Past Imperfect*. On the later period, see Gavin Bowd, *L'Interminable Enterrement: Le Communisme et Les Intellectuels Français depuis 1956* (Digraphe, Paris, 1999).

48   *Harry Pollitt Speaks* (CPGB, London, 1935), p. 33. For some of the background to the 1930s' generation, see Noel Annan, *Our Age* (Weidenfeld and Nicolson, London, 1990); Valentine Cunningham, *British Writers of the Thirties* (Oxford University Press, Oxford, 1988).

49   Branson, *History*, pp. 169-71.

50   Haldane undertook 'a phased withdrawal' from the CPGB at the time of the Lysenko controversy and officially resigned in 1956. Bernal, who left in 1933, worked closely with the party in the 1950s: see Gary Werskey, *The Visible College* (Free Association Books, London, 1988), pp. 166, 302-30.

51   John McIlroy, 'The Demise of the National Council of Labour Colleges', in Brian Simon (ed), *The Search for Enlightenment: The Working Class and Adult Education in the Twentieth Century* (Lawrence and Wishart, London, 1990), pp. 188-89, 203 nn 86, 87.

52   James Klugmann, *From Trotsky to Tito* (Lawrence and Wishart, London, 1951); Eric Hobsbawm, *Interesting Times: A Twentieth-Century Life* (Allen Lane, London, 2002), pp. 122-24. See also Geoff Eley, *Forging Democracy: The History of the Left in Europe, 1850-2000* (Oxford University Press, Oxford, 2002), p. 309.

53   The flavour of Klugmann's work, and the ethos of a party in which nobody challenged it, can be seen from the following passage, typical of many: 'When you read of the secret agreements between the Trotskyites and German fascism, the plans for the internal sabotage of the Soviet regime, for the assassination of the Soviet leaders and for the restoration of Russian capitalism subservient to German imperialism, you read of the precursor of the Titoite agreements with the successor of German fascism – American imperialism ... Between the Trotskyites and the Titoites there are the closest links – links of person, links of purpose, links of method. In many cases, the Titoites of today are the Trotskyites of yesterday.' (Klugmann, *From Trotsky*, p. 85)

54   See the comments in Hobsbawm, *Interesting Times*, p. 209.

55   Arnold Kettle arguably overstated the problem: 'Their principal trouble is a persistent desire to have the best of both worlds, to have their cake and eat it – to retain the privileges of their position in bourgeois society while at the same time attacking bourgeois society and associating themselves with the socialist movement.' (Quoted in John Saville, 'The XXth Congress and the British Communist Party', in Ralph Miliband and John Saville (eds), *Socialist Register 1976* (Merlin, London, 1976, p. 22) The problem could be resisted but it was always present.

56   Ken Alexander, 'Democratic Centralism', *The Reasoner*, no. 1, p. 9.

57   For example, Hobsbawm's main activity after 1951 was in the Historians' Group to the exclusion of 'branch work – organisation, canvassing, selling the *Daily Worker* ... for which I had no natural taste or suitable temperament. From then on I operated entirely in academic or intellectual groups.' (Hobsbawm, *Interesting Times*, p. 190) Brian Simon had similar recollections – conversations with author. See also John McIlroy, 'A Communist Historian in 1956: Brian Pearce and the Crisis of British Stalinism', *Revolutionary History*, Volume 9, no. 3, 2006, pp. 84-145.

58   'Marxist' [Brian Pearce], 'Letters', *New Statesman*, 19 May 1956.

59   Hobsbawm, *Interesting Times*, p. 202.

60   Despite its limitations, Kenneth Newton, *The Sociology of British Communism* (Allen Lane, London, 1969), contains some insights.

61   Thompson, 'Edgell Rickword', pp. 238-39. Thompson is writing about the period 'from the mid-1930s to the late 1940s'.

62   Branson, *History*, p. 176.

63   Malcolm MacEwen, *The Greening of a Red* (Pluto Press, London, 1991), pp. 179-80.

64   Quoted Terry Brotherstone, '1956: Tom Kemp and Others', in Terry Brotherstone

and Geoff Pilling (eds), *History, Economic History and the Future of Marxism: Essays in Memory of Tom Kemp* (Porcupine Press, London, 1996), p. 297.

65   Hobsbawm, *Interesting Times*, p. 204, quoting 'Letter', *World News*, 26 January 1957.

66   Hobsbawm, *Interesting Times*, pp. 192-93.

67   See, for example, John Saville, *Memoirs from the Left* (Merlin, London, 2003), p. 91; John McIlroy, 'John Saville and Stalinism', in this volume. Thompson 'had a number of expressed disagreements with the full-time officials of the Yorkshire District'; see John Saville, 'Edward Thompson, the Communist Party and 1956', in Ralph Miliband and Leo Panitch (eds), *Socialist Register 1994* (Merlin, London, 1994), p. 26.

68   'Interview with E P Thompson', in Henry Abelove *et al* (eds), *Visions of History* (Manchester University Press, Manchester, 1983), p. 11. See also Scott Hamilton, *The Crisis of Theory: E P Thompson, the New Left and Postwar British Politics* (Manchester University Press, Manchester, 2013), p. 87 n. 6.

69   'Letters', *World News*, 4 August 1956; Michael Barratt Brown, *Seekers: A Twentieth-Century Life* (Spokesman, Nottingham, 2013).

70   *The Times*, 23 April 1957. 'Those of us who have a special knowledge of the Soviet Union have a grave responsibility for not speaking out about things we knew or suspected – and that goes for me as well as for Andrew Rothstein. But the leadership bears the gravest responsibility of all.' (CPA, CP/Cent/Cong/10/06) See Hill, 'Stalin and the Science of History'; KE Holme (Christopher Hill), *The Two Commonwealths* (George Harrap, London, 1945).

71   Doris Lessing, 'A Letter to the Editors', *The Reasoner*, no. 2, p. 12.

72   MacEwen, *Greening*, p. 179. Unlike others, MacEwen protested to Pollitt, without success.

73   Hyman Levy, 'The Place of Unorthodoxy in Marxism', *The Reasoner*, no. 2, p. 15.

74   Meek, 'What Should We Do …?' p. 8.

75   Alison McLeod, *The Death of Uncle Joe* (Merlin, London, 1997), pp. 12, 154.

76   For the speech and its context, see Service, 'The Road to the Twentieth Congress'; William J Tompson, *Khrushchev: A Political Life* (MacMillan, London, 1995), pp. 114-60; William Taubman, *Khrushchev: The Man and His Era* (Free Press, New York, 2003), pp. 270-91; Vittorio Vidali, *Diary of the Twentieth Congress of the Communist Party of the Soviet Union* (Journeyman, Hassocks, 1984).

77   See Paul Flewers, 'The Unexpected Denunciation: The Reception of Khrushchev's "Secret Speech" in Britain', *Revolutionary History*, Volume 9, no. 3, 2006, pp. 31-71.

78   Fred Westacott, *Shaking the Chains* (Joe Clark, Chesterfield, 2002), pp. 296-97.

79   Quoted in Francis Beckett, *Enemy Within: The Rise and Fall of the British Communist Party* (John Murray, London, 1995), pp. 139-40.

80   Donald Filtzer, *Soviet Workers and De-Stalinization: The Contradictions of the Modern System of Soviet Production Relations 1953-1964* (Cambridge University Press, Cambridge, 1992); Donald Filtzer, *The Khrushchev Era: De-Stalinization and the Limits of Reform in the USSR 1953-1964* (MacMillan, Basingstoke, 1993); Polly Jones, *The Dilemmas of De-Stalinization: Negotiating Cultural and Social Change Under Khrushchev* (Routledge, London, 2006).

81   'Secret Speech of Khrushchev Concerning the "Cult of the Individual", Delivered at the Twentieth Congress of the Communist Party of the Soviet Union, 25 February 1956', in *The Anti-Stalin Campaign and International Communism* (Columbia University Press, New York, 1956). See also NS Khrushchev, *The Crimes of the Stalin Era: Special Report to the Twentieth Congress of the Communist Party of the Soviet Union* (New Leader, New York, 1956).

82   Khrushchev, 'Secret Speech', pp. 29-89.

83   See, for example, Bill Lomax, *The Hungarian Revolution 1956* (Alison and Busby, London, 1976); György Litvan (ed), *The Hungarian Revolution of 1956* (Longmans, London, 1996); 'Special Issue: Remembering 1956', *Revolutionary History*, Volume 9,

no. 3, 2006; Keith Flett (ed), *1956 and All That* (Cambridge Scholars, Newcastle, 2007); Simon Hall, *1956: The World in Revolt* (Faber and Faber, London, 2015).

84   Khrushchev and Mikoyan referred in the open meetings to the CPSU Central Committee's condemnation of 'the cult of personality' as 'alien to Marxism-Leninism'; Khrushchev's four-hour presentation in the closed session was based on his own treatment of an earlier report to the CPSU Central Committee by the Pospelov Commission: see Taubman, *Khrushchev*, pp. 270-91. Pyotr Nikolayevich Pospelov, chief ideologist of the party, 'had been a great supporter of Stalin until he became a great supporter of Khrushchev', see Julian Barnes, *The Noise of Time* (Jonathan Cape, London, 2016), p. 148.

85   *World News*, 3, 11 and 17 March 1956.

86   Wood, *Communism*, p. 195.

87   MacEwen, *Greening*, p. 181.

88   For an account of reactions across the political spectrum, see Flewers, 'Unexpected Denunciation'.

89   CPA, CPGB/Cent/Cong/09/02, Resolutions and Proceedings of the Twenty-Fourth Congress of the Communist Party.

90   Robert Service, *A History of Twentieth-Century Russia* (Penguin, Harmondsworth, 1998), pp. 338-41; McLeod, *Uncle Joe*, pp. 68-70.

91   CPA, CP/Cent/Cong/09/03, Notes for Report on Twenty-Fourth Congress.

92   MacEwen, *Greening*, p. 183. Pollitt's state of mind at this point is illustrated by McLeod's account of a meeting on 12 March: 'Pollitt shouted back at his hecklers, "Defending the Soviet Union gives you a headache? You think I don't know that? All right – if it gives you a headache take an aspirin"' (McLeod, *Uncle Joe*, p. 57)

93   Saville, 'The XXth Congress', p. 30.

94   Margot Heinemann, '1956 and the Communist Party', in Ralph Miliband and John Saville (eds), *Socialist Register 1976* (Merlin, London, 1976), pp. 45-46. Heinemann exaggerates Togliatti's critical stance; see Tobias Abse, 'Palmiro Togliatti and the Italian Communist Party in 1956', *Revolutionary History*, Volume 9, no. 3, 2006, pp. 182-207.

95   MacEwen, *Greening*, p. 183.

96   Hobsbawm, *Interesting Times*, p. 209.

97   MacEwen, *Greening*, pp. 181-82. Cf McLeod, *Uncle Joe*, p. 101: 'Campbell said he had been in Moscow during the purges of the 1930s, he had known what was going on but what could he do? How could he say anything in public when the war was coming and the Soviet Union was going to be attacked?' McLeod continues: 'This might have been some excuse for silence. However Campbell was not silent. He wrote a book, *Soviet Policy and Its Critics*. In this he defended every action of Stalin and argued that the purge trials were genuine.'

98   Geoff Andrews, *Endgames and New Times: The Final Years of British Communism 1964-1991* (Lawrence and Wishart, London, 2004), pp. 166-77 n. 120.

99   Including apparently suicide, see John Callaghan, *Rajani Palme Dutt: A Study in British Stalinism* (Lawrence and Wishart, London, 1993), p. 270.

100   Flewers, 'Unexpected Denunciation', pp. 65-67.

101   *The Dethronement of Stalin* (Manchester Guardian, Manchester, 1956); *The 20th Congress (CPSU) and World Trotskyism* (New Park, London, 1957); Branko Lazitch, *Le Rapport Khrouchtchev et Son Histoire* (Éditions du Seuil, Paris, 1976). Ron Thompson, a Lancashire miner and member since 1951 of the Young Communist League, recalled: 'I remember reading the *Observer* and I was devastated as it shattered all the conceptions of Stalin as the great leader, and the Soviet Union as the leading force for socialism.' (Quoted in Bill Hunter, *Lifelong Apprenticeship: The Life and Times of a Revolutionary* (Index Books, London, 1997), p. 337)

102   Eric Hobsbawm, '1956: Gareth Stedman Jones interviews Eric Hobsbawm', *Marxism Today*, November 1986, p. 19.

103 CPA, CP/Cent/Cult/05/13, Minutes of the Historians' Group, 8 April 1956. This resolution was passed to the party's Executive Committee.
104 Thompson, *Poverty of Theory*, p. i.
105 CPA, CP/Cent/Org/98/04, Thompson to Klugmann, 15 and 22 March 1956.
106 There is an insightful description of their relationship in Michael Newman, *Ralph Miliband and the Politics of the New Left* (Merlin Press, London, 2002), p. 69. The comment that Saville was 'an experienced organiser, having spent the whole of his adult life in political and trade-union work of one kind or another' is, nonetheless, an exaggeration.
107 The CPGB leaders maintained their restrictive stance, even after Pollitt, Gollan and the Yorkshire organiser, Bert Ramelson, had consulted the CPSU leaders in Moscow; *Daily Worker*, 17 July 1956. Unless otherwise indicated, the following account is based on Saville, 'XXth Congress'; Saville, 'Thompson', pp. 20-31; Saville, *Memoirs*, pp. 101-27.
108 Saville, 'Thompson', p. 24.
109 Saville, 'XXth Congress', p. 4.
110 CPA/CP/Cent/Org/98/04, Thompson to Klugmann, 2 May 1956; Thompson to Ramelson, 28 May 1956.
111 E P Thompson, *The Making of the English Working Class* (Victor Gollancz, London, 1963), p. 407 n. 2.
112 'Editorial: Why We Are Publishing', *The Reasoner*, no. 1, p. 3.
113 'Editorial: Taking Stock', p. 4.
114 McLeod, *Uncle Joe*, p. 102.
115 McLeod, *Uncle Joe*, p. 117.
116 McLeod, *Uncle Joe*, p. 102.
117 Bryan Palmer, 'Reasoning Rebellion: E P Thompson, British Marxist Historians and the Making of Dissident Political Mobilization', *Labour/Le Travail*, no. 50, 2002.
118 Discussion in the literature is typically brief. For perceptive comments see Dennis Dworkin, *Cultural Marxism in Postwar Britain* (Duke University Press, London, 1997), pp. 48-51.
119 E P Thompson, 'Though the Smoke of Budapest', *The Reasoner*, no. 3, November 1956, Supplement, p. 6.
120 'Editorial', *The Reasoner*, no. 3, Supplement, p. 4.
121 Harvey Klehr and John Earl Haynes, *The American Communist Movement: Storming Heaven Itself* (Twayne, New York, 1992), pp. 141-47; James R Barrett, *William Z Foster and the Tragedy of American Radicalism* (University of Illinois Press, Urbana, 1999), pp. 252-72.
122 Sam Bornstein and Al Richardson, *Against the Stream: A History of the Trotskyist Movement in Britain 1924-1938* (Socialist Platform, London, 1986), pp. 62-96.
123 Cultural journals, such as *Left Review* in the 1930s, had been produced by party members. But they were broadly orthodox and ultimately amenable to direction. There was no specific rule in the CPGB constitution prohibiting independent publication, but the leadership relied on the catch-all Rule 27 which accorded them the final say in interpreting the constitution.
124 Parsons, 'Nineteen Fifty-Six', p. 7.
125 Saville, 'Thompson', p. 30; Saville, *Memoirs*, p. 113. Thompson was concluding that it would prove impossible to reach a compromise by which *The Reasoner* would be replaced by open discussion in the party press even before the 31 August meeting at King Street: see CPA, CP/Cent/Org/98/04, Thompson to Howard Hill, 20 August 1956. The conservatism of some members was highlighted by Fred Westacott: '... the most serious loss in the East Midlands was from our thriving Eckington branch where almost all the members, including Horace Kay, our only Communist Councillor, left in protest at the criticism being made of Stalin.' (Westacott, *Shaking the Chains*, p. 301)

126 Saville, 'XXth Congress', p. 15. In his first letter to Saville in early April, when he initially suggested publication of a discussion journal, Thompson stated: 'If necessary we shall have to leave the Party and found a small Marxist educational league. I hope this will never have to take place but it is more important that we should remain loyal to our intellectual integrity as Marxists than to the Party under all circumstances.' (Quoted in Saville, 'Thompson', p. 23)

127 Samuel, *Lost World*, p. 133.

128 Samuel, *Lost World*, p. 134.

129 The best accounts of Communist trade unionists in 1956 are Steve Parsons, *Crisis in the British Communist Party: The Impact of the Events of 1956 on the Membership with Particular Reference to Trade Unionists* (Unpublished MA Thesis, University of Warwick, 1981); and Richard Stevens, 'Cold War Politics: Communism and Anti-Communism in the Trade Unions', in Alan Campbell, Nina Fishman and John McIlroy (eds), *The Postwar Compromise: British Trade Unions and Industrial Politics 1945-1964* (second edition, Merlin, Monmouth, 2007), pp. 173-81. The only leading union activists to become associated with *The Reasoner* group were Lawrence Daly, the Scottish miner who had quit the CPGB after Khrushchev's speech, and, to a lesser extent, Bert Wynn of the Derbyshire miners.

130 'Letters', *New Statesman*, 1 December 1956.

131 'Letters', *Daily Worker*, 9 November 1956. See also Peter Fryer, 'Once Again on Hobsbawm's Protest', *Workers' Press*, 10 March 1990; John McIlroy, 'Founding Fathers', *Labour History Review*, Volume 70, no. 2, 2005, pp. 231-38; John McIlroy, 'Communist Historian', p. 95 n. 52.

132 Fryer was expelled from the CPGB in January 1957 after being interviewed in the *Daily Express* and writing to the *New Statesman*; see Peter Fryer, *Hungarian Tragedy* (Dobson, London, 1956; enlarged edition, Index, London, 1997).

133 *World News*, 12 January 1957; CPA, CP/Cent/EC/04/03, Report of the Delegation to the Soviet Union, October-November 1956; Werskey, *Visible College*, pp. 309-10. For the CPGB's Jewish Committee in 1956, see John Callaghan, *Cold War Crisis and Conflict: The CPGB 1951-1968* (Lawrence and Wishart, London, 2003), pp. 67-68.

134 Levy was further demoralised by the hostile reception he received at the CPGB's Twenty-Fifth Congress. He was expelled in 1958 after the publication of his book *Jews and The National Question*, but remained ready to discuss rejoining the party: Werskey, *Visible College*, pp. 311-13.

135 The CPGB even attracted new members. A group around John Lawrence, who had left the party to join the Trotskyists in 1939, entered the CPGB, inspired by illusions in Khrushchev: see John McIlroy, 'The Revolutionary Odyssey of John Lawrence', *Revolutionary History*, Volume 9, no. 2, 2006, pp. 105-93. Outside the party, the theory of 'self-reform' was personified by Isaac Deutscher, who supported the invasion of Hungary as regrettable but necessary, although he eventually documented 'the failure of Khrushchevism': Isaac Deutscher, *The Unfinished Revolution: Russia 1917-1967* (Oxford University Press, Oxford, 1967).

136 *Daily Worker*, 17 December 1956; Heinemann, '1956', pp. 48, 57 n. 2.

137 Saville, 'XXth Congress', p. 16.

138 CPA, CP/Cent/Cong/09/02, Resolutions of the Twenty-Fourth Congress of the CPGB; ARL, 'Letters', *Daily Worker*, 25 April 1956.

139 Parsons, 'Nineteen Fifty-Six', particularly pp. 79-83.

140 *World News*, 23 February 1957.

141 Quoted in Wood, *Communism*, pp. 212-13.

142 Quoted in Wood, *Communism*, p. 213. Wood also quoted an evocative response from a worker – the Communist shop steward Johnny McLoughlin: 'You are the enemy, you lying old swine.'

143 *World News*, 12 January 1957.

144 Randall Swingler, who had quit the party in April and was in close touch with Thompson, described himself as '… shocked, horror-struck, paralysed. The whole thing is an emotional nightmare which I can't yet cope with.' (Quoted in Andy Croft, 'Mapless in the Wilderness: Randall Swingler and 1956', *Socialist History*, no. 19, 2001, p. 56)

145 *Newsletter*, 10 May 1957, reproduced in David Widgery, *The Left in Britain 1956-68* (Penguin, Harmondsworth, 1976), pp. 78-85; *Forum*, July-September 1957.

146 Malcolm MacEwen, 'The Day the Party Had to Stop', in Ralph Miliband and John Saville (eds), *Socialist Register 1976* (Merlin, London, 1976), pp. 29-30; *Report to the Executive Committee by the Commission on Inner-Party Democracy* (CPGB, London, 1957); Thompson, *Good Old Cause*, pp. 106-10. A London branch objected unsuccessfully to Reid's appointment and its members subsequently resigned *en masse*: see Bob Potter, 'Special Work', in Widgery, *Left in Britain*, pp. 76-77.

147 Unless otherwise indicated this section is based on the sources cited in note 146.

148 Hill retrospectively referred to doubts on the part of Klugmann; see Kate Hudson, *The Double Blow: 1956 and the Communist Party of Great Britain* (unpublished PhD thesis, School of Slavonic Studies, University of London, 1992), pp. 199-200; Callaghan, *Cold War, Crisis*, pp. 77, 84 n. 104.

149 MacEwen, 'The Day', p. 31.

150 *Report to the Executive Committee*, passim.

151 *Report to the Executive Committee*, pp. 58-59.

152 Communist Party, *Twenty-Fifth Congress Report* (CPGB, London, 1957), p. 18.

153 Communist Party, *Twenty-Fifth Congress Report*, p. 66.

154 Communist Party, *Twenty-Fifth Congress Report*, p. 15.

155 Communist Party, *Twenty-Fifth Congress Report*, p. 22.

156 Communist Party, *Twenty-Fifth Congress Report*, p. 123.

157 Communist Party, *Twenty-Fifth Congress Report*, p. 24; CPA, CP/Cent/Cong/10/06, Documents and Reports on the Special Twenty-Fifth Congress.

158 Thompson, *Good Old Cause*, p. 109, emphasises the small proportion of paper membership that the delegates represented, given the small numbers in attendance at the meetings which elected congress delegates.

159 'A Congress of Re-Stalinisation', *Congress Special* (issued by the Editors of *Labour Review*), no. 3, 21 April 1957.

160 Parsons, 'Nineteen Fifty-Six', pp. 74-75.

161 Judt, *Past Imperfect*, p. 283.

162 Communist Party, *Twenty-Fifth Congress Report*, p. 24.

163 Beckett, *Enemy Within*, pp. 216-21.

164 Thompson, *Good Old Cause*, pp. 134-90; Andrews, *Endgames and New Times*, pp. 201-46.

The Communist Party and 1956

Defending the Soviet Union gives you a headache? ... if it gives you a headache take an aspirin.

Harry Pollitt

DOCUMENTS

* * *

I: Harry Pollitt, The Twentieth Congress of the CPSU – And the Role of Stalin[1]

From *World News*, 21 April and 5 May 1956.

* * *

The Twentieth Congress of the Communist Party of the Soviet Union recorded immense achievements within the Soviet Union and adopted the Sixth Five-Year Plan which by 1960 will have taken the Soviet Union a great step further along the road to Communism.

It seems almost incredible that, in the short historical period since 1917, such a vast transformation could have been carried out.

A backward peasantry, mass illiteracy, almost no industry and few skilled workers; civil war on eleven fronts, armed intervention by the capitalist world, famine over large areas – such were the conditions of the early years of the Soviet Union. In addition, many holding leading positions in the Communist Party, lacking confidence in their own people, thought that the revolution could only be saved by revolutions in other countries, while others wanted to slow down the pace of industrialisation and appease the rich peasants.

Such gigantic problems and difficulties could only be overcome by a strong Central Committee and a disciplined Communist Party, guided first by Lenin and, after Lenin's death, by Stalin: great personalities with outstanding abilities as organisers, leaders and theoreticians, understanding events more profoundly than others, and for that reason playing a leading role.

Although we attended the Twentieth Congress of the CPSU, no foreign guests attended the Closed Session of the Congress which discussed the new assessment of the role of Stalin.

It should be remembered that the Communist International was dissolved in 1942[2] and no connections between our party and other parties have existed since that time. The Communist Information Bureau was established in 1947; we have never been members of it or attended any of its meetings.

After Lenin

In the critical period after Lenin's death, Stalin gave a pledge to the CPSU that he would endeavour to overcome some of the weaknesses which Lenin had drawn attention to, and in the following years he did so. Under his leadership, Trotsky and Bukharin were defeated, the basis for industrialisation and collective agriculture was established, and his drive for carrying through the First Five-Year Plan prepared the ground for the future successes of the Soviet Union in peace and in war.

After the defeat of the internal enemies at the Seventeenth Party Congress in 1934, Stalin more and more began to turn away from the principles of collective leadership, and his personal methods created a position where the security organs could misuse their powers and increasingly place themselves above the party and the state.

A series of purgings and wrongful arrests took place, 'confessions' of guilt were made under pressure; the party rules were violated and members of the Central Committee who were arrested were denied the right to place their case before meetings of the Central Committee. In fact, meetings of the Central Committee were only called at infrequent intervals, and no meetings of the Central Committee of the CPSU took place throughout the war.

In connection with Hitler's attack on the Soviet Union in June 1941, the general theory to be found in Soviet literature is that there was a sudden unexpected attack by Hitler on the Soviet Union.

This does not correspond to the facts. Firstly, the Soviet government had been warned of the forthcoming attack by the whole history of Nazism; secondly, by Churchill through Cripps;[3] thirdly, through the Soviet Military Attaché in Berlin; and fourthly by German deserters who came over to the Russians.

It would appear that, after the war, Stalin kept complete control of foreign policy, in some cases aggravating the international situation, as for example when differences arose with Yugoslavia which could have been solved on the basis of fraternal discussion.

Serious Damage

For all these reasons it would be wrong to underestimate the damage that has been done, and the seriousness of the task of overcoming it.

When Stalin placed himself above the CPSU, the Soviet government and the people, it was inevitable that future investigations would reveal what the consequences of such a policy were bound to be. That is what we are now seeing as a result of the examination into the last twenty years of Stalin's personal rule.

Rise of Fascism

At the same time, we have to take into account the whole character of the period which has been under review, and in doing so, we have to recognise our responsibilities in failing to be able to mobilise the British people to have played a more positive part in stemming the advance of fascism.

They were the years which saw the rise of fascism; the civil war in Spain, in which Britain adopted the policy of non-intervention in a struggle for democracy in Spain, which was openly recognised as a dress rehearsal for the Second World War. There was the betrayal of Czechoslovakia by Chamberlain[4] in 1938, the refusal of Chamberlain to take part in a Nine-Power Conference of European states to form a united front against fascism; the refusal of the British Military Mission which went to Moscow in August 1938[5] to make a united front with the Red Army against any aggression by Hitler.

By this time fascism had become a nightmare to world civilisation, and with the outbreak of war in 1939, it looked as if Hitler would stride roughshod over the whole world.

This does not excuse what Stalin's mistakes resulted in, because Lenin faced similar grave problems after the Russian Revolution in 1917, but he always preserved party democratic practices and collective leadership. But it helps to explain how it could have happened and the difficult problems involved in putting it right.

The victory over fascism and all the great political consequences which have flowed from it, have undoubtedly laid the basis for the great new vista opened out by the Twentieth Congress of the CPSU.

They could have been won, however, at a lighter cost, but for the damage and mistakes arising as a result of the policy of Stalin in the last twenty years of his rule.

Since its very first days, the Soviet Union has been subjected to capitalist intervention, sabotage, wrecking and espionage. There were, and still are, internal and external enemies of the Soviet Union who aim to realise imperialism's policy of trying to destroy the socialist world. They had to be fought then, and they have to be fought now. Strong security forces were needed then, and are needed now, to prevent this from taking place.

Theory of Class Struggle

Stalin, however, did not himself realise the profound changes which the transformation of the Soviet Union had brought to the Soviet people. In spite of the victory over the capitalists and landlords which had been fully achieved by 1934, he failed to realise the great new forces that had developed within the Soviet Union and the increasing attraction of the socialist system for those who had formerly supported capitalism. His theory was that the class struggle must continue to grow more intense; and on the basis of this theory he turned more and more to the false outlook that the dictatorship of the proletariat meant, in those circumstances, greater and greater dependence on the security forces instead of on the people.

On this question of the way in which the class struggle would develop in the Soviet Union, Stalin put forward a viewpoint which conflicted with that of Lenin. Lenin declared that:

The abolition of classes not only means driving out the landlords and capitalists – that we accomplished with comparative ease – it means also abolishing the small commodity producers, and they cannot be driven out, or crushed, we must live in harmony with them; they can (and must) be remoulded and re-educated, but this can be done only by very prolonged, slow, cautious organisational work. (*Selected Works*, Volume 10, p. 83)

Whereas Stalin stated:

Take for example the question of building a classless socialist society. The Seventeenth Party Congress declared that we are advancing towards the formation of a classless socialist society. Naturally, a classless society cannot come of its own accord, as it were. It has to be achieved and built by the efforts of all the working people, by strengthening the organs of the dictatorship of the proletariat, by intensifying the class struggle, by abolishing classes, by eliminating the remnants of the capitalist classes, and in battles with enemies, both internal and external. (*Collected Works*, Volume 13, p. 357)

Thus, while Lenin stressed that with the defeat of the landlords and capitalists a new approach would be necessary, in order to remould and re-educate other non-proletarian elements, Stalin saw only continued and intensified class struggle and 'strengthening the organs of the dictatorship of the proletariat' – the security forces.

Such a doctrine was bound to breed distrust and suspicion, and when applied after the successes of industrialisation and collective agriculture took no account of the change in class forces that had resulted, and the narrowing basis for foreign intervention among the people. Nor, after victory in the Second World War, could such a doctrine lead to appreciation of the great change in the relationship of international class forces resulting from the defeat of fascism. Hence at each stage in the last twenty years of Stalin's life the carrying through of the correct general line by the party and the people was accompanied by mistakes, abuses and injustices arising from Stalin's increasing dependence on the security forces instead of on the party and the people.

On the basis of this wrong theory of Stalin's, Beria[6] and other capitalist agents who had wormed their way into the CPSU and the security forces were able to use their influence to increase this distrust and suspicion on Stalin's part, to build up unfounded accusations and take measures of persecution and repression against innocent comrades.

All this was necessarily associated with Stalin's personal methods. He had won his great authority and prestige because, after Lenin's death, he had around him the best supporters of Lenin, and because the successful defeat of the enemies of the CPSU in building socialism was identified with his name, above all. His error was to place himself, stage by stage, above the rest of the leadership of the CPSU, gradually substituting personal power for collective leadership.

The Cult of the Individual

The cult of the individual creates the impression that men can perform miracles without the help of the party and the people. It belittles the role of the party and provides the basis for serious political mistakes to be made. Marxism teaches us that great individuals can play a role in history only if they are at one with history, the party and the people.

The cult of the individual leads to the stultification of intellectual life. If it is left to one great man to make the pronouncements in every field, then there is bound to be an absence of independent thought and creative work. This was reflected in certain aspects of the work of Soviet economists, historians, writers, film producers, etc.

When Stalin died the capitalists gloated that there would be a new struggle for personal power in the Soviet Union, that there would be acute dissension, divisions and disruption, and that internal weaknesses would develop.

On the contrary, what has happened is that the Leninist principle of collective leadership has been fully restored, Soviet democracy and protection of the legal rights of every Soviet citizen put into operation, and justice done to all who had to suffer from the mistakes and abuses of Stalin's personal rule. And measures have been taken to make it impossible for a similar situation to arise again.

These steps were of vital importance not only for the development of the Soviet Union, but also because of the far-reaching consequences they would have (and already are having) on an international level. This can be clearly seen in the way that the influence of the Soviet Union is today increasing all over the world.

Collective Leadership

The full collective leadership of the CPSU is today showing its strength, as seen in the freshness and boldness of its recent policies and approaches.

It is to be seen in every aspect of foreign policy, in the principle of European collective security, in the present Soviet disarmament proposals, in the reduction of the Soviet armed forces, the return of the Porkkala base to Finland, the resumption of friendly relations with Yugoslavia, in the great perspectives of the Sixth Five-Year Plan. It is to be seen in the opening up of wider contact abroad, in the visit of Khrushchev and Bulganin[7] to India, Burma, Afghanistan and now to Britain, in the visit of Malenkov[8] to this country, in the visit of Mikoyan[9] to Pakistan and India, and in the visits of so many prime ministers and social-democratic leaders to the Soviet Union.

It is to be seen also in the important pronouncements at the Twentieth Congress, on the question of peaceful coexistence, that war is not fatalistically inevitable, that peaceful roads to socialism are opened up by the change in international forces, and the new emphasis given to the importance of seeking a united front of Communist and Social-Democratic parties.

As far as the Soviet people themselves are concerned, there is now bound to be a terrific upsurge of initiative, led by the CPSU, opened up as a result of the re-establishment of Soviet legality, with the state and party in control of security and with the full functioning of Soviet democracy.

There will also be an intellectual renaissance, with a loosening up and development of Marxist thought in all directions, with concrete and analytical examination of problems and the production of new theoretical works in the fields of economy, philosophy, history, etc.

Above all will these new developments have profound and enormous effects on the possibilities for peace.

It is in this light that we can proudly proclaim our confidence in the Soviet Union, its Communist Party and its people.

Yugoslavia

In connection with Yugoslavia, it is now evident that whatever criticisms were made of the political line of the Yugoslav party in 1948, these could have been discussed in a fraternal way without the break that was made; and that in the following period the position was greatly aggravated by the unfounded accusations against the Yugoslav Communist leaders on the basis of material fabricated by Beria and his associates.

It is now clear that Yugoslavia remained an independent country, that today only 10 per cent of trade is in private hands, and that all the efforts of the USA to shake Yugoslavia out of its independent position failed.

We, in the Executive Committee of the British Communist Party, were misled by evidence that is now stated to have been fabricated, and we now withdraw our previous attacks on Tito and Yugoslavia, including the statement made by myself at the London membership meeting in 1948, and James Klugmann's book *From Trotsky to Tito*.[10]

Marxist Principles Confirmed

The enemies of the Communist Party are trying to pretend that the reassessment of Stalin proves that everything that they have said about the Soviet Union was correct, and everything we said was wrong.

Whatever the mistakes made and the abuses associated with Stalin's personal methods, however, the great historic achievement of the Soviet people and the CPSU is that they have proven, for all the world to see, the superiority of the socialist system over the capitalist system. Despite the faults, weaknesses and mistakes, all the basic Marxist principles have been proven correct, and confirmed again and again, above all in the indestructible socialist system in the world today.

There is no doubt that the new estimation of the role of Stalin has come as a profound shock to the members of every Communist Party in the world, precisely because of what Stalin has stood for and his outstanding contribution to the building of socialism in the Soviet Union – the base for all the further advances of socialism in the world.

But we must remember what Lenin wrote in 1915:

The experiences of the war, like the experiences of every crisis in human history, of every great calamity and every sudden turn in human life, stun and break some people, *but they enlighten and steel others*.[11]

The enemies of socialism are trying to make the most of this situation, precisely in order to 'stun and break' some people; but for us, the thing is to appreciate not only the facts which have been revealed but also the conditions which gave rise to them, and to draw the lessons both of theory and organisation which can help to 'enlighten and steel' the party and strengthen its work.

In Britain

We have collective leadership in the British Communist Party. There are regular meetings of the Executive Committee, a sharing out of the preparation of reports, the widest participation in the discussion and the decisions, and regular reporting of its decisions. We need, however, to develop this still more. Our leading committees, from top to bottom, suffer from a narrow, practical approach and we do not analyse our problems sufficiently deeply. We have to develop our theoretical basis, applied in British terms and conditions, and we must develop still further the basic principles of our programme *The British Road to Socialism.*[12]

And we shall do this effectively only to the extent that at the same time all of us are constantly on the alert to protect and develop every aspect of party democracy, and to ensure that the authority and political life of the party branch is enhanced, because this is the key to the development of a live party democracy.

While there is need for widespread discussion of all the implications of the new situation, it is in their application to our party that the experience gained can really help to strengthen our work. The more specific and concrete the criticism and self-criticism that comes from our discussion is, the more useful it will be, the more it will help the leading committees to improve their work.

The class struggle goes on. The full development of mass work to bring down the Tories becomes ever more urgent. The balance of forces on a world scale is changing in our favour. Ours is the party that must act to bring about the unity of the British working class and its allies for victory over capitalism. Despite all our mistakes and weaknesses, ours is a record that neither capitalism nor right-wing Labour can destroy. We must draw fresh strength for the battle from all our discussions, and go forward along the path mapped out by the Twenty-Fourth Congress of our party.

Since the Twentieth Congress and particularly since our Twenty-Fourth Congress there has been a widespread and searching discussion in the party, in the branches, membership meetings, conferences and committees. More comrades have been involved in these discussions than at any recent period.

Now, as a result, we can put forward some further considerations arising out of the reports and experience of these meetings.

What Is the Background To Our Discussions?

It is natural that a great discussion should be taking place arising out of the reassessment of Stalin's role, for this raises questions of the greatest importance and has profound lessons for Communists everywhere.

At the same time, it is vital that we should not be thrown off balance in such a way as to prevent the full mobilisation of the party in the new situation which is opening up.

The very developments which have led to such widespread discussion are also responsible for some of the most important new factors in the world situation. The Twentieth Congress did not only reassess the role of Stalin and examine the experiences of the past twenty years. Equally important were its adoption of the Sixth Five-Year Plan, its discussions on foreign policy and its contributions to Marxist-Leninist theory.

This is well understood in certain capitalist circles, who know what the restoration of collective leadership means, and will mean, in strengthening the Soviet Union in every respect.

I have previously remarked that when Stalin died the capitalist world rubbed their hands in glee at the prospect of what was going to happen in the Soviet Union. This was expressed editorially in *The Economist* (7 April 1956), which wrote that the news was greeted by the 'free world' with 'a certain complacency, anticipating a murderous struggle for power among Soviet leaders'.

The whole world now fully understands that no such struggle did take place, and that Stalin's death was the signal for an immediate return to collective leadership.

In an important article in the magazine *The Twentieth Century*, of April 1956, entitled 'Where Does Russia Stand?' the author gets down to the root of the question. She spends little time on the role of Stalin because, quite rightly, she sees the results of the Twentieth Congress of the CPSU as a whole, stating:

For the tone of the congress is one of tremendous confidence, both in the domestic and foreign domains. It is clear that the Russian leaders now believe that they are approaching, if they have not yet achieved, equilibrium of power with the West. Against this, other aspects dwindle into comparative insignificance. It is a waste of time for commentators on Soviet affairs to pursue their speculations about who is going up and who is coming down in the Kremlin hierarchy: who is a Khrushchev and who is a Malenkov man … It would be well to get in our heads, before the

Russian leaders arrive in this country, that they come as representatives of an immensely strong power which is looking forward confidently to further accretions of strength.[13]

I quote this because I have felt at every meeting where a report has been made on the Twentieth Congress of the CPSU that the principal aims of this historic congress have not been listened to, understood, or their present and future positive significance for the working people of the entire world been realised. It may be perfectly natural that this should be the case because of the esteem in which we all held Comrade Stalin, but we must frankly state that this lack of a balanced approach has been a political weakness, which has not characterised responsible capitalist reactions to the congress, in which the full significance for the whole capitalist world therein represented has been understood.

I make this point at the outset because it would be a tragedy if, in their natural preoccupation with aspects of the Soviet situation in past years, some comrades failed to see that opportunities are now opening up before our party such as we have not seen for many a long day. To fail to grasp them, to fail to give leadership to the working people who are now engaged in battle with the Tories, would be irresponsible in the extreme.

Therefore, in discussing these questions let us do so in a responsible manner, remembering that we are above all a fighting party aiming at ending Tory rule and helping the British people advance along the British road to socialism.

Some Questions Arising From the Discussion

a) **How Could It Happen?** Grave dangers and problems *inevitably* beset the first country in the world where the working people won political power and began the historic task, against almost unbelievable odds, of building socialism. They came under the bitter fire of the whole of world capitalism and the former ruling classes of their own country. Threats, blackmail, economic boycott, continuous plots, and war itself – nothing was too grim or ruthless for world reaction.

The Soviet people, government and Communist Party had to steel themselves to beat back these ferocious attacks, and a degree of bitterness and ruthlessness, which was not their choice but which was imposed on them by world reaction, became necessary in this struggle, for without it the revolution could not have survived.

It was on this background of capitalist encirclement and later of fascist threat that, within the framework of a wonderful socialist advance, there crept in step by step a number of mistakes and then of evil abuses, including grave violations of socialist democracy.

It is precisely because of our love of socialism, and of our profound gratitude and admiration for the amazing accomplishments of the Soviet revolution, that we say that these abuses were alien to socialism. They weakened and hampered the socialist advance in many ways.

We are all deeply shocked to learn that many of those who were represented as traitors to the people's cause, were, in fact, devoted Communists, victims of what are now revealed as deliberately organised violations of justice. As Communists we feel these events acutely just because of our Communist outlook.

But at the same time we consider that the fact that these errors and abuses have been fearlessly laid bare by the leaders of the CPSU, despite the shock that this has inevitably meant, is a proof of their great courage and Communist honesty. The actions that they have taken to put things right, publicly and openly, gives the world a powerful demonstration of their political integrity, sense of justice, unreserved intention of repairing injustices and determination to see that such grave violations of collective leadership and socialist legality cannot be repeated.

On the basis of information now stated to have been fabricated, we mistakenly supported things shown subsequently to be wrong.

We must never forget that when the errors and abuses occurred, they occurred within the framework of a profound socialist advance and transformation, which has radically altered the balance of forces in the world and opened up new and more favourable roads of advance to socialism in all countries.

In condemning errors and abuses now exposed, we must never lose our sense of historic proportion. And we know that the very exposing and remedying of mistakes will accelerate the triumph of socialism and communism throughout the world.

b) **What Were They Doing?** The question 'Where were the other members of the Central Committee of the CPSU when all this was going on?' has been asked repeatedly. The only people, of course, who can fully answer this question are members of the Central Committee of the CPSU themselves, and we can only put forward our views in the light of the information which has been made available, and of our own understanding and study of the period.

Stalin not only refused to call full meetings of the Central Committee, but also introduced the method of dividing the members of the Central Committee into working groups, each working in separate compartments; the result being to strengthen the personal control of Stalin over the Central

Committee as a whole. Moreover, his methods had brought things to such a position, and his prestige in the eyes of the people was such, that any inner or open fight against his wrong methods would have divided the people and the nation, at the most critical moments in their history, risking divisions that could have proved fatal.

It may be judged, therefore, that the other Soviet leaders regarded it as their duty to preserve the unity of the party as a whole, and rally the Soviet people behind its general correct line of policy, and by so doing were able to defeat fascism and lay the basis for the present epoch-making developments which have been opened by the Twentieth Congress.

c) **Criticism and Self-Criticism**: The question is also being asked, 'Where is the criticism and self-criticism of the other members of the Central Committee of the CPSU?'

We need to remember that the essence of self-criticism is not breast-beating, but in putting wrong policies right, at the same time as the mistakes have been publicly acknowledged. This is what has been taking place during the last three years and is being continued at the present time. It is being done boldly and publicly and not being hushed up as happens in the capitalist world.

What happened at the Twentieth Congress and what has happened since constitutes self-criticism of the most concrete kind, namely the boldest and frankest admission and exposure of past mistakes, and equally bold and determined efforts to correct them and ensure that they cannot happen again.

d) **What Guarantees for the Future?** We are also being asked, 'What guarantees have we that such things cannot occur again?' We think the answer is, first, in the fact that in the last three years the Soviet Constitution has been enforced, Soviet law strengthened, and the unconstitutional aspects of the work of the security forces have been ended.

Second, and most important, the drawing into a nation-wide discussion of the whole membership of the CPSU and the entire population of the Soviet Union, not only to discuss the past but the whole of the decisions of the Twentieth Congress of the CPSU, has led to a deeper political understanding, drawn all the people closer than ever before around the CPSU and its collective leadership and new methods of work, and made them determined to prevent the possibility of similar happenings in the future.

It is necessary, also, to understand that the conditions in which the past mistakes and abuses took place no longer exist. The early Soviet Union, weak and isolated, threatened from all sides, is a thing of the past. Today the mighty Soviet Union, reinforced by the People's Democracies and China, and with important former colonial countries also taking a stand against aggressive imperialism, has not to face the dangers of the earlier period. There is confidence in the future, the line of advance is clear, and the people are playing an increasing part; while there is increasing interest in and support for the socialist countries and the policy of peaceful coexistence.

e) **International Solidarity**. We are proud of the record of our party in the field of international solidarity.

We have played a leading role, since our first foundation, in developing solidarity with the USSR, defending the achievements of the Soviet revolution – often against overwhelming odds. We have a record second to none in Britain in solidarity with the struggle of the colonial peoples.

We cannot and will never give up our internationalist standpoint. As I said at the Twenty-Fourth Congress, there is no contradiction between international working-class solidarity and true patriotism. On the contrary, the one demands the other.

There are enough hostile capitalist forces in the world attacking the USSR without our bringing grist to their mills.

It is an historical fact that the Soviet Union emerged as the leading force of the world's workers, because it was the first country to build socialism. Its existence has given enormous help, making it easier for other countries to advance to socialism. Recently other powerful parties have developed; each with its own policy based on conditions in each country on the common ground of Marxism; each contributing to the experience of all, and developing better opportunities to help the common advance.

In this connection I would like to make four main points.

First, we have never said that there was nothing wrong in the Soviet Union or claimed that it was a paradise. This is one of the caricatures of our attitude towards the Soviet Union that the capitalist press is always accusing us of. We have been only too conscious of the tremendous difficulties and obstacles which the Soviet people have had to overcome on their way to socialism.

Secondly, we stated at the Twenty-Third Congress of our party[14] that it was wrong to try to impose Soviet discussions and lines of thought regarding scientific and cultural questions on comrades in Britain.

Thirdly, in respect of this country in our judgement of the situation and the policy of our party and working-class movement, we have always been a responsible and independent political party and have never hesitated to uphold and stand by our judgement when occasion arose.

Fourthly, the issue in question is our attitude to the general world political situation and the role of the Soviet Union within it. On that we have been right to act in solidarity with the Soviet Union against its capitalist enemies, and we shall continue to do so. We are engaged in the class war, and international solidarity is absolutely essential.

This does not mean that we have in the past defended mistaken policies knowing them to be mistaken, or that we will do so in the future. What it does mean is that we cannot be 'neutral' or 'objective' in the class war. We have to defend our class and our brother parties, in whatever country, against capitalist attacks, distortions and slanders. And since we are a political party engaged in a day-to-day battle we cannot wait for the judgement of history on every event – we have to decide our attitude on the basis of the facts as they are known to us.

It is entirely wrong to say, as some have said, that our past support of the Soviet Union is the main reason for the fact that the party has not been strengthened as much as we would have liked. The logic of this argument, carried to its final conclusion, would be that we would be nearer socialism in Britain if there were no Soviet Union. The point has only to be put in this way for its absurdity to be plain.

The victories of the Soviet people, and our popularisation and explanation of them, are a great positive factor in the fight for socialism in Britain. The reasons for our failure to build the party are deeper and more complex than the comrades who use this type of argument would have us believe. We cannot make the fact that mistakes and abuses have occurred in the Soviet Union an alibi for our own weaknesses.

Our support for the Soviet Union is based on international working-class solidarity. No working class in the world understands such solidarity better than the British working class, or has a finer record in its support. Anyone who thinks that our position amongst the British working class would be strengthened if we joined in with the capitalist and right-wing Labour criticism of the Soviet Union does not understand the working class.

f) Intensification of the Class Struggle After Power is Won. The issue of the intensification of the class struggle was put in a one-sided way by Stalin. It is true that in any country where the people win political power the old ruling class fights back harder than ever before. It is equally true on an international scale that when a socialist country and then a group of socialist countries emerge, world reaction tries to destroy those conditions by every method.

But this is only one side of the question.

On the other side, when the working people have power and begin to build socialism, socialism has an ever-growing *attractive force* and new opportunities arise to win allies from those who previously hesitated, and even, through re-education, from the ranks of those classes who have lost power. Equally, on an international scale, the new socialist world exercises a *tremendous attractive power* on the part of the world which has not taken the path of socialism.

The danger lies in seeing one side of the question only, and therefore in seeing enemies everywhere and nothing but enemies, and underestimating the possibility of winning friends and allies at home and throughout the world.

Lessons For Us

But still more important than all these questions is the issue of what can *we* learn in Britain and in our own party from the discussions on the Twentieth Congress. The Soviet comrades are looking after the position in the USSR, our responsibility lies here.

And out of all our discussions there is very much we can learn and use to improve our own work.

Improve Our Theoretical Understanding: It is quite clear that we need to take steps to improve the general theoretical level of our party from top to bottom. Reflecting a general historic weakness in the British labour movement, we are too prone to concern ourselves with immediate problems and insufficiently with questions of principle that underlie immediate struggles and immediate tactics.

We have made some important progress in recent years in applying Marxist principles to the specific problems of Britain, but we still have a long way to go in this field.

We need to develop still further our study of British labour history, including the history of our own party, of British democratic traditions. We need to initiate work on the class structure of Britain. We need to give more thought to the transition period from the present position to the election of a People's Government.

Improving Party Democracy and Collective Leadership: We have nothing to be ashamed about in the field of party democracy or collective leadership. Our right-wing Labour critics would do well to learn from our methods and to begin to put their own house in order.

Our Executive Committee is very far from a 'one-man band'. For example, in the past two years, with an EC membership of forty-one, twenty-two different comrades have given opening reports, eleven of whom were not on the Political Committee; and all the remaining members take part in discussions – we have no silent members.

But we would be wrong if we did not see that there is plenty of room for improvement. We have to consider how to improve collective leadership at all levels – and it would be good if all EC, District, Area and Branch Committee members began to think how to improve their committees in this respect.

The reluctance to consider new ideas which did not seem to fit into practical day-to-day work in which we were engaged, has led in many cases, and at all levels of party organisation, to a reluctance to give serious consideration to points of view put forward. We have not listened sufficiently sympathetically or carefully to points and criticism raised.

The whole party, starting with the EC, must make it its concern to change such methods, and not only to practise criticism and self-criticism, but also to listen patiently to all points of view and to realise that Marxism requires all-round consideration of each problem in its actual setting and development, and that collective discussion helps to bring out the many aspects of the problem and so helps in finding the correct solution.

We need to create the atmosphere in which the greatest discussion can take place, where comrades have no fear when they raise points of being branded as 'deviators'. This approach is all the more necessary because of the need to get rid completely of dogmatism and sectarianism so that we can really apply the principles of Marxism-Leninism to the problems of the British people.

The British Road to Socialism: Already in 1951 we were able to put forward, in relation to Britain, what the Twentieth Congress of the CPSU stated generally on the possibility of a peaceful transition to socialism. We were the first party outside the socialist countries to draft such a programme; and it was a help to the Communist parties in the Scandinavian countries and the Dominions, as the fraternal delegates said at our congress.

But we have not done enough to carry the analysis further, and to examine a number of actual problems which will face us.

There is a gap in our work. We have an immediate programme, which was last outlined at our Twenty-Fourth Congress,[15] and also a long-term programme in *The British Road to Socialism*. But we have not seriously tackled the relation between the two, and the concrete ways of developing towards the unity of the Labour movement and the building up of the broad alliance.

Our congress set the course for Labour unity. It showed the urgent need for this in the fight for peace and against the Tories. It set the objective of the removal of the bans and proscriptions as the key next step in the fight for unity. We should not underestimate what is involved in this. It will require a tremendous effort and a great campaign, which as yet has hardly begun, and which it is now urgent that we develop.

At the same time we need to examine the relation of the party to the wider labour movement in a concrete way, and to work out the future political developments in the working-class movement in such a way that we have a clear perspective and an understanding of the necessary steps in order to bring about these developments.

Similarly, we must study more closely the detailed class structure and relation of political forces in Britain, both now and in the development towards a People's Government, so that we can better appreciate the conditions in which the struggle for socialism has to be conducted.

In this, great attention requires to be given to developing and extending the democratic rights and liberties which have been won in Britain as a result of generations of struggle. The great political developments in Britain necessary for the advance to a People's Government mean also a great extension and flowering of democracy. Here we have to consider, for example, the problem of party political life and relations under a People's Government in Britain to other political parties. The preliminary thoughts on this issue in the political report to the Twenty-Fourth Congress require to be discussed and elaborated.

We also have to consider the questions connected with the concept of the 'fraternal alliance' with the former colonial peoples, in the light of what is taking place in India, Burma and Ceylon, the constitutional changes in Malaya and parts of Africa, and the whole disintegration of the colonial system.

Then there is a very important group of economic questions with a bearing on *The British Road to Socialism* – questions of where our supplies come from, our own resources, the possibilities of foreign trade, and all the problems associated with the building up of industry to serve a socialist Britain.

In connection with the broad political alliance that we see as a condition for a People's Government, we have only a general idea of the relations between the working class and professional workers and the middle sections generally; we have not made a deep examination of all that is involved. We also need to develop our work on Marxist lines, closely linked with the British background and contemporary British developments. Excellent work has been done by some comrades – but more has to be done in every field.

The New Situation Before Us

I end on the same note as I began on. The entire world situation gives us grounds for immense confidence, and this should be the keynote of all our discussions and actions.

Within the Soviet Union the reassessment of the role of Stalin did not take place against a background of crisis and decline. On the contrary, things in the Soviet Union have been going from strength to strength. Both internally and externally the position of the Soviet Union was never so powerful, and its influence in the world today is greater than it has ever been.

It is at this moment that discussions have been taking place, and whatever temporary problems they may have created for us they have certainly strengthened the position of the Soviet Union, which in the last analysis means strengthening the cause of Communism all over the world.

It is not out of place to draw attention to some of the important events which have taken place since the Twentieth Congress of the CPSU and *after* the discussions on the role of Stalin. No serious student of politics would say that they were accidental.

In the Soviet Union itself a new wave of enthusiasm for the carrying out of the Sixth Five-Year Plan has developed; a new confidence in the Communist Party of the Soviet Union and its collective leadership, putting into practice already some of the social gains as indicated by the shortening of working hours without loss of pay, better maternity services, more building of houses and extension of educational services.

Abroad, the speech of Pineau,[16] France's Foreign Secretary, and the interview of Mollet,[17] France's Prime Minister, in an American magazine; both Pineau and Mollet being very critical of Anglo-American foreign policy. The more friendly tone of Eisenhower's[18] last letter to Marshal Bulganin. The sacking of Glubb Pasha.[19] The decision of Iceland to send out of the country all American troops and end all American bases in Iceland.

The tremendous significance of the general election result in Ceylon. The welcome given to Malenkov during his recent visit to Britain, and the welcome that has been given to Bulganin and Khrushchev. The coming visit of an important delegation of French Socialist Party leaders to the Soviet Union.

And it is our opinion that these events are only a foretaste of bigger events to come.

Unity of all working-class forces on the basis of agreed demands and policies is being discussed on a wider scale than ever before. True, so far no positive results have accrued, but the big thing is that it is being seriously discussed. Our own programme *The British Road to Socialism* has shown that our approach is based on the conditions and traditions of Britain, and further helped the efforts to obtain working-class unity.

Greater support than ever before is being won to remove bans which prevent members of the Labour and Communist Parties from working together in defence of living standards and peace, and for the right of the trade unions democratically to elect those they think are best fitted to represent them at all conferences of the labour movement at all levels.

One of the outstanding lessons we can learn from the present discussions taking place is the importance of stressing at every stage of the class struggle the leading role of the Communist Party.

It is the Communist Party of the Soviet Union which has enabled the Soviet people to overcome every crisis and problem since the Russian Revolution in November 1917 – to conquer in civil war on eleven fronts – to overcome the horrors of the famine in 1921 – to defeat all its internal and external enemies – to build socialism and now pass on the road to Communism – to admit mistakes openly and put them right – to demonstrate at every turn its profound sense of real working-class internationalism.

The Communist Party in Britain is animated by the same Marxist ideas as those of the CPSU. It, too, has the duty of strengthening the ranks of the working people in every phase of their struggle against capitalism and speeding up the developments towards socialism. How urgent these tasks are has been shown in what has been said about the situation in Britain today. If we make a strong appeal for working-class unity it is in order to strengthen the fight against capitalism, and the development of working-class unity and the mass fight against the Tories will take place to the extent that we strengthen the Communist Party and the YCL and build the circulation of the *Daily Worker*.

We need from now on to go into the battle as never before. Yes, we shall learn from the discussions on the Twentieth Congress of the CPSU and from those which took place at our own Twenty-Fourth National Party Congress. There will be deeper thinking and study on the part of all our members; they will take due heed of the character of the self-criticism which the Executive Committee made of its own work since the Twenty-Third Congress. There will be continued examination and improvement of our methods of work, leadership and education, and from out of it all will come better mass work, a greater desire to win new members for the Communist Party and the Young Communist League and more regular readers for the *Daily Worker*.

The test of whether we learn from life, experience and mistakes is how far we accomplish these aims and so bring nearer the day when we will play our part in building a socialist Britain.

* * *

II: The Lessons of the Twentieth Congress of the CPSU

Resolution of the Executive Committee of the Communist Party of Great Britain, adopted on 13 May 1956.
From *World News*, 19 May 1956.

* * *

I

The reports and discussion of the Twentieth Congress of the CPSU revealed the vast progress made in recent years by the forces of socialism.

Side by side with the capitalist world is a socialist world system embracing one-third of the world's population. The colonial system is disintegrating as country after country wins independence from imperialism. Great economic, social, cultural and political advances are being achieved in the USSR, People's China and the people's democracies.

On the solid foundation of these advances that profoundly change the balance of class forces in the world, the Twentieth Congress expressed its complete confidence in the possibility of preventing a third world war. New and more favourable roads to socialism open up to the peoples of the capitalist world. New opportunities emerge for achieving working-class unity.

The successes of the USSR have laid the basis for such a transformation of the world that, with all the hard struggles that lie ahead, the future for every country becomes easier.

Stalin, as an outstanding Marxist leader, made a great contribution to the building of socialism in the USSR, and to the development of the international working-class movement.

At the same time, the Twentieth Congress, within the framework of the colossal Soviet advances in every field, revealed a number of serious mistakes and grave abuses that had developed within the period 1934–53 and were connected with the cult of the individual and lack of collective leadership.

It was shown how the fact that Stalin had progressively in this period put himself above the party and above the state had led to the belittling of the party and the people, to serious lapses in the democratic functioning of the party, to violations of socialist law and grave injustices to loyal comrades, to a certain stultification in intellectual life, and to some serious mistakes in home and foreign policy.

The Soviet leaders at the congress courageously laid bare these mistakes; and have taken resolute steps to correct the mistakes, to repair injustices done, and to ensure that they cannot recur.

II

It was inevitable that grave dangers and problems would beset the first country in the world where the working people won political power and began to build socialism.

Under the bitter onslaught of the whole of world capitalism with every foul means – including war, espionage and economic boycott – the Soviet people, led by the Communist Party, had to fight back bitterly and ruthlessly if the revolution was to be defended and socialism built. Strong security organs were essential, as was the inner-party struggle against those whose wrong policy would have wrecked the revolution.

It was on this background that the mistakes, abuses and grave injustices arose. It is necessary to see them in their historical perspective, for this helps to explain how they could have happened, though it does not justify or excuse them.

It is precisely because of our love of socialism and our admiration for the vast achievements of the USSR that we say that the abuses and injustices that arose were alien to socialism. They occurred within the framework of gigantic socialist advances, but they weakened and hampered these advances.

We were shocked to learn that a number of those arrested in the Soviet Union as traitors to the people were in fact devoted patriots and Communists; and that a number of those tried and convicted as traitors in the people's democracies were the victims of deliberate provocations and fabricated evidence.

We welcome the fact that errors, abuses and injustices have been so fearlessly laid bare by the present leaders of the CPSU. We see this as a demonstration of Communist honesty and integrity. We give full support for the measures they have taken and are taking to correct mistakes and repair injustices.

It is clear now that on the basis of false information we, in all good faith, made a number of mistakes, as in our support for the accusation against the Yugoslav Communist leaders as traitors, and our condemnation of a number of those falsely convicted.

Where we have made such mistakes, we profoundly regret them, and unreservedly withdraw our mistaken attacks.

But while we openly acknowledge and regret mistakes, we are proud of our long record in the field of international working-class solidarity.

It is the capitalist and right-wing Labour critics of the Soviet Union who have been continually wrong about its socialist achievements, while we, despite errors, have been overwhelmingly correct in our defence of the Soviet Union.

It was our party that took the lead in defending the achievements of the USSR from those who waged the war of intervention and prepared further wars.

It was our party, above all, that made known the Soviet achievements in the field of industrialisation and collectivisation of agriculture.

It was our party that showed the strength of the USSR when others denied it, and that ceaselessly led the fight for peace and friendship and for close economic and cultural relations with the Soviet people.

We shall continue to fight for the closest relations of friendship with the USSR and to defend it from capitalist aggression. We shall continue to make known its socialist achievements.

There is in the future bound to be a more critical examination of policies, from whatever quarter they come, but our attitude to the policies of other Communist and workers' parties will be based firmly on the principle of international solidarity.

Our support of this principle does not mean that in the past we have defended mistaken policies in the knowledge that they were mistaken, or that we will do so in the future.

It does mean that we recognise that we are engaged in the class war, and therefore cannot be neutral. We have to defend the working class and our brother parties, in whatever country, against capitalist attacks. There is no contradiction between international working-class solidarity and true patriotism – the one demands the other.

We have always been a responsible and independent British political party, deciding our own policy and activities in the light of our knowledge and estimate of the situation. The influence of our party has been developed in service to the British working people and the British labour movement, from which our party sprang.

We will assist in all efforts directed towards developing more exchanges and views between the various Communist and workers' parties.

As the Communist parties throughout the world grow in strength and maturity each party through its theoretical and practical work will make a greater, more independent contribution to world socialist understanding and experience. To the extent that we strengthen the work of our party in Britain *our* contribution will be the more fruitful.

III

Following the report and discussions at the closed session of our Twenty-Fourth Congress, a whole series of discussions on the Twentieth Congress of the CPSU have taken place throughout our party organisations.

We welcome the good attendance at these discussions; we welcome the thought, initiative and independent approach that has been given to the problems arising; we welcome the fully free atmosphere in which all points of view, however critical, have been put. Our party can only be strengthened by such live inner-party discussion.

At the same time the discussions have shown that some comrades have tended to concentrate on the weaknesses revealed at the Twentieth Congress rather than to discuss these within the context of the great advances, new perspectives and new theoretical approaches.

It is quite wrong to refuse to face up to the errors and injustices revealed, to refuse to acknowledge them, to try in any way to cover them up. If that is done we cannot appreciate the important steps already taken in the USSR to correct them and to repair them. If we refuse to accept and acknowledge weaknesses, we can never learn from them, nor appreciate the positive influence of their exposure and correction.

But it is equally wrong to see nothing but the errors and abuses, to examine them out of the context of the tremendous total human advance. For if that is done there results a purely negative attitude, a lack of balance and proportion.

It would also be wrong not to see the very great effects which the Twentieth Congress has already had on wide circles outside our party and especially within the British labour movement. Its significance for the future development of working-class unity on a national and international scale is becoming increasingly clear.

The main purpose of all our discussions must be to learn both from achievements and mistakes in the USSR, and from our own achievements and errors, to improve the work of our party in a situation which presents so many new problems but is also so extremely favourable.

IV

It has become clear in the course of discussions both at and following our Twenty-Fourth Congress that we need to take steps to improve the work and thinking of our party from top to bottom. We have been and are far too prone to neglect discussion of the questions of principle on which our immediate decisions and tactics must be based.

A certain dogmatism, rigidity and sectarianism in our approach and thinking have created unnecessary obstacles to united work and discussion within the labour movement.

Our Twenty-Fourth Congress drew attention to difficulties of our own making in this respect and called for the necessary steps to put this right.

We need to carry through discussion on three main lines:

1) **Problems of Unity:** The immediate line of work in connection with working-class unity is contained in the decisions of our Twenty-Fourth National Congress. Our task is to try to put these into operation as a matter of urgency so as to develop the struggle against the Tory government and the capitalist offensive. In addition, every success we can register in the struggle to remove bans and proscriptions will pave the way for even bigger and more important developments of unity. At the same time the Executive will indicate[20] a discussion on the longer-term issues of unity, particularly the relations of the party with the Labour Party, and of the political movement with the trade unions, how to develop the popular alliance, etc.

2) **The British Road to Socialism:** Ours was the first Communist Party outside the socialist countries to put forward a programme for the peaceful transition to socialism through the establishment of a broad popular alliance, election of a People's Government and the transformation of parliament and the state.

We did this in the light of the new balance of class forces in the world and the traditions, customs and institutions that are proper to Britain.

But we have not done enough to carry the analysis further. We need to study how the democratic liberties won in generations of people's struggle can be maintained and extended in the transition to socialism, to consider the problems of party political life and the relations of other political parties under a People's Government, and to examine the methods of guaranteeing socialist legality.

We need more study, thought and development of the section of our programme dealing with peaceful coexistence.

We have, in the light of the great new advances to independence of the colonial peoples, to examine more deeply the future relationships of a People's Britain and the liberated colonial countries.

We have to study the future of local government, and how the traditions and gains through popular struggle in that field can be developed and extended.

The Executive Committee will initiate a party discussion on all these matters, with the aim of preparing a new edition of the *British Road to Socialism* for presentation to the party branches and to the next party congress.

3) **The Communist Party:** The Twenty-Fourth Congress put forward the aims of 50,000 members of the party and 5000 members of the YCL as the next stage in our development. We need to strengthen and improve our party-building efforts and to give continual attention to the steady and sustained growth of our party branches, factory and local. Our congress

drew attention to serious shortcomings in relation to building the party and developing working-class unity. We must overcome these weaknesses in the course of improving our public work and inner-party life and strengthening the fight for unity. The further development of our collective work at every level, from the Executive Committee to the branches, must be seriously tackled.

A special commission has been established to examine the methods and working of our party congress, its committees, methods of discussion and election, criticism and self-criticism, and the improvement of inner-party democracy. The views of all party organisations on the report of this commission will be invited when it is published.

We need at all levels to learn to listen more attentively to those who raise points, suggestions, criticisms. We need to create the atmosphere in all party branches and committees where points, however critical, are freely raised and listened to in a comradely manner.

We need more controversy and discussion of a positive and constructive character in our party periodicals.

V

The Twentieth Congress of the CPSU showed that socialism is the hope of humanity. It should inspire us to new efforts to defeat the Tories and end capitalism and exploitation in Britain.

Never has the position been more favourable for the work of our party in Britain. Never has our party been more urgently needed by the working class and the working people.

Following the visit of Bulganin and Khrushchev there has been a considerable relaxation of international tension, and many long-established prejudices against the Soviet Union and the People's Democracies have been weakened and broken down.

There is a great wave of struggle developing on economic and social issues, a mounting anti-Tory feeling and determination to oust the Tory government. There are new opportunities for working-class unity and for a broad alliance of the people against Toryism. But in this favourable situation the official Labour leadership is not putting forward an alternative policy nor developing a campaign against the Tories. The role of and need for our party is clearer than ever before.

Our party is a fighting party, striving to unite the working people for the defeat of the Tories and the victory of socialism in Britain. Let our discussions be directed towards improving the fighting capacity of our party, inspiring all its members with our socialist aims, turning outwards to the people and leading them into action.

* * *

III: Rajani Palme Dutt, Notes of the Month: The Great Debate[21]
From *Labour Monthly*, May 1956, article dated 16 April 1956.

* * *

> Everyone recognises that change is in the air, and that the old Western policy is obsolescent, if not obsolete.
>
> Joseph Harsch, *Christian Science Monitor*, 10 January 1956.

> The need in this new and changed situation of discarding the old ways and trying new ideas and a fresh approach to peace.
>
> Alfred Robens,[22] House of Commons, 27 February 1956.

On this May Day of new hope and promise for the world – despite all the problems and dangers still with us – a fresh current is stirring and is changing all the old landmarks. The old problems still clamour for solution; the inheritance of the Cold War still dogs our steps. But on all sides there is recognition of a new world situation and a new balance in the world. Among representatives of all political sections, equally in the sphere of international relations, and within the labour movement, a fresh wind is blowing. The search goes forward to chart a new course for the second decade after the war such as will replace the dark clouds and threats of the first decade by happier omens. The Great Debate has opened.

Three Themes

What are the essential themes of the Great Debate? Not about Stalin. That there should be spots on any sun would only startle an inveterate Mithras-worshipper. Not about the now recognised abuses of the security organs in a period of heroic ordeal and achievement of the Soviet Union. To imagine that a great revolution can develop without a million cross-currents, hardships, injustices and excesses would be a delusion fit only for ivory-tower dwellers in fairyland who have still to learn that the thorny path of human advance moves forward, not only through unexampled heroism, but also with accompanying baseness, with tears and blood. The Great Debate that has opened is about larger issues, which spring from the swiftly moving new world situation, and which were spotlighted by the Twentieth Congress of the Communist Party of the Soviet Union. Three above all. First, the future of mankind in the nuclear age, of East-West relations, of peace and peaceful coexistence. Second, the future of the labour movement to meet the challenge of new conditions. Third, the future of the transition to socialism, for the completion of national and social liberation throughout the world.

Five Years of Change

Five years ago in these Notes in August 1951, we wrote already of the first stage of the Great Debate which had begun with the opening of the cease-fire negotiations in Korea as the initial sign of the turning point in the international situation. But the signs then were still weak and early. It took two years even for the cease-fire to be achieved in Korea. Since then the transformation has moved forward at an accelerating rate. Cease-fire in Korea; cease-fire in Vietnam; the leading independent role of India in the cause of peace; the Bandung Conference[23] of states representing the majority of mankind for peaceful coexistence; the Geneva Conference of Heads of State;[24] the upsurge of the Middle East and victories of independence of Egypt and the Sudan; the soaring economic achievement of the socialist world; and then the Twentieth Congress, with its tremendous new perspectives. Attempted counter-measures in plenty have not been lacking: Nazi rearmament, South-East Asia Pacts and Baghdad Pacts.[25] But these have had to be pushed through in the face of overwhelming popular resistance; they bear already in the sight of all the character of desperate rearguard actions to turn the tide of history. The caravan moves on.

Quickening Pace

Since the Twentieth Congress the pace has quickened. Consider the events of the mere six weeks of March and the first half of April. France, on the basis of the new leftward majority in parliament, moves to open official criticism of the entire Western military policy of the past years, and prepares for the visit of the French Premier to Moscow. The British people, breaking through all the police iron curtain barriers, boisterously welcome Malenkov; and the diehard campaign to cancel the Bulganin–Khrushchev visit fails. Iceland's parliament calls for the withdrawal of American troops. Morocco and Tunis win independence. Jordan expels Glubb; and the last British troops leave the Canal Zone. Pakistan proclaims a Republic. Ceylon's people clear out the discredited flunkey Kotelawala[26] and align their country with the progressive international orientation represented by Nehru.[27]

Socialist Aid

The Indo-Soviet Steel Agreement, finally signed in the beginning of March for the erection of a giant steelworks with Soviet aid, is followed a month later by an Indo-British Steel Agreement for the construction of a similar giant steelworks with British aid. Imitation is indeed the sincerest form of flattery. A new conception of the relation of advanced industrial countries to underdeveloped countries whose economy has been kept backward by imperialism is now extending from the socialist sphere to beyond its boundaries. President Eisenhower may still be demanding astronomical figures of dollars from Congress for the old type of so-called 'aid', four-fifths of which is officially described as 'military aid' (pouring in guns and subsidising troops for counter-revolution to uphold reactionary regimes which would otherwise collapse in a day without such aid), while the remaining one-fifth of so-called 'economic' aid is officially defended to Congress as subservient to the political and strategic purposes of United States foreign policy. The old familiar type of export of capital, investment, loans, credits or grants from imperialist countries to colonial or underdeveloped countries (sometimes mis-described as 'economic aid') may still continue, which is directed, not to make possible the independent economic development of the country in question, but to maintain its dependence, facilitate commercial penetration and pump out its raw material resources, while leaving the people in abject poverty.

A New Revolutionary Principle

But the new revolutionary principle of aid from an advanced industrial country to an underdeveloped country to enable that country to establish its own independent economy by industrialisation, this new principle, first practised in history within the Soviet Union in the relations with the Central Asian Soviet Republics and other former backward colonies of Tsarism, then extended during the last decade in the relations of the Soviet Union with the People's Democracies of Europe and with the Chinese People's Republic, is now extended beyond the frontiers of the socialist sphere to countries in Asia and the Middle East. More. Under the beneficial stimulus of competitive peaceful coexistence this principle begins to force itself even on the imperialist countries, so that industrialisation – the indispensable basis for independent economic existence and therefore for full and effective independence from imperialism – begins to go forward in these countries, not only with Soviet aid, but, under its stimulus, also with what the Twentieth Congress ironically and not unjustly called 'indirect Soviet aid' from the imperialist countries. This is a very striking concrete measure of a changing world.

Socialist International and Communism

Within the Socialist International two successive meetings of the Bureau and of the Executive of the Bureau have taken place to discuss the outcome of the Twentieth Congress and the proposition of cooperation with Communist parties. True, the immediate outcome is negative; the emphasis in the public statement is placed on the old dogmatic abstractions of alleged irreconcilable opposites, without regard to the immediate common interests for peace and the defence of living standards, which in real life are felt and recognised and acted upon by Socialist and Communist workers together in all countries. But differentiation already appeared at Zurich between the British Labour Party, French Socialists and Canadians on the one hand, and the Austrian–Dutch–Scandinavian majority on the other, when the Labour Party moved a minority amendment against the majority extreme view; and again at the London meeting when the document prepared by the Labour Party appears to have been ignored by the majority ('Transport House prepared a document, but little use seems to have been made of it', *The Times*, 9 April 1956). The issue will not be so easily settled. The very fact of these two meetings of the Bureau means that the discussion has opened; the question is on the agenda. In Italy cooperation exists. In France the whole pressure of the political situation drives towards it. In the special conditions of Britain the Twenty-Fourth Congress of the Communist Party has made its fresh approach to the aims of cooperation. On every side new questions are arising.

From Fear to Hope

'The trouble is', wrote the correspondent of *Time*, Jim Bell, in April, 'that the Geneva summit meeting killed the fear on which NATO was based.' A penetrating judgement which goes further than its proponent may have realised. For if mankind turns from being driven by fear to being moved by hope, there is no limit to the horizons which now open. Why this change in the mental climate of the world which all can now feel? What underlies this new world situation which is so visibly transforming the whole question of East-West relations, of the relations between the old minority world of capitalism and the rising majority world of socialism and national liberation? Many factors may be indicated. Underlying all is undoubtedly the manifest advancing peaceful economic and constructive strength of the socialist world (from less than one-tenth of world industrial production to nearly one-third today), the advance of socialism from one country to a world system, with the ceaseless peaceful initiatives of the socialist world. Closely allied with this, and arising from the extending weight of socialism in the world and the consequent end of the monopolist domination of the world by imperialism, is the advance of four-fifths of the former colonial and semi-colonial majority of mankind to the establishment of independent states, and to increasing open differentiation from the policies of their former imperialist overlords and to friendly cooperation with the socialist world for peace. All this has manifestly changed, and is further changing, the balance of the world.

A Revolution of Thought

The new conceptions which arise from this changed world balance, and which have rendered obsolete all the old assumptions of the Western system of military alliances as the 'bulwark against communism', may be briefly indicated. First, it is now universally recognised that there is no question of military superiority of either camp. From this has followed the collapse of the old Western 'policy of strength' with its dream of the eventual 'showdown' or dictated solutions in place of negotiation. Second, it is now universally recognised that the entire nuclear strategy is suicidal, and that in this sense the 'Great Deterrent' is the Great Illusion. The Defence White Paper may still seek to brandish the nuclear weapon as the lynchpin of Western strategy (now also for 'limited wars'); the government may proclaim the 'plan' to evacuate twelve millions of the population to fictitious 'safe areas'; while the official Labour Party pamphlet in reply may retort that the real solution is not 'evacuation' but 'dispersal'.[28] But the majority of intelligent people have long reached the conclusion that all this is mania, even though still dangerous mania. Third, it is now universally recognised that the Soviet leaders and all the leaders of the socialist world want peace, just as the Soviet leaders have recognised at their Twentieth Congress that there is today no aggressive state in either Europe or Asia which could launch a new world war. The special question of the United States, which now stands at the crossroads of its policy to face the new world situation, and is at the moment in this presidential year torn between conflicting currents, needs separate consideration.

'This Is All Rather Different'

Walter Lippmann[29] has graphically described the perplexity of American policy in face of this new world situation which has begun to make its vast panoply of military alliances inherited from the previous decade look obsolete:

> In the past few months Mr Dulles[30] has found himself entangled in an extraordinary series of dilemmas – in issues in which he is damned if he does and damned if he doesn't. He has been caught in the Goa dilemma between Portugal and India, in the Jakarta dilemma between the Netherlands and Indonesia, in the North African dilemma between France and the Algerian Arabs, in the Palestine dilemma between Israel and the Arabs, in the Baghdad dilemma between Iraq and Egypt, in the Cyprus dilemma between Britain and Greece, in the Persian Gulf dilemma between Saudi Arabia and Britain, and so on and on.

This is all rather different from what it used to be in the pre-Geneva phase of the Cold War. Then the issues were between Communists and anti-Communists. The line of leadership was self-evident. But now the issues which plague Mr Dulles are very often primarily among our allies and the peoples that we are courting …

The old, much simpler days are past when there was one great adversary and leadership consisted in opposing him. (Walter Lippman, *New York Herald Tribune*, 7 April 1956)

Similarly Mr Dulles himself reported in Washington on 23 March, after returning from his tour of ten countries in the Middle East and Southern Asia, and discovering the marked contrast of the frigid reception he received from the enthusiastic mass reception to the Soviet leaders: 'While we think first of the dangers that stem from international Communism, many of them think first of possible encroachments from the West.' Herein is expressed the present dilemma of American policy, reflected equally in the present doldrums of NATO, from which General Gruenther,[31] after three years of vainly belabouring and berating his European 'allies' and seeing his 'grand army' dwindle under him, has thought it wisest to retire. In the United States also there is going to be need for thought, even though the atmosphere of a presidential election may temporarily arrest its public progress.

Britain, France and Germany

What of Britain? France has led the way among the Western powers in taking the first initiative to begin to break free from old conceptions and respond to the new world situation. The bold declaration of Foreign Minister Pineau on 2 March, criticising the 'gigantic error' of Western policy over the past few years, has been followed up by the no less emphatic declaration of Premier Mollet on 2 April when he said, with reference to the disarmament negotiations: 'Each time No is said by the United States, we lose a battle in world opinion. People conclude: "Well, then, it is Russia that wants peace. It is the United States that doesn't want it."'

He went on to emphasise that German unity could only be realised in a framework of general disarmament, in place of the other way round – precisely the thesis maintained by the Soviet Union at the Geneva October meeting of Foreign Ministers and then rejected by the Western representatives. France has moved ahead of Britain. But there is reason to believe that Britain, simultaneously involved in many difficulties with the United States, has found the initiative of France not unwelcome:

The rogue elephant tactics of M Pineau have compelled France's allies to look afresh into the whole question of relations with the Communist half of the world. While France is moving a bit too fast for Britain, and much too fast for the United States, she is moving in a direction that begins to look inevitable. (*Sunday Times*, 25 March 1956)

Shades of the inevitability of gradualism! When a leading Conservative organ begins to speak in these terms, the signs of new currents are inescapable.

Britain's Policy Straddle

British policy, hamstrung by the preoccupations of its obstinate losing battle to maintain its old monopolist hold in the Middle East against both Arab and Cypriot national liberation and American penetration, has not been ready so far to move with the same freedom of action as France in the European sphere. French preoccupation with the war against Algerian national liberation actually sharpens the hostility to NATO, which in the eyes of French colonialists has diverted French armed forces from their colonial tasks to an inappropriate military training, equipment and immobilisation under American command against an imaginary Soviet menace. Hence the most varied streams in French policy drive to the new orientation. British official policy, on the other hand, remains torn between the past and the future. On the one hand, the British Ambassador in Paris, Sir Gladwyn Jebb,[32] sang the old gramophone record of the inevitable conflict with world Communism in order to rebuke France on 6 March: 'By definition Communism must pursue its efforts to destroy capitalism. Conflict is the natural state of relations between East and West.' Similarly the *New York Times* correspondent in London, Drew Middleton, reported on 22 March a 'senior official' in London as declaring: 'Almost without noticing it we have passed from the postwar into the prewar era. We know it. I hope you know it in Washington.'

On the other hand, the British Ambassador in Washington, Sir Roger Makins,[33] emphasised the significance of Soviet economic aid as 'without strings or conditions' and went on to criticise the Western Cold War strategy in terms closely similar to those of Mollet and Pineau: 'On our side there is a tendency to stress guns rather than butter.' In short, from the British point of view, both France and the United States are out of step.

Sir Anthony's Two Voices

As befits a British Prime Minister, Sir Anthony Eden[34] sings both tunes on successive occasions in order to keep his disparate flock in hand. On the one hand, he seeks to appease his anti-Soviet diehards by proclaiming in public speeches at Conservative rallies all the old provocative shibboleths of the Cold War, as in his speech at Bradford on 28 January:

> The character of the contest between the Communist powers and the Western democracies has changed, not for the better … The address of the power which dragoons and dominates its satellites is 'The Kremlin, Moscow'.

And similar stuff to delight the High Tory gallery and charm away their suspicions. On the other hand, his actions are in certain respects more important than his words. Having removed the extreme anti-Soviet Macmillan[35] from the Foreign Secretaryship after the latter's dismal servility to Dulles and consequent fiasco at Geneva in the autumn, he has firmly resisted the very considerable clamour of the anti-Soviet Tory sections (reflected in the normally loyal Conservative organ, the *Daily Telegraph*) to cancel the Bulganin–Khrushchev visit. Indeed, he went so far as to achieve a (for him) relatively infrequent epigrammatic brilliance when he tartly replied to Air Commodore Harvey's[36] enquiry on the 'cost' of the visit: 'Very much less than a millionth part of one hydrogen bomb.' The significance of the differentiation in Conservative ranks should not be underestimated.

What Is a 'Great Power'?

Sir Anthony Eden's dilemma of policy, reflecting the contradictions of the present position of British imperialism, found expression in his speech to the Central Council of the National Union of Conservative and Unionist Associations on 16 March, when he sought to defend the 'unpopular' economic measures which the government felt compelled to impose by the argument:

> Only a solvent and prosperous Britain can shoulder the burdens of a Great Power. History and geography have combined to give us a special position in the world. We cannot, and will not, abdicate from this … The logical conclusion of abdication would be a policy of neutralism, and to be neutral for Britain is a slow death.

But supposing the 'logical conclusion' of this imperialist conception of a 'Great Power', with the consequent crippling colonial wars and overseas commitments, making Britain the most heavily taxed and militarised major country in the world in proportion to population, leads to economic strangulation and a consequent alternative form of 'slow death'. What then?

No wonder that one Conservative MP has already jumped to the opposite conclusion:

> Mr Osborne[37] (Louth, Conservative) said that we were trying too much to keep up with the Russians and the Americans. We did not have the resources to keep up with the Joneses and the Browns. Was it not time to recognise that Britain had come down in the world, and was no longer the Great Power she had been. (*The Times*, 1 March 1956)

Between these two extremes of Conservative utterance is typically expressed the present crisis of British imperialism.

How Britain Can Lead

But is it really true that these are the only two alternatives before Britain? Either to perish of economic strangulation in the desperate attempt to maintain a doomed imperialist system of power. Or to give up the unequal struggle and sink to the level of an insignificant country with little voice in world affairs. The two alternatives are equally preposterous. Never had Britain such an opportunity as today to play a foremost progressive role in world affairs, equally beneficial for peace and security in the world, and for the solution of Britain's problems at home. Let us recall the words of *The Times* on 22 June 1942:

> The structure of European peace must be truly international, and must be founded on the freedom and cooperation of the peoples of Europe. But Great Britain and Russia will remain the essential pillars on which the whole framework rests. So long as they are intact and erect, the structure of peace will stand unshaken. If they fall asunder, nothing else will avail.

It is precisely because Britain during the decade after the war, in the desperate attempt to maintain a doomed empire, and falling a victim to the Hitlerite anti-Communist bogey, fell away from this policy, entered into unhealthy dependence on the United States, and agreed to the partition of Europe and the remilitarisation of the old forces of Nazism in Western Germany, that Britain has fallen deeper in the mire. Britain, France and the Soviet Union, as the leading powers of Europe, have the responsibility to cooperate for peace and security in Europe; and on this basis the peaceful reunification of Germany can be achieved. More. Britain has the decisive opportunity for world leadership for peace today. An independent and consistent initiative of Britain for peace today alongside France, the Soviet Union, India and

China, for collective security in Europe and Asia, for the ending of colonial wars, for the peaceful reunification of Germany outside sectional military alliances, and for disarmament, would rally all Europe and Asia in support, and hasten the indispensable revision of United States policy.

National Independence and Working-Class Leadership

But such a development requires decisive changes and a positive step forward in the whole orientation of Britain's policy. It requires a change in political direction in Britain. Its fulfilment requires in the first place the effective national independence of Britain. When Sir Anthony Eden last went to Washington he pleaded for permission to relax the embargoes on trade with China in order to assist in meeting Britain's desperate market problems. Permission was not granted. Is that what Sir Anthony means by the status of a 'Great Power'? Toryism may manoeuvre an election in Britain, not on the basis of confidence in its own merits, but on the basis of the wave of disillusionment with the shortcomings of past Labour leadership and policy. But Toryism cannot lead Britain along the path of peace, progress and economic reorganisation required by the present situation. The responsibility of leadership to win a new future for Britain rests and can only rest with the organised working class, representing the majority of the nation and potentially capable of drawing to its banner the widest sections of the people for a new policy which could give them hope. But the fulfilment of this responsibility requires the policy, the leadership and the unity which can alone make it possible. The problems of policy and leadership can only be solved on the basis of the fullest democracy within the political labour movement, such as is at present hampered by the bans on representation and expression of key sections. The problem of unity of the political labour movement turns on the relations of the Labour Party and the Communist Party. To these problems the Twenty-Fourth Congress of the Communist Party directed its main attention.

Do the Communists Matter?

At this point the critics commonly explode. How ridiculous! To talk of unity of the political labour movement as turning on the relationship of the Labour Party and the Communist Party. But the Communist Party, they repeat with tireless iteration, is insignificant. As well talk of uniting the fly and the elephant. The Communist Party, proclaims the pontifical *Times* editorial, with its mere 34,000 members and minute electoral vote, is 'derisory' in point of size, and 'of little immediate consequence'. 'The British Communist Party has no political influence in this country whatsoever', thunders the *Daily Herald*.[38] It represents only a 'nuisance value'. It is a 'fifth column', screams the *Daily Herald* a few days later. 'Never in its chequered history', shrieks *Tribune*,[39] 'has the Communist Party been nearer to complete demoralisation.' In fact, quite a remarkable amount of heat appears to be engendered by this insignificant object. A striking unanimity of apoplexy appears to extend from the Carlton Club to *Tribune* at the mention of British Communists or the British Communist Party. But why does this apoplexy need to be so constantly buttressed by the ceaseless iteration of the assertion that its occasion is really quite too utterly unimportant for anyone's attention?

Communist Congress and the Press

For such a negligible object, a remarkable amount of space and attention was given by the press to the recent congress of the Communist Party. Of course it is true that the press had conjured up a 'crisis' in the Communist Party and was gleefully awaiting its outbreak. The contrast between the screaming headlines on the day that the congress met, and the sudden somersault and discomfiture two days later when the press had to creep away with its tail between its legs, deprived of its 'crisis', affords an amusing example of modern high-power publicity. Before the congress the attentive reader learned that 'British Reds Slam Their Leaders' (*Daily Express*), 'British Communists Snipe At Their Own Leaders', 'Executive Committee Under Fire' (*Manchester Guardian*), 'Reds Rebel' (*Daily Mail*). After the congress, when the bewildered press table had had to observe the unanimous adoption of the political resolution by the free vote of the delegates, the gloomy headlines proclaimed 'Communist Crisis? Oh No' (*News Chronicle*), 'Communist Leadership "Get Away With It"' (*Daily Express*), 'Don't Write Off the Reds Yet' (*Daily Express*). *The Times* ponderously sought to explain the inexplicable by blandly asserting that 'it was evident that the rules enforcing discipline in the party still stand firm' (what 'rules' or what 'discipline' governed the free vote of the delegates was left discreetly unexplained). But this amusing example of current press methods carries also a certain lesson for the politically observant. Would there be so much excitement about an alleged internal 'crisis' of a minute organisation if it were really so politically insignificant?

Misleading Appearances

The truth is that the 'insignificant' line of argument can have a certain temporary effectiveness at the moment, but it can be overdone. The Communist Party is still one of the smaller parties, though its membership already represents a greater organised strength than the old socialist parties which founded the Labour Party. The electoral system, designed to maintain the monopoly of two parties, gives to a certain extent a misleading effect; the 'British' system was deliberately imitated in Western Germany in order to wipe out all Communist representation in the traditional Marxist strongholds of the Ruhr and the industrial West; its adoption has been openly advocated by reaction in France as a means to reduce the Communist representation of a quarter of the electorate to a fragment. Still the electoral weakness is so far a fact. There is no need to exaggerate the present stage of strength of the Communist Party in order to prove the value of cooperation of Communist and Labour Party workers in order to exert the fullest united strength of the working class and the political labour movement.

The Industrial Working Class and the Communist Party

The politically important question for those seriously concerned with the future of the working-class movement is not the comparison of the relative size of two parties, but the real situation in the working class. Even the noisiest peddlers of the 'political insignificance' of the Communist Party stress its 'industrial' influence in the factories, in the key industrial areas and in the trade unions – as if this were not 'political'. Hence the foolish talk about 'infiltration', 'troublemakers', 'fifth columns', etc. But it is precisely this influence that is *political* in its significance and importance for the whole working-class movement. When the Communist Party led the campaign in the trade unions against Nazi rearmament, and a real majority was won to reverse the official policy of support, this was a political campaign. When the progressive alliance of Communist and non-Communist trade unionists in the Trades Union Congress win an average of three to three and a half millions for resolutions denounced by the platform as 'Communist-inspired', and with Communist spokesmen as the principal advocates, this is a political phenomenon. When the same or corresponding left policies receive only from one to under two million votes at the Labour Party Conference, despite the addition of the largely leftward votes of the constituency parties, but where Communist spokesmen are excluded, this would clearly indicate that the political influence of Communist spokesmanship and leadership within the labour movement is not negligible. The maintenance of the *Daily Worker* now for over a quarter of a century, as the principal organ of left opinion in the labour movement, entirely on the basis of working-class support, when the Labour Party and Trades Union Congress combined, with all their resources, found it impossible to maintain a daily newspaper, is also a political phenomenon of our era which no serious student of working-class politics, with any knowledge of the history of the movement, will underestimate.

Realist Conclusions

Every trade-union official, Labour Party organiser and serious political observer is perfectly well aware – whatever fairy tales they may feel compelled to offer on the platform or in syndicated press articles – that there exists a significant body of Communist opinion within the key sections of the industrial working class, and that the Communist Party and *Daily Worker* express and voice this body of opinion. But the industrial working class is the decisive basis of the Labour Party. From this situation three conclusions follow. First, the industrial working class, as in every capitalist country, but above all in such a country as Britain where the wage-earners are the majority of the population, represents the political future in Britain and the leader of the transition to socialism. Second, the Communist Party representing the aim of socialism, already exercises a sizable and growing political influence and leadership within the most active key sections of the industrial working class, especially in major industry. Third, and as the inescapable consequence of the foregoing, it follows that, if the two foregoing propositions are true, then for any serious socialist or Labour Party member concerned for the future of the political working-class movement the question of the relationship of the Communist Party and the Labour Party, and of the possibility of cooperation of Communist and Labour workers is no minor subsidiary question, but the key question for the effectiveness and unity and future victory of the political labour movement and socialism in Britain.

Trade Unions and the Labour Party

The trade unions are the basis of the Labour Party, thereby differentiating it from the type of social-democratic party based on a set of political doctrines. They supply five-sixths of its membership and the main proportion of its central finance. The policies of the majority of unions are thrashed out at conferences with the participation of Communists in preparation for the Labour Party Conference. The constitutions of important unions require the participation of their leading officials in delegations to the Labour Party conference. In given cases the leading officials may be Communist. They participate in the discussions of the delegation determining its vote outside the conference hall, and then are illogically excluded from presenting the viewpoint of their membership inside the conference hall. What is the use of talking about the 'menace' of the 'Communist embrace'? The 'Communist embrace' is already there; only the normal healthy democratic functioning is hindered which would facilitate the common thrashing out of policy with democratic representation and decisions to express the wishes of the membership.

Mr Gaitskell Kisses Death[40]

When the Labour Party leadership need more finance for the Labour Party
– and they need it badly, as the so far unsuccessful wooing of the cooperative
societies for affiliation has indicated, thus revealing that the problem of
unity is in fact a problem affecting all sections of the movement – they
inevitably have to go to the general secretaries of the trade unions to ask
for it. So Mr Gaitskell[41] and Mr Morgan Phillips[42] travelled up to Southport
before the last Trades Union Congress to meet the general secretaries of the
unions and ask for more money. But the general secretaries of some of the
most important major unions are leading Communists. Did Mr Gaitskell
blench before the 'kiss of death'? On the contrary. He positively rushed
forward into the embrace with the laudable aim of securing more cash for
the Labour Party. All that he forgot for the moment was that there is an old
English democratic principle of 'no taxation without representation'. Mr
Gaitskell is a realist. Perhaps he may even yet learn, if Communist influence
continues to extend in the main trade unions, and he wishes to maintain the
indispensable basis of the Labour Party. But Mr Robens will have to beware
of contamination from association with Mr Gaitskell and Mr Morgan
Phillips. For kisses can be infectious. And Mr Robens' 'kiss of death' was Mr
Gaitskell's 'kiss of life'.

Liberating Mr Zilliacus

Mr Zilliacus[43] has sought to defend the maintenance of the iron curtain
between Communist and Labour Party workers by exhuming the somewhat
hoary MacDonaldite[44] fallacies that there exists some supposed irreconcilable
antagonism between the Marxist theory of the conquest of political power
by a united working class leading the majority of the people for the purpose
of establishing socialism and the theories of the Labour Party. True, Mr
Zilliacus has to admit that the Communist Party stands for the achievement
of socialism by democratic means. But he endeavours to argue that this is
only since the Twentieth Congress of the Communist Party of the Soviet
Union in February 1956, after which 'the British Communist Party with
disciplined unanimity became lightning converts to democratic socialism'
– 'a lightning conversion'. It would be an insult to so well documented
a scholar as Mr Zilliacus to suggest that, without needing to go into past
controversies, he was unaware that the Communist Party programme *The
British Road to Socialism* in 1951 propounded this same path. Five years
would make a somewhat curious 'overnight conversion'.[45] Indeed, Mr
Zilliacus could construct a much prettier argument, if he were so inclined,
to 'prove' that the Communist Party of the Soviet Union slavishly follows

the British Communist Party. But we sympathise with Mr Zilliacus and would not dream of accusing him of being unaware of the facts belying his allegations. He knows that he is under very sharp surveillance on these matters, and that unless he were to repeat somewhat vociferously the ancient MacDonaldite fallacies he might again be in danger of finding himself on the mat under the somewhat precarious democratic structure of the Labour Party. We sympathise with Mr Warbey[46] and the rest of the thirteen Labour MPs who found themselves caned for endeavouring to hold a conference on suggested democratic improvements of the Labour Party's constitution. We regard Mr Zilliacus, Mr Warbey and their friends as good men in bondage. The Communist Party is endeavouring to liberate them and all other socialists in the Labour Party to be free to fulfil the aims of the pioneers.

A Voice From the Past

After all, the aims of the pioneers were to try to establish unity of all sections of the working-class movement, socialist parties and trade unions together, Marxist and non-Marxist, for the democratically-agreed common objectives of the working class. Listen to the address of the Chairman of the Labour Party Conference in 1917 (when the Labour Party was still a federation of socialist parties and trade unions):

> From the very first the ties which bound the party together were of the loosest possible kind. It has steadily, and in my opinion, wisely, always declined to be bound by any programme, to subscribe to any dogma or to lay down any creed ... On the contrary, its strength has been its catholicity, its tolerance, its welcoming of all shades of political and even revolutionary thought, provided that its chief object – the unifying of the workers' political power – was not damaged or hindered thereby.

No doubt conditions have changed. We cannot go back to the past. But is it not desirable to try to find the way to fulfil the same basic aims in the new conditions of today, as the pioneers did in their day? They also had to wrestle with many obstacles in the path of unity. But they found a solution in terms of their day, on the basis of 'catholicity', 'tolerance' and 'welcoming of all shades of political and even revolutionary thought', to combine all sections, without destroying the identity of each, for the common objective of 'unifying the workers' political power'. Has this no message for us today?

Why Not Try To Cooperate?

Let us be modest in our first steps towards the aim of unity, recognising that the inheritance of the past will not be overcome in a day. What is in question today is an immediate objective for immediate political needs. It would be idle phantasy to imagine that the present conditions are ripe for settling the ultimate questions of the long-term future relationship of the Labour Party and the Communist Party as we know them today, or the path to the final aim of a united political party of the working class. It would be as out of place to denounce the Labour Party as bankrupt because many of its leaders have moved away from socialism, as to demand the dissolution of the Communist Party because its members sincerely believe that the whole history and experience of the labour movement demonstrates the necessity of an active party of socialism within the broad labour movement of the mass organisations of the working class. What is in question is to seek the first steps to cooperation of all workers, Communist and non-Communist, in the immediate political field as they cooperate already in the economic field; to remove the artificial barriers which at present hinder such cooperation; and to facilitate the democratic functioning of the political labour movement by the participation of all sections through the democratic election of delegates with equal rights from the mass organisations. These objectives are not unattainable. The whole situation requires them and will further require them. The plain issue is before us. The debate has opened. Even Mr Robens' 'kiss of death' speech was a contribution to the debate, however negative; for he recognised that the issue now stands before the movement for discussion. Let the debate continue. We can be confident that the good sense of the working class, the urgent needs of the situation and the deep desire for unity will prevail in the end against all the forces of division.

* * *

IV: John Saville, Problems of the Communist Party
From *World News*, 19 May 1956.

* * *

What are the main problems facing the British Communist Party?

1) The Twentieth Congress of the CPSU revealed that there had been many miscarriages of justice and many crimes committed that went far beyond what can be explained by that convenient term 'historical inevitability'. Associated with these crimes were certain major political mistakes, especially in the realm of foreign policy. The present Russian leadership has suggested that the main, indeed the only, reason for these

mistakes was the assumption of personal power by Stalin.

2) These revelations meant that many of the policies of the CPSU which we had supported were wrong. In international politics Yugoslavia is the obvious example. More important, we were shown as having vigorously denied that arbitrary arrests, deportations and executions could occur in a socialist democracy. It is important to remember that, as a party (whatever individuals may have said in private), we did deny such things, and we argued that, in all respects, socialist democracy, as it had established itself in the Soviet Union, was superior to bourgeois democracy. In most other matters (the exceptions are trifling) we followed the line of the CPSU.

3) When not only our enemies, but many of our friends, suggest that our blind faith has led us to support many things which violate the socialist ideas of brotherhood and fraternity, it seems to me that we can say two things only in reply. Firstly, that political support of the USSR is the basic principle of working-class internationalism, and this we will always adhere to. Secondly, that the error we fell into was not defending the USSR despite its mistakes but defending the mistakes themselves.

4) Where does the division of opinion arise? Why are we faced with a number of comrades seriously questioning whether they can remain within our ranks? The division has arisen because the leadership, or a majority of the leadership, are apparently not willing to recognise that here is a major problem for us. They are not willing, that is, to admit that we shall stand discredited before the labour movement unless we honestly and frankly state where we went wrong and that we will ensure, as far as we can, that similar errors are not made in the future. This is not an academic issue, as some pretend. It is our political honesty as a political party that is at stake. Both inside and outside the labour movement, the question of how we envisage the transition to socialism is of crucial importance. Belief in our intentions and our assurances will inevitably be judged, and rightly so, by our attitude towards these recent revelations which have come out of the Soviet Union.

We have, surely, to convince many socialists, let alone the millions outside the labour movement, that the establishment of socialism, while by no means painless, will not be accompanied by the 'knock on the door at 4am', guilt by association and judicial murder. This is what Comrade Dutt has quite failed to understand in the current *Labour Monthly*. He writes:

> To imagine that a great revolution can develop without a million cross-currents, hardships, injustices and excesses, would be a delusion fit only for ivory-tower dwellers in fairy land who have still to learn that the thorny path of human advance moves forward, not only through

unexampled heroism, but also with accompanying baseness, with tears and blood.

If the crimes we now know of were historically necessary, the man in the street is entitled to say 'Not for me, brother!', and I would agree with him. It is not, I think, unfair to remind Comrade Dutt that the greater number of those arbitrarily executed were leading Communists.

5) There are many fundamental problems of theory and practice which require the most thorough and widespread discussion. I would mention only three. Firstly, and to my mind the most important, the question of our attitude to the Soviet Union in the future; secondly, the political forms within which the transition to socialism will take place; thirdly, the preservation and active extension, both now and in the future, of inner-party democracy.

6) I believe that the tradition of controversy within the party has become much weaker in recent years. Of late, we have become much more conformist. At the present time questioning is more widespread than it has been for well over a decade, and only the widest debate will re-establish confidence. I trust that the argument that 'we must really get on with the job, because the class struggle never stops and we cannot afford to waste time on debate, etc' will never again be heard. If similar arguments had been adopted in 1928 and 1929 Comrades Pollitt and Dutt would not have defeated the old leadership when they did. Our need for theoretical discussion and political debate is not less than it was in the 1920s, and it is the responsibility of our party leadership actively to encourage the development of political unity out of the present clash of ideas.

* * *

V: Rajani Palme Dutt, Notes of the Month: New Times, New Measures

From *Labour Monthly*, June 1956, article dated 16 May 1956.

* * *

The world changes and in these days it changes rapidly. A policy that was good six months ago is not necessarily now of any validity. It is necessary that we find better, more effective ways of keeping ourselves in tune with the world's needs. – President Eisenhower, 21 April 1956

From Fulton to Aachen is geographically many leagues. In the span of time it is ten years. In the measure of world politics it is the journey from the abyss of darkness to the first rays of sunrise. Ten years have passed since

Sir Winston Churchill, in the words of the *Daily Telegraph* (10 May 1956) 'in his courageous Fulton speech of 1946 declared the Cold War open'. Already within seven years, by 1953, in face of the visible bankruptcy of the Western dreams of military and nuclear superiority to impose dictated solutions, and in face of the impregnable peaceful strength and staggering constructive advance of the socialist world, the author of Fulton led the way among Western political leaders in publicly advocating a new perspective for top-level negotiations for peaceful coexistence. But this year at Aachen the premier veteran statesman of the Western world went further.

Portent of Aachen

On 10 May 1956, Sir Winston Churchill at Aachen, in the presence of Premier Adenauer[47] (to whom his speech gave, according to the *Manchester Guardian*, 'his biggest headache since his visit to Moscow in September'), launched a direct offensive against the basic Cold War conception of the division of Europe into opposing military camps. With one blow he shattered the whole mythology of presenting the truncated torso of a bloc of Western European states as 'United Europe'. 'In a true unity of Europe', he declared, 'Russia must have her part.' With regard to all the forms of so-called 'European unity' expressed in NATO, Western European Union, OEEC, the 'Council of Europe', etc, he declared that 'the spirit of this arrangement should not exclude Russia and the Eastern European states'. 'The great issues which perplex us', he went on, 'of which one of the gravest is the reunification of Germany, could then be solved more easily than by rival blocs confronting each other with suspicion and hostility.'

The Wheel Turns

Two years ago the Soviet Union offered to join NATO, in order to bring to the test of practice whether it was really a defensive alliance, as alleged, or in its essential character an anti-Soviet military coalition, and met with a refusal. Last year at the Foreign Minister's Conference at Geneva the Soviet Union proposed a united European Collective Security Pact, which should draw together and eventually replace both NATO and the Warsaw Pact, and thus end the dangerous confrontation of opposing military blocs. This proposal was rejected by the Western Foreign Ministers. The Soviet Union equally proposed that the unification of a peaceful Germany could best be achieved within such a framework of European Collective Security (as, indeed, the original Directive from the Heads of States Conference had plainly implied, by placing the question of German unification several paragraphs down in the agenda after the question of European security). This was no less absolutely refused by the Western Foreign Ministers, who insisted on their 'take it or leave it' terms of German unification in a partitioned Europe as the first condition for any settlement and as their non-negotiable ultimatum on the basis of which they broke up the conference. Now the broad conception underlying the Soviet proposals has been presented in general outline with dramatic emphasis by Sir Winston Churchill as the path to a peaceful solution. No wonder the *Daily Telegraph* warns against the 'overriding danger of regarding the Churchillian policy as practicable in the present'. But even the gutter press has not so far dared to present Sir Winston as the Gramophone of Moscow. When the Cold Warmaker of Fulton has become the Grand Peacemaker of Aachen, this is a measure of the transformation that is taking place in the world.

Churchillian Barometer

For the Churchillian initiative does not stand alone. The elder statesman may still be, as often before on some of the wider strategic-political issues of world relations, a little ahead of the main body of the politicians and generals of the capitalist world, the Montgomerys,[48] Ismays[49] or Macmillans today, or the Neville Chamberlains and Hoares[50] of yesterday. This wider strategic conception in viewing the world outlook from the standpoint of his class has on occasions led him in an extreme reactionary direction. As the main protagonist of the wars of intervention, he was profoundly conscious of the new world era which was opening with the first victory of the working class and socialism, and desired to strangle it at birth. Similarly his recognition of the far-reaching world significance of Indian freedom led to his desperate rearguard diehard fight against it. As the author of Fulton, he was no less conscious of the new balance of world relations with the extension of socialism to a world system, and once again hoped to use superior military nuclear power to turn the tide of history. But the same wider conception has also on occasions led him to stand in the forefront for conclusions of progressive significance. Before the Second World War he was the first of the capitalist politicians to recognise the danger of the policy of promoting Hitler's rearmament and expansion as the supposed grand weapon against Communism, and during the war he took the lead in embracing the alliance with the Soviet Union which saved the world – even though not without ulterior very different calculations for the future. So today since 1953 he has taken the lead among capitalist politicians in recognising the new balance of the world situation, the bankruptcy of the Cold War policies, and the necessity to advance to meet the Soviet Union halfway in order to realise a positive policy for peaceful coexistence.

British-Soviet Talks

But in varying degree the same new tendencies have made themselves felt in all the countries of the Western alliance. The British Conservative government has welcomed Bulganin and Khrushchev for the most important talks since the Geneva summit meeting to carry forward the meeting of heads of states on both sides. The frank and friendly interchange, and the constructive communiqué, have demonstrated the positive significance of these talks as a step forward on the path of peaceful coexistence. This positive significance has only been underlined by the failure of the reactionary diehard campaign to cancel or sabotage the talks. It is regrettable that the true feelings of the labour movement were misrepresented by the dinner episode, which succeeded in creating the impression that, at a moment when the Tory government was striving to improve friendly relations with the Soviet Union, Labour appeared to be ranged with the most hostile anti-Soviet Cold War forces.[51] Had the full strength of the labour movement been mobilised for constructive aims, there is no doubt that more positive results could have been won from the talks. As it is, on the key issues of disarmament, the trade bans and European collective security the battle has still to be fought and won. Nevertheless, the outcome of the talks, the concrete trade offer, and the character of Sir Anthony Eden's subsequent broadcast and agreement to make a return visit to Moscow represent a serious step forward along the road.

Ferment in the West

Nor does Britain stand alone in thus taking the first tentative steps towards a new response to a new world situation. France's Premier Mollet has left for Moscow, following the visit of the French Socialist delegation and its talks with the representatives of the Central Committee of the Communist Party of the Soviet Union (in practical contradiction of the Socialist International Bureau declaration attempting to veto such talks). France proposed through the Pineau plan to transform the emphasis of NATO to the economic plane, supported the Soviet proposal for a ban on arms exports to the Middle East, and has welcomed Tito to Paris. In Western Germany, even at the same time as the rearmament plans have now openly drawn in Hitler's principal generals such as Halder[52] and the convicted war criminal Manstein[53] to guide them, the flood of public expression rises against the bankruptcy of the Adenauer policy of relying on the power of NATO to force unification on the Western terms, and the demand gathers for direct negotiations with the Soviet Union as the path to peaceful reunification. Even in the United States, the confusion and controversy on future policy in the midst of the partial paralysis of a presidential election year is accompanied by signs of new trends. In relation to the discussions on the future of NATO at its Council meeting the *Observer* reported on 13 May:

> … the product of a pre-conference working group in which America played a leading role – the idea of a general European security group which might embrace both NATO and the Warsaw Pact. To put it bluntly, the American view is that NATO has grown stale.

Disarmament Deadlock and Disarmament Practice

This new climate in Western opinion and discussion has not yet found reflection in the necessary positive advance to new policies, corresponding to the far-reaching advance carried out by the Soviet Union and the socialist world. The Western powers still cling to the entire structure of the old Cold War policies, even at the same time as their increasingly visible bankruptcy in the new conditions is recognised. This was shown in the breakdown of the Disarmament Sub-Committee negotiations, where the Western representatives aroused the biting sarcastic comment of their own supporters by successively obstructing every one of their own proposals as soon as the Soviet Union accepted them, and finally sought to introduce unlimited new conditions by demanding settlement of every political question all over the world before disarmament. But here, too, these tactics have proved a boomerang. To the mortification of the Western representatives, the Soviet Union has proceeded to cut the knot of the deadlock, so far as it can be cut from its side, by entering on large-scale unilateral disarmament, with the slashing of its armed forces by 65 divisions and 1,200,000 men, on top of the previous reduction of 640,000, or a net reduction of 1,840,000. A crash of shares on Wall Street followed this alarming news. The armaments tycoons very well understood that this practical example will overwhelmingly reinforce the popular campaign in the Western countries to compel a corresponding large-scale reduction of armed forces and a disarmament agreement.

What To Do With the Dinosaur?

Similarly the NATO Council meeting in May revealed the same crisis of Western policy. 'Confusion', 'frustration', 'fundamental differences', 'deep divergences' – such are the terms the most responsible press reporters have used to describe the meeting. On the one hand, it was recognised that the ancient imaginary bogey of an impending Soviet military onslaught could no longer be maintained or effective to induce the peoples to put up with the burdens of rearmament whose costs had totalled some 300 billion dollars or £107,000,000,000. On the other hand, as soon as it was proposed to endeavour to put a more reasonable face on the monster, and to present its purpose as mainly economic, insuperable difficulties were discovered. For not only did such economic projects cut across and duplicate the proliferation of West European and Atlantic economic organs already established. Still more decisive, it was obvious that the assumed main source of funds would need to be from the United States; and the United States had made abundantly clear, first, that it would never allow its foreign 'aid' funds to pass from its own control into the hands of any international body; and second, that the purposes of its foreign 'aid' were, and would remain, overwhelmingly military and strategic. Of the current vast figures of foreign 'aid' appropriations at this moment being demanded by President Eisenhower from Congress (figures often quoted by innocent, or perhaps sometimes less innocent, commentators as 'proof' of how far more abundant is American 'aid' than the socialist economic aid to under-developed countries), 83 per cent is officially declared to be military aid, while the remaining less than one sixth of so-called 'economic' aid (mainly to bolster up Rhee,[54] Chiang[55] and Diêm[56] and other dictators) is expressly declared to be subservient to the strategic aims of US foreign policy.

From Words to Deeds

Hence the monster remains in fact as before. After all the discussions about face-lifting for dinosaurs, the only reality of NATO remains the gigantic military machine of costly installations, bases, pipelines and airfields sprawling across half the world, occupation divisions and planned Nazi rearmament, all under American command, with the openly proclaimed aim of nuclear warfare even in 'minor' wars. All this, no less than the breakdown of the disarmament talks, shows how serious the fight for peace still is. But there is no doubt that the entire climate of discussion has changed. The formerly so aggressive apostles of the Cold War and arms race are now on the defensive and apologetic. More and more, all serious and responsible opinion is seeking for an alternative course. It might be said that the battle for the principle of peaceful coexistence has already been won, even though the consequent essential practical changes in policy (disarmament, banning of nuclear weapons, ending of colonial wars, removal of strategic trade bans, recognition of China in the United Nations, replacement of sectional military alliances by European and Asian collective security, etc) are still resisted in practice and have still to be achieved. But the road towards these aims has opened out more favourably than at any previous moment.

The new world situation has brought within the view of all the practical possibility of the fulfilment of the aim of peaceful coexistence and the banishing of the menace of a third world war.

Harvest of the Twentieth Congress

If it is asked what has made possible these striking changes in the climate of international relations, discussion and opinion, which have made themselves felt at an accelerating pace over these past three years, and which today are universally agreed to be opening out new and hopeful perspectives, there can be no question of the answer. The answer lies in the profound underlying changes of the world situation which were highlighted at the Twentieth Congress of the Communist Party of the Soviet Union. The answer lies in the increasing peaceful strength, manifest invincibility, success of economic construction and scientific advance of the socialist world, constituting close on two-fifths of mankind. The answer lies in the sweeping advance of the former colonial peoples, with India in the forefront, to fulfil an independent world role on the side of peace and the extension of friendly relations with the socialist countries for peace and economic cooperation. The answer lies, not least, in the positive and constructive response of the Soviet Union and the countries of the socialist world to the new possibilities and opportunities arising from this changed balance of the world situation: the bold new initiatives for peace and the improvement of international relations; the far-reaching and imaginative planning for new economic achievement and the extension of international economic aid; and, as an integral part of this, the most drastic self-criticism and review in the internal field to lay bare and correct whatever required correction from the preceding period, in order to liberate the fullest creative forces of Marxism and the peoples for the era before us.

The Great Renewal

This gigantic process of review, correction and renewal, extending to every field, of political and legal structure and administration, of party organisation and methods of leadership, of ideology and research, and also of policy, both economic and in the field of international relations, has been developing over the past three years in the Soviet Union since the death of Stalin, and reached a high culminating point at the Twentieth Congress in February, in a way which has held the attention of the world. It has extended, and is extending, through all the countries of the socialist world. Every day brings significant new developments. A mighty process has been set in motion, which is itself a reflection of the maturity of socialism that such changes (including corrections of certain serious deformations and violations of essential principles of socialist and party democracy) has become possible, and possible without internal convulsions. The process that has been set in motion is still sweeping forward, and will assuredly bring many further and beneficial changes. It is of profound significance, not only for the socialist world, but for the whole international working-class movement and for the entire field of international relations. This renewal and correction is not only helping the development of the socialist world. It is also encouraging and stimulating a new attitude on the part of the non-socialist world to promote a more favourable atmosphere for friendly relations and peaceful coexistence. The Twentieth Congress has itself become a powerful factor in the new world situation.

Indivisible Whole

This review, correction and renewal is an integral and indispensable part of the whole new approach and vast new perspectives opened by the Twentieth Congress. It is evident from correspondence received that some incidental remarks made in last month's Notes (page 191, lines 2–10),[57] referring to this aspect of the congress, were unfortunately worded in such a way as to give rise to justifiable criticism. It was not the purpose of these very incidental remarks in nine lines to deal with this aspect of the congress, but only to explain why the broadest mass issues of the 'Great Debate' now opening, which it was the subject of last month's Notes to discuss, turned on the 'larger' questions of the future of peace, the transition to socialism, and unity of the labour movement, and that the special questions of the analysis of the past in relation to the role of Stalin or the abuses of the security organs in a preceding period, however intense the discussion of them among more limited sections, should not be emphasised at the expense of the great issues of the present and the future.

A Welcome to Criticism

But it is clear from letters of criticism received from valued readers, to whom we express our thanks, that the character of these remarks caused offence and that it was unsatisfactory to treat the question in this fashion. The attempt to correct one unbalance led to another. The treatment created the impression first, of counterposing the self-critical aspects of the congress to the 'larger' issues of the future perspective; second, of summarily brushing aside the grave questions involved under cover of historical generalities; third, of discounting or appearing to treat contemptuously the shock caused by the gravity of the revelations and the inevitable emotional feelings aroused; and fourth, and most serious, of appearing to treat the questions as only questions of the past and therefore to underestimate the profound present and future significance of the questions of principle involved and the lessons to be drawn for the whole working-class movement. We accordingly owe all our apologies to our readers for having unwittingly created such an impression by these incidental remarks, and hasten to endeavour to repair the damage by treating a little more fully some of the major questions involved.

From the Past to the Future

It would be undoubtedly mistaken and misleading to endeavour to separate the drastic review of the past and self-criticism at the Twentieth Congress from the inspiring and breath-taking perspectives for the future of socialism, peace and human advance held out at the same congress, as if they were negative and positive aspects of the congress. There can be no question here of saying that 'on the one hand' the congress presented most grievous revelations with regard to a past period which could only cause pain, but that 'on the other hand' the congress presented with a sure and factually justified self-confidence most positive perspectives for the future, both for Communist construction, and for peace and the prospects of the working-class movement and socialism, which could only cause joy. The two aspects are inseparable parts of a single whole. It is precisely the drastic review and self-criticism that helps to lay the basis, not only for the practical correction of defects, malpractices and shortcomings revealed in the preceding period, but for the reassertion of the basic principles of Marxism and Leninism, the enormous strengthening of socialist and party democracy, and thereby the liberation of all the creative forces of the people and their Communist Party, and of living Marxism, with its inherent ceaseless criticism and discussion, from certain straitjacket conditions which had grown up in a specific period and had become a dangerous impediment to growth and to the true freedom which is the heart of Communism.

Indispensable Review

Hence it was essential to carry through the drastic review, the reassessment in relation to the role of Stalin in his later period, and the ruthless uncovering of serious evils, violations of certain essential principles of party collective leadership and functioning, and of socialist legality, and arising out of these conditions, the criminal misdeeds which accompanied and stained an era of heroic achievement and basically correct policy. This review was no mere post-mortem on the past. It was the indispensable basis for the approach to the tasks of the present and the future. History will deal in due time, through the successive work of future historians, with the final assessment, or attempted final assessment (for it may well be that controversy will long rage, and pass through many phases yet) of this era of two decades of such unique significance for the future of humanity, its achievements and shortcomings, its policies and personalities, its glories and its shames.

Verdict of History

Future history will assuredly not fail to pay tribute to the epic accomplishment of this period, the completion of the construction of socialism, the withstanding of the onslaught of the Nazi blitzkrieg before which every other army had fallen, the joint victory over fascism, and the speed of reconstruction from the heaviest devastation ever known, under the conditions of the perpetual menace and harassment of the Cold War from the war-enriched and unscathed United States. Future history will not fail to pay tribute to the heroism, unity and heaven-storming achievement of the Soviet people through these ordeals, the policy and leadership of the party, and the genius, unyielding courage, steadfastness and devotion to the revolution of Stalin, also in this later period when black pages blotted the record, and when some of his very virtues turned to defects, his steel-hardness to harshness, his unwavering shouldering of responsibility to methods of personal leadership, and his vigilance and suspicion, indispensable in every true revolutionary, to an increasingly violent frenzy which caused executions, not only of counter-revolutionary enemies and agents, but also of friends and comrades.

Great Principles at Issue

It was not the task of the Twentieth Congress to anticipate the final verdict of history. The task of the Twentieth Congress was to bring out and emphasise precisely what was negative in the record, because it was this that required to be corrected and to be made known in order that it should be corrected. Hence the misleading appearance of an unbalanced emphasis, as has sometimes been suggested in some criticisms of the treatment, of the negative aspects of Stalin's record (although in fact it is evident, from the summaries which have been made available, that the report to the private session of the congress did in fact pay full tribute to the role of Stalin as the strongest Marxist leader after the death of Lenin, and to his leading role in maintaining the unity of the party against disruption and faction, in the accomplishment of industrialisation and in the collectivisation of agriculture). There was no unbalanced emphasis in relation to the task in hand. The task of the congress was not to make the final balanced assessment of the scholar in his study, but to fulfil an urgent practical need, to complete the review and correction of shortcomings and grave abuses which had already been conducted by the Central Committee during the preceding three years, to draw in the entire membership of the party and the Soviet people to full knowledge and participation in this review, reassessment and correction, and thereby to re-establish essential principles of Marxist-Leninist theory and practice which had been violated. It is these principles, of collective leadership and functioning of the party, of inner-party democracy and the methods of democratic centralism, of socialist democracy and legality, of the combination of freedom with planned organisation and unity, and of the creative critical spirit of Marxism as against dogmatism and routinism, that are brought into the forefront of attention by this review and the discussions arising therefrom, and that are of such vital urgency, not merely within the countries of socialism, but in the working-class movement of all countries, for the fulfilment of the tasks of the present and the advance to the future.

Personal Rule?

Was Stalin a 'dictator', a 'tyrant', or (as the *Daily Herald*, somewhat oddly 'summarising' the recent British Communist Executive statement on the issues, announces) a 'scoundrel'? Were those associated with him or Communists in other countries 'servile sycophants' prostrated before a supposed 'infallible idol'? This current melodramatic press picture is a travesty of the most serious, critical and, incidentally, iconoclastic movement in human history, the revolutionary Communist movement. The real situation and problem which arose, and which was summarised in the Twentieth Congress formula as the 'cult of the individual', was of a very different character from these novelette-style vapourings. There was here no parallel with the traditional forms of one-man rule, with Bonapartism or the Führerprinzip or fascist dictatorship. There was here no question of a proclamation of a constitution placing all power in the hands of one man, of an Emperor or a Leader, as the sole repository of power, from whom all authority is declared to spring (the authoritarian principle). On the contrary. The unique and peculiar character of the situation which arose during this period was that nothing was changed in the basis of class power, the socialist soviet power of the working people who had expropriated the capitalists and landlords, constructed socialism and were advancing to communism. The party continued to lead the people. Nor was the main basic policy incorrect. This was the very period when the Webbs[58] were describing the 'multiform democracy' of the Soviet Union as the widest participation of the largest numbers of ordinary men and women in the administration of their affairs that had ever been evolved. And it was true. Without this the gigantic creative achievement of the Soviet people throughout this period would never have been possible. The evils that arose affected primarily the functioning of the apparatus rather than the essence of the class power of the working people, although the violation of collective leadership had also harmful effects in particular spheres of policy, as in relation to agriculture and the break with Yugoslavia. Throughout this period, despite all the evils, the masses of the people were continuing to enjoy and exercise self-rule in running their affairs to a degree unknown in any capitalist democracy, and continuing to justify Lenin's description of Soviet democracy as the highest form of democracy yet known.

Personal and Collective Leadership

What, then, went wrong? What happened was that in a period of heavy strain after the rise of fascism, of continual war or threat-of-war conditions, the practice of leadership began to depart from the correct constitutional forms. During this period after fascism – not previously, not therefore inherently in the system of Soviet democracy or democratic centralism – Stalin, on the basis of the unique and well-earned theoretical and practical authority and mass influence he had won through his previous record of wise and successful Marxist leadership in the battle against disruption and for the victorious construction of socialism, began to operate new methods of working which departed from the methods of Lenin and the previous practice of the Communist Party. The change developed, not in a moment, not by decree, but step by step, at first without general realisation, after the Seventeenth Congress in 1934. With close lines of direct contact with the masses (the collective farms, factories, shock brigades, etc, began to send their messages and reports and pledges directly to him as the embodiment of the party instead of to the Central Committee), and with the widest party and non-party masses looking to him as the wisest and ablest revolutionary leader in whom they felt full confidence, Stalin entered on the dangerous path of beginning increasingly to take major decisions in his individual capacity, without waiting for the endorsement of committee consultations. The machinery of the meetings of the Central Committee and congresses ceased to function regularly. This was the essence of the 'cult of the individual' which is often distorted in the vulgarised press treatment as if it were expressed in the 'adulation' of a great individual. The sometime moving, sometimes flowery and distasteful eulogies were a symptomatic excrescence (though not without considerably more solid foundation than is usual in such cases). But the essence of the 'cult of the individual' was the violation of collective leadership.

Collective Leadership and the Security Organs

This situation, which could have been corrected under normal conditions by reference to the rules, was complicated in these emergency conditions by the fact that the role of the security organs was correctly and necessarily enlarged to meet the increased menace of enemy penetration, but that, under the influence of Stalin's theory of the intensification of the class struggle after the victory of socialism, these powers began to be exercised in extreme forms, and with illegal means, and fell into the hands of criminal controllers who used them, not only against enemy agents and traitors, but against all elements expressing or suspected of opposition or criticism, including some of the finest revolutionary comrades with outstanding records who were unjustly executed or imprisoned. Once this combined situation had developed, of Stalin's personal methods of leadership, his overwhelming mass influence and popularity, the abuse of the security organs, and the constant external menace and emergency conditions, a unique problem had arisen in which to have opened a direct battle against the character of Stalin's personal leadership could have meant the visible danger of a factional fight disrupting the party, tearing the country in two, opening the front to the enemy and wrecking the revolution. Hence it was not until after a very serious prolongation of this phase that the problem could be effectively tackled. But the essence of the problem was the violation of collective leadership, and the question of the abuses of the security organs should not be separated from this. Once collective leadership was restored there was no difficulty in establishing full control over the security organs and restoring and strengthening the effective functioning of socialist democracy.

Was it Inevitable?

'To understand all is to forgive all', says the French proverb. But in the revolutionary movement there can be no forgiveness for what goes wrong, even where its causes can be understood. It is inevitable in general that no revolution in real life can correspond to some idealist dream of one hundred per cent perfection, that in every revolution there will be, not only achievement, but also excesses and abuses, not only heroes, but also malefactors. We can glory that the revolution has conquered in spite of all. But no particular evil, shortcoming or abuse in its course is therefore inevitable or to be excused, least of all, such serious abuses as took place during the twenty years under review. It is sometimes suggested that the elements of social backwardness inherited from pre-revolutionary Russia, with the still recent advance to the victory of socialism, created the conditions for the retrogressive tendencies expressed in the 'cult of the individual'. There is a measure of truth in this, but only in part. For the survivals of backwardness were even more present during the period 1917-34, during which these evils did not arise.

External Backwardness

Hence we must also see the external conditions of backwardness in Western and Central Europe expressed in the victory of fascism, which created an unparalleled problem and ordeal for the new socialist state, a menace compared to which the wars of intervention were child's play. It was under those conditions that it was evidently judged necessary to weld and strengthen the solidarity of the entire people, including the peasant masses most recently emerging from backwardness to socialism, not merely with the appeal of socialism, and soviet loyalty and the party, but with every appeal, the national and patriotic appeal, the religious appeal for all attached to the church, and the personal symbol of the regime of the working people embodied in the leadership of Stalin. The name of Stalin inspired confidence and heroism among countless millions. But experience revealed that this method of political leadership, however understandable in the period in which it arose (and when it bore a corresponding significance as an expression of the solidarity of the international Communist movement) entailed grave shortcomings in practice, which required to be corrected. These corrections have now been made.

Our Responsibility

Let us never forget that fascism arose, not through the fault of the Soviet people, but through our weakness, in our movements in Western and Central Europe, that we never carried through the socialist revolution alongside them, but opened the gates to the fascist monster, and then depended on their strength and sacrifice to vanquish it. They were the first to carry through the socialist revolution, to chart the unknown paths, to face and pass through limitless ordeals. Our path of transition may be easier, thanks to them, but to our shame, not to our honour. It is sometimes suggested that we should have criticised them more in the midst of their ordeals to give them the benefit of our advice on how to run things. Perhaps they might have answered: 'Show us first, dear comrades, that you know how to lead the masses, to win and hold power, and we shall be glad to learn from you.' Our responsibility was not that we failed to join the ranks of their critics (there was no lack of such); or even that we in good faith repeated mistaken charges emanating from sources that alone had the means and the opportunity to judge them, but which subsequent review proved to be unfounded; or that we sought so far – as was in our power to inspire the enthusiasm and solidarity of our peoples for the first socialist revolution and the first socialist state. Our responsibility above all was that, with all the objective conditions ripe for socialist revolution in Western and Central Europe, such as would have solved all the problems alike for the Russian and all the peoples of Europe to march forward together in happy and peaceful construction, we were not successful to mobilise our peoples and left them to struggle alone until their own strength opened the way to the first victories of socialism beyond the Soviet Union and the beginning of the world system of socialism.

Pains and Shocks

There are those who say that to find joy and thankfulness in the frank review, however ugly the facts revealed, in the reassessment and the new perspective opened by the Twentieth Congress is to show callousness to the pain which must be felt for those who died unjustly, or indifference to the horror which must be felt for the revelation of criminal actions and violations of justice in a socialist society. Their vision is too short. We know also the pain of the millions who have died through capitalism, and the daily million-fold injustice of capitalist society, and we know on which side we stand. We know that the path of revolution is not without sorrow, not merely from the external enemy, but also from within.

Darkness and Sunrise

How far does the memory of some of these questioners go, to whom these revelations seem to be felt like the first shock and anguish on a hitherto stainless shield, until they almost seem ready to join the hapless ranks of those who denounced 'the god that failed'? It was pain and anguish during the 1920s to see that goodly company, as it had seemed at the time, which had led the first victorious socialist revolution break up in mortal division, with successive factional fights led against the party, until the unity of the steadfast leaders around Stalin saved the party. It was no less pain and anguish during the 1930s to see so many dear friends and comrades, some of whom, like Béla Kun,[59] have since been cleared of their sentences, revealed and proclaimed as traitors and enemy agents, until the movement seemed honeycombed with treasonable corruption. And if now the Twentieth Congress has revealed that the party was not seething with traitors and agents, that it was, on the contrary, the security organs that had got out of hand and gone wrong, that many of these dear friends and comrades were not traitors and agents, that although they suffered cruel and unjust deaths their revolutionary honour stands high, then some younger comrades must forgive the 'callousness' of some of us longer in the movement that this feels, not like the end of the world, not like 'the god that failed', but like the sunrise breaking through the clouds and the dawn of a new day.

Learning the Lessons

Above all, let us learn the lessons and strive to apply them for our own movement and for the future. The review and the reassessment at the Twentieth Congress, no less than the positive perspectives held out, have undoubtedly a very wide international significance for the working-class movement in all countries. It has emphasised, not only the new world situation and the new opportunities that are opening out, but the fresh and flexible and imaginative approach that is necessary, with ruthless self-criticism of our own weaknesses, in order to respond to the new opportunities. It has given a stimulus to the development of creative Marxism in place of superficial routine thinking and clinging to ready-made formulas. It has helped to remove many obstacles to closer mutual understanding and cooperation of all sections of the working class, at the same time as its whole teaching has emphasised, not in opposition to this aim of unity, but in integral association with it, the indispensable role of a strongly-based Marxist-Leninist party of the working class, the Communist Party, to act as the vanguard for the whole movement. Within Britain we can feel the new tide that is stirring, not only in the field of industry, with the marked militant advances, but also, despite the difficulties of the present situation within the political labour movement, in the political field, as partially shown in the local elections. There is the beginning of a new climate, not only in international relations, but within the labour movement in Britain. Within the Communist Party the process of renovation and democratic strengthening is sweeping forward. Within broad sections of the labour movement the discussions for cooperation and a new policy extend. The recent contribution of G D H Cole, rebutting the contention of the Socialist International Bureau that socialism and communism have nothing in common, is a welcome sign of the times.[60] If Sir Winston Churchill in his eighty-second year can respond, from his standpoint, along new and constructive lines to meet a new world situation, let us hope that we in the British labour movement can also respond in a new and constructive fashion to the much greater opportunities that are within our reach in order to advance with united strength to the fulfilment of the tasks before us.

* * *

VI: Edward Thompson, Winter Wheat in Omsk

From *World News*, 30 June 1956.

* * *

> The staff of the Agricultural Research Institute in Omsk, in support of Comrade Lysenko[61] and ignoring the obvious facts, proved the unprovable in hothouse conditions on the institute's plots.
>
> As a result, tens of thousands of hectares sown under winter wheat in the Omsk district alone went to waste year after year. (*Daily Worker*, 29 May 1956)

John Saville (*World News*, 19 May 1956) has referred to the weakening tradition of controversy in the Communist Party. This is true. How often has the routine of the unanimous vote, the common front against the class enemy, the search for the 'correct formulation', inhibited the development of sharp controversy?

Year after year the Monolith, from its cave, somewhere inside *For a Lasting Peace, For a People's Democracy*, has droned on in a dogmatic monotone, without individual variation, without moral inflexion, without native dialect.

> We do not see [wrote Milton][62] that, while we still affect by all means a rigid external formality, we may as soon fall ... into a gross conforming stupidity, a stark and dead congealment of wood and hay and stubble, forced and frozen together.

We have even jargonised the need for controversy itself, under the label 'criticism and self-criticism'. We need now to dig up some other good English words: argument, debate, polemic. The danger beneath the label is shown by Maurice Thorez:

> The party of the working class requires experienced leaders, vested with authority, and as Lenin said, seeing more clearly and more profoundly in certain cases. The aim of criticism from below is to help these leaders themselves, thus to help the party. (*World News*, 26 May 1956)[63]

In certain circumstances this attitude contains dangers, by limiting criticism to the criticism of given statements and actions of the leadership, within limits defined by these leaders.

Holy Church, in medieval times, also encouraged disputations on the dogma of the priesthood. But woe to those heretics who were unmasked as having acted for many years as agents of the Devil!

The aim of controversy is more fundamental: it is to arrive at truth out of the clash of opposing views. This is the first meaning of dialectics.

Our party must create the conditions for a rebirth of real controversy in our press and throughout our organisation. We might recall Marx's demand for 'ruthlessness – the first condition of all criticism'. Or some more words of Milton: 'Let Truth and Falsehood grapple; who ever knew Truth put to the worse, in a free and open encounter?'

Certainly we must bear this in mind when building socialism, or we will all find ourselves in Omsk.

Russian Wheat in Britain

As a critic of our leadership, I have space to ask two or three questions.

I choose to ask, first, how much winter wheat (from seed matured in Omsk, Tomsk and Irkutsk) have we been ploughing into British furrows in the past thirty years? How much devotion and sacrifice has gone to the raising of a thin and straggling crop of dogmatism and opportunism – with here and there some sturdy growth – when, if we had attended more closely to our own conditions, our own climate, we might have grown rich crops?

How often have we neglected our native socialist seed in favour of seed bred for Siberian conditions? Education classes based on the *History of the CPSU(b)*. Russian texts on political economy. Even Comrade V Rubin (*World News*, 28 April 1956) on 'Britain's Writers Today'.

How often have we used hothouse tests to prove our theory 'correct', ignoring the test of the unsheltered open field? How often do we deduce what we want to deduce, exaggerating our victories and refusing to analyse our defeats?

The Moral Climate

First, there is a moral climate in Britain. Traditionally, battle after battle of the British people has been fought out in moral terms. The very names of popular leaders carry this quality: Lilburne,[64] Winstanley,[65] Cobbett,[66] Oastler,[67] Ernest Jones.[68] The propaganda of Morris,[69] Hardie[70] and Tom Mann[71] was imbued with this passionate moral protest against capitalism.

We have always seen this characteristic as a source of weakness. Rightly so. Two generations of careerists have fattened on sentimental moral guff. But if we do not also see it as a source of strength, then we are damning up sources of energy in ourselves, we are cutting ourselves off from our people.

Monolithese has forgotten how to strike this chord. It has become so concerned with 'correct formulations' that it has no language for right and wrong. When certain revelations were made, it was painful to watch the way our press gradually (under pressure from below) jacked up its words: from 'errors' to 'mistakes' to 'malpractices' to 'abuses' to 'crimes'.

We need not veer over and debate ethical instead of economic realities. But it is high time that we rid ourselves of inhibitions against discussing moral issues in political decisions: of the silly, mechanical view that morality is something to do with 'idealism': and of the more dangerous view that all Communists are good by nature, or because our ends are good, and that moral questions can look after themselves.

Arnold Kettle[72] criticised at our congress the tendency among some comrades to imagine that:

> … it is possible for us to keep our hands and our consciences absolutely spotlessly clean, to imagine there is some absolute and ideal integrity which everyone – East and West, socialist and capitalist alike – will recognise and respect. This is not so. You keep a pure, white conscience in this world only by keeping your thoughts out of the way of your actions and the implications of your actions. (*World News*, 21 April 1956)

Comrade Kettle does not help us by knocking down his own ninepins. His warning might be needed at another time: but it is a sorry business when it is used now to quieten the honest and healthy moral concern felt by thousands in our labour movement.

We are concerned not with pure consciences, but with honesty and good faith in our actions: not with absolute and ideal integrity but with Communist principle in our methods, socialist integrity in our political relations. Without this it is possible (as we have recently learnt) to preach a pure, white dogma while keeping one's actions out of the way of one's sense of principle or professions of principle.

It should be clear now to all that conscious struggle for moral principle in our political work is a vital part of our political relations with the people. The British people do not understand and will not trust a Monolith without a moral tongue. It is also clear that the best of formulations can conceal shame and unreason: that we must still read Shakespeare as well as Marx.

The Democratic Climate

Second, there is our democratic climate. Our Executive has promised to lead a discussion touching this in some months' time, in connection with *The British Road to Socialism*. Of course, the discussion has been going on for some time – for three or four hundred years – and I hope that the EC Commission will take evidence from such witnesses as Cobbett and

Hetherington.[73]

Recently I was invited to take part in a National School on the History of our Labour Movement. I suggested that one of the twelve sessions might be called 'The Free-Born Englishman' – a discussion on the illusions and the realities of our democratic tradition. Several friendly letters were exchanged. At length it was decided that there was no room for such a session in the formal syllabus – but that provisionally an extra, optional session would be put in on the last afternoon.

When I speak of our democratic climate I mean that the British people will not trust a party that regards its democratic liberties as an optional or extra item.

This is not meant as a cheap jibe. It is certainly not meant as a slick historical judgement upon the vastly different historical problems of the Soviet Union – a country about which I know little, and very much less than I had once been led to think. Nor is it meant as any sort of excuse for our denial of liberties to the colonial peoples.

But when all this is said, I must still return to Milton: 'Give me the liberty to know, to utter, and to argue freely according to conscience, above all liberties.' Or to the words of Lilburne in his 'Just Defence':

> ... for what is done to any one, may be done to every one: besides, being all members of one body, that is, of the English Commonwealth, one man should not suffer wrongfully, but all should be sensible, and endeavour his preservation; otherwise they give way to an inlet of the sea of will and power, upon their laws and liberties, which are the boundaries to keep out tyranny and oppression ...

Or to John Citizen's deep-rooted dislike of anyone who pushes him around.

Bourgeois democracy, we know, is a liar and a cheat. But it is a libel on our proudest history to say that all our liberties are illusions, the 'fig-leaf of absolutism'. It is a libel upon the British working class to suggest that they would exchange these liberties for a higher standard of life. Those (and there are such) who travel on delegations to the East only to gape enviously and to belittle our own traditions do no good to our cause. They bring back, not the true seed of solidarity, but a strange seed which will never thrive in our culture.

These questions are not academic. So long as our attitude towards these liberties is in doubt, we may win from the workers their *industrial* support, but not their *political* confidence. How many comrades secretly believe that only slump or catastrophe will win the British working class to our side?

Is socialism such a savage medicine as this, that the people will turn to it only at the point of death? Let us shatter this caricature of our case: and as a necessary condition for winning clarity, and as a proof to the people that we have no fear of the free clash of ideas, let us drop this fetish of the Monolith and get some real controversy into our midst.

* * *

VII: George Matthews, A Caricature of Our Party[74]
From *World News*, 30 June 1956.

* * *

In his legitimate desire to stimulate controversy, Edward Thompson has presented a picture of our party which most members will feel to be a caricature. If he thinks it over he will discover that he has unconsciously echoed all the most familiar anti-Communist jibes and sneers of the enemy press – that Communists repeat dogmas like Holy Church, have little regard for morality, are un-British, not much concerned with democracy, and so on.

All this is put forward in Comrade Thompson's own jargon, in which 'criticism and self-criticism' become 'controversy', which means something quite different, as any dictionary will tell him; and jargon itself becomes 'monolithese'.

He asks:

How often has the routine of the unanimous vote, the common front against the class enemy, the search for the 'correct formulation', inhibited the development of sharp controversy?

This way of putting the problem creates the impression that the search for unity of policy, for the common front, for the correct way of expressing the policy, are comparatively unimportant, are 'routine'. What *is* important is controversy. Thus the controversy is presented more as an end in itself than as a means to an end.

But would it not be truer to say that we *need* unity and a common front in support of a correct policy, and in order to get it we need, amongst other things, more discussion and controversy?

Later on Comrade Thompson tells us that the aim of controversy is 'to arrive at truth out of the clash of opposing views'. Certainly it is sometimes possible to arrive at truth in this way. But no 'clash between opposing views' will arrive at truth if *neither* view is based on fact and on a scientific approach.

Marxist Approach

To arrive at truth it is necessary first to make a scientific examination of phenomena, their history and development, and their inter-relationship, to elaborate theories on this scientific basis, and to put the theories to the test of practice.

This is the Marxist approach to social and political questions.

The Communist Party is a Marxist Party. When we speak about controversy within the Communist Party, therefore, surely the first thing to make clear is that what is required is controversy in the spirit of Marxism, aimed at strengthening the Marxist understanding of the party, and at uniting the party for the heavy tasks of the class struggle.

We need more of such controversy and discussion, as the Executive Committee in its resolution of 13 May declared, while at the same time it criticised our neglect to discuss questions of principle and our tendencies to dogmatism, rigidity and sectarianism.

It is not clear to me from his article whether Edward Thompson would agree with what I have said. If he does, there is little difference between us. If he does not, his emphasis on controversy almost for the sake of controversy could result in our party ceasing to be a Communist Party and becoming merely a discussion group, or even dividing into a number of tiny sects – certainly engaged in 'controversy', but getting nowhere as a result.

Communists and Britain

Comrade Thompson can see that there have been wrong tendencies to try to transplant methods and policies suited to Soviet, but not British, conditions.

But some other things he apparently does not see.

It is a fact that we produced *The British Road to Socialism*.

We produced our own textbook of political economy just because existing publications were unsatisfactory.

Of the education syllabuses produced by our party in the past few years, the overwhelming majority have been based on *British* conditions, *British* history, our policy for *Britain*, and the position of the *British* labour movement: and such books as Dutt's *Crisis of Britain and the British Empire*,[75] and Gollan's *British Political System*[76] have been published, not to mention Thompson's *William Morris*.[77]

Why, then, put a series of rhetorical questions creating an exaggerated and one-sided picture – the caricature of our party as a 'Russian Party' that we so often see in the capitalist press?

Morality

No discussion about morality will get us far unless we are clear what we mean by it. Comrade Thompson says it is high time that we rid ourselves of the view that morality is something to do with 'idealism'. But he doesn't tell us what it *is* to do with. He doesn't mention classes, or the basic position of Marxism as expressed by Engels in *Anti-Dühring*:

> Men, consciously or unconsciously, derive their moral ideas in the last resort from the practical relations on which their class position is based – from the economic relations in which they carry on production and exchange.

Engels preceded that sentence by saying:

> Certainly that morality which contains the maximum durable elements is the one which, in the present, represents the overthrow of the present, represents the future: that is, the proletarian.

Comrade Thompson says that we have 'inhibitions against discussing' moral issues when we are taking political decisions. But for Marxists every political decision is good or bad according to whether or not it serves the interests of the working people and the cause of socialism. In this sense, it is impossible for Marxists to separate the moral from the political aspect of decisions – every political decision involves a moral judgement.

We condemn what Edward Thompson calls 'certain revelations' – that is, the abuses and injustices in the Soviet Union – because they were both morally and politically wrong and against the interests of the working people and of socialism.

Lack of Moral Principle

I suspect that what Comrade Thompson is really getting at, though he does not say it openly, is that our past attitude to the Soviet Union has shown a lack of moral principle – that our party knew that wrong and criminal things were happening and deliberately refused to condemn them.

If this is his view, he is utterly and completely mistaken. It is now obvious to all that we made serious errors in our estimate of certain aspects of the position in the Soviet Union. But these errors were not due to lack of principle, but to lack of information, or to wrong information. Comrade Thompson can legitimately argue that we should have made more effort to get accurate information; but he is not entitled to imply that our party was unprincipled, dishonest and immoral.

This, however, is the effect of Comrade Thompson's argument, which he caps by implying that the party is a 'Monolith without a moral tongue'. Even the *Observer* would find it difficult to rival this. Does Edward Thompson really believe it? Does he think that everything our party has done in the fight against imperialism, for colonial freedom, for civil liberties, and against fascism justifies the use of such a phrase?

He says that the British people do not understand and will not trust 'a Monolith without a moral tongue'. Nor would 35,000 amongst the best of the British people have joined such a party. Sometimes it seems that Comrade Thompson has even less respect for the members than for the leadership of our party.

I do not know if he is proud of our party. I am. But I should not be if it were like his picture of it.

Democracy

To complete his description of our party, Comrade Thompson implies that it is a party which 'regards its democratic liberties as an optional or extra item'.

It is characteristic of his 'polemical' method that this fantastic charge is hung on to a point about a syllabus for a school.

He tells us that 'it is a libel on our proudest history to say that all our liberties are illusions'. This from one who accuses Arnold Kettle of knocking down his own ninepins! Is Comrade Thompson implying that the Executive Committee has said this?

Let us quote from *The British Road to Socialism*:

> The democratic rights, won by years of working-class struggle, must be defended with the utmost strength against the attacks of the capitalists and warmongers and their agents.

We do not ask the working class to defend illusions.
'It is a libel upon the British working class', says Comrade Thompson, 'to suggest that they would exchange these liberties for a higher standard of life.'

Libel

It is a libel on the party to imply that we have ever suggested anything of the sort. The working class won its democratic liberties in the course of struggling for a higher standard of life. We have always said that economic and political freedom go hand in hand, and that socialism should mean a vast extension of both for the working class.

Certainly the popular leaders whom Comrade Thompson mentions had no doubts about this. And it was our British democratic poet, Shelley,[78] who asked, 'What are thou, Freedom?', and answered:

> For the labourer, thou art bread
> And a comely table spread,
> From his daily labour come
> In a neat and happy home.
> Thou art clothes, and fire and food
> For the trampled multitude.[79]

I agree with Comrade Thompson that we need to do more to learn from and popularise the democratic traditions of the British working people. But in view of the general tone of his article, perhaps a warning against a type of narrow nationalism which can be anti-international would not be out of place. Blatchford's[80] example is a warning here. For we must also learn from the experiences of the working people of other countries.

Nor should our recognition of the merits of the great Englishmen from whom he quotes blind us to the fact that in their time they could not see the way forward so clearly as Marx was later to see it; they were not, and could not be, scientific socialists.

We should be, and are, proud of the British working people, their traditions of struggle and their fight for liberty. We are proud that our working class took the lead in establishing trade unions and the Cooperative movement.

But it is not wrong also to feel glad that the people of the Soviet Union, China and the people's democracies have got rid of capitalism.

When we do, we shall hope to do a better job than they, but not only because of different conditions here. It will also be because of *their* sacrifices, *their* pioneering work, and because we shall learn from the mistakes that have caused them so much pain and anguish, as well as from their heroic achievement.

* * *

VIII: Khrushchev's Report

Statement issued by the Political Committee of the Communist Party of Great Britain on 21 June 1956, from *World News*, 30 June 1956.

* * *

The Political Committee of the Communist Party has had under consideration the unofficial published version of Comrade Khrushchev's report to the private session of the Twentieth Congress of the CPSU, together with the discussion in our party.

At the private session of the Twenty-Fourth National Congress of our party on 1 April, a resolution was passed and conveyed to the Communist Party of the Soviet Union, regretting that a public statement on this question had not been made by the Central Committee of the Communist Party of the Soviet Union, which could have enabled members of all Communist parties and staunch friends of the Soviet Union to have understood fully the seriousness of the issues, and helped them to a better understanding of everything that is involved. Our party has not received any official version of the report of Comrade Khrushchev.

The continued absence of an official report has led to the publication of unofficial versions through gradual leakages and by sources hostile to socialism. This has made many Communists outside the Soviet Union dependent on such enemy sources for information on these vital matters, and thus added unnecessary difficulties to the estimation and discussion of the facts.

In the light of the unofficial text now published, which, in the absence of official denial may be regarded as more or less authentic, we reaffirm the general lines of the resolution of our Executive Committee of 13 May. We consider that the Twentieth Congress of the CPSU was correct in condemning the cult of the individual and in endorsing the return to Leninist principles of collective leadership and inner-party democracy. We consider that the Twentieth Congress was correct in frankly exposing all the evils which followed from the departure from Leninist principles, in order to put an end to these evils.

All Communists, in common with all democratic and progressive people, are deeply shocked by the injustices and crimes which, during the period under review, violated the essential principles of socialist democracy and legality and dishonoured the noble cause of Communism. We repeat that such evil practices are totally alien to socialism and Communism.

At the same time, we recognise that these evils arose not as a necessary accompaniment of working-class rule and Soviet democracy, as the enemies of socialism pretend, but as a result of the violation of socialist principles and during a specific period of abnormal strain between 1934 and 1953. This was the period of the rise of fascism abroad, the preparation of war, the Second World War and the Cold War.

The Soviet leaders have exposed the evils and abuses of this period in order to correct them and make a decisive turn to the fulfilment of the principles of Leninism, collective leadership, socialist democracy and creative Marxist work in all the fields of science, literature and art.

Successes

We recognise that, in spite of the grave harm caused by these abuses, the Soviet people achieved very great and historic successes. In face of terrible difficulties they established socialism, withstood and defeated the Nazi onslaught, and reconstructed their country after the unparalleled devastation of the war. This achievement deserves the admiration of all and shows the superiority of the socialist system over capitalism, and the creative possibilities it opens up for the people.

The Twentieth Congress of the CPSU itself recorded the historic fact that socialism had now become a world system. It made major contributions to Marxist theory, and helped the working-class movement in all countries, by its declarations on the possibility of preventing world war, the peaceful transition to socialism, and the new opportunities for developing working-class unity.

The discussion arising from the Twentieth Congress and from the revelations regarding the 1934–53 period in the Soviet Union is stimulating fresh and fruitful thought and endeavour in every field of Communist work and practice.

It is clear that further review and discussion is needed of the questions opened up by the report to the private session of the Twentieth Congress of the CPSU.

We agree with the observations of Comrade Togliatti[81] and the French Communist Party[82] that it will be necessary to make a profound Marxist analysis of the causes of the degeneration in the functioning of Soviet democracy and party democracy; that it is not enough to attribute these developments solely to the character of one individual; and that a more adequate estimate of the role of Stalin, both in its positive and negative aspects, will be necessary.

It is clear that the steps taken for strengthening the operation of socialist legality and safeguarding the rights of citizens will lead to further examination of all problems of the functioning of socialist democracy and legality.

Those responsible for past violations of socialist democracy and crimes against the people are being punished, and this is just and necessary. At the same time it is understandable that concern has been expressed at the application of the death penalty in a recent trial in the Soviet Union. We express the view that in the light of the present world situation and the strengthened position of the socialist camp it should now be possible to bring about the abolition of the death penalty in peacetime in all countries, and we recognise that we have a special responsibility to work for the fulfilment of this aim in Britain and the colonial countries under British rule.

Discussion

Within our own party we shall need to carry forward and encourage the widest and most thorough discussion, as already begun, of our political and organisational methods, the functioning of party democracy and the tackling of the problems before us, our relations with other sections of the labour movement and the aims of unity, as indicated in the Executive Committee resolution.

We shall also carry forward the work on a new edition of *The British Road to Socialism*, in which, amongst the many questions which will come up for review, we shall need to expand that section which shows how the democratic liberties won by the people can be maintained and extended, and how socialist legality will be guaranteed.

The enemies of our party hope that this discussion will weaken the party and open the way for attempts to smuggle anti-Marxist, anti-Communist bourgeois conceptions into the party, striking at the roots of Communist principles and organisation. On the contrary, our party members and organisations will know how to conduct the discussion so as to strengthen every aspect of our party's work and activity.

The democracy of our party is the widest democracy of any party in Britain. The freedom of discussion and democratic functioning which is possible in our party, and which the leaders of other parties fear to permit in theirs, is possible because of the essential unity of our party's Marxist outlook and our determination to reach, in the light of Marxism, unity on the policy which is in the best interests of the British working class.

Let us never forget, throughout this discussion, that the cause of Communism, of national independence, freedom and peace, is advancing with giant strides throughout the world. All the conditions are present here in Britain for a great advance of the labour movement. Given the correct policy and leadership, the British people will defeat Toryism and move forward to socialism. It is the mission of our Communist Party to help achieve these aims, and it is in this spirit that, while discussing the urgent and important issues raised by the Twentieth Congress of the CPSU, we work to develop the greatest united movement of the people for the policy put forward by our Twenty-Fourth National Congress.

* * *

IX: Derek Kartun, Ideas and Methods of Work[83]
From *World News*, 14 July 1956.

* * *

I attended my first party class in 1942. I remember the tutor's first question. 'What do we mean', he asked, 'when we say cadres decide everything?'

We didn't know. We didn't even know what cadres *were*. It was our first introduction to the sectarian jargon which bedevils our work, and to the way in which we have abdicated thought and taken our ideas and methods ready-made from the USSR.

Things have changed – but not very much. I still sit beneath a portrait of Stalin in military uniform (and look at a poster of Lenin) when I attend meetings at our local premises.

Has there been genuine discussion in the party? Edward Thompson says no; George Matthews points to the EC resolution welcoming discussion and denouncing rigidity. But what happens in practice?

Some of us have been critical of our leadership's reaction to the Twentieth Congress. In reply to a mildly critical resolution moved in West London, the EC representative said three things: we were hysterical; were setting up our consciences in place of the needs of the working class; were turning our backs on urgent political tasks to indulge in private debates. Loudest applause went to a comrade who announced that the working class awaited us while we were being asked to turn inwards.

Are such comrades now telling each other that Togliatti has turned inwards and set up his conscience ... etc? Do they think our own EC is hysterical, now that it is paying attention to these things?

They don't – and that is precisely what's so disturbing. For here indeed, despite George Matthews, is Holy Church – disputation on the dogma and only on the dogma.

In reply to Edward Thompson, George Matthews denounces as a slander the assertion that many regard us as a foreign party. He points to our achievements. We all know about our achievements. But we should guard against using them as alibis for our failures, which are substantial.

What has passed with us as discussion is the kind of mock-debate which has been standard in the international movement for over twenty years, in which all the really controversial questions are treated as established truth at the outset.

A slander? Consider how many readers the *Daily Worker* has driven away for the sake of Stalin's sometimes disastrous and often crude foreign policy. An outrageous remark? Be careful – Khrushchev or Togliatti may say something in a week or two, and lo! it won't be outrageous any more.

All this is relevant to the current discussion on unity. We shall never get it until we rid ourselves of the religious approach to politics, start speaking English, and re-examine what international solidarity really means (it *doesn't* mean vociferously defending the indefensible). Until, in short, we rid ourselves of the practices we borrowed from the Russian Social-Democrats, working in illegal conditions.

Now is our chance to do it. I hope George Matthews won't say this is a one-sided picture. Of course it is – the bad side – the one that has to be changed.

NOTES

1   Harry Pollitt (1890–1960) was born into a working-class family in Droylsden Lancashire; he became a boilermaker and was a shop steward at the age of 21. He joined the Independent Labour Party at the age of 18, and joined the Openshaw Socialist Society upon its foundation in 1906. This group joined the British Socialist Party in 1912. He opposed the First World War. He joined the CPGB upon its foundation in 1920, became its General Secretary in 1929, and served in this post, with a break during 1939–41 as a result of his publicly-admitted demurral from the Comintern's anti-war stance following the Molotov–Ribbentrop Pact of August 1939, until 1956. He attended the Twentieth Congress of the Communist Party of the Soviet Union, but not the session at which Khrushchev delivered his 'Secret Speech'. Suffering from ill-health, he resigned from his post in the spring of 1956, just after the CPGB's Twenty-Fourth Congress, and took up the newly-created post of party Chairman.
2   The Communist International was actually dissolved in 1943.
3   Richard Stafford Cripps (1889–1952) was a barrister and Labour MP for Bristol during 1931–50. He helped form the Socialist League, a left-wing faction in the Labour Party, in 1932. He was expelled from the Labour Party in early 1939 for publicly advocating in his 'Memorandum' that it support the Communist Party's unity campaign, and rejoined it in 1945. He was appointed British Ambassador to the Soviet Union in 1940, in which post he unsuccessfully attempted to warn Stalin of the impending threat from Nazi Germany, was a member of Winston Churchill's wartime coalition government, and held senior posts, including Chancellor of the Exchequer, in Clement Attlee's postwar Labour government.
4   Neville Chamberlain (1869–1940) was a Conservative MP during 1918–40, Minister of Health during 1923, 1924–29 and 1931, Chancellor of the Exchequer during 1923–24 and 1931–37, and Prime Minister during 1937–40, heading the coalition National Government which declared war on Germany in September 1939.

5   The British Military Mission to the Soviet Union was in August 1939.

6   Lavrenty Pavlovich Beria (1899–1953) joined the security apparatus of the Azerbaijan Democratic Republic in 1919 and transferred to the Bolsheviks' Cheka sometime in 1920–21, joining the Cheka in Georgia after the Soviet takeover in 1921. He became Secretary of the Georgian Communist Party in 1931, and joined the CPSU Central Committee in 1934. He became deputy head of the People's Commissariat of Internal Affairs in August 1938 and oversaw the winding down of the Terror after his appointment as its head in November 1938. He played a key role during and after the Second World War in several governmental fields, including overseeing the Soviet atomic bomb project. In 1946 he became Deputy Prime Minister and a full member of the Politbureau. After Stalin's death, he was seen as a threat by his colleagues in the Soviet leadership, and he was arrested, tried on a series of dubious charges, and executed.

7   Nikolai Alexandrovich Bulganin (1895–1975) joined the Russian Communist Party in 1918, and worked in the Cheka and electrical supply. He became a full member of the CPSU Central Committee in 1937, held military posts during the Second World War, and became a full member of the Politbureau in 1948. He became Premier of the Soviet Union in 1955, and at first supported Khrushchev's reforms, but subsequently backtracked and was dismissed from the party leadership in 1958. He accompanied Khrushchev on an official visit to Britain in 1956.

8   Georgy Maximilianovich Malenkov (1901–1988) joined the Red Army in 1918 and the Russian Communist Party in 1920, and from the mid-1920s worked in the party's Organisational Bureau. He joined the party's Central Committee in 1939, and became a full member of the Politbureau in 1946. He was one of Stalin's close associates, and he played a key role in various state concerns during and after the Second World War, including the nuclear industry and economic reconstruction. He was centrally involved in the purge of the Leningrad party in the late 1940s. He was widely tipped to be Stalin's successor, and he delivered the main report to the CPSU's Nineteenth Congress in 1951. He was rapidly sidelined after Stalin's death, especially after he plotted against Khrushchev, and he was expelled from the party in 1961 and thereafter lived in obscurity.

9   Anastas Ivanovich Mikoyan (1895–1978) joined the Bolsheviks in 1915 and worked in the Caucasus; he was the only survivor of the infamous massacre of the Baku Commissars in 1918. He joined the Russian Communist Party's Central Committee in 1923 and the Politbureau in 1935. A supporter of Stalin, he was slightly less sanguine than his colleagues during the Terror. He delivered a speech at the Twentieth Congress that was critical of Stalin, and helped Khrushchev prepare his 'Secret Speech'. He opposed Soviet military action in Hungary in 1956. He played an important role in Soviet diplomacy under Khrushchev, including helping to defuse the Cuba missile crisis.

10   See *World News and Views*, 17 July 1948. Norman John 'James' Klugmann (1912–1977) joined the CPGB in 1933 whilst studying at Cambridge University; he become Secretary of the World Student Association in 1935, and after joining the armed services in 1940 was seconded to the Special Operations Executive, working in the Middle East, Italy and Yugoslavia. He was later mainly concerned with party theoretical and educational work, edited *Marxism Today* during 1957–77, and wrote many books, including the first two volumes of the CPGB's official history. Klugmann wrote *From Trotsky to Tito* (Lawrence and Wishart, London, 1951) at the request of the CPGB's Political Committee. It was hailed by the party's Assistant General Secretary George Matthews as a 'brilliant success' in its task of providing 'a thorough and systematic exposure of Titoism from both the theoretical and the practical standpoints'. Matthews added that Klugmann – who must have known by dint of his position as a Major in the Yugoslav

section of the SOE that what he was writing was a work of insidious fiction – had 'produced a weapon of inestimable value in the fight for peace and socialism'. This book was no academic by-way: Matthews considered it 'the duty of Communists to campaign around' the book, and called for a 'really big sale' and for 'discussion and study' of it to be 'carried through on the widest basis in Britain' (*Communist Review*, December 1951).

11   V I Lenin, 'The Collapse of the Second International', *Collected Works*, Volume 21 (Progress, Moscow, 1974), p. 216.

12   *The British Road to Socialism* was the programme of the CPGB; the first edition was published in 1951, its text having been approved by Stalin. Subsequent revised editions appeared in 1952, 1958, 1968 and 1977.

13   Pollitt refrains from naming the author of this article, Jane Degras, perhaps as her promotion of the Cold War viewpoint at this juncture was a far cry from her attitude to the Soviet Union during the 1930s when she was a member of the Soviet Communist Party and worked in the Marx–Engels Institute in Moscow.

14   The CPGB's Twenty-Third Congress was held in April 1954.

15   Pollitt announced this programme in his speech to the congress: '1) Wage increases in every industry. 2) Refusal to accept short time and unemployment. The government must reverse its policy of cuts, increased interest charges and hire-purchase restrictions. For a 40-hour week without reduction of pay, no sackings, full pay, restoration of the home market and East-West trade. 3) Defend the social services. Reduce interest charges; restore the housing and food subsidies. Cut military expenditure and tax the rich. 4) Increase the old age and disablement pensions and all social service payments now.' (Harry Pollitt, 'The People Will Decide', in *The People Will Decide: Speeches at the Twenty-Fourth National Congress of the Communist Party* (CPGB, London, 1956), p. 12)

16   Christian Pineau (1904–1995) was a Socialist member of the French National Assembly during 1946–58, minister in various postwar French governments, Prime Minister for two days in February 1955, and Foreign Minister from February 1956 to May 1958 and was responsible for handling the Suez crisis.

17   Guy Mollet (1905–1975) was the leader of the French Socialist Party during 1946–59, and was Prime Minister from February 1956 to June 1957, during which time he oversaw the Suez crisis and greatly increased repression in Algeria.

18   Dwight David 'Ike' Eisenhower (1890–1969) was a US career army officer, the Supreme Commander of Allied Forces in Europe from January 1944, and in April 1951 became Supreme Commander of NATO. He was elected President on a Republican ticket in January 1953, and re-elected in November 1956. Cold War tensions continued throughout his period as President, with his endorsement of the 'rollback' of Communist regimes in Eastern Europe and of the 'domino theory' of the threat of Asian states falling to Communist insurgencies, the threatening of China with atomic weapons, and, later on, arranging an invasion of Cuba, which was unsuccessfully attempted after his retirement in 1961.

19   Sir John Bagot Glubb (1897–1986) was a British career army officer and the commander of Transjordan's Arab Legion during 1939–56, known as Glubb Pasha; he was dismissed by King Hussein of Jordan in March 1956.

20   Sic – the word 'initiate' seems to have been meant here.

21   Rajani Palme Dutt (1896–1974) was born in Cambridge to an Indian father and Swedish mother. He joined the Independent Labour Party in 1914, and opposed the First World War, which led to his being rusticated at Oxford University. He joined the CPGB upon its foundation, joined its Executive Committee in 1923, and was its main theoretician until the mid-1950s. After backing the wrong horse with his glowing review of Trotsky's *Where is Britain Going?* in 1926, he was an unerring

supporter of the Moscow line, often coming to the fore when a potentially unpopular change in orientation was imposed upon the CPGB, such as in October 1939 when the Communist International declared that the Second World War was now an imperialist conflict. After 1956, with the CPGB's gradual distancing from Moscow, he slid into the background, leaving the Executive Committee in 1965. He was a prolific author, with many substantial books to his name, and he edited *Labour Monthly* from 1921 to 1974.

22   Alfred Robens (1910–1999) worked for the Manchester Cooperative Society, became an official of the shop-workers' union in 1935, served on Manchester City Council, and was elected Labour MP for Wansbeck, Northumberland, in 1945. He held junior posts in the Ministry of Transport and Ministry of Fuel and Power in the Attlee government, and became Minister for Fuel and Power in 1950. He was later Shadow Foreign Secretary, but was thwarted in his desire to become party leader, and he was appointed Chairman of the National Coal Board in 1960.

23   The Bandung Conference was held on 18–24 April 1955 in Bandung, Indonesia, and was organised by Indonesia, India, Pakistan, Burma and Ceylon and held under the auspices of the Indonesian Ministry of Foreign Affairs. A total of 29 countries, including China, were represented, and the conference was intended to promote African–Asian economic cooperation and to oppose colonialism. It carried a 10-point declaration that emphasised racial equality, national self-determination and peaceful resolution of differences. Subsequent conferences were held in Cairo in 1957 and Belgrade in 1961, at which the Non-Aligned Movement was formed.

24   The Geneva Conference of Heads of State took place in April–July 1954. Attended by Britain, China, France, the Soviet Union and the USA, it attempted to deal with the aftermath of the Korean War and the fighting in Vietnam. No declaration was agreed in respect of the former; Vietnam was divided along the seventeenth parallel.

25   The South-East Asia Treaty Organisation was set up in February 1955; it was a parallel organisation to NATO and consisted of Australia, Britain, France, New Zealand, Pakistan, the Philippines, Thailand and the USA; it was dissolved in June 1977. The Central Treaty Organisation or Baghdad Pact was set up in February 1955; it was a parallel organisation to NATO and consisted of Britain, Iran, Iraq, Pakistan and Turkey; it was dissolved in 1979 after several years of inactivity.

26   Sir John Lionel Kotelawala (1895–1980) was a career army officer and a member of the United National Party; he was Prime Minister of Ceylon from October 1953 to April 1956, when the UNP was defeated by the Sri Lanka Freedom Party led by S W R D Bandaranaike.

27   Jawaharlal Nehru (1889–1964) studied law in Britain and became a leading member of Congress after his return to India; he was Prime Minister of India from August 1947 until his death.

28   Labour Party, *Civil Defence: Report of the Labour Party Joint Committee on Civil Defence* (Labour Party, London, 1955).

29   Walter Lippmann (1889–1974) was a noted US journalist, foreign affairs commentator and analyst of the problems of the relationship between mass culture and democracy.

30   John Foster Dulles (1888–1959) was a US lawyer specialising in international law. A Republican and virulent anti-communist, he was the main advocate of rollback in the Eastern bloc, as against the containment strategy favoured by the Democrats, and was Secretary of State from January 1953 to April 1959.

31   Alfred Maximilian Gruenther (1899–1983) was a US career officer, and was the supreme allied commander in Europe and commander-in-chief of the US European Command from 1953 to 1956.

32   Hubert Miles Gladwyn Jebb (1900–1996) was a British career diplomat and Ambassador to the United Nations during 1950–54 and to France during 1954–60.

33   Roger Mellor Makins (1904–1996) was a British career diplomat and Ambassador to

the USA during 1953–56; he was quick to recognise that the USA would not support Britain in the Suez crisis.

34 Robert Anthony Eden (1897–1977) was the Conservative MP for Warwick and Leamington during 1923–57; he held many ministerial posts, including Foreign Secretary from October 1951 to April 1955, then served as Prime Minister until January 1957.

35 Maurice Harold Macmillan (1894–1986) was Conservative MP for Stockton-on-Tees during 1931–45 and Bromley during 1945–64; he held many ministerial posts, including Foreign Secretary from April to December 1955 and Chancellor of the Exchequer from December 1955 to January 1957, then served as Prime Minister until October 1963.

36 Arthur Vere Harvey (1906–1994) was a career Air Force officer and businessman; he was Conservative MP for Macclesfield during 1945–71.

37 Cyril Osborne (1898–1969) was Conservative MP for Louth, Lincolnshire, during 1945–69; he was later a member of the right-wing Monday Club group of MPs.

38 *The Daily Herald* reflected the opinion of the leadership of the Labour Party, that is, a right-wing social-democratic standpoint.

39 At this juncture, *Tribune*, the left-wing Labour weekly, was incredibly optimistic about the possibilities of de-Stalinisation within the Soviet bloc, whilst remaining hostile to the CPGB.

40 On 3 April 1956, Alfred Robens (see note 22) warned that were the Labour Party to 'fall' for Moscow's propaganda for a popular front, 'we shall find the embrace of the Communist Party is the kiss of death to social-democracy'.

41 Hugh Todd Naylor Gaitskell (1906–1963) became interested in politics whilst a student at Oxford in the mid-1920s, worked in the Ministry for Economic Warfare during the Second World War, and was elected Labour MP for Leeds South in 1945. In Clement Attlee's governments he became Minister for Fuel and Power in 1947, and Minister of Economic Affairs and then Chancellor of the Exchequer in 1950, where his tax increases and introduction of NHS prescription charges to help cover expenditure on the Korean War led to resignations from the Cabinet. He became Leader of the Labour Party upon Clement Attlee's retirement in 1955, and fought for right-wing policies, not least on the question of nuclear weapons.

42 Morgan Walter Phillips (1902–1963) was a Welsh colliery worker, he joined the Labour Party at the age of 18, was active in the party in London from the late 1920s, became a full-time party worker in 1937, and was appointed party Secretary in 1944. He advocated a less working-class-based approach for Labour and called for an appeal to the middle class. He was Chairman of the Socialist International during 1948–57. He retired as Labour's General Secretary in 1961.

43 Konni Zilliacus (1894–1967) was born in Japan to a Finnish father and US mother, and raised in Britain. He worked for the League of Nations, and for the Ministry of Information during the Second World War. He was elected Labour MP for Gateshead in 1945 and was a staunch critic of Labour's Cold War foreign policy orientation. Expelled from the party with three other Labour MPs after voting against NATO membership in 1948, they joined D N Pritt, the MP for Hammersmith North who had been expelled from the Labour Party in 1940, in the Labour Independent Group, but Zilliacus fell out with them over his support for Tito in the Soviet-Yugoslav dispute (the others sided with Moscow). He was readmitted to the Labour Party and was MP for Manchester Gorton from 1952 to 1967. He was a founder member of the Campaign for Nuclear Disarmament. Although the Soviet dispute with Yugoslavia had been patched up by the time this article was written, Zilliacus was still *persona non grata* with the CPGB, although relations between them subsequently improved.

44   James Ramsay MacDonald (1866–1937) was Labour Prime Minister during 1924 and 1929–31, when he became Prime Minister of the first National Government, resulting in his being expelled from the Labour Party.

45   Since the above was written Mr Zilliacus has offered the explanation (*Daily Worker*, 17 April 1956) that he regarded *The British Road to Socialism* programme of 1951 as a proposal to establish 'a pale imitation of the People's Democracies' which he defines as 'broadly based revolutionary dictatorships which came to power by violent means'. Since *The British Road to Socialism* proposes that a united labour movement, rallying its support from the majority of the people, should elect a parliamentary majority in order to carry through the change to socialism, it is difficult to see how even the scholastic powers of Mr Zilliacus can 'interpret' this proposal as contrary to the conception of a democratic transition to socialism – Author's note.

46   William Noble Warbey (1903–1980) was a school-teacher, and was elected Labour MP for Luton in 1945, but lost his seat in 1950. He was elected MP for Broxtowe, Nottinghamshire, in a by-election in 1952, and was MP for Ashfield, Nottinghamshire, from 1955 until his retirement in 1966. He stood on the left of the party and was critical of Labour's Cold War policy orientation, he was later an opponent of the US war against Vietnam.

47   Konrad Hermann Joseph Adenauer (1876–1967) was a member of the Catholic Centre Party and the Mayor of Köln during 1917–33; after the Second World War he was a leader of the Christian Democratic Union, and was elected Chancellor of West Germany in 1949, 1953, 1957 and 1961.

48   Bernard Law Montgomery (1887–1976) was a British career army officer. He played a prominent role in the British Expeditionary Force in France in 1940, commanded the British ground forces in North Africa, and played a leading role in the invasion of France in 1944 and the ensuing advance into Germany. After the war, he was Chief of the Imperial Staff and Chairman of the Western European Union's commanders-in-chief committee, and helped Eisenhower in the establishment of NATO.

49   Hastings Lionel Ismay (1887–1965) was a British career army officer. He was Secretary of the Committee of Imperial Defence at the outbreak of the Second World War, and was Winston Churchill's primary military assistant. He served as NATO's Secretary-General during 1952–57.

50   Samuel John Gurney Hoare (1880–1959) was a Conservative MP during 1910–44, and held ministerial posts in various Conservative and National Governments, including Home Secretary during 1937–39.

51   Leading members of the Labour Party asked Khrushchev at a dinner in April 1956 about the fate of members of social-democratic parties in Eastern Europe, only to be met with a surly rebuff. It should be added that the behaviour of the senior Labour figure George Brown gave the impression that he was out for a fight with the Soviet visitors.

52   Franz Halder (1884–1972) was a German career army officer; he was appointed head of the General Staff in 1938, and was involved in a plot to remove Hitler were he to declare war over Czechoslovakia that year. Although lukewarm about waging war in the west, he was central to the plans to drive eastwards; he became pessimistic about the possibility of an Axis victory in the east, and was retired. In the 1950s he helped to rebuild West Germany's armed forces, and worked for the US Army's historical division.

53   Erich von Manstein (Fritz Erich Georg Eduard von Lewinski, 1887–1973) was a German career army officer and a senior commander on the Eastern Front during the Second World War; he was tried for war crimes, receiving an 18-year sentence, reduced to 12 years, of which he served only four; on his release he helped rebuild West Germany's armed forces.

54 Syngman Rhee (1875–1965) was a Korean nationalist politician with strong ties to the USA; he was elected President of the Republic of Korea in July 1948, and was re-elected in 1952, 1956 and 1960. His rule was notorious for repression and corruption, and an uprising in April 1960 forced his resignation.

55 Chiang Kai-shek (1887–1975) was a Chinese nationalist leader and head of the Kuomintang; his relations with the Chinese Communist Party ranged from collaboration to harsh repression, and although elected as President of China in May 1948 Communist forces rapidly defeated those of the Kuomintang, and Chiang retreated to Taiwan, where was repeatedly elected as President until his death.

56 Ngô Đình Diêm (1901–1963) was a civil servant in French-run Vietnam and a lifelong anti-Communist; for a while in the 1930s he was Interior Minister, but came into conflict with the colonial regime. When in exile, he forged close connections with the USA, and, returning after the partition of Vietnam in 1954, he was elected Prime Minister of South Vietnam in June 1954, and then President in October 1955, holding the post until deposed in a US-backed coup in November 1963.

57 See Document III, p. 77.

58 Sidney James Webb, First Baron Passfield (1859–1947) and his wife Martha Beatrice Webb, Lady Passfield (née Potter; 1858–1943) were Fabian socialists and prolific writers on social reform and welfare. Hostile to Bolshevism, they became greatly enamoured with the Soviet Union in the 1930s. A Labour MP during 1922–29, Sidney Webb was both Secretary of State for the Colonies and Secretary of State for Dominion Affairs in the Labour Government elected in 1929.

59 Béla Kun (Kohn, 1886–1938) became a Bolshevik when he was a prisoner-of-war in Russia in the First World War, fought in the Civil War, and founded the Hungarian Communist Party upon returning to Hungary in late 1918. He played a leading role in the Hungarian Soviet Republic of March–August 1919; after its collapse he was imprisoned in Austria and then exiled to the Soviet Union. He worked with Zinoviev in the Communist International apparatus, at first promoting ultra-left, putschist tactics. He was arrested in June 1937 in the Great Terror, tried in secret and executed, and was rehabilitated in 1956.

60 G D H Cole, 'World Socialism Restated', *New Statesman*, 5 May 1956; 'Three Questions for Communists', *Daily Worker*, 14 May 1956. George Douglas Howard Cole (1889–1959) was a British Fabian, socialist theoretician and historian; he was a guild socialist aiming at a decentralised form of society based upon workers' control; a prolific author, he is best known for *The Common People, 1746–1946* (co-written with his brother-in-law Raymond Postgate) and the seven-volume *A History of Socialist Thought*.

61 Trofim Denisovich Lysenko (1898–1976) was a Soviet biologist; he rejected Mendel's theories of genetics and elaborated his own theories, which were adopted in the Soviet Union in an attempt to overcome the problems resulting from the collectivisation of agriculture. He became the Director of the Institute of Genetics of the Soviet Academy of Sciences in 1940, and his ideas were championed by Stalin, leading to the persecution of mainstream biologists in the late 1940s. His ideas were repudiated during the 1960s. The CPGB championed Lysenko's ideas, see James Lattimer Fyfe, *Lysenko is Right* (Lawrence and Wishart, London, 1950).

62 John Milton (1608–1674) was an English poet and pamphleteer; a supporter of republicanism, he openly supported the execution of Charles I and wrote in defence of the Commonwealth; his most famous work was *Paradise Lost*, published in 1667.

63 Maurice Thorez (1900–1964) was a coal-miner and a foundation member of the French Communist Party; he became Secretary in 1923 and General Secretary in 1930, holding the post until his death. He was in Moscow from late 1939 to November 1944; he helped ensure that the resistance forces in France were disarmed. He was Vice-Premier of France during 1946–47 and a parliamentary deputy during 1946–58. In

1956, Thorez informed party member Jean Pronteau, who had seen the text of the 'Secret Speech' whilst in Poland: 'There is no secret report ... Besides, soon it will never have existed. We must pay no attention to it.' (*Socialist Register 1976* (Merlin, London, 1976), p. 59) Thorez must therefore have been expecting that Khrushchev would soon be removed from his post.

64   John Lilburne (c1614–1657) was a radical campaigner who fought for the Parliamentary forces in the English Civil War, but was prosecuted by the Parliamentary regime when he criticised it; his writings were influential amongst the Levellers.

65   Gerrard Winstanley (1609–1676) was a leader of the True Levellers, or Diggers, an egalitarian group, in the English Civil War, and was the author of *The New Law of Righteousness* and *The Law of Freedom in a Platform*.

66   William Cobbett (1763–1835) was a noted British writer and campaigner for political and social reform.

67   Richard Oastler (1789–1861) was a 'Tory radical' who campaigned for improved working conditions in factories and against repressive Poor Law measures.

68   Ernest Jones (1819–1869) was a prominent Chartist, a poet and writer, and editor of several Chartist newspapers.

69   William Morris (1834–1896) was a poet, writer and textile designer; he formed the Socialist League in 1884 after splitting from the Social Democratic Federation; Morris left this group in 1890 after it turned towards anarchism.

70   James Keir Hardie (1856–1915) was a founder of the Independent Labour Party in 1893, and helped form the Labour Coordinating Committee in 1900; he was an MP during 1892–95 and 1900–15, and was leader of the Labour Party from its foundation in 1906 until 1908.

71   Tom Mann (1856–1941) was centrally involved in many militant workers' struggles in Britain, including the London dock strike of 1889. A member of, in turn, the Social Democratic Federation, the Independent Labour Party and the British Socialist Party, he was a foundation member of the CPGB and headed its National Minority Movement in the 1920s.

72   Arnold Kettle (1916–1986) joined the CPGB in the 1930s when studying at Cambridge University, and was subsequently a professor of literature. He played a major role in establishing *Marxism Today* as the party's theoretical journal, and he remained a party member until his death.

73   Henry Hetherington (1792–1849) was a printer and was influenced by the ideas of Robert Owen; in 1830 he wrote the *Circular for the Formation of Trades Unions* and in 1831 he launched *The Poor Man's Guardian* in London, which led to harassment from the authorities. He helped form the London Working Men's Association in 1836, and subsequently became a leading figure in the Chartist movement.

74   George Matthews (1917–2005) was born into a wealthy liberal agricultural family. He joined the CPGB in 1938, joined its Executive Committee in 1943 and became Assistant General Secretary in 1949. He attended the CPSU's Twentieth Congress in 1956, and later that year became Deputy Editor of the *Daily Worker* and its Editor in 1959, overseeing its transformation into the *Morning Star* and continuing as Editor until 1979. After then he oversaw the party's archive. He was a strong supporter of Eurocommunism and of proposing major re-evaluations of certain aspects of the party's history, including its opposition to the Second World War in October 1939, and he was also prominent in revealing the party's financing from Soviet sources.

75   Rajani Palme Dutt, *Crisis of Britain and the British Empire* (Lawrence and Wishart, London, 1953).

76   John Gollan, *The British Political System* (Lawrence and Wishart, London, 1954). John Gollan (1911–1977) joined the Young Communist League and the CPGB in 1927, and in 1935 became the YCL's General Secretary and was elected to the CPGB's Central

Committee. He became the party's Assistant General Secretary in 1947 and National Organiser in 1954, and he was General Secretary during 1956–76.

77   E P Thompson, *William Morris* (Lawrence and Wishart, London, 1955).

78   Percy Bysshe Shelley (1792–1822) was a leading English epic poet and political radical.

79   From Shelley's poem, *The Mask of Anarchy: Written on the Occasion of the Massacre at Manchester.*

80   Robert Peel Glanville Blatchford (1851–1943) was a socialist activist and journalist most famous for writing the popular introduction to socialism *Merrie England*, which sold over two million copies, and for inspiring the Clarion propagandist movement. He was also strongly nationalistic and an outright jingo during the First World War, and drifted away from any form of socialism after then.

81   Palmiro Togliatti (1893–1964) was a founding member of the Italian Communist Party in 1921. He became its General Secretary in 1927, holding the post until his death. In exile from 1926 to 1944, he played after his return the leading role in moving the PCI towards a parliamentary strategy. Several of his statements on Khrushchev's 'Secret Speech' are contained in *The Anti-Stalin Campaign and International Communism* (Columbia University Press, New York, 1956).

82   Probably a reference to Palmiro Togliatti, '9 Domande sullo Stalinismo', *Nuovi Argomenti*, 16 June 1956; 'Statement of the Political Bureau of the French Communist Party', *l'Humanité*, 19 June 1956; both reproduced with other statements of that time in *The Anti-Stalin Campaign and International Communism* (Columbia University Press, New York, 1956).

83   Derek Isidore Kartun (1919–2005) was born into an artistic Jewish family. He joined the CPGB in the late 1930s after meeting the journalist Claude Cockburn whilst working as a script-writer for MGM films. He subsequently became the European Correspondent of the *Daily Worker* and was a prolific author. He wrote the notorious book *Tito's Plot Against Europe: The Story of the Rajk Conspiracy* (Lawrence and Wishart, London, 1949) with its immortal starting line: 'So very much stranger than fiction is this narrative …' He left the CPGB in 1956, and subsequently joined the Labour Party, became involved in the clothing business, and in retirement wrote several crime novels and other works.

Reasoning and *The Reasoner*

I commenced to reason in my thirty-third year and despite my best
efforts, I have never been able to shake the habit.
E P Thompson

THE REASONER
A JOURNAL OF DISCUSSION

Edited by
JOHN SAVILLE and E. P. THOMPSON

"To leave error unrefuted is to encourage intellectual immorality" - *Marx*

First Number   July 1956

Why We Are Publishing

THE REASONER is a journal which is, in the main, written by and addressed to members of the Communist Party.

It is a discussion journal. Our first aim is to provide a new forum for the far-reaching discussions at present going on within and close to the Communist Party - on questions of fundamental principle, aim, and strategy. Nothing in these pages should be taken as the expression of official Communist positions.

We shall judge our success by the number of serious and well-argued contributions to this discussion which we receive. While we are likely to place our emphasis upon contributions critical of views which have come to be accepted as orthodox, we shall welcome letters and articles from every source.

           x   x   x   x   x   x

Our second aim will be to provide in each number copies and translations of documents published in the Communist and Socialist press of other countries, and not readily available in Britain.

Readers will realise that this aim cannot be fully met in the first number. This is why we are on this occasion drawing upon American Communist sources for three of our documents. We are building a monitoring service to cover French, Russian, Czech, and Polish sources. The assistance of readers with access to Italian, Chinese, and other journals will be welcome.

           x   x   x   x   x   x

The Reasoner: A Journal of Discussion
Edited by John Saville and E P Thompson

To leave error unrefuted is to encourage intellectual immorality. – Marx

First Number

July 1956

Why We Are Publishing

The Reasoner is a journal which is, in the main, written by and addressed to members of the Communist Party.

It is a *discussion* journal. Our first aim is to provide a new forum for the far-reaching discussions at present going on within and close to the Communist Party – on questions of fundamental principle, aim and strategy. Nothing in these pages should be taken as the expression of official Communist positions.

We shall judge our success by the number of serious and well-argued contributions to this discussion which we receive. While we are likely to place our emphasis upon contributions critical of views which have come to be accepted as orthodox, we shall welcome letters and articles from every source.

* * *

Our second aim will be to provide in each number copies and translations of documents published in the Communist and Socialist press of other countries, and not readily available in Britain.

Readers will realise that this aim cannot be fully met in the first number. This is why we are on this occasion drawing upon American Communist sources for three of our documents. We are building a monitoring service to cover French, Russian, Czech and Polish sources. The assistance of readers with access to Italian, Chinese and other journals will be welcome.

* * *

We also hope that this journal will perform a practical service in loosening up the constricted forms within which discussion between Communists has taken place in recent years.

We believe that the self-imposed restrictions upon controversy, the 'guiding' of discussions along approved lines, the actual suppression of sharp criticism – all these have led to a gradual blurring of theoretical clarity, and to the encouragement among some Communists of attitudes akin to intellectual cynicism, when it has been easier to allow this or that false proposition to go by than to embark upon the tedious and frustrating business of engaging with bureaucratic editorial habits and general theoretical inertia.

* * *

This inertia has been broken through, not by any fresh polemic arising out of British conditions, but by the revelations following the Twentieth Congress of the Communist Party of the Soviet Union.

Since that time, discussion has grown in increasing volume, bursting through the normal restraints in our press. The discussion has revealed two things. First, a fear of ideas on the part of some members – and even leading members – of our party, who have been for too long cushioned from the give-and-take of polemic. Second, the veritable crisis of theory which has resulted from this long Ice Age.

Of the first we will say nothing at this moment.

Of the second it must be said that these discussions have revealed deep disagreements on the very meaning of 'Marxism'; the presence of grossly irrational and authoritarian attitudes intermingled with claims to a 'scientific analysis': the hardening of theory into dogma, of socialist education into indoctrination: the absence of a clear common understanding, indeed at times of any common terminology, on fundamental questions of democracy, political morality and party organisation.

Not only writers and artists, but every one of us, must reflect upon the tragic words of *Alexander Fadeyev*,[1] a few days before his suicide: 'For us writers ideology should have been a helpmate and an inspiration. By our excesses and our stiffness we made her a cross-grained shrew.'

This is no ordinary disagreement over the 'political line'. All agree upon the need for peace and for the unity of the labour movement in the common struggle against the Tories. The present disagreements touch deeper (although not more urgent) questions than these. They concern such questions as: 'Is there a need for a Communist Party in Britain? Should its structure be changed? What are the full implications of the aim of our party to become an affiliated unit of the Labour Party? Is our present theory adequate to deal with the problems of democracy, morality, justice, which events have brought forward? What is socialism?'

* * *

A crisis demands crisis measures. It is now clear to all that the fullest discussion is a necessity. It should also be clear that theoretical clarity can never be won unless disagreements are brought to the point of written expression.

To those comrades who welcome this discussion, but who argue that it should be kept within the acknowledged journals of the Communist Party, we say this:

We welcome the greater freedom of controversy at present evident in our publications. We hope it will be used to the full.

But we doubt whether the existing journals, with the limited space at their disposal, can give adequate expression to the storm of ideas of the coming months.

Nor can there be any trimming to the dictates of expediency. The first need of our movement is a rebirth of socialist principle, ensuring that dogmatic attitudes and theoretical inertia do not return.

We accept the need, as do all members of the Communist Party, for a degree of self-imposed discipline in action, based upon discussion and collective decisions. It may be that this concept of discipline has been interpreted too rigidly in the past; and it is certain that the democratic processes within the party are in need of attention. But we must state emphatically that we have no desire to see the party degenerate into a number of quarrelling sects and self-opinionated individuals. It is no part of the aim of this journal to encourage the formation of political factions.

It is now, however, abundantly clear to us that the forms of discipline necessary and valuable in a revolutionary party of action cannot and never should have been extended so far into the processes of discussion, of creative writing, and of theoretical polemic. The power which will shatter the capitalist system and create socialism is that of the free human reason and conscience expressed with the full force of the organised working class. Only a party of free men and women, accepting a discipline arising from truly democratic discussion and decision, alert in mind and conscience, will develop the clarity, the initiative and the élan necessary to arouse the dormant energies of our people. Everything which tends to cramp the intellect and dull their feelings weakens the party, disarms the working class, and makes the assault upon capitalism – with its deep defences of fraud and force – more difficult.

Neither the reason nor the conscience of man can be confined within the discipline and procedures appropriate to decisions of action: nor can great theoretical issues be solved by a simple majority vote.

* * *

We take our stand as Marxists. Nothing in the events of past months has shaken our conviction that the methods and outlook of historical materialism, developed by the work of Marx and Engels, provide the key to our theoretical advance and, therefore, to the understanding of these events themselves; although it should be said that much that has gone under the name of 'Marxism' or 'Marxism-Leninism' is itself in need of re-examination.

History has provided a chance for this re-examination to take place; and for the scientific methods of Marxism to be integrated with the finest traditions of the human reason and spirit which we may best describe as Humanism.

This opportunity may be of short duration. Once passed it may not soon return. It would be treason to our cause, and a betrayal of the strivings, past and present, for a classless society, to let it pass in silence.

* * *

Taking Stock

Communists all over the world are today being forced to consider the shattering implications of the Khrushchev speech. The fact that Communists have at last publicly recognised many things which those outside their ranks have long been saying has naturally led to a widespread and general questioning of the Communist position.

National Communist parties, both in Eastern Europe and in the rest of the world, have shown very different official reactions to the disclosures at the secret session, although there is evidence that beneath the surface disquiet among Communists is world-wide. To explain why, for example, the American Communist Party has reacted much more passionately to the revelations than the French, or why Poland has developed a much freer public discussion and instituted more far-reaching measures to eliminate past injustices than either Czechoslovakia or Romania, would take us beyond the boundaries of this preliminary statement. Yet at some point such an analysis has to be made unless we are to succumb once again to the error which has dogged us for so long – that of failing to make a Marxist analysis of the developments in Communist movements in general and in the socialist countries in particular.

* * *

Our chief concern at the moment is with Britain, where our public voice has been both muffled and confused. How weakly and inadequately our moral feelings have been expressed will be appreciated by a reading of the letter which *Steve Nelson* sent to the New York *Daily Worker* on the occasion of their editorial on the Rajk[2] trial (both documents in this number). Is it not shameful, in a country whose labour movement has found so many eloquent and passionate spokesmen, from Cobbett to Tom Mann, that our own powers of speech would appear to have deserted us? Are the American Communists, who have spoken with such vigour and honesty of feeling, betraying their heritage? Or is it not that we, who have procrastinated, who have shuffled and dragged our feet behind events, who have waited for the safe 'formulation', are betraying a moral nihilism out of keeping with the ideals for which our pioneers struggled?

Or – if we turn to our political appraisal – and compare RP Dutt's analysis in the May and June issues of *Labour Monthly*[3] with the recent statement of Togliatti,[4] it is unfortunately clear that the seriousness of the situation has not been matched by our understanding. And our failure is shown as much by those who have kept silent as by those who have spoken.

* * *

It is no accident that our moral and political reactions have been so feeble, for the one involves the other, and the weakening of the moral basis of our political life necessarily makes less vigorous our practical judgements and our practical activity. If we, in this journal, raise such problems as these, we do so with some humility, since we ourselves share responsibility for the failures which we analyse.

The shock and moral turmoil engendered by the revelations were the result of our general failure to apply a Marxist analysis to socialist countries and to the Soviet Union in particular. The absence of such an analysis is an admission of naivety, or worse. This failure bred Utopianism, and encouraged attitudes of religious faith amongst us. When, as often happened, there came a recognition of the gulf between myth and fact, the disillusion which followed turned in many cases to bitterness. Our irrational approach to the Soviet Union, and our hostile attitude towards those who were not prepared to accept our myths, have brought some socialists to the point of doubting our integrity, have been a factor contributing to the disunity of our labour movement, and have helped to drive others into anti-Soviet attitudes dangerous to the cause of peace and socialism.

Certainly, the establishment of Soviet power is the greatest historical event of this century. From the moment of its foundation, the defence of the Soviet Union from the attacks of the capitalist world was rightly at the centre of working-class internationalism. The debt which all humanity owes to the Soviet people, the heroism of the Soviet people in the Second World War, can never be forgotten. But the balance sheet cannot be closed at this point. Our responsibility to our own labour movement is no less heavy. To argue, as has so often been argued, that 'we do not believe [that] the interests of the British working class and people conflict with the interests of the working class and people of other countries' (Gollan, *End the Bans*, p. 11) is to include the complexities of the real world within a platitude. Argument begins at the point where the phrase ends: and we must still interpret these interests in terms of political action. In practice, the interests of the British working class have been interpreted in such a way that we have identified them with the acceptance of the foreign policy of the Soviet Union, and at the same time we have been indignant at accusations of blindly 'following Moscow'.

* * *

The discussion cannot rest here, for the uncritical character of our public support for the Soviet Union was carried over into other fields. Certain recurring themes in the history of our party demand particular attention. One is the chequered history of Communist–Labour relations; another is the ever-present problem of our sectarianism and dogmatism: a third is the slow growth of a native Marxist tradition. In future numbers we will discuss these problems in more detail.

The roots of sectarianism will be found in our movement long before the Russian revolution. Inevitably (and leaving aside the particular influence of *HM Hyndman*)[5] in a country with strong empirical traditions, with a trade-union movement already strongly entrenched and shot through with petty-bourgeois radicalism, the young Marxist movement of the 1880s developed strong tendencies towards purism and sectarianism. By 1914, the weak Marxist tradition, although it had achieved practical results far beyond its numerical strength, was already cast in a dogmatic mould. Upon this there was imposed, after 1917, the strong tradition that had grown up within the Russian movement; and here, as elsewhere, the advice and guidance of the Communist International was coloured by the experience of the Russians.

This is not to belittle the historic importance, for the world movement, of the establishment of the Third International. But in countries with advanced democratic forms and weak revolutionary traditions, as in Britain and America, the impact of a tradition derived from very different historical circumstances, aggravated the tendencies, already powerful, towards dogmatism and sectarianism. As late as 1935 the programme of the British party was entitled *For a Soviet Britain*.[6] In 1938 and in subsequent years there was a major campaign to popularise *The Short History of the CPSU(b)*[7] – a work which, leaving aside its gross distortions, had only little relevance to British conditions.

We cannot, however, escape responsibility for the weakness of the Marxist tradition in Britain by reference to historical circumstances. This is the escape by the formula of 'historical inevitability' which we have too often used in the past. We ourselves have been active agents in the historical process, and the shallow growth of Marxist scholarship as well as the failure of Marxism as a body of ideas to stimulate and excite, must be accepted as our own failure.

* * *

This is the time to examine our mistakes. Their effect has been to isolate us from the labour movement, to diminish our political influence, and to hinder the devoted work for socialism of a generation of Communists. But this work has gone forward nonetheless. Our record in the fight against imperialism, the great services rendered by our party to colonial movements, the leadership of the unemployed workers before 1939, the fight in defence of the Spanish Republic, the constant struggle for working and living conditions – these also are part of British history.

We are confident that the men and women who have sought to remain true to the principles of internationalism throughout all the pressure and confusion of the Cold War, whose errors have flowed, in the main, from the desire to believe only the best of their comrades who are engaged in the building of socialism in other countries: and whose steadfastness has won the respect of many of our most militant workers in our workshops and mines – we are confident that a party made up of such men and women will have the courage to look squarely at our failures, and will find the initiative to return to the main highway of British revolutionary traditions.

* * *

Ken Alexander, Democratic Centralism[8]

In recent discussions many have raised the questions of the organisation and structure of the Communist Party. How far is its structure well adapted to its tasks and to its national and political environment? Would a revision of its organisational principles increase its political effectiveness?

The Communist Party is based on the principles of democratic centralism. The nature of these principles and their historical origins

have not been widely discussed by British Communists. An article in the
·*Communist Review* of January 1951 is one of the few recent British writings
on the subject.[9] The standard sources to which readers are referred for
detailed elaboration of the case for democratic centralism are Lenin, *One
Step Forward, Two Steps Back*;[10] Stalin, *Foundations of Leninism*, especially
Chapter VIII;[11] Liu Shao-Chi, *On The Party*, especially Chapter V.[12] There is
also an outline of some working principles of democratic centralism in the
Rules of the Communist Party.

The principles of democratic centralism were first clearly set out by Lenin,
in part to enable a revolutionary party to fulfil its functions, particularly
the function which Stalin named 'acting as the organised detachment of
the working class',[13] and in part because of the environment of Tsarist
oppression, illegality and eventually civil war in which the Russian party
was working. The idea that the degree of centralism was dependent upon
the ruling environment was expressed by Lenin:

> In the present epoch of acute civil war a Communist party will be able to
> perform its duty only if it is organised in the most centralised manner,
> only if iron discipline bordering on military discipline prevails in it, and
> if its party centre is a powerful and authoritative organ, wielding wide
> powers and enjoying the universal confidence of the members of the
> party.[14]

To devoted revolutionaries anxious to prosecute class war to a successful
socialist conclusion the appeal of a centralised, disciplined organisation
is obviously strong. Rosa Luxemburg was among the few who called
attention to the disadvantages which might be set against the advantages
of such a tightly-knit organisation. In 1904, she opposed what she called
Lenin's ultra-centralism, arguing that old forms of centralism appropriate
to conspiratorial organisations without a mass basis were harmful for a
movement which depended for everything on the independent actions of
the masses of the people. Luxemburg also argued that 'to provide a party
leadership with such absolute powers of a negative character, as Lenin
suggests, would artificially and most dangerously intensify the conservatism
which naturally belongs to every such body'.[15] She opposed rules permitting
the Central Executive to dissolve and re-form branches and otherwise
interfere in their affairs, as providing a means by which what might become
focal points of different viewpoints could be eliminated, and opposition
weakened before the calling of elective conferences.

The historical success of the Bolsheviks in 1917 provided a further and compelling argument in favour of a highly centralised party structure – although the extent to which central leadership was in fact able to function in the early and crucial stages of the revolution is in some doubt. The environmental features of most countries at that time – with many parties working in illegal or semi-legal conditions – strengthened the view that a Marxist party must necessarily adopt a highly centralised structure.

In Britain the parties and groupings which united in 1920 to form the CPGB were not centralist in structure. 'The parties were based on the geographical constituency with its branches, or group of branches. Their activities combined the propaganda of socialist ideas with the local municipal or parliamentary electoral campaign.' (Tom Bell) Acceptance of a centralist structure was amongst the twenty-one conditions of affiliation to the Third International. The imposition of new forms of organisation presented problems in the first year of the British party's existence. Tom Bell, the first national organiser, recalls:

> Our first job was to get the branches together as units of the new party and link them up into districts with district committees, each with its own organiser, and each unit organised on the principle of democratic centralism. But it was not an easy job getting the comrades to understand the meaning of centralised direction. Time after time, on the Executive Committee, we had to combat the 'federalist' and 'constituency' notions of the comrades who came from the provinces, and try to get them to think 'executively'. At the opposite extreme we had amusing cases of local secretaries and organisers who interpreted centralised direction to mean that they were, like sergeant-majors, to give orders and every member had to spring to attention and obey.[16]

The *Thesis on Organisation* adopted at the Third Congress of the Communist International (1921)[17] led to a further reorganisation. A special commission of R P Dutt, H Inkpin[18] and H Pollitt was appointed as a result, 'to examine the whole party organisation and make proposals for bringing it into line with the Thesis of the Third Congress'. The report of this commission was presented to the British Congress of October 1922,[19] and, as a result, 'collective direction was entrusted to a central committee, with a political bureau and an organising bureau' (Tom Bell). 'When the authoritative history of the party comes to be written', comments Pollitt, 'it will have to pay great attention to this report and the turning-point it represented for us all.'[20]

In the absence of an authoritative history, and even of authoritative sources (Tom Bell's narrative, in *Pioneering Days*, stops short at the General Strike; Pollitt's, in *Serving My Time*, at 1929), it is impossible to trace the influence upon British concepts of centralised leadership of developments within the Third International in the 1930s. The threat to the international working-class movement presented by the rise of Fascism, together with the tendencies towards ultra-centralism, associated with Stalin, gave rise to the theory of a world-wide centralised discipline. The Sixth Congress of the Communist International (1928) adopted in its programme a concept of Communist duty which remained in force throughout the 1930s:

> The coordination of work and revolutionary actions and their correct direction imposes on the international proletariat an *international class discipline*, of which the essential condition is the most strict international discipline in the ranks of the Communist parties. This international Communist discipline must be expressed by the subordination of partial and local interests of the movement to its general and lasting interests, and by the strict application of all decisions of the leading organs of the Communist International by all Communists.[21]

The Statutes of the Comintern gave almost unrestricted authority to the Executive over the national sections. 'The decisions of the Executive Committee are obligatory upon all sections and must be carried out immediately by them.' It had powers to ratify programmes of national sections, reverse decisions of national congresses, and no congress could be called without its authority. At the time of the Seventh Congress (1935), according to the recent statement of Togliatti:

> The parties which had gained strength, were united and well directed, already felt that an international centre could do no more than lay down general lines on the situation and on the duties of our movement, but that decisions of practical policy and their implementation should be the work of the individual parties ... This is how things went, above all in France and Spain ...[22]

When the authoritative history of the British party comes to be written, it will be of interest to learn how far the concept of international centralised leadership was modified in practice during this period. Certainly the dissolution of the Comintern was not followed by any radical change in the working of democratic centralism as applied to the organisation of the British party itself.

* * *

The questions which must be asked about democratic centralism are:

First, has democratic centralism any general disadvantages which may hold back the movement for socialism?

Second, has it any particular disadvantages in British conditions?

Third, has it any possible disadvantages in the post-revolutionary period when socialism is being built?

Already in 1918, Rosa Luxemburg was expressing her doubts on the third point. She wrote:

> The suppression of political life throughout the country must gradually cause the vitality of the Soviets themselves to decline. Without general elections, freedom of the press, freedom of assembly and freedom of speech, life in every public institution slows down, becomes a caricature of itself, and bureaucracy rises as the only deciding factor. No one can escape the workings of this law. Public life gradually dies, and a few dozen party leaders with inexhaustible energy and limitless idealism direct and rule … In the last resort cliquism develops a dictatorship, but not the dictatorship of the proletariat: the dictatorship of a handful of politicians, that is, a dictatorship in the bourgeois sense, in the Jacobin sense …[23]

Inside the young Soviet republic there were at least three groups, including several prominent Bolsheviks, organised in opposition to centralism. When one of these groups secured a majority on the Central Committee of the Ukrainian party the committee was disbanded. Recent admissions about the degeneration of party life in the Soviet Union and in other countries in which Communist parties have become the main political force require some reassessment of the force of the case against democratic centralism.

Nenni has suggested that the Khrushchev Report 'strikes not only at the Stalinist but at the Leninist notion of a workers' party'.[24] Togliatti has written: 'Perhaps we are not wrong in asserting that it is from the party that the damaging limitations of the democratic regime originated with the gradual substitution for it of bureaucratic forms of organisation.'[25] The CC of the CPSU, in its resolution on the matter, does not explicitly state that there was a connection between the organisation of the party and the growth of tyranny in the Soviet system, but it does recognise that 'stringent centralisation of leadership could not but have had an adverse effect on the development of some democratic forms'.[26] In the absence of alternative and convincing explanations, the most reasonable explanation of how the limited democracy of democratic centralism was supplanted by tyranny is that democratic centralism so weakened democracy as to make this possible.

What are the disadvantages of a highly centralised political structure for a Marxist party in a capitalist country?

The general objections of Rosa Luxemburg have already been quoted. She opposed the idea of rigid boundaries between leadership, membership and masses. The effective participation of Communists in mass movements on economic, social and political questions has often been held back by their adherence to principles which require that:

> Lower party organisations should not exceed their powers by publicly issuing their views in place of or prior to the Central Committee on issues which should and must be decided upon and made public by the Central Committee. No responsible party leader, including members of the Central Committee, should publicise their views without the Central Committee's approval. They may discuss their views at the meetings of lower party committees and make suggestions to the Central Committee. But it is impermissible for them to make public, either inside or outside the party, views not yet made known by the Central Committee or to circulate these views among other lower party committees. (Liu Shao-Chi)

It seems certain that the tendencies to dogmatism in Marxism – recognised by Marx – are encouraged when what political discussion there is takes place within a highly centralised and disciplined structure. Amongst the explanations of the lack of imagination in political work and of apathy about political activity to be found amongst many Communists is surely the effect of a political organisation erected and operated in the belief that 'an organised party implies the establishment of authority, the transformation of the power of ideas into the power of authority, the subordination of lower party bodies to higher party bodies' (Lenin).[27]

Whatever the counterbalancing emphasis placed from time to time on inner-party democracy, criticism and self-criticism, and now, collective leadership, is it not a sad fact that political controversy within the British Communist Party has been barely discernible at most times, and that unrelieved dullness has repelled many who are otherwise sympathetic to Marxism, and encouraged many others to remove themselves from the maw of 'the Monolith'? Methods of discussion within the party usually result in any opposition viewpoints being dissipated rather than concentrated, and in stagnation instead of clash and dialectic producing better policies. Methods of voting do not encourage elections being used to reflect the support for differences of opinion which might exist, and thus a main means by which such differences can be crystallised and resolved by the membership is thwarted.

A socialist movement thrives on controversy and withers when it is absent. An idea on the way up can neither be developed nor win through to practical application without the cut and thrust of argument about the idea itself, just how it can be applied, and so on. Marxists have imprisoned themselves in a political structure which has constricted the development of their theory and severely limited their political effectiveness. The regular admonitions in all Communist parties to overcome bureaucratic tendencies and dogma miss the point that these tendencies are in part rooted in the soil of a centralist political structure.

The disadvantages of a highly centralised and disciplined political structure have particular force in Britain. A political movement which places such stress on authority and in which political argument and decision are circumscribed lacks appeal to a working class which is amongst the most politically conscious and experienced in the capitalist world. In addition the possibility in Britain of uniting Marxism with the existing labour movement has been made more remote by the adoption by British Marxists of a repugnant political structure, and a philosophy of authority which accorded to a foreign political party a 'leading role' and which ultimately led to public manifestations of idolatry not even excused, as it appears to have been in some other cases, by being performed under pain of death.

The historical circumstances of the period now opening weaken the arguments in support of democratic centralism. An environment of peaceful coexistence rather than of capitalist encirclement, the possibility of a peaceful transition to socialism for some countries, and the recognition that it may be possible for some countries to reach socialism without Communist parties being in the lead, all call into question the case for centralism. When into the scales are put the disadvantages accompanying democratic centralism even in an environment in which it has advantages more obvious than at the present time, the case against it looks even more substantial. Add to this the lessons to be learnt from those countries which have begun to build socialism with parties based on democratic centralism at the helm – the degeneration of party life, the persecution of oppositions and minorities, and the widespread constriction of democratic participation in the making of key decisions – and the case against democratic centralism becomes overwhelming.

Some Communists, recognising that democratic centralism is brought into question by experience near to and far from home, argue that the principle is sound but that its practice has been imperfect, that the centralism has grown out of proportion to the democracy. First, it should be noted that in the term itself 'centralism' is the noun and 'democratic' the qualifying adjective – emphasising that the structure must be centralist, with some democratic features compatible with centralism. Second, the fact that all Communist parties have shown evidence of these 'imperfections' indicates that there is a strong tendency, to say the least, for such a structure to operate in the way it has done. It can be argued that whether or not party structure should be based on democratic centralism is a matter of degree only, and that all political organisations if they are to be effective require some centralism, some degree of authority in their structure. But truly democratic political institutions – those which have at least a good chance of functioning democratically and of remaining democratic irrespective of the weaknesses and motives of the individuals who temporarily come to hold some degree of authority in them – must provide checks and balances to authority, not checks and balances to the very means by which the actions of such authority can be brought into question.

The argument that the new emphasis on collective leadership and on criticism introduces sufficient safeguards for democracy founders on the experience of several parties in which, at different times, collective leadership has given way to rule by small groups and even individuals. Although the CPSU now regards collective leadership as the prime and 'supreme principle' of party leadership, whereas previous statements have given greater emphasis to centralised control, the failure to examine how previous collective leaderships were transformed into tyranny leaves little confidence that the current return to collective leadership is by itself a sufficient guarantee against future tyranny. The especial danger of democratic centralism is that once accepted it provides a rationale by which intelligent men themselves limit their own right to question and criticise, so that eventually they either lose the faculty or facility, or both, altogether. Collectives have provided examples of this already. What guarantee is there that they will not do so again?

Many practical changes could be suggested to meet these dangers. The clear-cut right to know what disagreements there are on party committees, to make all disagreements public, to publish independent of central control – these, with an overhaul of electoral methods, could make a beginning within the Communist movement. Outside it, freedom of the press, freedom of assembly and free choice at elections would be essential. This is not the place to argue such proposals in detail. Central to all reforms and all proposals must be the realisation that the linking of the ideas of authority and leadership has to be replaced in our theory by the concept of democratic control and initiative.

This is not to jettison the idea of a disciplined political party, but to argue for discipline based on argument, democratic decisions and conviction, rather than on a centralised structure within which the decisions are generally taken at the top and the traffic of ideas flows in one direction only. Bringing such a new concept of discipline to life will have its difficulties; at times the yearning for the old centralism will be very strong. But only if the change is made will the grip of dogma on Marxist thought and of apathy and lack of initiative in Communist political action be broken, Marxism eventually be united to the broad labour movement, and the job of winning and building socialism be advanced.

* * *

E P Thompson, Reply To George Matthews

In *World News*, 30 June 1956, there was published an article by E P Thompson, 'Winter Wheat in Omsk', together with a reply, 'A Caricature of Our Party', by George Matthews. The article below was submitted to *World News*, but was rejected on the grounds that many other contributions had been received, and 'it is reasonable to give these comrades space to put their viewpoint rather than to publish a further article by yourself'. In view of the limited space at the disposal of the Editor of *World News* we do not consider this decision unreasonable. On the other hand we think it of general interest to allow this polemic full opportunity for expression: and we shall be glad to find space for a further reply from George Matthews, if he wishes to write one for our September number – Editors.

* * *

Comrade Matthews writes that I have 'unconsciously echoed all the most familiar anti-Communist jibes and sneers of the enemy press – that Communists repeat dogmas like Holy Church, have little regard for morality, are un-British, not much concerned with democracy, and so on'.

He is quite wrong. I was consciously and openly suggesting that our party, and especially our leadership, has – from time to time – laid us open to all these very serious accusations.

It is a feature of dogmatic and irrational thinking that all criticisms are dismissed with the defensive emotional cry, 'enemy propaganda'. If the capitalist press accused us of being 'against Property, against the Queen, against the Empire', we would have little need to be disturbed. But when it makes charges of an altogether different order – that we are *not* rational Marxists or principled British revolutionaries – then we must examine seriously our opponents' case. The more that we find that honest friends in the labour movement are influenced by such accusations, the more urgent this self-examination becomes.

Let us look more closely at these charges.

Dogma

Holy Church, as we know, was founded upon an apostolic succession, with supreme doctrinal authority vested in the Pope and College of Cardinals. It excommunicated heretics, pronounced anathema on those who sought to smuggle heresies into the Church, and sought to establish the truth or falsity of doctrines by referring to a self-consistent system of thought, founded upon authority and Biblical texts, rather than by constant reference to facts.

What, then, are we to make of the following comments by R P Dutt on the occasion of the seventieth anniversary of the death of Marx? Dutt describes the 'succession of four figures of incomparable genius to lead mankind through the most hazardous and critical transition of human development' as 'without parallel in the historical record'. After quoting the noble tribute which Engels paid to Marx on the day following the death of his friend, Comrade Dutt continues:

> It is timely to recall this estimate by Engels of the role of Marx, not only as the founder of scientific socialism, the theoretical genius, 'the greatest head of our time', but equally as the practical leader, the guide of the whole international movement, the 'central figure to which Frenchmen, Russians, Americans and Germans spontaneously turned at critical moments to receive always that clear uncontestable counsel which only genius and a perfect understanding of the situation could give' … It is timely to recall these words today, when the corresponding recognition of the role of Lenin and Stalin in our era arouses the special fury and reviling from all the pygmies and enemies of socialism … who denounce such recognition as 'personal idolatry' which from the heights of their superior Marxist wisdom they are pleased to proclaim as 'wholly alien to Marxism'.

Comrade Dutt next declares:

> Marxism is no textbook of ready-made formulas and recipes to be applied by fools. Marxism is a science alike in the field of theory and of

action; and precisely because it is a science, and all the more because it represents the highest level of science, it requires mastery; and mastery implies a master. For this reason living Marxism finds its expression in the living person, and its highest expression in the 'greatest head', the 'central figure', the 'genius and perfect understanding' whose theoretical and practical leadership most effectively carries forward the fulfilment of Marxism. (*Labour Monthly*, March 1953)

The passage concludes with references to Stalin.

The Method of Marxism

Here, then, is our apostolic succession, our fount of doctrinal purity. It is easy to be wise after the event. I do not suggest that Comrade Dutt was the only – or even the worst – offender. I wish only to emphasise that in our discussions on the 'cult of the individual' it is high time that we brought our examination nearer home – and enquired into our own modes of thought and attitudes towards doctrinal authority. To the degree that we have all allowed such attitudes as those expressed by Comrade Dutt to pass in silence, we must now examine ourselves.

Nor do I suggest that this tendency towards dogmatism is the whole story, nor could it be in a party made up of men and women who have joined it because they have seen through the frauds and immoralities of capitalist society.

But how does our total record square with Comrade Matthews' definition of Marxist method?

To arrive at truth it is necessary first to make a scientific examination of phenomena, their history and development, and their interrelationship, to elaborate theories on this scientific basis, and to put the theories to the test of practice.

Fine words. Is this what we did in the case of Yugoslavia? Has this guided our attitude towards the Soviet Union? No, we have been guided by faith – or 'wrong information'.

Have we examined the history of our own party according to these precepts?

If practice, action, is the test of our theory, do not the Khrushchev revelations, and their implications, suggest that we must conduct the most searching re-examination of some part of our theory?

Have we not talked too glibly often of Marxism as a 'science', suggesting to outsiders that we claimed sole possession to a potent form of magic? Should we not talk more often of the need for deep and detailed knowledge, close study, intelligent analysis, sharp discussion?

Perhaps Engels had foresight when he wrote:

> The materialist conception of history has a lot of friends nowadays to whom it serves as an excuse for *not* studying history. Just as Marx used to say … 'All I know is that I am not a Marxist.'[28]

As an historian I can only feel shame that, in the name of 'Marxism-Leninism', we have so far departed from the high critical temper, the constant return to reality, of Marx and Engels. Increasingly we have emphasised an arbitrary selection of conclusions (some derived from nineteenth-century or Russian conditions) rather than the method of historical materialism: have sought to make 'correct formulations' within a schematised system of doctrine, rather than to return again and again to social realities. Add to this the rigidities of democratic centralism, the absence of real controversy, the growth of a special jargon, a hierarchy of authority, a foreign fount of doctrine, and we get, do we not, some analogy with Holy Church?

Democracy

But are we so innocent of the other 'enemy' charges? It is true that we have recently paid more attention to our own history as a source of inspiration. But this is not the same thing as deriving our own policy from a deep study of our own traditions and conditions.

In this connection I would ask whether we are fully satisfied that our policy can truthfully be called *The British Road to Socialism*: or whether certain passages in it might not be better entitled *The Russian Road to Socialism, Done into English*? Certainly I hope that the 'formulations' about 'people's democracy' will be re-examined in this light.

It does not impress me when Comrade Matthews quotes this or that resolution to prove our respect for democracy. What impresses the British people is that for twenty-odd years we have been eagerly justifying as 'the highest form of democracy' a society in which there is no real freedom of the press – whether for the publication of information, opinion or creative writing – no freedom from arbitrary arrest, and no contested elections.

It may be true that in the historical circumstances of the Soviet Union much of this – but by no means all – can be seen as inevitable.

But this is not what we have been saying, as a brief reference to our press and propaganda will prove. Nor is it true in any sense whatsoever that we were unaware of these facts, whatever mental evasions or glosses we may have made.

Moreover, Comrade Matthews' quotation from Shelley leads me to doubt the sincerity of his own self-criticism. When Shelley described freedom for the labourer as meaning 'bread' and a 'neat and happy home', he showed profound insight into his own society, and stated an important aspect of the truth. When Comrade Matthews quotes this in 1956 in order to reply to my article, he displays either a failure to understand what the great debate going on throughout the world is about: or an attitude of dangerous patronage to the working class.

Is he suggesting that intellectual liberty is an unimportant foible of 'intellectuals', of little real concern to working people? If I thought that this was the case, I could not remain a Communist. But in fact the British working class have proved on a hundred occasions that they consider intellectual liberty to be their own concern. Many hundreds of labourers were imprisoned, in the time of Bunyan[29] and before, for liberty of conscience. Thousands took part in the struggles for a free press: supported Darwin:[30] campaigned for and voted for Bradlaugh.[31] And some went homeless and without bread for their principles.

In our own day the disgust aroused by McCarthyism, both in the United States and in England, prove that our people have not forgotten these traditions. And we must face the fact that we have alienated many British workers because they have suspected us of indifference towards these liberties.

Can Comrade Matthews not see that this problem – of combining economic and social with political and intellectual liberty – demands more than a few platitudes for its solution? If not, I must believe that most British workers have a truer respect for these liberties than do some leaders of the 'vanguard of the working class'.

Morality

As for Matthews' remarks on the question of morality, I am frankly appalled:

> For Marxists every political decision is good or bad according to whether or not it serves the interests of the working people and the cause of socialism.

Has he been reading the same facts as I have been during the past three months? Can he cover over the crack in the walls of our theory with this piece of soiled wallpaper?

Who is to judge what serves these interests? *How* is he to judge? On the basis of obvious political expediency? Or on deeper and more considered grounds, which take into account the effect of certain actions upon the moral sensibilities of the ordinary people? And if the latter, then how can this political judgement be made without consciously raising moral issues?

The quotations used by Matthews from *Anti-Dühring* do not take us very far in the solution of these problems, although in *Ludwig Feuerbach* Engels takes us further: and I have suggested elsewhere that William Morris also made a very great contribution to these problems which we have neglected to our peril. This is not the place to examine these problems: nor do I think that they will be capable of easy solution. But the least that I expected of Comrade Matthews was that he would now recognise that they exist.

If he does not, then Expediency is still King, and Stalinism may yet return.

Pride In Our Party

Finally, Comrade Matthews asks me rhetorically if I am proud of our party. Let me give a straight answer.

I believe that our party contains within its ranks many of the best, most self-sacrificing, intelligent and courageous representatives of the British people. I am proud of what our party has done for the British working class, for the colonial peoples, and against Fascism and the threat of war. I respect those comrades who have given the best of their lives to the party, even where I think that some of their actions have been mistaken.

I am *not* proud of our failure to root ourselves more deeply in British life, of our failure to interpret creatively our democratic traditions, of our confusion of the true principles of internationalism with a servile attitude to the leadership of the Soviet Union. I am *not* proud of the way in which we have alienated many thousands of the best of the British people by our rigidity and our folly. I am *not* proud of the vacillation which our present leadership has shown during the last three months. I am *not* proud of the silence which I and others have kept too long over these and other matters. One thing only will give me back that sense of pride – when we find once again principled socialist policies and a leadership truly representative of the best of the British working class.

* * *

CORRESPONDENCE
What Is Socialism?

Dear Comrade

The essential features and requirements of the basic law of socialism might be formulated roughly in this way: the securing of the maximum satisfaction of the constantly rising material and cultural requirements of the whole of society through the continuous expansion and perfection of socialist production on the basis of higher techniques. – Stalin, *Economic Problems of Socialism in the USSR*[32]

We want bread! – Slogan shouted by workers demonstrating in Poznań

The recent riots and demonstrations in Poznań and official admissions of the justness of the demands and grievances of the strikers have given a further jolt to the thinking of most Communists and Socialists, already studying seriously the implications of the Khrushchev speech. The discontent expressed by the workers of Poznań is not the only internal evidence of serious economic failings in the 'People's Democracies'. The following are extracts from a poem by a young Hungarian Communist poet, Károly Jobbágy,[33] which appeared in a Budapest journal in April 1956. The title of the poem has been translated as *Mudville.*

> Don't talk to me about spaceships,
> a trip to the moon or Mars,
> about life in the atomic age …
> The oxcarts, like a fleet on shoals,
> are caught in a shoreless sea of mud,
> Mud is our roads, yards, pasture.
> When winter comes and the rain, like this,
> men if they could would turn into beasts and hibernate, and see nothing.
> Darkness comes early; there is no electricity here.
> Beside a cold lamp, the mind sputters
> vainly sparking behind the forehead.
> Kerosene? More expensive, five times as expensive as a matter of fact,
>   than gasoline of which during the summer one can easily burn up five
>   gallons on joyrides.
> But kerosene, sometimes there's not a drop, besides at that price, who
>   can afford to burn half a litre a day, enough to light the house?

We're at the point we can't even believe the good – no point to tell us that
    they think of us, consider our needs.
We live like this. In darkness, in mud, far away.

We too are 'heroes', all of us
Who, crowded into tiny rooms,
chew pumpkin seeds and lie around like garbage.
Don't tell me it is worse in Africa.
I live in Europe, my skin is white.
Who will embrace me to make me feel that I am human?

The following extract is from an article which appeared in the Cracow
(Poland) journal *Życie Literackie*, 19 February 1956. The article retails a
conversation between the author, a party activist agitating for collectivisation
in the countryside, and an old friend of his, an average middle peasant who
had refused to join a collective. The author had visited his friend at his home
when the temperature was 25°C below zero. He started to say something
about socialism when he was interrupted:

Suddenly my friend, making a sharp gesture towards the stove, said: '*This
is your socialism.* The stove is cold as ice. Tell me, when before had there
ever been no coal in my house? Go around Chadów, and you will see for
yourself: *nobody has any coal.* I bought some coke but it wouldn't burn in
the stove. The railwaymen did not get their coal allowance either.'
    My position weakened. I tried to speak about the general difficulties
connected with the period of socialist construction, about the fact that
the situation improves year by year. My friend was looking at me with
indignation, the veins on his hand swelling … He turned his glass upside
down, his face flushed. 'You speak of the Plan. A year ago it was for much
more coal, and now? How can I believe all those plans? Every time I tried
to believe, something bad happened to me: every time I reached out my
hand for justice, I got my fingers burned …'

The change in the intellectual climate has not yet gone far enough and the
press is still too monolithic in the Soviet Union for it to be possible to obtain
a less one-sided picture of economic conditions there; but already it is clear
that rethinking is required on the economic no less than on the democratic,
political and cultural aspects of socialism. It has been claimed that despite
the monstrous distortions in the 'superstructure' in the Soviet Union, the
immense basic economic achievements of socialism remain and are being
further developed, that this is the central fact about the Soviet Union,

against which the Stalinist excesses must be seen as a temporary distortion; and that this fact justifies the unconditional and unqualified support which foreign Communist parties have always given to the Soviet Union. This claim, however, will inevitably be subjected to the same new critical scrutiny that is now being applied to other aspects of Soviet socialism.

It seems possible in fact that the problem of the definition of socialism may come up for discussion again in a new way. It is interesting to recall that some issue of this kind received a momentary public airing in the Soviet Union before it was overshadowed by the Twentieth Congress. Molotov confessed to a theoretical error in *Bolshevik* in which he had talked of the foundations of socialism having been laid in the Soviet Union. He had apparently been convinced by the Central Committee that it was wrong to imply that the building of socialism had not been completed in the Soviet Union, and he agreed that this stage had been reached – *as early as 1936* – and that the country was now on the road to Communism.

If in the past the Morrisonian[34] type of definition of socialism – 'the assertion of social responsibility for matters properly of social concern' – has been dismissed as too ridiculously vague, abstract and unscientific, I feel that the revelations of the Twentieth Congress and the state of affairs disclosed in Eastern Europe must lead us to consider whether the classic definitions themselves are not also inadequate. In the light of the full facts of the Soviet experience, can it be said that 'From each according to his ability, to each according to his work' adequately defines what socialists are striving for? Or can this be said even of the more precise and 'scientific' definition of socialism – the common ownership of the means of production, distribution and exchange – or of such expressions as 'the ending of exploitation of man by man'. The disturbing thing is that these definitions would all seem to have been satisfied by the regimes in the Soviet Union and Eastern Europe during periods when profoundly serious anomalies existed in their social and economic life.

'From each according to his ability' tells us nothing of what methods of coercion, if any, are used in obtaining from each his work, or what methods of 'labour discipline' are employed. 'To each according to his work' tells us nothing of how differentials are fixed between skilled and unskilled workers, between bureaucrats and technicians, or of what determines the relative incomes of industrial workers and peasants. 'The common ownership of the means of production', etc, implies nothing with regard to the amount, pace or direction of industrialisation or the efficiency of economic planning. If it is argued that these difficulties are secondary and that these definitions, together with 'the ending of exploitation of man by man', are the only truly scientific ones, since they describe the real essence of socialism – the new 'relations of production' between men in society – then I would reply that it is nevertheless essential never to lose sight of what we are trying to gain by changing the 'production relations'. That these objectives can be distorted by wrong methods of changing people's relations or can be lost sight of by over-doctrinaire leaders should now be evident to all socialists.

We do not want to establish new production relations which are relations of bureaucracy, disincentive and stagnation. There are important lessons in the opinion of a Polish worker in Poznań, put to the *Daily Worker* correspondent after the riots: 'We are not interested in capitalism and not all of us are interested in socialism. What we want is a better standard of living.'

Above all, none of the classic definitions imply anything as to how the decisions on all the questions raised above are to be taken. The chief lesson of the Twentieth Congress is that the preservation and expansion of democracy in every sphere of life must be regarded as an integral part of socialism.

Yet despite the negative features in the Soviet Union and Eastern Europe there can be no doubt that impressive increases in material production have taken place. This raises a problem for socialists. Within the conditions for 'expanded reproduction of commodities' there can be a more or less fast rate of expansion of capital goods (heavy industry) relative to consumer goods. How far is it possible or desirable to force the pace of investment at the expense of consumption? How far should a socialist government force its people to postpone consumption to an indefinite future? This problem can only be discussed within its due historical context, but the problem still remains.

There are other problems that need examination. Even after the firm establishment of a people's government, at what speed and to what extent should nationalisation be carried out? Is it possible that the interests of maximum social production might make it desirable to maintain a capitalist sector, under socialist control, for a period? How can the problem of incentives and of quality production be solved in a system of centralised planning? How can a correct and sensitive response to consumer demand be ensured under socialism? It is not suggested that all these problems are new, but the effect of the Twentieth Congress and of its aftermath must be to reopen discussion on these lines, between Socialists and Communists. It is possible that these new discussions about the different ways to socialism may also give rise to new discussions on the ends.

Yours fraternally

A L

London

* * *

An Open Letter From a 'Premature Anti-Stalinist'

Dear Comrade

The opportunity of a new beginning is given to few political parties. Such an opportunity was given to the party in Britain, as to the other Communist parties of Western Europe, within the last few months.

The Twentieth Party Congress attack on Stalin and Stalinism was a belated recognition by the Soviet party leadership of the fact that their postwar policies had led the Soviet Union into a blind alley. The Talmudic legalism and subtleties of the Stalin line – exemplified by the obstinacy and stupidity of the decision on the 'Soviet wives',[35] the Berlin blockade, the 'walk-out' at the United Nations which made the Korean War possible – had contributed to bringing humanity to the brink of war. Internally, the Stalin tyranny had alienated whole sections of the community and created widespread disaffection, shown by the flight to the West of thousands of Soviet citizens, including valuable political and scientific cadres. The large numbers of political prisoners, coupled with the remorseless liquidation of all dissident opinion, made the possibility of a Thermidor not unlikely. At the same time the real revelations as well as obviously manufactured atrocities of the escapees supplied ammunition as well as justification for the external enemy, the open advocates of a Holy War against Communist dictatorship.

Although we still lack a Marxist analysis of the economic causes either of the tyranny or of the attack on the 'Stalinist' cult of personality, it is possible that the continuing crisis of Soviet agriculture and the political crises associated with arguments about the level of industrialisation forced the new–old policies of collective leadership on a frightened, and therefore receptive, leadership.

As a Marxist, it is clear to me as to you, that in this interpretation a large number of factors have been left out. You may say that this is no more than a series of 'hunches'. Perhaps, perhaps not! Someday Khrushchev or anti-Khrushchev may reveal the detailed mechanics of the construction and dismantling of a political tyranny; but the general picture is clear.

It is not a 'hunch' unfortunately, but a clear fact, that the party in Britain, as well as non-party sympathisers like myself, have been compromised, even humiliated, by the exposure of Stalinism in *our* midst. Like Stalin, the party in its day has rendered great service to the working-class movement. We can be justifiably proud of the record of defence of the Russian Revolution, of the fight against colonialism and imperialism, of the defence of the living standards of the people of Britain, year in, year out, of the struggle for peace and social justice. Your leaders, individually and collectively, have shown a power to resist corruption, both ideological and material, for which we must go back more than a century in British working-class history to find a parallel.

But we have been corrupted in other, perhaps subtler and more dangerous ways. As an active worker on the fringes of party activity I must accept a certain amount of responsibility; although my resignation was a direct consequence of refusing to stomach the Stalinist methods of leadership of the postwar period, I too have been forced into equivocal situations, for tactical reasons I too failed to protest effectively over policies of invasion of human rights and at obvious stupidities which endangered all our lives. But on the question of anti-Stalinism both at home and abroad, my conscience is clear: my activity since leaving the party was always consciously devoted to the defence of the Soviet people against the slanderous attacks of the yellow press; my defence was presented without party blinkers, presenting facts as I knew them in a positive way, admitting human imperfections, indeed emphasising them in order to assert the essential brotherhood of the Soviet peoples with the rest of erring humanity.

But your party worshipped the great man; you became a generation of irresponsible political innocents, relying on the loyalty of your members and the solidarity of the working class to cover your political nakedness when you made nonsense of all previous analyses and policies by overnight changes in the 'line'. The 'dialectic' worked in mysterious ways, the 'logic of history' gave an alibi to justify any political gymnastics. You saw every question through Stalinist blinkers and presented every situation in the same way. You became adepts at making the worse appear the better reason. Worst of all, you tampered with your own conscience so that honest human dealings with political opponents and even with your friends – indeed the very idea of 'conscience' itself – appeared to you to be 'bourgeois claptrap'. You tried to build a movement out of the working class, but in relation to the potentialities of the situation you failed. You failed because you underrated our intelligence. You lost our trust in a multitude of minor ways.

But history, or Khrushchev, has presented you with your great opportunity to break with the past, and to become wise through past mistakes. Call to mind the hundreds, nay thousands of comrades who have left the movement because of their disagreement with policies which all can now see to be wrong; trace the disagreements back to their roots, and see that these mistakes were bound up with the Stalinism which has corrupted the party, both its inner life and its relations with potential allies in the workers' movement.

So far we have not had a real collective comradely discussion and public renunciation of Stalinism in the party; so far the party has not come to terms with the past errors of the leadership and of the individual member; so far the party has not grasped the initiative in this historical stage of the workers' movement, it is waiting for events which are rapidly leaving it behind. There are a large number of party sympathisers, ex-members, who are waiting for the public disavowal of Stalinism in *our* party before applying for readmission. If you could regain the loyalties of the thousands of ex-members who left on the basis of this issue or that, but whose essential criticism was the lack of real party democracy and of political honesty, you would already have the basis for a mass party which could bring socialism to pass in Britain in our generation. We need 'a party of a new type', flexible in action, learning from and criticising our mistakes as Lenin taught us to do, a party imbued with a real democratic spirit, one that can speak for the people of Britain, one in which the policies are decided by the membership rather than by ukase followed by a phoney discussion in Stalinist blinkers. The Soviet party, by the method it has chosen to renounce its Stalinist past, has given the initiative to the British and other parties to do this in an independent way, suited to the particular needs of each national party. I suggest that the above way is the necessary, uncomfortable but positive path the party must follow in Britain if it is to win the confidence of the British people.

Yours fraternally
John McLeish

* * *

Where Do We Stand Now?

Dear Comrade

This surely must be the question of the day for all members of the Communist Party.

The Twentieth Congress and the no-longer secret report of Khrushchev has given rise to the greatest crisis of socialist thought since the birth of Marxism.

This is happening not in a time of political defeat or retreat but just when it appears that the working-class movement is about to take giant strides towards its goal of emancipation. But where are we going? What kind of civilisation are we going to build? Where do we stand now?

I hope it will be the function of *The Reasoner* to raise, and attempt to answer, fundamental questions such as these. For me it is impossible to proceed with the smallest party task, even the stamping of my card, until a beginning is made with an evaluation not just of Stalin, but of the whole concept of Marxist theory and practice.

Indeed, we must go further and deeper. We must not only examine socialist theory from the Marxist standpoint, but also the reverse – examine Marxist theory from what, according to our most fundamental moral and ethical beliefs, is a rational and defensible position.

This may involve discarding some long-cherished beliefs and accepting others once considered outside the bounds of the Marxist philosophy.

It may be that we might create, thereby, a theory and practice more acceptable to wider groups of Socialists and Communists than contemporary Marxism has proved to be, at least in our country.

We must reject charges of weakening the struggle for peace and social advance by launching this controversy, for it is only by such a searching examination of our policy that we will win the respect of working-class and middle-class groups, and create that broad unity needed for the defeat of the Tory government and the building of a People's Democracy in Britain.

Yours fraternally

K Hughes
Taunton

* * *

Needed: A Party of a New Type

Dear Comrade

That part of Togliatti's statement which I welcome and agree with is – I think – part of the sum of the strong criticism rising from the Italian rank and file. The part I quarrel with is, in my opinion, a bit of the old narrow paternal attitude.

Yes, I agree with our Italian comrades that each national Communist party should be absolutely independent. The path to socialism in each remaining country should be the one chosen by the people themselves, not by something calling itself a 'vanguard'.

Touching on this vanguard question – remember 1939. After years of anti-fascist propaganda, thought and feeling, given out by sections of the Labour Party, Co-op and trade-union movements, and especially by our party – we were instructed by our National Executive that the reverse was now the 'correct, historical, scientific, Marxist' thing to do! Terrible oafish blunder, wasn't it? Vanguard, eh?

Come the end of the war, with fascism in most of Europe defeated. The people of Europe and Britain showed a strong desire to move left. It must have been obvious in the factories, docks, camps, pubs, queues at home. It certainly was in the army in France and Belgium. But what did we, the Communist Party, advise the people at this truly historic moment? A National Government, including Churchill! We were in the van – the guard's van!

The great need is for truly national Communist parties, and Communist parties which reflect and crystallise the will of the people.

If Marxism teaches us that it is the interplay or fight between positives and negatives that makes progress in nature, in science, in the destruction and birth of economic and social systems – then surely this clash between opposite or oblique views is needed inside the Communist Party as well. What's progress for one is progress for the other.

Some sources, trying to 'explain' the causes of the cult of the individual, harp on 1934 as being the starting-point of the decline and fall of Stalin.

Myself, thinking of the rigid, militaristic organisational system known as Democratic Centralism as being the root-cause of all the filthy mess – and not the rudeness of a Joe Stalin – would suggest that, say, 1922 would more likely be the date. My theory is that Democratic Centralism started to cause a festering in the Soviet Communist Party from the day that party became fully legal and above ground.

Should general secretaries, members of central committees, and so on, serve for brief periods, say five years, only? Should a new Communist International be formed – to meet, say, twice a year, in a different country each time, rotating chair, all equal, press invited?

All silly jargon should be slung out. Why not talk of Socialism and Communism instead of 'Marxism-Leninism'? Why not just the CP, a Workers' Party, instead of 'the glorious vanguard of the indestructible irresistible proletariat'?

Plain English, common sense, the right of publication within the party, differing views, a Communist Party of a new type – that's what's needed.

R Cocker
Halifax

* * *

DOCUMENTS

I: Editorial: The Rajk Case, *Daily Worker* (New York), 2 April 1956

The execution of innocent persons is a crime anywhere and by any standards. In Hungary it was also a betrayal of the socialist revolution which swept away the hated Horthy[36] dictatorship and proclaimed a people's government.

No explanation and no mitigating circumstances can excuse the terrible miscarriage of justice uncovered with the announcement that László Rajk and his associates were executed by the Hungarian government on false and framed-up charges.

The overthrow of the Horthy regime in Hungary was a great and liberating development. It removed an ally of Hitler who had fought Americans fighting fascism.

It placed Hungarian people's divisions at our side as allies in America's war for survival. It ended the abomination of Horthy rule, whose anti-Semitism, whose savage and constant murder of labour leaders, socialists, communists, liberals, for decades had become a by-word.

At this moment reactionaries are trying to use the admissions on the Rajk case as a means for furthering the Cold War and the crusade to overthrow all socialist governments by force and violence. It is the height of hypocrisy for them to pretend anguish about Rajk, since they supported the murders of the Hungarian Horthy regime. How hollow their outcries since they sponsored and supported frame-up in our country, from the Haymarket martyrs[37] to Ethel and Julius Rosenberg,[38] from the Molly Maguires[39] to Sacco and Vanzetti,[40] from Joe Hill[41] to Willie McGee.[42]

But none of this explains, none of this excuses the adoption, by a socialist government, of the age-old capitalist method of frame-up, sending innocent persons to their death or to prison.

Frankly, this newspaper and people everywhere do not have the facts of how this miscarriage of justice came about. To blame it on just one or two individuals is unworthy. No explanation has been given, but the public is entitled to know how so-called 'confessions' in open court were rigged. Not one, not some, but all those responsible should be brought before the bar of justice.

This we do know. The frame-up of Rajk and other Hungarian Communist leaders was a result of the false charges brought against Tito in 1948 by Soviet leaders.

It is noteworthy that the Soviet leaders have undertaken a huge review of the operations of their system of justice with an aim to restoring completely the rights guaranteed to the individual by socialist law. We trust that such a review will be carried out everywhere in the socialist countries without fear or favour.

Such a review has never been carried out by capitalist governments. Who has ever heard of capitalist regimes admitting they had wronged and persecuted countless victims of the fight for social justice? All the world knows that Sacco and Vanzetti were innocent. But under capitalist rule not a thing is done to admit the wrong.

To those hypocritical supporters of reaction who taunt us, advocates of socialism, for admitting that injustices took place in socialist lands, we say: Look to the victims at home. Look at the dungeon at Alcatraz that still holds Morton Sobell,[43] whose innocence of any crime now causes even anti-communists like Bertrand Russell[44] to cry out for rectification of this injustice.

But in demanding justice at home we who have supported socialism as a system which brings real justice and freedom to all are doubly justified in condemning departures from these principles in socialist countries.

We who protest each day against the continued murder of Negroes seeking the simple right to vote have every right to demand that the investigations in Hungary and the Soviet Union shall be full and complete and shall bring to book those responsible for injustice, no matter how high their position was or is.

At the same time we derive great satisfaction from the effort of the socialist countries to drastically overhaul their procedures and bring their legal system into line with socialist principles.

Murders like those of Willie McGee, the Martinsville Seven,[45] Joe Hill and the Rosenbergs are typical products of capitalist class rule and of racism produced by such rule. But socialism is a system based on the fullest expansion of democracy. It means government of the people, by the people and for the people to an extent impossible for capitalism because socialism creates an economic democracy enabling individual rights to flourish.

Any departure from the rule and practice of justice and equality, any violations of human rights, are alien to socialism. We therefore express our most profound indignation and protest against the frame-up and murder of László Rajk and his associates.

We also take this opportunity to reaffirm a demand we made in the past – that our country and all other countries shall abolish capital punishment. We urge that our government take the initiative in the United Nations to secure a world covenant ending capital punishment.

* * *

II: A Letter from Steve Nelson,
Daily Worker (New York), 12 April 1956[46]

3 April 1956

Dear Johnny[47]

Since this is a day when most of our friends are rejoicing over the victory in my case, you would think that my letter to you would deal with that event. Actually, I'm writing you about something that I consider of even greater importance. I want to congratulate you and the paper for the departure from past practices in your editorial of 2 April, dealing with the Rajk case. This is an important historical step for our movement and for our paper, and despite momentary joys on the part of our enemies and confusion on the part of some of our supporters, this is a great historical advance.

Last Friday I tried reaching you by telephone, to urge you to write an editorial, and to speak out along the lines that you did. In reading your editorial this morning, you have literally taken the words out of my mouth on the things I wanted said.

Obviously you have drawn the same conclusion I have as a result of the current discussion, for we have been making many mistakes in the past, in our desire not to hurt those who are basically fighting for correct aims, socialism. Actually, our silence and uncritical acceptance helped the enemies of socialism.

Also, we developed the wrong concept of internationalism, which some of the discussion articles on the *Daily Worker* seemed worried about; that is, that a critical criticism of the socialist countries and some of its actions will lead to a weakening of internationalism. Those who think thus have not comprehended the full meaning of this struggle. They are still living in the past.

Criticism of wrong methods or wrong policies does not weaken one's belief in socialism but rather strengthens socialism. Therefore your editorial in sharply criticising those responsible for the ugly Rajk frame-up and in calling for an end of such capitalist methods, will strengthen internationalism.

We must explain that those remnants from the capitalist past, even if carried through by people who call themselves Communists, will not be condoned, even if momentarily the bourgeoisie will be happy with joy at such criticism.

The whole Soviet experience with the cult business cries out against silence on these matters, and condemns the notion that we ought to be quiet when obviously wrong things are being done.

One of the conclusions I have come to out of this discussion is that self-criticism was forgotten and its very essence destroyed, and centralism remained without democracy. Thus they developed the 'great man theory' and forgot the essence of socialist democracy and collective leadership, and the role of the common people.

Remember Lenin's admonition that 'every cook must learn how to operate the state'. Remember the paintings of Lenin carrying logs with other workers who donated their free labour on their off days for special projects. He did not sit behind the Kremlin walls. Likewise, recall the paintings of Lenin sitting in his office, with scores of peasants around him making complaints and criticism. This was later forgotten by false claims of security.

Constructive criticism of leaders and policies and methods in socialist lands by supporters of socialism in capitalist lands is a *must* rather than the opposite which we have followed till now.

Leaders in socialist countries must stand accountable for mistakes, not only before their own people, but before supporters of socialism everywhere. This, in my opinion, would lead to more solid internationalism on the basis of facts and knowledge and understanding, and not just blind loyalty; which is counter to Marxism.

I like your point that even within this ugly admission where a socialist country admits a serious crime as in the Rajk case, one can see something new, something which no capitalist country has ever done (admitted its own criminal mistakes). However, I agree with your editorial that this is not enough: that everything cannot be thrown on a 'Beria misled us' proposition.

I wish to conclude by congratulating you as the editor of the paper for making this very important first step in the direction of a new Marxist, realistic attitude towards weaknesses in socialist countries. My own steam has been pent up on this subject for quite a while, and your editorial sort of gave vent to it.

I'm not saying that I saw these things years ago and I see them now, but I'm sure it's the same with you and others. The important thing is that we don't allow events to pass us by now that we see the problem. Thus I urge you to continue in your bold step. This will be to the good of the Marxist movement throughout the world.

Sincerely yours

Steve Nelson

* * *

III: Statement by the Editorial Board, *Jewish Life*, American Communist Paper, June 1956[48]

The wiping out of Soviet Jewish culture, confirmed in the past few months, horrified us. The revelations also impose obligations upon us. Why did this magazine in the past eight years fail to raise questions concerning the shutting down of Jewish cultural institutions in the Soviet Union? Why did we not suspect foul play in the disappearance of leading Soviet Yiddish writers? Why did we not detect the anti-Semitism injected in the Prague trial?

Answers to these questions constitute our form of apology to our readers for having failed them in these important respects.

We feel sorrow and resentment – but these are not enough. Understanding and perspective are just as necessary …

To regard these anti-Semitic manifestations in isolation from the evil condition of which they were one expression would be a distortion. For not only were crimes committed against Jews. Other nations and nationalities also suffered from the one-man rule that afflicted the Soviet Union for some 20 years. These manifestations, so harmful to the East European countries, were profoundly anti-socialist in character, for they violated socialist principles of democracy and equality.

The leaders of the socialist countries are taking steps not only to repair whatever damage can be remedied, but also to avoid recurrence of these evils. Our anguish and anger do not blind us to the efforts made during the past three years to uncover the malignant growth on a state that is advancing the cause of peace and equality of peoples. The disclosures by the socialist countries themselves of anti-national and undemocratic practices are signs of the determination to prevent a recurrence of the evils exposed.

But why were we so insensitive to anti-Semitism as to ignore or to deny outright the reports published in the press about measures taken against Jews and Jewish culture in the Soviet Union in the five years before 1953? …

Again why did we not perceive that the campaign against 'cosmopolitanism', which was directed preponderantly against Jews, was a thinly disguised form of anti-Semitism? …

Our disbelief of charges of anti-Semitism in socialist countries was based on our belief that the basic socialist policy of equality of nations made highly improbable the brazen violations charged. Like many others we knew that the tsarist 'prison-house of nations' had been dissolved in the Soviet Union, that formerly oppressed and backward nations had in an incredibly short time developed into modern states and had achieved equality ... More specifically, it was well known that all barriers to equality for the Jewish people had been demolished in the Soviet Union. Anti-Semitism itself was outlawed. Educational and vocational opportunity was opened to all Jews. Jews played an important role in Soviet life at all levels and in all fields. Yiddish culture itself flourished. Yiddish literature, theatre, schools and press blossomed in a land where Jews had been ghettoised and oppressed for centuries.

When all this was suddenly stopped in 1948 – and this we, like everyone else, knew – it was hard for us to believe that this earlier policy had been discarded. But we had no authentic information beyond the bare fact that the institutions had been shut down. We should have suspected foul play and made a noise about it. Our confidence in the Soviet nationalities policy led us to disbelieve that charges of anti-Semitic intention had a valid basis.

There was another reason why we tended to disbelieve the press reports of anti-Semitism in the Soviet Union. They seemed to us to be, and often were, used as a means of heating up the Cold War and of intensifying the anti-communist, anti-democratic, anti-peace hysteria that flourished in our country in those bitter years ...

These reasons help to explain but not to excuse our failure to protest against the anti-Semitism revealed in some reports and activities that should have been apparent to us.

Yet the revelation of anti-Semitism and suppression of Jewish culture in the Soviet Union should not distort our understanding of the large degree of freedom gained by Jews under socialism. Jews did win the right to live where they pleased, to equal opportunity in jobs, education and religion. This freedom was gravely undermined by some anti-Semitic elements in the socialist countries and full recovery of these rights is still to be reached. For some years Jews in the Soviet Union suffered from intimidation and anti-Semitism, and Yiddish culture was all but obliterated in the Soviet Union. Yet equality of all nationalities is so basic to socialist principles that these crimes were finally admitted by the Soviet leadership itself, and correction undertaken ... In addition, information has reached us, which we have published in this magazine, that gives promise of a revival of Jewish cultural activity in the Soviet Union ...

Despite these signs of recovery and the revelations gradually being unfolded about crimes against Jews and others in the socialist countries during the period the security police were above the law, much needs to be ascertained.

With respect to the Prague trial,[49] the situation is not wholly clear. Even if the trial is valid, as Czech authorities maintain, precisely how does this case differ from those of László Rajk in Hungary and Traicho Kostov[50] in Bulgaria, both of which have been declared as frame-ups by their own governments? The same type of confessions were presented at the Prague trial, as in these cases. Further, which defendants in the Prague trial, most of whom were Jewish, were actually guilty and which innocent?

Does the reported release of the three Slánský co-defendants Artur London, Vavro Hajdů and Evžen Löbl,[51] mean that they were innocent or not? Other witnesses at this trial who were themselves tried and imprisoned, such as Edward Goldstuecker,[52] former Czech ambassador to Israel, have been released. Who was guilty and who was framed? What is the situation regarding Mordecai Oren,[53] a leader of the Israel Mapam Party, who was implicated in the Prague trial and sentenced to fifteen years, and was just released? To what extent have the charges against the Zionist movement made in the Prague trial been sustained by the recent review of the case? We believe that these questions should be answered by the Czech government.

The shocking information concerning the anti-Semitic closing down of Jewish cultural institutions in the Soviet Union and execution of leading Yiddish writers came in a statement from Poland ... Why has no word on this terrible series of events come from the Soviet Union itself? We believe that it is incumbent upon the Soviet government to make known through its own channels the full truth about the crimes against the Jewish culture and the Jewish writers. The world is entitled to know just who was affected, what exactly did happen in this series of events, who was responsible, and what punishment has been meted out to the perpetrators of these crimes. Even at this late date too much is obscure, and obscurity harms the cause of peace.

At the same time, we believe that the radical turn of events in the Soviet Union in the past three years and especially in the past few months indicate that the genuine socialist national policy will be resumed.

We expect to observe the resumption of Jewish cultural activity in the Soviet Union in accordance with the socialist principle of the rights of nationalities. We hope the government will actively encourage the Jews in re-establishing a Yiddish press and theatre and any other forms of cultural expression the Soviet Jews themselves may desire. Whatever degree of integration Soviet Jews have reached up to now, numbers of them desire cultural expression in Yiddish. This is attested by reports of crowded and enthusiastic audiences for concerts of Yiddish song and poetry held in the past months in many Soviet Russian and Ukrainian cities. So long as such an audience exists, socialist policy requires satisfaction of this desire.

The correction of the violations of the rights of Soviet Jews is further demanded in the interests of peace. For with such remedial action the socialist countries not only fulfil the socialist policies that were permitted to be violated, but they also make a contribution to peace. The removal of this justifiable grievance will greatly facilitate the unification of all the forces labouring for peaceful coexistence.

* * *

IV: Andrzej Braun, A Polish Self-Examination[54]

From *Nova Kultura*, the weekly publication of the Union of Polish Writers, 22 April 1956, translated by Alfred Dressler[55] – Editors

Together with other papers, journals, the Polish Radio and all other 'propaganda institutions' that are part of the so-called 'ideological front', we have received hundreds of readers' letters. At the present moment we are simply snowed under with such letters. This testifies to the immense agitation of public opinion aroused by the facts presented by the Twentieth Congress of the CPSU, or rather by the conclusions drawn from a consideration of these facts. For, after all, the facts only partly represent something new. The majority of our people – as is proved once again by these very letters – knew many of the individual facts. We only differed in our attitudes to these facts and some of us did not accept them as facts. A new element in the present situation is that we can now draw conclusions, connect isolated facts, perceive and understand a series of disconnected dramas, crimes, deceits, mistakes and falsehoods as one complex interconnected whole, as a system subject to an inevitable logic of its own.

This wave of activity, of discussion, this sense of involvement, is a most encouraging and cheering manifestation, quite apart from the tone, the point of view and the world outlook of the people who express their views. Even offensive invective, even hatred and contempt, by the very fact that they are addressed to editors, newspapers and writers show that the public does favour us with confidence of a sort. The more so, because they are in a way typical reflections of the feelings, doubts and needs of public opinion – of our youth, of the older generation, of our 'active' as well as of the average honest man-in-the-street.

In this issue we publish – with certain cuts – three of the most characteristic letters of this type, written by different people and different in tone, ranging from despair and bitterness to sarcasm and optimism.

As these letters were addressed to me, I shall try to answer them. I confess that this is a most difficult task. Most of these letters (one might say) are written in blood. To reply in ink is insufficient. They usually conclude with an avalanche of questions. Publication of these questions would require the expression of an attitude towards them, would demand replies to them. To many of these questions we – that means myself also – are not in a position yet to give an answer. In the first place this refers to questions about a number of facts concerned with the last war, with the past. Up to now misleading answers are being given to these questions, answers that explain nothing, that contradict the facts as we ourselves remember them, that contradict the truth and our own experience. As long as these problems are not honestly re-examined and clarified, we feel incompetent to answer them and therefore it is not worth raising them at the present time …

Yet we have the right to demand revision of the interpretation of whole periods of our history, particularly of the history of the last war. But more about this later. We can and must now pose a whole series of questions concerning the last ten years, that is, about the conduct of government and the realisation of the revolution in People's Poland. And first of all we must consider the evil that has existed and that still exists even today, lay bare the reasons for it, draw conclusions, seek out and demand changes which would guarantee that none of the old crimes could be repeated, honestly and openly expose the criminals and demand their punishment.

Comrade Michael Bruk![56] You are right to protest against a situation in which a man has to change his view every few years, has to tear from his heart, trample and spit on what was most precious to him. You are right that unjustly we blame you for cynicism and lack of principles and ideals while we ourselves 'remember with tears in our eyes the years of our idealistic youth'. You are ashamed for us and for your own credulity, you cannot 'stand in the ranks with your head held high', because there is no reason why you should trust us.

I shall be as sincere in my reply as you were in your letter. I understand your exasperation. I myself have felt the same about certain matters, and about others I feel it now. You have had too much faith. The theses of your faith had been worked out for you 'scientifically'. It is obvious that this 'scientific' didacticism is pernicious for young people: it only helped to confirm you in your faith whenever you came up against real problems. You did not try enough to understand, to test your faith against the truth of reality or even the experience of your young life. I am one of your Lechs[57] – maybe by a few years older – who survived. I was also taught that the cause for which I was prepared to lay down my life was unjust. But I didn't fully believe it. Nothing can convince me that a war of liberation is a crime or counter-revolution. 'Theories' put forward could only torture but could not clarify the matter. And that these theories were unconvincing was proved not only by one's own memory of the actual circumstances but also by the fact that these theories were soon turned into 'bad marks' in testimonials and biographies, into instruments of abuse, blackmail and violence.

I only mention this as an example. All theories must first of all be confronted with life, with reality, with actually existing relationships to which they are intended to be applied or which they are to explain. It seems to me that this disregard for life, for concrete reality, lies at the root of most of our mistakes and abuses.

This danger existed from the very moment of the establishment of people's power in Poland. When we undertook the revolution in our country we paid too little attention to the concrete, existing situation, the real, and not imaginary, relationships and structure of our society. We ignored the fact that this is the only country in which before the war the Communist Party had been dissolved by the Comintern, and that consequently we had been deprived of our own, our best revolutionary traditions; that this is a country that for six years had been engaged in an heroic war with the occupationists; that this country has genuine anti-fascist forces, resistance fighters, uniting the best of our young people, all that was best in our nation; that these forces in one way or another carry on our typical national traditions of independence, romantic traditions maybe, some better, some worse, yet immensely popular traditions; that this is a predominantly Catholic country; that then it was still in the main a backward, peasant country.

But it was not such considerations as these that determined certain moves of the newly-established people's power. As a model was taken a pattern of revolution, a pattern of a system of people's democracy and of the dictatorship of the proletariat defined in too theoretical and too dogmatic terms and, moreover, measured exclusively by the standards of practical application in the Soviet Union. Disregard for certain features of concrete reality, adherence to narrowly theoretical principles (often wrong principles as, for instance, the theory about the growing class struggle during the period of the construction of socialism) caused certain mistakes which in time – to the extent to which the results of these mistakes became evident – began to create a chasm between the theoretical postulates and theses on the one hand, and reality on the other, between truth and propaganda, between the apparatus of power, its ideologues and the public, between words and deeds. Oversimplified interpretation of the class structure of the anti-fascist forces, of forces of resistance in Poland during the occupation was accepted; hostility was aroused; honest, patriotic young people, members of the underground armies were arrested; but at the same time support was found in servile (because guilty) executives devoid of any moral standing.

The dogmatic approach to the religious problem (in spite of the existing agreements between church and state, which laid the foundation for a growing secularisation of our society and in particular of our youth) ignores the vitality of the moral and traditional attraction of Catholicism in our country, led to duplicity, hypocrisy and artificial conflicts. Whenever the new, theoretical patterns of morality were discredited in practice, traditional morals or religious ethics experienced a revival.

The false, abstract assumption that, with progress in the building of socialism, the class struggle would sharpen, led to the expansion and autonomy of the security apparatus which soon – in the absence of real enemies in sufficient numbers – needed to fabricate fictitious enemies. This demoralised the apparatus, caused its degeneration, because in the end it no longer knew which cause it was serving. Falsehood and deceit required concealment, secrecy and removal from public control. The removal of whole spheres of state activity from the control of the party and the nation, the profusion in the levels and degrees of 'initiation' favoured again the growth of abuse and falsehood.

The homage paid to certain dogmatic views and concepts of the revolution – which today go by the name of Stalinism – deepened this crisis of confidence, this chasm between words and deeds, this indifference for the real needs of the broad masses of the people who lived in poverty for the sake of an ever more remote vision of the future; it injured, deformed and made fools of our young people who increasingly relied on their faith only, without understanding, without testing their convictions and assumptions by the realities and practice of life; it confirmed the irritation of adult people who were immersed up to their ears in day-to-day reality.

The separation of the practice of government from the concrete needs of the nation, its adaptation to false concepts of the revolution, produced the formula that 'if reality does not fit into theory – the worse for reality', that 'the end justifies the means'; it became the source of violations of the law, of the throttling of liberty and criticism. This bred more deceit, more falsehood and more abuse, and produced widespread cynicism; nothing any longer was what it should have been. The Constitution was violated, confessions and verdicts were falsified, government institutions and courts at all levels of jurisdiction were turned into fictitious mechanisms for the repetition and confirmation of 'suggestions' made at the top. Even the life of the party changed, little by little, into a system of circles of the initiated peculiar to Freemasonry: the principles of inner-party democracy, of criticism, of eligibility became practically unrealisable and were subordinated to a lifeless unanimity. Principles and ideals have become a fiction, what has remained is merely the external trappings and mechanisms.

The generalised notion of the 'cult of the individual' is not very helpful in such a situation. It is more important to find out which elements of this cult existed in our own thinking, in our institutions, in the mechanism and the routine of our life, and which still exist today. We must be clear about this in order to change it and to prevent the return of the past and to do away with present evils.

The bitterness and irony of our second reader who writes about his 'servility' is understandable. But his hopelessness is incorrect. Communist idealists existed not only in works of fiction. If they 'committed evil precisely because they are idealists and felt they had to submit to majority decisions', that does not alter the fact that they were mistaken. The point is that they should not have submitted to formal decisions of formal majorities but to the genuine needs of the genuine majority of their nation. They should have been with the nation, shared and experienced the people's conditions of life. They should not have elevated themselves above the nation. They should not have hidden from the nation what it was the right of the nation to know.

Dear readers! The fact that you put these matters so sharply, that you so deeply experience the crises and tragedies of our life, testifies to your sincerity and courage, to your sense of dignity as citizens of People's Poland. It seems to me that, for the first time in years, the concept of the national front in Poland is growing into something real and ceases to be just a nebulous phrase. For the first time we see the overwhelming majority of our nation uniting in face of these very problems, in face of matters that concern their life, their destiny, their country, their history, past and present, their rights and their personal dignity. The demand for truth and honesty, for legality and democracy is growing. But this national front ought to be guided by the party. Confidence must be restored in the people's government, in the party, in the administrative apparatus, the law, the truth we proclaim. This truth must be purged of the excrescences of falsehood. We must return to an honest interpretation of our history; we must speak openly and frankly about the truth of our present position; we must repair injustice, punish the guilty, restore confidence in justice.

What, then, are the most important things we must do today in order not to waste this great experience, this chance given to us by the unity of our nation, in order to rectify the mistakes of the past, to re-establish full confidence, to defeat deceit (even if it was practised from the noblest motives)?

First of all, full publicity is necessary. We must speak publicly and frankly about all matters that concern the whole nation. We must reply to questions and requests. We must submit to the control and judgement of our nation and recognise this judgement as the most important factor for us. We must either liquidate those institutions that are only trappings and that long ago ceased to serve their original purpose, that only functioned to mislead the public, or we must return to them their proper administrative functions. We must revise as far as possible our history, reject fanciful concepts and return to hard facts, destroy all sources of blackmail and deceit. We must abolish – by exposing them to the public – anti-democratic privileges and inequalities, the sources of injustice and abuse. We must publish and discuss freely statistical data about material conditions and the standards of life of the broad mass of the people; pay more attention to how the people really live and what they really feel and less to speculations as to what things will or will not be like under Communism. We must transform the press and the propaganda apparatus into representative democratic institutions and restore them to their proper function as forums for public opinion, for frank and public discussions, for frank and public criticism.

We must put an end to the state of affairs when official propaganda, official measures, publications, theses always trail a long way behind public opinion and often clash with it. We must allow literature and art to return to the sacred sources of their inspiration, the thoughts and emotions of the people, the destiny and the sorrows of the nation. The arts must breathe the free air of the people's true life; we must release them from the straitjacket of static, didactic formulæ, of abstract, theoretical models.

We must stop treating the people like a bunch of foolish, blind and gullible children who have to be guided by the possessors of higher knowledge, of higher reason, allegedly for their own good.

Only in this way can mutual trust be restored, can the nation be united around the party which will become the true guiding force of the national front. Only thus, it seems to me, can the results of the Twentieth Congress of the CPSU lead to the liquidation of the sources and manifestations of the evil that existed and still exists in our country, the evil which we call the 'cult of the individual'. *There can be no return to the old methods and the old attitudes.* If we do not take advantage of this great chance to rehabilitate our principles, the present crisis of confidence will deepen immeasurably. We shall waste again the idealism of great sections of our society. And the results would be catastrophic.

I do not know how far my readers will be satisfied with what I have been able to say at the present time. I don't know whether I am right. But if I am not, further discussion will help to clarify these matters. But in the first place let us all say frankly and sincerely what we think. And then let us demand facts.

* * *

Culture-As-a-Weapon & Heritage Corner

Conscious of impotence, they soon grow drunk
With gazing, when they see an able man
Step forth to notice; and, besotted thus,
Build him a pedestal, and say, 'Stand there,
And be our admiration and our praise.'
They roll themselves before him in the dust,
Then most deserving in their own account,
When most extravagant in his applause,
As if, exalting him, they raised themselves.
Thus by degrees, self-cheated of their sound
And sober judgement, that he is but man,
They demi-deify and fume him so,
That in due season he forgets it too.
Inflated and astrut with self-conceit,
He gulps the windy diets; and ere long,
Adopting their mistake, profoundly thinks
The world was made in vain, if not for him.
Thenceforth they are his cattle: drudges, born
To bear his burdens, drawing in his gears,
And sweating in his service, his caprice
Becomes the soul that animates them all.

William Cowper, *The Task*, Book V[58]

* * *

Smugglers' Cove: 'New collective is but old cult writ large.' – J Milton[59]

* * *

Note To Our Readers

The next number of *The Reasoner* will be published in mid-September. Please send your subscription with the enclosed form. This number has raised many general problems. The next will pass on to more detailed and constructive analysis and we hope will include articles on 'Why We Need a Communist Party' (by Jim Roche); on aspects of British CP history; and on Marxism and Humanism. All letters, documents and proposals for articles should be sent to J Saville, 152 Westbourne Avenue, Hull.

* * *

Published by J Saville, 152 Westbourne Avenue, Hull.

NOTES

1   Alexander Alexandrovich Fadeyev (1901–1956) joined the Bolsheviks in 1918, and fought in the Red Army during the Civil War. He wrote several novels, the most famous being *The Young Guard* about Soviet resistance during the Second World War. He was Chairman of the Soviet Union of Writers during 1946–54. He was a staunch supporter of Stalinist cultural policies. He shot himself in protest against the policy of de-Stalinisation.
2   László Rajk (1909–1949) joined the Hungarian Communist Party in the 1930s and fought in the Spanish Civil War. He became Minister of the Interior in the postwar Hungarian government in 1946, and Foreign Minister in 1948. He was arrested, falsely accused of treason, and executed after a show trial. He was rehabilitated in March 1956.
3   See Documents III and V.
4   Several of Togliatti's statements on Khrushchev's 'Secret Speech' are contained in *The Anti-Stalin Campaign and International Communism* (Columbia University Press, New York, 1956).
5   Henry Mayers Hyndman (1842–1921) was a journalist who became a socialist after reading Marx's writings. He formed the Democratic Federation (later Social Democratic Federation) in 1881, and was a foundation member of the British Socialist Party in 1911. He was a strong supporter of Britain's involvement in the First World War, which led to his departure from the BSP to form the National Socialist Party in 1916, a small group whose members largely drifted into the Labour Party after his death.
6   CPGB, *For a Soviet Britain* (CPGB, London, 1935).
7   *History of the CPSU(b): Short Course* (Collets, London, 1938).
8   Kenneth John Wilson Alexander (1922–2001) was at the time of this article an economics lecturer at Sheffield University. He later lectured at Dundee University and became Professor of Economics at the University of Strathclyde. He also served on the board of both Fairfields and Upper Clyde Shipbuilders, and was appointed Chairman of Govan Shipbuilders. After a stint from 1976 as Chairman of the Highlands and Islands Development Board (and receiving a knighthood in 1978), in 1982 he became the Vice-Chancellor of the University of Stirling, and in 1986 the Chancellor of Aberdeen University. He wrote or co-wrote several books on the topics of trade unions and industrial relations, wages policy, economic policy, industrial management, regional development, and adult education.
9   Reuben Falber, 'Democratic Centralism', *Communist Review*, January 1951.
10 V I Lenin, 'One Step Forward, Two Steps Back: The Crisis in Our Party', *Collected Works*, Volume 7 (Progress, Moscow, 1964).
11 J V Stalin, 'The Foundations of Leninism', *Works*, Volume 6 (FLPH, Moscow, 1953).
12 Liu Shao-Chi (Liu Shaoqi), *On The Party* (FLPH, Peking, 1950).
13 J V Stalin, 'The Foundations of Leninism', *Works*, Volume 6 (FLPH, Moscow, 1953), p. 180.
14 V I Lenin, 'Terms of Admission into Communist International', *Collected Works*, Volume 31 (Progress, Moscow, 1965), p. 210.
15 Rosa Luxemburg, 'Leninism Or Marxism', in *The Russian Revolution and Leninism Or Marxism* (University of Michigan Press, Ann Arbor, 1961), p. 94; the original title of

this article is 'Organisational Questions of the Russian Social Democracy'.

16   Thomas Bell, *Pioneering Days* (Lawrence and Wishart, London, 1941), p. 194. Thomas Bell (1882–1944) was born in Glasgow; he joined the Independent Labour Party in 1900, moved to the Social Democratic Federation, and, with several others expelled from the SDF in 1903, formed the Socialist Labour Party. He was a leading militant in Glasgow during the First World War. He was a foundation member of the CPGB, its first National Organiser, and a Central Committee member during 1920–29. He stayed with the party until his death.

17   Republished by the Prometheus Research Library, *Guidelines on the Organizational Structure of Communist Parties, on the Methods and Content of Their Work* (Prometheus Research Library, New York, 1988).

18   Harry Inkpin was the brother of Albert Inkpin, the CPGB's first Secretary; he had been a member of the BSP, and was Chairman of the CPGB's Control Commission during the 1920s.

19   See L J Macfarlane, *The British Communist Party: Its Origin and Development Until 1929* (MacGibbon and Kee, London, 1966), p. 78.

20   Harry Pollitt, *Serving My Time: An Apprenticeship to Politics* (Lawrence and Wishart, London, 1940), p. 155.

21   See *The Programme of the Communist International* (CPGB, London, 1932), p. 65.

22   See Palmiro Togliatti, '9 Domande sullo Stalinismo', *Nuovi Argomenti*, no 20, 16 June 1956, in *The Anti-Stalin Campaign and International Communism*, p. 136.

23   Rosa Luxemburg, 'The Russian Revolution', in *The Russian Revolution and Leninism Or Marxism*, pp. 71–72.

24   See Pietro Nenni, 'Le giunte e il resto', *Avanti!*, 17 June 1956, in *The Anti-Stalin Campaign and International Communism*, p. 145. Pietro Sandro Nenni (1891–1980) joined the Italian Socialist Party in 1921; he was in exile from 1926 until 1943, during which time he became party Secretary. He led the PSI after his return to Italy, and held various government posts until 1947, and working closely with the PCI until the events of 1956 led to his estrangement from it.

25   See Palmiro Togliatti, '9 Domande sullo Stalinismo', *Nuovi Argomenti*, no 20, 16 June 1956, in *The Anti-Stalin Campaign and International Communism*, p. 122.

26   See 'Resolution of the Central Committee of the CPSU', *Pravda*, 2 July 1956, in *The Anti-Stalin Campaign and International Communism*, pp. 286–87.

27   V I Lenin, 'One Step Forward, Two Steps Back: The Crisis in Our Party', *Collected Works*, Volume 7 (Progress, Moscow, 1964), p. 365

28   Friedrich Engels to Carl Schmidt, 5 August 1890.

29   John Bunyan (1628–1688) was a Baptist priest and author of many works, most notably *The Pilgrim's Progress*; he joined the Parliamentary army during the English Civil War, and was jailed for 12 years under the restored monarchy for illegal nonconformist preaching.

30   Charles Robert Darwin (1809–1882) was the pioneer of scientific evolutionary biology.

31   Charles Bradlaugh (1833–1891) was a pioneering British secularist and Liberal MP; he founded the National Secular Society in 1866.

32   J V Stalin, 'Economic Problems of Socialism in the USSR', *Works*, Volume 16 (Red Star Press, London, 1986), p. 333.

33   Károly Jobbágy (1921–1998) was an Hungarian poet. He was drafted into the Hungarian army in 1943, captured in 1945 and imprisoned in the Soviet Union until 1948; his poems started to be published after Stalin's death. He supported the Hungarian uprising in 1956; he subsequently worked as a Russian-language teacher and librarian.

34   After Herbert Stanley Morrison (1888–1965), a Labour MP during 1923–24, 1929–31 and 1935–59, and Deputy Prime Minister during 1945–51. He also headed the London

County Council in the early 1930s. He was an advocate of municipal corporations and nationalisation of industry.

35   A small number of British servicemen married Soviet women whilst they were in the Soviet Union during the Second World War; about half of the women were allowed to leave for Britain, but the remainder were forbidden to do so. A press campaign calling for the release of the 'Soviet Wives' caused some embarrassment to the CPGB.

36   Miklós Horthy de Nagybánya (1868–1957) was a career naval officer in the Austro-Hungarian Navy; a conservative nationalist, he was head of state of Hungary throughout the interwar period, implemented repressive policies, and forged an alliance with Nazi Germany. He was deposed in late 1944 after he declared Hungary's surrender and withdrawal from the Axis bloc.

37   The Haymarket Martyrs were four anarchists who were executed in November 1887 for their alleged role in a bomb attack on the police at a labour demonstration in Haymarket Square in Chicago on 4 May 1886.

38   Julius Rosenberg (1918–1953) and Ethel Rosenberg (neé Greenglass, 1915–1953) both joined the US Young Communist League in the 1930s; they were convicted in March 1951 of conspiracy to engage in espionage on behalf of the Soviet Union and were executed in June 1953.

39   The Molly Maguires were self-defence teams set up in the 1870s by Irish miners in the Pennsylvania coalfields who were facing appalling working conditions.

40   Nicola Sacco (1891–1927) and Bartolomeo Vanzetti (1888–1927) were Italian-born US anarchists; they were found guilty in 1921 of murdering a guard and a paymaster during an armed robbery in 1920; successive appeals proved unsuccessful and they were executed in 1927.

41   Joe Hill (Joel Emmanuel Hägglund, 1879–1915) was an activist in the Industrial Workers of the World; he was executed after being found guilty of the murder of a shopkeeper and his son despite there being no evidence of his being involved in their deaths.

42   Willie McGee (–1951) was a black American found guilty of the rape of a white woman in 1945; he protested his innocence, protests led to two retrials, both of which returned the same verdict, the juries in all the trials being all-white.

43   Morton Sobell (1917–) fled to Mexico after being accused of espionage for the Soviet Union. He was kidnapped and returned to the USA, where he served 17 years of a 30-year sentence. He later admitted that he had been involved in espionage.

44   Bertrand Arthur William Russell (1872–1970) was a British positivist philosopher, author and political activist; his latter-day activities were mainly concerned with civil liberties and anti-war campaigning.

45   The Martinsville Seven were seven black men from Martinsville, Virginia, who were all found guilty of the rape of a white woman in 1949, and executed in 1951; there was a campaign by civil liberties groups to ensure that they were given a proper trial on the basis that black defendants rarely received one.

46   Steve Nelson (Stjepan Mesaroš, 1903–1993) was born in Croatia and moved with his family to the USA after the First World War. He joined the Young Workers League, the youth section of the CPUSA, in 1923. He worked in industry and was a trade-union activist, and became a full-time worker for the CPUSA. He was a political commissar in the Abraham Lincoln Brigade during the Spanish Civil War, and joined the top leadership of the CPUSA during the 1940s. He was arrested in Pittsburgh in August 1950 and sentenced to 20 years in prison under the Pennsylvania Sedition Act. Released after seven months, he was sentenced in 1953 with five other party members to five years under the Federal Smith Act. This was successfully challenged in 1956. He left the CPUSA in 1957 in the aftermath of the Khrushchev revelations, returning to manual employment, and remaining active in radical politics. In 1963 he became the National Commander of the Veterans of the Abraham Lincoln Brigade, serving in that post for

the next 40 years.

47   John Gates (Solomon Regenstreif, 1913–1992) was born in New York into a Polish-Jewish family. He was a political commissar in the Lincoln-Washington Battalion during the Spanish Civil War, and became head of the Young Communist League on his return. He was sentenced in 1949 with 12 other party members to five years under the Federal Smith Act, and was released in 1955. He was appointed Editor of the *Daily Worker* upon his release. The paper under his editorship championed the Khrushchev revelations and opposed the Soviet suppression of the Hungarian uprising. He left the party in January 1958, and subsequently worked as a senior research assistant for the International Ladies Garment Workers Union.

48   *Jewish Life* subsequently severed its connection with the CPUSA, and has since appeared under the name *Jewish Currents*. A more complete version of this article appears in Tony Michels (ed), *Jewish Radicals: A Documentary Reader* (New York University Press, New York, 2012). When this article was published in an abbreviated form in *The Reasoner*, several words were accidentally omitted from the paragraph starting 'With respect to the Prague trial', thus garbling the text; these have been restored.

49   Fourteen senior members of the Czechoslovakian Communist Party, including the General Secretary Rudolf Slánský, were put on trial in November 1952, accused of being involved in a Titoite–Trotskyite–Zionist conspiracy. Eleven defendants were immediately hanged, and three were given life sentences. The show trial had decided anti-Semitic overtones: 11 of the 14 defendants were Jewish. Rudolf Slánský (1901–1952) joined the KSČ upon its foundation in 1921, joined its Politbureau in 1929, and became General Secretary in 1946.

50   Traicho Kostov (1897–1949) was General Secretary of the Bulgarian Communist Party and President of Bulgaria; he was removed from his posts and denounced as an anti-Soviet nationalist, and later put on trial with 10 other defendants on a number of trumped-up charges. He repudiated his confession, the trial was staged without his being present, and he was executed, the others being jailed. The verdicts were overturned in 1956, and all the defendants were rehabilitated.

51   Vavro Hajdů (1913–1978), Artur London (1915–1986) and Evžen Löbl (1907–1987) were all prominent members of the KSČ and senior government officials. They were all arrested in 1951 and sentenced to life at the Slánský show trial in 1952. They were all released in 1955 and rehabilitated in 1963.

52   Eduard Goldstücker (1913–2000) joined the KSČ in the 1930s, and was the Czechoslovakian ambassador to Israel when he was recalled, tried and given a life sentence. He was released after the death of Stalin, took part in the Prague Spring, and went into exile in its aftermath.

53   Mordecai Oren (1905–1985) was born in Galicia and joined Hashomer Hatzair; he emigrated to Palestine in 1929, was a founder member of Mapam in 1948, and was in its pro-Soviet wing. He was arrested in 1951 whilst travelling through Czechoslovakia, charged with crimes against state security, and sentenced to 15 years. He was released after the death of Stalin, and cleared of all charges.

54   Andrzej Braun (1923–2008) was a Polish novelist and journalist. He was a partisan with the Home Army during the Second World War, joined the Polish Communist Party in 1947, worked in its Central Committee's cultural department from 1949, and subsequently was on the editorial board of *Nova Kultura* and worked in academia, film and television.

55   Alfred Dressler (1916–1964) was born in Chemnitz, Germany, was educated in Germany, Poland and Czechoslovakia, and arrived in Britain as a refugee in the late 1930s; he was fluent in several languages and taught in the Department of Russian at the University of Leeds from 1948; he was subsequently a member of the Editorial Board of the *New Reasoner* and the *New Left Review*.

56 The author of the letter – Translator's note.

57 Lech is the name of Bruk's brother who was killed fighting the Germans as a member of the non-Communist Polish Underground Army – Translator's note.

58 William Cowper (1731–1800) was a pioneer English romantic poet. *The Task* was his most famous work; published in 1785, it variously attacked slavery, blood sports, fashionable frivolity, unenthusiastic clergy and despotism in France.

59 A parody of a line from John Milton's *On the New Forcers of Conscience Under the Long Parliament*: 'New Presbyter is but old Priest writ large.'

THE REASONER

A JOURNAL OF DISCUSSION

Edited by
JOHN SAVILLE and E. P. THOMPSON

" To leave error unrefuted is to encourage intellectual immorality " _ Marx

Second Number   Price 2/-   September 1956

MAIN CONTENTS

THE CASE FOR SOCIALISM

WE PUBLISHED our first number in mid-July. It sold out in three weeks. We have now received close on three hundred letters from readers, the great majority welcoming the journal. All voice disquiet, self-questioning, the need for fresh Marxist analysis, for Socialist discussion with a new temper and direction. All have helped us, and we thank those who have written.

But the letters also raise a question. In our first number we emphasised that this is a discussion journal, written, in the main, by Communists and addressed in the first place to Communists. Why have so many readers written to us, but without thought of publication? Why have so few sought to address other readers, to take up and carry forward the discussion?

     x x x x x

We think there are two main reasons. First, the discussion is still in a primitive, a negative and partially destructive, stage. Cherished illusions have been shed. But they have not yet been replaced by new and positive affirmations. Problems are seen more clearly; but practical solutions have yet to be presented. And the first number of The Reasoner reflected this negative phase of the discussion.

     x x x x x

TOGETHER.

The Reasoner: A Journal of Discussion
Edited by John Saville and E P Thompson

To leave error unrefuted is to encourage intellectual immorality. – Marx

Second Number

September 1956

Statement

This number of *The Reasoner* was already printed when we received the resolution of the EC of the Communist Party (9 September) calling on us to cease publication.

We wish to make it clear that we have at all times been willing to find a solution to the problem of our unofficial publication, provided that this gave effective guarantees that means will be found whereby minority views in the Communist Party can be fully posed, developed and sustained: and whereby full and frank discussion, of the type to be found in this number of *The Reasoner*, can continue. In our view the present facilities in the official press are quite inadequate to meet this crisis in Communist theory; and the editorial control is not such as to give confidence that minority rights can be safeguarded.

Up to this time the leadership of the party has refused to enter into any discussion with us on the various proposals which we have made, nor have they offered any compromise on their behalf. We are confident that if the leadership will suggest means by which full and frank discussion can continue, and minority rights be safeguarded, a solution can be found which will end the present danger of dissension. We, on our behalf, are – and always have been – willing to give way to an official discussion journal (with certain obvious safeguards), and would be glad to discuss turning *The Reasoner* outwards, to fight the intellectual battles for socialism among the people in the manner of the old *Left Review*,[1] with a broader and more representative editorial board.

After studying the statement of the EC which is to appear in *World News* we will be willing to submit further information, and answers to specific questions, to any branch or committee of the Communist Party.

Finally, we wish to make clear two points. 1) None of the contributors to this number are in any way committed to the above statement. 2) We state categorically that we were not responsible – directly or indirectly – for releasing information disclosed in a *Tribune* report of last week.[2]

E P T and **J S**
11 September

The Case For Socialism

We published our first number in mid-July. It sold out in three weeks. We have now received close on three hundred letters from readers, the great majority welcoming the journal. All voice disquiet, self-questioning, the need for fresh Marxist analysis, for socialist discussion with a new temper and direction. All have helped us, and we thank those who have written.

But the letters also raise a question. In our first number we emphasised that this is a *discussion* journal, written, in the main, by Communists and addressed in the first place to Communists. Why have so many readers written to us, but without thought of publication? Why have so few sought to address other readers, *to take up and carry forward the discussion?*

* * *

We think there are two main reasons. First, the discussion is still in a primitive, a negative and partially destructive, stage. Cherished illusions have been shed. But they have not yet been replaced by new and positive affirmations. Problems are seen more clearly: but practical solutions have yet to be presented. And the first number of *The Reasoner* reflected this negative phase of the discussion.

* * *

In the second place, *The Reasoner* has almost been drowned in infancy by the waters of argument about discussion itself: what is the *place* for discussion, *how* do ideas grow and develop, how can theoretical controversies (which can never be decided, initially, by majority decisions) take place within the structure of a party of action where, rightly, the discipline of majority decisions must prevail?

The contributions in this number from Ronald Meek,[3] Doris Lessing[4] and Professor Hyman Levy[5] show the very wide implications of this controversy: indeed, the discussions around the rights of minorities, and this unofficial publication, have revealed a central place of conflict between the needs of united, disciplined action on the one hand: and the claims of honest and unrestricted discussion and enquiry on the other.

In this controversy, we have been guided by one main consideration: *the discussion must continue*. And it must be more frank and searching than any at present being conducted in official Communist journals. For example, the Communist Party cannot effectively pursue its aim of unity if Communists are unwilling to enter an honest and self-critical discussion of the serious criticisms of Communist method and theory put forward by socialists who hold the general position of Professor G D H Cole. The discussion must take place across the barriers of party loyalties: for this reason, we publish among the documents in this number certain views of two non-Communists, Paul Sweezy[6] and Leo Huberman,[7] interpretive of the Soviet Union, which pose questions which Communists must consider and discuss. Further, we publish a letter from Lawrence Daly,[8] until recently a member of the Scottish District Committee of the Communist Party, who has recently resigned his membership of the party. We regret his decision. But is it possible to consider realistically the problems of recruiting, the need for a party of 50,000, questions of unity, etc, if we are unwilling to receive and reply to the arguments of responsible Communists who have left the party on political grounds?

The discussion must continue: it must be honest; it must cross party barriers. *How* the discussion shall be conducted: the personal position of the editors: the continued existence of *The Reasoner* as an unofficial publication – all these are secondary questions.

* * *

It may be that discussion of the right way to discuss must be carried to some conclusion before the discussion itself can begin in earnest.

But let us be clear *what this discussion is about*. There are some Communists who are so concerned with urgent day-to-day struggles that they mistake the discussion for a distraction of energies. They are prepared to admit full discussion on certain immediate tasks and problems: and, within defined limits, discussion on certain questions of organisation and verbal alterations of programme. Discussion which does not have an immediate bearing on these tasks and questions they regard with impatience.

We do not agree with the view, implied by a correspondent in our first number, that individuals must cease political activity while fundamental review of theory and policy takes place. The shock of the 'revelations' had this initial effect upon many of us: but this phase is now surely passing?

Events such as the BMC[9] strike and the Suez crisis underline the fact that activity and discussion must go together and strengthen each other.

* * *

But this is no argument for any *limitation* of the discussion. Even questions of the most general theory, such as the nature of dogmatism, have the most direct bearing upon our political work: first, because they concern the very processes by which we interpret reality, decide policy, and conduct discussion: second, because they have important bearings upon the political relations of Communists with the labour movement.

Questions of general attitude, good faith, political honesty and party history, *even when they have no obvious bearing on the immediate political line,* can be of the first importance in our political, as well as personal, relations with people. When Engels condemned the early SDF[10] it was not because of major disagreements with its political line, but as a result of the abstract, didactic opportunism revealed in its approach to the working class: 'People who pass as orthodox Marxists have turned our ideas of movement into a fixed dogma to be learnt by heart … and appear as pure sects.'[11] And William Morris elevated the same question of attitude to a similar level of political importance:

> I sometimes have a vision of a real Socialist Party at once united and free … but the SDF stands in the way. Although the individual members are good fellows enough … the society has got a sort of pedantic tone of arrogance and lack of generosity, which is disgusting and does disgust both Socialists and non-Socialists.[12]

The Communist Party does not share the faults of the early SDF, nor does it express its sectarianism in the same way or to the same degree: certain aspects of sectarianism are the inevitable result of isolation during the Cold War, and will be shed not through discussion but through breaking this isolation, through activity among the people: but discussion will hasten this process and is necessary to it.

* * *

This is not the heart of the question. The discussion, surely, is first and foremost about *socialism*. Second, it is about the political honesty, independence and effectiveness of the Communist Party as a party capable of leading the British people to socialism.

British Communists have taken note of Engels' warnings against purism and abstract propagandist sects: have studied *Left-Wing Communism*, and have learnt from Lenin that Communists must carry on activities '*right in the heart* of the proletarian masses', participating in every struggle for living standards, peace and social advance.

But in place of the clear analysis of imperialism, the agitational explanation of the socialist alternative, which Engels and Lenin, Morris and Tom Mann, knew must be carried on alongside and in the heart of every struggle, we have increasingly substituted, for the first, an over-simplified myth of the 'two camps', and for the second, utopian propaganda about the Soviet Union as the land of socialism-realised.

Communists have won industrial strength through the courage, militancy and intelligence of their members in day-to-day struggles: but the Communist Party has failed to emerge as a political influence corresponding to the energy and quality of its membership – despite repeated betrayals both of working-class interests and of socialist principles by reformist Labour leaders – precisely because the British people did not believe or trust this central political message.

* * *

Into this situation there comes the speech of Khrushchev, setting out in all its grotesque barbarity the political distortions and violations of human rights which have taken place – and which we have for so long denied – in the country which, to a great degree, we have substituted in our propaganda for the explanation of socialism in general and in British terms.

For months Communists have been seeking to disentangle many confused issues in their minds: those aspects of Soviet history which can be seen as predetermined by conditions at the time of the Revolution, or made inevitable by the problems of holding power in the face of internal and external threat: those arising from the general problems of building socialism in any country: those deriving from specific Russian traditions and culture: those aspects of degeneracy which arose in specific conditions of acute conflict and threat, but which outlived those conditions in certain ideological, moral and institutional forms: those deriving from the particular qualities and failings of individual leaders: those organisational or theoretical manifestations of the 'Stalin era' which have in their turn been reflected in the theory and practice of other Communist parties. We have now reached a point where all agree that far more detailed knowledge, more detailed analysis, is necessary. But in all this there has run a common thread: the problem of disentangling the understanding of the essential character of socialist society from the specific and concrete historical problems of the Soviet Union – of achieving an understanding of socialism both enriched and chastened by the experience of the Soviet people – and of returning with fresh eyes to our own people, our own problems, our own traditions.

To suggest that we have now 'had' the discussion, that this or that statement 'answers' these problems, that we can forget these unpleasant matters and return to our old tasks in the old way, is to retreat from socialist theory itself.

No Communist party, no party aiming at socialism, can maintain the enthusiasm of its members if there is to be an inhibition, a 'close season', in the discussion of its very aims and reason for existence. And – while the discussion must focus more and more on British problems – this surely is why discussion of 'the Stalin business' must and will go on.

* * *

But this is not only a question of the enthusiasm of Communists and Socialists – of the inner conviction which generates activity in a hundred day-to-day struggles. It is surely impossible that any can fail to see that the Khrushchev revelations – while it is true that they present problems which only the Soviet people can solve; while it is true that they do not touch the pockets or jobs of British workers – affect the whole political standing of the British Communist Party, and its relations with the British people.

A reader from Glasgow expresses this:

Two people have recently put it briefly. One lives in a Lancashire cotton town, and asked what the neighbours were saying about the Stalin business, replied angrily but honestly: 'They're laughing their heads off.' Another is a university lecturer in Scotland, who when asked the same question about his colleagues, replied: 'They're not saying much, but they're all thinking: "Let's see you talk yourself out of this one."'

The primary datum of the discussion is that we are proposing to promote political and economic change among people who regard us with amusement, tolerance and a kindly contempt. They are also quite prepared to use us, at least individually, if we can serve their ends, for example, in doing the donkey-work in trade unions and other organisations.

This is not an issue of sudden origin: nor is it one which will 'soon blow over'. It is ridiculous to say that the British workers 'are not concerned with "the Stalin business"'. The fact that they are concerned, and were concerned long before the Twentieth Congress, is revealed every time a Communist – often with wide respect and industrial influence – goes to the polls. So long as the British workers suspect the independence, the honesty and the authoritarian tendencies of the Communist Party, this discrepancy between industrial and political influence is likely to remain.

The records of any TUC or Labour Party conference during the past ten years show how 'the Stalin business' has been used by reformist leaders to divide the movement, and how the quarrel about human rights and liberties, in which more than once we have taken the wrong side, has become embedded in the history and even in the structure of our labour movement.

Nor have the Khrushchev revelations in any sense 'rehabilitated' Communists on those questions where we have been mistaken; although they have created a situation within which, if we ourselves draw the right lessons and take the right initiatives, we can regain our honesty and independence of judgement and action.

But 'the Stalin business' is here to stay. It will not be forgotten next year nor in ten years' time. At the worst, *the capitalist class will see to that.* Nor will Communists, in ten years' time, be able to look with indifference upon those aspects of the history of the first socialist revolution which destroyed – by torture, death and slander – many of its own best sons. The 'business' is part of socialist history: it forms a central experience to which socialist theory must constantly return.

So long as we refuse to face these facts, honestly and publicly, we are self-defeated in our work, and the return from every political action of Communists is diminished. Fine comrades will redouble their efforts and expend their energies in day-to-day struggles: they will succeed in alleviating suffering here, and in restraining imperialism there, but few results will accrue in the deepened political consciousness of the British people and the direct *political* influence of the party. The goal of socialism will be brought little nearer.

* * *

What is necessary?

First, we must jerk our explanation and agitation for socialism sharply out of the old ruts of pro-Soviet propaganda: we must dissociate our propaganda of fraternal solidarity with the people of the Soviet Union, our explanation of their problems and achievements, from the old uncritical acceptance of particular leaders, particular actions, particular forms of political and social expression.

Second, we must recreate – and first of all within ourselves and our party – a much clearer understanding of the character of socialist society, not only in its economic basis but also in its social relations and political institutions, and in relation to *contemporary* British conditions. This is not at all a question of writing certain democratic safeguards into our programme. It is a question of rekindling enthusiasm and imaginative understanding, of commencing an analysis of social reality with fresh eyes and open minds.

Third, we must take our refreshed socialist understanding, and carry the agitation for socialism in Britain into the heart of every day-to-day struggle, raising the question of socialism with a new bite, urgency and confidence: not as a peroration to our speeches, nor as a gleam to warm our hearts in a hopeless time: not as the ultimate target blue in the distance beyond foothills of new Labour Governments and People's Governments, but as a practical, common-sense, desirable and (within political reason) immediate possibility.

* * *

This is *not* what we are already doing. Our Communist Party still has peculiar elements of economism in its thought and practice.

Starting from the understanding that socialism is not won by propaganda speeches, some Communists have come to elevate the day-to-day struggles to the exclusion of the fight to win the minds of the working class. There has gradually entered the tendency to view the party as a small and disciplined élite, in possession (as Marxists) of a correct understanding of the needs, interests and way forward for the working class. To some degree the purity of the party's doctrine has been ensured by an exacting orthodoxy and a highly centralised structure, which has acted as a barrier to the growth of the party itself, and hedged round the initiatives of its members among the masses. Stalinism, and the cult both of authority and of the party associated with it, have hardened these attitudes in Britain also. Hence, the Communist tends to see his role as being largely that of building influence and connections with the masses and within mass organisations, for some period when economic crisis or external pressure will bring a mass following which the élite will steer to power.

Certainly, we should not slacken in any way our mass activity around industrial and social issues. Certainly, socialism will not come by converting twenty million people to Marxism by lectures and street-corner propaganda. But we do suggest that it is urgent that we break sharply with the outlook which sees these struggles as ends in themselves, as means for building the party, as incidents within a never-ending perspective of defending living standards within a capitalist framework, alongside many years of peaceful coexistence and peaceful competition.

It is necessary now to mount a propaganda such as has not been seen in this country for many years *to win the minds of the British people for socialism*: and it is necessary to mount it in ways that take fully into account the intelligence, experience, democratic traditions and organisational maturity of the British working class.

It is imperative to rebuff the actions of British imperialism in Cyprus and at Suez: but at the same time to explain as never before the nature of imperialism and its general weakness.

It is necessary to resist in every way the suffering brought upon the British workers by the introduction of automation: but it is also necessary to explain in a new, sharp and imaginative manner the general character of monopoly capitalism and the perspectives opened to a socialist society by automation and nuclear power.

It is necessary to struggle to defend and improve existing living standards: but it is necessary to generate anew – and especially among our youth – the understanding that socialism is not to be measured in living standards alone, but in new social relations, new values and opportunities, a new, more generous, more just and less selfish way of life. We should recall more often the words of Maxim Gorky:

> It is well known that a characteristic and inherent peculiarity of bourgeois society lies in the fact that the overwhelming majority of its members must expend all their energy in obtaining the most primitive necessities of life. People have become used to this accursed and humiliating 'peculiarity' of their existence and although it drives them to concentrate on themselves and think only of themselves, only a very few understand the monstrous nature of such a social order.

It has been this clear conception of a new society which has given inspiration and staying-power to Socialists and Communists in earlier years. It is the violation of important aspects of this vision which – half-suspected, half-understood – has blurred the vigour of our imaginative appeal in recent years: and which, now fully known but still imperfectly explained, has caused some Communists to stop dead in their tracks.

* * *

We have no ready-made solutions to this problem which events have forced upon us. We claim only that the problem must be faced: and there must be discussion. The result of this discussion, we hope, will be the liberation of great political energies, the re-emergence of socialist principle with a new vigour in Britain.

A reader from Colchester gives us encouragement:

As for 'unity', is there no one sufficiently Marxist to ask: 'Unity for what?' Unity for unity's sake seems as uninspiring a slogan as it is sterile. I think the unity of conscious and informed purpose in the struggle for socialism and communism is the only unity worth having, and that can only be promoted by such important and basic debate as I see in *The Reasoner*.

We think he is right. Clearly, he – and all readers – know the urgent need for common unity in action of all possible sections in immediate struggles against the Tory government, around Suez, in the coming industrial battles.

But this is not the same as questions of organisational and political unity of socialists. This can come only through open discussion, in good faith. It will not come by slurring over past or present disagreements.

The crisis of British imperialism is real enough now, and laid open before all eyes: its repercussions upon British industry may soon provoke a rapid sharpening of political consciousness among the British working class: the abatement of the Cold War has given us a brief breathing-space. The seriousness of immediate, and impending, political and industrial issues makes it *more*, and not less, urgent that we get the equipment of our socialist theory sharp and into good order. The gathering threat to British living standards makes it *more*, rather than less, urgent that we should contest all propaganda which seeks to fool the British people into the belief that there is any long-term solution to their problems within the framework of monopoly capitalism. If the mock battles of Gaitskell on the one hand, and the 'Stalin business' on the other, have brought the ideals of socialism into discredit with sections of our working people, it becomes our first duty to reassert them in their full truth and power.

The unity required is that of the gathering of socialist forces, the renewal of socialist understanding, for the final assault upon British imperialism itself. Such an assault can only be carried by those who, like Cromwell's soldiers, 'know what they fight for, and love what they know'. It is our hope that *The Reasoner* will strengthen their number.

* * *

We urge readers to encourage bookshops to stock *The Reasoner*. Wholesale terms are 25 per cent discount on a sale or return basis, postage both ways being paid by us. These terms have been available from the first issue.

* * *

very large number of rank-and-file members whose opinions are reflected – although sometimes in a very distorted way – in *The Reasoner*. In saying this, I have no wish to undervalue the growing degree of independence and maturity which our press and public statements have displayed since the Twentieth Congress, or the fairness with which the public controversy seems to have been so far conducted. I feel personally that the accusations against the leadership made by some of the contributors to the first number of *The Reasoner*, although every now and then they rang a distinct bell, were grossly exaggerated. Nevertheless, it does seem to me that the leadership has not yet shown a sufficient appreciation of the magnitude of the problems which have to be solved and the rethinking which has to be done – in other words, that it has underestimated the extent of the crisis in our party of which the appearance of *The Reasoner* is one of the most spectacular and important reflections.

What then should we do about *The Reasoner*? I do not think that we should dismiss out of hand the idea that a journal like *The Reasoner* can continue to exist and circulate within the party, providing room for contributions to the present discussion which our official press, with its limited space, is unable to accommodate. The principle of independent publication involved here ought to be the subject of party-wide public discussion before any decision is arrived at. Nor do I think that we should concentrate too much attention on the somewhat unorthodox manner in which *The Reasoner* made its appearance. Personally, I believe that its editors have acted irresponsibly, and that their tactics have been incredibly bad. But to concentrate on this aspect of the matter, and to ignore the fact that the editors, to put it mildly, are not speaking for themselves alone, would be criminal folly. To suppress *The Reasoner*, or to take disciplinary action against its editors and contributors, would not be to suppress the crisis of which it is a reflection, but to exacerbate it greatly, and to do incalculable harm to the unity and reputation of our party. It is precisely because I believe this very strongly that I have written the present article.

What is required on the part of the leadership, I suggest, is a frank and open recognition of the fact a) that the crisis in our party is rather more serious than has hitherto been acknowledged, and b) that the space in the existing party press which can be allotted to controversy and discussion is nowhere nearly sufficient to enable the problems involved to be properly solved. If these facts are admitted, I do not think that the question of *The Reasoner* will be very difficult to deal with. If the right of independent publication be permitted, then *The Reasoner* can continue to fulfil its present function so long as there is a demand for it, preferably with the addition to the editorial

Ronald L Meek, What Should We Do About *The Reasoner?*

Whether one approves of *The Reasoner* or not, one can hardly ignore it. To brush it aside as unimportant, or to deal with it as if it were merely an expression of the views of a handful of disgruntled intellectuals, would be the height of stupidity. Anyone with a smattering of Marxism (to say nothing of eyes and ears) must surely recognise that the appearance of *The Reasoner* reflects a very real crisis in our party – a crisis which, as the evidence of several party aggregates shows, extends far beyond the ranks of the intellectuals.

What then should be our attitude towards *The Reasoner*? This question cannot be answered without saying something about the reasons for the growth of the great concern and bewilderment which exists in our party today.

It would be quite wrong to date all of this concern and bewilderment from the Twentieth Congress. The waters had been accumulating behind the dam for many years: Khrushchev did not do very much more than open the flood-gates. It was not at all easy to be a Communist in the days of the purges, the Nazi–Soviet pact, the anti-cosmopolitan campaign, the break with Yugoslavia, the Rajk trial and the 'doctors' plot'. All too often our press and propaganda discussed events such as these in terms which gave colour to the claim that our party represented Russian interests rather than British. All too often it exaggerated the achievements of the Soviet Union, covering up its blemishes and talking about it as if it were a sort of outpost of British liberalism. And all too often those of us who criticised these practices were treated somewhat coldly (to say the least of it) by the leadership, and our criticisms remained largely unpublished.

All this, together with the prevailing tendency towards dogmatism and doctrinal rigidity, lost our party a number of members and a great deal of support. Those of us who remained loyal to the party, and continued to work for it, did so for a number of different reasons. Some of us, no doubt, were ignorant of the real facts about the unpleasant things which were going on in the Soviet Union: it was not at that time quite as easy as some comrades now assume it to have been to separate fact from fiction. Others of us, possibly the majority, knew some of these facts and were very worried about them, but remained loyal to the party because of the apparent lack of any alternative party capable of leading the British working class to socialism, and because of the continuing need to defend the great achievements of the Soviet Union against capitalist attack. A small minority of us gradually came to know most of the facts and protested about them, but at the same time tried to look at them from a Marxist viewpoint, realising that many of the errors and abuses and restrictions on liberty had their roots in certain objective conditions, and foreseeing that they would begin to wither away when these conditions disappeared.

As the facts became more and more widely known, the solidarity which the party continued to display in public came to conceal a greater and greater volume of doubt and scepticism. This should on no account be exaggerated: there was no disagreement over such things as the need to defend peace, end colonialism, defeat the Tories, and work for socialism in Britain, which were and remain our most important practical tasks. But the accumulation of doubt and scepticism was at any rate sufficiently great, when it was finally released and intensified by the Khrushchev revelations, to bring about a real crisis in our party – a crisis in which many of us are being forced to undertake agonising reappraisals not only of the Soviet Union but also of some of the very fundamentals of Communist theory and practice.

The reactions of our comrades during the past six months have been very varied. A few, disgusted at having for so long defended certain things which now appear to them indefensible, have left the party. Others, at the opposite extreme, have stolidly refused to discuss 'the Stalin business' and its implications at any length, on the grounds that it is not relevant to the party's struggle in Britain. The majority, however, have stayed in the party and worried about 'the Stalin business' a great deal. Amid all the confusion and scepticism, certain fairly definite attitudes have emerged, which may perhaps be classified under the two headings of 'conservative' and 'radical'. On the 'conservative' side are ranged those who believe that the amount of rethinking that has to be done is not really very great; that although certain things which happened in the Soviet Union were deplorable, our general attitude towards the Soviet Union in the past was not all that wrong and does not need to be changed very much in the future; that the structure and methods of organisation of the party are basically correct, although no doubt in need of some modifications; and that the existing body of Marxist theory is quite capable, with perhaps a little development here and there, of dealing adequately with the problems of liberty and morality which recent events have brought into prominence. On the 'radical' side, the views are much more diverse, although there is fairly general agreement that the amount of rethinking and self-criticism that has to be done is much greater than the 'conservative' side is at the moment prepared to admit. On the question of the Soviet Union, some comrades concentrate on blaming themselves and others on blaming the leadership; others feel

that the exposure of past errors has not gone far enough; others again seek the basic cause of our wrong attitude towards the Soviet Union in our failure to use Marxism in the analysis of developments in that country. On the question of party organisation, views range from that which suggests that the principle of democratic centralism is anachronistic and should be discarded, to that which suggests that while the principle itself is still basically correct we need a great deal more democracy and a great deal less centralism. On the question of the adequacy of Marxist theory, we again meet a variety of views, but the majority of the 'radicals' would agree that the development of Marxism has to a large extent been inhibited in the past by the various practices which are nowadays subsumed under the title 'the cult of the individual'; that facile solutions to the problem of liberty under socialism are greatly to be deplored; and that something like a renaissance of creative Marxism is an urgent necessity if our party is to be able to fulfil what we have always regarded as its historic task.

The tragedy of all this is, of course, that the differences of opinion which I have been describing might have been greatly minimised, and the crisis largely averted, if the affair had been properly handled. If our party had had its ear to the ground a little more during the past three or four years, and taken a little more notice of those who spoke of the important developm taking place in the Soviet Union, the Khrushchev speech would have as less of a shock. If that speech had been less one-sided and superfici had contained fewer exaggerations, half-truths and personal trivia, i gone even part of the way towards a Marxist interpretation of the fac it disclosed, and if the Soviet party had taken brother parties mor confidence about it, we would have been better prepared to meet and to turn the feeling which it was bound to arouse into more c channels. If the early statements of our own press and leadershi more self-critical, if they had not taken Soviet documents quite their face value, if … but one could multiply these 'ifs' almos without helping very much to get us out of the present crisis. stage of socialism did not always develop in the way we sho so the transition to the new and higher stage of socialism i in a way which is very different from what most of us exp The habits of thought of a lifetime, whether in the Soviet cannot be completely altered overnight. The essential po we like it or not, whether it could have been avoided o and it is the duty of every comrade to help the party to

In this crisis, I think it is fair to say that the 'conservat that of the majority of the leadership, and the 'radica

board of one or two comrades nominated by the Executive Committee. If the right of independent publication be not admitted, then alternative channels must be made available for the adequate public expression of the views reflected in *The Reasoner*. A substantial enlargement of *World News* might possibly meet the need, but a preferable arrangement would be for the Executive Committee itself to issue a special journal devoted to inner-party discussion, similar in aims and format to *The Reasoner*, with the latter's present editors included on the editorial board. Above all, let us realise that *The Reasoner* cannot possibly be dealt with in the way in which it would have been dealt with, say, five years ago. The principle of solidarity is a good and essential one. But solidarity which conceals widespread disagreements on basic points is surely worse than no solidarity at all.

Glasgow
27 August 1956

* * *

We urge readers to encourage bookshops to stock *The Reasoner*. Wholesale terms are 25 per cent discount on a sale or return basis, postage both ways being paid by us. These terms have been available from the first issue.

* * *

Doris Lessing, A Letter To the Editors

Comrades: The fact that you felt impelled to publish an independent Communist journal seems to me of more significance even than the material you print – which I find valuable.

The basic conflict in the party now in Britain is between those comrades who immediately respond to statements such as (I quote from your first issue) 'there is a fear of ideas on the part of some members – and even leading members – of our party, who for too long have been cushioned from the give-and-take of polemic', and 'we believe that the self-imposed restrictions upon controversy … have led to gradual blurring of theoretical clarity and to the encouragement … of attitudes akin to intellectual cynicism' – and those comrades who react with angry and even puzzled surprise, as to an unjustified attack.

Recently I was at a meeting of a party group where a member of the party administration was present to hear criticisms by comrades of party policy since the Twentieth Congress. For some two hours we were sharply demanding, in various forms, new thinking, a fresh approach, a return to honest intellectual conflict. The comrade from King Street listened patiently, and replied in a series of defensive platitudes which reflected all the attitudes of mind we had been attacking. The point is that this comrade, an intelligent and devoted man, had not the faintest notion what we were talking about.

This has been going on in various ways in the party for some months: a battle between those of us who believe that deep issues of principle are raised by the 'revelations'; and those who think of what has happened in the Soviet Union and other countries as 'mistakes', or who are shocked by them but think any open or sharp debate will split the party. This fear by the leadership of splitting the party has been responsible for their lack of leadership, for their dragging behind events; of admitting nothing until they were forced into it by pressure from the rank and file or by statements in the capitalist press.

Your journal has come into existence because of a feeling of deep frustration, which I understand only too well.

But, comrades, I feel there is a danger in the form of your protest – for it is, in fact, a protest.

One of the most interesting and frightening of the reactions to the 'revelations' is the attitude of mind, expressed by the phrase 'you intellectuals'. It is a phrase which inevitably emerges during the course of a conversation with any of the comrades in leading positions; and is only yet another of the defensive rationalisations against clear thought.

After the meeting I mentioned above, during which I attacked this concept of intellectuals being concerned with abstract ideas of liberty, as opposed to the honest workers who were only concerned with the basic and important bread-and-butter principles, the comrade from King Street insisted that any gulf between workers and intellectuals was dangerous, suggesting that I was trumping up an imaginary grievance. The moment the meeting was over, he turned to the person sitting next to him, and said: 'We are having terrible trouble with our intellectuals.'

We all know that the British working-class movement has an instinctive anti-intellectual bias, which we need not go into here. We all know that intellectuals in our kind of society tend to be isolated from the ordinary people. This is particularly true in Britain. Above all, the Stalin era was deeply anti-intellectual in the sense that it suppressed the emergence of ideas that were not of immediate service to the business of survival.

But I do not think the way to break down this barrier is to separate ourselves off, as intellectuals, from the conflicts inside the party now. I think it would be a pity if *The Reasoner* became a sort of sniping post from the tree of liberty at the body of the party.

I believe your motive for starting *The Reasoner* was the admirable and necessary one of trying to restore intellectual conflict and real Marxist thinking into the party. But it could easily be interpreted as an attack against the party leadership as such.

At the moment, a lot of comrades are going around saying: 'We've got to get rid of the old gang, get fresh men in, the old ones are discredited.' But this is nothing more nor less than the business of looking for scapegoats, which, on another level, has led to the whole sickening business of trials and frame-ups and murders in the Communist countries. Admittedly the phrase 'you intellectuals' is pure scapegoatism; but there is no reason why we should do the same thing in reverse. Our job as intellectuals is to think.

It seems to me naive, and bad politics, and even dishonest to suggest that all we have to do is to kick out the old gang and put in a new one.

The fact is that the British party, together with the other Communist parties, is deeply marked by the attitudes of mind of the Stalin era; that all the party members, including ourselves, have been formed by them – whether in acceptance or in reaction – and this is bound to be so for some time. The sharp and angry demand for a new approach is just as much a part of the process as the defensiveness and the rigidity.

What we have to demand, I think, is not scapegoats, confessions and breast-beatings, but a re-examination of our basic thinking; and this should be done at a full party congress devoted not to pious platitudes and affirmations of support for Communism, which surely should be taken for granted by now, but to hard thinking. I am in absolute disagreement with the attitude that open conflict will split the party; on the contrary, I believe that it is only open conflict resulting in a policy reflecting the various trends in the party which will save it from disintegrating into ineffective little splinter groups. If the attitude of mind represented by *The Reasoner* (with which I am in full agreement) can make itself felt at such a congress, then I think its publication will be justified. But you should do everything you can to prevent it from becoming something like 'a revolt of the intellectuals'.

There is only one remark in your first issue which I found disquieting – and indeed, comrades, dishonest.

You said: 'I am not proud of the silence which I and others have kept too long over these and other matters.'

The facts are that, up to the Twentieth Congress, if those of us who knew what was going on – and it was perfectly possible to know, if one kept one's mind open and read the plentiful evidence available – if we had said what we thought, in the only place open to us, the capitalist press, we would have been cast out by the party and branded as traitors, and inevitably isolated by bitterness and recrimination from a world movement in which we believed, and of which we wished to remain a part.

That is why we kept silence. We believed that Communism had a vitality and a moral vigour that would triumph over the brutality and intellectual dishonesty that had undermined it. We were right to think so. But we *did* keep silence, knowing exactly what we were doing; and for precisely the same reasons that made the leadership of the Communist parties of the West absolutely right about the great economic advances of Communism, and absolutely dishonest about the defeat of liberty and decency that was the price paid for these advances. What is the use of saying: 'We should have done this – or that.' The fact is, that we did keep quiet, and if the same situation arose, we would probably keep quiet again. What we have to do is to make it impossible for the same situation to arise.

But above all, we must accept our responsibility for having been part of the thing, our responsibility for the good and for the bad.

As long as groups, or individuals, hurl abuse at each other, trying to fasten the blame on each other, it shows we have not begun to accept the implications of what has happened.

We have all been part of the terrible, magnificent, bloody, contradictory process, the establishing of the first Communist regime in the world – which has made possible our present freedom to say what we think, and to think again creatively.

London
29 July 1956

* * *

Hyman Levy, The Place of Unorthodoxy in Marxism

Marxism is the natural offspring of capitalism. When the violence to human values which early capitalism inflicted on its men, women and child workers was wedded to the science and technology of the industrial revolution, a rational analysis of society was ready for birth. Yet Marxism was an unorthodoxy. It still is. It seeks to extend scientific principles beyond the limited range of inanimate matter to social groups; it sets out deliberately to transform the capitalist society from which it sprung. It is new and creative because it is, and sees itself, as an expression of a necessary contradiction in capitalism. The vital distinction between the Labour Party and the Communist Party lies in the tendency of the former to compromise with capitalist orthodoxy, and the insistence of the latter to retain its unorthodoxy. This difference in behaviour lies in the nature of the Marxist exposure of the contradictions of capitalism.

The respective creative roles of orthodoxy and unorthodoxy stand out clearly in the field of science and technology. For example, the destruction of the belief that the earth was the centre of the universe, and that man was specially created as the focal creature in that scheme, marked the end of an old orthodoxy. So also at a later date did the denial of the indivisibility of the atom, the repudiation of action at a distance and of the existence of the ether, the concept of space-time, and the theory of relativity. These unorthodoxies were creative activities that paved the way to a new level of orthodox science. They were primarily theoretical advances. Technology, on the other hand, is the detailed working out of orthodox science in social practice. It helps to change the physical environment in which people live and so helps to change their outlook. Unorthodoxy, when it is correct, jerks the mind of man forward suddenly; orthodoxy, when correctly applied, marks a steady indirect advance.

Marx and Engels deliberately absorbed everything possible in science, both in fact and in methodology, and used it as an instrument in the social struggle. They, like Lenin, were acutely aware of the possible creative role of unorthodox ideas. Today therefore, a century later, when Marxist parties are consciously organised social institutions, we have to ask how far they also are aware of this, and pursuing it into practice, how far they have even set up machinery deliberately to encourage intelligent unorthodoxy to express itself in word and deed.

Within the Communist Party there does not at present exist a really adequate machinery of self-criticism. By this I do not mean the breast-beating and the rending of garments by miserable sinners; if it gives him satisfaction anyone can indulge in this in the privacy of his own apartment. I mean the public analysis of policy in the mood in which a matter would be discussed at a scientific gathering; the examination of where the party has been right and where wrong in the past; whether the falseness, if any, has arisen simply from a wrong analysis of existing facts or from the emergence of new facts that could not have been known; the careful drawing of scientific lessons. This is a necessary step for effecting the readjustment of the minds of Marxists to meet the changing situation. Scientific education demands this at least. Party press is not adequate in space alone to meet this; nor is it broad enough, perhaps as a consequence, to allow for a wide latitude of divergence of views. I, like many others, claim the right to be wrong. It is not possible to find the right without blundering through the wrong.

There are difficulties here. There is, for example, an intense loyalty among members, an easy because loyal acceptance of policy, a tendency to be critical of those who are critical, and therefore a ready acceptance of the line as officially sponsored. There is a case for this, the history of the Soviet Union is scarred deeply by the wounds inflicted by *irresponsible* unorthodoxy during the revolutionary struggle. But today we have had exposed to us the infinitely deeper wounds inflicted on the body of a would-be socialist society by an unrelenting and inflexible orthodoxy.

The consequences could have been foreseen, and should have been anticipated by professing Marxists. How can an unorthodox party leave no room for unorthodoxy within its own ranks, and expect to survive without doing violence to its best values, to its imagination and therefore finally to its own integrity? To a scientific body integrity is its very life-blood. Truth demands integrity. That is why I am writing this article for *The Reasoner*; not because I necessarily agree with the content of its articles – that is irrelevant – but *because at a critical moment when a public expression of faith in human decency was called for, it dared to take the unorthodox step of challenging an impossible silence.*

It is important to examine the nature of the confusion that now exists in the minds of many members. Let us realise in the first place that no one joins the Communist Party for social advancement. To the social climber the first step on the ladder is the rung of orthodoxy. We must assume therefore that members are honest genuine people, who have certain values in common. But values do not exist in a vacuum. They must be periodically asserted, justified and developed. Every change in circumstances demands their reassertion and reassessment. From them spring loyalties, and danger begins with the persistent rationalisation of loyalties that have become uncritical. The first historic experiment in socialism called forth an intense upsurge of enthusiasm and an immense fund of loyalty. This had its place and was of great importance while the Soviet Union was struggling against internal and external enemies. Capitalist agencies throughout the world were watching hawk-eyed for any weak spot that might be exploited to decry and to destroy the great experiment. For every truth these enemies of socialism may have uttered there were a thousand fabricated lies, and so the loyal supporters swept both truth and falsehood indiscriminately into the refuse can. That was natural, and I personally have no regrets. If I have been uncritical, it was the damage done to me by anti-socialist propaganda. I lick these wounds and start again.

Today the situation has been transformed. While British capitalism, in spite of its decay, is still strong enough to permit the existence of a Communist Party in its midst, the Soviet Union is now so strong that its decisions tend to dominate the political world scene, and it can easily dispense with any aid that the British Communist Party may give it. This in no way reflects on the need for the international solidarity of the socialist movement. But a dialectical change has taken place on the world political stage, and this must be reflected in the thoughts and feelings of Communists if their minds are to keep pace with the physical world.

Let me illustrate the kind of difficulty I meet. Khrushchev makes a public statement exposing a vast network of unsocialistic degeneracy that has existed in the Soviet Union for many years. If the economic exploitation of man by man has been swept away, apparently there still did exist that other form of human exploitation that under physical pressure extracted false confessions from individuals. Marxists have been adamant in denying that they hold any brief for the purely economic interpretation of history. Economism is no part of their outlook. Because the economic exploitation of man by man has been eliminated from the Soviet Union, this does not therefore in itself imply that socialism has been achieved – and the Khrushchev revelations underline this. They do more. They lead the way in public self-criticism. They now throw the door wide open to socialists the world over to see for themselves what has been happening, and to draw the lessons. Anything less than this would not be worthy of scientific Marxists. The progress of an experiment has to be reported regularly and systematically so that the understanding of the scientific thinker may proceed step by step with the development of the experiment.

But here a curious contradiction begins to arise among many comrades. Their socialist loyalty during the many years of Soviet construction under the most terrible of conditions has become a conditioned habit of thought, a suppression of judgement and a danger to their integrity. The demand that the Communist Party shall give leadership not only on political and economic matters but also on ethical and moral issues, seems to them to smack of heresy and treason, if it involves condemning the very things that Khrushchev has himself exposed. In remaining loyal to everything without exception in the past they necessarily condemn the present exposures; but this also they do not do, again out of loyalty. Such a contradictory attitude has no meaning and no place surely among Marxists, and those who seek to retain it are in fact becoming mental and moral reactionaries. Their minds and feelings are becoming atrophied, and they are losing the capacity for critical and constructive judgement.

To condemn or blame them for this is itself a stupidity. The problem is not to blame – that is merely to approach the problem through individual sinfulness – but to remedy and to rectify. The violent upsurge of feeling within the party during the past few months is both a sign of vigour and evidence of a dangerous malady that had grown unawares in our midst. This malady is the creeping paralysis of orthodoxy, and must be deliberately and carefully handled. Because we are an unorthodox party composed of members who renounce social advantage, we tend to hold the respect of outsiders. We must beware lest we become the object of ridicule and contempt. All this is of first importance in relation to the immediate future.

This country is on the edge of tremendous changes. Countries like Britain and France with their industries rooted largely in the first industrial revolution are facing the oncome of a new industrial revolution with futile unavailing gestures intended to retain a hold on a rapidly crumbling colonial empire that belongs to a past epoch. A fundamental reconstruction of the whole industrial structure of the country is now called for. When we talk of a new level of production of scientific and technical men comparable with what is being done in the USSR to meet the needs of the new age we are talking of the release of enormous potential thought and activity from the working class, for from no other source can these men come. In such a situation the Communist Party has a great role to play if it can mobilise the creative energies of brains and youth and can use its Marxism in a constructive way.

How is it to win the youth? In the 1930s the universities of the country were alive with young men and women eager and anxious to understand the world in which they lived. Many of the best laid down their lives in Spain; others have slipped away into disillusionment or become stiff and doctrinaire in their attitude. The fire of unorthodoxy has burnt out, partly I think because the Communist Party has not known how to feed the flame. Today a new generation has come into being consumed with new problems ... the ethics of the atom bomb, the constructive use of science and technology, the apparent contradiction between specialisation and cultural interests, etc, etc. In the prewar years when the dangers of fascism and war loomed on the horizon, the Left Book Club channelled the mental and moral energies of young men and women in the right direction, but today the issues that agitate them arise sporadically as individual problems, and the party has lost its punch and its attraction for them. If the Khrushchev revelations have indeed jerked the CPSU out of the desperate path it was treading, once more onto the true path of socialism, how far will a corresponding salutary effect have been produced on the British Communist Party? What is to be the consciously planned readjustment that will draw in the new blood so urgently needed today? Above all these young people need discussion, open and frank discussion with people whose *bona fides* they can trust. Those of us who move in academic circles know how anxious they are for clarity and guidance, and how easy it is for institutions that trade in mysticism to lead them captive and mentally bound up their blind alleys. I intend here to mention only one or two relatively simple steps, if only as a beginning.

The first is to admit openly and publicly that we do not have all the answers to all the questions. This is merely to state a fact that is apparent to everyone whose mind is not petrified. The disclosures about the USSR in themselves point to a hundred factors on which we have been wrong. Are we satisfied that the USSR is already a socialist country now treading the path to Communism? Did we understand the practical working of Soviet democracy? Can we examine the vicissitudes of Soviet art, its music, its literature, its theatre, its cinema, honestly and frankly? What are the lessons for Marxism to be drawn from what has occurred? What is meant by socialist ethics in theory? In Soviet practice? In the world of capitalism? These and a thousand other questions are on the lips of many people.

The second point is to attempt to implement in practice the principle I have tried to propound earlier that there is both a 'line' to be followed and there is not a 'line'. I will not expand this further except to say that it implies an easier, more accommodating, less rigorous attitude to publication within the party press. We expect to have the right to be wrong without the assumption that the party necessarily endorses our wrongness. We expect a specific admission periodically that the party may have been wrong, by putting its policy publicly and critically to the test, in its own press. A policy is correct if it predicts the outcome of action or if those who predict wrongly can lay their finger on the previously unknowable factors that have falsified the prediction. A scientific party must act like a scientific society.

The third point is concerned with the problem of mobilising the younger generation of intellectuals. The two previous points, it seems to me, are necessary preliminaries to this, and without them the problem is insoluble; the party will remain defunct as far as they are concerned, and they will not listen to any rational analysis of the multitude of problems that confront them today. At every university and in most major towns there is required an open forum, at which party members and such of their friends as can be guaranteed by party members (in order only to exclude the cranks and the quarrelsome) can meet for unfettered discussion of political, social and ethical issues without let or hindrance, and without previous briefing. By this I mean that although the party should sponsor the meetings, it should make no attempt to 'steer' the lines of the discussion, to select topics, or to keep party members on the correct 'line'. The important thing is for those who are seeking a way out, to fight through to the solution, along with those who think they already know. The atmosphere is at present ripe for a Battle of Ideas. If the party believes in itself all it requires to do is to provide the battleground, sweeping aside its habitual tendency to work out the strategy and the tactics to the minutest detail. To those not already convinced a staged and directed discussion can easily defeat itself. This ought to be obvious to those who watch the dialectical process at work.

Such open forums would show not only that the party is fearless in its approach to the truth, but that it is the only party that is fearless. Let it then incorporate the best of the outcome of such discussions into its own outlook. Along some such lines – and only minor ones have been suggested here – unorthodoxy can be nourished and encouraged within the party itself. This, I believe, is one of the necessary conditions for the renewal of its life-blood.

* * *

Bertolt Brecht, To Posterity

Indeed I live in the dark ages!
A guileless word is an absurdity. A smooth forehead betokens
A hard heart. He who laughs
Has not yet heard
The terrible tidings.

Ah, what an age it is
When to speak of trees is almost a crime
For it is a kind of silence about injustice!
And he who walks calmly across the street,
Is he not out of reach of his friends
In trouble?

It is true: I earn my living
But, believe me, it is only an accident.
Nothing that I do entitles me to eat my fill.
By chance I was spared. (If my luck leaves me I am lost.)

They tell me: eat and drink. Be glad you have it!
But how can I eat and drink
When my food is snatched from the hungry
And my glass of water belongs to the thirsty?
And yet I eat and drink.

I would gladly be wise.
The old books tell us what wisdom is:
Avoid the strife of the world, live out your little time
Fearing no one,
Using no violence,
Return good for evil –
Not fulfilment of desire but forgetfulness
Passes for wisdom.
I can do none of this:
Indeed I live in the dark ages!

I came to the cities in a time of disorder
When hunger ruled.
I came among men in a time of uprising
And I revolted with them.
So the time passed away
Which on earth was given me.

I ate my food between massacres.
The shadow of murder lay upon my sleep.
And when I loved, I loved with indifference.
I looked upon my nature with impatience.
So the time passed away
Which on earth was given me.

In my time streets lead to the quicksand.
Speech betrayed me to the slaughterer.
There was little I could do. But without me
The rulers would have been more secure. This was my hope.
So the time passed away
Which on earth was given me.

Men's strength was little. The goal
Lay far in the distance,
Easy to see if for me
Scarcely attainable.
So the time passed away
Which on earth was given me.

You, who shall emerge from the flood
In which we are sinking.
Think –
When you speak of our weaknesses,
Also of the dark time
That brought them forth.
For we went, changing our country more often than our shoes,
In the class war, despairing
When there was only injustice and no resistance.

For we knew only too well:
Even the hatred of squalor
Makes the brow grow stern.
Even anger against injustice
Makes the voice grow harsh. Alas, we
Who wished to lay the foundations of kindness
Could not ourselves be kind.

But you, when at last it comes to pass
That man can help his fellow man.
Do not judge us
Too harshly.

This poem, written in 1947, is translated by H R Hays, and reprinted here
with acknowledgements to the *National Guardian*.

* * *

John Saville, *World Socialism Restated*: A Comment

G D H Cole, *World Socialism Restated* (New Statesman Pamphlet, 1/6d)

The stand that Cole has made for labour unity, in his articles in the *New
Statesman* of 5 May and in the *Daily Worker* of 14 May have been much
welcomed in our press and in our propaganda. The present pamphlet is
a more thorough working out of his position and is, I believe, his most
important pronouncement for years. Since he lays so much emphasis upon
the importance of the unity of the labour movements throughout the world,
this present statement will be widely commented upon, and quoted by all
of us.

It will be widely quoted. Yes, indeed. I can see already the letters in *World
News* and I can hear our speakers – 'As Professor Cole so rightly says in

his *World Socialism Restated*, page 46: "Socialism cannot be reinvigorated unless the working-class movement in each country can be reunited solidly in its support."' And yet if we stop at this point, and lean too heavily upon Cole's general support for labour unity, we shall not only be falsifying Cole's position but we shall be deceiving ourselves.

Our party is rightly much heartened by this support for unity from such a respected member of the British labour movement, and we are certainly not wrong in our emphasis of its importance. But we have to consider *all* that Cole has said in this context. For Cole, after acknowledging that socialism in Italy and France cannot be achieved without the Communist parties in these countries, goes on to say this about us in Britain:

> In Great Britain, where the Communist Party is negligible as a political force, there is no case for a united front – the more so because the party is peculiarly sectarian and doctrinaire. But there is a case for recognising the plain fact that the Communists are a quite considerable force in a number of trade unions and will continue to be a disruptive and trouble-making force as long as the attempt is made to ostracise them. I am not unaware of the mischief that a small, highly disciplined, unscrupulous minority out to make trouble can do to an organisation consisting quite largely of rather apathetic adherents. Nevertheless, I am against the adoption of rules excluding Communists from trade-union office, and still more against the tendency of some trade-union leaders to brand every left-wing trade unionist as a Communist or 'fellow-traveller'. I believe that the way to build a strong, democratic movement is to decentralise power and responsibility and to combat Communism, not by exclusions, but by increasing the numbers who can take an active part in trade-union affairs and by carrying out a really big campaign of trade-union education in economic and political matters. (p. 14)

There are many things in this quotation to be argued about. I take strong exception to the statement that our industrial comrades are 'a disruptive and trouble-making force', and I believe this to be a distortion of the situation in British trade unionism. I am sure that Cole would not deny the importance of the trade-union struggle and the day-to-day fight on the factory floor; and who more than the Communists engage in these battles? And on another level, it is our Communist trade unionists who have consistently raised colonial questions at the TUC – issues about which Cole writes so passionately in this present pamphlet. I cannot in any way accept these comments upon a group of men without whose personal sacrifice, guts and political courage the working-class movement in this country would be immeasurably weaker.

I am not however concerned in this comment with any detailed discussion of what, to me, are weaknesses in Cole's argument. What does concern me here are those points of criticism which strike home. It is all too easy for Communists to write off hostile comment with a catchphrase, and to accept a rounded and tight analysis that refutes all error to our own satisfaction. We roll 'self-criticism' off our tongues at the least provocation. But self-criticism demands not just a *general* recognition of error but *particular* analysis and *detailed* discussion. When one of our leading comrades writes that 'we are acknowledging our mistakes openly and trying to repair them', I want to know where we have done this except in the most general terms.

Is it true, for example, that the British Communist Party is 'peculiarly sectarian and doctrinaire'? In two limited respects I would argue that it is not true. I certainly do not find the British more doctrinaire than the French party or more sectarian than the Australian. And I believe that as a party we have greatly matured in political experience and Marxist understanding over the past twenty years. In what then does our sectarianism consist, and how far is Cole justified in commenting upon our attitudes in these contemptuous terms?

I will confine myself to one important aspect of sectarianism – and one of which Cole, as an historian, will be very much aware. This is our attitude to our own history, our refusal to analyse fully, frankly and honestly past mistakes and failures, alongside past achievements. And not our history alone. We must look afresh at the whole history of the labour movement. It is not simply a matter of estimating the degree of error in our own past policies, if we believe mistakes have been made, but of analysing these mistakes in the whole context of the political situation in which they occurred. If we were wrong, or partially wrong, then others – groups, parties, individuals – may have been right. Simply to acknowledge our mistakes without recognising that a more correct policy may have been advocated or practised by others, is to overcome a sectarian attitude only in part.

Take, for example, the crucial matter of Communist–Labour relations. We are working today to remove bans and proscriptions in order that Communists shall take their place in the organisations of the labour movement. That is our short-term aim. Our long-term perspective is a united labour movement whose exact form it is impossible yet to foresee.

But these bans are rooted in history. We know the role of those who profited by our mistakes, who sought to drive us into isolation and to perpetuate the division in our labour movement. But what of our own part? When Cole, for instance, writes that after 1918 the 'Comintern ... deliberately split the working-class movement in every country', this is a statement that cannot be answered by platform rhetoric but must be examined in all its complexity. Again, we must examine the whole period of 'social-fascism'. Were we correct in applying the 'New Line' in this country after 1928, in which social-democracy was characterised 'as the mainstay of imperialism in the working class'? I have not forgotten that the political background included a Labour Party leadership, a section of which sold out to the class enemy in 1931. But this is not the whole story; and it is from this time especially that there developed much of the bitterness that still finds political expression in the movement at large. We may have been right in our general line, but sectarian in its application. But the examination must be made.

Or consider what is a more vivid memory to us all – the change of line to the war of 1939. There is not a shred of doubt that this question is still exercising a considerable political effect. Many of our own members are now convinced that we were wrong to switch to the policy of the imperialist war, many more are confused, and most are no doubt hoping that we can get by without the painful business of analysis.

Comrades will ask: why should we get involved in this detailed criticism of ourselves, which may give joy to our enemies and embarrass our friends? Why dig up issues long laid to rest? Will not the impression be created that the whole of our past is to be thrown out of the window? Have not other sections of the labour movement made more serious and prolonged mistakes of policy, whose effect was to weaken working-class opposition to fascism and imperialism, and to contribute to the drift to war? Is not social-democracy a trend in the labour movement which, because it is based on the theory of class collaboration, has disarmed the workers and delivered them up to the Butskells?[13] And are not our mistakes paltry beside these, and ones for which we need make no apology?

These arguments are commonly used. They stem, I believe, from a refusal to appreciate the deeper implications of our sectarianism. Whatever mistakes others have made, and whatever wrong tendencies they reveal, there is no substitute for honest enquiry into our own shortcomings. To claim to be the vanguard, to emphasise on all occasions the need for Marxist theory to become the guiding principle of our whole movement, and yet to exhibit an attitude of smugness and complacency towards our political activity, past and present, is a contradiction that will have disastrous effect upon our practice.

The political health of our party depends upon the maintenance of a critical, questioning attitude towards ourselves. I can sum it up most easily in the words of Palme Dutt, written in 1929 on the occasion of another major crisis in our history:

> … the mistakes of the past two years have already cost us too much. The easy-going attitude which is satisfied to 'recognise' mistakes and pass on, without deeper analysis or drawing lessons for the future, and with the inevitable consequence of repeating these mistakes in new forms, must end … It is no longer sufficient merely to 'recognise' a mistake after it has been pointed out, and pass on. It is necessary to draw out by the roots the *tendency* revealed by the mistake and brand it.[14]

* * *

I have concentrated upon this matter of self-criticism and our party history because, as I read it, this pamphlet by Cole is above all else a call to all sections of the world labour movement to look again at themselves and to ask in the most serious and responsible way whether much more cannot be done on all sides to end the tragic divisions which have cost us so much these past forty years. But there are many other matters of importance that must be considered in a more detailed discussion. I believe, for example, that Cole underestimates the part that imperialism plays in the British economy, and that on another matter he does not underline with sufficient emphasis the strength of the reactionary elements in Britain and their ability to manipulate the media of communication and not least the state machine. I am today, however, a good deal less dogmatic in denying his analysis than I might have been half a dozen years ago. One of the worst features of the past decade is that Marxism has ceased to be the exciting intellectual body of ideas that it was in the 1930s. In the field of economics, for example, we have not yet succeeded in developing our ideas to meet the changing structure of postwar society; and when Cole writes as he does of imperialism, I can only reply, despite the important work of R P Dutt, that we have as yet little to offer in criticism except generalities.

By focussing on our own problems in this way, I have done less than justice to this pamphlet by Cole. His unequivocal attitude to the colonial question, his refusal to be associated in any way with the world crusade against Communism, his recognition of the deficiencies in the theories of social-democracy, his insistence upon the importance of equality in a socialist society – these represent encouragement and hope to all Socialists of whatever persuasion. There are important arguments to which Communists cannot assent, but used imaginatively this statement could become an important landmark in the history of our movement.

We must not for one moment underestimate the extent to which this present situation allows us to establish fraternal relations between all sections of the world movement, and the real possibilities that exist to end the divisions between us from which only our enemies have benefitted. Unity is not an historical process that will take place easily. It is the gritty, difficult business of comradely discussion and practical action in the course of which many setbacks will be experienced. What must keep us going along this road is our common belief in the socialist commonwealth. G D H Cole has provided us with a start.

* * *

Though a lie may serve for the moment, it is inevitably injurious in the long run; the truth, on the other hand, inevitably serves in the end even if it may hurt for the moment. – Diderot

* * *

Readers' Round-Up

'Long legs to the baby', writes a Lanarkshire reader, and the mass of letters echo this welcome: 'a welcome life-line to hang onto' (Tunbridge Wells), 'expressed the feelings of many comrades' (Bromley), 'our integrity has been saved' (Hertfordshire), 'feelings of mounting elation and tremendous relief' (West Yorks). 'My first reaction was one of great joy and wild excitement, so accustomed had I become to the severe limits imposed on self-expression by the dogmatic, sectarian and authoritarian tradition of our own press.' (London) A Cambridge reader goes overboard (we think): 'the first number … will prove to be an historic document in the annals of international socialism.' We prefer an assessment from SE London: 'The most hopeful thing to come out of the discussion – which so far hasn't really been a discussion but grumble, complaint and assertion with no sense of direction or even of common language.'

We find no difference between the welcome of industrial and professional comrades. From Nottingham: 'I took it to work and showed it to a couple of comrades … it has become so battered and soiled that I hardly dare take it back to the owner! … Nothing particularly "intellectual" about any of us – we are just ordinary crazy mixed-up party members clutching at straws – so I foresee a great future for *The Reasoner*.' Old stagers and young hands join the welcome. 'I am concerned with adjusting the numerous defects of the CP of which I have been a member for 32 years', writes a Londoner – adding: 'If I am really convinced this to be impossible, then I shall chuck politics.'

Another reader who joined the party last year writes that *The Reasoner* has given new hope and helped him to reverse a decision to leave. 'The first bright spot I have found in *this* country … almost since I joined the party in 1932', writes another Londoner, with wilful exaggeration: 'So good to get some genuine material from other countries, other than the sickening usual blurb about the magnificent achievements, the superb leadership, the comfort and happiness of the masses, etc.'

There are many general comments of interest. 'Some members who managed to swallow Khrushchev's speech are finding great difficulty with Nina's Hats.'[15] (London) 'Those of us who most prided ourselves on our independence and criticism are horrified to find the extent of the tyranny and abuse of power which we have in a sense supported; we are ashamed and angry with ourselves for having been deceived.' (Birmingham) A Londoner writes (and we regret it) that he and his wife have recently resigned a long membership of the CP, 'a reading of your magazine … has taken the edge off our bitterness'. 'I am glad that you make it clear that you are not encouraging factionalism. If factions arise as the result of such *honest* and fundamental discussion then the party itself will be responsible for it.'

Other readers are critical. 'Valuable … but shrill and negative also.' (Manchester) The article on democratic centralism 'touches on all the points that are worrying many of us but does so without attempting to lay even the foundations for a discussion on what shall take its place'. But a Somerset reader finds the article 'brilliant', and one from Hertfordshire writes: 'Is the organisational system which Lenin advocated for a military task in illegal conditions necessarily the best for Britain in 1956? And did "democratic centralism" in Lenin's day include open discussion of fundamental policy in the party, or didn't it? These … questions need to be *raised* first, before they can be answered; good luck to *The Reasoner* for starting the ball rolling.'

Some readers are worried about our independent publication. From Edinburgh comes a long letter concluding: '*The Reasoner* has done this much good: it has raised very urgently the question of the need for fundamental rethinking and controversy. But it remains for recognised party machinery to be used to the full, as it can and should be, so that the job can be really carried out.' 'Could not such valuable fundamental polemical discussions be conducted within party journals and organs?' (Glamorgan) But a Londoner thinks 'it should serve perhaps to give a bit of a kick to some other of our publications', and another that it is capable 'of acting as a powerful lever' to make more open the official press. A few letters reveal more definite opposition. 'The person who first showed it to me, unfortunately refused to let me borrow it on the grounds that "it would be bad for me"!' A reader from King Street, London, 'considered that, whatever your intentions, this was a harmful step'. 'Most interesting ... though I hope it will *not* be necessary to make it a *permanent* publication.' (Bradford)

Most readers would like to see the question of official/unofficial publication cleared up in a comradely way. So would we. But all are determined that discussion must not be put 'in the old strait-jacket again' (Somerset).

For the future? Several readers send suggestions. 'Communist morality has got to be restated and made worthy of respect.' (Worcestershire) 'I think there should be an article exposing the way in which consistently over a long period, writers and artists have been alienated by bureaucracy and foolishness.' (Essex) 'I hope it will grow into the controversial cultural journal which we all so desperately desire.' (Another Essex reader) Whatever the long-term perspective, we like the summing-up of a Londoner: 'May it bear fruits in the form of getting more people to think, clarify their ideas, stop talking jargon and cease to be hundred-percenters, and to formulate scientific and correct theories of socialism in all the spheres of human knowledge.' A big order. But we hope that we have made a small start.

* * *

CORRESPONDENCE
Democratic Centralism

It is too early to say whether a Communist can welcome the publication of *The Reasoner*, because it is not clear in which way it will develop. Personally I am in favour of free and open discussion of all the fundamental issues that have been thrown in our faces by the Twentieth Congress and its repercussions, and if this cannot be contained in our standard party publications, then by all means let us have another one, official or unofficial.

However, I cannot say I am very impressed by the first issue of *The Reasoner*, since there is a sniping snarling tone about it that I for one don't want to see inside our party. Of course, many of us are still on the rebound from the Twentieth Congress, and it is natural if not very Marxist for unbalanced viewpoints to develop. Certainly I hope the editors will rapidly drop their avowed policy of giving priority to 'criticism of views which have come to be accepted as orthodox', and use their new journal instead for an extended examination of our profound problems, contributions being accepted on their merits. In this process, 'orthodoxy' and 'the leadership' (and of course ourselves) will indubitably receive thoroughly well-earned criticism, and if it comes to pass that a few well-known heads roll, and some new blood appears on the Executive Committee, who can say that won't be beneficial? But this is a different approach from setting up as a primary aim the lashing of the party leadership and the rejection of 'orthodox' ideas – an approach I find peevish, negative and quite undesirable.

I want to take issue with the contribution of K Alexander on democratic centralism. It is a contribution sloppy in argument and a little sly in approach, it seems to me; certainly nothing in it will cause the orthodox to shake in their boots, though it nevertheless represents a certain trend of thought current at the moment.

To begin with Alexander nowhere defines what he means by democratic centralism; nor does he outline the sort of organisational principles that should replace those holding the field now; nor even does he examine the kind of problems we face in trying to achieve socialism in this country, in order to find out what sort of organisation is *necessary* in a socialist party for the job in hand. While he should be addressing himself to these problems Alexander takes us instead on a world quotation tour. After this we are introduced to the inner meanings of the phrase (not the thing itself) 'democratic centralism'. We should note, says Alexander, that the word 'democratic' is only the adjective qualifying the noun 'centralism'. This emphasises 'that the structure must be centralised, with some democratic features compatible with centralism'. It does nothing of the kind of course, but how silly can we get? Would Alexander be any happier if the phrase we used was 'centralist democracy' – if that phrase has any meaning? It is to be doubted, for in this case don't you see, 'democracy' is only the noun, and the essential thing is that this noun is qualified by the word 'centralist', which emphasises that the democracy can never be real or true democracy.

By centralism in a political party I mean 1) that minorities shall accept the decisions of majorities, and 2) that lower party organs shall accept the decisions of higher party organs. These definitions are of course taken from the printed rules in the Communist Party membership cards – Rules 12c and 12d respectively.

If these two principles of organisation are not accepted, then either the majority accepts the decisions of the minority (and surely Alexander would be against *that*), or else no one necessarily accepts the decisions of anyone. Similarly, if we don't accept the second principle then either higher party organisations shall accept the decisions of lower ones, or else all party organisations are free to do as they like. If the second alternative in each of these instances is adhered to in practice, then the Communist Party would be turned into a debating society.

Does anyone, even the bitterest opponents of democratic centralism, think the achievement of socialism in this country now a matter of debate only? If so let them say so openly, but I refuse to argue the point seriously here. I am merely going to assert that even assuming that socialism will be achieved purely on the basis of victory at the polls, we are engaged in a fundamental all-embracing struggle that will go on for a very long time; that we shall be faced throughout this struggle with huge political and organisational problems, with the need for great flexibility of tactics combined with consistency of purpose, and that we shall never succeed until the Communist Party becomes the active day-to-day leadership of the working class in all its activities, linking this with the struggle for socialism. In this struggle we need ideas, organisation and cohesion. No debating society or anything like it could conceivably do the job.

From all this I conclude we do need centralism in the Communist Party, as indeed you do in any serious political party. (And which one, when it comes to the test, hasn't got it?) As a matter of fact centralism as I have defined it is very well understood throughout the labour movement in this country, and nowhere more than in the trade unions. It is in fact the basic organisational principle on which the unions have been built up, and they could not have been built up without it.

The only question really up for discussion is in fact, not whether we should have any centralism or not, but what sort of centralism we should have, and how much. As to the type of centralism I imagine few would opt for any other than democratic centralism. For a socialist party the democratic side of its organisation is as indispensable as the centralist side. Alexander argues that you cannot have the two because the centralist bias must always dominate the democratic one. Is this inherently so? Alexander doesn't attempt to show it is; he merely alludes to the results of democratic centralism in the Soviet Union. We can all have our theories just now about what precisely went wrong over there, but for my part I believe the overwhelming failure has been, not in organisation (though that has played its part), but in attitude or ideology.

Over here it is primarily a matter of attitude too. After all we have a lot of democratic rights of which the chief are the right to elect and to be elected to all party committees, and to take part in the discussion and formulation of party policy. These and others are contained in Rules 11, 12a and b, and 13. They can and should be added to, but the basic thing is how we use them or don't use them.

Much emphasis is being placed on the indispensability of collective leadership just now. This is very welcome, but the change in attitude that is needed has to go further than that. We have to accept for example that free discussion and debate (they are not the same thing) inside our party on our policies, tactics and ideological concepts is also indispensable. Such discussion can go hand in hand with political activity, and the taking of decisions on all those matters on which they have to be taken. Of course in ideological matters decisions about what is right or wrong cannot be taken; what we have to do here is to try and work out among ourselves what is the proper Marxist *approach* to any given subject. This is a process which mustn't be forced or judged by how well it keeps up with a timetable.

In matters of policy and tactics decisions have to be taken daily. These should be taken as they are now and should be loyally supported and adhered to: but, provided this is done, there must be no discouragement, through attitude or the use of 'the machine', of minorities wishing to get decisions reversed, however many times they try (at the appropriate times and places, naturally).

An important corollary of all this is that our party publications must in future be open all the time to minority viewpoints on all questions, and must cease (as they have done already) merely to carry *ex cathedra* statements of policy, and explanations and factual justifications of policy. This is not however a plea for minorities to be given most of the space.

Then our National Congresses must cease to be the empty and dreary parades that they have been of late and must become what they should be: bodies which lay down policies after debating them, thrashing them out on the floor, one by one. A number of procedural alterations are required to allow this to happen. But as with other organisational changes the really important thing is the extent to which we use them in the right manner.

To make the democratic part of democratic centralism work, therefore, the indispensable requirement is the unflagging determination to *make* it work, organisational improvements though there must be. This determination will be aided by an understanding that the vigorous functioning of democracy is essential to correct policy-making and that in itself, when it comes to be observable to those outside the Communist Party, it is a reassuring demonstration of our good faith and sound principles. I am sure that the Communist Party will never become the mass party of the working class until it can plainly be *seen* that while it is disciplined, centralised and self-sacrificing, it is also thoroughly democratic in terms of the experience and traditions of our own labour movement.

Yet it must be democracy 'plus', just the same.

J Lyons
London

* * *

Discussion and Democracy

Heartiest congratulations on your initiative in publishing *The Reasoner*. My only regret is that it wasn't done years ago.

The discussions taking place in the Communist Party are the most important in its history. Our job is to make sure that this discussion results in the strengthening of Marxism in Britain. This is not inevitable: the reverse could happen – we could degenerate into a sect like the SPGB.[16] This discussion will be fruitful to the extent to which it draws in the rank and file, makes them feel that it's their party, that they take a part in formulation of policy, that theory and policy are not just the affair of the leaders. Once that atmosphere develops then you'll get the enthusiasm and the élan of long ago.

Of course we want a party of 50,000, but we want quality as well so that we keep all those recruits we make. In my opinion our most important job is to win back all those people who have been driven out of the party or resigned in disgust. (I could name 50 from Nottingham alone.) Then we'll have our mass party, mass in influence and links with ordinary people.

To make this discussion as wide as possible and to bring in all these ex-party members I suggest discussion groups are set up in every town. This way we will all have an opportunity to let our hair down without some bureaucrat telling you that you're undermining the leadership.

Pat Jordan[17]
Nottingham

* * *

'The Long Road Back'

The Reasoner fulfils a vital need at the present time when we so much require the widest and most thorough discussion – in a free, frank, honest and serious way – of the fundamental questions which flow from the Twentieth Congress. The anti-Stalin criticisms – whatever their validity – have revealed deep divergences of opinion between many members of the British Communist Party on the one hand and the party leadership on the other.

These differences have led in not a few cases to resignations, rightly or wrongly, from the party. As one of these, I would like the chance to say my piece, knowing that most comrades will respect my sincerity; as I do theirs.

It should be realised that misgivings about the party leadership's attitude are not confined to what we call 'the intellectuals', though an attempt was made to give this impression, here, when reporting the Twenty-Fourth Congress.

I am no 'intellectual', having been a coal-miner all my life; and I have been a party member for 16 years (since the age of 15). Others in this area who agree with me, including coal-miners, cobblers and housewives, are as deeply concerned as any 'intellectual' with the political and *moral* issues arising from the Khrushchev speech. Their attitude is simply expressed by saying: 'We can't go round the doors and state an *honest* case for the party now. *We are still playing "about turn" when the Soviet leaders say so*, and the workers feel, therefore, that we can quite easily defend similar mistakes and crimes in the future as readily as we did in the past. They will not trust us, unless we change our attitude – and the party leadership shows no sign of doing so.' Such comrades realise that, whether we like it or not, the mass of the workers are concerned about the issues which were spotlighted at the Twentieth Congress, *and, indeed, were concerned about them years before that congress took place.* However inadequate and hypocritical British capitalist democracy may be, the average worker does feel that he has the right, more or less, to express his own opinion freely on political and other affairs, worship freely in his own way, get a fair trial if he is arrested, listen to different points of view and make up his own mind, travel almost where he likes (if he can afford it) and so on.

Workers cherish these rights, however restricted, and have refused to give any substantial political support to the CP largely because they feared that many of these rights would disappear if it came to power.

It would now appear that their fears were justified. That this has now been officially confirmed will make them more, not less, suspicious of the CP in this respect, unless we can show in future, not by words, resolutions, etc, but by *deeds*, that we genuinely regret our mistakes; and carry through certain measures to ensure that they will never occur again. The workers respect Communists as individuals, agree with 90 per cent of their policy, and admire their militancy – hence the CP's industrial support. But they steadfastly refuse to send them to Parliament or to organs of local government (with a very few exceptions) because they fear abuse of political power. It will be objected that what they really fear is the split vote and that it is the 'two-party system' which prevents the CP's advance. Those who do will have to explain why it is that the Labour Party had substantially overcome the same obstacle in 30 years whereas the CP hasn't made the slightest progress in this respect in 36 years! Comrades ask: 'Well, what should be done now?' Here are only a few of the measures which, I believe, if carried out would help to convince British workers that we had begun to put loyalty to socialist principles before blind loyalty to the Soviet leaders.

1) Object to assertions in the Soviet press that the Soviet people *unanimously* approve the anti-Stalin revelations, when this is plainly untrue. (Mikoyan: 'Some people took it badly' – interview in India.)

2) Demand freedom of expression of opinion in the Soviet press, for example, for those who disagree with the criticisms of Stalin. Why not the same kind of controversy in *Pravda*, etc, on these questions, as there was in the *Daily Worker*?

3) Invite to Britain Communists, Socialists and others imprisoned during the Stalin era, in order to make some assessment ourselves as to events in the Soviet Union, etc, in past years.

4) Demand an open hearing of the evidence against Beria (and those executed and imprisoned as members of the 'Beria gang'). To date we have much less proof that Beria was an 'imperialist agent' than we had about Tito. But, as with Tito, we have swallowed the allegations against Beria without question. No lessons learned, no real change of attitude. What if Khrushchev is the 'imperialist agent' tomorrow?

5) Request the publication of critical contributions from brother Communists (for example, Togliatti's statement) and *Socialists* in the press of the Soviet Union, in order to develop the atmosphere of free, frank and democratic discussion.

6) Call an international conference of all Communist and workers' parties (including the Yugoslavs) to discuss questions of common interest, and especially the question of international working-class unity.

In general the Communist Party must demonstrate in every possible way that it will approach questions of concern to the movement in the spirit of honest enquiry and respect for the facts. No more blind loyalty, based on false conceptions of international solidarity.

The operation of *some* of the above proposals at least would be a first step on 'the long road back'. There is room for hope, but *only if* the CP begins to show the workers by *deeds* that a genuine change has been made. Can the leadership respond to the challenge? My opinion is that it cannot, but I hope it will yet prove me wrong.

Lawrence Daly
West Fife

* * *

Labour–Communist Relations

The *Tribune*, reporting your first issue, deliberately sought to present the journal as that of an opposition group in the party.[18] If that were true, I would consider it a bad thing. I see however that the *Tribune* report was incorrect, and was simply an expression of the aim of certain elements on that journal, which is to disintegrate the Communist Party. However, I had hoped to see a letter from you in *Tribune* repudiating the suggestion.

I am rather worried that *The Reasoner* seems to be supported mainly by intellectuals. That is, of course, not surprising. It is the intellectuals who have had to do much of the work as publicists in justification of various phases of Soviet and British Communist policy. But the danger of a split between workers and intellectuals in the party on our attitude to our past mistakes seems to be real. When arguing that we need to be self-critical, not only among ourselves, but to our friends in the labour movement, I was attacked by party comrades as showing the typical weakness of an intellectual, remote from the class struggle (as though any open Communist during the Cold War period was ever allowed to forget the class struggle!). But more serious, the same comrades suggested that the party's main political task had been, and should continue to be, propaganda for the USSR. The conception of the party as little more than a British-Soviet Friendship Society is bound to lead to the assumption that it has no function in the transformation of British society. With this attitude, our failure to carry weight as a political body in the local labour movement is not surprising.

It seems to me that the key to the situation, that is, not only the question of relations between workers and intellectuals in the party, but also the wider political issues precipitated by the Twentieth Congress, is the relation of Communists to non-Communists in the labour movement. The failure to make any headway on this question is much more serious than the failure of our leadership and press to show any positive reaction to the destruction of the myths that have borne them up so long. R P Dutt, analysing the motives which make Labour men suspicious of Communists, wrote about democratic methods, the use of force, and all the old subjects of division between reformists and revolutionaries. But he evaded the real point, namely that Labour men and women who should be our closest allies and friends have become convinced that we are incapable of independent thought. They have concluded, with some justification, that Communist policy, even if made in Britain, was done under Moscow patent.

The point now is to prove that this is no longer the case. The labour movement judges our attitude largely by the party press, and by this standard little would seem to have happened. Surely events such as Poznań should make it obvious that sunshine stories about happy workers in Karlovy Vary are no substitute for realistic Marxist estimates of the progress – or lack of it – made towards socialism in the Popular Democracies. In fact the *Daily Worker* and *World News* have become simply boring on the subject of economics and politics in the socialist half of the world. 'Enemy' discussions about Soviet and Eastern European trends, such as those in the *Observer*, are readable simply because they discuss problems, even though in an unfriendly way. Our press admits no problems until they cause a crisis which cannot be concealed, and consequently is incapable of discussing them.

And so it is my hope that *The Reasoner*, for lack of any other Communist expression of opinion, may perform the all-important function of a bridge between us in the Communist Party and the thousands who see the need for the British revolutionary tradition to be embodied in a Marxist political party. It doesn't have to be a bridge across which Communists leave the party, and it shouldn't be a bridge flung out to seduce Labour workers from their present allegiance. But it could be a bridge for ideas to cross about the creation, in whatever forms, of the unity of the labour movement.

Rodney Hilton[19]
Worcestershire

* * *

Beware of Attempts to Stifle the Discussion

From various sources are appearing subtle threats that the discussion flood released by reports from the Twentieth Congress must not wander any further from orthodox streams.

The *Daily Worker* of 23 July reports Bulganin in Poland attacking 'opportunists and wavering elements' who came out of their corners inside socialist countries and sowed their inimical seeds in the press, including the press of Poland …

In Budapest the debates at the Petőfi Circle[20] have been praised by the Communist newspaper *Szabad Nép* as contributing 'to the formation of sincere public opinion to be listened to, which we have unfortunately gone without for years'. *Szabad Nép* continued with the democratic viewpoint that: 'People don't want to be the dumb extras of history, but people who take a role thinking with their own heads.' Afterwards the Central Committee of the Hungarian Communist Party attacked 'enemy, demagogic views' expressed at the meeting and declared that the Petőfi Circle was a focal point for reactionaries attacking the party.

Editorial comment in the *Daily Worker* on the resignation of Rákosi[21] contained the warning paragraph: 'In all Communist parties the greatest freedom of discussion needs encouraging and welcoming, but freedom to tear parties apart would be the denial of freedom to all who wish to advance the cause of scientific socialism and strengthen the party which is its organised expression.'

Possibly it is true that there are 'wavering elements' in the Communist parties and socialist countries, but it is the leadership responsible for many grave errors who share a great responsibility for any existing disunity and any further attempt at suppression of criticism will only lead to the gap between the party and the people widening.

Nikita Khrushchev may get away with it when speaking in the Urals but I doubt whether he would convince British people that the quelling of the Poznań demonstration which was under the slogan 'We want bread' was a crushing defeat for *reaction*. Here is a clear example of our need to be objective in our policy towards socialist countries and while retaining solidarity with socialists everywhere, we must revoke sectarianism disguised as support for the governments of these countries.

The Communist Party is, as we often describe it, 'standing at the crossroads'. Our only opportunity in winning a following in the ranks of the working class and its allies is by continuing the great discussions unrestricted, boldly admitting and then correcting errors.

To build unity there also needs to be a radical elimination of the conception, previously dominant at all levels in the party, that those leaders of the labour movement who did not agree entirely with Communist Party methods were either partly or completely reactionary.

I think that the most effective reply to any critics of the existence of *The Reasoner* should be that we certainly have nothing to lose by debate, and there are the minds of the millions of members of Britain's labour movement to gain.

Jim Johnson
Northumberland

* * *

Marxism: Science and Dogma

It is time we seriously examined our claim to be guided by a scientific study of politics. Whether we drop the last part of the Marxist-Leninist-Stalinist title or the last two parts, does not affect the point that we do claim to be in sole possession of a certain body of scientific knowledge and technique.

I would make three points about this claim.

Firstly, Marxism is certainly the only science which in the last hundred years has not completely changed its fundamental theories several times. Modern physics, though it may have developed from the physics of 1848, would appear completely unrecognisable to a scientist of that date. It would be universally admitted that modern physics does provide a great deal more accurate picture of reality than did nineteenth-century physics, and the picture will be more accurate still in 2056. Any science that does not develop like this is no more valid than astrology.

Secondly, a science develops by the constant examination of newly-observed facts, fitting them into the framework of the existing theories, if necessary by enlarging or remaking the framework to fit the facts. Sciences which aim at changing the world, as well as explaining it, like medical science or political science, develop by constant examination of results – 'the operation was successful and the patient died an hour later' is a grim joke, not a picture of a soundly-based science.

Let us, therefore, examine two recently-observed facts, results of the application of Marxism in the Soviet Union. First fact: of 1966 delegates to the Seventeenth Party Congress, 1108 were later arrested on charges of anti-revolutionary crimes. Second fact:

Last year the amount of housing space per person in the Soviet Union was only 23 square feet, which is only the equivalent of the 1913 level and lower than the 1926 level … the allocation [of new building] is still largely on the basis of one family one room with two or three families sharing kitchen and bathroom.

It may be objected that these two unfavourable facts are arbitrarily selected from a number of more creditable facts such as the increased industrialisation of the Soviet Union in spite of a hostile world. But I am interested in ends more than means. Industrialisation is only a means to an end – to higher profits in a capitalist country, to higher standards of living in a socialist country. If personal security and decent living accommodation are not regarded as priorities in the aims of the Russian Communist Party, I can only reply that the British worker does so regard them and I suspect the Russian worker does too.

What is particularly disturbing is that these two aims have in fact been largely achieved, under capitalism, by a British labour movement in the course of its struggle, a struggle not guided by Marxism. But they have not been achieved after 39 years of working-class power in the Soviet Union.

Thirdly, even the most up-to-date and carefully checked body of scientific knowledge often has the most dangerous effect on its practitioners. The scientist sometimes regards himself as a sort of high priest of revealed truth and expects ordinary mortals to bow down to its splendour. So long as he can argue like this, 'I believe so-and-so is correct because this-and-that supports the belief', then he may be a useful citizen with a contribution to make to society. But when he begins to say, 'I know this is correct because it is plainly set forth in such a textbook on such a page', then he is no better than the man who claims ultimate authority for the utterances of a Pope or a chapter in the Bible. At best he is a fool, at worst a dangerous maniac.

Let us not share the colossal conceit of the scientist pilloried long ago by our own Shaw. We Communists are not in possession of any supreme knowledge or mighty weapon beyond those of human reason. There are no such weapons. Our reason – yours and mine and all of us – is adequate for the task before us. We can only fail if we cease to trust it.

E Sleight
Yorkshire

* * *

A Lesson from History

The panic which seized upon all classes of men during the excesses consequent upon the Revolution is gradually giving place to sanity. It has ceased to be believed that whole generations of mankind ought to consign themselves to a hopeless inheritance of ignorance and misery, because a nation of men who had been dupes and slaves for centuries were incapable of conducting themselves with the wisdom and tranquillity of freemen so soon as some of their fetters were partially loosened. That their conduct could not have been marked by any other than ferocity and thoughtlessness, is the historical fact from which liberty derives all its recommendations, and falsehood the worst features of its deformity.

Such a degree of unmingled good was expected, as it was impossible to realise. If the Revolution had been in every respect prosperous, then misrule and superstition would lose half their claims to our abhorrence, as fetters which the captive can unlock with the slightest motion of his fingers, and which do not eat with poisonous rust into the soul.

The revulsion occasioned by the atrocities was terrible, and felt in the remotest corner of the civilised world. But could they listen to the plea of reason who had groaned under the calamities of a social state, according to which one man riots in luxury whilst another famishes for want of bread? Can he who the day before was a trampled slave, suddenly become liberal-minded, forbearing and independent? This is the consequence of the habits of a state of society to be produced by resolute perseverance and indefatigable hope, and long-suffering and long-believing courage, and the systematic efforts of generations of men of intellect and virtue. Such is the lesson which experience teaches now.

But on the first reverses of hope in the progress of liberty, the sanguine eagerness for good overleapt the solution of these questions, and for a time extinguished itself in the unexpectedness of their result. Thus many of the most ardent of the worshippers of public good have been morally ruined, by what a partial glimpse of the events they deplored, appeared to show as the melancholy desolation of all their cherished hopes.

Hence gloom and misanthropy have become the characteristics of the age in which we live, the solace of a disappointment that unconsciously finds relief only in the wilful exaggeration of its own despair. This influence has tainted the literature of the age with the hopelessness of the minds from which it flows. Metaphysics, and inquiries into moral and political science, have become little else than vain attempts to revive exploded superstitions, or sophisms calculated to lull the oppressors of mankind into a security of everlasting triumph. Our works of fiction and poetry have been overshadowed by the same infectious gloom. But mankind appear to me to be emerging from their trance. I am aware of a slow, gradual, silent change.

Percy Bysshe Shelley
Parnassus

PS: I send these reflections, which I wrote in the Preface to my *Revolt of Islam* in 1817. The parallel between the French and Russian upheavals is not close: but I thought they might be of use in characterising those features of revolutionary disillusionment in the culture of your time, and in warning against those revulsions of disappointed hope which can only lead on to states of mind beneficial to the oppressors of mankind.

* * *

> We had fed the heart on fantasies,
> The heart's grown brutal from the fare;
> More substance in our enmities
> Than in our love ...

W B Yeats[22]

* * *

DOCUMENTS

I: Helena Eilstein, Problems of Free Discussion in Poland[23]

This contribution by Helena Eilstein was originally published in *Przegląd Kulturalny* (the weekly organ of the Polish Council for Culture and Art), no 29, 26 July 1956. *Przegląd Kulturalny*, no 30 published a further letter from the author protesting against cuts the editor had made in her article, and quoting in full the missing passages. In the present translation these have been restored. The ambiguities, obscurities and contradictions are in the original; no attempt has been made by the translator to tamper with the style or arrangement of the article, with one or two minor exceptions. The article reflects, in the translator's view, the struggle between 'the old and the new' not only in the author's mind but also in the ranks of the Polish Workers Party. All emphases in the translation are those of the author. Translated by Alfred Dressler – Editors.

* * *

The return to democracy in our party and country, to public discussion of our national affairs, raises for Marxists a number of specific problems.

Post-Stalinism is a difficult period in the life of a Marxist-Leninist party. It is a time of intense maturing of party cadres and of the growth in the political consciousness and activity of party sympathisers. At the same time this is a difficult period of re-education, of painful processes of moral revival.

In this situation a clash of ideas and attitudes in the party itself is unavoidable. There are bound to be differences in the level of people's understanding of the distortions of the past. There will even be differences in the degrees of sincerity and enthusiasm with which people will welcome the revival: it is quite understandable that there exist certain sections among the followers of the party who adapted themselves to past errors – who, to tell the truth, profited by them.

Take, for example, this matter of the 'cult of the individual'. It is by no means restricted exclusively to the sphere of ideas and conscience. This cult, as all other similar cults, created its own specific priesthood which in its turn strove to maintain the cult as the basis for its own existence.

The creation – during the period of Stalinism – of the *social institution of the 'classic' as the universal and infallible authority whose utterances must for ever determine our solutions of theoretical and practical problems*, finds its counterpart, in the material sphere, in the existence of groups of dogmatists, drones of science, art and philosophy – in short, of a priesthood which itself becomes a real force and a social institution of great influence. This priesthood – as any other priesthood – can even agree, if need be, to the overthrow of a hitherto revered deity, but it cannot agree to the destruction of such ingredients of the 'religionisation of public life' as the sibylline books, the infallible oracles, the excommunication of the erring believers, and the complete submission of the faithful.

The struggle with dogmatism is first and foremost a struggle for the intellectual growth of the mass of the party membership, and the sympathisers with Marxism – for their re-education towards a proper understanding of the interrelationship of theory and reality. But an essential and inescapable first step is the removal of dogmatic drones from positions of influence – from editorial offices, from educational institutes, from university chairs, in the countries of the socialist camp.

Similar considerations could be applied to any other sphere of life, for example, to the search of the party for methods of economic management appropriate in a people's state.

It would be naive to think that the dictatorial, oracular, presumptuous and therefore irresponsible methods of work of so many people in the economic field was a sign of their personal 'conceit'. It was the result of the working of Stalinism in the structure of our economic institutions, and in their rules and customs; the result of the concept – nowhere formulated, and consciously-held, maybe, by only a few, although inculcated into our party *active* – of the substitution of government *by* the people by guardianship *over* the masses, in whose name declarations are made from the top, *who are not allowed to think for themselves, from whom vital facts are concealed, and on behalf of whom decisions are adopted.*

It is obvious that this made it easy for callous and careerist elements to infiltrate into the party *active.* Stalinism in economic management as in all other spheres led to a process of natural selection and breeding of people for whom Stalinist methods became second nature, and whose attitudes, mentality, positions and interests fitted well into the struggle for the complete realisation of the 'model' of the dictatorship of the proletariat which was proclaimed as a form of people's government.

The struggle for democratisation of party and state must aim at ending the careers of all 'busybodies' who fail to gain in their own fields of work personal, moral and political authority indispensable for the representation of the moral and political authority of the party and the people's government. The recently initiated changes in our life constitute a serious threat to those representatives of the apparatus of party and state who have become bureaucratised and demoralised by Stalinist perversions … But it must be strongly emphasised that this is only one of the elements in our present situation – to regard this as the heart of the matter would be a serious vulgarisation. The great revival of our party and state must inevitably be accompanied by a struggle of ideas and attitudes within the party itself. Precisely the best, the purest, the most zealous party members, officials, civil servants and intellectuals feel especially deeply the need to overcome in their *own* attitudes the distortions created by some aspects of party education during the period of Stalinism. It is precisely the most devoted people with the clearest conscience who wage a difficult – and uncompromisingly self-critical – struggle to understand the reasons for the perversions and crimes, and for the party's blindness in regard to these; they struggle for a new moral and political attitude, for a clearer understanding of the problems and tasks of our epoch. In the course of this struggle, *the concept of democracy and of people's government becomes more concrete and more comprehensive.* However, not all fetishes and taboos can be eradicated even from the minds of those who most warmly welcome and approve of the direction of the changes initiated in our life. Recently we could more than convince ourselves of the fact that the destruction of elements so deeply rooted in our life must go hand in hand with the overcoming of fatal political immaturity, of the tendency to rash, irresponsible, elemental attempts at protest that open the gates to criminal and counter-revolutionary acts.

In view of this we must, even while we carry on our vital discussion, combat panic and revisionism.

The matter is, however, complicated by the fact that the process of exposing the errors of the past and their fatal results, the process of reaching the stifled voice of public opinion, is often abused by those who would prefer 'to liquidate' all our present troubles by silencing protest rather than by mobilising the nation to wage a deliberate, uncompromising struggle with our present difficulties. This is the pernicious attitude of those who have recently been accused by official pronouncements of our party of attempting to stop the process of democratisation.

From all these points of view this is a most difficult period for Marxist parties. In addition to all this they must relearn the Leninist methods of struggle for the leading role of the party in the nation's life. The ability *to convince in conditions of freedom of speech*; the ability to put forward genuine arguments based on the fullest acquaintance with the facts of the masses, and not on concealment and political deceit serving the 'good cause'; the ability to gain influence in the activities of various societies, organisations, clubs, in conditions of the true democratisation of public life – this is an art, a science and a system of habits which to a large extent must be relearned and perfected by the party *active* at all levels …

The democratisation of public life which just now is meeting with certain objective difficulties puts the party into a position which Stalinism tried to prevent with all the means at its disposal (weakening in the process the party's political skill and flexibility); into a situation in which postulates can be advanced 'from below' which the leadership considers to be incapable of immediate realisation, but the correctness of which the party leadership neither can nor wants to deny. And how the unity of public opinion is to be achieved in a situation when Communist self-criticism has given rise in certain individuals and circles to resentment because we shut our eyes to altogether monstrous things, because we could not prevent them, because we kept silent; it has created doubts whether we shall be able to make up for all the injustices (at least for those that can still be repaired) and to protect the nation against a return to the old methods in the future.

These are the 'dark sides' of our present situation. *But the essence of the past can in no way be encompassed in the words 'the era of Stalinism'.* On the contrary, 'the era of Stalinism' is a conscious and completely one-sided *abstraction*, an abstraction which is useful if in one word one wants to express the complex accumulation of errors and monstrous perversions connected with the Stalinist methods of government …

And yet this past epoch belongs to history as one of the periods of the victorious struggle of the popular masses for a society free of oppression. The post-Stalin period finds our country in a fairly advanced stage in the building of socialism … Irrevocable changes have taken place in the economic basis of a society engaged in building socialism, the political, economic, educational and cultural achievements of a revolutionary decade have resulted also in irrevocable changes in the nation's consciousness. Under the leadership of the party great, decisive successes have been achieved in regard to the socialist transformation of the political consciousness of the popular masses and the creation of a real, *not a sham*, not an idyllic moral and political unity of important sections of society. Fundamental structural changes have already been accepted by the nation. That does not mean, of course, that an intensive struggle for the mobilisation of the masses around the party's programme for further advances has become unnecessary. It only means that the preconditions for such an *ideological* struggle are given; that the party can wage a real struggle for mobilisation in support of its programme *in the conditions of democratisation.*

Poznań has shown how *very* necessary this *ideological struggle of the party for the masses* is today; how indispensable it is to demonstrate to the masses that *the party* is the only, the true, the national advocate of their interests, how indispensable is the ability of explaining difficulties, of winning confidence based on understanding.

As soon as the 'paralysis of free speech' gave way to *free discussion* between the party and the nation, Communists discovered that they had to listen to many criticisms, not only about the past but also about the present, far-from-impressive, tempo of reform in many spheres of life and in many areas of the country. All these avalanches of harsh resentment, reproaches and impatient prodding to which the Communists are exposed have one strikingly uniform point of departure. All critical discussion starts from a comparison of Communist practice with the ideal *proclaimed by the Communists themselves*: a social and moral ideal the basic features of which are approved even by the critics. These people recognise the new basic features in the Communist programme, the new economic structure of society, and the new relationship between people … Severe criticism of the activities of our party was recently voiced in the columns of our press by people who, maybe, have not much to say for us Communists but who have quite unambiguously proved, both at home and abroad, that they '*prefer us*', that they have 'chosen' us and that they are determined to stick to their choice. It is not a matter of complimenting these critics but of understanding the attitudes which they represent. Against their errors we must wage an *ideological struggle*, that is, through *honest and public discussion*. But the difference between ideological and armed struggle is that the latter is waged *against somebody* while the former often is waged for somebody …

The conviction that these principles must as fully as possible be realised in our life is not based on the assumption that there are no longer enemies in our midst who would exploit freedom of speech for their own aims, but it is based on the assumption that if *the enemy puts his views in open discussion we shall be able to mobilise public opinion against his demagogy* …

The hypocrisy bred during the era of Stalinism presented the ideological unity of the Marxist-Leninist party and the moral and political unity of a nation engaged in building socialism as something embodied in the heart and the mind of a single '*corpus mysticus*' (it was hypocritically proclaimed that the 'word had become flesh' in our country); hypocrisy even succeeded in combining this view with the thesis put forward at the same time about the sharpening class struggle.

Unity of the party on theory, unity in action, the working out of an agreed party view on current political problems (a matter of course amongst people linked by a common idea), and the moral and political unity of the masses rallying round the party is real only because, *to say the least, such unity does not degenerate into an idyllic 'harmony of souls', because it is not a miracle of unanimity in all matters, and attained at a moment's notice without exchange of views or struggle of ideas.* The public discussion of the problems of our social life will often fail to delight our ears with the divine harmony of angelic choirs; freedom of public expression cannot depend on whether all people write exclusively about important and timely matters, though *everybody* will consider his contribution important, intelligent and correct.

The introduction of principles of maximum public discussion is *bound* to lead to people (who objectively or subjectively are the allies of the party) criticising the party's actions in a manner not always just or well-considered. And the Communists, while not breaking the alliance, while not questioning the critics' place in the moral and political unity of the nation, will nevertheless have to refute them for the sake of the common cause and the strengthening of national unity ...

Maximum freedom of speech for our citizens will lead again and again to questions and problems being raised publicly to which the leaders of the party and its leading organs will not be able to give immediately a satisfactory reply. *After all, they are not councils of omniscient gods,* but a group of the most experienced workers whose task it is to study the life of our society with the utmost application of theoretical competence, based on their knowledge of the facts, in order to work out and arrive at mature decisions. Characteristic of our present position is the charging and synchronising of many such 'circuits' linking the masses and the leadership, but so far they have not yet gone into action. But this, after all, is *the correct way in which democracy should function.*

The errors of the period of Stalinism can only be overcome if the party and its leading organs prove able to rely not on the stifling of the voices of those who have 'evil thoughts' but on the ideological strength of the Marxist front, on the continuous raising of the intellectual level of its cadres; on its growing ability to mobilise the membership whenever necessary; on the experience and skill of the leading party *active* to resolve doubts, to recognise difficulties, and to transmit correct analyses convincingly and without delay. The renunciation of the contempt – characteristic of Stalinism – of the intellectual potentialities of the masses (this attitude was much more widespread among the party *active* than was its indifference for the needs of the masses) requires new methods in the struggle to establish the authority of the party and its leadership. The Stalinist method was based on the spreading of fairy-tales about the good uncle or the devil who had abundant surprises in store for the humble masses. But when Leninist norms of democracy are observed and the masses are released from their 'submissiveness', and are allowed not only to express their gratitude but also their views and demands, the authority of the leadership cannot be based *only* on initiative from 'above' to satisfy the needs of the masses and to improve the methods of government. It will also have to be founded on an attitude to criticism from 'below' in accord with party and state legality, on a proper attitude to the postulates and projects that are an expression of the political activity of society. A 'proper attitude' does not at all mean that all such critical views or even those at one time or another most popular must be accepted.

The authority of the leadership depends also on its ability to *convince* the party and the nation of the impossibility of acceding to certain demands. The Stalinist method of safeguarding authority was based on the principle of infallibility. In the conditions of democracy, the authority of the party and its leading organs must be based both on the correctness of their policy and on their self-criticism and ability to declare publicly that it has no solution to offer for certain problems – that these must be discussed and solutions found with the help of public opinion.

The Stalinist method which relied on treating the masses as political adolescents, actually reduced them to that level. In conditions of democratisation the method of strengthening the authority of the party and its leading organs must be based on an appeal to reason. The first maxim of all systems of education is that by appealing to reason, and only in this way, can the mind be formed and developed.

* * *

II: An American Assessment of the Stalin Era

We publish below extracts from the editorial comments, 'After the Twentieth Congress', in the July–August number of the American socialist journal, *Monthly Review*, edited by Leo Huberman and Paul M Sweezy. Readers will find the entire issue valuable, including a 'Critique of the Stalin Era' by Anna Louise Strong[24] – Editors.

* * *

The theory that what has been happening in the USSR is a case of a socialist democracy correcting its errors is not satisfactory. The problem here ... lies in the idea of 'error' as an historical concept. Undoubtedly errors do happen and have a place in historical explanation. In wars, particularly, crucial decisions can often be traced to one or a few people, and if they go wrong they can only be described as errors which would not have been committed if their consequences had been correctly foreseen. But in making use of this kind of explanation, we must be sure that we can pinpoint the crucial decisions and identify those who were responsible for making them. And we must certainly *not* attempt to explain gradual and cumulative historical processes as the result of a long series of 'errors' committed by many different people, for used in this way the notion of error loses any definite meaning and becomes a mere substitute for serious analysis …

During the 1920s, the Soviet Union was a backward peasant country with few friends and many powerful enemies. The leadership was divided three ways: there were those who looked to a world revolution for salvation (Trotsky), those who favoured going slow and hoping for the best (Bukharin), and those who called for a tremendous effort to develop the country's own resources and strength to enable it to come through whatever tests might lie ahead (Stalin). After bitter political struggles which left their mark on everything that was to follow, the third group won out and pursued its chosen policy with ruthless determination. The country was industrialised at break-neck speed; a vast educational programme was improvised and strained to the limit; discipline was literally forced upon a new and untrained working class. To these ends a huge bureaucracy was hastily built up, and the whole lumbering machine was kept in order and whipped on by a ubiquitous secret police. The gamble succeeded. The great testing came in World War II, and the Soviet Union survived. But the time of troubles was still not over. To the vast burdens of reconstruction were added those of a cold war in which the USSR, while no longer isolated, was now faced with the menace of unilateral atomic annihilation. Under these circumstances the forced march under the discipline of the knout continued. Even the mastery of atomic weapons and the gaining of a giant ally in China brought no immediate release from strain and tension, for hard on these events came the Korean War, with its ever-present threat to explode into World War III.

Such was the Stalinist state at the time of the death of Stalin himself. It embodied a gigantic contradiction: in its aims and achievements it can fairly be described as superhuman, in its methods and attitude towards the rights and dignity of the individual it was subhuman. Or to put the matter in other terms: on the one hand, the Soviet Union had become the world's second industrial power, with an educated citizenry and surrounded by friends and allies; on the other hand, it was governed by the methods of an oriental despotism rather than of a modern civilised society. This contradiction was driven to the breaking point by three events of 1953 – the death of Stalin, the end of the Korean War, and the Soviet achievement of the H-bomb. Something had to give, and something did give. There was apparently a short, sharp crisis which ended with the downfall of Beria. Thereafter, the new leadership, following the logic of the situation in which it found itself, rapidly set about mending the country's international fences and redressing the balance of its internal structure. The Twentieth Congress can be taken as an official proclamation to the Soviet people and the world at large that the USSR is on the way to regaining its equilibrium and, barring accidents, intends to continue along its present course for a long time to come.

The essence of this theory is that 'Stalinism' was an extremely dynamic and profoundly self-contradictory phenomenon. Growing up under one set of conditions, it completely altered those conditions and thereby made its own continuation impossible. The analogy with the Marxian theory of capitalism is striking but should not be pushed too far: Stalinism is not a social system but rather a socio-political superstructure which arose in a backward mixed society which had to choose between going forwards to socialism or backwards to capitalism. It was shaped by the decision to go forward and became the instrument of the advance to socialism. But socialism, as a higher form of society, is quite incompatible with Stalinist methods. At this stage, the requirements of further progress called not for a social revolution in the Marxian sense of a complete change in underlying property relations, but rather for bringing the socio-political superstructure up to reasonably civilised standards. Conceivably, this might have entailed a *political* revolution more or less comparable to certain bourgeois political revolutions of an earlier period, but fortunately it did not. The Soviet leadership was, to be sure, trained in Stalinist methods, but it also retained its basic Marxian ideas and perspectives (this, indeed, is one of the many internal contradictions of Stalinism), and when the time came when change could no longer be put off, the leadership showed itself capable of adapting to the new situation ...

How far, then, is the liberalisation process now under way in the Soviet world likely to go? Our theory gives every reason for believing that the process is genuine and important, but it also contains an implicit warning against exaggerated hopes or expectations.

Stalinism incorporated the methods of oriental despotism – murder, mendacity, duplicity, brutality and above all arbitrariness. This was no accident. These are the methods which are often found in the governing apparatus superimposed upon a backward, primitive society. And it was precisely these methods that were rendered intolerable by the industrialisation and education of the Soviet people. Modern science and technology, as Veblen[25] repeatedly emphasised, have a logic of their own: in particular, they inculcate a respect for facts, for order, for predictability and reliability. Not only would a people with these attitudes be repelled by Stalinist methods; perhaps even more important, their productivity would be increasingly impaired. On the latter point, Khrushchev was very explicit in his secret report to the Twentieth Congress:

> We should also not forget that due to the numerous arrests of party, Soviet and economic leaders, many workers began to work uncertainly, showed over-cautiousness, feared all which was new, feared their own shadows, and began to show less initiative in their work.

In other words, the continuation of Stalinist methods was undoubtedly alienating the leadership from the people, and opening up a widening gap between the actual and potential performance of the Soviet economy. We may be sure that it was these problems, rather than abstract humanitarianism, which motivated the Soviet leaders to change their course in the last three years.

But if this is right, it suggests that at this stage of the game we would be wrong to expect more from de-Stalinisation than the abolition or rectification of methods which were most obviously in conflict with the present needs and attitudes of the Soviet people. We may expect an end of arbitrary police rule, but certainly not an end of the secret police. We may expect an end to the frame-up, but not an end to the conception of political crime. We may expect an end to the deliberate falsification of history, but not an end to the party-line interpretation of history. The Stalin cult is dead, but not the Lenin cult. Above all, there is no ground for expecting an abandonment of the one-party state or any abdication of its monopoly of leadership by the Communist Party ...

The Soviet dictatorship is cleaning house, not abolishing itself. But we hasten to add that from our point of view, to say this is in no way to belittle the importance of what is happening. We believe that present reforms, despite their limited scope, will indeed set in motion or accelerate certain trends in Soviet society which *in the long run* will make further and more basic changes necessary and inevitable. Here we can do no more than suggest the general nature of the processes at work.

The key to power in a modern society – an industrialised, urbanised society of mass education and communications – is control over the public mind ... This implies that democracy in the sense of government by the people can be genuine only to the extent that public opinion is free of manipulation or tutelage by a small minority, whether that minority be a ruling class in the Marxian sense or a self-perpetuating political élite in the manner of the Communist dictatorships. In other words, *genuine democracy means that public opinion is in a real sense self-forming.*

The USSR started as a backward country in which public opinion was as yet too amorphous to play a decisive role. The function of the Stalinist state might be said to have been not to divert public opinion from its 'natural' course (that *is* the purpose of the fascist state under capitalism) but rather to create public opinion and to press it into the service of socialist construction. In order to do this, Stalinism used much the same techniques as the capitalist thought-control systems, including physical coercion, deliberate falsification, hiding or glossing over contradictions, and so on. But its purpose was diametrically opposite: not to preserve a system in perpetual and deepening crisis but to build a new system with limitless possibilities for expansion and progress. This was a thoroughly rational goal and to the extent that the Soviet thought-control system served it, the result was to produce an increasingly rational and enlightened public opinion. *At a certain point, this process of public opinion formation came into conflict with the methods that were being used to promote it …*

At this point, the Soviet leadership faced a choice: either adapt to public opinion and modify the old methods, or try to make use of the old methods to curb the further growth and enlightenment of public opinion. The logic of the system as a whole dictated the former course: an attempt to pursue the latter would have led to increased tension and eventual crisis, with possibly disastrous results not only for the Soviet Union as a country but also for the leadership itself. Giving up the old methods, however, does not imply any changes in the forms of rule at this time. These have worked in the past, and are still intact. But giving up the old methods does necessarily imply that the element of autonomy in the formation of public opinion will be increased. And this, in our view, is a cumulative process which will sooner or later result in the emancipation of public opinion from the tutelage of a self-chosen political élite. Then, but not until then, we shall see in the USSR a genuine socialist democracy, one in which a *rational and enlightened* public opinion is supreme and the political leadership is merely its chosen instrument …

It must be stressed, however, that this is a *long-run* perspective. Soviet public opinion is still a long way from being genuinely well-informed or sophisticated, to say nothing of self-forming. Most Soviet citizens have still had no more than primary schooling; secondary schooling for the upcoming generation will not be universal until 1960; in the universities, there is as yet room for only about one out of every 15 to 20 candidates; what is taught under the heading of Marxism-Leninism is for the most part crude and mechanical; reporting of world events in the Soviet press is far from complete and often misleading; available accounts of the USSR's own history still suffer from all the falsifications and distortions of the Stalin period ... Conditions are being improved in all these respects; and particularly in the field of education, Soviet plans are incomparably more far-reaching and ambitious than anything ever envisaged by a capitalist society. Sooner or later, there is hardly any doubt, the Soviet public will rise far above the highest capitalist level both in knowledge and culture, and when that time comes genuine socialist democracy will become not only possible but inevitable. But this is at best a slow process ... Methods are changing, but the system of tutelage itself, which has very deep roots both in Russian and Communist history, will remain for a long time to come – probably until, like Stalinist methods, it has not only outlived its positive functions but has become an obvious and obtrusive barrier to the further development of Soviet society.

* * *

Note to Our Readers

Advertising space in the *Daily Worker* has been refused to us, and we do not intend to advertise elsewhere. We rely on our readers, who know the importance of this discussion, to see that *The Reasoner* gets around. Send us addresses of likely readers: better still, buy extra copies (buy soon) and sell them yourself.

From start to finish the entire work of producing and sending out the journal is done by the editors and their friends. That is why we haven't been able to reply to all letters, and why orders may sometimes get delayed. If in doubt, send us a postcard reminder. We wish particularly to thank those readers who sent us donations over and above the price of their copies.

The last number of *The Reasoner* in this form will come out in November. All letters, documents and proposals for articles should be sent to J Saville, 152 Westbourne Avenue, Hull. We shall announce in the November number any plans for carrying forward the discussion in a new form. Meanwhile, if you are not a regular subscriber send us a postal order for 2/– to ensure that you receive the November number on publication – J S & E P T.

* * *

Published by J Saville, 152 Westbourne Avenue, Hull, Yorkshire.

NOTES

1   The *Left Review* was a Marxist cultural journal that was set up under the auspices of the International Union Of Revolutionary Writers (or Writers' International), and ran from 1934 to 1938. Although its editorial board contained a majority of CPGB members, it was not promoted as a party journal.

2   Mervyn Jones, 'King Street Fears Pressure From Rank and File', *Tribune*, 7 September 1956. This article gave information of the moves by the CPGB's leadership against *The Reasoner* that must have been provided from within the party, including details of decisions taken by the Political Committee at a meeting attended by Saville and Thompson on 31 August. The article was clearly intended to intensify the tensions within the CPGB, even at the cost of making the position of Saville and Thompson more precarious; indeed, they subsequently wondered if this was the intention; see their letter '*Reasoner*', *Tribune*, 14 September 1956.

3   Ronald Lindley Meek (1917–1978) joined the Communist Party in his native New Zealand, moved to Britain in 1946, and joined the CPGB. He taught economics at Glasgow University from 1948, and at Leicester University from 1963. His first major work, *Studies in the Labour Theory of Value*, was published in 1956 by Lawrence and Wishart. He left the CPGB in 1956, remained a Marxist, and wrote several further books on economics and economists.

4   Doris May Lessing (1919–2013) was born in Iran and grew up in Rhodesia (Zimbabwe). She became interested in left-wing politics during the early 1940s, and joined the CPGB after moving to Britain in 1949. She left the CPGB in 1956, and drifted away from political involvement. She started writing fiction as a teenager; her early works reflected her political views, a later one, *The Good Terrorist* (1985), has been seen as a negative verdict upon her earlier outlook.

5   Hyman Levy (1889–1975) was born into a Jewish family in Edinburgh; he worked at the National Physical Laboratory and was later a professor of mathematics at Imperial College in London, and wrote extensively on that subject. He joined the Labour Party in 1920, and left it for the CPGB in 1931. He was deeply distressed by the resurgence of anti-Semitism within the Soviet Union, and was expelled from the CPGB in 1958 after publishing the pamphlet *Jews and the National Question* (Hillway, London, 1958).

6   Paul Marlor Sweezy (1910–2004) was a US economist and author. He taught economics at Harvard University and worked for various New Deal organisations in the 1930s, and for the Office of Strategic Services during 1942–45; in 1949 he and Leo Huberman founded the independent socialist journal *Monthly Review*; he wrote widely on economic matters, his most famous work being *Monopoly Capital: An Essay on the American Economic and Social Order*, co-written with Paul Baran.

7   Leo Huberman (1903–1968) was a US journalist and author. He co-founded *Monthly Review* and wrote several noted works, including *Man's Worldly Goods: The Story of The Wealth of Nations* and *We, The People: The Drama of America*, and several others on labour history, Cuba and China.

8   Lawrence Daly (1924–2009) started work as a miner in Scotland at the age of 15; he was active in the miners' union and joined the CPGB. He left the CPGB in 1956, worked with the New Left, and helped to form the Fife Socialist League, joining the Labour Party upon its dissolution in 1964. He became General Secretary of the Scottish area of the miners' union in 1965, and was the national union's General Secretary from 1968 to 1984.

9   The British Motor Corporation, formed in 1952 by a merger of the Austin and Morris motor-vehicle manufacturers.

10   The Social Democratic Federation was formed in 1884 from the Democratic Federation which had been formed by Henry Hyndman; it had a Marxist orientation, unlike its

chief rival the Independent Labour Party. Splits in 1903 and 1904 produced respectively the Socialist Labour Party and Socialist Party of Great Britain. In 1911, it merged with the left wing of the ILP and several socialist societies to form the British Socialist Party. The BSP split during the First World War, with Hyndman's pro-war minority forming the National Socialist Party, which in 1919 renamed itself the SDF.

11   Friedrich Engels to Karl Kautsky, 12 August 1892.

12   William Morris to John Bruce Glasier, 9 March 1892.

13   A popular term at the time, along with Butskellism, drawing on the similarities of the policies of right-wing Labour and the Conservatives, as personified in the Labour leader Gaitskell and Richard Austen Butler (1902–1982), the Conservative Chancellor of the Exchequer and Home Secretary in the 1950s.

14   See R P Dutt, 'The Fight for Independent Leadership', *Communist Review*, September 1929, p. 495.

15   Nina Ponomareva, a Russian discus-thrower with the Soviet athletics team at the White City Games in London, was arrested for stealing hats from an Oxford Street shop, and the Soviet government withdrew its team from the games in protest. The CPGB publicly disagreed with Moscow's actions.

16   The Socialist Party of Great Britain was formed in 1904 from a split in the Social Democratic Federation. It is most noted for its insistence upon a full socialist programme to be implemented peacefully by way of a parliamentary majority.

17   Pat Jordan (1928–2001) joined the CPGB in the mid-1940s; he left the party shortly after the debacle of 1956, was then active in independent left-wing politics in Nottingham, then joined a Trotskyist group, the Revolutionary Socialist League, led by Ted Grant. In 1961, he split from the RSL and helped form the International Group, later the International Marxist Group. He was expelled from the IMG in the early 1980s, and remained a Marxist operating in the Labour Party in Hackney until stricken by ill-health.

18   Richard Clements, 'Opposition Group Start Paper in CP', *Tribune*, 20 July 1956. The relationship between *Tribune* and the CPGB at this juncture was very hostile, and the wording of this article shows that the former intended to portray *The Reasoner* as the journal of a faction, with all that this would imply within the party. The following was almost inviting the party leadership to clamp down on the journal and thereby hopefully provoke a factional response: 'The group which has assembled round *The Reasoner* already has strong support. They openly state that they are seeking out like-minded Communists both in England and abroad to continue the discussion which they have started. Their policy is to stay inside the party and fight it out with the "monolith". And nothing less than complete freedom of discussion is their aim.'

19   Rodney Hilton (1916–2002) joined the CPGB in the late 1930s and was later a member of its History Group; he lectured in mediaeval history at Birmingham University from the late 1940s; he left the CPGB in 1956 and remained a Marxist historian, writing many works on early British history

20   The Petőfi Circle was set up by members of the Dolgozó Ifjúság Szövetsége (DISZ – Union of Working Youth); it played an important part in the intellectual ferment during 1956. It was named after Sándor Petőfi (1823–1849), a leading Hungarian poet and revolutionary.

21   Mátyás Rákosi (1892–1971) joined the Hungarian Social-Democratic Party in 1910, and the Hungarian Communist Party in 1918; he served in the revolutionary government in Hungary in 1919, moved to the Soviet Union after its fall, and returned to Hungary in 1945. He became General Secretary of the Hungarian Communist Party in 1945, and was Deputy Prime Minister during 1945–52, and Prime Minister during 1952–53, periods which were marked by political repression and economic hardship. Soviet pressure led to his removal from his party post in June 1956, and he lived in

retirement in the Soviet Union.

22   From William Yeats' poem *Meditations in Time of Civil War*.

23   Helena Eilstein (1922–2009) was a Polish philosopher; she held leading positions in the Polish Academy of Science, emigrated to the USA in 1969 after being victimised in an anti-Semitic campaign, and returned to Poland in 1993.

24   Other articles included Paul Baran, 'On Soviet Themes'; Joshua Kunitz, 'Khrushchev and the Jews'; Alexander Leslie, 'Has the Communist Party a Future?'.

25   Thorstein Bunde Veblen (1857–1929) was a US economist and sociologist, best known for his *The Theory of the Leisure Class*, a critique of waste under capitalism.

The Communist Party and *The Reasoner*: Documents

* * *

I: Communist Party Executive Committee Statement on *The Reasoner*
From *World News*, 22 September 1956.

* * *

At the meeting of the Executive Committee held on 14 and 15 July, it was reported to the Executive Committee that a duplicated journal entitled *The Reasoner* had been published and circulated by Comrades EP Thompson of Halifax, and John Saville of Hull.

The Executive Committee was gravely concerned at this action, and decided to ask the Yorkshire District leadership to discuss the matter with Comrades Thompson and Saville and to report back to the Executive Committee in September.

The Yorkshire District Committee at its meeting on 22 July elected a commission of four comrades to meet Comrades Thompson and Saville. This meeting took place, and a report on the discussion was made to the Yorkshire District Committee on 18 August, attended by twenty-one members. Arising from the report and the discussion, at which Comrades Thompson and Saville were present and in which they both spoke, the following resolution was adopted by the Yorkshire District Committee: 'This District Committee asks Comrades Thompson and Saville to cease the publication of *The Reasoner*.'

The resolution was passed with one vote against and no abstentions. (The vote against was that of Comrade Thompson, who is a member of the Yorkshire District Committee, which Comrade Saville is not.)

Comrades Thompson and Saville were asked if they would like to consider the resolution and their attitude to it after the meeting, and all comrades urged them to accept the resolution. They replied that they would not need further time for consideration and declared their intention to refuse to abide by the decision of the District Committee.

On 26 August a further meeting of the Yorkshire District Committee was held to discuss the position arising from the decision of Comrades Thompson and Saville not to accept the District Committee resolution. Twenty-four members were present.

The following resolution was passed by fifteen votes to five, with two abstentions, two comrades having left the meeting before the final vote:

> The Yorkshire District Committee at its August meeting called on Comrades Saville and Thompson to cease publishing *The Reasoner*. The District Committee takes a grave view of the declaration made by these two comrades that they will not carry out the decision of the District Committee.
>
> The continued publication of *The Reasoner* constitutes a breach of party rule, practice and discipline, harmful to the party.
>
> As the principle involved is of national importance and there are comrades involved with the journal outside Yorkshire, we bring these facts to the notice of the Executive Committee, and ask them to deal with this matter.

The party leadership decided that while discussions with Comrades Thompson and Saville were proceeding, we should not give publicity in the party press to the question involved, in order not to prejudice the discussions.

The Executive Committee has no responsibility for the information which has in fact appeared in the non-party press.

Meeting with the Political Committee

When the Political Committee received a report of the 18 August meeting of the Yorkshire District Committee, it decided to request Comrades Thompson and Saville to attend a meeting of the Political Committee prior to the September meeting of the Executive Committee, in order that the Political Committee could be fully acquainted with the views of the two comrades, and could also convey its opinions to them.

This meeting took place on 31 August.

Comrades Saville and Thompson were asked to put their point of view, and the following are the principal points which they made.

1) They were two comrades with a long record of active work in the party taking a stand on a question of Communist principle.

2) They believed that there was a political crisis in the party which was not being reflected in the party press or in the statements of the party

leadership. The number of letters they had received — approximately 250 — as a result of publication of *The Reasoner* had further supported them in this belief.

3) The comrades in charge of official party organs had shown a reluctance to publish fully and freely the doubts of many party comrades.

4) For democratic centralism to operate properly, there must be free and open discussion. They recognised that the party has a degree of discipline quite different from any other organisation. They recognised that the view of the majority must prevail. But ideas were not developed by majority decision. Therefore theoretical problems must be thrashed out, and minority views must be allowed to be sustained and developed.

5) They therefore considered that there must be within the party a genuinely open forum — a journal in which discussion should take place free from direct intervention by the Executive Committee.

6) They were not engaged in factional activity because a faction involved a difference in policy and approach. Comrades Thompson and Saville also said that they could not discontinue publication of *The Reasoner* because of pledges which they had given to others, and that even if they ceased publishing it, there were others who would do so.

7) They put forward the following proposals as the basis for what they said they were ready to accept as 'a compromise':

a) That after the second issue, further issues of *The Reasoner* should be suspended until the party conference, where a vote will be taken defining rule and practice, or urging revision of rule; and that they would determine their future action in the light of that vote.

b) That in lieu of the third issue of *The Reasoner*, there will be published in November a duplicated journal/booklet (not entitled *The Reasoner*) containing articles and letters debating the question of the right of publication. Such a publication to be edited jointly by Comrades Thompson and Saville and two members appointed by the Executive Committee or Yorkshire District Committee; to be of a length not less than *The Reasoner*; and the Executive Committee actively to encourage its circulation and discussion in the party.

They also considered that ex-party members who have not engaged in anti-party statements or activities should be allowed to contribute to the journal. They further expected some pledge of good faith from the Executive Committee that they would permit a full and fair discussion of the issue at the conference and would not bulldoze it from the platform.

(These proposals were made prior to the Political Committee meeting in letters to Comrades Bert Ramelson[1] and Howard Hill[2] from Comrade Thompson.)

8) If disciplinary action against them was contemplated, they asked the Executive Committee to consider what would be the consequences of such disciplinary action on other party members and on the wider labour movement.

The Political Committee explained to Comrades Thompson and Saville that they had been guilty of a grave breach of party rule, practice and discipline, and that whatever their motives, the results of their actions were doing grave harm to the party.

First, they had produced a political journal dealing with Communist Party policy, without any consultation with, or any decision by, any elected committee of the party. Not even their own party branches had been consulted, nor had the Yorkshire District Committee or the Executive Committee been approached.

No one had elected them, and they were responsible to no one but themselves.

They had placed themselves above the party and had acted purely as individuals and without any regard for the collective leadership of the party at any level.

At a time when the party was endeavouring to improve collective leadership at every level and learn the lessons of the Twentieth Congress of the CPSU, they were in practice repudiating collective leadership.

Second, they had not only not observed party rules and procedure in bringing out the first number of *The Reasoner*, but they were now declaring that they refused to accept a decision of the Yorkshire District Committee, arrived at after prolonged and democratic discussion, and voted for by twenty members of the District Committee with only Comrade Thompson voting against.

Third, the Political Committee pointed out to Comrades Thompson and Saville that if they claimed the right to publish their own political journal, they could not deny that right to others. Any individuals or groups of individuals, disagreeing with any aspect of the democratically-decided policy of the party at any time, would be entitled to produce their own political journals and circulate them.

Far from being democratic, this situation would be the negation of democracy. For such journals would be completely beyond the control of the party membership, and would be produced by individuals not elected by or responsible to the membership, but who had the necessary time and money to produce the journals and distribute them.

Thus the right of the membership as a whole would be gravely damaged as a result of the individuals concerned insisting on their 'individual right' to produce political journals. Such a position could lead to the growth of a whole series of factional groups, and disrupt the unity of the party.

The only way to protect the rights of all members, including those who disagree with existing party policy, is for the party press to be the responsibility of the elected committees of the party, which have the duty to ensure full and adequate discussion and can be called to account by the membership if they do not do so.

The Executive Committee must have regard to the party membership as a whole, by whom it was elected through the National Congress, and must safeguard the rights of the members as laid down in the party rules.

It was also pointed out to Comrades Thompson and Saville that if they had the right to defy majority decisions, that right could not be denied to all other party members, at all levels of the party. They might argue 'special circumstances'; but everyone who ever defied a majority decision considered that there were 'special circumstances' justifying it.

Fourth, the question of factionalism was not as presented by Comrades Thompson and Saville. The essence of factionalism is the taking of steps which cut across the democratic organisation of the party. Once steps are taken which ignore or by-pass the party branches and the elected committees of the party, then whatever the motives of those taking such steps, inevitably a separate organisation begins to be built up, and tendencies are set in motion which in the end can lead to different leaderships, different centres, and different policies appearing in the party.

Already, as was clear from the statement of Comrades Thompson and Saville, a network of correspondence had been created around *The Reasoner*. At least one meeting had been held involving party members other than Comrades Thompson and Saville. Comrade Thompson had circularised all subscribers to the first issue.

Irrespective of the motives of the initiators, to publish a journal without reference to the elected committees of the party was bound to lead to the development of a faction.

The party can only have one leadership — that which is democratically elected by the party members.

It can only have one policy — that which is democratically decided by the members through the party organisations and in accordance with the party rules.

To abandon these fundamental principles of Communist organisation would be to render the party impotent to carry through the tasks and responsibilities placed upon it in the course of the class struggle.

Fifth, the Political Committee pointed out to Comrades Thompson and Saville that full facilities for discussion existed in the party.

The Executive Committee has established two commissions, one on inner-party democracy and the other on *The British Road to Socialism*. The first of these is dealing precisely with such questions affecting democratic centralism as Comrades Thompson and Saville wish to have discussed. They have the same right as every other member of the party to put their views to the commission, but they have not done so. Nor have they put their views to the commission on *The British Road to Socialism*.

Not only are the commissions meeting, but discussions have been or are on the point of being initiated in the party press on working-class unity, inner-party democracy and *The British Road to Socialism*. It is difficult to imagine any aspect of party policy or practice not covered by these three subjects. But no contributions to any of these discussions have been received from Comrades Thompson and Saville.

The Political Committee pointed out that the Executive Committee was showing by its actions that it was desirous of stimulating the most thoroughgoing and serious discussion on party policy and organisation, to which every member and party organisation had the duty to contribute, and in which differing points of view should receive expression.

But Comrades Thompson and Saville were in practice refusing to participate in this discussion. It was they, and not the Executive Committee, who were operating in a completely undemocratic way.

Comrades Thompson and Saville spoke of 'free discussion' as if everything anyone cared to write must automatically be published. But every publication has to be edited, and a choice has to be made as to what shall appear and what shall not appear. They, in fact, stated that they had decided that a certain article should not appear in *The Reasoner*.

Thus they were admitting the necessity of 'control', but saying that the control should be exercised by self-appointed individuals rather than elected committees of the party.

Sixth, if Comrades Thompson and Saville objected to the principles of democratic centralism or to its operation as laid down in the party rules, they had every right to express this view and work within the party to secure the amendment of the rules at the next party congress. The way in which all party members can put their views forward on all questions of policy and organisation is laid down in the party rules, and constitutes a democratic procedure which no other political organisation in Britain can equal. But in the meantime, they had the duty to abide by the rules.

But they could not expect the Executive Committee to give them extra rights denied to all other members, including the right to defy majority decisions, and then expect the Executive Committee to discuss possible future developments of party policy and organisation with them on that basis. They were in fact asking the Executive Committee to put itself in the position of saying that party rules and discipline had been infringed, but that it would accept this breach pending a discussion on whether or not it is permissible to flout the rules and discipline of the party. For the Executive Committee to do this would be a failure on its part to fulfil one of the most important responsibilities entrusted to it by the membership — the safeguarding of the rules and principles on which the party is based.

The Political Committee therefore asked Comrades Thompson and Saville to cease publication of *The Reasoner*. The meeting was adjourned to give them the opportunity to consider this.

After the adjournment Comrades Thompson and Saville said that they could not agree to the decision of the Political Committee.

They were asked to consider the matter further during the next few days, and to write in prior to the September meeting of the Executive Committee.

The following letters were received.

5 September 1956

This is to confirm our statement at the conclusion of the special meeting of the Political Committee last Friday.

We consider it to be in the fundamental interest of the party that the fullest and frankest discussion shall continue. Since you were unable to give us either assurances or effective guarantees that it shall continue in other forms, we regard it as a question of Communist principle to continue publishing *The Reasoner*, and the second number is in active preparation.

EP Thompson

5 September 1956.

You asked us individually to write to you as Chairman of the PC concerning the matter of *The Reasoner*, and whether we still abide by our decision.

I have to inform you that the answer we gave the PC on Friday last has not changed, and that we stand by our decision.

I should like to express my personal appreciation of the way in which the PC received us, and the hearing which was given to our case. We could not have been treated more fairly and sympathetically.

John Saville

A full report on the above facts and discussions was made to the 8-9 September meeting of the Executive Committee.

After discussion the following resolution was unanimously passed:

> The Executive Committee has received a report on the discussions which have taken place between Comrades EP Thompson and John Saville, the Yorkshire District Committee and the Political Committee regarding the publication of *The Reasoner*.
>
> It regrets that the comrades concerned refused to agree to the request of the Yorkshire District Committee and the Political Committee to give an undertaking not to produce any further issues of *The Reasoner*.
>
> The Executive Committee now instructs Comrades Thompson and Saville to cease publication of *The Reasoner*.

In the event of Comrades Thompson and Saville agreeing to abide by the rules of the party and accepting the same responsibilities as all other party members, any question or any proposal whatever which they wish to put before the Executive Committee will receive the utmost consideration.

The Executive Committee publishes this statement in order that all party members and organisations can be aware of the position in relation to *The Reasoner*.

* * *

II: *The Reasoner*: Statement by Communist Party Executive Committee
From *World News*, 27 October 1956.

* * *

The Executive Committee of the Communist Party has issued the following statement.

After the meeting of the Executive Committee on 8 and 9 September a letter was sent to Comrades EP Thompson and John Saville conveying to them the instruction of the Executive Committee that they should cease publication of *The Reasoner*. They were subsequently sent a copy of the Executive Committee's full statement on the question.

On 19 September Comrades John Gollan and George Matthews met Comrades Thompson and Saville, discussed with them questions arising from the decision of the Executive Committee, and urged them to accept this decision.

On 11 October the following letter was received from Comrades Thompson and Saville.

7 October

Dear Comrade Gollan

Thank you for your letter. We are sorry not to have replied before about *The Reasoner*. After our discussions with you we thought about the matter once again very carefully, and it is only in the last few days that we have come to a decision.

While we appreciate your general assurances about the intention of the leadership to promote and extend discussion, we are not at all satisfied that this can in fact take place adequately in the present forms: nor are we satisfied that within the present very serious political context, the power of judgement as to what should or should not be discussed and the way in which discussion should be conducted, can or ought to be left in the sole control of the Executive Committee, without effective safeguards of one sort or another defining and protecting the rights of minorities in written discussion. The discussion on the central questions — which can best be defined for the moment as 'Stalinism' and its influence upon our own theory and practice — has scarcely even begun in our party, and it would be a very serious setback for our movement if it was now curbed or guided into channels decided beforehand by considerations of expediency. Whatever may be said about recent practice, this would seem to us an infringement of the understood right of all comrades to discuss basic questions of theory and practice, and would be regarded as such by ourselves and many others.

However, we recognise at the same time that owing to the uncompromising attitude of the EC, and its unwillingness even at a time of theoretical ferment like the present to provide (as yet) adequate facilities or safeguards, there may be some danger that the attention concentrated upon the particular issue of *The Reasoner* may divert comrades from the general question of securing their basic rights within the party.

We therefore propose to bring *The Reasoner* to a close at the third number. We hope that there is sufficient concern throughout the party to enforce the continuation of the discussion; and we ourselves have several proposals which we would like to put to you after the closure.

We hope that this decision will make it possible for comrades to continue their efforts to extend and safeguard their rights, without any diversion into secondary or personal issues.

Yours fraternally

Edward Thompson

John Saville

The following reply was sent to Comrades Thompson and Saville on 16 October.

16 October 1956

Dear Comrade

I received your letter of 7 October on 11 October, and its contents have been communicated to the members of the Executive Committee.

The Executive Committee has asked me to reply to you as follows.

The September meeting of the Executive Committee, for the reasons given in its statement (a copy of which was sent to you), instructed you to cease publication of *The Reasoner*. At the time of the Executive Committee meeting you were in process of bringing out a second number, and you did in fact publish this after the Executive Committee meeting.

You now inform the Executive Committee that you propose to bring out a third number. This is a clear and deliberate refusal to abide by a decision of the Executive Committee. It indicates that you have no intention of abiding by the rules of the party and accepting the same responsibilities as all other party members.

For two individual members to disregard the democratic procedure of the party, refuse to abide by the decisions of its elected committees, and act without responsibility to anyone but themselves and without guidance or control by any committee elected by the party members, is the reverse of democratic practice.

We urge you accordingly very seriously to reconsider your position, and to accept your responsibilities as party members at the same time as you avail yourselves of the rights and opportunities of party members to raise and discuss any points of difference within the party, and help to improve and develop its methods of work and policy.

The Executive Committee is giving full facilities for discussion in the party press, is encouraging the maximum discussion of party policy and organisation in every party organisation, and has convened a National Party Conference to take place in March 1957. It has asked the whole party to discuss and make proposals for the better democratic functioning of the party, and the question of party democracy will be one of the two main items for discussion at the National Conference.

If, despite all this, you are not satisfied with the present forms and organisation of discussion within the party, you have the same rights as all other party members to make proposals for changing them.

The Executive Committee has the duty to protect the party, uphold its rules, democracy and discipline, and safeguard the rights of the party membership as a whole.

In accordance with its decision in September, the Executive Committee therefore specifically instructs you not to bring out a third number of *The Reasoner.*

We shall be glad to receive your undertaking that you intend to carry out this instruction of the Executive Committee.

Yours fraternally

John Gollan

General Secretary

III: Statement by the Executive Committee of the Communist Party on *The Reasoner*

From *World News*, 17 November 1956.

* * *

The following statement was unanimously adopted by the Executive Committee at its meeting on 10-11 November.

The Executive Committee of the Communist Party has considered the position of Comrades EP Thompson and John Saville in the light of the publication of the third number of *The Reasoner.*

This has been published in defiance of repeated decisions of leading committees of the party that publication of *The Reasoner* should cease.

Members of the party knew that for many months the Executive Committee has made patient efforts to solve by agreement the difficult problems created by the decision of Comrades Thompson and Saville to publish *The Reasoner.*

At its July meeting the Executive Committee asked the Yorkshire District Committee to discuss the publication of *The Reasoner* with Comrades Thompson and Saville, arising from the first issue.

The Yorkshire Committee asked them to cease publication. They refused to agree. The Political Committee met them on 31 August and asked them to cease publication. They again refused, and published a second issue early in September.

The September meeting of the Executive Committee then instructed them to cease publication of *The Reasoner.* They replied on 7 October, saying that they proposed to produce a third number. The Executive Committee then specifically instructed them not to publish a third issue. They did not answer.

They have now produced this third number, in spite of these repeated instructions not to do so.

Further, in this third number they have advanced a number of demands to the Executive Committee in an editorial statement, in connection with the events in Eastern Europe, and follow up these demands by saying:

> If these demands are not met, we urge all those who, like ourselves, will dissociate themselves completely from the leadership of the British Communist Party, not to lose faith in socialism, and to find ways of keeping together. We promise our readers that we will consult with others about the early formation of a new socialist journal.

Thus, not only have they refused to accept majority decisions and carry out the same responsibilities as other Communist Party members, but they now make a statement which can only be interpreted either as an intention to try to form alternative leadership within the party to that of its elected committees (that is, a faction), or as advice to party members to leave the party and rally to an alternative grouping.

They are attempting to influence the policy of the party by this threat. In the first number of *The Reasoner* they said: 'It is no part of the aim of this journal to encourage the formation of political factions.' In the third number they announce their intention to form one.

In the first number they emphasised that *The Reasoner* was purely a *discussion* journal. But the last number is utilised for a full-scale attack on the current policy of the party and a call to others to join in an organised effort to prevent that policy from being operated.

The issue here involved is not disagreement or otherwise with the policy of the party. Members have the right to disagree, to maintain their disagreement and to endeavour within the party, in accordance with its democratic procedures, to win the majority for their point of view.

But Comrades Thompson and Saville have shown that they are not prepared to work democratically to change the policy of the party. They have operated outside the party organisation and procedure, without reference to the party membership, and without responsibility to the party's elected committees, and declare their intention now to organise with others to defy the party unless the Executive Committee accepts their particular demands.

The gravity of the present position, and the discussions going on in the party, make the discipline of the party and the observance by all members of party decisions more important than ever.

The Executive Committee cannot, therefore, ignore the undemocratic, undisciplined and disruptive activity of Comrades Thompson and Saville.

It decides to suspend them from the Communist Party for a period of three months for refusal to carry out party decisions, and for conduct detrimental to the party; and to review their position at the end of that period of suspension.

NOTES

1 Bert Ramelson (Baruch Ramilevich Mendelson, 1910-1994) was born in Ukraine, grew up in Canada, and settled in Britain in 1939 after fighting in the Spanish Civil War. He became a full-time worker for the CPGB after his military service, and became its Industrial Organiser in 1966. He was a staunch opponent of the Eurocommunist trends that developed in the CPGB from the 1970s.
2 Howard Hill (1913-?) was an electrician and a member of the Labour Party in Sheffield; he joined the CPGB in 1940 but maintained Labour Party membership until he was expelled in 1946. He was the Secretary of the Sheffield CPGB branch until 1975.

THE REASONER
A JOURNAL OF DISCUSSION

Edited by
JOHN SAVILLE and E. P. THOMPSON

"To leave error unrefuted is to encourage intellectual immorality" - Marx

Final Number   Price 2/-   November 1956

MAIN CONTENTS

EDITORIAL

This final number of The Reasoner was planned several weeks ago: most of it was typed and duplicated before the events of the past fortnight in Poland and Hungary.

Three days before publication, Eden launched his brutal aggression against Egypt. Every one of our readers will be fully occupied in organising protests and demonstrations of every kind, to end this war and to bring down the Government. Our first thought was to withdraw or postpone this number while the emergency lasts.

But even while we considered, Soviet forces surrounded Budapest and, as we write these lines, we hear the tragic news of the attack on the city.

Even the urgency of the Egyptian crisis cannot disguise the fact that the events of Budapest represent a crucial turning-point for our Party. The aggression of British imperialism is uglier and more cynical in degree than previous imperialist aggressions. But the crisis in world Communism is now different in kind.

"And furthermore I don't know why you take up this position
regarding Democratic Centralism."

-from the Rumanian satirical magazine STERCHEL

The Reasoner: A Journal of Discussion
Edited by John Saville and E P Thompson

To leave error unrefuted is to encourage intellectual immorality. – Marx

Final Number

November 1956

Editorial

This final number of *The Reasoner* was planned several weeks ago: most of it was typed and duplicated before the events of the past fortnight in Poland and Hungary.

Three days before publication, Eden launched his brutal aggression against Egypt. Every one of our readers will be fully occupied in organising protests and demonstrations of every kind, to end this war and to bring down the government. Our first thought was to withdraw or postpone this number while the emergency lasts.

But even while we considered, Soviet forces surrounded Budapest and, as we write these lines, we hear the tragic news of the attack on the city.

Even the urgency of the Egyptian crisis cannot disguise the fact that the events of Budapest represent a crucial turning-point for our party. The aggression of British imperialism is uglier and more cynical in degree than previous imperialist aggressions. But the crisis in world Communism is now different in kind.

The intervention of Soviet troops in Hungary must be condemned by all Communists. The working people and students of Budapest were demonstrating against an oppressive regime which gave them no adequate democratic channels for expressing the popular will. The fact that former fascists and those working for the restoration of capitalism joined the revolutionaries does not alter this central issue. The criminal blunder of unleashing Security Police and Soviet forces against these crowds provoked the mass of the people to take up arms, in the name of independence, liberty and justice, against an oppression that was operated in the name of Communism. Those Hungarian comrades of ours who were innocent of the corruptions and abuses of the Rákosi regime were placed in a horrifying and tragic dilemma. The Soviet intervention unleashed the counter-revolution – the mob violence, ultra-nationalist passions – which it was designed to prevent. No doubt Western agents were hurried into Hungary and we do not doubt the reports that a White Terror was beginning in Budapest, but the responsibility for these developments lies squarely on the shoulders of the former Stalinist Party of Hungary and of the Soviet generals and political leaders who sanctioned the use of their forces.

During the critical days when it seemed possible that the situation might be stabilised and Hungary find a similar way forward to that of Poland, the continued presence of Soviet troops added fuel to counter-revolutionary flames. One thing only might have restrained the Soviet forces from their final criminal action – an outspoken call for restraint from the Communist parties of the world.

In this crisis, when the Hungarian people needed our solidarity, the British Communist Party has failed them. We cannot wait until the Twenty-First Congress of the CPSU, when no doubt the attack on Budapest will be registered as another 'mistake'. The international Communist movement, and also the World Peace movement, must exert its full moral influence to effect the immediate withdrawal of Soviet troops from Hungary: at the same time demanding the neutralisation of Hungary and resisting all Western attempts to turn the situation to their military and political advantage.

The EC of the British party must at once:

1) Dissociate itself publicly from the action of the Soviet Union in Hungary.

2) Demand the immediate withdrawal of Soviet troops.

3) Proclaim full and unequivocal solidarity with the Polish Workers Party.

4) Call District Congresses of our party immediately and a National Congress in the New Year.

If these demands are not met, we urge all those who, like ourselves, will dissociate themselves completely from the leadership of the British Communist Party, not to lose faith in socialism, and to find ways of keeping together. We promise our readers that we will consult with others about the early formation of a new socialist journal.

In attacking Budapest the Soviet Union has struck a blow at the moral authority of the international working-class movement. Only the political demands outlined above will give the right to Communists to play a part in ending British aggression in Egypt, and in restraining those Western generals and politicians who will see the present situation in Eastern Europe as an opportunity to unleash a new war.

Sunday, 4 November 1956

E P Thompson, Through the Smoke of Budapest

Stalinism has sown the wind, and now the whirlwind centres on Hungary. As I write the smoke is still rising above Budapest.

It is true that dollars have also been sown in this embittered soil. But the crop which is rising will surely not turn out to be the one which Mr Dulles expected – some new Syngman Rhee for Eastern Europe, backed by a fraudulent Chancellery and a Papal Junta?

By an angry twist of history, it seems that the crop is coming up as students', workers' and soldiers' councils, as 'anti-Soviet' soviets.

I do not know how things will be when this is published. Will Russian troops withdraw soon enough to prevent the country from being engulfed in waves of nationalist fury and anarchy? Will a new, honest government of Communists and others succeed in wresting calm from the passions of the moment – calm enough to ensure some justice, more mercy, and that the will of the people finds expression?

It is all that we dare hope for. But – leaving aside such groups of counter-revolutionaries as there must have been – those youths and workers of Budapest who first threw up barricades against the Soviet tanks, surely they did not wish to embrace the 'American Century'? Nor can they then, unless in desperation, have found comfort in the hypocritical appeal to the Security Council of governments blooded to the elbow from their exploits in Kenya, Cyprus, Algeria – and now Egypt.

No chapter would be more tragic in international socialist history, if the Hungarian people, who once before lost their revolution to armed reaction, were driven into the arms of the capitalist powers by the crimes of a Communist government and the uncomprehending violence of Soviet armies.

And so I hope that the Communist Party, my party, will regain the support of the working people. But *where* is my party in Hungary? Was it in the broadcasting station or on the barricades? And *what* is it? Is it a cluster of security officials and discredited bureaucrats? Or is it a party 'rooted in the people' of town and countryside, capable of self-purification and new growth?

We will read the answer in its actions. I hope we will hear less about 'rooting out' this and that, 'ruthlessly smashing' this and that, and more about learning from the people, serving the people, and honouring Communist principle.

I know that our Hungarian comrades will recall the prayer of their great patriot, Kossuth,[1] over one hundred years ago:

> Send, O God! the genial rays of the sun, that flowers may spring from this holy blood, that the bodies of my brethren may not perish in lifeless corruption … As a free man, I kneel on the fresh graves of my brethren. Sacrifices like these sanctify the earth, they purge it of sin. My God! a people of slaves must not live on this sacred soil, nor step on these graves!

* * *

I had intended in this article to attempt some definitions of Stalinism, to enter into some questions of theory which our British leadership refuses to discuss, and to consult with readers upon the best way to rid our own party of Stalinist theory and practice.

But these points of theory have now found dramatic expression in the great square of Warsaw and amid the smoke of Budapest. It is difficult to speak at all in the teeth of a whirlwind. And if we have helped, in small degree, to sow that wind, do we have the right to speak?

And yet someone must speak. The *Daily Worker*, in its editorial columns, has done nothing to express our thoughts or to assert our honour in the past few weeks.

One week before the fighting commenced in Hungary, it published an editorial, 'No Vengeance'. This declared that 'the difficulties created by the past violations of socialist legality are being patiently solved'. A crowd of 200,000 had attended the reburial of László Rajk, and voices were raised calling for the trial and punishment of those responsible for his execution:

> The anguish of the kinsmen and friends of these dead Communists is understandable; but it would be distressing to Hungary's friends throughout the world if new trials were to disturb the life of the Hungarian people and blot the 'clean, new page' that their party has now embarked on. Surely the time has come to temper justice with mercy and to look, not to the past, but to the bright future that a hard-working people and a party united as never before can build together.[2]

Good little hard-working people! We do not wish to 'disturb' your life. Your party has embarked you on a new page. You may rest content.

But the population of Hungary is nine million. And a crowd of 200,000 does not often assemble from the whole of Britain.

What thoughts passed through the minds of these people as they stood by this seven-year-old grave at this strange funeral?

Did they recall that Béla Kun, leader of the Hungarian Soviet Republic of 1919, had found an obscure and wretched death in the Soviet Union in the 1930s? That the Comintern had acquiesced in this betrayal and laid its botching hand upon their revolutionary movement while Horthy's White Guards stamped through their capital city?

Did they wonder how it was possible for their leaders – Rákosi, Gerő,[3] Farkas[4] and the rest – to allow their comrade László Rajk, ex-International Brigader and victim of Nazi concentration camps, to be dragged through public execration to a traitor's shameful death?

'One cannot plan human consciousness', says our Comrade Gomułka.[5] I think that this is a good thing, despite the tragic outcome in this case. Certainly, the same men cannot switch off 'violations of socialist legality' and switch on a 'clean, new page' like an electric light. Nor can the moral responses of a people be switched by government edicts.

And what is 'socialist legality', by the way? Is it justice? Or is it as much justice as is expedient when the people are very angry?

Apart from the Poznań trials, I cannot remember any recent examples of 'socialist legality' which can be recognised as acts of justice.

And what was this justice which (in the editorial view of the *Daily Worker*) had been so stern and unrelenting that 'the time has come' to temper it with mercy? I do not recall any trials of those responsible for 'violations of socialist legality' in Hungary or elsewhere, although Beria seems to be dead and I have read of some cursory shootings in Azerbaijan. Whether these were just or not, neither I nor the Editor of the *Daily Worker* know.

And why should the *Daily Worker* assume that any *just* trial would *blot* any 'clean, new page'? And why should Hungarian party members assume that their party *had* embarked on such a page, when they had not been consulted through any congress? Why should it assume that the party was 'united as never before' when the members had recently learned that one part of its Central Committee had butchered the other part to placate a man whom we are now told was all along the agent of the 'Mussavat intelligence service'?

And why should the Hungarian people be confident that such a leadership was about to build them a 'bright future'?

And why should the *Daily Worker* call for 'no vengeance', in the interests of hushing up truth and perverting justice in a case where the facts were becoming unpleasantly clear, when – so far as my memory goes – it had never before called for 'no vengeance' in any of the more dubious trials in socialist countries?

Why – and this is the real question – did the *Daily Worker*, which has for so long rejected letters and trimmed editorials to ensure that we do not 'intervene' in the affairs of a brother party, suddenly speak in the name of British Communists to assure the Hungarian authorities that 'it would be distressing to Hungary's friends throughout the world' if these guilty men were brought to trial?

I do not want to see vengeance. We have all had our fill of executions. But justice demands that criminals are tried for their crimes, and their associates shown out of public life.

I know very well that the knots tied by Stalinism cannot be untied in a day. But the first step on the road back to Communist principle is that we tell the truth and show confidence in the judgement of the people. After the Twentieth Congress (said Gomułka) 'people began to straighten their backs, silent enslaved minds began to shake off the poison of mendacity. Above all, the working people wanted to know all the truth, without embellishments and omissions.' Our own need for truth is no less.

On 29 October, almost a week *after* the Budapest rising, the *Daily Worker* found a new editorial explanation:

> It is a tragedy that the leadership of the party and the government did not act more promptly in putting right those economic and political wrongs that were causing such deep discontent among the masses.

Too true. And if the Stalinists in Hungary attended to the advice given to them by the *Daily Worker* ten days before, it will have contributed to that fatal delay which triggered the revolt. And in that case, a part of the bloodshed in Budapest lies on British heads.

* * *

In the next few days, with the dramatic events in Poland, the *Daily Worker* sat awkwardly on the fence, with its editorial legs on the wrong side.

I can think of few moments so moving, so significant for the future of the international working-class movement, as those when our courageous comrade Władysław Gomułka emerged from gaol and calumny and found for the Polish people a narrow passage through to a creative future, between the rocks of counter-revolution on the one hand and of armed intervention on the other. All honour to the maturity, self-discipline and confident initiative of the Polish people!

But the *Daily Worker* could see none of these things. It could not (editorially) even see the excellent reports of Gordon Cruickshank[6] in its own columns. For two days running it could see nothing but speeches by Eisenhower, 'wild rumours … in the capitalist press', 'divisions in the popular ranks', new 'Piłsudskis':[7]

> The imperialists may see some cause for rejoicing, but they might well be seeing things, things that are not there. Time, of course, will resolve doubts as it will dispel hopes. We are not astrologers, but we have faith in the working class, and that includes the working class of Poland. (23 October)

Time (of course) has dispelled doubts in the shape of half a million people demonstrating peacefully in Warsaw's greatest square. Time has not yet dispelled doubts as to the competence of our Editorial Department of Failed Astrology.

The only serious doubts (apart from these) of that weekend have now been partially dispelled: would the Soviet Union commit the crime of launching a cold or hot war against the new Polish Communist government? If the *Daily Worker* had advice to give, it should have sent it to this quarter. Editorials in the international Communist press, calling for restraint from the Soviet party, might have had a salutary effect, here and on events in Hungary. Such advice would have been endorsed by the great majority of British Communists.

But from start to finish, our paper – in the name of all of us – has sent the *wrong* advice and sent it to the *wrong* address.

* * *

Back to Hungary. On Tuesday night, 23 October, demonstrations by students and others led on to general rioting and bloodshed in Budapest. No facts were clear. Had counter-revolutionary groups, aided from outside, laid sparks on the tinder of an embittered population? Where did the working class of Budapest stand? We anxiously awaited information.

On Thursday morning the answers were given:

> Counter-revolution in Hungary staged an uprising in the hours of darkness on Tuesday night. The Hungarian working class rallied around its government and party and smashed this attempt to put the clock back. The capitalist press rejoiced too soon and what it rejoiced about was the shooting of shop stewards, Socialists and Communists by armed detachments of terrorists. (25 October)

No evidence was given for these statements. Our Department of Failed Astrology had learnt nothing from the Twentieth Congress, Poznań, Warsaw in October.

It is a small point, but I cannot find in any reports references to the murder of shop stewards. Perhaps this was only a harmless device to rouse the indignation of British trade unionists?

It is also a pity that the *Daily Worker* showed few signs of editorial indignation when it was first revealed that under Rákosi's regime a great many Communists, Socialists and trade unionists were imprisoned and shot.

> Soviet troops have answered the call of the Hungarian government for assistance precisely because those troops are acting in solidarity with the Hungarian people to defend the socialist system. (26 October)

It is comforting to know that history is always so 'precise' in its movements. In fact, the Soviet intervention vastly aggravated the situation and greatly embittered the people. If we are to use Stalinist terms, the Soviet tanks were 'objectively' inflaming 'counter-revolution'.

I find it a profound source of shame that a Communist government should have become so corrupt, so isolated from the people, that in a time of crisis it could find no protection in the arms of its own working class.

> Let every local Labour Party and Communist Party branch, every trade-union branch and executive committee, every Labour MP, send telegrams to the Hungarian government condemning the counter-revolutionary violence and standing by the government and people ... (25 October)

No, no, no, no! This is not work for us. Shame on this indecent haste, shame on this breach of solidarity, shame on those who wished to rush in the moral armaments of the British working class behind Gerő's security police, to destroy these students and young workers in the streets!

Is our party leadership bent on making a miniature Poland or Hungary out of our party? How far from reality, from our labour movement, must they be to print such an appeal at such a time? Our membership has had enough.

* * *

It is time that we had this out. From start to finish, from February onwards, our leadership has sided (evasively at times, perhaps) with Stalinism.

This is not to say that they have defended the memory of Stalin, or seriously questioned the dishonest attempt to make one man a scapegoat for the sins of an historical epoch.

On the contrary, they have run two lines of argument. First, all these 'wrong things' (which we 'could not know about') were associated with the influence of one man in Russia, and the 'cult' of his 'personality': second, Stalin's theory was admirable but (unknown to us) an alarming gap grew up between his theory and his practice.

Convenient arguments, these, for our leadership: since they absolve us from all responsibility for having passed 'wrong information' and justified 'wrong things': since they absolve them from all need to drive out the influence of Stalinism upon their own theory and practice, and that of our party.

But there *is* one 'wrong theory' of Stalin's which we are licensed to criticise: the theory of the intensification of the class struggle. All right, let us look at it. The theory derives, in fact, from Lenin – thrown out in a fluid situation of revolutionary crisis, and, like so much else, wrested out of context by Stalin and turned into a stone axiom:

> Certain comrades interpreted the thesis on the abolition of classes, the establishment of a classless society and the dying out of the state, to mean justification of laziness and complacency, justification of the counter-revolutionary theory of the subsiding of the class struggle and the weakening of state authority. Needless to say, such people cannot have anything in common with our party. These are either degenerates, or double dealers, who must be driven out of the party. The abolition of classes is not achieved by subduing the class struggle but by intensifying it. The state will die out not by the weakening of state authority, but by strengthening it to the utmost necessary for the purpose of finally crushing the remnants of the dying classes and for organising defence against the capitalist environment ... (Stalin, *Report to January 1933 Plenum, CPSU(b)*)[8]

Take out this one 'wrong theory' and this whole passage falls apart, and shows itself to be corrupt. The theory of the all-powerful, centralised state is wrong – our comrades in Poland and Yugoslavia are proving this in life. The attitude towards the role of the party, and towards party comrades, is wrong.

And the Stalinist theory of the dictatorship of the proletariat is wrong. Once again, Stalin made out of Lenin's words a stone axiom:

> The dictatorship of the proletariat is the domination of the proletariat over the bourgeoisie, untrammelled by law and based on violence and enjoying the sympathy and support of the toiling and exploited masses. (Stalin, *Foundations of Leninism*)[9]

As we learn from Hungary, such a dictatorship need not for long command the sympathy of the toiling masses: nor would it do in Britain. This is indeed a far cry from Engels' definition of the 'two infallible expedients' which distinguish this phase of transition: election to all positions by universal suffrage, with the right of recall residing in the electors; and all officials to receive workers' wages (Introduction, *Civil War in France*).

And the identification of all disagreement, all opposition, all hesitation, with 'objective' counter-revolution is wrong. It permeates Stalin's writings and the *History of the CPSU(b)* (upon which a generation of our full-timers have received their education) from end to end:

> The opposition has ideologically broken with Leninism ... and has objectively become a tool of counter-revolution against the regime of the proletarian dictatorship ... To attain victory, the party of the working class, its directing staff, its advanced fortress, must first be purged of capitulators, deserters, scabs and traitors. (*History of the CPSU(b)*, pp. 289, 360)

And the military vocabulary of Stalinism is wrong, and strange and offensive to the ears of the British working class.

And the attitude to discussion is wrong. This should have been clear when, in 1931, Stalin branded the editors of a journal which had permitted a discussion of certain prewar theories of Lenin, for 'rotten liberalism', for 'stupidity bordering on crime, bordering on treason to the working class': 'Slander must be branded as such and not made the subject of discussion.'[10]

And the theory of the party is wrong, the theory that 'the party becomes strong by purging itself', the theory of the party's paternal, self-appointed mission and infallibility, the 'cult of the party' which submerges all loyalty to people, to principle, to the working class itself, in loyalty to the party's 'iron discipline'.

And the mechanical theory of human consciousness is wrong: the theory that historical science 'can become as precise a science as, let us say, biology': the subordination of the imaginative and moral faculties to political and administrative authority is wrong: the elimination of moral criteria from political judgement is wrong: the fear of independent thought, the deliberate encouragement of anti-intellectual trends amongst the people is wrong: the mechanical personification of unconscious class forces, the belittling of the conscious processes of intellectual and spiritual conflict, all this is wrong:

> The superstructure is created by the basis precisely in order to serve it, to actively help it to take shape and consolidate itself, to actively strive for the elimination of the old watchword basis, together with its superstructure … Desperately the old superstructure rallies to the defence of the basis that gave rise to it. (Stalin, *Marxism in Linguistics*; Klugmann, *Basis and Superstructure*)[11]

All these theories are not altogether wrong. But they are wrong enough to have brought our movement into international crisis. And it was mechanical idealism such as this, mounted on Soviet tanks, which fired through the smoke at the workers and young people of Budapest.

* * *

Stalinism is socialist theory and practice which has lost the ingredient of humanity. The Stalinist mode of thought is not that of dialectical materialism, but that of mechanical idealism. For example:

> … if the passing of slow quantitative changes into rapid and abrupt qualitative changes is a law of development, then it is clear that revolutions made by oppressed classes are a quite natural and inevitable phenomenon.
>
> Hence the transition from capitalism to socialism and the liberation of the working class from the yoke of capitalism cannot be effected by slow changes, by reforms, but only by a qualitative change of the capitalist system, by revolution.
>
> Hence, in order not to err in policy, one must be a revolutionary, not a reformist. (Stalin, *Dialectical and Historical Materialism*)[12]

The gap between Stalinist theory and practice is inherent in the theory. 'Truth is always concrete', wrote Lenin: but from the fluid movement of Lenin's analysis of particular social realities, Stalin plucked axioms. Stalinism is Leninism turned into stone.

Instead of commencing with facts, social reality, Stalinist theory starts with the idea, the text, the axiom: facts, institutions, people, must be brought to conform to the idea. Wheat is grown in hothouses to 'prove' a scientific theory: novels are written to 'prove' the correctness of the party line: trials are faked to 'prove' the 'objective' treason of the victims.

Stalinist analysis, at its most degenerate, becomes a scholastic exercise, the search for 'formulations' 'correct' in relation to text but not to life. And how often is this 'correct formulation' poised, mid-way between two deviations, one to the left, one to the right? 'To the question, which deviation was worse, Comrade Stalin replied, "One is as bad as the other ..."' Do the real choices of life present themselves in this mechanical way?

'He had completely lost consciousness of reality', declares Khrushchev. And he was not alone. This gap developed everywhere. It was this gap which defied Khrushchev's analysis: 'Not only a Marxist-Leninist but also no man of common sense can grasp how it was possible to make whole nations responsible for inimical activity.' Precisely so. But this is the irony of Stalin's career. Emerging as the most 'realistic', the 'strongest' Marxist, he limited his vision to the single task of holding and extending the power of the Soviet state. Tearing his severe, textual path through unprecedented complexities and dangers, he allowed one part of reality to escape him – the thoughts, prejudices, aspirations, of living men and women. Stalinism is at the opposite pole to common sense.

* * *

But never free from the restraint of common sense: rather, the Stalinist oscillates between the axiom and '*realpolitik*': dogmatism and opportunism. When the axioms cease to produce results, a 'mistake' is 'recognised'. Khrushchev's speech is made: the tanks withdraw from Budapest. But the theory is little changed. For Stalinism prevents a serious critique from emerging within the borders of its rule. And we, outside those borders, have also failed.

Stalinism was not 'wrong things' about which 'we could not know', but distorted theories and degenerate practices about which we knew something, in which, to some degree, we shared, and which our leadership supports today. Who does not know that our moral atrophy, our military vocabulary and structure, our paternalist outlook upon the people and their organisations, our taste for disseminating 'wrong information', our fear of popular initiatives independent of our guidance, our dislike of criticism, our secrecy and occasional bad faith with our friends – all these have crippled our propaganda, isolated us, and robbed our work of its right reward? And who does not know that it was our rank and file that was tainted least with these things, and our leadership most?

Our leaders do not wish to discuss this because they do not wish to change. At heart, they have always feared the 'thaw'. Their hearts lie with the Soviet tanks. After all, tanks are mechanical things, which will answer to controls and can consolidate power. 'Marxism-Leninism' is safe with them. But if people take initiative into their own hands … it is too great a risk.

And on the other side of the smoke, what do we hope for from the people of Poland, the workers and students of Budapest, when their wounds are healed and their national pride assuaged? First, I hope, a new respect for *people*, permeating the whole of society, its institutions, its social relations. And then, a new respect for truth, for principle. A democracy which does not limit its action within narrow limits defined by a paternal party, pronouncing anathema on all who stray outside, but one based on real confidence in the people's initiatives. A new understanding of the continuity of human culture. And finally, a new internationalism, based (among socialist countries) upon true independence and respect: and (among Communist parties) upon truthful exchanges and fraternal controversy – exchanges in which the membership, by personal and published contact, can take part.

* * *

The Polish and Hungarian people have written their critique of Stalinism upon their streets and squares. In doing so, they have brought back honour to the international Communist movement. These revolutions have been made by Communists; not it is true by those who arrogated to themselves all wisdom and authority, but by Communists just the same. Wherever this wind of Stalinism has been sown, Communists have also sown good socialist seed. The crop of human brotherhood will prevail, when the winds have passed away.

I recall a 'Christmas message' from my brother, which he wrote after meeting Communist partisans, in December 1943:

> There is a spirit abroad in Europe which is finer and braver than anything that tired continent has known for centuries, and which cannot be withstood. You can, if you like, think of it in terms of politics, but it is broader and more generous than any dogma. It is the confident will of whole peoples, who have known the utmost humiliation and suffering and who have triumphed over it, to build their own life once and for all.

It is the crime of Stalinism that it crabbed and confined this spirit, while many of those who are now greeting, with complacent self-approval, the exploits of the Polish and Hungarian peoples, themselves were feeding Stalinism with each strident anti-Communist speech, with the rearmament of Germany, with each twist of the Cold War.

Stalinism confined this spirit, but it was never killed. Today it walks abroad again, in full daylight, on Polish streets. It was present on the Budapest barricades, and today wrests with anarchy for the future of Hungary. Never was there a time when comrades of ours were in so great need of our solidarity, in the face of the blind resistance of Stalinism, the black passions of reaction.

This socialism of free people, and not of secret speeches and police, will prove *more* dangerous to our own imperialism than any Stalinist state. Its leaders will make mistakes enough, but not such 'mistakes' as destroy their own honour and the good name of the party.

We British Communists have a right and duty to greet our comrades in these lands of reborn principle.

Shame on our leaders for their silence!

Greetings to the Polish people! Honour to the working people, and students, who shed their blood at Budapest! May they regain mastery over their own future, and curb the mob passions unloosed by their ordeal!

And may it prove that Communist need never fire on Communist again! 1 November 1956

* * *

Three Letters on *The Reasoner*

Since the publication in September of the EC's statement on *The Reasoner*[13] we have received many letters on this case. The first two letters below were – like many others – submitted to *World News*, but rejected on the grounds that there could be no discussion on the statement in the party press until the editors had replied to the Executive. However, in the three or four weeks since the editors' reply was sent, no letter on the subject has yet appeared in any section of the party press, and we therefore publish these with the permission of the authors – Editors.

* * *

I have no doubt that Comrades Thompson and Saville behaved in a thoroughly undisciplined way in producing *The Reasoner* in the way they did.

But how was it possible for the EC to discuss the question and produce a 5000-word document about it which does not contain one single word of self-criticism?

What is the reason for *The Reasoner*? I should have thought it was perfectly clear: the official channels of discussion in this party have been blocked ever since the Twentieth Congress, and inevitably the ideas and feelings provoked by that congress have overflowed into unofficial ones.

Here are all the Communists in the world, engaged in the greatest, most self-critical debate since the days when Lenin founded the Party of a New Type. And what has been our official policy, till very recently?

Anybody who re-reads the successive statements made by our party leaders since the Twentieth Congress must see how unwillingly they have been pushed, by the feeling of the members, from uncritical, all-covering support for the Soviet Union right or wrong, hushing up crimes against socialism and talking about 'mistakes', to 'regretting lack of information', then publicly asking for explanations, and then making condemnatory comments about some of the terrible injustices that have occurred.

Anybody who has had anything to do with the party press, or has written letters to it, knows how discussion has been limited and clamped down there. It is only since the first appearance of *The Reasoner* that *World News* itself launched a discussion on 'democratic centralism', with a pitiful article which could not even do justice to the power that democratic centralism has given our movement, because it was so determined to ignore its difficulties and dangers.[14]

Meanwhile discussion has seethed in the branches and wherever two or three Communists have gathered together. Thompson and Saville have not started anything: their crime is simply to commit some of the best, most thoughtful contributions to this discussion to the duplicator.

Serious leaders cannot dismiss such activity as 'factionalism': it is a symptom of their own failure to lead in a crisis such as we have never faced before.

I have been told: but this sort of thing, even if started with the best intentions, is dangerous, because it can lead to disruption in the party. That of course is true.

But isn't it also true that discipline imposed with the fine intention of protecting the unity of the party, also has its dangers? Didn't one man rule, in the name of party unity in the Soviet Union, while others, in the interests of party unity, sat and looked on at a new Inquisition?

Yet we don't talk of the need for 'nipping discipline in the bud', because we know that organisation and discipline are essential weapons of the working class.

When the international Communist movement was young, democratic centralism imposed international discipline upon all brother parties: that discipline no longer exists, because it is realised that the Communist parties of the world are sufficiently mature to work together in the spirit of internationalism without anybody having to give orders.

If the parties are more mature, their members are also more mature, more experienced and less likely to fall into all kinds of capitalist booby traps. Then let's trust each other a bit more, and not rely on orders from above to create wisdom, discipline and loyalty.

A truly free-for-all discussion just now, leading up to the recall conference next year (the demand for which, again, came from the branches), is the only method by which we can clear up the confusion the Twentieth Congress inevitably created, and enable us to become a healthy, united party once again on the basis of deeper understanding.

Sheila Lynd[15]

* * *

The resolution on *The Reasoner* which was published in *World News* gives a number of reasons why that journal should cease publication. However, all these reasons presuppose that there is free access to the official journals for all points of view. If this had been so, the content of *The Reasoner* would have appeared elsewhere, for example in *World News* or the *Daily Worker*.

It is precisely because such free, democratic discussion has disappeared that *The Reasoner* has unfortunately become necessary. I regret that it has become necessary, not that it has appeared. And the reaction of the Central Committee is further proof of their fundamental error.

If they truly tried to represent the membership of the party, their first step should have been to try to determine how far *The Reasoner* represented the views of that membership. (But I suspect that if a free vote were taken, after free and equal access to party communications, it might be the banners who were banned. That is, if bans are necessary.)

The only true guarantee which the working class can have is a party where the real power lies with the rank and file. I am a Communist because only the Communist Party offers that as a possibility. But I am only too well aware that it is not always a reality, even in the Communist Party. And it does not exist where the leadership exercise the power of censorship.

The opposition to *The Reasoner* speaks in the sacred name of unity. We shall not achieve unity by the forcible suppression of differing points of view. And I want no more of unity on the basis of revealed truth from 16 King Street.[16] Marxists are not developed that way.

Let us instead have the truth; when it is good, when it seems bad, when we don't know what to make of it. And let us have all the interpretations and points of view which develop. Then the party members will buy *World News*, and the working class will buy the *Daily Worker* – even if it hasn't any sex or sadism.

Leslie Sewell

* * *

The reasons adduced by the EC for the banning of *The Reasoner* may be summarised as follows:

1) The authority of the party is vested in its elected leadership.

2) The view of the majority must prevail and between congresses the view of the EC must be taken as representing the view of the majority.

3) No individual member or group must express opinions in print except in the party press, which may or may not publish them. To bring out an independent journal for the discussion of political theory and the ventilation of opinions for which space cannot be found in the party press is undemocratic and does the party grave harm.

4) Criticism can be expressed by means of party branches and committees.

I should like to examine these points in more detail.

1) That the party leadership has authority in all matters involving political activity has been challenged, so far as I am aware, by nobody, and certainly not by *The Reasoner*. Where party action is called for, that action must be unanimous. This has never been in dispute.

2) It may and does happen that a view expressed by the leadership is not the view of the majority of the membership but is, as far as one can tell, accepted by the majority only after it has been promulgated by the leadership. This was the case in 1939 when the leadership pronounced the war to be not anti-fascist but imperialist. It is doubtful whether the membership ever wholeheartedly accepted this view.

3) The EC holds that for an individual or group to express its political theories in an independent journal is to do the party grave harm.

Just *how* does it do the party harm to publish a journal dealing not with political activity but with theory? No Marxist can accept the view that his political philosophy must necessarily accord with majority opinion or that he must subordinate his reasoning to the demands of a leadership, whether democratically elected or not. It is his duty as well as his right to observe, study and think for himself and to express the conclusions at which he has arrived. In what way is an independent journal published by Communists for Communists a 'negation of democracy'? May it not rather be a much-needed stimulus to our membership to devote thought to the questions raised, and does not this conduce to better Marxist understanding?

The argument that all expressions of opinion can find place in the party press is one that we all know to be untrue. What serious articles, for example, appeared in the party press giving a critical assessment of the value of the work of Lysenko, in opposition to the ill-informed, uncritical enthusiasm which was the party 'line'?

4) A comrade, so the EC tells us, may express his views to his party branch, or to one of the party committees, and, it would appear, if he is in a minority he must henceforth keep quiet. He must not publicise his opinions in an independent journal in order to have them answered and provoke discussion in the party press and discover whether there are other comrades who agree with him. This seems to me the negation not only of democracy but of intellectual effort.

Either the independent journal contains a contribution to our political understanding or it does not. If it is of no help to us in arriving at a solution of the problems which are causing many of us so much anxiety at the present time it will be a flop and the leadership can ignore it. If, on the other hand, it contains valuable and thought-provoking material, as, in my opinion, is the case with *The Reasoner* then its banning is a thoroughly bad thing smelling of heresy hunting and the prohibition of 'dangerous thoughts'. Heresy hunting has had appalling consequences in Communist parties.

Comrades Thompson and Saville should, I agree, have informed the EC of their intention to publish as a matter of loyalty and of courtesy, and it certainly seems regrettable that they have not put their views before the Commissions on 'Inner-Party Democracy' and *The British Road to Socialism*, but on this matter I cannot form an opinion without knowing more of the circumstances.[17] I am, nonetheless, convinced that *The Reasoner* is doing a valuable job in provoking much freer and more lively discussion in the party press than we have been used to, and in stimulating many comrades to think more for themselves than they have been in the habit of doing. If this creates a 'faction' the fault lies not with *The Reasoner* but with the motives which have led to its banning.

For these reasons I shall support *The Reasoner* and urge all the party comrades whom I meet to do the same.

Ursula Cox

* * *

Derek Kartun, Seeing the Trees For the Wood

No one doubts, I imagine, that the international Communist movement is in the midst of the most serious crisis in its history. One of the difficulties about crises of historic significance is that it becomes difficult to see the trees for the wood. The sense of history in the making weighs heavily on the mind. One feels, very properly, the need to re-examine fundamental beliefs and to reappraise basic texts and teachings. One takes a closer look at neglected things like one's conscience, like the actual, irreducible, incontrovertible *facts*; one becomes suddenly sceptical, inquisitive and, like the citizens of Missouri, one finds a new slogan: 'Show me.'[18]

In a situation of this kind people change their minds or fail to change them at varying rates, in varying degrees. It becomes impossible to sink one's differences because suddenly one's differences have become more important than one's agreements. It can become a time of dangerous bitterness. Certainly we are all brothers. But we could be like the brothers in Douglas Jerrold's phrase – all Cains and Abels.[19] And so an effort is needed to see some of the trees; to try to reduce to black-on-white what precisely one feels is wrong, outdated, unacceptable in the Communist Party's methods of work today. And doing this is without prejudice to the larger task of analysing the historical processes which are at work.

Here, then, are some of the things which, to me at any rate, must disappear henceforth from our work. And to condemn them now does not imply that some of them have not had their rightful place at some earlier time.

* We must break with a marked preference for conspiratorial methods – a legacy from the writings of the leading Russian revolutionaries.

* We must try saying what we have to say in plain English, since it is the language of the population of these islands.

* We must stop once and for all abusing the meaning of the phrase 'international solidarity'. It has made puppets and parrots of us in the past. It has been bad for the Russians and disastrous for us.

* We must rid ourselves of a certain grandiloquence in our political work – a kind of idiot optimism which leads us solemnly to predict the unattainable, to make noises out of all proportion to our size, to delude ourselves and very often to make ourselves ridiculous.

* We must take our consciences out of pawn. They have been in the safe-keeping of the leadership for far too long. The experience has not been fair to the leadership and has not been good for any of us. And what has a conscience to do with politics? More than we have been ready to admit.

* We must adjust our organisational forms in a number of ways. To enable us to know, at election times, not only what a candidate's record of mass work may be, but also what his or her political opinions and capacity are too. To enable us more easily to give expression to views which the existing leadership may not accept or like.

* We must overcome a certain philistine mistrust of professional standards of work which has been creeping up on us for a long while.

* We must start the painful process of developing a brand of Communism which is not dogma sprinkled with Holy Water, but a rational conviction rationally held.

All this implies, I think, a very different kind of party.

It won't be such a cosy party, since everyone will no longer think alike. It will not be half as easy to lead, since the inner play of democracy will create for it some at least of the problems that other parties have. It will not be as capable of the kind of disciplined, high-speed actions we have been good at in the past. It will be a little less efficient, less adept at exerting an influence out of proportion to its size. It may not, I think, be quite such a happy and inspiring place as our party has been in the past.

But perhaps some people will join it. I no longer believe they will join the old kind of party in numbers of any serious political significance whatsoever. I speak, of course, of Britain.

We can, of course, go on in the old way. The party will survive all right. We can make a few democratic noises, modify a rule or two, revise *The British Road to Socialism*. We shall be suffused with self-righteousness, a tight little, right little party, the vanguard of an army marching in another direction, a leadership without followers, a party without serious political influence. It would be a pitiful waste of the devotion, efforts and sacrifices of the party's members, and it would deny to the people of Britain their most important weapon in changing the social system. Nor is it good enough to say to them: 'Here we are; it is up to you to join us.' They won't – until they begin to feel we are people like them.

Is such a view a sign of mere frustration or vulgar panic? I don't think so. We live and work in a country with a long socialist tradition. The party has been here through good times and very bad times. It has been right – repeatedly. It stands for the noblest ideas and it contains thousands of the finest people one can find anywhere. It is marching with history. What it says makes sense. Yet its political appeal has been negligible and is still negligible.

Why? Because of what happened in Russia? Because the Labour Party is standing in the light? Because the time isn't ripe? These are elements in the situation; they are not replies to the question. The reply lies primarily elsewhere – on our own doorstep. People have seen in us a disciplined force, an effective weapon of history (though a blunt weapon), a determined band of devoted revolutionaries. They have not seen in us a truly British party, nor one which intended to safeguard the freedoms we have in order to build wider freedoms in a socialist order of society. They have admired and respected us: they have not trusted us. Until they change that view – until we give them some solid cause for changing it – they will go elsewhere for their politics. They may yet come to us for an honest, hard-working trade-union leader or two, or for a rip-roaring campaign on some short-term issue. But they'll take their politics from a different shop.

It seems to me that there is no point in having such a Communist Party any longer. Therefore – since we must have a Marxist party in Britain – there must be a change.

It may be that a successful demonstration in Poland and Hungary of the proposition that socialism and freedom are not incompatible would have a salutary effect here and throughout the world. But regardless of what our friends there may do, there's a great deal we can and should do here and now ourselves.

* * *

We have received a review copy of *Russia Reviewed*, by Stanley G Evans. Readers can obtain this thoughtful and stimulating pamphlet, price 9d, from the Rev E Charles, Arlesey Vicarage, Beds.

* * *

G D H Cole, Reflections On Democratic Centralism

What is 'democratic centralism'? I have recently read a definition of it, or rather of the term 'centralism' as applied to a political party, as meaning 'i) that minorities shall accept the decision of majorities, and ii) that lower party organs shall accept the decision of higher party organs'. These two requirements, I am told, appear in the rules of the British Communist Party. If this were all, I imagine most of us would be ready to accept the label of 'centralists'; but clearly it is not all. One wants to know what are the majorities and minorities in question – majorities and minorities of what precisely? And one also wants to know what are the 'higher' and 'lower' party organs; for this is not a matter on which agreement can be taken as a matter of course.

Does majority in this connection mean majority of all the members of the party, ascertained by referendum or ballot vote? If so, it has to be admitted that by no means all issues can be settled in this way. Some are too technical for mass voting to be appropriate; in other cases there is no time, or no opportunity, to take a ballot vote. Even if major questions of principle are settled as far as possible by referendum, some other agency has to be used for taking the secondary decisions. There has to be an *executive* body able to do this; but an executive, even if it is democratically chosen, is not a 'majority', and its decisions are not majority decisions which all members can be required to obey on that ground. In practice, questions of principle are more often decided at a congress or by delegates or representatives than by referendum; but a congress, however democratically chosen, does not constitute a majority, or even necessarily express the majority's will.

After all, then, it cannot be simply that minorities are required to accept the decision of majorities. It turns out that what is meant is that, except in case of referendum, majorities are being required to accept the decisions of minorities that are deemed to represent them (congresses) or to have some special authority to prescribe a correct line of conduct (executive committees). It is clearly reasonable to give representative congresses a large power to decide on matters of principle or high policy where the use of the referendum is felt to be inappropriate, or where it cannot be used; but it is a very different matter to endow an executive, which cannot be representative in anything like the same degree, power to issue orders to the majority – in effect, to almost everybody concerned – even if the executive is limited to acting in what it holds to be in accordance with congress decisions. For one thing, there will inevitably be many issues on which congress has not given judgement; and, for another, even when it has there may be wide differences of opinion concerning the right way of applying such judgements to particular cases or situations, above all in a situation that is not static, but subject to rapid development.

Thus, the first real and substantial point that arises in relation to the claims of centralists is this. How much power is the *executive* to be given to issue orders binding the members and branches or regional organisations? If the executive is given virtually complete power in this respect, subject only to obeying decisions of congress, this amounts to a very great subjection of the majority to the executive – that is, to a very small minority deemed to be in some sense its representative. Clearly, in any party organisation, the executive must be given considerable powers, and must be able to rely on its orders being for the most part carried out by the members. But must a branch or regional body always obey the executive, whatever it orders and even if it regards the executive as acting in violation of congress decisions? Or should there be limits, in addition to those involved in congress decisions, on what the executive can order? For example, should the executive (or only the congress) have the right to expel, or to suspend, a member or branch accused of 'subversive' practices or opinions? Should the executive have a right to lay down a 'party line', and to require all members to conform to it, and to switch the line when and as it thinks fit?

In the case of Communist parties there is a further problem. Under the constitution of the Comintern (now defunct) each national party was required to regard itself as a branch or section of the Comintern and to accept the orders, not only of an international congress, but also of the Executive Committee of the Comintern (ECCI). Thus, the international *executive* was treated as 'higher' than even the *congress* of a national Communist party.

It may be said that, since the dissolution of the Comintern, this situation has ceased to exist; but how far was the place of the ECCI taken in practice by the central organs of the CPSU? It seems clear that well before Stalin became a dictator – indeed, while Lenin was still active – the principle that an international *executive* was 'higher' than a national party *congress* was laid down as an essential principle of centralism. This was indeed largely what centralism meant when the term first came into widespread use.

The conception of 'higher' and 'lower' party organs is not simple. A national executive is obviously higher than a local executive, but is it 'higher' than a regional congress, or even than a widely attended branch meeting?

So far, I have been dealing only with the term 'centralism', and not with the qualifying adjective, 'democratic'. What does 'democratic' mean, in this context? Clearly, it must mean that the persons who, as congress delegates or executive members, lay down policies and issue orders are chosen by the members so as to represent their views. Does this mean that all such persons ought to represent the views of a majority of the entire membership, or is it consistent with some of them representing local or sectional majorities whose views are not those of a majority of the whole party? If the former, it seems to exclude all real debate either on the executive or in congress itself, and to involve that both should be 'monolithic' bodies so chosen that no minority spokesman can secure election to them. This would exclude all forms of election to represent particular localities or groups, and would imply that the majority view was known already before the elections took place. In the case of congress delegates it would involve empowering the executive to decide who should get elected, by excluding all candidates standing for 'deviationist' views, and, up to a point, this does seem to have occurred, though not by any means completely. In the case of executive members, it would seem to involve election not by rank-and-file nomination or by mass vote, but by a congress already sufficiently hand-picked in the way described.

Is this 'democratic', even if it does result in a congress and an executive that represent the view of a majority? Or does 'democracy' require some recognition of the rights of minorities? My conception of democracy does include such a recognition, which I regard as inconsistent with the conception of centralism that has so far been accepted, at any rate in most cases, by the Communist parties. For, if minority views (including those of local or sectional majorities) are not to be represented, real free discussion is made impossible, and in practice too much power is put in the hands of those who represent the majority at a particular time, not only in conducting party affairs without regard for minority views, but also to perpetuate their power after they have ceased really to represent the majority view. *New* views, including adaptations of policy to meet changing circumstances and opportunities, are bound in most cases to be at the outset minority views; and to prevent such views from being expressed and taken notice of is to condemn a party to utter dependence on the personal qualities and the adaptability to new situations of those who represented the majority when they were chosen, under conditions which make it difficult for them to change their minds – for were they not chosen to carry out a determined monolithic policy? Free discussion is indispensable for the discovery of new truths or working hypotheses; and the monolithic conception of leadership is therefore wholly unscientific, as well as contrary to any constructive conception of democracy.

'Democratic centralism' could mean, and was presumably meant at least in part by its originators to mean, something widely different from 'monolithicity'. It could mean that throughout the party, the fullest opportunity was given for free discussion in framing and reframing policies, but that when, after such discussion, a definite decision had been reached by the party as a whole, such decision (until revised) should be binding on all its members. This, I think, could be called 'democratic' only if the power to make such binding decisions was reserved exclusively for congresses so elected as to give thorough scope for the representation of minority views and to exclude all central pressure designed to influence the electors. It is not 'democratic' for an executive to be allowed to take such binding decisions, or even for a congress that is not freely elected in such a way as to ensure due representation of minority views.

There remains a further question. Even when these conditions of 'democracy' have been satisfied, is a party congress entitled to lay down decisions binding as orders on all the individual members of the party? I think not. Clearly, such a congress must have the right, in the last resort, to expel an individual, or a group, that it considers to be acting seriously against the party's interest and well-being. But it should invoke such power only in the very last resort, and never merely because of what may be merely temporary disagreements on tactics, or even on fundamental policies, except after every possible attempt to work with the dissentients, or allow them to go their own way, as long as their actions do not threaten actually to disrupt the party, as distinct from causing trouble or inconvenience to the persons actually in control of its affairs for the time being. The other side of this is that the individual member must never be called upon to *act* in support of any policy to which he objects on grounds of morality (conscience), though he may, in certain circumstances of this order, be strongly urged *not to act* against such a policy, except by using his right as a member to agitate for getting it changed – and to join with fellow-members in any such agitation; for to deny this right to act with others is to deny the right to agitate to any real purpose. It is a fundamental moral principle that no man should be required to act against his conscience, either by condoning for reasons of party expediency things of which he morally disapproves or by being made to do things which revolt his sense of justice or fair dealing.

This degree of respect for the rights of the individual is indispensable among socialists, in whatever sort of society they are living. For any other attitude involves sacrificing the individual's rights, not to those of his class, but to the conception of class-rights held by a particular body of persons who find themselves for the time being in command of the party machine.

Really free discussion, such as the continual discovery of new truths or working hypotheses requires, is not possible unless it exists at every level of party organisation, and cannot work democratically unless policies are allowed to find their way upwards and outwards from the smaller – local or sectional – groups to the higher levels. It is not *democratic* centralism when policy is allowed to emerge only from the centre, even if *some* criticism of the central proposals is thereafter allowed before final and binding decisions are arrived at. In practice, the more control an executive is allowed to have over the framing of policy, to the exclusion of the smaller groups, the less democratic the process is – above all, if the executive is so constituted as to exclude, or nearly exclude, representation of minority views.

Where parties, like the CP in Czarist Russia, have to operate under conditions of police persecution and cannot meet and discuss freely at all levels, it is made impossible for them to work in thoroughly democratic ways and, especially in revolutionary situations, there may be no alternative to the adoption of undemocratic centralist methods. But the recognition of this necessity provides no reason for regarding as desirable in themselves methods which inevitably involve great dangers of the party falling into the hands of a dominant clique or of a masterful individual intent on enlarging his own power.

* * *

Democracy and Dissent

A full-scale discussion is now underway in the American Communist Party. The party leadership is assisting this discussion by providing special facilities. The piece below, by 'B S', is taken from a Special Discussion Issue of *Party Voice*, the bulletin of the New York State CP. This 32-page bulletin is entirely devoted to problems and policies of the party. It contains several second principle, the subordination of lower to higher organs. This is an equally unacceptable test of centralism because here everything turns upon how the functions of higher and lower organs are defined. Comrade Lyons will not find any organisation in which the lower organs are not subordinate to the higher, but he will find great differences in the degree to which the competence of higher bodies is restricted and the autonomy of lower bodies secured.

It is not surprising that armed with such a definition of centralism as this Comrade Lyons should find centralism everywhere and like a great many other comrades he declares it to be the 'basic organisational principle upon which the unions have been built up'. Thus, he makes short work of the immense variety of forms, the tremendous diversity, which characterises the government of British trade unions. But not only does his treatment of the subject divert our attention away from a valuable field of experience, it makes it impossible for us to understand a large percentage of the writings of Marx and Lenin. For example, on Comrade Lyons' reading of centralism what are we to make of Marx's assertion that '*centralist* organisation [Marx's emphasis], although very useful for secret societies and sectarian movements, goes against the nature of trade unions'?

Marx has turned in his grave and Lenin would turn in his mausoleum if he knew that the defenders of democratic centralism resorted to arguments based on – of all things – trades union practice. Indeed, the failure to go back and look at the conditions under which democratic centralism arose and the terms in which Lenin advocated it is one of the principal weaknesses of the discussion up to date – not excluding Comrade Mahon's contribution.[20] But before considering this question, it is well to attempt a brief and provisional characterisation of democratic centralism.

Having disposed of centralism, Comrade Lyons deals with the remaining part of the question with characteristic simplicity and brevity. As to the type of centralism, he says: 'I imagine few would opt for anything other than democratic centralism.' Let us see whether we cannot do a little better than this. First, democratic centralism – like undemocratic or despotic centralism – concentrates power in the hands of a small leading group. Decisions between congresses are made at the centre and they are all absolutely binding upon the membership, who are called upon to accept an 'iron discipline'. If local officers are elected (there may be various forms of intervention from above) they are responsible to the higher bodies and not to those who elected them. Second, democratic centralism distinguishes itself from despotic centralism, by virtue of the unique relationship which it establishes within a monolithic structure between the leadership and the

transcripts from the short-hand record of discussions of the New York State Committee, of which this is one. This method might well be used here also, to assist busy comrades who find it difficult to get their ideas onto paper – Editors.

* * *

That section of Comrade Dennis' report which deals with collective leadership, democracy, criticism and self-criticism, is, in my opinion, an important opening to an area of our thought which needs much further development. Perhaps it was Comrade Dennis' intention to provide the opportunity for such development and for a more fundamental probing into the essential features of democracy. I hold that where we have failed in inner democracy cannot be simply laid to the attacks of the past years or to the fact that our party's mass ties have seriously diminished. Nor can we simply exhort our people to be more democratic in their ideas and their ways. We must trace any failures in democracy to the important left ideological concepts that we have lived by for the last twenty to thirty years.

The determinant for us, in the US, as to the scope of our inner democracy must be based on a clear outlook as to what we want to be on the American scene.

For myself, I prefer to be a part of an important trend in the labour and mass movement rather than a purist sect. Is it sufficient to say that all we have to do is to show and develop skill in our approaches to the mass movement that we will become such a trend? This does not conform to an analysis of the worst features of our undemocratic practices which ultimately had to lead to one broken mass tie after another, to the resolution of internal differences by vilification, slander and expulsion, to the ideological purification processes which were literally brainwashing, and to the cardinal crime of all, the extreme stultification of our party membership and a certain level of our cadre …

It is my opinion that we cannot simply say that we will improve the situation by a more balanced development of democratic centralism with a greater emphasis on democracy. We must know what democratic centralism is – does it apply to the American scene today? …

What has been the main ideological weapon that has militated against the practice of democracy in our party? Each 'prosecutor' at an expulsion knew full well that there were a series of standard charges that had to be put into each case in order to make it stick: anti-leadership, undisciplined, anti-working-class, and for the poor soul who would dare to attempt to argue his or her case, the cardinal crime of breaking the unity of the party and in reality wanting it to degenerate into a debating society. It is the concept of monolithic unity which we must examine.

In the name of monolithic unity we have learned to stand by while important dissent was expunged from our ranks. Most members today … would honestly like to see a situation in our party in which important dissent could be expressed without our falling apart at the seams. Isn't it true that we borrowed literally from the CPSU on this question of monolithic unity? …

Because scientific thinking … can only take place in an atmosphere in which ideas flow and reflect wide mass experience, we must stress the value and importance of dissent and difference. As long as we have a section organiser or a club organiser or anyone who, when unable to convince a member of the correctness of the line, can take recourse to the need for monolithic unity, then you must run the risk that the party's ears are closed to the masses. As long as our party committees consider it an important principle to submerge differences in unanimous reports so that neither the membership nor the masses can know what we are debating, then we must run the risk that the line of our party is the property of the few.

So long as we place major emphasis on the danger of our becoming a debating society and the danger of the influx of bourgeois ideas, then we must run the risk that somewhere honest and correct opinion will be characterised as an effort to do that.

For many years now we've cultivated a contempt for bourgeois democracy, unable to separate those aspects of bourgeois democracy which the people had struggled for and won, from the practices of the bourgeoisie, the distortions and the efforts to go back historically. We fail to consider that rules we very often advance for the labour and mass movement are rules which we somehow think do not apply to us. We are supposed to be the possessors of a science which eliminates the need for trends in finding the path towards socialism. Yet life has shown that where you have a hard-fisted, iron-bound line, you can't seriously have a market-place of ideas … Aside from the danger of classifying dissenting ideas prematurely and incorrectly as bourgeois ideas, we reflect a great lack of faith in the masses both within and outside our party to reject ideas that are harmful …

On the American scene, monolithic unity – which I contend is far different from majority rule – is alien. The people first are testing many, many ideas and are not buying a single line. They are even suspicious of ultimate or 'ulterior' objectives. Those who have had contact with us are also repelled by our inability to stand dissent and differences. As soon as difference arises we get panicky and must expunge it …

The 'party of a new type', in my opinion, will not be suited to the

American scene. We will have to provide guarantees for democracy which can compete with any organisation in America. We will be impelled to establish rules which will protect dissent and prevent by design simplified expulsion methods. We need not delude ourselves about the degree of unity in our party today. We must adjust to the idea that a minority, not understanding or agreeing with a line, may very well choose not to apply it too well. By proving in life and struggle that a line or a leadership is largely correct, then we will win *voluntary* unity and the fullest acceptance of the rule of the majority.

* * *

P H, On Democratic Centralism

Although the controversy on democratic centralism has continued for some time, both 'sides' have so far failed to come to grips with the problem and to present it in a systematic and helpful way. To satisfy oneself on this point it is only necessary to look at the recent articles that have appeared in *The Reasoner* and in *World News*. In the last issue of *The Reasoner* we find Comrade Lyons taking another comrade to task for some criticisms of democratic centralism. Because the position taken up by Comrade Lyons is representative of a very powerful tendency within the party, as revealed at aggregate meetings and in branches, it is worth considering it in some detail.

Lyons begins by reprimanding the earlier writer for failing to make clear what he means by democratic centralism. This is a perfectly just reproach, but Comrade Lyons himself does no more than attempt to elucidate the meaning of centralism, and this he does in a far from satisfactory way.

He tells us that it means '1) that minorities shall accept the decisions of majorities, and 2) that lower party organs shall accept the decisions of higher party organs'. Despite the fact that these definitions are taken from the party rules they tell us nothing at all about whether the party or any other organisation which happens to accept these principles is centralised or decentralised: except that in paramilitary and other ultra-centralist organisations the converse of the first proposition holds: that is, majorities shall accept the decisions of minorities.

Consider the first principle, the principle of majority rule. Everything depends upon how this principle operates. Upon how often (and under what conditions) what fraction of the total membership is enabled to participate in reaching a majority decision. It is with reference to precise consideration of this sort and not by vague, general formulæ, that one distinguishes practice between centralised and decentralised organisations. Consider t

rank and file. Instead of despotically imposing decisions upon the rank and file, the leadership seeks the agreement of the membership, it seeks to be informed about rank-and-file opinion, and it takes its decisions in the light of such opinion.

The reader may protest that no reference has been made to the democratic process of the congress and the election of the executive. But in my opinion this is not a defining condition of democratic centralism. Where election takes place it does so under such conditions of restricted choice as to make it a merely formal matter whether elections are held or whether the ruling oligarchy replenishes itself by direct selection. (Let the outraged reader who has no more patience to continue turn to the article by Joliot Curie[21] in *World News*, 18 August, where he will find it stated that: 'The accession to successive responsibilities in our party is made on the basis of proofs given in action, and without forgetting as one of the criteria of selection [sic] the leadership's own practice, which results in inestimable experience.')

However, an attempt to characterise democratic centralism in a series of bald statements is of very limited usefulness. No organisation can be evaluated satisfactorily without considering it historically, without taking account of its purposes and the conditions under which it had to work. Now, as everyone knows, democratic centralism is an organisational conception to which the name of Lenin is most closely linked. In the early years of this century he waged a relentless struggle against elements who stood out for a loosely-organised party, against all those who wanted the party to be based on 'broad democratic principles' and who would have reduced what Lenin termed the organisation of revolutionaries to the level of the 'organisation of workers' for trade-union purposes. Lenin boldly championed 'bureaucracy' against 'democracy'. He distinguished between conditions in 'politically free countries' and in Tsarist Russia, the main bulwark of European and Asiatic reaction. As far as Russia was concerned:

> The one serious organisational principle for workers in our movement must be strictest secrecy, strictest choice of members, training of professional revolutionaries. Once these qualities are present something more than democracy is guaranteed: completely comradely confidence among revolutionaries.[22]

But by what was this complete comradely confidence, this responsibility of leaders guaranteed? Only by the presumed capacity, honesty, selflessness and incorruptibility of *the established oligarchy which stood at the head of this secret organisation, chose* its members and *selected* its leaders. Under the conditions of Tsarist absolutism there could be no question that Lenin's views on organisation were absolutely correct; that to adopt the democratic procedures of control from below was to deliver oneself up to the secret police. Under the terrible conditions of Tsarist oppression it *was* likely that the oligarchy would have the qualities needed to guarantee 'something more than democracy'. But what happens once the party is victorious? Is it desirable or possible for it to change its oligarchical character? Or will the character of the oligarchy, in the absence of the old pressures which made for purity and devotion, be changed?

Plekhanov was absolutely wrong as against Lenin on the organisational question in 1904. In relation to the immediate necessity for organising the revolutionary struggle he had nothing to offer, but it is central to the contradictions of the Russian Revolution that Plekhanov, from this thoroughly muddled position, could still observe that if Bolshevik methods prevailed then 'everything will in the last resort revolve round one man who *ex-providentia* will unite all the powers in himself'. (A religious interpretation of Marxism poorly prepares us for the tragic dilemmas which history may have in store for us.)

I am suggesting that the whole Communist world has taken over from Russia a system of organisation which is democratic not in the sense of involving rule by the members, but rule by an élite sprung from the members, and that conditions are so dissimilar in England from those ruling in the past in Russia that steps must be taken to develop a new theory of organisation.

The starting-point for the development of thoroughgoing ideas on organisation must be a serious and fresh study of the origins and growth of democratic centralism in Russia, and a comparison of present-day conditions in Britain with those prevailing in Russia before 1917; a steady recognition of the inescapable implications of our own revolutionary purposes; a new realism in our approach to problems of party and political organisation in general; a constant attempt to state clearly the principles of an alternative organisation of Communists in Britain.

Consider what has happened in the absence of this procedure. Lenin, considering that the class struggle was on the point of assuming the form of civil war in all the advanced countries of the world, made democratic centralism a condition for parties wishing to affiliate to the Third International. In the course of time British Communists were obliged substantially to modify and adjust the classic Leninist conceptions to British conditions. But they did this gradually, empirically, in a piecemeal way, so that the Bolshevik tradition always tended to come into conflict with the intended changes. Thus the pretensions to democratic electoral practices were off-set by the tradition of 'the accession to successive responsibilities … on the basis of proofs given in action'; the desire to build the mass party by the Leninist tradition of a small party of professional revolutionaries.

We all see, or ought to see, that we need a party which is capable of striking quickly and effectively against opponents who still command immense resources and who have had tremendous experience. Such a party must be highly centralised, but we must have the courage and honesty to recognise that this creates grave dangers, tends always to promote oligarchy or rule by a few. (The religious Marxist does not like to face these dilemmas, he is disinclined to admit that they exist and this makes the danger all the greater.)

All organisation tends to lead to oligarchical control. There are technical and other factors which make for this, but with the passage of time, the growth in membership, and the degree of centralism, this tendency becomes more pronounced. Is it not possible even at this stage to see the outlines of this process in the history of the CPSU? The power of Stalin and Beria grew more subtly, more dialectically, than the Ukrainian funeral mounds referred to by Khrushchev. Can we not see how Plekhanov's prediction was fulfilled through the unchecked advance to the most perfect and absolute centralism? The creation of the Soviet Control Commission in 1934: the concentration of the work of selecting cadres from top to bottom in the hands of one body, so as to raise it to a 'proper', 'scientific', 'Bolshevik' level in 1939, and so forward to the final set-up which was fit only to be described in 'card player's terminology'?

Plainly we are duty bound to take steps to prevent the recurrence of the abuses which are made possible by the concentration of power in the hands of a few leaders, but the first step is to get rid of the childish notion that the perfect democracy of a band of brothers is attainable or (worse) attained under democratic centralism, or any other form of organisation.

Any party which is to be an effective fighting force must be highly centralised, must have a monolithic structure, must concentrate the power of decision in the hands of a very few men. However, I am of the opinion that, without weakening the revolutionary fighting power of the party, certain safeguards can and should be introduced to prevent the abuse by the leadership of its power and the isolation of the leaders from the rest of the party. I do not believe that party policy can be safely left to develop spontaneously from below: there are many occasions on which a leadership must ensure prompt action without prolonged discussion at branch level. But there are many questions of policy where immediate decision is not necessary – or desirable – and there must be opportunities for the members to participate to the full in forming such policies. So that the rank and file will not degenerate into mere 'decision accepters', new forms of organised expression of opinion inside the party, but outside its centralised, decision-taking and decision-enforcing chain of command, might be established. In every party, rank-and-file opinion differs to some extent from leadership opinion. The creation of 'Journals of Discussion' inside districts at which editorial boards would be elected at periodic conferences of representatives from the branches would be an important step towards ensuring a more open, a more healthy conflict of ideas, which, far from damaging the party, would help to raise the level of political understanding of the members. This principle is closely bound up with the second, which is the necessity of ensuring that there are opportunities for leaders to arise in the party even if these men and women do not possess the qualities which the existing leadership think to be desirable. If centralism is to be qualified by democracy it must be possible for such alternative leaders to arise and this will not happen – as far as the Executive Committee is concerned – until the present system of panels commissions (the instruments *par excellence* of oligarchical control) are replaced by a system of election through a number of geographical and occupational constituencies.

Finally, it is a pleasure to find one point of agreement with Comrade Lyons: I think that he is correct in suggesting that democratic party life depends ultimately upon the attitudes and the political maturity of the membership as a whole. However, this problem of attitudes in relation to democracy goes deeper than he thinks. We fear that, at bottom, the issue is between those who imagine that they can exchange the consolations of religion for the materialist conception of history, and those for whom the party is not 'Holy Church', but an important means to a greater end. Thus, I do not believe that the absolute minimum of democratic restraint upon oligarchy is compatible with Comrade Joliet-Curie's suggestion that we can attain a sort of state of grace by being 'concerned to be deeply in agreement' with our leaders. He tells us that: 'One must be in that state during the carrying out of a decision, so that the action will be the result of a conviction so deep that it appears to us almost as if it emanated from ourselves.' I am firmly convinced that this is an attitude with which neither Marxism, nor Science, nor Democracy can live. It is such thinking which leads to Stalinist degeneration.

* * *

Ronald L Meek, Notes From a Polish Diary

The author visited Poland recently with a group of fifteen British economists
– Editors.

I

They are very proud of their thaw in Poland. It is a bigger and better
thaw, one is constantly told, than that taking place in the other People's
Democracies and in the Soviet Union. One Polish economist who discussed
it very frankly with me in the privacy of his home described it as a 'new
revolution'. 'We can talk about things quite freely now', he said, 'not only in
private, but also in public and in the press. There's a great ferment of ideas
going on, reaching out into all branches of thought, and it's impossible to
tell where it's going to lead.'

How genuine is the Polish thaw? We visited the library of one of the
leading Institutes of Economics. Most of the British visitors looked for one
another's books in the catalogue, found them, and were very satisfied. I
looked for Bukharin and Trotsky, didn't find them, and asked about it. 'Ah
yes – the prohibits', they said, and the story came out. Apparently at the
beginning of what many Polish people now call 'the bad period' (roughly
1949–54), decrees were issued putting certain books on a prohibited list,
so that students couldn't borrow them except upon presentation of a chit
signed by a professor. 'It was really very silly', someone said. 'The list of
prohibits even included the works of Hitler and Mussolini.' Then, fairly
recently, public criticism of this policy was voiced in the party press. So now,
although the decrees haven't yet been formally annulled, the 'prohibits' are
gradually finding their way back into the catalogues at the institutes and
universities, and the majority of students are now able to borrow them
quite freely. 'At last!', said one of the librarians, and I remember well the
expression on his face as he said it.

What do the Poles themselves regard as the most important features of
this 'new revolution'? Whenever I asked anyone about this, 'free speech'
was almost invariably put first. 'Polish literary papers are very liberal', said
someone, 'they are still prohibited in East Germany.' On several occasions
people remarked, with some pride, that Poland was the only People's
Democracy to publish Togliatti's article. After free speech there usually
came the release of political prisoners and the curtailment of the powers
of the secret police. And treading close upon these came the changes which
are taking place in central planning – changes in the direction of greater
decentralisation and a more extensive use of what British (and Polish)

economists call the 'price mechanism'. The thawing process had started, I was assured, two or three years ago, but it had of course been greatly accelerated in recent months as a result of Khrushchev's famous speech on Stalin, which was very widely distributed in Poland.

This doesn't mean that the Poles have accepted Khrushchev's speech literally. Most of the people to whom I spoke – mainly but by no means exclusively economists – were glad that the speech had been made, and emphasised what they called its 'tragic' aspects, but at the same time deplored its general tone and much of its content. 'It was sheer idiocy to describe it all in personal terms', said one economist. 'Why did Khrushchev have to put in that nonsense about Stalin planning the war on a globe?', asked another, 'I've spoken to generals who had personal contact with Stalin during the war at the time when the front line was in Poland, and they said that he knew the names of every little village.' Most of the portraits of Stalin have disappeared (the only ones I saw were in a school and a planning institute), but the Poles whom we met seem to be resisting any attempts to throw out the baby with the bathwater. Some of the economists who are advocating a more extensive use of the price mechanism in economic planning regard themselves as continuing the job begun by Stalin in his *Economic Problems of Socialism in the USSR*. Others describe this work as 'naive', but all agree that the issues Stalin raised ought to be thoroughly discussed. 'Stalin himself began the de-Stalinisation of economics', one man said. ('And of linguistics', another added.) 'The real trouble was the prevailing dogmatism, which led people merely to accept his important new ideas as ultimate truths instead of developing them creatively.'

One of the most welcome features of the Polish thaw is the intense interest being shown in developments in the West. Among the economists this is particularly noticeable. During 'the bad period' contacts with the West were strictly limited, and now that communications are being opened up again the economists are making the most of it. At a session in Warsaw at which our group of British economists answered questions put by our Polish colleagues, we were besieged with questions about the nationalised industries in Britain. What are the main principles of economic administration in your nationalised industries? In analysing the effectiveness of investments in your nationalised industries, how far do you use the tools of analysis put forward in your textbooks? (A tough one, that!) How far is decision-making in your nationalised industries decentralised? And their interest in recent developments in British economic theory, particularly those associated with the name of Keynes, is just as great as their interest in the field of practice.

Of course, most of the intellectual discussion is taking place within the formal framework of Marxism. Most, although by no means all, of the economists we met (including those who were Catholics) would probably describe themselves as Marxists, and many were members of the party. But it soon became clear to us that 'Marxism' was a rather ambiguous term, and that the Marxist framework was regarded as being sufficiently wide to permit discussion of almost the whole range of problems which are being currently debated in the West. For example, one of the main questions now under discussion among the Polish economists is that of the relation between Marxist economics and bourgeois economics. How far can the tools and techniques developed by bourgeois economists be used to supplement Marxist economics where it is deficient? Do Marxist economics and bourgeois economics play separate roles in helping us to understand and control economic reality, or is some sort of integration possible? Those of us who lectured to different audiences of economists in Poland found that this problem, in various shapes and forms, was seriously exercising the minds of both students and teachers alike, and that they appeared to be quite uninhibited in the expression of their views on it. And sometimes their questions put one in a rather embarrassing position. What does one reply, for example, when one is asked (as two of us were at an Institute of Social Sciences run by the party) what researches British Marxist economists have recently done on such matters as the general crisis, state capitalism, inflation, interest rates, and the subject-matter of political economy?

It is true that many of the new ideas which are now being so widely and strenuously debated in Poland are still in the field of theory and haven't yet been translated into practice. When we asked a high government official what he thought of the various proposals which the economists were putting forward for a greater use of the price mechanism in economic planning, he replied – rather delightfully, I thought – that: 'The majority of the proposals are taken seriously, with the exception of those which go too far.' I don't think that any very startling changes in the field of economic and political practice are likely to occur in the immediate future. Various important policy proposals are under discussion, but that is about all that can really be said. The vital point, however, is that the discussions which are taking place are widespread, profound and relatively unrestricted, and that most of those taking part in them are largely putting forward their own personal points of view rather than any very definite 'party line'. The present direction of the Polish thaw would not be at all easy to reverse.

My feelings about the thaw were neatly summed up, oddly enough, by a rather superior joke which was perpetrated at my expense by a prominent Polish economist. Mrs Joan Robinson[23] gave a lecture at Cracow University to an audience consisting mainly of economists of that city – a lecture which I, by special dispensation, was granted leave to attend. It was a very stimulating lecture. The argument was, briefly, that Marx had been wrong in his description of the contradictions of capitalism; that capitalism was indeed subject to contradictions, but that they were different from those which Marx had described, and capitalism was quite capable of overcoming them; and that the socialist advocates of peaceful coexistence must therefore get used to the idea that capitalism was probably going to coexist for quite a long time. There wasn't much discussion afterwards, partly because of the language difficulty, but partly also, I suspect, because the majority of the audience agreed substantially with the speaker. At dinner that night I happened to be sitting opposite to Mrs Robinson and next to a prominent Polish economist. 'How many orthodox Marxists would you say were present at my lecture this afternoon?', Mrs Robinson asked the PPE. 'Well', he replied, 'there was Mr Meek …' Full stop. It was a very good joke, and I like to think that I enjoyed it as much as my colleagues did. But it was a joke from which others besides myself may possibly have something to learn.

II

The road had been blocked with lorries, so we got out of our bus and made our way through them on foot. On the other side of the lorries a small crowd of people was looking at a notice which had been erected in the middle of the road. On one side of the notice was written 'A free Poland, more bread, and higher wages', and on the other side was 'Down with Bolshevism'. Nearby, a street was strewn with the wreckage of the equipment of a jamming station. The Poznań riots had begun.

The battlefront is rarely the best place to find out the causes of the battle, and Poznań was no exception. The rumours flew around like wildfire. 'The people of Cracow and Stalinogrod are joining us', an elderly worker told us as we stood watching some tanks move into position near the security police building. 'It's started in Czechoslovakia and Hungary too', we heard from someone else later. Where did the men who attacked the security police building get their arms? What was the exact role of the army in the morning? Had the workers' representatives in fact been imprisoned? There were so many answers being given to questions like these that an answer was impossible.

The question of the basic cause of the Poznań riots, however, is perhaps rather easier to answer. Insofar as such a complex series of events can be said to have had a single cause, it lay in the extremely high rate of investment in the Polish economy during the recent Six-Year Plan. Rightly or wrongly, the Polish authorities decided to embark upon a hurried and intensive programme of capital investment, in order to lay the foundations of a socialist society in the shortest possible space of time. The use of resources for this purpose – and for purposes of rearmament during the worst years of the Cold War – meant of course that they weren't available for other uses. The labour and capital employed in building the great new steel town of Nowa Huta couldn't be used to increase the supply of consumers' goods available to the people. The labour and capital used in reconstructing the fine administrative buildings and the 'Old Town' in Warsaw couldn't be used to alleviate the housing shortage. That is the reason why they told us at the Warsaw Institute of Town Planning and Architecture that they regarded British housing with great envy. And it is also the reason, at second or third remove, for Poznań.

It's important to note that the main aims of the Six-Year Plan were in fact fulfilled. A great stride was taken in transforming Poland from an economically backward and weak country into a major industrial power. Nowa Huta has to be seen to be believed; the reconstruction of Warsaw is immensely impressive and moving; and the Silesian industrial basin, as we saw during our tour of that area, has been extensively developed and re-equipped. Poznań, then, should be regarded not as something apart, but as in a certain sense a *cost* of this remarkable and rapid industrial development.

In this process of swift transformation, grave difficulties were bound to occur. It meant a high degree of centralisation, with its inevitable accompaniments of bureaucracy, over-use of administrative as opposed to 'economic' methods, and waste of resources. It meant the growth of serious disproportions in the economy between the development of agriculture and industry, capital investments and raw material supplies, and so on. But most important of all, it meant the failure to carry out the plan for raising the standard of living of the people. The analogy with developments in the USSR, although it shouldn't be pressed too far, is an interesting and important one, and is sometimes drawn by the Polish economists themselves. The best short analysis yet to appear of recent events in the socialist world was in fact made by the well-known Polish economist Oscar Lange[24] in a speech to a conference of Polish economists which took place just before our visit.[25]

It was primarily as a result of these difficulties and contradictions, then, that Poznań arose. The difficulties were made more intense, of course, by the general atmosphere of the Cold War and the severe restrictions on personal freedom which it was thought to necessitate. Nor were things made easier by the traditional anti-Russian feeling which is clearly still quite widespread in Poland, or by the increase in certain types of criminality which is the usual accompaniment of a rapid influx of peasantry into cities. Under these conditions, and given the existence of a large-scale thaw, Poznań can be quite readily explained without having recourse to any 'external' causes. There may well be some truth in the claim that an underground organisation cashed in on the events; the destruction of the jamming station, for example, was possibly inspired by such an organisation. It is also true that there was at least *some* preparation: the lorries which blocked several of the streets near the security police building didn't look as if they'd got there by accident. On the other hand, it was clear to all of us who moved among the people of Poznań and spoke with them during those two days that popular support not only for the general strike but also for the accompanying attacks on public buildings was very widespread indeed, at any rate among the many people who voiced their opinions to us. To try to explain what happened at Poznań primarily in terms of the machinations of imperialist agents would be childish and absurd, and one of the most convincing indications yet of the genuineness of the Polish thaw is the fact that in the trials which are currently proceeding no attempt is being made to explain it in such terms.

Contrary to reports appearing in the West at the time, the serious fighting was mainly confined to one very small sector of the city, and the Polish authorities seem on the whole to have behaved with considerable restraint in an extremely difficult situation. The great majority of the people remained quite calm. I remember that when I saw an old woman in a peasant shawl feeding pigeons right under the guns of a tank, I felt that this was not at all inappropriate. The amount of looting, except at the railway station, didn't appear to be very great: we saw several unguarded shops where windows had been smashed but the goods lay untouched. I was vastly amused on my return to Britain to see a photograph in one newspaper of what was described as 'a tank protecting a bank from an angry mob'. The tank in question was indeed protecting a bank, which happened to be next door to our hotel; but the 'mob' confronting it never consisted of anyone but orderly citizens of Poznań, many fraternising quite happily with the soldiers, together with fifteen British economists who were not, as I recall, very much angrier than usual.

But perhaps the most impressive thing about Poznań was this: never once during those two unhappy days, when tongues were loosened and people were very free in saying what they thought about it, did we hear anyone suggest that *socialism* ought to be done away with in Poland. 'Down with Rokossovsky'[26] – yes; 'Higher wages and more freedom' – yes; but never anything that could honestly be interpreted as 'Down with socialism'. If

Poznań was a grim reminder of the human cost which has been involved in the building of socialism in Poland, it was also a confirmation of the fact that the majority of Poles do not reject the basic idea of socialism itself.

The great debate which is being carried on in Poland today is not about whether or not socialism as such is a desirable system. The majority of the participants in the debate agree that it is. The main question at issue is simply that of the reconciliation of socialism and freedom. It takes on different forms, and is fought out in different ways. But at bottom, what the Poles are doing is to begin the basic rethinking which is necessary both in Poland and elsewhere, if a socialist system is to be built which shall be characterised by a rising standard of living, personal liberty, and freedom from outside interference. On an overturned tramcar in Poznań, near the spot where the fighting was most fierce, there appeared the slogan 'Down with *false* communism'.

Glasgow
10 October 1956

* * *

The Soviet Union: Respect For Truth Is Returning

The Soviet writer Konstantin Simonov,[27] in his obituary of Fadeyev published in the Moscow magazine *Novy Mir*, June 1956, refers to the pressures that were brought to bear on Fadeyev to rewrite his novel of the Second World War, *The Young Guard* – Editors.

* * *

The first edition of *The Young Guard* certainly did not deserve the criticisms it received. This criticism stemmed from the wrong desire to see in every episode of the war what one wished to see instead of what really happened … History – and not only the history of literature, but history in general – shows that only truth is really of service to the people: both when the truth is triumphant and lovely and also when it is hard and cheerless. The honey of comforting, lying speeches is eventually, sooner or later, exposed as false, and the same applies to the honey of comforting, lying books. The justice of one's cause is inseparable from the truth of one's words, and a literature that upholds a just cause cannot write falsehood about life, for such falsehood is incompatible with it.

It may be asked: why bring this up now? It is a reproach that weighs on the consciences of many, including the writer of these lines; but the party teaches us that where mistakes are concerned which are very much greater than these, and by no means merely concerned with literary criticism, it is better to speak out late than never.

The facts [about Fadeyev's alcoholism] were stated in the announcement with a painful but necessary respect for truth – a truthfulness which, thank God, has again generally been taking root in our country in the last few years.

* * *

Ursula Wassermann, Hungary: Fighting for Socialist Democracy

This report, reprinted with grateful acknowledgements to the *National Guardian* (1 October 1956), may be left behind by the rapid pace of events in Hungary by the time it reaches our readers. But we believe the principles debated will still be of the widest interest – Editors.

* * *

Of the three people I wanted to see most during a brief visit to Hungary, I was lucky enough to see two. If I did not see former Premier Imre Nagy,[28] it was due more to lack of time than lack of cooperation. But I saw and talked at length with Tibor Déry,[29] perhaps Hungary's greatest contemporary writer, at his home in Budapest; and Tibor Tardos,[30] journalist, at the beautiful Writers' House on Lake Balaton – Count Esterhazy's former palace.

These three share more than the experience of having been expelled from the Communist Party within the last eighteen months: as the symbols of democratisation they are the most talked about people in Hungary today.

The expulsion of Déry and Tardos followed their famous appearance at the last meeting of the Petőfi Circle on 27 June – by odd coincidence a day linked to Poland's Black Thursday at Poznań. The Petőfi Circle, originally founded by Hungary's Youth Movement, had been holding frequent discussion meetings since March. At one of these meetings Mme Rajk,[31] widow of the executed László Rajk, made her impassioned plea on behalf of the then unrehabilitated victims.

The 27 June meeting was held at the Budapest Officers' Casino – an unusual place for highly critical discussion. The subject was freedom of the press. The audience, close to 8000, was unexpectedly large since the Circle appealed to select groups as a rule. Overflow meetings were connected to the main hall by loudspeakers. The meeting lasted until 4 a.m. Tardos, as a journalist, confined himself to the press, but Déry – whose latest novel, *Niki*, the story of the life of a dog set against the political background of the Rajk trial, is today's Hungary's best-seller – spoke on the freedom of the written word as such. Further, he discussed the basic causes for the ills of present-day socialist society where, he said, 'individual freedom finds far fewer advocates than social duty'. Not only personalities, he said, but theory must come under scrutiny. There were many, he added, who wanted to stop such criticism as had been expressed during the Nagy regime and has been given voice again after the Twentieth Soviet Congress. These people, he said, in their attempt to hinder socialist democracy, were even willing to call in the police. These forces might be willing to talk about methods, but not about a basic re-evaluation of theory.

Discussion to date, he said, had been possible only with permission from above; those participating were like actors in a play not staged by themselves. A few thousand – usually the same few thousand – were discussing and arguing only within the framework of a well-conceived psychological plan: to permit a limited letting off of steam as a safety valve. But a safety valve, he said, does not eliminate brakes.

Déry directly attacked those whom he considered the embodiment of false theories. He accused Márton Horváth,[32] editor of *Szabad Nép*, CP central organ, of changing his position constantly. Déry remarked: 'I say position, not opinion, because I do not know his opinion regarding the views he represents.' (Asked at the general meeting of the Writers' Association last April why he had changed his stand so often, Horváth replied that, as a member of the Central Committee, he was obliged to represent the party's stand at any given time.) 'I have no confidence in Horváth', Déry said, 'I dare not leave literature in his hands.'

He said former Minister of Culture Révai[33] was ignorant of the realities of contemporary Hungarian literature:

> I maintain that he is personally responsible for the deterioration in our art and literature which began in 1948 and has continued until just recently … Dogmatism always speaks of the so-called successes of our so-called younger writers. Our literature is not young; it is at least 800 years old, and this so-called ten-year-old literature is of no merit. If any good books have been written during this decade, it is not because of but in spite of our literary policy.

Déry held József Darvas,[34] present Minister of Culture, more responsible than the rest since Darvas, as a writer, should have foreseen the dangers. Always acting against his better knowledge, Déry said, Darvas inevitably decided in favour of policy and against the interests of art and literature. As a result of errors, policy and literature lacked a common basis.

'I am a Communist', Déry said, 'I cannot deny my profound sympathy for those confronted with this conflict. But in my view, the conflict still remains unsolved.' Then he said (and this was most responsible for Déry's expulsion from the party):

> Here we are confronted with structural errors [in our society] which unnecessarily limit the rights of the individual … As a writer my main concern is man. My criticism begins when I see man unhappy, especially when I see men and women suffer unnecessarily.

The greatest fault of the present leadership, he said, was their distrust of the people:

> They build and function on suspicion and distrust. They underestimate the people's sense of honour and its moral force; its capacity to think and to create. But we who have always believed in our people … have the duty to create conditions under which love of life and love of work can once again function normally. The prerequisite for such conditions is honest thinking.

In conclusion Déry said criticism should be directed where it belonged: to the top leadership. 'We must have no more scapegoats', he said, 'small fry who by carrying out orders were sure they were serving the party loyally.' He asked Hungary's youth not to forget their revolutionary ancestors of 1848: 'We used to call them the Youth of '48. As for me, I shall want to see a "Youth of '56" who will aid the people in their conquest of the future.'

As Déry finished, the audience went wild with enthusiasm. The party's answer was expulsion. And despite the fact that almost all writers and journalists formerly discredited have recently been rehabilitated – editors are returning in force to their former jobs – Tardos and Déry remain unrehabilitated. They write, they publish – any story of Déry's appearing in a periodical is sold out almost before it hits the news-stands – they live in great comfort. Déry had without difficulty obtained a passport and was preparing for a holiday in Italy and Switzerland.

But the impasse continues; the party apparatus has not yet been thoroughly reformed and there remain certain people who have neither the will nor the courage to change, I was told with some impatience. I would add that these people possibly have neither the ability nor the knowledge. It takes a long time to reconstruct a cumbersome and complicated machine, heavily weighted with bureaucracy, and with old loyalties which are hard to throw overboard.

The party insists that rehabilitation will be considered only if Tardos and Déry petition to this effect. But Déry, an old-time Communist, made it quite clear that he would not go to Canossa.[35] Other forces presumably will have to act as mediators. The Writers' Union in August, in a unanimous resolution, demanded the readmission of the two. The Hungarian Writers' Congress was expected to act as conciliator too. The impasse cannot continue for long, because nothing is static in Hungary today. There is a fresh wind blowing across the Pusta – the wind of 1848. Déry told me:

> The fight today is concerned with the concept of socialist democracy. The fight is hard and all the harder because we ourselves have not yet completely clarified this concept. I trust that we will reach our goal in the best and, I believe, the only possible way: through the closest contact with the realities of life …

* * *

John Saville, On Party History: An Open Letter To Comrade R Page Arnot[36]

Dear Comrade Arnot

I understand that you have been given the responsibility for writing the party history, although this was not made clear in the *World News* statement which announced the establishment of an Editing Commission.[37] I suppose you had mixed feelings when you received this invitation. I am not thinking, when I say this, of the reception given to the previous attempt at a party history by Tom Bell, whose book was so devastatingly taken apart by Allen Hutt in the *Labour Monthly* of June 1937, and subsequently withdrawn, but rather that as an historian of our labour movement who has taken an active share in party work since the earliest days, you are in a better position than most to appreciate what is involved in terms of critical reassessment of past policies and practices.

Most of our membership today however have been in the party for less than twenty years. And since the important reasons for writing a party history are the practical ones of inspiration and instruction I think it most necessary that the Editing Commission do not conduct their discussions behind closed doors. This means, I suggest, two things. First, because so many basic documents are obtainable only in specialist libraries, that the Commission undertake to publish as much material as possible; and second, that before a definitive assessment is arrived at, the Commission must be prepared to conduct its debates in public.

Let me give an example of what I have in mind, and consider the question of 1939, the character of the war and our change of line within a month or so of its commencement, from support to opposition, on the grounds that it was a struggle between rival imperialisms in which the workers had no interest.

Now it is widely recognised that this is a political issue that is far from being academic but is very much alive politically at the present time. Many of our friends in the Labour Party, in the absence of any new evaluation by ourselves, still regard 1939 as a touchstone by which they judge the subservience, as they see it, of our party to the Soviet Union. And among party members there is considerable confusion and uncertainty. Many, including myself, who at the time wholeheartedly supported the 'imperialist war' thesis, have now come to the conclusion that we were disastrously wrong (in my own case – like many others – I had arrived at this position by the end of the war). These differences in political approach and appraisal keep dogging us. You will recall the TV interview that Harry Pollitt gave a few months back. In that interview, in answer to a question by Frank Owen,[38] Comrade Pollitt said:

> In 1939 I thought it was an anti-fascist war. I thought it then and I think it now. But I was outvoted by the majority of our party and being a democrat, I advocated the policy of the majority of our party.

The interview in which this comment was made was reported at some length in the *Daily Worker* of 2 May 1956. Since, as the recent statement by the party's Executive has forcefully pointed out to the editors of *The Reasoner*, 'every publication has to be edited, and a choice has to be made as to what shall appear and what shall not appear' we can agree that the prominence given to these remarks by Comrade Pollitt was not accidental. The question of 1939 is therefore to be regarded as an open one, contrary views may be freely expressed and the whole matter is ready for political argument and debate. The Commission on Party History should encourage this debate which I believe will enhance the political standing of the party in general. I would suggest that the Commission could usefully sponsor a collection of documents on 1939 and initiate a full-length written discussion in which the different points of view can be adequately expressed.[39]

This brings me to the point which I want to make central to this letter – the imperative need to encourage and develop lively political discussion within our party. During the past decade or so we have lost the stamina for such discussion and nowhere is this more noticeable than in our press. A comparison of the writings and controversies of the past decade with those of any previous period in our history brings out very clearly our intellectual and political sloth – and one of our central tasks, following the earthquake of the Khrushchev report, is to shake off the conditioned attitudes of the past and restore political argument and debate to its central place in our party. In encouraging and sustaining this discussion the Commission on Party History can and should play a most important part.

My conviction in these matters has been given renewed emphasis by a study of what is the most important crisis in our history – apart, that is, from the last six months. This was the political crisis of 1928–29, the split in the leadership and the application of the 'social-fascist' thesis. This period, in which you yourself were one of the leading spokesmen for what began as a minority, is of extraordinary importance for us today. It illustrates and illuminates the whole problem of sectarianism – it is the only large-scale example of a fundamental cleavage within the leadership – and it affords instructive examples of the workings, and the failings, of inner-party democracy. It is, in short, a period rich in historical experience and one that must become part of the political heritage of all our activists.

You will remember that the discussion within the party leadership and the differences between the majority – which included Inkpin (General Secretary),[40] Campbell,[41] Rothstein,[42] Horner[43] – and the minority – led by Pollitt, Dutt and yourself – developed rapidly towards the end of 1927. Early in 1928 the Ninth Plenum of the Executive Committee of the Communist International (ECCI) devoted a considerable part of its time to the British situation. For the minority you were the main speaker and for the majority there was J R Campbell. All the documents and speeches are published in a volume entitled *Communist Policy in Britain*, to which my page references refer.

At this Ninth Plenum, Campbell, for the majority of the Central Committee of the British party, argued that Lenin's advice in 1920, set forth in *Left-Wing Communism*, was still broadly valid. After strong criticism of the Labour Party, Campbell summed up the majority approach:

Still, we believe that so long as the Labour Party is based on the trade unions, so long as there is a drift of the workers to the left, so long as new opposition forces are growing in the trade unions, it is a mistake to simply lump the whole as a third capitalist party and not examine the peculiarities which still exist in the composition of the Labour Party.

That being the situation, we believe that at the present moment it would be a mistake to modify the previous party policy of affiliation to the Labour Party. We believe that that policy should be continued because of the obvious advantages which it gives the Communist Party as a means of explaining its policy and winning over the workers. (p. 12)

Later in the plenum Willie Gallacher[44] spoke along similar lines. Following directly after Campbell, you then spoke for the minority. Your thesis was that Lenin's advice could no longer be accepted because of certain crucial changes in the years since 1920. These were:

… the growth and influence of the Communist Party, the whole seven years of capitalist decline and capitalist offensive, and the resulting revolutionisation of the British working class; His Majesty's Labour Government; and, following after the Labour Government, His Majesty's Labour Opposition; last of all, the General Strike, on which very little stress is laid in the thesis of the Central Committee. (p. 21)

The Labour Party had undergone a number of 'organisational changes' which had transformed it into a 'centralised social-democratic party'. The lefts in the Labour Party – including Lansbury[45] and Purcell[46] – had now swung behind Macdonald and Thomas.[47] Within the working class there was 'the beginning of an upward movement'. 'At such a moment as this', you continued, 'the Communist Party policy must be one of the sharpest and clearest antagonism to the British Labour Party. Anything which hides the cleavage between the Communist Party and the Labour Party, whether it be an organisation or whether it be a policy, is detrimental to the future of Communism in Great Britain.' (p. 23)

You asked for a 'sharp turn', and not least in electoral policy, where we had to get across 'the effect that we are standing absolutely opposed to the Labour Party'. This involved putting up candidates wherever possible, especially against the Labour Party leaders and not excluding 'Lansbury in Poplar and Purcell in the Forest of Dean'. Your approach to electoral policy can be summed up by another quotation taken from your closing remarks:

Where the party has no influence, where no Communist Party members exist (and there are many such constituencies) there it is our business to put forward in the strongest possible way the Communist Party policy, to carry out the strongest possible propaganda to put forward our point of view and to keep this up until the worker is clear as to the antagonism between ourselves and the Labour Party. In such a case, finally, we should adopt the demonstrative vote and advise workers to spoil the ballet papers by writing across some such slogan as 'To Hell with the Lot'. (p. 26)

I have no space to follow through in the detail that it requires the bitter inner-party struggles of the next two years – how the resolution at the conclusion of this Ninth Plenum gave substantial endorsement to the views of the minority – how the resolution was accepted formally but without enthusiasm or conviction by the majority on the Central Committee – how the minority continued to wage a most vigorous campaign against the majority of the leadership – how the Tenth Party Congress in January 1929 by no means resolved the crisis (Wally Tapsell,[48] of the minority, later killed in Spain, noting that 'if ever there was a party leadership obstinately determined *not* to be self-critical it was the party leadership at the Tenth Congress') – how throughout 1928 and 1929, with a steadily falling membership, bitterness and sectarianism steadily increased among those who remained – how without the intervention of ECCI it is unlikely that the minority would have had full access to the party press – how the reluctance of the majority of the Central Committee to publish critical resolutions was at least in part overcome by their publication in the journal of the international movement – how the Tenth Plenum of ECCI (July 1929) gave full support to the minority and how this was followed by the replacement at the highest levels of certain of the majority by the minority (Harry Pollitt taking over General Secretary from Inkpin) – and finally, how the emergency congress at Leeds at the end of 1929 confirmed the existing changes of personnel already made, gave endorsement to the 'New Line', and made nearly a clean sweep of the old majority leadership (only twelve members of the old Central Committee being re-elected, with twenty-three new comrades being brought in).

This is an inadequate summary, as I am well aware – and on many points there will be differences, and often sharp differences, of opinion. To enable all of us to participate in this discussion we need not only a full selection of documents but as many personal accounts by participants as we can obtain. As I read the story Arthur Horner gave only perfunctory support to the new policies of the Leeds Congress, and Comrade Horner has a duty to set down for the record what his position was then and what his analysis is today after twenty-five years. Andrew Rothstein in those days was high in the leadership of the party. He belonged to the majority of the Central Committee and his account, unvarnished and untrimmed, would be a valuable historical document. The same is true of J R Campbell, also a member of the majority. Above all, when we have the documents and the personal stories, we need honesty in our reappraisal of these years. And an honest story and an official history are rarely one and the same thing. But honesty we must have, whatever the personal heartaches and the political misgivings. Honesty in our estimate of the part (the crucial part, as I read the evidence) which the Communist International played in this internal crisis – honesty, too, in the factual account of the internal processes of the struggle. I get the impression – and from the cold print alone I can get no further – that the minority engaged in quite considerable factional activity on their own behalf. I am not relying for my evidence upon the statements of the majority of the Central Committee who continually accused the minority of factional activity – for this, as we all know, is the first accusation of any leadership when critics and criticism develop. There *is* evidence of factional work on the part of the minority, but whatever the story, in this as in other connections, let us have it straight.

More important, however, than anything that has yet been mentioned, is the political analysis which has to be made. The 'New Line' as it developed was based upon the theory of 'social-fascism' – and the first necessity in the approach to these years must be an assessment of this theory. Stalin provided an early formulation in September 1924 when he wrote that 'social democracy is objectively the moderate wing of fascism'[49] – a thesis which was worked out in detail in the years which followed and which was elaborated at the Sixth Congress of the Communist International in 1928 and the Tenth Plenum in 1929. Here we get the full-blown theory which the advocates of the 'New Line' in Britain accepted and applied to British conditions. In the *Programme of the Communist International,* adopted by the Sixth Congress, social democracy was characterised as 'the mainstay of imperialism in the working class'. The right wing of social democracy was avowedly counter-revolutionary while 'the left wing is essential for the subtle deception of the workers. While playing with pacifist and at times even with revolutionary phrases, "left" social democracy in practice acts against the workers … and is therefore the most dangerous faction in the social democratic parties.' As late as 1934 R P Dutt was repeating this analysis at great length in his *Fascism and Social Revolution.* A footnote on page 155 says this:

> Left Social Democrats often say of Communism: 'Our aims are the same, we differ only in methods.' It would be more correct to say of Social-Democracy and Fascism: 'Their aims are the same (the saving of capitalism from the working-class revolution), they differ only in their methods.'

This, then, was the starting point for the New Line in Britain. The Eleventh Congress at Leeds (November–December 1929) which saw the victory of the Pollitt–Dutt line, approved a resolution which said that the main political task of the party was:

... to rally masses of workers around a programme of struggle against the Labour Government and against the so-called 'lefts' (Maxton,[50] Cook[51] and Co) binding together all the struggles into the central political fight against the Labour Government. The party, which aims at winning over the majority of the working class, must come out as the independent leadership of the proletariat in all its struggles, leading and initiating strikes, and must give clear political character to every fight and show their revolutionary significance. In the fight against the Social-Fascist government, as a government of armed attack on the Soviet Union, and on the colonial revolt, the party must mercilessly expose the pseudo-lefts, the main prop of the MacDonald Government.

The results of the 'New Line' were disastrous. The very considerable potentialities of rallying the many thousands of honest socialists in the Labour Party against MacDonaldism disappeared beneath the waves of sectarianism that engulfed the party. The National Left-Wing Movement (made up originally of Labour Parties disaffiliated for refusing to accept the ban on Communists) was deliberately broken, on the grounds that there could be no third party between the social-democratic masses, 'now rapidly moving leftwards', and the Communist Party. The Minority Movement, of considerable significance in the trade-union field, was undermined and seriously weakened by sectarian mistakes. Party membership fell from an official registered figure of 3200 in December 1929 (it had been 10,000 three years earlier) to 2555 in November 1930. By the middle of 1931 it was just over 3000, and at the time of the Twelfth Congress in November 1932, a year after the collapse of the second Labour Government, membership had only risen to 5600, of whom, moreover, 60 per cent were unemployed. All this while the economic background to these years included the most serious economic crisis in British history, with unemployment being counted in millions.

Sectarianism went all along the line and affected decisions on minor as well as major issues. J T Murphy,[52] who in 1929 had been one of the most vociferous of the 'lefts', was expelled in 1932 for advocating the development of trading relations with the Soviet Union – a political argument which the Political Bureau characterised thus:

J T Murphy's childish argument that international trading relations reduce the danger of war is nothing but vulgar capitalist propaganda ... to put forward the demand for trading relations as an alternative or supplementary form of fight against armed intervention means to completely disguise the whole character of the life and death struggle now going on between the two world systems.[53]

The results of the 'social-fascist' policy were not just disastrous in the short run – and as so often happens, the day-to-day application of the policy was more rigid than the policy itself – but in the long term it had two major consequences. In the first place, it gravely worsened the relations between ourselves and the rest of the labour movement, and the political effects are still with us today, and secondly it strongly reinforced the sectarianism which our party inherited from the pre-1914 Marxist groups. Sectarianism is the strongest conditioned attitude within our movement – and whenever the political going begins to get tough, sectarianism stiffens our backs and provides us with a too easy solace in our struggle 'against the stream'. At our Twenty-First Congress in 1949, for example, James Gardner[54] reported on 'The Battle of Ideas and the Importance of Theory'.

> The more the class struggle develops [he said] and the more the workers begin to see through the right-wing reformist leaders, the more capitalism will throw out various breeds of leftists, mouthing revolutionary phrases to capture the workers and keep them in the capitalist net. It is not by chance that we see the 'rising star' of Aneurin Bevan.[55] It is not an accident that Harold Laski[56] and G D H Cole, old reserves of capitalism, are being thrown into the limelight.

The comments that James Klugmann recently made (*Marxist Quarterly*, July 1956) concerning personal sincerity and political disagreements are apposite here. Allen Hutt,[57] in a completely different context and certainly from a very different point of view, put the matter more vigorously when he wrote (in his critique of Tom Bell's attempt at a history of the party) of 'the rotten sectarian suspicion of everyone else's motives that has for half a century had such disastrous effects on our movement in this country' (*Labour Monthly*, June 1937). The point I want to make is this. The sectarian tendency in our thinking and our practice is very deeply rooted in all of us. We fluctuate in our attitudes to the Labour left between an analysis which sees the left as the most dangerous enemy (which in its many variations is at bottom the Sixth CI Congress line) and that which takes hold of the statements of the Labour left and boosts them in our unity campaigns – as we are doing at the moment. But we have to do more than protest our sincerity if not only the Labour left but the whole labour movement are willing to accept our united front approaches as anything but a tactical manoeuvre.

I have concentrated upon two of the difficult periods in our history because they bear directly upon current discussions and problems – both in the issues at stake and in the conduct of controversy itself. There are other periods about which there will be less controversy and where our record is an example to the whole labour movement. The need for close and honest analysis is, however, no less great. The story of our struggle against unemployment, the record on colonial issues, the years of rising membership and increasing political influence – such as 1935–39 and 1941–45 – are all rich in examples of political and organisational flexibility, intellectual vigour and of a lively political life close to the people. There are lessons here which, if taken to heart, can help us once again to breach the walls of sectarianism. The recital of these things will enthuse both our latest recruits and our foundation members. We can learn what has helped our party to advance and what has held it back – the *causes* of both our achievements and our failures. It is the task of the History Commission, and not least of yourself, to ensure that we get a party history that our movement deserves – one that will teach and instruct, one that will inspire, and above all, because of its honesty and integrity, one that will play a not inconsiderable part in the furtherance of the unity of our labour movement in Britain.

Yours fraternally

John Saville

* * *

Bob Davies, Some Notes on the 1937–38 Purges[58]

In their assessment of the 1937–38 purges of Soviet party, professional and administrative personnel, British Marxists have hardly ever been more than superficial. Until the publication of Khrushchev's speech to the private session of the Twentieth Congress, we ignored (in our *publications* at least) the facts about the widespread nature of the purges, we defended the system of arrests and trials as fully justified, and the charges against the accused as accurate.

Since June, on the other hand, we seem to have found it extremely easy to accept the view that the whole purge was a simple case of easily avoidable injustice. This has been common ground between the 'liberal' and 'conservative' extremes of our party. R Palme Dutt put it from his point of view as follows:

> The Twentieth Congress has revealed that the party was not seething with traitors and agents, that it was, on the contrary, the security organs that had got out of hand and gone wrong. (*Labour Monthly*, June 1956)

And liberal-minded intellectuals, who had always felt doubts about the whole business, now also tend to condemn 'the evil crimes of 1937–38' as a blot on the name of socialism, without serious analysis of what lay behind them.

I believe that the purges had profound historical causes, and that British Marxists must make a careful investigation of these causes if we are to draw any lessons for the future. These notes are no more than the beginning of an approach to this investigation.

Perhaps it almost goes without saying that the original official Soviet explanation, couched primarily in terms of Stalin's personal idiosyncrasies, is inadequate and unhistorical. Stalin did not act alone in 1937–38: he was *actively* backed by many of the present Soviet leaders, and by at least a large section of the industrial working class. Thus Molotov made the main report on wrecking to the February–March 1937 Plenum of the Central Committee of the CPSU (*Bolshevik*, no. 8, 1937); Zhdanov[59] was the co-signatory of the letter demanding the appointment of Yezhov[60] as Commissar of Internal Affairs (Zhdanov, had he lived, would undoubtedly have held a leading position after Stalin's death) and Khrushchev publicly supported the purge, including the purge of people such as Yenukidze[61] who did not go far enough in dealing with 'enemies of the party' (see quotation in *Manchester Guardian* text of Khrushchev's speech, p. 11; he made many similar public statements).

An explanation in personal terms, as Togliatti said, means that 'the true problems are escaping. These are how and why Soviet society could arrive at certain forms removed from the path of democracy and legality.'[62]

Here I suggest, as raw material towards an eventual historical analysis, four major factors which need to be taken into account.

I: The Contradiction in Soviet Life Which Was Overcome By the Purges

a) For historical reasons, a very high proportion of leading positions in the party had tended to be held by intellectuals rather than by industrial workers. After the Lenin enrolment of 1924, there was a substantial improvement in the class composition of the party, but even by 1934 (below Politbureau level) very many posts were held in the party by intellectuals whose experience had been gained in factional struggles before and after the revolution, rather than by the new forces of the working class trained in the

Five–Year Plans and experienced in socialist construction at factory level.

b) This contradiction within the party also extended to industrial and state administration generally, in which top posts tended to be in the hands of Civil War heroes and intellectuals rather than of the young engineers from the working class, trained in 1925–32.

After the purges, this contradiction had been resolved:

> After the purge, the administrative personnel of the whole *combinat* was almost 100 per cent young Soviet engineers. There were almost no prisoner specialists, and the foreigners had virtually disappeared. Yet by 1939 the work of certain departments had become better than ever before. (Scott, *Behind the Urals*, p. 163)

> From 1937 a general purge of the whole administrative and economic apparatus of the country set in and with it the removal from business posts not only of Trotskyists but of many other party members, who held their positions in the economic system on the strength of former party 'services' and not because they knew their job ...
>
> The subsequent developments in industry show that the campaign against wrecking and the party purge of 1937, with the numerous changes in the personnel of industry's managerial and production-administrative machinery which they entailed and the promotion to administrative posts of new cadres trained in special schools and grown to manhood during the first and second five-year periods, exercised not an adverse but a beneficial influence on the development of industry. (Baykov, *Development of the Soviet Economic System*, p. 281)

II: The Structure of Soviet Judicial Machinery

a) Tsarist Russia had a long background of injustice. In the 1920s, the use in Soviet conditions of the continental system of judicial investigation, based on the Napoleonic Code, led to the development of a pattern of public political trials in which the accused made elaborate confessions, based on fact, but often only *partly* based on fact.

The trials of bourgeois specialists and of counter-revolutionary politicians in the 1920s were succeeded, as it were, by a 'natural' process of growth, by the big public trials of enemies *within* the party in 1937–38.

b) The injustices which resulted were not prevented by the Soviet state machinery because the Soviet Union had not proved able to develop a proper system of checks and balances in its constitutional and legal structure. There was much tacit assumption that Lenin's dictum that the proletarian dictatorship 'is not subject to any laws', and the Marxist view on the divisibility of powers, meant that special attention did not have to be devoted to elaborate constitutional devices for safeguarding the citizen against bureaucracy and injustice emanating from the working-class state.

Thus though much was done in the 1930s to improve civil law, etc, nothing was done to protect the citizen against the political police of the socialist state.

III: The Ideology of the Party and the Working Class

a) The struggle against the opposition in the late 1920s and early 1930s had left great bitterness in its wake in the party. The mass of party members, and the leadership associated with Stalin, found it easy to believe that these people were traitors, and that anyone (like Postyshev)[63] who wanted to compromise about destroying them physically was a traitor too. The extent of this bitterness is indicated by Khrushchev's remark (State Department version, my italics): 'At present, *after a sufficiently long historical period*, we can speak about the fight with the Trotskyists with complete calm and can analyse this matter with sufficient objectivity.' This implies that at the time calm and objectivity were difficult if not impossible.

b) Thus on the ideological side we can sum up the position by saying that the Soviet proletariat had not at that time achieved a sufficient understanding of the political developments then taking place in the USSR to be able to distinguish between political errors, objective treachery and subjective treachery. (This was a feature of the whole international Communist movement in the early 1930s, as the term 'social fascist' indicates, though outside the USSR it began to be overcome after the 1935 Comintern Congress.)

Why was the Soviet proletariat insufficiently mature to be able to make this distinction between treachery and political error? In the first place, it must be remembered that the Soviet working class was largely a new working class, made up of largely semi-literate ex-peasants, who brought a peasant's outlook on affairs into the working class and somewhat diluted the socialist consciousness of the working class as a whole. The Soviet party paid great attention to the political education of this new working class, but this education inevitably took dogmatic and simplified forms. The position was made worse by the fact that the issue involved was one on which even a more advanced working class might tend to take up an oversimplified position: the Bukharinites and Trotskyites were thought of in the same way that a factory on strike thinks of its scabs and blacklegs, and with a considerable amount of justification.

Secondly, and this is of great importance to us, little attempt was made by the more educated (if much less revolutionary) working class in the West to check or correct what was going on in Russia. In Britain, for example, the average Labour worker was bewildered and uncomprehending; and he was utterly unconvinced by our attempts to explain the purges in the terms used by the Russians themselves. Moreover, the speeches by British Communist leaders and left-wing lawyers defending the purges were reproduced at length in the Soviet press, and helped to quiet what doubts there were among the Russians themselves, by giving the impression that the solid body of British progressive opinion was on their side. (I am not attempting to argue here that it was really possible in the circumstances for the British party to act differently, though I tend to think that it was; nor am I saying that it is certain that things would have been radically different in the USSR if Western Communists had acted differently. But I do think that these possibilities deserve serious examination and discussion.)

IV: The International Situation and the Policy of the Soviet Leadership

Thus in the USSR in 1936 there existed: 1) the social contradiction in soviet and party life; 2) the one-sided structure of the judicial apparatus; 3) the general ideology of the party and the working class on the question of enemies of the working class.

In this situation the majority of the Soviet leadership in the Politbureau, led by Stalin, supported or launched the 1937–38 purge. The theoretical basis for this was the view that the war danger meant that the potential fifth column danger in the USSR must be eliminated:

The more we progress, the more successes we have, the more inimical the remnants of the exploiting classes will become, the more rapidly will they move to sharper forms of struggle …

It must be borne in mind that the remnants of the defeated classes in the USSR are not alone. They have the direct support of our enemies outside the USSR. It would be mistaken to think that the sphere of the class struggle is limited by the frontiers of the USSR. If one end of the class struggle operates within the framework of the USSR, its other end stretches into the bourgeois states which surround us. The remnants of the defeated classes are bound to know this …

Tens of thousands of workers have to be set to work to build a Dnieper Dam, but it requires perhaps not more than a few dozen men to blow it up. Several Red Army corps may be necessary to win a battle during wartime. But it needs only a few spies somewhere in the army headquarters, or even in a divisional staff, to steal the plan of operations and pass it on to the enemy. Thousands of people are required to build a big railway bridge, but a few people are sufficient to blow it up ... Consequently, we must not comfort ourselves with the fact that we are many, while they, the Trotskyite wreckers, are few. We must bring about a situation where there is not a single Trotskyite wrecker left in our ranks. (Stalin, *Bolshevik*, no. 7, 1937)[64]

Thus the purges of 1937–38 are most complex in their origin. It is now our job, without in any way minimising these events, or underestimating the injustices involved, to study their underlying causes, so that we can learn from Soviet experience and minimise injustices in the development of socialism in Britain.

* * *

CORRESPONDENCE
Bright Memories Will Remain

In February of this year, the *Daily Worker* reported briefly that *Pravda* had published an article by Eugene Varga[65] commemorating the seventieth anniversary of the birth of Béla Kun, the great Hungarian revolutionary who led the short-lived Hungarian Soviet Republic of 1919.

One reader was curious and asked the *Daily Worker* when and where Béla Kun died and what was the history of his latter years. The Assistant Editor replied that they had no information at all and suggested that the Hungarian Information Service might help.

The Hungarian News and Information Service knew only that he was a refugee in the Soviet Union for a great many years and understood that he died there.

The British-Soviet Friendship Society had no information as to when and where he died, but the General Secretary confirmed that 'it certainly was in the Soviet Union'. How did he know Béla Kun died 'certainly' in the Soviet Union as he did not know when or where? He knew Béla Kun was in the USSR in the 1930s as he saw him then when Kun working in the Communist International. As far as he knew, he 'dropped out of activity' round about the time that Dimitrov[66] became Secretary. After that he knew nothing, but mentioned – significantly – that 'Béla Kun was already quite old in the 1930s'.

Was he suggesting that Béla Kun, having 'dropped out of activity', died quietly of old age about that time? Perhaps he was looking old but in, say, 1937 he was only 51. Could the BSFS use their good offices to address enquiries as to the fate of Béla Kun to the appropriate body in London or

Moscow? No, he could not help any further and he did not think it was any business of us in Britain to spend time 'fishing about for details of things like this because surely it is a matter primarily for the Hungarian Communists rather than for us'.

Continuing the search, the Society for Cultural Relations with the USSR were asked the same questions. The Secretary provided a translation of the original *Pravda* article which added little information except in the phrase '… people's democracy was established in Hungary, but only after Béla Kun's death'. So he died before 1945 and no one commemorated the sixtieth anniversary of his birth in 1946. The Secretary of the SCR suggested that 'many things will clearly emerge into the light of day during this year' and one should wait a little. But why wait? Could she address enquiries somewhere to find the answers now? Frankly, she did not know and had not the slightest idea how one could find out. The patient enquirer suggested that the editor of *Pravda* might know. But no reply.

In the July issue of *Labour Monthly*, RPD referred to 'so many dear friends and comrades, some of whom, like Béla Kun, have since been cleared of their sentences …' Hoping this meant what it said, would he kindly quote details of the sentence Béla Kun received? But RPD had no further information other than 'the official statement'. What official statement presumably only he knows.

Only one other avenue was unexplored. A letter was sent to Eugene Varga, c/o *Pravda*, Moscow. A reply is still awaited, but with diminishing confidence.

Apart from the *Daily Worker*, the Hungarian Information Service, the British-Soviet Friendship Society, the SCR and *Labour Monthly*, the whole world knows that Béla Kun was one of the victims of Stalin's purges, probably in 1937 when press reports to this effect were first circulated. Even as recently as last December, he was being slandered as a traitor and the hangman of the Hungarian revolution by Rákosi.

Why this mystery about this particular crime when so much more has already been admitted? Is the difficulty this – that because the Russians have not themselves said anything about what did happen, we in Britain may not ask?

But why bother about it all? Partly because this man's life and death are not less important to us than, say, the Rosenbergs' or Sobel's.[67] But more than this, because it is one example (and there are many, many others) where a great crime has been committed which, with the others, sullies the name of the Soviet Union and international socialism. What is the proper attitude to such a crime? Surely to act as Lenin said Communists should when mistakes were made (Lenin didn't envisage the commission of deliberate crime), namely to admit things openly and fully (not in secret sessions), analyse how they happened, see they cannot recur. Has the present Soviet leadership taken any of these steps in the case of Béla Kun? More important still is the attitude of British Communists and others who think themselves friends of the Soviet Union who, even now, will criticise the Soviet leadership only up to the point that they are prepared to criticise themselves, deeming loyalty to them more important than truth, than socialism itself.

Varga wrote: 'Bright memories of Béla Kun will remain forever in the hearts of the Hungarian people and the minds of Communist fighters in all lands.'

J Young[68]
London
1 October 1956

* * *

Blinkers

Not all revolutionary movements are fully democratic in the sense that power resides with the membership; it is quite possible to have a 'government of the saints', *for* the people not *by* the people. I do not wish to raise here the organisational question – how far has our party been a democratic one – but rather to look at the spirit behind our organisational practice, in other words our methods of thought.

Discussions in the party are often lively and hard-hitting, and this has given the appearance of the greatest possible participation in party decisions. In fact these are usually on the basis of how policy is to be carried out, rather than on actually framing it; and within terms of reference set from above. There are two symptoms of this limitation; first, there is a tendency for political discussion to be dull, that is, not to make demands on the mind so much as the memory. How many discussions can we remember of really basic political issues? None in our party press, certainly. This lack has produced a compensating tendency; there has been less rigidity where cultural questions are concerned, and these when raised have often struck the sort of intellectual sparks untouched by politics.

Far more serious is the effect of this paternalism, and the thought-patterns that go with it, on our integrity. If limits are drawn to our mental horizons, then there are going to be difficulties on both sides. On the side of those who draw the limits, a false sense of responsibility will argue, 'It would not be good for them to know *that*', and facts will be evaded. A series of such exercises in responsibility, and we can find ourselves utterly out of touch with reality. On the other side, the acceptance of these limits leads to a dangerous nullity of Marxist thought – to otherwise acute minds harbouring blind spots. For instance, many of those capable of perceiving the positive historical merits of Ivan the Terrible have been quite unable to see the importance of the Labour Party's post-1945 reforms. Or there are those who still believe Beria to have been an American agent since 1920, and that only reluctance to disturb relations with America prevents the publication of the full evidence.

The existence of these intellectual blinkers naturally cramps initiative, and this is one of the most noticeable lacks of our party today. Indeed, it may be asked if initiative now is regarded as a political virtue. The initiative for the two most vital postwar discussions, the question of 'seizing the banner of democratic freedoms' and the present Great Debate, have both come from successive Russian party congresses.

Finally, we should not be puzzled by the gap which divides us from the Labour left. How often we speak of them 'supporting our policies, but not *us*': it is not any particular policy or lack of policy on our part which repels so many Labour friends, so much as our way of thinking, our style. Paternalistic ideas are especially alien to the left wing of the Labour Party, as they should be to us; even in Russia, where they have more of an ancestry, they are clearly on the way out.

Without claiming that this is necessarily the key to the complex of problems which we now, mostly, recognise to exist, we should examine our shortcomings in every activity, including that of *thinking*. This will make good our claim to be a party in which the membership are participators rather than followers.

E Martin
Hertfordshire

* * *

Democratic Centralism

This letter was submitted to *World News* some weeks ago, but has not yet been published. The author has now added two sentences at the end of the first paragraph – Editors.

* * *

Comrade Mahon's article on 'democratic centralism'[69] asserts that this system is essential for political effectiveness; but he brings forward no serious arguments to support this opinion, and our experience in this country during the last twenty years has shown its weaknesses rather than its advantages. For instance, it has failed to secure a vigorous intellectual life in the party, and our publications on intellectual subjects have catastrophically declined; and it has failed to bring forward new leaders able to adapt our policy and attitude to changing circumstances. Both these faults can probably be ascribed to the absence of organised, publicised opposition to executive authority. This absence of opposition has resulted in an Executive composed of ageing men and women, who remain sectarian whilst decrying sectarianism, and who advocate self-criticism for everyone except themselves. If there are promotions of younger men, for instance to the Political Committee, they are of party officials who have received ten years' discipline in loyalty to the Executive.

When I attended a national congress as a delegate from my branch I became convinced of the undemocratic character of election by the Panels Commission and list method. Indirect election (and the panels method amounts to this) always tends to be undemocratic. Panels Commission members were most of them inevitably established leaders of the party and their influence partly derives from the esteem of party officials, who are themselves profoundly influenced by King Street. The right of appeal to the commission is made ineffective (except perhaps as a psychological safety-valve) because a member who goes to the commission is unaware of the points made by other comrades, and cannot know whether his disagreement is limited to himself and his delegation, and is therefore insignificant, or is widely supported and therefore politically important. The list which emerges, whatever the successes or failures of the party during the preceding two years, is almost precisely the list proposed by the retiring Executive. Our Executive is very nearly a self-perpetuating body, reinforced by cooption.

Comrade Mahon's point that an unbalanced Executive results from a free vote is often used as a defence of the panels system. If the panel system were the only possible alternative to a free vote the defence would be valid. But it is not the only possible alternative. It would be possible to elect the Executive by some such means as the following: a) each district elect one member by a free vote at an aggregate meeting; b) the remaining places to be elected at congress, these places to be grouped, a certain number allotted to industrial workers, a certain number to professional workers, and so on. A well-balanced Executive could be obtained on a free vote by this means.

The essential factor in 'democratic centralism' which makes it so centralist and so little democratic is that it consistently isolates the individual who disagrees. This is shown by his isolation when he goes to the Panels Commission, unaware of the support which he might receive from other comrades. It is shown in a much more important respect by the monolithic character of the party press, which until recently gave no place to serious opposition. Even now, when the shock of an external event has broken the front of orthodoxy, we suspect that certain criticisms are not published. How is the comrade with a new or different point of view to publicise it within the party? How is he to get in touch with other comrades who share his ideas? How are these members to find their natural leaders and elect them on to the Executive? All they can do is to natter about their point of view in their branches until an official is sent along to a branch meeting to deal with their 'weaknesses and difficulties'. The authority given to the officials by our movement and the unanimous weight of party literature stifles movements for change and reassessment at their inception.

I have little sympathy for Comrade Mahon's attempt to lay the blame for our lack of democracy upon the shoulders of our members and his charge of 'lethargy'. It is true that we have been too acquiescent, but in designing institutions we must take account of human characteristics. Our institutions demand a more than human degree of energy, independence and conviction before democracy can be effective within the framework they provide.

Stella Jull
Birmingham

* * *

The Basis of Stalinism

When I joined the YCL in 1941 at the age of 14, I was taught that in the maxim 'look for the class basis' lay the key to understanding human affairs. I will never forget the new world which opened to me through the use of that key.

Now, however, I find that fashions change even in Marxism. We have been told of monstrous perversions of justice, freedom, academic life, history, of the suppression of national minorities and, in one case at least, of a minority culture. No one to my knowledge seems to be looking for the *class* basis of these aberrations.

We now know that Stalin was not Lenin's Siamese twin; that his role in the revolution and Civil War was, to say the very least, exaggerated in the text books; that his reactionary activities against his own people were denounced by Lenin; even that he supported the Provisional Government in 1917! Yet we not only fail to apply Marxist analysis to the rise and development of Stalinism but we accept as gospel the characterisation of his opponents and the analyses of their ideas from the same tainted source as gave birth to these lies.

In our reappraisal is it not time we looked to original sources and went back to the very beginnings? Is there any Marxist reason for accepting 1934 as the demarcation line of our reappraisal – if so, what day?

Is it possible that Stalin represented the bureaucracy against which Lenin warned? That the theory of Socialism in One Country was the expression of the wish of that bureaucracy to consolidate its position in a period of exhaustion and disillusion in the revolutions of the West? That the swelling of the party membership by fifty per cent in 1924 and the purge, mainly directed against opposition elements, which was simultaneously carried out, were the beginning of the consolidation of the power of the bureaucracy? The lifting of the wage restriction of party members – the development of a fantastic differentiation in earnings – the reactionary developments in the judicial field – were these part of the same process which culminated in the annihilation of the Bolshevik Old Guard?

Was the invention of foreign intrigue which was used as the excuse for the Moscow Trials merely a device to condemn by guilt through association and thereby avoid the public discussion of opposition programmes?

Were the anti-Semitic outrages a product of the Great Russian chauvinism of the Stalinist bureaucracy or were they due to the condition of one or two men? If the latter, then Jews are evidently unsafe even thirty years after a socialist revolution and the Zionist thesis that the Jews can only trust Jews emerges strengthened at the expense of the Marxist class analysis of anti-Semitism!

How much of the present turmoil is caused by the absence of a convincing, trustworthy Marxist explanation of the horrors revealed (or partly revealed?) by Khrushchev and subsequent developments?

Perhaps I am completely wrong – perhaps we must now explain history on the basis of individuals and exterior stresses rather than classes and interior pressures. I do not claim to know all the answers – all I can say is that I am determined to study these questions – and not from the sterility of the Stalinist view of Stalin's enemies, their role in history, their ideas.

M D
Penge
13 September 1956

* * *

'The Cult of the Individual'

The reaction to the Twentieth Congress has been expressed in party circles throughout the world in the phrase 'the cult of the individual'. That these words should have been chosen as the banner under which we should fight what is wrong with the party seems to me a sign of the corruption in our thinking.

For they suggest that what caused the breakdown of inner-party democracy was an excess of individualism. But the opposite is the truth. What was bad is not that one man was a tyrant, but that hundreds and thousands of party members, inside and outside the Soviet Union, let go their individual consciences and allowed him to become a tyrant.

Now we are discussing what sort of rules we should have in the party to prevent the emergence of bureaucracy and dictatorship. A lot of worried and uneasy people are pinning their faith in some kind of constitution which will ensure against tyranny. But rules and constitutions are what people make them. The publication of the Constitution of the Soviet Union, an admirable document, coincided with the worst period of the terror. The party rules in the various Communist parties are (I believe) more or less the same; but the development of the different Communist parties has been very dissimilar.

I think that this talk about changing the rules is a symptom of the desire in all of us to let go individual responsibility on to something outside ourselves, something on to which we can put the blame if things go wrong. It is pleasant to have implicit trust in a beloved leader. It is pleasant and comfortable to believe that the Communist Party must be right simply because 'it is the vanguard of the working class'. It is pleasant to pass resolutions at a conference and think that now everything will be all right.

But there is no simple decision we can make, once and for all, that will ensure that we are doing right. There is no set of rules that can set us free from the necessity of making fresh decisions, every day, of just how much of our individual responsibility we are prepared to delegate to a central body – whether it is the Communist Party, or the government of the country we live in, be it a Communist or a capitalist government.

It seems to me that what the last thirty years have shown us is that unless a Communist Party is a body of individuals each jealously guarding his or her independence of judgement, it must degenerate into a body of yes-men.

The safeguard against tyranny, now, as it always has been, is to sharpen individuality, to strengthen individual responsibility, and not to delegate it.

Doris Lessing
London
19 October 1956

* * *

We regret that recent events in Poland and Hungary have necessitated the inclusion of additional material in this *Reasoner*. The correspondence section, which is one of the last to be typed, must therefore be cut. We apologise to correspondents whose letters have not been included. Extracts from several letters appear below – Editors.

* * *

J A Wilson (Essex): There has been a lot of talk of how the party, by its methods, has turned away potential support. As one who joined at the height of the Cold War (January 1950), I think it would be equally useful to find out why people *joined* the party during these difficult years. My reasons were somewhat as follows: i) Communist economics are incontrovertible, ii) the British CP was based on democratic lines, iii) the worst accusations against the Soviet Union were unproved, and circumstantial evidence seemed to disprove them ...

The Khrushchev 'revelations' therefore seem to have affected me differently from both (what Ronald Meek divides into) 'conservatives' and 'radicals'.

My first reaction was to consider K & Co conscious traitors, because they had taken a grievance (that is, the cult of the individual) and magnified it into a crime. It does not require my detailing the un-Marxist distortions which flowed from Soviet sources in so unorthodox a manner. My second reaction was contempt for our leadership who did nothing to subject the new 'line' to a critical analysis. This did make me look back and think that (what I still consider) our correct line on international matters was perhaps 'accidental' in that the leadership followed the SU which at this stage was correct ... But how can one really feel at ease when the party is officially supporting a policy which in the next decade (or sooner!) may become the discredited line in the SU? About turn again! What I feel is needed is neither the 'official' British CP attitude to the question, nor an exaggerated lamenting, but a speedy critical examination of the present Soviet leadership.

HR (London, N16): I should like to comment on the 'theory' that *The Reasoner* represents a revolt of the 'intellectuals'. This theory, which in my opinion has been sedulously fostered in the party, is to put it bluntly an unprincipled piece of demagogy. It exploits the anti-intellectualism and aversion to theory prevalent in the British labour movement, including the British Communist Party, to attack new ideas (and very often *old* ideas which have been forgotten or, at best, to which mere lip service has been paid) without venturing on an examination of these ideas as such. This is, of course, McCarthyism in reverse and is only a short step from the characteristic Stalinist method of attacking a person whose ideas you don't like (if necessary by frame-up, torture and assassination) rather than the ideas themselvesb... My experience is that the ferment of thought and feeling is most definitely *not* confined to 'intellectual circles' in the party. The real situation is, I think, something like this. Among the general mass of party members there is a great deal of frustration, unhappiness, worries, questionings on isolated points, etc – in brief, a diffused, amorphous atmosphere of disaffection and resentment. On the other hand, the more theoretically inclined members (the 'intellectuals') are by their very nature more articulate in expression and systematised in their thoughts. They are therefore acting as a barometer, and a very sensitive barometer at that! ... As a matter of fact all the evidence is that the real line of demarcation is not that between the intellectuals and non-intellectuals, but between the *officials and rank and file* of the party. This is a highly significant fact which will merit careful study from a number of angles (for example, the officials of the party apparatus have become bureaucratised partly because of the structure of the party and partly because of ideological vested interests developed over the course of years, if not decades, in relation to what we may now fairly call Stalinism – a system of thought, insofar as it deserves the name of a system – for many of its ideas are I feel purely empirical and opportunist – which in many respects marked a most radical departure from Marxism.

* * *

John Saville and E P Thompson, Statement by the Editors

Branches and individual members of the Communist Party have asked for our comments on the EC resolution and statement instructing us to cease publication of *The Reasoner* (*World Views*, 22 September 1956). Since we have not been permitted to present our case, nor even to correct errors of fact in the EC statement, in the official press, we present our own statement below.

* * *

The case of the Executive Committee against our action in publishing *The Reasoner* rests upon a single line of argument: that, irrespective of content or political context, the *act* of independent publication constitutes a 'grave breach of party rules, practice and discipline': that in conformity with rule, we have been called upon to cease publication by the Yorkshire District Committee and Executive Committee: and that, in disobeying this majority decision, we have broken the principle that 'minorities shall accept the decisions of the majority'.

It is therefore astonishing that the rule in question, prohibiting independent publication – upon which the whole constitutional case of the EC is based – is nowhere quoted in their statement. In fact, there is no such rule.

In answer to enquiries, the EC has fallen back upon the explanation that under Rule 27 the EC is empowered to interpret the other rules as it sees fit: and it has found it possible to interpret several rules to mean what in fact they do not say. The constitutional case of the EC rests upon this interpretation.

However, the act of our publication, and the very active controversy which has developed around it, can only be understood if it is regarded as a serious *political*, and not a simple *constitutional*, issue. Such an analysis is absent from the EC statement. The case of *The Reasoner* must in fact be judged in relation to i) the *political context* within which it has been published, ii) the *rights* of members of the party to take part in discussion, iii) the *facilities* available for this discussion, and their *editorial conduct*.

Political Context

The Khrushchev revelations and their aftermath have precipitated a fundamental debate among all Communists and Communist parties on questions of theory, history, structure, policy and method.

Nineteen fifty-six will be seen as a major landmark, a turning-point for the international working-class movement. Our actions and those of the EC must be judged against the background of a world Communist movement in which the volume of discussion continues to grow and to intensify, and which can be correctly described as a crisis.

Discussion Rights

The right of members of the Communist Party to discuss fundamental questions of Communist theory, history, policy and organisation should not be in question.

This right of discussion should not be confused with the right of independent publication, which may be in question.

If this right of discussion is not to be an empty phrase but is to be an *effective* political right, then it becomes a first duty of the leadership to ensure that adequate facilities exist in which written discussion can take place. Adequate facilities entail the existence of journals in which views at variance with those of the EC can be presented free from the censorship of the EC, and in which minority views can be posed, developed and sustained. This is a different matter from a journal (such as *World News*) under the direct and immediate control of the Political Committee, in which critical views may from time to time be given room for expression as a *safety valve* for discontent, rather than in a form suitable for serious theoretical confrontation.

The right to discuss cannot be taken away by majority decisions. Comrades who are confused by this constitutional argument must examine it more closely. No comrade will dispute the right of the majority (through its committees) to take decisions on questions of policy or action. But no comrade should agree that any committee has the right to enforce *opinions* upon the membership, to discipline the *minds* of comrades. Opinions are not effective opinions unless they can find expression, and the attempt to deny their expression, or to refuse facilities for their expression, constitutes a violation both of political and personal rights, which must be resisted by all members.

In the event of the violation of basic political rights (which we believe to be the case at present) then comrades are justified in asserting their rights in unofficial form.

The Conduct of the Discussion

The first incomplete reports of the Khrushchev speech led to a vigorous correspondence in the *Daily Worker* (early March). This was arbitrarily closed by the Political Committee but reopened under pressure from the readers. Our Twenty-Fourth Congress met in an atmosphere of confusion, one day after the announcement that the Rajk trial had been a frame-up, with many delegates believing press stories of the Khrushchev speech to be gross exaggerations. At the private session several strongly critical speeches were made, none of which were published later in the party press. Delegates left the congress convinced that a searching continuation of the discussion was to be encouraged throughout the party.

They were mistaken. Correspondence was severely restricted in the *Daily Worker* once again. Letters were refused by *World News*, and – over several weeks – only three or four letters were published arising from Comrade

Pollitt's two articles (21 April, 5 May). Comrade Dutt's 'Notes' (*Labour Monthly*, May) in which Stalin's 'errors' were compared to 'sun spots' led to a flow of highly critical letters and resolutions, not one of which was published in that journal, although Comrade Dutt later revised certain statements.

Mounting concern at aggregate meetings formed the background to the EC resolution of 13 May, which contained certain self-criticisms, elevated Stalin's 'mistakes' to the status of 'abuses and injustices', and announced the setting up of commissions (at first to be composed exclusively of members of the EC) to examine inner-party democracy and *The British Road to Socialism*. But so far from initiating discussion, this resolution was regarded as 'definitive', and District Committees were encouraged to 'endorse' it. Following upon it a further attempt was made to bring all wide-ranging discussion to a close, and (9 June) Comrade Burns opened a discussion in *World News* on 'Unity' and it was hoped to divert discussion into this more limited field.

The publication by the US State Department (June) of the text of the Khrushchev speech led to renewed and more profound concern throughout the party: and this was followed by the emergency resolution of the Political Committee (21 June) which represents the furthest point yet reached in critical analysis in any official document. At the same time the PC took the excellent step of publishing Togliatti's statement.

Even so, there are grounds to suppose that the 21 June resolution was intended to quieten criticism rather than to encourage further analysis. It contained the threat of a prohibition of discussion outside certain undefined bounds:

> The enemies of our party hope that this discussion will weaken the party and open the way for attempts to smuggle anti-Marxist, anti-Communist bourgeois conceptions into the party, striking at the roots of Communist principles and organisation.

In practice, a severe limitation of discussion continued in our press. To take one example, most of our Jewish comrades know of the two month's fight to get the *Volkstimme* article (giving facts on the decimation of Jewish political and cultural life in the Soviet Union in Stalin's last years) published. Even now, after six months, the facts contained in it have only appeared in the *Jewish Clarion*. Many letters on this question to the *Daily Worker* went unpublished. On other questions, censorship, especially in the key periodical *World News*, was so prolonged and sustained that many comrades ceased writing in despair; others, in the absence of frank and open discussion, resigned from the party. Where critical letters or articles did appear, it was only after intensive pressure.

Early in July a modification in the leadership's approach towards the question of discussion took place. This followed upon the return of Comrades Pollitt, Gollan and Ramelson from the Soviet Union, and coincided with the long resolution of the CPSU on the role of Stalin (*Daily Worker*, 7 July) which challenged Togliatti's reference to 'certain forms of degeneration' in the Soviet state during the last years of Stalin. *The actions of our EC must be seen against the world background of an attempt to stem discussion and reassert the hegemony of the Soviet party.*

At the 14–15 July EC a resolution was passed endorsing the resolution of the CPSU (with an undefined clause referring to 'some issues still not fully clarified') and calling for the main discussion to take place on 'our own policy and problems'. Comrade Matthews presented a report, a paragraph from which was given special prominence in a box on the correspondence page of *World News* (21 July):

> We should recognise that in our own party we are at a new stage in the discussion. There has been a great deal of discussion about the past, and this will continue. But our most important task now in discussing the lessons of the Twentieth Congress of the CPSU is to review our own problems and examine our own policy and activity.

What did this 'new stage' mean in practice, in the conduct of our press? 1) The direction of general discussion into two main channels – inner-party democracy and *The British Road to Socialism*. 2) The prohibition of discussion on 'the past', on Stalinism, on present problems of democratisation in the Soviet Union and East Europe, on our own party history, etc.

The permitted discussion was to take place within closed commissions or in letters of 500 words to *World News*. No further facilities were provided.

Moreover, there are grounds for believing that the Political Committee did not intend to permit any fundamental discussion of principle even within these constricted forms, but discussion only on minor questions of tactics, modifications of structure, and amendments to the phrasing of our programme.

For example, at a branch meeting in Halifax subsequent to this EC, Comrade Ramelson, a member both of the Political Committee and of the delegation to the Soviet Union, stated that it would be 'criminal' to bring into question the principles of democratic centralism within the party.

Other leading comrades are known to have stated that those who wished to question such fundamentals might do so – 'outside the party'.

It should be noted that the discussion now taking place in *World News* on democratic centralism took on a serious character only *after* the first number of *The Reasoner*, which included a long article by K Alexander on the subject.

Therefore, it was proposed to conduct a 'discussion' of inner-party democracy without discussing the theoretical principles upon which the party is based.

It was proposed to conduct a 'discussion' of *The British Road to Socialism* without permitting discussion of central problems of socialist theory (the state, the dictatorship of the proletariat, etc) and without analysis of the history and present problems of socialist countries.

It was proposed to conduct a discussion on 'unity' without discussing the history of the party or of the international movement, without examining those causes of working-class disunity upon which the 'revelations' threw light.

It was proposed to permit discussion, provided it did not depart from the framework laid down by the party leadership, and did not conflict on any point of substance with their views.

It was within this context that *The Reasoner* was first published.

Why We Published

We published *The Reasoner* because there was a political crisis both within the party and in international Communist theory which was not being reflected in the statements and actions of our leadership; because the *rights* of comrades to take part in fundamental discussion were being violated by the EC: because the *facilities* for this discussion were inadequate and their editorial control not such as to safeguard the expression of minority views.

First, our leadership had failed in their responsibility to initiate discussion, and to assist the membership in a period of political confusion and shock. The only two serious attempts to analyse the Stalin era, and its legacy in theory and practice, made by leading members of the party, have been the articles by Comrade Pollitt (*World News*, 21 April, 5 May) and Comrade Dutt (*Labour Monthly*, May, July). Both were quite inadequate.

No member of the leadership has carried forward the discussion opened by Togliatti, discussion of which has been discouraged since the return of our delegates from the Soviet Union. Members have been left to deal with a host of problems, ranging from the reassessment of Trotskyism to the problems of relations between Communist parties, without any contribution from their political leadership. From the beginning of the discussion until the present time our General Secretary, Comrade Gollan, has remained silent. Comrade Klugmann, head of the departments of propaganda and education, has said not one word of explanation concerning the sources of 'wrong information' in his book *From Trotsky to Tito*. Our experts on Soviet Russia, well-known names, have shown no public indication of the results of recent events upon their own thinking or upon their published work of the last two decades.

Second, not only were the leadership unwilling to take part in the discussion, *they were also unwilling to see the discussion take place at all.* So far from welcoming the ferment among the members, the Political Committee regretted it and were afraid of the consequences: envisaged discussion in terms of a series of safety-valves and diversions: responded reluctantly to pressure from the rank and file: and did not disguise their hope that the general concern would soon 'blow over' without serious political re-examinations.

Third, there was sufficient evidence of actual censorship, together with suppression of information, to indicate a general violation of members' rights and of the processes of inner-party democracy.

It must be remembered that at the time of our first publication the leadership held absolute control over the only media of written inner-party communication. Critics were isolated from each other. No one could have any precise knowledge of the extent of the censorship.

The publication of the first *Reasoner* answered these doubts and confirmed our assessment. Within two or three weeks we received over 200 letters, from every part of the country, revealing a ferment which reached to every corner. Many of these letters quoted instances of censorship or of the active discouragement of discussion.

The EC Statement

Thus the EC statement, by confining itself to legalistic arguments, evades any analysis of the real political issues.

Even so, several corrections of fact and comments must be made. It is not true that we have ever given 'pledges' to others to continue publication: nor that we had 'circularised all subscribers' on any question; nor that we had made any attempts to build a 'separate organisation' around *The Reasoner*: nor that we have used it to promote the emergence of an alternative leadership or of factional policies.

The Reasoner has been used for one purpose, and for one purpose only: to break open the discussion on subjects prohibited or restricted by the leadership: and to restore to members their rights of discussion.

The EC accuses us not only of infringement of rule (unspecified) but also of 'practice' – whereby, presumably, journals must be controlled by elected committees of the party. But 'practice' is by no means clear. Past practice (*Left Review, Our Time*, etc) contradicts this statement, while present practice in relation to *Labour Monthly* is undefined.[70] Our evidence suggests that this journal is, in the last resort, independent of any control by any elected committee: the 'Notes of the Month' are not submitted to the editorial board: and critical correspondence is refused publication on the authority of the Editor. We do not object to this position (although we deplore the ban on letters): but it suggests that the Political Committee has one law for its own members and another for ourselves.

Finally, a more serious question has been put to us, both in the EC statement and by some of our own readers. Why, if we believed that violations of the rights of members were taking place, did we not take up the matter fully through the recognised machinery of the party before publishing *The Reasoner*?

1) Both of us, for several months prior to publication, had been engaged in active political discussion within our own branches and areas, with the Yorkshire District and Party Centre. As a result of these active contacts, we were aware that the party leadership were 'playing for time' in the hope of avoiding serious inner-party controversy, and were using the machinery of the party, and particularly the loyalty of full-time workers, to silence and isolate criticism. So long as the leadership maintained its censorship over all national discussion, it was impossible for the effective demand for discussion rights to break through this silence.

2) Verbal and written requests from ourselves to members of the EC for a definition of minority rights had met with no satisfaction or had remained unanswered.

3) In our view no prohibition of independent publication exists in our rules, and therefore no prior permission was necessary if we were to put this question to the test. We made no secret of our intention to publish, and announced it widely beforehand. Members of the EC knew of our intention.

4) We already had had experience of the attitude of the leadership towards the 'democratic procedures' of the party. Both our own branches, before the May EC, had gone on record for a special congress. Five other branches had made the same demand. The procedure for calling a special congress is laid down in the party rules – Rule 14f – that such a congress shall be convened on the request of not less than one-third of the District Committees or one-fifth of the branches. At its May meeting the EC decided that it was not in

the interests of the party that a congress should be convened, and it brought pressure to bear on branches to withdraw their demand. Three branches withdrew, and in the meantime eight further branches and organisations went on record for a congress. At the July meeting of the EC it was agreed that a two-day National Conference, with a restricted agenda and without any power to determine policy, should be convened: and only after this was the party membership informed (*World News*, 28 July) that the demand for a special congress had been made.

Thus three and a half months were allowed to pass after the first demand for a congress, and in the meantime the EC had sought to persuade all branches to withdraw their resolutions, and had itself taken a decision on the question without permitting any national discussion. When the *fact* of the resolutions was finally published, the *text* of none of them was released, and to this day no branch or individual has been permitted to publish reasons for demanding a congress, although letters and statements have been submitted.

Thus we had experience of the leadership's respect for the 'democratic procedures' of the party, on a question relating to the rights of basic units of the party, as set out in the rules. Can it be doubted that demands for an open and honest forum, if raised through the 'recognised machinery', would have been subject to the same evasion and delay, so that today we should still have been arguing, at some point on the official ladder, while events passed us by?

'A crisis demands crisis measures', we wrote in our first editorial in July. We were not prepared to stand by any longer while members' rights of discussion were violated: nor to allow such a question of basic right to become the subject of interminable delay and prevarication.

The Present Position

Events subsequent to the publication of *The Reasoner* have confirmed our judgement as to the crisis in the party and the attitude of the leadership.

From the hundreds of letters which we have now received, we believe that *The Reasoner* – so far from spreading confusion – has helped to rally and encourage readers, has prevented their falling victim to apathy and disillusion, and has given them – and us – new confidence that we can solve our problems and find new ways forward to socialism.

These comrades did not join the Communist Party in order to abandon their minds and consciences into the hands of the Executive Committee, but in order to devote them more effectively to the work of winning socialism through the democratic, collective decision of the party.

They are not content to have their attempt to analyse and understand the present world crisis in theory met by the Executive with exhortations to turn their backs upon it and discuss the details of British policy, important as these may be.

A leadership which ignores the needs and feelings of members who over many years have devoted themselves to the work of the party, often in the face of hostility or victimisation, is in danger of losing their confidence.

The Executive's instruction to us to cease publication has aroused among these readers understandable anger.

At the same time the Executive's response to our publication has revealed their true attitude to the rights of discussion. Had it been sincere in its professed desire to promote far-reaching discussion, it could have welcomed *The Reasoner* as a part of the preliminaries leading up to the national conference. If it had felt it essential to vindicate its interpretation of rule on independent publication, it could have censured us for our action, while at the same time providing alternative discussion facilities, with safeguards for minority rights.

It could certainly have considered one of the several compromise proposals which we put forward after our first meeting with the Yorkshire District Committee.

In fact the leadership – from the time of our first publication – has been guided by two aims only: to silence *The Reasoner* unconditionally, and to regain unrestricted control over all the means of discussion.

In defence of their position, the EC statement claims that adequate discussion facilities already exist:

> Not only are the commissions meeting, but discussions have been or are on the point of being initiated in the party press on working-class unity, inner-party democracy and *The British Road to Socialism*. It is difficult to imagine any aspect of party policy or practice not covered by these three subjects.

It is surprising that the 'imagination' of the EC should have been so little agitated by the events of this year.

The question of *what* may be discussed is as crucial as the question of *how* discussion is conducted: our difference with the EC turns upon this point.

Why was all discussion in our press on the question of *The Reasoner* banned for two months, despite the fact that scores of letters had been received? District committees and branches have been encouraged to pass resolutions on the subject. How could they form a true judgement if no statement of our case could be published in the party press, if they did not know from where to obtain copies (since all advertising has been banned in party journals, and no sales allowed in party bookshops), and if all correspondence has until this time been refused?

Why can branches and committees not secure publication of their resolutions, on *The Reasoner* or on any other subject, in the party press? If space is insufficient, why are not summaries published?

Can we discuss the question of international Communist relations, Togliatti's views on 'polycentric' leadership, Stalinism in its many implications?

Can we discuss our own history? Or is discussion of this to be bottled up in the privacy of the editing commission for the next five years?

Can we reach *any* realistic and well-considered conclusions on our policy: our programme: our organisation, and our international relations – if discussion on the bases of our theory is to be prohibited, or conducted in such a way that minority views are not safeguarded and the EC is empowered to guide the membership to a predetermined conclusion?

Conclusion

We made it clear in our discussions with the Yorkshire District Committee and the Political Committee that, in the present political crisis, rights of discussion must be asserted as a matter of Communist principles: and that so long as rights are disregarded, the EC has no moral or constitutional authority to enforce duties.

We also made it clear that we did not claim any special privileges for ourselves: that in the event of these rights being safeguarded, and adequate facilities being provided, *The Reasoner* would cease publication. We inserted a statement to this effect in our second number, after receiving the EC instruction.

Neither safeguards nor new facilities have yet been provided.

We appreciate that since the appearance of *The Reasoner* – and especially during the past two months when the EC has been attempting to silence it – a considerable improvement has taken place in the correspondence columns of *World News*. At the same time we recognise that this constitutes absolutely no guarantee that even this protection for the rights of the membership will continue: that it remains absolutely within the power of the Political Committee to open or close discussion here at will; and that it may decide to do so once *The Reasoner* is closed.

Therefore there is no case for closing *The Reasoner*. The EC has written to us since its last statement, specifically instructing us not to produce a third number. This instruction is quite unacceptable to us, since a) the EC showed a total disregard of the interests preserving the unity of the party, with due regard to the interests of a large section of the membership, by ignoring our decision to close at the third number – which had already been communicated to the leadership; b) it was necessary for us to publish this statement, in order to put the issue of discussion rights squarely before the membership; c) we believe it necessary to open up certain key problems for discussion – and this has been done in this number.

But this remains our final number. We planned only three numbers in this form, and there are two important considerations which we have borne in mind.

1) The indefinite continuation of *The Reasoner* in this form might make it possible for the 'Case of *The Reasoner*' and of ourselves to be turned into a diversion from the central issues of the discussion rights of the whole membership.

2) There is an urgent need now for a serious Socialist journal, freed from the atmosphere of dissension, with a wider and more representative editorial board.

By our ceasing to publish *The Reasoner*, the EC has the opportunity to take steps adequate to the political crisis and itself to initiate the formation of such a journal.

If the EC does take this step, it will bring to an end the situation within which individuals have been forced to act upon their own initiative. The EC has already lost much of its moral authority over the membership; it is its duty to begin to remedy a situation which is now critical.

31 October 1956

Note

We apologise to those many readers whose letters remain unanswered. Further copies of this number are obtainable, 2/– post free. Our costs and most of our expenses have been met by subs and donations: many thanks. If you think any refund is due, or if you know of a subscriber whose copy has not arrived, please let us know. All orders to address below. Printed and published by John Saville, 152 Westbourne Avenue, Hull, Yorkshire.

NOTES

1   Louis (Lajos) Kossuth (1802–1894) was the leader of the Hungarian Revolutionary Government of 1848–49 and of the Hungarian national struggle against Austria.
2   *Daily Worker*, 16 October 1956.
3   Ernő Gerő (Singer, 1898–1980) joined the Hungarian Communist Party when he was a student, went to the Soviet Union after the fall of the Hungarian Soviet Republic

in 1919, and worked in the secret police, gaining a notorious reputation during the Spanish Civil War for the repression of non-Stalinist left-wingers. He returned to Hungary in late 1944, held various ministerial posts, including Minister of the Interior, and worked closely with Rákosi. He became Prime Minister after Rákosi's fall in June 1956, but was replaced by János Kádár in October 1956. He went into exile in the Soviet Union, and returned to Hungary in 1960, but was expelled from the Communist Party.

4   Mihály Farkas (Hermann Lőwy, 1904–1965) joined the Communist movement in the 1930s, and went to the Soviet Union after fighting in the Spanish Civil War. He returned to Hungary in late 1944, and worked closely with Rákosi. He was expelled from the Communist Party and jailed in 1956, and worked as an editor after his release in 1961.

5   Władysław Gomułka (1905–1982) was a Polish industrial worker and labour activist who joined the Polish Communist Party in 1926. Arrested in 1936, he avoided the deadly purge of the party in Stalin's Terror by being in a Polish jail; he became party Secretary in 1943 and was the leading Polish Communist until his removal by Soviet loyalists in 1948. Jailed in 1951, he was released in 1954, and as a result of the political unrest and calls for liberalisation after Khrushchev's 'Secret Speech', resumed his post as First Secretary in October 1956. His record in the process of de-Stalinisation, however, was decidedly patchy, and the violent suppression of strikes by his government in 1970 led to his removal and retirement.

6   Gordon Cruickshank was the Warsaw correspondent of the *Daily Worker* during the 1950s; he also worked for the Polish national wireless station.

7   Józef Klemens Piłsudski (1867–1935) was born into a Polish noble family in Lithuania, and joined the Polish Socialist Party in 1893. His advocacy of a combination of socialist and nationalist ideas led to a split in 1906, and he subsequently led the PPS Revolutionary Fraction. He became the Head of State of independent Poland, having dissociated himself from any vestigial links with left-wing politics, and adopted an expansionist foreign policy, which led to the abortive Soviet invasion of Poland in 1920. He staged a coup in May 1926, and was informally head of state until his death, ruling in an increasingly authoritarian manner.

8   J V Stalin, 'The Results of the First Five-Year Plan', *Works*, Volume 13 (FLPH, Moscow, 1954), p. 215.

9   J V Stalin, 'The Foundations of Leninism Bolshevism', *Works*, Volume 6 (FLPH, Moscow, 1953), p. 118.

10   J V Stalin, 'Some Questions Concerning the History of Bolshevism', *Works*, Volume 13 (FLPH, Moscow, 1954), p. 88.

11   J V Stalin, 'Marxism and Problems of Linguistics', *Works*, Volume 16 (Red Star Press, London, 1986), p. 197; James Klugmann, 'Basis and Superstructure', *Essays on Socialist Realism and the British Cultural Tradition* (Fore Publications, London, 1952).

12   J V Stalin, *Dialectical and Historical Materialism* (FLPH, Moscow, 1951), p. 16.

13   It appeared in *World News*, 22 September 1956.

14   John Mahon, 'Inner-Party Democracy', *World News*, 1 September 1956. John Mahon (1901–1975) joined the CPGB in 1920, and soon became a full-time party worker. He joined the Executive Committee in 1948, and was the party's Industrial Organiser and later the Secretary of its London District. He wrote a biography of Harry Pollitt.

15   In 1956, Sheila Lynd was a journalist working for the *Daily Worker*; she left the CPGB in 1958.

16   The address of the CPGB's national headquarters in London WC2.

17   At our meeting with the Political Committee on 31 August this point was put to us, and we assured the PC that we intended to submit contributions as soon as time allowed. Comrade Thompson in fact submitted a very long statement to the Commission on Inner-Party Democracy early in October – *Reasoner* Editors' note.

18   The 'Show Me State' is an unofficial name for the US state of Missouri; why it is so called is unclear.

19   '… when men deal with men, how often do they go to work like so many Cains and Abels …', from *Mother Earth* by Douglas William Jerrold (1803–1857), an English radical playwright and author.

20   See note 14 above.

21   Jean Frédéric Joliot-Curie (1900–1958) was a French physicist; he supported the Popular Front in the 1930s, and joined the French Communist Party in 1943 whilst he was active in the French Resistance.

22   V I Lenin, 'What Is To Be Done?', *Collected Works*, Volume 5 (Progress, Moscow, 1977), p. 480.

23   Joan Violet Robinson (1903–1983) was a leading British Keynesian economist and Cambridge academic; she was the author of many works on the subject of economics. She was greatly interested in Mao's China and made several visits there.

24   Oskar Ryszard Lange (1904–1965) was a Polish economist. He was born in Poland, emigrated to the USA, was head-hunted by Stalin, returned to Poland in 1945, and served in diplomatic and other government posts as well as working at Warsaw University. He disagreed with Marx's theory of value, and was a pioneer of market socialism.

25   An English translation of this speech has been published in the September 1956 number of the *Economic Bulletin*, issued by the Economic Committee of the British Communist Party. Reference should also be made to Lange's stimulating article in the May 1956 number of *Cahiers Internationaux* – Author's note.

26   Konstantin Konstantinovich Rokossovsky (1896–1968) was born into a Polish noble family. He joined the Bolsheviks in 1917 and fought in many areas in the Red Army during the Civil War. He was arrested in the Great Terror, but did not confess, and was subsequently released from jail in 1940. He played a leading role in many key areas of combat during the Second World War. In 1949 he was appointed Minister of Defence in Poland; he took a hard line against protests in Poznań in 1956, and was removed by Gomułka. In 1958, he was appointed chief inspector of the Soviet Ministry of Defence.

27   Konstantin Mikhailovich Simonov (1915–1979) worked as an engineer until the mid-1930s, when he went to university. He was an army officer and war correspondent during the Second World War. He had various poems and novels published and plays performed, and he was the editor-in-chief of *Novy Mir* during 1946–50 and 1954–58, editor-in-chief of *Literaturnaya Gazeta* during 1950–53, and Secretary of the Soviet Writers Union during 1946–59 and 1967–79.

28   Imre Nagy (1896–1958) was a prisoner-of-war in Russia during the First World War, he joined the Soviet Communist Party and the Red Army, returned to Hungary in 1921, but moved back to the Soviet Union in 1930. He held ministerial posts in postwar Hungarian governments, and advocated a reformist 'new course' after 1953, which led to his dismissal from his post as Chairman of the Council of Ministers in 1955. He was reinstated in that post in October 1956, attempted to move towards a multi-party system and announced the withdrawal of Hungary from the Warsaw Pact. He took refuge in the Yugoslav Embassy during the Soviet invasion, but the promise of free passage proved false, and he was arrested, secretly tried and executed.

29   Tibor Déry (1894–1977) was a leading Hungarian writer and translator. He was expelled from the Communist Party in 1953, and was a spokesman for the opposition during 1956, for which he was tried in 1957 and imprisoned until 1960.

30   Tibor Tardos (1918–2004) was an Hungarian journalist, translator and writer. Living in France after 1938, he worked with the French Resistance during the Second World War, and returned to Hungary in 1947. In 1956 he was active in the Petőfi Circle, and as a result was sentenced in 1957 to six months in prison. He emigrated to France in 1963.

31 Júlia Rajk (Földi, 1914–1981) joined the Hungarian Communist Party prior to 1945, she was arrested with László Rajk in 1949, jailed for five years, and rehabilitated in 1954. She was interned in Romania after the suppression of the Hungarian Uprising.

32 Márton Horváth (1906–1987) joined the Hungarian Communist Party in 1931, and he held several important posts in the postwar government up to 1956, but was relegated afterwards to cultural posts.

33 József Révai (Lederer, 1898–1959) joined the Hungarian Communist Party in 1918, and lived in the Soviet Union during 1934–44. He edited the party paper *Szabad Nép* during 1945–50, was appointed Minister of Culture in 1949, although his influence waned after 1953, and he resumed his place in the leadership of the party after 1956.

34 József Darvas (Dumitrás, 1912–1973) was an Hungarian poet and writer. He was in touch with the Hungarian Communist Party in the 1930s, and by 1945 he was a leading member of the National Peasant Party. He was Minister of Religion and Education during 1950–51, Minister of Education during 1951–53, and Minister of Culture during 1953–56. He held various political and cultural posts after 1956, and became President of the Writers Association in 1960.

35 Canossa is an Italian town where in 1077 the Holy Roman Emperor Henry IV stood in penance in the snow for three days in order to reverse his excommunication: the term is often used to describe an humiliating climb-down.

36 Robert 'Robin' Page Arnot (1890–1986) was a member of the ILP and headed the Labour Research Department during 1914–26. A foundation member of the CPGB, he was a member of the party's Executive Committee during 1927–38. He wrote a large number of historical works, including a multi-volume history of the miners' union in Britain.

37 *World News*, 22 September 1956.

38 Humphrey Frank Owen (1905–1979) was a journalist and author, and the Liberal MP for Hereford during 1929–31. He worked on the *Daily Express* and edited the *Evening Standard* during 1938–41 and the *Daily Mail* during 1947–50; he assisted Michael Foot in writing *Guilty Men*.

39 The situation of the CPGB in 1939 was subsequently discussed in J Attfield and S Williams (eds), *1939: The Communist Party of Great Britain and the War* (Lawrence and Wishart, London, 1984); the minutes of the CPGB Central Committee meeting at which the new line was discussed can be found in F King and G Matthews (eds), *About Turn: The Communist Party and the Outbreak of the Second World War: The Verbatim Record of the Central Committee Meetings, 1939* (Lawrence and Wishart, London, 1990).

40 Albert Inkpin (1884–1944) joined the Social Democratic Federation in 1906 and then the British Socialist Party in 1911. He opposed the First World War, joined the CPGB upon its foundation, and was its General Secretary during 1920–22 and 1923–29, after which he headed the Friends of the Soviet Union, later the Russia Today Society, until his death.

41 John Ross Campbell (1894–1969) joined the British Socialist Party in 1912, and then the CPGB upon its foundation. He was a member of its leadership and held several key posts, including Assistant Editor of the *Daily Worker*. His disagreement with the Communist International's 'imperialist war' line in October 1939 led to a temporary period of disgrace. He was Editor of the *Daily Worker* during 1949–59.

42 Andrew Rothstein (1898–1994) joined the CPGB upon its foundation; he was removed from its leadership in 1929 because of his opposition to the ultra-left 'Third Period' line. After then he wrote extensively on the Soviet Union, and translated Russian material into English. His academic career was cut short in 1950 when he was dismissed from the School of Slavonic and East European Studies in London in a Cold War purge.

43 Arthur Horner (1894–1968) was a miner and active trade unionist; he joined the

CPGB upon its foundation, he was removed from its leadership in 1929 because of his opposition to the ultra-left 'Third Period' line, but returned to it in 1935. He was President of the South Wales Miners Federation during 1935–46, then was General Secretary of the National Union of Mineworkers during 1946–59.

44   William Gallacher (1881–1965) was a member of the Social Democratic Federation and President of the Clyde Workers Committee during the First World War, and was sentenced to six months' jail for publishing an anti-war article in the CWC's journal. He joined the CPGB in 1921, was an MP during 1935–50, and was President of the party during 1956–63.

45   George Lansbury (1859–1940) was a Christian socialist and pacifist on the left of the Labour Party. He was an MP during 1910–12 and 1922–40, and leader of the Labour Party from 1932 to 1935.

46   Albert Arthur Purcell (1872–1935) was a left-wing trade unionist and a member of the Social Democratic Federation; he was later a Labour MP during 1923–24 and 1925–29, and was elected President of the TUC in 1924. In 1925 he headed a TUC delegation to the Soviet Union.

47   James Henry 'Jimmy' Thomas (1874–1949) was Secretary of State for the Colonies in MacDonald's first government, then Lord Privy Seal and later Secretary of State for the Dominions and Colonial Secretary in his second Labour and National Governments, and was duly expelled from the Labour Party.

48   Walter Thomas Leo 'Wally' Tapsell (1904–1938) was an early member of the CPGB, and became Secretary of the Young Communist League. He was backed by Moscow because of his support for the policies of the Third Period. He was the Political Commissar of the British Battalion in the Spanish Civil War, and was killed when the battalion was ambushed by Italian forces after the Battle of Belchite.

49   J V Stalin, 'Concerning the International Situation', *Works*, Volume 6 (FLPH, Moscow, 1954), p. 295.

50   James Maxton (1885–1946) was Chairman of the Independent Labour Party during 1926–31 and 1934–39, and MP for Glasgow Bridgeton during 1922–46.

51   Arthur James Cook (1883–1931) was a long-standing militant in the miners' union, and was General Secretary of the Miners Federation of Great Britain during 1924–31.

52   John Thomas Murphy (1888–1965) was a shop steward in the engineering industry who joined the Socialist Labour Party in 1917 and then the CPGB upon its foundation. He was the party's Industrial Organiser and helped run its National Minority Movement. He moved the expulsion of Trotsky from the Communist International in 1927. He developed differences with the CPGB in the early 1930s, was expelled in 1932, worked for a while in the Socialist League, and then dropped out of political activity.

53   'Statement of the Political Bureau on J T Murphy', *Communist Review*, Volume 4, no 6, June 1932.

54   Jim Gardner was a foundation member of the CPGB; he was a member of the party Executive Committee from the late 1940s, and was elected General Secretary of the National Union of Foundry Workers in 1944.

55   Aneurin Bevan (1897–1960) was a miner and trade unionist activist; he was elected as the Labour MP for Ebbw Vale in 1929 and held the seat until his death. A noted left-winger, he was Minister of Health in the first postwar Labour government, overseeing the creation of the National Health Service.

56   Harold Joseph Laski (1893–1950) was an influential left-wing academic and writer; he was Chairman of the Labour Party during 1945–46.

57   Allen Hutt (1901–1973) was a journalist and writer who joined the CPGB in the mid-1920s; he worked on the *Daily Worker* from its inception, and was its chief sub-editor for many years. He was a leading member of the National Union of Journalists.

58   Robert William 'Bob' Davies (1925–) was at this point a lecturer at the University of Birmingham; he subsequently wrote extensively on the Soviet economy, co-authored

with EH Carr one of the final volumes of *The History of Soviet Russia*, and wrote several large volumes on the initial Soviet Five-Year Plans.

59   Andrei Alexandrovich Zhdanov (1896–1948) joined the Bolsheviks in 1915; he worked in the Soviet Communist Party's organisational apparatus, he joined the Politbureau as a candidate member in 1934 and a full member in 1939, and he oversaw Stalin's restrictive cultural policies from 1946 until his death.

60   Nikolai Ivanovich Yezhov (1895–1940) joined the Bolsheviks in 1917; he worked mainly in the Soviet Communist Party's apparatus. He became head of the NKVD in 1936 and oversaw the Great Terror; he resigned in disgrace from his post in late 1938, and was tried and executed.

61   Avel Safronovich Yenukidze (1877–1937) was a founder of a social-democratic group in Baku in 1900 and helped to run its clandestine printing-house; he was Secretary of the Central Executive Committee of the Soviets from 1918 to 1935. In the 1930s he was accused of downplaying Stalin's pre-revolutionary role in his writings, fell out of official favour, and disappeared in the Great Terror.

62   See Palmiro Togliatti, '9 Domande sullo Stalinismo', *Nuovi Argomenti*, no 20, 16 June 1956, in *The Anti-Stalin Campaign and International Communism* (Columbia University Press, New York, 1956), p. 120.

63   Pavel Petrovich Postyshev (1887–1939) joined the Russian Social-Democratic Labour Party in 1904, and sided with the Bolsheviks. He headed the Communist Party in Ukraine during the late 1920s and from early 1933, and was notorious for purging oppositionists. Although an enthusiastic participant in the Great Terror, he was arrested in 1938 and executed.

64   J V Stalin, 'Defects in Party Work and Measures for Liquidating Trotskyite and Other Double Dealers', *Works*, Volume 14 (Red Star Press, London, 1978), pp. 268–69.

65   Eugen Samuilovich Varga (1879–1964) was active on the left in Hungary prior to the First World War, and was Minister of Finance in the Hungarian Soviet Republic of 1919. He moved to the Soviet Union in 1920, and over the subsequent decades wrote many works on the world economy.

66   Georgi Dimitrov (1882–1949) joined the Bulgarian Social-Democratic Workers Party in 1902, and adhered to the 'Narrow' faction when it split away in 1903. He remained with this group when it became the Bulgarian Communist Party in 1919. Whilst living in Germany, he was framed by the Nazi government for the burning of the Reichstag in 1933; he defended himself vigorously at his trial, and was acquitted. He became Secretary of the Communist International in 1935, and was the leading spokesman for the Popular Front strategy. He became General Secretary of the Bulgarian Communist Party and the Prime Minister of Bulgaria in 1946, remaining in both posts until his death.

67   Perhaps a reference to Morton Sobell (see note 43, *The Reasoner*, no 1), although he was not executed.

68   Joe Young of London SE3 praised the new Trotskyist paper *The Newsletter* for its 'great contribution to the awakening socialist movement in Britain' (*The Newsletter*, 7 June 1957).

69   See note 14 above.

70   *Labour Monthly* was launched in 1921 as a nominally independent magazine. It was edited by Rajani Palme Dutt, who contributed a lengthy 'Notes of the Month' to most issues, until his death in 1974. That he used it for factional purposes in the CPGB came to light in 1928 when he openly promoted in its pages the minority view in the party leadership on the Labour Party; for this he was censured by the party Executive, although this censure was subsequently overturned by the Executive Committee of the Communist International, which was backing the supporters of this line. It ceased publication in 1981.

RONALD MEEK

The Marxist-Leninist's Song

The sixtieth anniversary of *The Reasoner* must not go by without the republication of this delightful view of the changes taking place in Communist parties in the light of Khrushchev's 'Secret Speech'. It is taken from *The Rhyming Reasoner*, no 2, November 1956. *The Rhyming Reasoner* was a somewhat scurrilous duplicated magazine published by Ronald Meek. It is sung to the tune of the famous air from Gilbert and Sullivan's *The Pirates of Penzance.*

M-L: I am the very model of a modern Marxist-Leninist,
I'm anti-war and anti-God, and very anti-feminist;
My thinking's dialectical, my wisdom's undebatable,
When I negate negations, they're undoubtedly negatable.
And yet I'm no ascetic – I am always full of bonhomie
When lecturing to classes on the primitive economy;
And comrades all agree that they have never heard a smarter cuss
Explain the basic reasons for the slave revolt of Spartacus.

Chorus: Explain the basic reasons for the slave revolt of Spartacus.

M-L: I'm fierce and unrelenting when I'm extirpating heresies,
Yet patient and forgiving to the comrade who his error sees;
In short, as propagandist, agitator and polemicist,
I am the very model of a modern Marxist-Leninist.

Chorus: In short, as propagandist, agitator and polemicist,
He is the very model of a modern Marxist-Leninist.

M-L: My love of party history comes very close to mania,
I teem with information on the Bund in Lithuania;
My speech on the Decembrists is replete with fun and pleasantry,
I know the different stages in collectivising peasantry.
With Russian Social Democrats I'm always glad to clench a fist

(While carefully distinguishing the Bolshevist and Menshevist);
But when I am confronted with a regular Bukharinite,
I get a rise in temperature (both centigrade and fahrenheit).

Chorus: He gets a rise in temperature (both centigrade and fahrenheit).

M-L: I know what Lenin said about the concept of the deity,
And why it's very dangerous to worship spontaneity;
In short, as propagandist, agitator and polemicist,
I am the very model of a modern Marxist-Leninist.

Chorus: In short, as propagandist, agitator and polemicist,
He is the very model of a modern Marxist-Leninist.

M-L: In fact, when I begin to try to fight against bureaucracy,
To criticise myself a bit, and practise more democracy;
When bringing Marx's teachings up to date I'm much more wary at,
And when I've done with phrases like 'impoverished proletariat';
When I have learned that workers think that nothing can be sillier
Than 'monolithic unity' and biased Russophilia:
Then people will exclaim: 'Hurrah! He's not a stupid sap at all.
'A better Marxist-Leninist has never studied *Capital*.'

Chorus: A better Marxist-Leninist has never studied *Capital*.

M-L: My policies and theories have an air of unreality
Because I am a victim of the cult of personality;
But still, as propagandist, agitator and polemicist,
I am the very model of a modern Marxist-Leninist.

Chorus: In short, as propagandist, agitator and polemicist,
He is the very model of a modern Marxist-Leninist

Essays

... this project can only be fulfilled on one condition: that the
agenda of 1956 is carried through to the bitter end.
E P Thompson

JOHN McILROY

John Saville and Stalinism: An Exploration

The 1956 crisis of British Communism has been identified with the exit of the intellectuals, particularly the 1930s generation. There is truth in this, but the judgement does scant justice to the efflux of workers and simplifies the response of party intellectuals. Many of the anti-fascist generation resigned from the CPGB, at the time or in the aftermath of the crisis, including Chimen Abramsky; Ken Alexander; Robert Browning; Michael and Eleanor Barratt Brown; Henry Collins; Royden and Pauline Harrison; Rodney Hilton; Bridget and Christopher Hill; Victor Kiernan; Doris Lessing; Ronald Meek; Malcolm MacEwen; Brian Pearce; Edgell Rickword; Raphael Samuel; John Saville; Randall Swingler; and Edward Thompson. Others remained – notably, Noreen Branson; Ron and Joan Bellamy; Alan Bush; Bill Carritt; Maurice Cornforth; Eric Hobsbawm; Margot Heinemann; Arnold Kettle; James Klugmann; John Lewis; Jack Lindsay; George and Betty Matthews; Max Morris; Betty Reid; Brian, Joan and Roger Simon; and Pat Sloan. Of the older generation, Rutland Boughton and Hyman Levy left, but Robin Page Arnot; Kay Beauchamp; Olive Budden; Emile and Eleanor Burns; Maurice Dobb; Rajani Palme Dutt; GCT Giles; Walter Holmes; AL Morton; Ivor Montagu; and Andrew Rothstein remained.[1] There was continuity as well as change.

This alerts us to the limits of generalisation. Despite a defining core of common political commitment, the term 'intellectual' fails to distinguish between the situations of architects, lawyers and artists or the personal experience of Communism of, say, Klugmann, a party functionary, Morris, a schoolteacher, and Lessing, a novelist. It does not differentiate between those employed by the CPGB, such as Reid or Cornforth, imaginative writers such as Randall Swingler and John Sommerfield, and those who worked in universities, although even in the academy we can distinguish between the experience of scientists, historians and literary critics, for example, JBS Haldane, Hill and Kettle. The point is underlined when we observe that within generations, roughly defined, members were of different ages, originated from different backgrounds, and joined at different times and, to some extent, for diverse reasons. The vast majority came from the bourgeoisie, but Levy, for example, came from an impoverished Jewish immigrant family and Montagu an aristocratic background, while Abramsky was an immigrant from Russia. Sloan, normally identified with the Popular Front generation, joined the CPGB in 1930; Levy, already in his forties, in 1931; Cornforth in 1932; Edward Thompson a decade later. Recruitment in the universities commenced in 1931 and took off in 1932 – when the party was still purveying ultra-left Third Period politics. Like Sloan, Levy and Cornforth, the journey to Communism of other intellectuals might just as easily be identified with economic crisis, middle-class insecurities, the split in the Labour Party and faith in the Soviet Union, as with the anti-fascism that influenced recruits of the late 1930s.[2] Moreover, John Saville suggested, most of the intellectuals who enrolled in the 1930s and during the war left during the immediate postwar years.[3]

The categories 'intellectual' and 'generation' help only at a general level. To probe further we need to examine individual experiences of Communism. Given his importance in 1956, I want to look at Saville's earlier history and his later evolution in order to explore what it tells us about one intellectual's engagement with Stalinism as both protagonist and antagonist.[4]

The Making of a Communist Intellectual

Saville wrote briefly about his early life in an essay in the 1990s and at greater length in his memoirs published in 2003.[5] His self-examination discloses little in his childhood and adolescence which might explain why he became a Communist as an eighteen-year-old student at the London School of Economics (LSE). Born in 1916, Saville passed his early life in 'a comfortable petty-bourgeois family milieu' in Romford, 'a small country town' near London, protected from the worst ravages of the interwar depression. His stepfather, Alfred Saville, was a master tailor, company executive and freemason; he met and married Saville's mother when she worked as his housekeeper. Unlike many middle-class Communists who were privately educated, Saville attended the local grammar school. He was a boy scout and a practising Anglican, although he ceased to believe in his teens. He enjoyed school, where he was not bookish but acquired a taste for the French language and culture.[6]

There was another side to this. His father was an upper-class Greek who died in the Great War, a year after Saville's birth. The son spent the first four years of his life with a friend of his mother, with whom he remained friendly through life, in Gainsborough 'in a working-class home', where, he stresses, he was offered love and security. This gave him some insight into how other people lived. Until he became John Saville as a Communist in the late 1930s – whether in empathy with the Popular Front stress on 'anglicisation' or for other reasons remains obscure – his name was Orestes Stamatopoulos.[7] He gives no indication that this had any impact on the identity of a boy growing up in a conventional English middle-class milieu – the family took the right-wing *Daily Mail* – or that it encouraged a sense of being an outsider. What he emphasises is that: 'It would not be appropriate to describe myself as politically aware when I first entered LSE ... I found myself ignorant of much of the detail of the political discussions I was listening to.'[8] On this account capitalist crisis, the Soviet Union, fascism, had negligible impact on his formation. The car factories, Briggs, Kelsey Hayes and Ford, on the nearby Dagenham Estate and the big strike of 1933 did not impinge on his consciousness, although in his last year at school he read more and developed anti-war feelings. Here, again, his story diverges from many contemporary 'induction into Communism' narratives where subversive attitudes emerge before contact with the party, sometimes during the subject's schooldays.[9]

Hobsbawm hazarded: '... something must have been germinating.'[10] Despite the absence of earlier manifestations of radicalism or political allegiance of any kind, within two months of his arrival at LSE, he joined the student Communist Party. Whether his lack of prior commitment to socialism or knowledge of alternatives against which to measure the Soviet surrogate affected his decision to enrol remains conjectural.[11] Young Communists he encountered, notably James Jefferys and Jean MacDonald, facilitated an epiphany consolidated by voracious reading. He recalled his conversion in prosaic, matter-of-fact terms, but remembered 'a growing sense of excitement at the widening intellectual horizons that Marxism offered'.[12] Despite his later disparagement of explanations which depicted recruits to Communism as fulfilling a need for authority and belonging, he appreciated being part of a disciplined international movement. He developed a powerful antagonism to capitalism, the National Government, fascism and Labourism, pride in the CPGB, and lifelong enthusiasm for the Popular Front.

Saville joined the Communist Party on the basis of politics different from those of the revolutionary 1920s. Through 1935 Communists moved beyond seeking a united front with mainstream labour movement leaders to soliciting a Popular Front which included 'progressive' Liberals and

Conservatives in order to foster alliances between the Soviet Union and the liberal democracies against Germany. The CPGB enthusiastically embraced change as an escape from the ultra-left Third Period with its Class Against Class line: it asserted its identification with the 'national interest', emphasised its English lineage, and accepted the blunting of the sharp edge of revolutionary politics and the veering towards reformism that cross-class policies demanded.[13] Popular Frontism mobilised the radicalised bourgeois consciousness of the early 1930s which identified with the condition of the working class and sought to transform it. The new line empowered middle-class intellectuals by providing them with a distinctive role in what they perceived as an emancipatory project. It furnished them with a 'sensible', palatable politics, further to the right than at any point since the CPGB's inception. Middle-class students were politically enfranchised: for the first time in the twentieth century an effective student organisation with strong traction at Cambridge, Oxford and LSE, but radiating out to other universities and colleges, attracted middle-class youth in significant numbers. The cell Saville joined in late 1934 had some 25 members, and more than eighty three years later.[14]

In a party striving to make itself hospitable to the bourgeoisie, the commitment of the 18-year-old was trained through practice: Saville became the London student organiser and acquired a grasp of how the CPGB functioned as secretary of its Romford branch for a spell in 1937-38. He spent brief periods working on the party's behalf in the 'progressive' Union of Democratic Control, where he was involved in the Comintern-orchestrated campaign for solidarity with China, and the National Unemployed Workers Movement, where he was inspired by Communists such as Wal Hannington and Don Renton.[15] Many young agitators have shed their radicalism when the freedoms of student life are superseded by the restraints of making a living. Saville's fidelity endured as he worked as a teacher and for the Dictaphone Company and British Home Stores in the late 1930s. Many Communists have defected when confronted with the twists and turns of party policy required by Russian interests. Saville demonstrated his stamina by maintaining his affiliation even when the Soviet Union and the CPGB deserted anti-fascism for the Hitler–Stalin Pact. He admired Harry Pollitt and Rajani Palme Dutt and became in every way a passionate young Communist. His faith was sufficiently strong for him to resist the 1939-40 efflux of intellectuals such as John Strachey, who had strongly influenced him, and it was reinforced by his wartime experience in the army. That 'toughened him', gave him greater insight into British workers and class relations, sharpened his insight into imperialism and provided an introduction to Indian Communism – as well as offering opportunities for further study.[16]

Saville vindicated the Jesuitical maxim, 'Give me the boy and I'll give you the man'. Despite his zeal for the party, the 'get good degrees and good jobs in the professions to further the cause' strand in contemporary Communist thinking prevailed over the path chosen by his friend, the academically gifted James Klugmann, who decided to work full-time for the CPGB.[17] By the time he was appointed as an assistant lecturer in economic history at Hull in 1947, Saville was in his thirties and part of a small group of Communist scholars who pursued academic careers in provincial universities. Recognised as a University College the previous year (and as a university in 1956), it remained an outpost of academe in a city 'on the edge of the world ... so far from anywhere else'.[18] Saville was a relatively isolated, self-contained, if collegial Communist. Most British academics he observed, 'are technicians ... the majority do not form part of an intelligentsia concerned with the wider cultural or political issues of the world'.[19] He defined himself against this as an intellectual and historian, determined to remain a Communist and an academic. His political identity centred on anti-capitalism, the Soviet Union and the labour movement. Henry Pelling and other mainstream historians of labour, Saville declared, suggesting how he conceived himself, were 'outside the orbit of the labour movement'.[20] In common with most Communist intellectuals, his relationship with organised labour was more aspirational than real, particularly in light of the marginality of the CPGB during the Cold War. A notable exception was a group involved in the growth of trade-union education in the universities and here party members were sometimes at the cutting edge.[21] Saville was active in the Lecturing and Administrative Staffs Association, tutored adult classes in Hull during the evenings as well as miners' schools in the North East of England, and sold the *Daily Worker*. Neither the university nor the city were strongholds of Communism, and he was not involved in a representative capacity in the CPGB; his main party work was organising a British-Soviet Friendship Society.[22]

Academic duties and raising a family absorbed time and energy, and in 1956, a year of stress, he experienced conflict between the claims of researching and writing history and engagement in politics.[23] In the first postwar decade he reconciled them through participation in the nineteenth-century section of the CPGB Historians' Group, an organisation which involved, inter alia, Hill, Hilton, Hobsbawm, Collins, Kiernan, Abramsky, Meek, Pearce and Dona Torr. Torr, to whom the volume of essays which Saville took a leading part in editing, *Democracy and the Labour Movement*, was dedicated, exercised a powerful influence on both him and Thompson. She nourished their Popular Front conviction that the CPGB was not a Russian intrusion into the British political landscape but the legitimate descendant of the British democratic tradition stretching back to John Ball and embracing the Chartists, William Morris and Tom Mann.[24] The Historians' Group provided Saville with an anchor and an intellectual network based firmly in the academy. Attempts to develop history beyond the walls and to engage directly with workers were limited. Lay historians who participated in the group felt that: 'The tendency to academic sectarianism prevalent amongst the academic members must be combated sharply.' There were complaints that the nineteenth-century section was insufficiently involved with the labour movement.[25] The academic trajectory of the group highlighted the fact that most CPGB intellectuals of the period operated in a specialist sphere, rather than making a more direct contribution to mainstream party activity.[26] Saville researched the early working class and Chartism, but his contributions to the party press were restricted to an article on 1848 in the *Modern Quarterly* and a short piece on Henry Fielding in *Labour Monthly*.[27] He never wrote on questions of party policy or general political issues. But he lived in the world of 'the two camps', of the Soviet Union as the face of the future and the inspirational genius of Stalin. The Historians' Group reflected and purveyed that ethos. Christopher Hill, a Fellow of Balliol College Oxford, Saville's collaborator in preparing *Democracy and the Labour Movement* and the scholar he regarded 'as the senior member of the Historians' Group, a historian of growing reputation and a man of notable integrity',[28] was fulsome in his praise of Stalin's qualities as an historian:

> First, because he was a very great and penetrating thinker, who on any subject was apt to break through the cobwebs of academic argument to the heart of the matter; secondly, because he was a highly responsible leader, who expressed a view only after mature consideration and weighing the opinion of experts on the subject. His statements, therefore approximate to the highest wisdom of the collective thought of the Soviet Union.[29]

Saville and the Experience of Stalinism, 1934-1956

Despite occasional expressions of his preference for history, Saville was always profoundly political. His memoirs begin, in Pauline fashion, with his conversion to Communism rather than with his early life. Two-thirds of the text is dominated by his 22 years as a Communist, and he briefly discusses his response to some of the central episodes in Stalinist history. The

Moscow Trials, 1935-38, seem to have possessed continuing significance for him. He wrote about them no less than four times between 1977 and 2003 and two of the accounts refer briefly to his own attitude.[30] Saville was striving to be fair. However, his comments are at times informed by a restricted Communist conception of who constituted 'the Left' and may appear contradictory. Addressing what he belatedly accepted were 'frame-ups', Saville claims that there was surprisingly little adverse comment in Britain.[31] Although 'some of the best minds of the labour movement were either sceptical or in firm opposition … the weight of evidence available to British readers on the Left was overwhelmingly in support of the trials'.[32] The examples he cites to support the latter judgement – the testimony of the fellow-travellers, Dudley Collard and DN Pritt, the American Ambassador to Moscow, Joseph Davies, who was infatuated with the Soviet Union, the Anglo-Soviet Parliamentary Committee, and the Moscow correspondent of the *Daily Herald,* are hardly conclusive.[33] On the other hand, Saville acknowledges the extent of criticism in the *Manchester Guardian,* the *New Statesman, Plebs* and *Forward*: 'The range and degree of scepticism on the left, even in Britain, was, however, greater than is sometimes recognised'[34] – although never as great as in America or France.

There is no mention of the role the CPGB played in the personal comments and only terse reference in his other accounts.[35] There is little inkling in these texts that the party, of which Saville was an enthusiastic activist – not a dispassionate assessor of evidence – mounted a sustained offensive to discredit critics, even threatening to withdraw from the Unity Campaign with the Independent Labour Party and Socialist League unless they desisted from attacking the Soviet Union.[36] The CPGB – the *Daily Worker* headline 'Shoot the Reptiles' was symptomatic – did not tolerate doubts: for the party this was the opposite of a debate designed to establish the truth. Communists were partisan players. The coverage, and spin, in the CPGB press exceeded that from any other single source. Its fabrications were justified in a *trahison des clercs* by party intellectuals, notably Ralph Fox, Allen Hutt, Douglas Garman, Pat Sloan and John Strachey. But the public relations campaign was marshalled from Moscow:

> The Comintern gave very firm instructions on how the party should present the major show trial of 1936 … The PB [Politbureau] was quick to pick up on the significance of this [1937] trial – presumably Pollitt had been briefed while in Moscow. The PB planned a special supplement to the *Daily Worker* and a special pamphlet … Pollitt did, however, ask

> Moscow to try to persuade Stalin to give an interview to the British press
> in order to explain the importance and validity of the trial ... [37]

Saville provides two major reasons, in addition to the weight of evidence,
to explain why the trials 'exercised so little influence on my generation'.[38]
The first was that the accused confessed and did not deny the charges or
retract their confessions in court; if they were innocent, this was baffling for
there was no evidence of torture and due process seemed to have occurred.
The second was the international situation and the perceived need on the
non-Stalinist left to join the Soviet Union in an anti-fascist alliance.[39] Any
definitive judgement on the weight of evidence and how it was perceived
is difficult. However, a recent survey of the press and personal statements
concludes that 'the purges were fiercely criticised across a representative
range of Labour and Left opinion'.[40] The implication is that there was
sufficient information for socialists with open minds to reach a critical
verdict.

In contrast with Saville, many contemporary observers found the
confessions eminently explicable. The socialist intellectual, HN Brailsford
stated at the time that: '... only terror could have extorted them ... Civilised
justice does not rely on confessions ... the whole procedure is a relic of the
Middle Ages, worthy rather of the Inquisition than of a Socialist Tribunal.'
The ILP's *New Leader* believed that 'physical and mental exhaustion plus the
hope of a possible reprieve influenced the minds of the defendants'. William
Gillies of the Labour Party claimed that 'the confessions were extracted by
the threat of torture'.[41] Saville pointed out that Koestler's hypothesis in
Darkness at Noon, which did not depend on torture – the party is always
right, the individual must capitulate to its dictates – was rejected in the
cases of Bukharin and Radek by their biographers.[42] However, he makes no
reference to the well-known case of Galileo, who, denying reality, confessed
as heresy to the Inquisition his belief that the earth revolved around the
sun, and never retracted his false confession.[43] Saville is on firmer ground in
relation to the stultifying impact of the international situation, although it is
questionable whether the end justified the means. Michael Foot recalled the
case of *Tribune*: '... all papers have their Achilles heels, their blind spots or
what less charitably may be called their streaks of cowardice ... Our excuse
was that we were engaged in a unity campaign.'[44]

The context was important but not determinant. That sufficient evidence
existed for LSE students to penetrate Stalinist propaganda and take a critical
view is clear. Saville remembered intense debate in the college and recorded:
'One of my contemporaries was Alec Nove with whom I argued for many

hours about the trials. He was right and I was wrong … '[45] He recollected: 'In personal terms what I learned from my Communist years at LSE was intellectual discipline and a strong commitment to party work.'[46] In the late 1930s his commitment to party discipline prevailed. He viewed the evidence and argument through the distorting lens of a youthful but intellectually disabling Stalinism.

The limits of the *Memoirs* as autocritique are underlined when, in contrast to the attention devoted to what he described retrospectively as 'a gigantic confidence trick',[47] Saville says nothing at all about the Hitler–Stalin Pact, or his reaction to it. He can hardly have been happy with the abrupt termination of the anti-fascist line, as the swastika fluttered over Moscow airport; or with CPGB insistence that Britain and Germany were equally pursuing imperialist war aims, although Britain was the aggressor. British workers, the party argued, should support neither but push for a negotiated peace with Hitler.[48] It was, nonetheless, a moment of personal as well as political significance. In his account of 1956 he recalls, in passing, that Constance Saunders, whom he met and married at LSE, left the party over the pact. The context did not guarantee a favourable reaction from CPGB members; but Saville chose to stay.[49] Some intellectuals quit on an individual basis. Those who remained stomached what for many must have been the unimaginable: '… at meeting after meeting the new line of the Central Committee was endorsed by overwhelming votes.'[50] If Saville harboured any misgivings he swiftly discarded them and 'wholeheartedly' espoused the new line. It was only in 1956, after long silence, that he referred in print to events which demonstrated the profundity of his allegiance to Stalinism and the Soviet Union:

> Many, including myself, who at the time wholeheartedly supported the 'imperialist war' thesis, have now come to the conclusion that we were disastrously wrong (in my own case – like many others – I had arrived at this position by the end of the war).[51]

After his break with the CPGB, he rejected the argument that '… in World War Two there was no difference in fundamentals between the bourgeois democracies … and the fascist powers, Germany most particularly … It would follow among many other consequences that which [sic] of the two blocs won, the working people could expect to be treated in broadly the same way.'[52]

There seems to have been a greater degree of continuity in Saville's understanding of the Cold War. In both his recollections of that period and later historical work, he considers American imperialism, the British

Labour government's subordination to it, and the anti-Communism of both, as the major cause of the conflict. In his memoirs he laments the 'incompetence' and 'stupidity' of Russian policy, noting the refusal to provide exit visas to women married to men outside Russia, Zhdanov's cultural policy, Lysenkoism, the postwar trials and Stalin's rupture with Tito, but he does not address the dynamics of Soviet foreign policy.[53] This is also absent from his 1993 monograph, *The Politics of Continuity*, which explores British foreign policy during 1945-46: 'The major issue of Soviet intentions after 1945 is not discussed at any length ... not least because availability of the Russian archives for research should become possible within a few years.'[54] Saville's views were made clear in his 1991 essay on the Communist experience:

> The Soviet Union was not expansionist beyond its requirements for a *cordon sanitaire* on its Western borders and the widely believed idea that Russia was waiting only for the opportunity to march across Europe or into the Middle East is no longer accepted by orthodox historians. It was the great lie on which the Cold War was nourished; but the ways in which the Soviet Union pursued its foreign affairs bear a considerable responsibility for its continued nourishment. The Soviet Union, it needs to be emphasised, was not, however, the major architect of the Cold War; that dishonour belongs firmly to the United States and the United Kingdom.[55]

Few would defend the idea that the Russians intended in 1945 to march across Europe or beyond; or ignore the longstanding, deep-seated hostility of imperialism and social democracy to the Soviet Union. The problem lies rather with Saville's assertion that Russia was not expansionist, apart from its requirement for a *cordon sanitaire*: the statement occludes the degree to which the *cordon sanitaire* demanded significant expansion. Unlike capitalism, the Russian system possessed no inherent imperialist dynamic. But for Stalin, security was inextricably bound up with extending Russia's boundaries and the geopolitics of the Romanovs; vindication of Marxism-Leninism-Stalinism was another factor.[56] The *cordon sanitaire* involved annexation of the Baltic states and parts of Czechoslovakia, Finland, Germany, Japan, Poland and Romania. The innocent-sounding phrase required Russian domination of Bulgaria, Czechoslovakia, East Germany, Hungary, Poland and Romania. Whether this 'requirement' was legitimate and acceptable divided not only Stalin from Truman but Communists from social democrats. From a socialist viewpoint, the major problem with the

Attlee administrations was surely Labour's imperialism and its support for American imperialism – rather than its not entirely disinterested antagonism to Russian aggrandisement, exploitation and atomisation of the working class throughout Eastern Europe. Communists, including Saville, saw this as the extension of liberty, not oppression, enthusiastically welcomed rather than resented by the workers. The hostility of the social democrats was more evidence-based: it was underpinned by the knowledge that Soviet expansion into Eastern Europe between 1939 and 1941 had been accompanied by dictatorship and mass murder and by historical awareness of the ruthless character of Stalinism – not to speak of Labour's lengthy first-hand experience of the CPGB whose policies Saville concedes 'could be regarded, with some justification, as an extension to Russian foreign policy'.[57] Stalin's expanded conception of security and his insistence on subjugating Eastern Europe was a major contributory factor to the initiation as well as the continuation of the Cold War.

If, as Saville suggests, the main responsibility of British Marxists was for Britain's actions,[58] Russian oppression of small nationalities should have attracted their opprobrium. Criticism of Anglo-American imperialism does not require suppression of criticism of the Soviet Union – as Saville illustrated when he condemned the invasion of Hungary *and* the invasion of Suez in 1956. Writing about the collapse of Communism in 1990, he observed: 'The evil deeds of the bourgeois democracies were many but this was no argument to set against the common knowledge of what was happening in the countries of professed socialism.'[59] But knowledge of what was happening in these countries *was* common during the early Cold War; the newspapers were full of it. Nonetheless, Saville maintained that very argument in the late 1940s and early 1950s, and swallowed his misgivings. The context, the Cold War, loyalty to the Soviet Union and the siege mentality in the CPGB, constituted a constraining factor. Some party activists were reluctant to throw the towel in and let the side down; others could not break out of a routinised way of life; others felt trapped. But agency and choice, which interact with context and can overcome it, were also part of the equation. Saville's friend Francis Klingender, an art critic who worked in the Sociology Department at Hull, chose to leave the CPGB in 1948. Saville chose to remain: 'I was much more concerned with the iniquities of British foreign policy in general.'[60] When anti-Semitism was raised: 'I took an uncompromising stand against any suggestion that it existed in Russia.'[61] In this he was influenced by the testimony of Jewish Communists: 'Why should I believe the bourgeois press and not my political comrades?'[62]

The years after the war were for Saville a 'very difficult period … much more difficult than is often appreciated'.[63] The excitements of his first decade in the CPGB had subsided; Popular Front politics and Dimitrov had been superseded by the Cominform line and Zhdanov; the party had peaked and was in decline. If the mood was darker and it was harder to be a Communist, Saville's conformity ensured he did not face the difficulties or attract the opprobrium of the apparatus in the way the poets and critics Edgell Rickword and Randall Swingler did. The latter reflected in 1956: 'I have had a long experience in the party of being sneered at, smeared and generally frozen-elbowed as an unreliable element, anti-party renegade and, yes, degenerate.'[64] In early 1956, Saville wrote to Pollitt reflecting on the past, affirming his faith and affiliation, but refusing for the future unquestioning acceptance and silence:

> I was much more critical of certain aspects of Soviet society than the official Party line (that is, in private I always admitted the existence of labour camps, disliked the Stalin cult and was appalled at the way people disappeared) but I never made these criticisms, except in milder form, public. I believe now, as I have always believed, that these were transitory phenomena and I have always had confidence in the long-term development of socialism in Russia.[65]

Even at this late hour his credo remained substantially intact and the communication confirms the extent to which, in company with the majority of Communists of his generation who remained in the party, he had disregarded the responsibility of the socialist intellectual to act as a critic of power. Subsequent months generated a dramatic change. Intensive reading, writing, thinking; focused discussion with fellow members; the reassurance of knowing that one does not stand alone; producing *The Reasoner*; the stubborn immobility of the leadership; and the support and stimulus that his partnership with Thompson offered – all played a part. Saville remembered: 'Most members of the British party were not in my own privileged position with access to good libraries, time to read and a group of acquaintances within the party with whom I exchanged facts and ideas.'[66] But that had been the position since 1947. Khrushchev made the difference. Surprisingly for such a self-conscious intellectual, Saville internalised the principle of authority. For all his strengths, he was a member of the 'We were not told' generation. It required an *ex cathedra* ordinance from the hierarchy in Moscow to spur him into action – although to his credit he not only acted decisively but provided leadership to others.[67]

Exploring Stalinism After 1956

The Reasoner, largely through Thompson's contributions, had presented the beginnings of a socialist humanist approach, a moral critique of Stalinism. Editorials also insisted that an historical and political assessment of the Soviet Union and international Communism was necessary. This was generally accepted, at least in the abstract – even by the Political Committee of the CPGB.[68] Saville's own contributions in 1956 were limited and did not address Stalinism as an ideology, politics and practice rooted in the trajectory of the Russian revolution. They focused on particular aspects of CPGB history, notably the Third Period and 1939-41. This was understandable – Saville and Thompson were themselves emerging from Stalinism and endeavouring to convince other members in an internal discussion journal.[69] Nonetheless, Saville exhibited little curiosity about how CPGB policy was moulded by the development of Stalinism in Russia and Russian domination of the Comintern. Party history was treated piecemeal. It was divided into 'good' – the Popular Front – and 'bad' – the Third Period – phases, rather than being integrated into an explanatory framework which addressed origins and causation.[70] Popular Front politics were decontextualized and singled out as exemplars for the future:

> ... the years of rising membership and increasing political influence – such as 1935-39 and 1941-45 – are all rich in examples of political and organisational flexibility, organisational vigour and of a lively political life close to the people. There are lessons here which, if taken to heart, can help us again to breach the walls of sectarianism ... We can learn what has helped our party to advance and what has held it back – the *causes* of both our achievements and our failures.[71]

Signs of softness on the CPGB sat uneasily with harsher verdicts elsewhere in *The Reasoner.* For example, in September 1956 Saville wrote: '... I believe that as a party we have greatly matured in political experience and Marxist understanding over the past twenty years.'[72] Had the CPGB really 'greatly matured in Marxist understanding' in the two decades after 1936? The contents of *The Reasoner,* Saville's critique of CPGB policy in the postwar period and the unfolding of events in 1956 argued the opposite. The only example Saville provided of 'mature Marxism' was the recent campaign to remove bans and prescriptions adopted by the labour movement against Communists. Perhaps he was thinking of the Popular Front. If so he was overlooking its provenance, its purpose and its demise; the fact it was every bit as Stalinist as the Third Period or the Cold War; its intimate relationship with and subordination to the policies of a despotic state; its singular failure in Britain; and its abrupt termination because it became redundant for the Russians in light of the Hitler–Stalin Pact.

By 1957, Saville was free of the constraints of attempting to develop opposition in a hostile party and at liberty to develop the examination of the national Communist parties and the evolution and nature of Stalinism that *The Reasoner* had considered vital:

> … at some point such an analysis has to be made unless we are to succumb once again to the error which has dogged us for so long – that of failing to make a Marxist analysis of the developments in Communist movements in general and in the Socialist countries in particular … The shock and turmoil engendered by the revelations were the result of our general failure to apply a Marxist analysis to Socialist countries and to the Soviet Union in particular. The absence of such an analysis is an admission of naivety or worse. The failure bred Utopianism and encouraged attitudes of religious faith.[73]

Launched that summer, the *New Reasoner* commenced this task. There were contributions by Levy on the Soviet Union and an extract from Sartre's examination of Stalinism, but subsequent debate centred on responses to Thompson's essay on socialist humanism. Alasdair McIntyre's critique pointed the way forward. It rejected Thompson's understanding of base and superstructure in the Soviet Union, the former socialist, the latter oppressive, an analysis that Thompson shared with others trying to think their way out of Stalinism. The two, McIntyre argued, were intimately related: considered holistically – and that was the essence of the Marxist method – neither base nor superstructure, neither Russia nor its satellites could be characterised as socialist.[74] Over the next two years the journal published articles on Russia and Eastern Europe. His editorial role aside, Saville did not write on these questions.[75] Valuable as it was, the *New Reasoner*'s coverage fell short of a systematic attempt to theorise and historically to explain Stalinism. Part of the problem, certainly on Saville's and Thompson's part, was reluctance to examine critically existing theoretical and historical analysis developed in what they had been taught was a schismatic anti-Communist literature. Perry Anderson reflected:

> … there was a very long tradition of Marxist analysis and discussion of Stalinism by revolutionary socialists. Its major current, of course was founded by Trotsky. The critique of the USSR that he constructed from

the mid-1920s onwards was charged with a burning moral and political indignation some three decades before the lights of 1956. But it was also an enterprise of materialist *social theory*, an attempt at a *historical explanation* of Stalinism. The fundamental hypotheses of *The Revolution Betrayed* (1936) remain unsurpassed to this day as a framework for investigation of Soviet society.[76]

As further examples of what he conceived to be a healthy heretical tradition, Anderson cited work by Isaac Deutscher, Boris Souvarine, André Gide and Victor Serge. Excavating this fertile vein of socialist thought would seem a necessary starting point for Marxists trying to make sense of Stalinism in the 1950s. It appeared to be an indispensable agenda, but was one which Saville minimally pursued. As early as the Wortley Hall conference of dissident Communists and the broader left which launched the Socialist Forum movement and the New Left in April 1957, he revealed a very British approach. In contrast with the many contributions on the nature of Marxism and the Soviet Union, he remarked:

> ... they must stop talking hot air and build a body of Marxist ideas that meant something to the British working class. That implied studying our own working-class movement and its history, about which far too little is known. We have not done anything yet to analyse our economy over the last thirty years. There is nobody here who can give an analysis of exactly how the working class are robbed by the Welfare State. We have not started yet to apply our Marxist tools of analysis to our contemporary society.[77]

Saville's predilection was for British issues, rather than studying the Marxist canon – although for Marxists both were necessary and intimately connected – and a detailed study of the Soviet Union did not figure among his priorities. Part of the problem lay with contemporary Trotskyists and their version of Trotskyism which confirmed prejudices carried over from the CPGB and acted as a barrier to exploring dissident thought. An editorial in the first issue of the *New Reasoner* condemned both 'Marxism-Leninism-Stalinism' and 'its stunted opposite, dogmatic Trotskyism'; Thompson, having recommended the writings of Trotsky and Deutscher, deprecated Trotskyism as 'the mirror image of Stalinism'.[78] The distinction was arguable but it went unelaborated. Saville retrospectively reflected: 'Trotskyism was anti-Stalinist ... but their creeds were dogmatic, inflexible and sectarian ... and it was precisely against the intellectual rigidity and dogmatism of the British Communist Party that *The Reasoner* had developed its central arguments.'[79]

He found the far left's avid interest in the nature of the Soviet Union and its clamorous small-group politics unappealing. Like Thompson he seemed to equate certain kinds of polemic, particularly polemic with which he disagreed, with 'sectarianism'. The attraction that the biggest Trotskyist organisation, 'The Club', held for Peter Cadogan, John Daniels, Peter Fryer, Brian Pearce, Cliff Slaughter and McIntyre, among others, he considered 'quite extraordinary'.[80] Nonetheless, in early 1957 he held a discussion with the leader of 'The Club', Gerry Healy; this confirmed the unfavourable impression Healy made at their first meeting three years earlier.[81] Saville's training, temperament and competing interests interacted with lack of empathy with the Trotskyists to close a relevant avenue of intellectual exploration. It engendered reluctance to collaborate or debate with Trotskyists supportive of the *New Reasoner*. In the end, the antipathy became mutual. Fryer's critique of Thompson's 'Socialist Humanism', powerful but hardly 'sectarian', cannot have helped, and relations were permanently soured when the *New Reasoner* refused to publish a Trotskyist contribution to the discussion on Stalinism, reviving memories of the CPGB leaders' attitude.[82] Fryer characterised 1956 as having produced two tendencies:

> Some wishing to remain Communists embarked on a study of earlier Marxist criticisms of Stalinist theory and practice and intensified their activity as industrial militants. Others, retaining from their Stalinist conditioning only the firm beliefs that Trotsky wrote nothing worth reading ... turned their back on revolutionary theory, especially its application to the history of the USSR and the world communist movement.[83]

If there was truth in the latter verdict, Saville's suspicion of Healy and 'The Club' proved prescient. Tendencies to ultra-leftism, impatience and catastrophism that were discernible in 1957 were full-blown by 1959 when the Socialist Labour League (SLL) was inaugurated. By the turn of the decade the large majority of the ex-CPGB contingent had quit the SLL or had been expelled, the organisation was dominated by Healy, and internal democracy was vestigial. The group's analysis of the Soviet Union and its satellites never progressed much beyond *The Revolution Betrayed*.[84]

The New Left itself, despite its creative contribution to the stock of socialist ideas, barely outlived the decade. It remained a loose network which created no permanent organisation. Moreover, its pertinent and influential emphasis on human agency, 'socialism with a human face', the young Marx, nuclear disarmament and neutralism, cultural renewal in Britain, and the English radical tradition, produced a reaction against the 'Russification' of the old left.[85] The ebb-tide of 1956 witnessed restricted theoretical engagement with the Soviet Union and the form a socialist society should take: '... with the cessation of the *New Reasoner* in late 1959, this interest dwindled away.'[86]

Interest in socialist humanism predominated and marked the New Left. Despite its limitations, it was a worthwhile attempt to reinterpret existing Marxism. What was more questionable was the attempt by Saville and Thompson to locate a version of socialist humanism, with minimal evidence, a great deal of assertion and, perhaps, a little nostalgia, in the CPGB during its Popular Front phases. In 1959, they offered as worthy of recuperation 'the rational, humane and libertarian strand within the Communist tradition with which men of great courage and honour – from Tom Mann to Ralph Fox have been identified'.[87] They argued: '... we still have no desire to disown our debt to the Communist tradition. For all its confusion, its mixed motives, its moral amnesia and doctrinal arrogance, it was the major carrier of humanist aspirations in Britain in the 1930s and early 1940s ...'[88] Aspects of the Communist tradition remained relevant, although: '... the elect of King Street have brought it into shifty disrepute.'[89]

Saville and Thompson invoked a 'Communist tradition' without explaining what that meant. One would deduce from reading *The Reasoner* that it meant Stalinism. In that journal they had detailed the CPGB's subordination of policy to the interests of Soviet despotism; the identification of terror and a police state with socialism; failure to apply a Marxist analysis; attitudes of religious faith; a false conception of the dictatorship of the proletariat; a mistaken idea of the party; an erroneous understanding of consciousness; fear of independent thought; and moral atrophy. If their articles from 1956 fell short of a full political and historical explanation, they portrayed the CPGB as a party permeated by Stalinism.[90] There was also, it has to be said, unfurnished reference to the fact 'it was our rank and file that was tainted least by these things and our leadership most';[91] and to an optimistic spirit of truth, principle and democracy on the left during the war which had re-emerged in Hungary after being 'cribbed and confined' by Stalinism.[92] More evidence than this was required from two historians to substantiate the existence of a meaningful rational, libertarian, humanist strand in the Stalinist tradition of British Communism.

In their 1959 statement, Stalinism, which still awaited a more detailed analysis from Saville and Thompson, was reduced to 'confusion', 'mixed motives', 'moral amnesia' and presumably 'the elect of King Street'. In a substantially rhetorical discourse, they said nothing concrete about the rational, humane and libertarian strand of the 1930s and early 1940s, where its postulates were to be found, how it had developed and how it had coexisted or conflicted with the Stalinism that dominated CPGB politics. There is no exposition of how and why this strand was allowed to shrink and wither in the later 1940s by Communists, including Saville and Thompson. Few would deny the courage of Fox and Mann. Few would have identified them without a lot more evidence as personifying a tradition of socialist humanism.[93] They functioned as part of a world dominated by 'the King Street elect' and were subordinate to it. Saville and Thompson seemed unaware of the hardly rational or libertarian role Fox played in legitimising Stalin as *the* authority on Marxism and justifying dogmatic intolerance of his fellow intellectuals in the CPGB. Mann by that time was a prestigious but ageing and marginal maverick, a figurehead for the party's industrial campaigns who drew a Comintern pension.[94] A handful of intellectuals, Edgell Rickword, Randall Swingler and Montagu Slater, did, ephemerally, stand up for humanist values in the field of culture in the late 1940s. They did so without challenging the party's Stalinist politics, while Thompson, on his own account, sided with 'the cultural police'.[95]

Saville and Thompson failed to retrieve a libertarian, humanist strand of any significance from the CPGB's history. At best, it was vestigial and subterranean, beating in the hearts, homes and cultural endeavours of a small minority who in public subscribed to Stalinism, the antagonist of socialist humanism. To echo Perry Anderson: where was this libertarian tradition at the time of the Moscow Trials – which Fox justified – or the Hitler–Stalin Pact? We can only denote the CPGB of the 1930s and mid-1940s as 'the major carrier of humanist aspirations in Britain' at the price of inflation, discounting socialists of other denominations, and neglecting the hegemony that Stalinism exercised over British Communism. Saville and Thompson seemed more intent on diminishing the sway of Stalinism rather than accounting for it. Their attempt to construct 'a useable past' for the New Left, linked to an alleged tendency in the CPGB's 'golden age' of the Popular Front, smacked more of 'the invention of tradition' than historiographical rigour. It suggested the influence that a sanitised version of CPGB history continued to exercise on their thinking and a desire to embed it in the New Left.

In subsequent years Saville neither expanded his thinking on socialist humanism nor pursued *The Reasoner*'s goal of a Marxist analysis of Russia.

He *did* explore other aspects of the history of British Communism. As he reflected: 'The previous history of the CP was unknown to most of the new recruits who joined in the anti-fascist years after 1933-34.'[96] To some degree, this was a tribute to the success of the injunction that members of the Historians' Group steer clear of researching the twentieth century after the formation of the CPGB with its troublesome controversies and questions about the CPGB's trajectory, and confine themselves to earlier periods.[97] Saville's curiosity was encouraged by Pearce, whose efforts in this regard stretched as far back as 1949.[98] They were focused on the commission established to oversee preparation of a party history in September 1956. Saville's open letter to Page Arnot, who had been nominated to write the history and who, with Pearce, was a member of the commission, urged a critical approach, particularly in relation to Class Against Class and the 1939 turn to the imperialist war line. It suggested the commission's deliberations should be open to all party members.[99] In April 1957, Saville published Pearce's examination of the CPGB and the Labour left in the 1920s as a *Reasoner* pamphlet. The rump of the Historians' Group had turned it down, but Saville wrote an introduction which emphasised the enduring damage that the Third Period had inflicted on the CPGB.[100]

Debating the History of the CPGB

Saville returned to that subject in 1959 in an acrimonious review of Henry Pelling's history of the party – the first book-length study by an academic. This brief essay is of interest here because it sheds further light on his attitudes three years after he left the CPGB and illuminates his indulgent orientation towards the history of the party. Perhaps surprisingly in relation to 1956, this favourable stance would endure. A recurring trope is Saville's stress on the sterling qualities of individual Communists and positive affirmation of his twenty-two years in the CPGB. Pelling, he asserts, depicted members as 'a sectarian band of dogmatists' suppressing their 'idealism', 'self-sacrifice' and 'passionate rejection of inequality and oppression'. Speaking for himself, 'membership of the Communist Party was an immensely exhilarating and enriching experience'.[101] If Pelling's political history is lighter on people and their experience of Communism than political analysis, Saville is equally one-sided.[102] For his characterisation of members divorces them from the politics that they practised and the way that those politics became part of their lives and infused their experience. Communists' attributes and experience are artificially insulated from their politics – so recently characterised by Saville in *The Reasoner* as 'sectarian' and 'dogmatic'. Much of the 'idealism' and 'self-sacrifice' was dedicated to defending the indefensible in the Soviet Union, and later the satellites, and implementing 'sectarian' or opportunist policies in Britain. To echo Ignazio Silone and Doris Lessing, idealists became Communists in order to fight for a better world but ended up countenancing the inhumanity against which they had rebelled.[103]

Equality and freedom are indivisible. Applying double standards, CPGB members campaigned for their extension in Britain while remaining silent or supporting their negation in Russia and, as *The Reasoner* had emphasised, alienating British workers in the process. Some of Saville's contemporaries may have found the struggle, the camaraderie, the solidarity and the education exhilarating and enriching. That experience was bound up with despotism in the Soviet Union and the Moscow Trials; the Stalinist terror in Spain; the Hitler–Stalin Pact; the invasion of Finland; mass murder in Poland – and much else – and giving workers the impression, as *The Reasoner* had pointed out, that socialism entailed a police state. The two strands of experience were inseparable.

Saville took things further. In 1956 he had deplored the failure of the CPGB in the postwar years to theorise imperialism and the Soviet Union and remarked upon the crudity of the 'two camps' approach. In 1959, he sounded a different note:

> The contribution the CP has made to the theory and practice of English socialism is in many respects considerable. While the CP in the interwar years was far from having the monopoly of progressive ideas and practice, as we so wrongly believed, at the time, its contribution to the development of Marxist ideas, its consistent struggle against imperialism, its leadership of the unemployed workers' movement – and the list is by no means complete – are important and significant items on the credit side of the balance sheet.[104]

The restriction of this statement to the interwar years – presumably excluding the Third Period, 1928-1933, which had earlier been savaged by Saville – implies that the degeneration of the CPGB took place during the Cold War. On this reading, the Stalinism of Saville's youth, the Popular Front and the war, was less toxic than the Stalinism of the 'two camps' and Cominform which had been excoriated in *The Reasoner*. But no examples of the party's contribution to 'the theory of English socialism' or to 'the development of Marxist ideas' between the wars are provided, and indeed it is difficult to think of any. Saville's estimation of the CPGB's achievements is grossly exaggerated. All the key concepts in party theory during the interwar years, the united front, social fascism, the Popular Front, came from the Comintern. Their exposition in Britain was sometimes effective, sometimes not; it was never theoretically novel. Saville's assertion that the CPGB 'consistently struggled against imperialism' – the claim overlooks 1941-45 when the Soviet Union was allied with imperialism – was effectively challenged when he repeated it in criticising another scholar.[105] That leaves us with the party's support for the unemployed movement. It is hardly a dazzling inventory – particularly as Saville proceeds to enumerate some of 'the unpleasant aspects of Communist history' – Russian funding of the CPGB, social fascism, 'above all the domination of the Communist International over the British party and the way that the internal struggles of the Russian party have been minutely reflected in the political line of the British party'.[106]

Few would disagree. But the judgement – note the '*minutely reflected*' – simply confirms the paucity of the CPGB's autonomous contribution to Marxist theory and practice. Moreover, the domination of the Comintern and the CPSU over the CPGB was not just one 'unpleasant aspect' of its history: it lay at its heart and determined all other significant aspects of that body's theory, politics and practice. Yet it is included as one item on a list, rubbing shoulders with secondary phenomena. And Saville's text is silent on the context and the content of the policy of the British party in the second half of the 1930s. What that policy 'reflected' was not the interests of British workers when that failed to coincide with the interests of the Russian state. It was the struggle of the Soviet bureaucracy to preserve 'socialism in one country', and maintain its privileged position and oppressive role in relation to Russian workers through internal terror and purges, external *realpolitik* and popular fronts with the bourgeoisie – at the expense of encouraging revolutionary advance in capitalist countries. This took precedence over everything else. Yet it goes unacknowledged. In Saville's article there is no reference to the forces driving the policy of the Russian party and, thus, the CPGB. Stalinism remains in the background and, in consequence, the historical picture is distorted.

Saville summed up Pelling's study as 'an anti-communist textbook'. Supplementing the publications of right-wing organisations like IRIS, it was 'shot through with the anti-communist attitudes of the past decade and there are no more degenerate and stultifying assumptions'.[107] Invocation of the Cold War, a technique used to devalue and skirt round the arguments of opponents, neglects the fact that stultification and virtue were not all on one side. There are further problems with Saville's inclusive conception of anti-communism. His version embraces not only right-wing social democrats such as Pelling but dissident communists. His two decades of devotion to the CPGB and the ideas it inculcated were reasserting themselves. He later recollected that 'we had personal experience of those who had left the Party to cultivate their own gardens, or of those who had left to become in our eyes renegades. One of the original sins for Communist Party members was to publish criticisms of the Party outside the Party press.'[108] The archetype of the renegade was Koestler, who condemned Communism in *The God That Failed*, renounced his hopes for socialist transformation and contributed to *Encounter*, which was subsidised by the Congress for Cultural Freedom. Others sometimes cited were Dennis Healey, Stephen Spender and John Strachey: 'At the centre of their political thinking was a committed anti-Communism.'[109]

Saville was no longer a member of the CPGB. But his continuing acceptance of the interdict on criticising it, what Communists branded as 'giving ammunition to the enemy' regardless, it seems, of whether that criticism was true or false, right or left, was now extended to his former CPGB comrade Pearce and the Trotskyists. Pearce, Saville notes, had described Pelling's text as 'useful but shallow', and continues disapprovingly, 'by which he means that its usefulness mainly consists in the harm it is capable of doing to the communist cause in this country'.[110] A critique of Stalinism and the CPGB, *The Reasoner* had argued, was essential to a renewal of socialist politics. That project, which was what 1956 was all about, would inevitably, and beneficially, undermine CPGB influence – or as Saville put it, 'harm' its cause. In 1959, the politics of 'official Communism' remained an obstacle to the regeneration of the left. It is difficult to understand why left-wingers should be criticised for welcoming new evidence, whatever its source, to develop the arguments of 1956. Then, of course, many in the CPGB believed that Saville, as much as Pearce, was harming the cause of Communism and giving ammunition to the enemy.

Saville's article could have been written by a critical CPGB member, such as Hobsbawm. It demonstrates softness towards 'official Communism' and indicates that he had not advanced on the critique offered in 1956. Strikingly, the word 'Stalinism' does not appear anywhere in his essay. He had left the party but the *mentalités* lingered on. Perhaps part of the problem lay with his failure to find a political replacement. He hankered after the cohesion and comradeship of the CPGB, despite its politics and lack of democracy. He was involved in CND, and in the 1959 general election campaigned with Thompson for Lawrence Daly, the candidate of the Fife Socialist League.[111] But he always retained his belief in the need for a party: 'I am fully aware that only a disciplined organisation can expect to offer the serious challenge to the powerful order of capitalist society that is so urgently required.'[112] What kind of party remained unclear. He rejected the Trotskyist version, did not believe that it was possible to create a tighter organisation out of the New Left, and, unlike Thompson, spasmodically, and other former CPGB members, more consistently, he dismissed the idea that something socialist could be built inside Labour's broad church: 'The Labour Party', he declared, 'was not for me.'[113]

His views on Labour developed, but they retained some of the emphases of his years in the CPGB: he was more analytical about social democracy and arguably harder on Labourism than he was on Stalinism. His antagonism to Attlee's foreign policy remained fierce. In contrast with former party friends, he questioned the achievements of the 1945-51 governments on the home front, highlighting their role in restructuring capitalism and downplaying the gains for workers.[114] For Saville, progress through parliament, to the exclusion of almost all else, except trade unionism and collective bargaining, insistence on the neutrality of the state, class harmony and the national interest, irredeemably flawed Labour's DNA. It was an approach he shared with Ralph Miliband, and their discussions informed the latter's *Parliamentary Socialism* published in 1961.[115] The Wilson governments of 1964 and 1966 confirmed Saville's suspicion of a party that won votes by mobilising the language of socialism and proceeded to administer capitalism. In comparison with his benign imprecision about the CPGB, his convictions were clear:

Labourism has nothing to do with socialism: that the Labour Party has never been nor is capable of becoming a vehicle for socialist advance; and that the destruction of the illusions of Labourism is a necessary step before the emergence of a socialist movement of any size and influence becomes practicable.[116]

By the 1970s, he was rehearsing another old Communist trope:

If the Labour Party is a massive institutional obstacle to the achievement of socialism in Britain then the Parliamentary left, and their many supporters outside the Commons ..., are the major stumbling block in the way of a serious reassessment of the means towards a socialist future.[117]

So what was the answer? As talk of a Marxist party revived in the optimistic climate of the early 1970s, pessimism persisted: the prospect was 'not yet on the horizon'.[118]

Saville remained indecisive, at least in specifics, as to which road the left should take, the politics and programme it should pursue. The concerns of the classical Marxists and those who had developed their ideas, Marxist theory, questions of reform and revolution, were rarely pondered in his writings. His reaction against the frequently abstract, sometimes esoteric and academic approach of *New Left Review*, Mark 2 was healthy.[119] Arguably he went too far in the opposite direction. He remained engaged in affairs at Hull, and with activities which bridged the academy and the labour movement. From 1960, he played a leading part in the Society for the Study of Labour History. Soon after, he began work on the major project which saw the publication of the first volume of the *Dictionary of Labour Biography* in 1972.[120] *The Socialist Register*, which appeared annually from 1964, and which Saville edited with Miliband, was a major contribution to socialist scholarship and the left. This kind of work was Saville's forte. He revered Harold Laski and admired GDH Cole who combined academic work with research and writing for the labour movement and had at times been ambivalent about Stalinism. His rejection of the Labour Party ensured he was unable to exercise the influence they had wielded. He never resumed activity in a political organisation or returned to the problems he had left unresolved in 1956. Anderson remarked at the end of the 1970s:

> … the momentum of '56 appears to have run out. For all the passionate polemics and self-questioning of the hour, it might be said that overall it is the dearth of sustained study of Stalinism that is remarkable, rather than any pattern of cumulative research. Did the levy of '56 produce a single book, or even analytic essay, on the USSR in the later Khrushchev years? Did it investigate the roots of the Sino-Soviet conflict?[121]

Communists who became party functionaries incurred costs, intellectual and material. Those who, with the blessing of the party leaders, took the academic path paid a more modest and comfortable price: they acquired good jobs with employment security, a degree of autonomy and new preoccupations; if they climbed the academic ladder they frequently had less time for political work. Saville was determined to pursue a career as an historian. In 1956, he expressed the pull this exercised – although even at a time of tension he emphasised the need to resist the lure of an escape from politics. He wrote to a fellow CPGB member:

> It so happens that I dislike politics – and even more after the last few months – and all I really want to do is to write history. What I have to

keep telling myself is that this is exactly the kind of attitude that bourgeois society inculcates, and that in the end if I accept it, it will and can only lead to stultification.[122]

Saville continued to find time for political writing, although his activity and campaigning was limited. As the years went by, he became increasingly involved in university governance: he was head of a growing department, a member of senate and faculty dean. Along with teaching and research, he devoted his energies to building up an archive. Beyond the university he chaired the Labour History Society and the Oral History Society and promoted their causes with the Social Science Research Council and its Economic and Social History Committee. Later he was engaged with *History Workshop Journal* and the Campaign for Academic Freedom. These activities could be seen as making a contribution to the left, while the *Dictionary of Labour Biography* and the *Socialist Register* certainly constituted political work. Saville spread himself widely in what some university colleagues saw as his 'search for the bubble reputation'.[123] But time does not appear to have been the primary problem. When he did find space in retirement he preferred to write on the British labour movement and the 1945 Labour government's role in the Cold War. Unlike that subject, rigorous investigation of Stalinism and its impact on the CPGB might entail painful re-examination and reassessment of his own past and its meaning. Whatever the reasons, it was something he declined to prioritise.

Saville, Stalinism and Spain: The Burden of the Past

Instead, Saville continued to contemplate the politics and personalities of his youth through the rose-tinted prism of remembrance of things past. One repentant Communist wrote: 'The truth is this: the day I left the Communist Party was a very sad one for me, it was like a day of deep mourning, the mourning for my lost youth ... Something of it remains and leaves a mark on the character which lasts all one's life.'[124] Saville was no fan of *The God That Failed*, but Silone's comments captures something of his experience. The political mark it imprinted was evident in his exchange in the early 1980s with the English Literature scholar Valentine Cunningham over the latter's discussion of the role that British Communists played in the Spanish Civil War.[125] Spain had been the great cause of the 1930s' left. AJP Taylor believed that for Saville's generation it provided 'the emotional experience of their lifetime', while later historians saw it as 'the one noble cause they could not let go ... an historical event never to be re-examined which was to serve as a source of never-ending inspiration'.[126] These attitudes were reflected in Saville's response to Cunningham which resumed his defence of British Communism in the 1930s. His emphasis on the nobility and self-sacrifice of Communists is flawed by failure to relate their actions to the ideas and the political framework which elicited them.

Cunningham challenged the representation of the war as a simple conflict between democratic values and socialism, on the one hand, and fascism, on the other, in which British volunteers and the CPGB played an unambiguously positive role. He was writing a commentary on the poets who enlisted to support the Spanish Republic and he placed them in the Orwellian paradigm of 'Stalin's betrayal of the Spanish revolution'.[127] Cunningham argued: 'The truth was indeed, as everybody sooner or later learned, being deliberately and cynically distorted ... the main agents of distortion in Spain, the Communists, seem from the first to have been infected with a queerly total disregard for truth ...'[128] The party leaders, and its press, mythologised and obfuscated the reality and complexity of the struggle and romanticised the International Brigades in which 'many volunteers got disgruntled and wanted simply to go home ... many fellow-travelling liberals felt sickeningly betrayed by the political ruthlessness they witnessed or heard about'.[129] Cunningham made a number of acerbic observations about the CPGB and disparaged its relations with the poet and student leader John Cornford, who died in Spain.

Saville deplored the 'denigration' of Cornford, the volunteers and the CPGB. He found what he described, *inter alia*, as Cunningham's 'gormless idiocy' and 'general nastiness' to be 'politically nauseating' and 'a disgrace to his publishers'.[130] Employing a memorandum drawn up by his old friend from the CPGB, and Cornford's companion, Margot Heinemann, in an aggrieved attempt to persuade Cunningham to revise his preface, Saville found little difficulty in establishing the inaccuracy of many of Cunningham's comments concerning Cornford and the implausibility of speculations about his relations with the CPGB.[131] Some ill-judged instances of the CPGB's and Harry Pollitt's perfidy were similarly despatched. However, as Cunningham pointed out in a detailed rebuttal, Saville failed to engage directly with his, Cunningham's, conclusions about the political role of Stalinism in Spain or dissatisfaction and disillusion among volunteers.[132] To expect a full-scale rehearsal of the arguments would be excessive. He demonstrated a reluctance even briefly to discuss the politics, criticise the CPGB or address the evidence buttressing Cunningham's perspective.

Saville dismissed it on the grounds that it was anti-Communist, ideologically biased, not just against the CPGB, but, incongruously and imperialistically, against 'the left in general'. Cunningham's introduction, he alleged, was the product of an outdated Cold War mentality. It read as if it had been written 'in the context of the years of the Cold War. His preface is one more addition to *The God That Failed* literature.'[133] As so often, the Cold War label seeks to dispense with the need to provide evidence to establish the validity or otherwise of Cunningham's critique. The work of André Gide, Koestler, Silone and now Cunningham, is excluded from consideration by employment of another label which tells us little more than that their sometimes over-imaginative, sometimes insightful writings were critical of Communism – but nothing about their truth. As Koestler reflected, it is possible to be right for the wrong reasons.[134]

Despite the enmity Saville and other former Communists continued to bear towards Orwell, he was widely respected, and his indictment of Stalinism in Spain remained popular and persuasive.[135] On grounds that are far from evident, Saville insisted that Orwell was not to be confused with 'Cold Warriors' such as Cunningham, although Orwell's indictments of Communism and Communists were frequently as caustic as those of Cunningham, and the similarities of substance regarding Spain are striking. Orwell, Saville agreed, did offer 'what to many contemporaries were unpalatable truths about the political divisions within Republican Spain'.[136] In consequence, *Homage to Catalonia* was 'derisively and abusively dismissed by Communists and their supporters'.[137] The reference to 'political divisions within Republican Spain' sanitises the situation. *Homage to Catalonia* was not simply 'abusively dismissed': left to the CPGB's fellow-travellers, there was a good chance that Orwell's classic would not have been published at the time.[138] Nonetheless, Saville claims, the scholarship of the 1960s and 1970s 'has now taken our understanding far beyond Orwell's interpretation, and it is inadequate and inaccurate to structure the discussion of the history of the civil war years in the terms in which they were discussed before 1950'.[139]

Precisely how recent scholarship had taken our understanding far beyond Orwell's interpretation is not explained. No citation follows that conclusion, and it is contentious. It was possible to argue in 1981 – and even more so today – that research has extended, deepened and contextualised, but not superseded, Orwell's interpretation. It is only at the end of his essay, and then without amplification as to whether they corroborate or question Orwell's approach, that Saville cites some of the texts then available.[140] Notable omissions – although he cites a chapter by Burnett Bolloten on the POUM in a collection – are Bolloten's *The Grand Camouflage* (1961) and the expanded version, *The Spanish Revolution* (1979), which put flesh on *Homage to Catalonia* and were inaccurately labelled as products of the Cold War; as well as the work of the Trotskyist historian Pierre Broué and his socialist collaborator, Emile Témime.[141] All these texts are critical of the Communists. Saville does reference another critic, Fernando Claudín, but Claudín contextualises Orwell rather than rendering him an anachronism. Claudín argues that to reconcile conflicting imperatives – showing solidarity with Spanish workers and keeping Britain and France on side in order to prosecute Soviet foreign policy – Stalin had simultaneously to offer limited support to the struggle and limit the struggle to defence of the republic and bourgeois democracy. This demanded coercion against those determined to fight for socialism. It meant exporting terror, in the form of the NKVD, as well as inadequate arms and Soviet military experts. It entailed crushing the POUM, CNT and the entire anti-Stalinist left, and suppressing the existing impetus towards revolution and occupation of the land and factories as 'fascist provocations', undermining the war effort.[142]

Since 1981 the Spanish civil war has remained controversial, but with the opening of the Russian archives a great deal of evidence supports the Orwellian or 'Cold War' interpretation of events.[143] Surprisingly for an historian, Saville never refers in his essay in any specific way to any of the issues, issues any historian or socialist interested in critically interrogating Stalinism would consider it imperative to explore briefly. He praises the people and passes on the politics: '… nothing has taken away from the people of the Republic the heroism of their struggle … nothing has diminished the bravery and commitment of those who went to Spain to assist in the struggle.' He glosses over the conflicts dividing 'the people of the Republic', the disputed basis of the struggle and the questions raised by Cunningham. The nearest he comes to these problems is the coy reference to 'internal political divisions' and evasive rhetoric: '… we have begun to set the agonies of the war, its nobility, its lies, its betrayals, into a more truthful historical perspective.'[144] What that perspective is remains opaque. The authors of 'the lies' and 'betrayals' remain unspecified.

These questions are indispensable to understanding the experience of the volunteers. They were animated by a sincere desire to defeat fascism. Immediate motivations, unemployment, domestic issues, a taste for adventure and so forth, were present but subordinate to that purpose. But illusions *were* shattered – it is hard to see how it could be otherwise in a vicious, unequal war whose ruthless conduct ensured that Stalin's secret service 'operated in Spain just as they would have done in the Mongolian People's Republic'.[145] Anti-Stalinist socialists such as Orwell were under surveillance, the ILP member Bob Smillie died in prison, Andreu Nin, the POUM leader, was tortured and murdered, and the CPGB and its direction of the British volunteers meshed into the Stalinist landscape. It is insufficient for Saville to discount Cunningham's cases of disillusionment with the dismissive statement that he 'scrapes up a half dozen or so examples but he has of course, no serious evidence to offer'.[146] Saville seems determined to defend the Communist legend almost in its entirety.[147] Subsequent work on the British battalion drawing on the Russian archives confirms that disenchantment was real.

Research in Moscow has turned up a British battalion blacklist with 400 names of deserters, drunks, cowards, Trotskyists, POUMists and the disaffected. It has been estimated that from a total of 2063 volunteers, 26 per cent were 'men whose behaviour and performance was considered worthy of condemnation'.[148] Another study based on Soviet sources prints documents which claim that 'the English battalion has fallen victim to a wave of collective desertions', and notes that in the spring of 1938, 460 out of 1806 volunteers had been sent home – although this might have been for a range of reasons.[149] The operation was in the hands of the Comintern and the CPGB, which was a loyal section of the Comintern in agreement with and responsive to its strategy in Spain. The Political Commissars and military commanders were almost all party members or sympathisers, and decision-making and political education reflected Comintern perspectives. The NKVD infiltrated the brigades, followed by the SIM, the Republican secret police: they reported on the behaviour and political reliability of volunteers with disciplinary consequences. The Communist press in Britain and Spain 'consistently misled or lied' about what was happening, although 'one must conclude that the British party leadership must have known, officially or unofficially, something of the increasing Russian terror in Spain'.[150]

We can argue about the dimensions of disillusion: it was significant. Hopkins provides case studies of dissenters and how they were dealt with by the Communists, remarking that 'those who disagreed with party decisions or simply were maladjusted to military service deserve their place in the history of Britons in Spain, a place they have not yet found in "official" accounts'.[151] He begins his monograph by stating: 'I will offer evidence that supports Valentine Cunningham's contention that "truth ... was deliberately and cynically distorted" in order to glorify the role of the Communist Party ...' After presenting persuasive evidence, he concludes: 'The Communist Party in practice stood in opposition to virtually every political instinct – democratic pluralism, the rights of the individual, freedom from oppression – that was incarnate in the British progressive tradition.'[152] This does not detract from the heroism of many volunteers. It points up the silences and absences in Saville's essay, an essay which evades fundamental issues and refuses the critical engagement with Stalinism promised in 1956.[153]

The terse treatment of Communism in Saville's survey of the British labour movement in 1988 followed a well-established pattern. The Third Period had a disastrous effect, but the CPGB made an impact in the later 1930s, before the Cold War 'brought to an end the *de facto* united front between the Communist Party and the Labour left'.[154] Thereafter, the party never exercised significant influence. An intriguing passage hints at a path that Saville never pursued. Noting that 'the impact of Stalinism in the Soviet Union and the countries of eastern Europe has been profound in western Europe', he observed that in consequence:

> Western European socialists and Marxists have found it difficult to elaborate new ideas ... What has eluded them has been the relationship between social ownership, central planning and individual freedom; and in the wider popular consciousness, it has been the absence of civil liberties in regimes that have styled themselves socialist that has been the most important single handicap in the creation of a vision of a socialist project that would take hold of the imagination of ordinary people.[155]

He never expanded on this: the promised Marxist analysis of Stalinism never materialised. With the fall of the Soviet Union he claimed that the time had come to discard the term 'Communist', which had ended in 'discredit and dishonour'.[156] It is unclear whether he is talking about 'official Communism' or the broader communist tradition. The absence of this distinction is suggestive of the extent to which he had continued to identify communism with the Russian surrogate. That the latter had brought 'discredit and dishonour' to socialism had been apparent in 1956 when on Saville's account he and Thompson had quit the CPGB 'believing that the Party was now wholly discredited'.[157] That Saville should write in this vein three decades later suggests an inability to settle accounts with Stalinism in the intervening years. Most of the article surveyed his personal experience and sounded familiar notes: the CPGB was an organisation to which 'one was proud to belong'.[158] The party's decline had continued after 1956 partly because of its 'refusal to analyse seriously the phenomenon of Stalinism in many aspects'.[159] That judgement, it may be argued, applied equally to Saville.

Conclusion

Saville's claim, made in 1991, that 'the enquiry ... into the nature and character of Stalinism and the extensive deformations occurring in countries which called themselves socialist ... began seriously in the year of Khrushchev's speech and has continued since',[160] is misleading. It neglects the significant explanations of Stalinism that the pathbreakers had developed before 1956; and it is in danger of overvaluing the contribution of those who broke with Stalinism at that time. It seems reasonable to include Saville in Anderson's assessment of Thompson and surmise that Saville, too, harboured 'the belief that the real work was already done – the *moral* critique of Stalinism had rendered painstaking sociological and historical inquiry into the dynamics of Eastern societies supernumerary or secondary'.[161] Much has been made of the relationship between its members' dedication to historical inquiry and the role that the CPGB Historians' Group played in 1956.[162] As an historian, Saville was well equipped to investigate Stalinism. Discussion of how it emerged; whether the USSR could have taken a different path; Stalinism's relationship to Leninism and Marxism; the question of 'socialism in one country'; the character of the Soviet Union as an economic and political formation; and its impact on the left and the working class in other countries, found little place in his writings. Accepting that the Russia he had revered had never existed, he left things at that. If Thompson was 'fascinated by the Soviet Union',[163] Saville demonstrated little curiosity about it after the myth dissolved in 1956.

Saville kept abreast of the literature on British Communism, although his own writing on the subject was slight and benign: CPGB history followed the contours of his experience and allegiance and justified them. The 'project of 1917' remained viable until the 1950s. It flourished in the anti-fascist years while the Hitler–Stalin Pact was overshadowed by pro-Soviet sentiment from 1941. In Britain, 'appreciation of the nature and character of Stalinism was confined to very few within the broad labour movement'.[164] Decline after 1945 climaxed in 1956: '… all the doubts and misgivings now came together … the smaller Communist parties, the British among them, started to fall apart.'[165] Saville continued to view the Popular Front phases of CPGB history as, relatively speaking, the 'golden age' of British Communism. He evaded or downplayed the extent to which, from the late 1920s, Stalinism enduringly structured the politics of the party, its activities and the experience of its activists. He believed that on balance, and despite its defects, the CPGB had been a force for progress before the late 1940s. He never came to terms with the fact that knowledge about Stalinism had been available from the mid-1930s; or that it convinced many in the labour movement; or the degree to which workers' trepidation about the hazards of revolution was intensified by apprehension that it would end up as badly in Britain as it had in Russia – to the advantage of Labourism. He never addressed the ways in which the CPGB's equation of Stalinism with Marxism contributed to discrediting socialism. Or the extent to which 'official Communism' dishonoured its intellectuals.

It is difficult for the historian to probe further. Writing about Saville's career, Miliband pondered on the complexity and ultimate unknowability of interior lives and motivations: '… the springs of action of every single man and woman are endlessly varied and deeply buried.'[166] What can be said is that in demonstrable ways Saville remained a man of the 1930s who retained a defensive pride in the role of a party he never completely left behind but remembered selectively. Perhaps this helped impede critical interrogation of its politics. The past persisted in small ways. He maintained his antipathy to Orwell, who personified the fact that it was possible to be a left-wing intellectual and speak out against Stalinism in the 1930s and 1940s.[167] He included student Communists of that period, Mohan Kumaramangalam and Ram Nahum, in the *Dictionary of Labour Biography*, although their role in the labour movement was negligible.[168] He reflected: 'I changed some parts of my general approach to the politics of the Left in the intellectual upheaval of 1956 but in certain crucial respects I remained fully conscious of what I owed to the Communist movement.'[169] Looking back to 1956, it seems evident that what was required was a more fundamental rejection of the past and a more comprehensive break with the entire tradition of Stalinism.

Defending Thompson's approach, Saville affirmed the importance of 'hard and firm polemic' among socialists.[170] This contribution is offered in the same spirit. It neither detracts from the exemplary and memorable role Saville played in 1956 nor diminishes his subsequent services to the left. His resignation from the CPGB constituted a powerful act of disassociation with widespread resonance. People are defined in moments of crisis. When others hesitated, he helped to push forward the momentum generated by Khrushchev's revelations and in doing so vindicated the good name of socialist intellectuals. People change, although rarely completely. Posterity will honour the influence of *The Reasoner* on the events of 1956 and the *New Reasoner*'s part in cohering the New Left. Saville will be remembered as an indefatigable organiser of socialist scholarship and a tireless pioneer of the history of the working class. *The Dictionary of Labour Biography* and the *Socialist Register* will endure as remarkable contributions to the left and the labour movement.

NOTES

1   There were time lags: for example, Levy was expelled in 1958, Collins and Kiernan left in 1959.

2   See Neal Wood, *Communism and British Intellectuals* (Victor Gollancz, London, 1959); John McIlroy, 'The Establishment of Intellectual Orthodoxy and the Stalinisation of British Communism 1928-1933', *Past and Present*, no. 192, 2006, pp. 188-226. Hobsbawm is frequently taken as the archetype of the Popular Front intellectual. Yet, in contrast with his peers, he was permanently marked by his experience of the preceding Third Period in Berlin and reaction against it. He conceived himself as 'the tail-end' of the previous generation of Communists: see Eric Hobsbawm, *Interesting Times: A Twentieth-Century Life* (London, Allen Lane, 2002), pp. 217-18.

3   John Saville, 'The Communist Experience: A Personal Appraisal', in Ralph Miliband and Leo Panitch (eds), *Socialist Register 1991* (Merlin Press, London, 1991), p. 114.

4   For an obituary focussed more on documenting his role as an historian than exploring his politics, see John McIlroy, 'John Saville, 1916-2009', *Labour History Review*, Volume 4, no. 3, 2009, pp. 330-38. See also David Martin, Dianne Kirby and David Howell, 'John Saville (1916-2009): Appreciation and Memories', *Labour History Review*, Volume 75, no. 1, 2010, pp. 114-27; David Howell, Dianne Kirby and Kevin Morgan (eds), *John Saville: Commitment and History* (Lawrence and Wishart/Socialist History Society, London, 2011). The latter deals largely with Saville the historian, the early New Left and the *Socialist Register*. Its treatment of Saville's Communism and his later politics is uncritical. What follows is based substantially on Saville's recollections, which are subject to the fallibilities of memory and personal reconstruction – of which he himself was aware.

5   Saville, 'Communist Experience'; John Saville, *Memoirs from the Left* (Merlin, London, 2003). In the latter (p 182), Saville states: 'These are memoirs of a political kind.' But they are patchy and uneven. Some things are remembered, some are not. For example, there is nothing about how he viewed controversial but important events such as the Spanish Civil War or the CPGB's stance on the Second World War. See also John Saville, 'May Day 1937', in Asa Briggs and John Saville (eds), *Essays in Labour History 1918-1939* (Croom Helm, London, 1977), pp. 232-84.

6   Saville, *Memoirs*, pp. 22-24.

7   Saville, *Memoirs*, pp. 21-26.

8   Saville, *Memoirs*, pp. 1, 3. Ralph Miliband, 'John Saville: A Presentation', in David E Martin and David Rubinstein (eds), *Ideology and the Labour Movement: Essays Presented to John Saville* (Croom Helm, London, 1979), p. 15. Miliband's introduction to the book is based on Saville's own recollections.

9   For political precocity at grammar school see 'Cambridge Communism in the 1930s and 1940s', *Socialist History*, no. 24, 2003, pp. 39-71. This was often a public-school phenomenon – a classic case is documented in Kevin Ingram, *Rebel: The Short Life of Esmond Romilly* (EP Dutton, New York, 1986). As a schoolboy E P Thompson read Christopher Hill and Christopher Caudwell. Together with his friend Arnold Rattenbury, he was disciplined while at Kingswood School for selling the *Daily Worker*: see Scott Hamilton, *The Crisis of Theory: E P Thompson, the New Left and Postwar British Politics* (Manchester University Press, Manchester, 2011), p. 45 n. 71. See generally James Klugmann, 'Introduction: The Crisis in The Thirties: A View from the Left', in Jon Clark *et al* (eds), *Culture and Crisis in Britain in the 1930s* (Lawrence and Wishart, London, 1979), p. 17.

10 Eric Hobsbawm, 'Obituary: John Saville', *Guardian*, 16 June 2009.

11 On prior commitment see ' Cambridge Communism', pp. 50, 55, 66, 72, 75. Cf David Caute, *Communism and the French Intellectuals 1914-1960* (Andre Deutsch, London,

1964), p. 275, where it is concluded that in many cases 'the decision to join the party was preceded by a long period of intellectual reflection within a Marxist framework'.

12   Saville, *Memoirs*, p. 9.

13   Fernando Claudín, *The Communist Movement: From Comintern to Cominform* (Penguin, Harmondsworth, 1975), pp. 166-241; David Beetham, *Marxists in the Face of Fascism* (Manchester University Press, Manchester, 1983).

14   Saville, *Memoirs*, p. 8; Wood, *Communism*, pp. 51-53; Klugmann, 'Introduction: The Crisis in the Thirties'; MY Lang, 'The Growth of the Student Movement', in Carmel Haden Guest (ed), *David Guest, A Scientist Fights for Freedom: A Memoir* (Lawrence and Wishart, London, 1939); Pat Sloan (ed), *John Cornford: A Memoir* (Jonathan Cape, London, 1938).

15   Saville, *Memoirs*, pp. 26-31.

16   Saville, *Memoirs*, pp. 37-72. Saville's rejection of the party convention that members in the armed forces should seek to become officers was a rare example of unorthodoxy.

17   Saville does not discuss this choice or whether he considered it, but Hobsbawm reflected: 'In the end, I reluctantly realised that the only desirable career, that of the "professional revolutionary", that is, the party functionary, was not for me and I resigned myself to earning my living in a less compromising way.' (Hobsbawm, *Interesting Times*, p. 113)

18   The comments are those of Saville's friend, the Hull University Librarian and poet Phillip Larkin, see Phillip Larkin, *Required Writing* (Faber and Faber, London, 1983), pp. 54-55; Rowan Moore, 'Hull's Big Chance to Win the Nation's Heart', *Observer*, 14 February 2016.

19   Saville, *Memoirs*, p. 1.

20   Saville, *Memoirs*, p. 118.

21   For example, John Hughes and Ken Alexander – later supported by Michael Barratt Brown and Royden Harrison – pioneered day-release classes for miners at Sheffield University from the late 1940s, while Jim Fyrth was involved in organising trade-union courses at London University. At the Oxford University Delegacy for Extramural Studies, the secretary, Thomas Hodgkin, and up to a third of the tutorial staff, were Communists before a purge at the end of the 1940s. John Vickers and Ronald Frankenberg worked as education officers at the Electrical Trades Union and the South Wales Area of the National Union of Mineworkers respectively; on this, see Roger Fieldhouse, *Adult Education and the Cold War: Liberal Values Under Siege* (University of Leeds, Leeds, 1985); and John McIlroy, 'The Triumph of Technical Training?', in Brian Simon (ed), *The Search for Enlightenment: The Working Class and Adult Education in the Twentieth Century* (Lawrence and Wishart, London, 1990), pp. 208-43. Edward Thompson taught adult education classes to a mix of students at Leeds University, but he was not involved in the trade-union courses there.

22   Saville, *Memoirs*, pp. 81-84, 97.

23   John Saville, 'The XXth Congress and the British Communist Party', in Ralph Miliband and John Saville (eds), *Socialist Register 1976* (Merlin, London, 1976), pp. 12-13, 19.

24   This was not, of course, simply an historiographical innovation but the party line after 1934. See John Saville (ed), *Democracy and the Labour Movement: Essays in Honour of Dona Torr* (Lawrence and Wishart, London, 1954). Pioneering chapters on British labour history occasionally reveal their provenance, as in the observation: 'Previous constitutions proclaimed the rights of man, *ad nauseam*; the Soviet constitution, however, guaranteed them.' (Christopher Hill, 'The Norman Yoke', in Saville (ed), *Democracy and the Labour Movement*, p. 60. Torr was viewed by Hilton and Kiernan as 'a party boss', recalled by Raymond Postgate as 'a fierce Stalinist', and by Hobsbawm as an exponent of hagiography: see Antony Howe, 'Torr, Dona (1883-1957)', in Keith Gildart and David Howell (eds), *Dictionary of Labour Biography*, Volume 12 (Palgrave Macmillan, Basingstoke, 2005), pp. 279-80. Cf the encomium in the introduction to

Democracy and the Labour Movement, and Saville, *Memoirs*, pp. 3-4, 88. For the group, see Eric Hobsbawm, 'The Historians' Group of the Communist Party', in Maurice Cornforth (ed), *Rebels and Their Causes: Essays in Honour of AL Morton* (Lawrence and Wishart, London, 1978), pp 21-47.

25   Minutes of the Historians' Group, 8 July 1950, cited in Dennis Dworkin, *Cultural Marxism in Postwar Britain* (Duke University Press, London, 1997), pp. 23-24. The counter-argument put by academics was that work in the universities would influence today's students and tomorrow's teachers and opinion-formers. For a contemporary view of the group and the need to make historical research 'politically useful', see Daphne May, 'Work of the Historians' Groups', *Communist Review*, May 1949, pp. 538-42.

26   Much of Saville's extended historical work – on the state and Chartism, the labour movement and the Cold War – appeared from the late 1980s. Harvey Kaye discusses the publications of Group members Dobb, Hill, Hilton, Hobsbawm and Thompson, but Saville is only referred to in passing: see Harvey J Kaye, *The British Marxist Historians* (Polity Press, Cambridge, 1984).

27   The list of his publications in *Memoirs* omits John Saville, 'Chartism in the Year of Revolution 1848', *Modern Quarterly*, Winter 1952, pp. 22-33. He also contributed a review essay to *Past and Present*, the journal animated by Communist historians: John Saville, 'A Comment on Professor Rostow's British Economy of the Nineteenth Century', *Past and Present*, no. 6, 1954, pp. 64-84. His main publication together with *Democracy and the Labour Movement* was John Saville (ed), *Ernest Jones, Chartist: Selections from the Writings and Speeches* (Lawrence and Wishart, London, 1952).

28   Saville, *Memoirs*, p. 104. Later in life Saville defended Hill against charges that he was a Russian agent: John Saville, *The Politics of Continuity: British Foreign Policy and the Labour Government 1945-46* (Verso, London, 1993), pp. 212-17.

29   Christopher Hill, 'Stalin and the Science of History', *Modern Quarterly*, Autumn 1953, p. 209. Cf, 'Bacon inaugurated the bourgeois epoch in science as Lysenko and his colleagues are inaugurating the new epoch today. In the Soviet Union the obstructive dogmas of bourgeois science have to be brushed aside ...' (Hill quoted in Raphael Samuel, 'British Marxist Historians, 1880-1980: Part One', *New Left Review*, March-April 1980, p. 75 n. 250)

30   Saville, 'May Day 1937', pp. 261-67; John Saville, *The Labour Movement in Britain* (Faber and Faber, London, 1988), pp. 62-67; Saville, 'Communist Experience', pp. 14-15; Saville, *Memoirs*, pp. 33-36.

31   For the trials and their reception, see Brian Pearce, 'The British Stalinists and the Moscow Trials' [1958], in Michael Woodhouse and Brian Pearce, *Essays on the History of Communism in Britain* (New Park, London, 1975), pp. 219-40; Paul Deli, 'The Image of the Russian Purges in the *Daily Herald* and the *New Statesman*', *Journal of Contemporary History*, Volume 20, 1985, pp. 261-82; Paul Corthorn, 'Labour, the Left and the Stalinist Purges of the Late 1930s', *Historical Journal*, Volume 48, no. 1, 2005, pp. 179-207; Paul Flewers, *The New Civilisation? Understanding Stalin's Soviet Union 1929-1941* (Francis Boutle, London, 2008), pp. 145-54.

32   Saville, 'Communist Experience', p. 14. His memoirs repeat points made in this essay.

33   Saville, 'May Day 1937', p. 267.

34   Saville, *Memoirs*, p. 34.

35   Saville, 'May Day 1937', p. 268.

36   Andrew Thorpe, *The British Communist Party and Moscow 1920-43* (Manchester University Press, Manchester, 2000), pp. 233-36.

37   Thorpe, *British Communist Party*, pp. 233, 236.

38   Saville, *Memoirs*, p. 34; Saville, 'Communist Experience', p. 14.

39   Saville, 'May Day 1937', p. 266.

40   Corthorn, 'Labour, the Left and the Stalinist Purges', p. 181; Flewers, *New Civilisation?*, pp. 145-54.

41   Quoted in Corthorn, 'Labour, the Left and the Stalinist Purges', pp. 189, 190-91, 197.

42   Saville, 'May Day 1937', p. 266. However, referring to the recantations of their line on the war published by Harry Pollitt and JR Campbell in 1939, Malcolm MacEwen, who went through similar experiences to Saville, recalled: 'It took me another 15 years to realise that they were moved by the same misplaced sense of loyalty to the Party and the Soviet Union that may have led Bukharin and others to confess to non-existent crimes …' (Malcolm MacEwen, *The Greening of a Red* (Pluto Press, London, 1991), p. 78) Of course there is a difference between death and humiliation. See MacEwen's testimony: 'Pollitt made the most extraordinary statement … that he respected revolutionaries who confessed to crimes they did not commit rather than "give in to the class enemy"!' And also see MacEwen's response in a letter to the party leader: 'A false confession only perpetuates the evil, sends more comrades to their deaths and hinders the advance to communism. It was the mistaken loyalty of this kind that led to Stalin's excesses … and yet you hold up this kind of thing as a model for all of us to admire. Presumably Tito should have confessed and knuckled under to Stalin …' (MacEwen, *Greening*, p. 183)

43   The parallel does not seem to have been remarked upon in the 1930s, but was raised in renewed discussion of the trials after 1956: Pearce, 'British Stalinists', p. 224 n. 243; Louis Marks, review of Giorgio Santillana, *The Crime of Galileo*, *Labour Review*, Volume 3, no. 3, 1958.

44   Quoted in Corthorn, 'Labour, the Left and the Stalinist Purges', p. 196.

45   Nove later became an eminent Sovietologist, see Saville, 'Communist Experience', p. 14. In the same essay, p. 21, Saville records he never encountered or argued with a Trotskyist before the 1950s – and only met a handful of ILP members. It was possible, however, to have been a Trotskyist at LSE in the 1930s. A number of students were recruited by Denzil Harber, a defector from the CPGB, but all seem to have graduated by 1934; see Denzil Harber, 'Seeing Soviet Russia', *Clare Market Review*, Volume 13, no. 2, 1933; Flewers, *New Civilisation?*, pp. 43-44; John McIlroy, 'John Archer (1909-2000)', *Revolutionary History*, Volume 8, no. 1, 2001, pp. 239-47.

46   Saville, 'Communist Experience', p. 14.

47   Saville, *Memoirs*, p. 34.

48   See the editorial, *Daily Worker*, 1 February 1940.

49   Saville, *Memoirs*, p. 97. 'Forty-three years on, Constance still liked to remind John that she had the foresight and sense to leave in 1939. John defended his past position vigorously … This was clearly a much revisited theme, which both addressed with good humour.' (Kirby, 'John Saville', p. 124)

50   Noreen Branson, *History of the Communist Party of Great Britain: 1927-1941* (Lawrence and Wishart, London, 1985), p. 268.

51   Saville, 'On Party History', p. 38. Saville's attitude towards the Hitler–Stalin Pact was different from some of the older Popular Front intellectuals. They broke with Stalinism in its wake as they digested the implications of its alliance with Fascism. Stalin's man in London, the Russian ambassador Ivan Maisky, recorded in his diary on 19 September 1939: '[Victor] Gollancz is in despair, in his view the Soviet-German pact killed off communism. [John] Strachey, in connection with the same pact, came to see Harry [Pollitt] with tears in his eyes.' (Gabriel Gorodetsky (ed), *The Maisky Diaries* (Yale University Press, New Haven, 2015), p. 226) Some younger intellectuals shared Saville's approbation. Christopher Hill, for example, publicly contested Strachey's crisis of conscience; 'Letters', *New Statesman*, 18 May 1940.

52   John Saville, 'Neil Redfern's Thesis: A Critical Comment', *Communist History Network Newsletter*, no. 7, April 1999, pp. 8-9.

53   Saville, *Memoirs*, pp. 90-92.

54   Saville, *Politics of Continuity*, p. 7. See also John Saville, 'Ernest Bevin and the Cold War 1945-1950', in Ralph Miliband, John Saville and Marcel Liebman (eds), *Socialist Register 1984* (Merlin, London, 1984), pp. 68-100.

55   Saville, 'Communist Experience,' p 51. For a restatement of the threat Labour politicians perceived, see Phillip Deery, '"A Very Present Menace": Attlee, Communism and the Cold War', *Australian Journal of Politics and History*, Volume 44, no. 1, 1998, pp. 69-93.

56   For the view that the Cold War commenced through mutual suspicion and misunderstanding of conflicting interests, see Geoffrey Roberts, *Stalin's Wars: From World War to Cold War 1939-1943* (Yale University Press, New Haven, 2006). For research which emphasises the role of Soviet expansionism, see Vladislav Zubok and Constantin Pleshakov, *Inside the Kremlin's Cold War: From Stalin to Khrushchev* (Harvard University Press, Cambridge, 1996); John Lewis Gaddis, *We Now Know: Rethinking Cold War History* (Oxford University Press, Oxford, 1997); Vladislav Zubok, *A Failed Empire: From Stalin to Gorbachev* (University of North Carolina Press, Chapel Hill, 2007); Jonathan Haslam, *Russia's Cold War* (Yale University Press, New Haven, 2011); Robert Gellately, *Stalin's Curse: Battling for Communism in War and Cold War* (Oxford University Press, Oxford, 2013). See also Melvyn P Leffler and Odd Arne Westad (eds), *The Cambridge History of the Cold War: Volume 1: Origins* (Cambridge University Press, Cambridge, 2010).

57   Saville, *Politics of Continuity*, p. 99; the comment is made in relation to Ernest Bevin.

58   Saville, 'Communist Experience', p. 20.

59   Saville, 'Communist Experience', p. 7.

60   Saville, *Memoirs*, p. 91.

61   Saville, 'Communist Experience', p. 21.

62   Saville, 'Communist Experience', p. 21.

63   John Saville, 'Edward Thompson, the Communist Party and 1956', in Ralph Miliband and Leo Panitch (eds), *Socialist Register 1994* (Merlin, London, 1994), p. 26. Miliband suggested that Saville was a man in whom adversity bred persistence: Miliband, 'John Saville: A Presentation', p. 23.

64   Quoted in Andy Croft, 'Mapping the Wilderness: Randall Swingler and 1956', *Socialist History*, no. 19, 2001, p. 56.

65   'I value more than I can say in a few words my membership of the British party but never again shall I accept any political line without question' (Saville, 'Thompson', p. 22)

66   Saville, 'XXth Congress', p. 4.

67   The phrase is Hobsbawm's. He appeared innocent of the implications and the contradiction inherent in intellectuals relying on authority: 'We were not told the truth about something that had to affect the very nature of Communist belief.' (Hobsbawm, *Interesting Times*, p. 204)

68   'Khrushchev's Report', *World News*, 30 June 1956.

69   For Saville's role in the events of 1956, see John McIlroy, 'Communist Intellectuals and 1956: John Saville, Edward Thompson and *The Reasoner*', in this volume. Saville emphasised that *The Reasoner* should consider the susceptibilities of its audience when he embargoed critical comments that Thompson proposed to include on Pollitt: 'He's washed up now, but the affection for Harry is tremendous among my generation. And your additional comment would be considered muck-raking of a type that would nullify the effect of the whole article ...' (Quoted in Saville, 'XXth Congress', p. 18)

70   John Saville, 'On Party History: An Open Letter to Comrade R Page Arnot', *The Reasoner*, no. 3, November 1956, pp. 23-27.

71   Saville, 'On Party History', p. 27, emphasis in original. However, Saville did agree that there was a need to examine 'in all its complexity' the creation of the CPGB and the

split it entailed in the labour movement; see John Saville, '*World Socialism Restated*: A Comment', *The Reasoner*, no. 2, September 1956, p. 20.

72   Saville, '*World Socialism Restated*: A Comment', p. 19. Within a few months, Saville had resigned from the party.

73   'Editorial: Taking Stock', *The Reasoner*, no. 1, July 1956, p. 4.

74   Alasdair McIntyre, 'Notes From the Moral Wilderness', *New Reasoner,* Winter 1959 and Spring 1959; E P Thompson, 'Socialist Humanism: An Epistle to the Philistines', *New Reasoner*, Summer 1957; Charles Taylor, 'Marxism and Humanism', *New Reasoner,* Autumn 1957; Harry Hanson, 'An Open Letter to E P Thompson', *New Reasoner,* Autumn 1957.

75   Bob Davies did attempt to carry on the work on Russia published in *The Reasoner;* see Bob Davies, 'The Soviet Economy', *New Reasoner*, Autumn 1959.

76   Perry Anderson, *Arguments Within English Marxism* (Verso, London, 1980), p. 117, emphasis in original.

77   *Newsletter*, 10 May 1957; David Widgery, *The Left in Britain 1956-1968* (Penguin, Harmondsworth, 1976), p. 80.

78   'Editorial', *New Reasoner*, Summer 1957, p. 2; Thompson, 'Socialist Humanism', pp. 108, 139. See Paul Flewers, 'E P Thompson and the Soviet Experience' in this volume. Thompson was in contact with Ray Challinor, a member of the Socialist Review Group, around this time and took a friendlier stance towards this neo-Trotskyist organisation. He later wrote that its magazine '*International Socialism* ... seems to me the most constructive journal with a Trotskyist tendency in this country ...' (E P Thompson, 'Revolution Again!', *New Left Review*, no. 6, November-December 1960, pp. 18-31). However, he never seems to have engaged with its characterisation of Russia as state capitalist, apart from two extremely brief asides rejecting the concept; see E P Thompson, 'Agency and Choice', *New Reasoner*, Summer 1958, p. 93; E P Thompson, 'The Poverty of Theory or an Orrery of Errors', *The Poverty of Theory and Other Essays* (Merlin, London, 1978), pp. 240-41.

79   Saville, *Memoirs*, p. 114.

80   Saville, *Memoirs*, p. 114. A further possible disincentive, given Saville's antipathy to Labour, was that 'The Club' conducted entry work in the Labour Party. For the view of 'The Club' towards 1956, see Bill Hunter, *Lifelong Apprenticeship: The Life and Times of a Revolutionary* (Index Books, London, 1997), pp. 333-53; Terry Brotherstone, '1956: Tom Kemp and Others', in Terry Brotherstone and Geoff Pilling (eds), *History, Economic History and The Future of Marxism: Essays in Memory of Tom Kemp* (Porcupine Press, London, 1996), pp. 293-350.

81   Saville, *Memoirs*, pp. 93, 114. They had met in Hull in 1954 when Healy was fostering a breakaway movement from the Transport and General Workers' Union to the Stevedores' and Dockers' Union – a policy which the CPGB opposed.

82   Peter Fryer, 'Lenin As Philosopher', *Labour Review*, September-October 1957; 'Editorial: An Unreasonable Reasoner', *Labour Review*, March-April 1958; Anonymous, 'Rejected by the *New Reasoner*', *Labour Review*, May-July 1958. *Labour Review* was the journal of 'The Club'.

83   'Unreasonable Reasoner', p. 34.

84   See John McIlroy, 'Healy, Thomas Gerard (Gerry) 1913-1989', in Keith Gildart and David Howell (eds), *Dictionary of Labour Biography*, Volume 12 (Palgrave MacMillan, Basingstoke, 2005), pp. 136-46; Harry Ratner, *Reluctant Revolutionary: Memoirs of a Trotskyist, 1936-1960* (Socialist Platform, London, 1994), pp. 220-45.

85   See Robin Archer *et al* (eds), *Out of Apathy: Voices of the New Left 30 Years On* (Verso, London, 1989); Lin Chun, *The British New Left* (Edinburgh University Press, Edinburgh, 1993); Michael Kenny, *The First New Left: British Intellectuals After Stalin* (Lawrence and Wishart, London, 1995); Paul Blackledge, *Perry Anderson and the New Left* (Merlin, London, 2004).

86   Anderson, *Arguments*, p. 119.

87   'Editorial', *New Reasoner*, Autumn 1959, reprinted in Widgery, *Left in Britain*, pp. 90-91 – the article is mistakenly assigned to *The Reasoner*.

88   'Editorial', *New Reasoner*, Autumn 1959, p. 90.

89   'Editorial', *New Reasoner*, Autumn 1959, p. 90.

90   For example, 'Editorial: Why We Are Publishing', *The Reasoner*, no. 1, pp. 1-3; 'Editorial: The Case For Socialism', *The Reasoner*, no. 2, pp. 1-7; E P Thompson, 'Through the Smoke of Budapest', *The Reasoner*, no. 3, Supplement, pp. 1-7.

91   Thompson, 'Through the Smoke', p. 7.

92   Thompson, 'Through the Smoke', p. 7. Cf T J Thompson and E P Thompson (eds), *There Is a Spirit in Europe: A Memoir of Frank Thompson* (Victor Gollancz, London, 1947); Frank was Edward's elder brother who inspired him.

93   Evidence related to this claim occurs in Thompson's discussion in 1971 of the CPGB cultural journal *Left Review* and Fox's contribution to it in 1935-36. But Thompson notes the pressure on the editors from 'the apparatus of the party at King Street which judged the usefulness of the review only as an organising medium', and observes 'a sense of growing doctrinal inhibition in the review' (E P Thompson, '*Left Review*', in E P Thompson, *Persons and Polemics* (Merlin, London, 1994), pp. 230-35. This is not much of a peg on which to hang the argument that Fox personified a strand of any significance in Communist tradition. The Popular Front politics of the 1930s granted Communist writers and artists what was always a limited licence. By 1938, the CPGB leadership was asserting control over *Left Review*, and, by 1939, 'the party's interest in culture suddenly looked as cynical and manipulative as its anti-fascism seemed shallow' (Andy Croft, 'Authors Take Sides: Writers and the Communist Party 1920-1956', in Geoff Andrews, Nina Fishman and Kevin Morgan (eds), *Opening the Books: Essays on the Social and Cultural History of the British Communist Party* (Pluto Press, London, 1995), p. 97.

94   For Fox, see McIlroy, 'The Establishment of Intellectual Orthodoxy', pp. 212-17; for Mann, see John McIlroy, 'The Revival and Decline of Rank-and-File Movements in Britain during the 1930s', *Labor History*, Volume 57, no. 3, 2016, pp. 358-61. Mann's humanitarian instincts were in play when he was the only CPGB member to protest against the imprisonment of the Chinese Trotskyists.

95   E P Thompson, 'Edgell Rickword', in E P Thompson, *Persons and Polemics* (Merlin, London, 1994), pp. 236-43.

96   Saville, 'May Day 1937', p. 280 n. 43.

97   Interview with Hobsbawm, in Henry Abelove et al. *Visions of History* (Manchester University Press, Manchester, 1983), pp. 33-34.

98   John McIlroy, 'A Communist Historian in 1956: Brian Pearce and the Crisis of British Stalinism', *Revolutionary History*, Volume 9, no. 3, p. 88. Pearce's 1949 piece was published three decades later, see 'From the Archives: Two Articles by Brian Pearce', *International*, Volume 3, no. 3, Spring 1977.

99   Saville, 'On Party History'.

100   Joseph Redman (Brian Pearce), *The Communist Party and the Labour Left 1925-1929*, Reasoner Pamphlet, no. 1 (Hull), April 1957, with an introduction by John Saville. Saville and Pearce had known each other since their student days in the 1930s. Pearce had helped with *The Reasoner*, contributing the quotation from Diderot on page 21 in the second issue: 'Though a lie may serve for the moment it is inevitably injurious in the long run; the truth, on the other hand, inevitably serves in the end even if it may hurt for the moment.' As 'L Hussey' he had contributed to the first issue of the *New Reasoner*. Relations between Pearce and Saville cooled with the tension between the *New Reasoner* and *Labour Review* and their different political trajectories (Pearce to author, 24 March 2006).

101 John Saville, 'A Further Note on British Communist History', *New Reasoner*, Spring 1959, pp. 99-101, quotes from pp 99 and 100. The book, which was attacked by the party even before its publication, had already been reviewed in the *New Reasoner* by the former leading Communist JT Murphy, but Saville obviously believed that Murphy's clement review was inadequate. For Pelling's response to Saville, see 'Correspondence', *New Reasoner*, Autumn 1959, pp 109-10.

102 In his review of Pelling, Dutt similarly emphasised the courageous, anti-capitalist rank-and-file member of the CPGB; see R Palme Dutt, 'Honour to Whom Honour: Some Reflections on Communist Party History', *Labour Monthly*, April 1959.

103 Ignazio Silone in Richard Crossman (ed), *The God That Failed: Six Studies in Communism* (Hamish Hamilton, London, 1950), p. 118; Doris Lessing, *Walking in the Shade: Volume 2 of My Autobiography* (Harper Collins, London, 1997), p. 52.

104 Saville, 'A Further Note', p. 100.

105 Saville, 'Neil Redfern's Thesis'; Neil Redfern, 'A Reply to John Saville', *Communist History Network Newsletter*, no. 8, July 2000, pp. 12-13. See also Neil Redfern, *Class or Nation: Communism, Imperialism and Two World Wars* (IB Tauris, London, 2005). For a more sombre view of the CPGB's role in the unemployed movement, see Alan Campbell and John McIlroy, 'The National Unemployed Workers' Movement, and the Communist Party of Great Britain Revisited', *Labour History Review*, Volume 73, no. 1, 2008, pp. 61-88.

106 Saville, 'A Further Note', pp. 100-101. IRIS, Industrial Relations Information Services, was a right-wing propaganda group which focused on trade unions.

107 Saville, 'Further Note', pp. 99-101.

108 Saville, 'XXth Congress', p. 7. Cf Hobsbawm, who states that he remained in the CPGB because he was 'repelled by the idea of being in the company of ex-Communists who turned into fanatical anti-Communists' (Hobsbawm, *Interesting Times*, p. 217).

109 John Saville, 'The Politics of *Encounter*', in Ralph Miliband and John Saville (eds), *Socialist Register 1964* (Merlin, London, 1964), p. 197; 'Editorial', *New Reasoner*, Autumn 1959. It was only later that CIA financing of *Encounter* was revealed. For different views of British intellectuals' independence in relation to 'Washington Gold', see Frances Stonor Saunders, *Who Paid the Piper? The CIA and the Cultural Cold War* (Granta, London, 1999); Hugh Wilford, *The CIA, The British Left and the Cold War* (Frank Cass, London, 2003).

110 Brian Pearce, 'Review of Henry Pelling, *The British Communist Party*', *Labour Review*, December 1958, p. 156; Saville, 'Further Note', p. 100.

111 Saville, *Memoirs*, p. 165.

112 Saville, *Memoirs*, pp. 117-18, 120-22.

113 Saville, *Memoirs*, p. 118.

114 John Saville, 'The Welfare State: A Historical Analysis', *New Reasoner*, Winter 1957; Dorothy Thompson, 'The Welfare State: Discussion', *New Reasoner*, Spring 1958.

115 Ralph Miliband, *Parliamentary Socialism: A Study in the Politics of Labour* (Allen and Unwin, London, 1961).

116 John Saville, 'Labourism and the Labour Government', in Ralph Miliband and John Saville (eds), *Socialist Register 1967* (Merlin, London, 1967), p. 68.

117 John Saville, 'Prospects For the Seventies', in Ralph Miliband and John Saville (eds), *Socialist Register 1970* (Merlin, London, 1970), p. 210.

118 Saville, 'Prospects For the Seventies', p. 212.

119 See Duncan Thompson, *Pessimism of the Intellect? A History of 'New Left Review'* (Merlin, London, 2007).

120 John McIlroy, 'The Society For the Study of Labour History 1956-1985: Its Origins and Its Heyday', *Labour History Review*, no. 75, 2010, Supplement, pp. 19-112; 'John Saville and the *Dictionary of Labour Biography* – Interview by Malcolm Chase', *Socialist History*,

no. 19, 2000, pp. 71-81. Credit is also due to Saville's co-editor of the *Dictionary*, Joyce Bellamy.

121 Anderson, *Arguments*, p. 119.

122 Quoted in Saville, 'XXth Congress', pp. 12-13.

123 David Rubinstein, 'John Saville: An Appreciation', *Bulletin of the Society for the Study of Labour History*, no. 48, Spring 1984, p. 3.

124 Silone in Crossman, *The God That Failed*, p. 118.

125 Valentine Cunningham, 'Introduction', in Valentine Cunningham (ed), *The Penguin Book of Spanish Civil War Verse* (Penguin, Harmondsworth, 1980), pp. 25-94.

126 Quotes from AJP Taylor, *English History: 1914-1945* (Oxford University Press, Oxford, 1965), p 395; Ronald Radosh, Mary R Habeck and Grigory Sevostianov (eds), *Spain Betrayed: The Soviet Union in the Spanish Civil War* (Yale University Press, London, 2001), p xvi. Lewis Mates disabuses readers of the notion that activism over Spain was the preserve of Communists by recuperating the part played by Labour Party members and trade unionists, many of whom were critical of the CPGB and its Popular Front politics; see Lewis H Mates, *The Spanish Civil War and the British Left: Political Activism and the Popular Front* (IB Tauris, London, 2007).

127 Cunningham, 'Introduction', p. 78.

128 Cunningham, 'Introduction', p. 74.

129 Cunningham, 'Introduction', p. 78.

130 John Saville, 'Valentine Cunningham and the Poetry of the Spanish Civil War', in Ralph Miliband and John Saville (eds), *Socialist Register 1981* (Merlin, London, 1981), pp. 277, 281, 278, 283.

131 John Saville, 'Valentine Cunningham', pp. 271-78.

132 Valentine Cunningham, 'Saville's Row with *The Penguin Book of Spanish Civil War Verse*', in Martin Eve and David Musson (eds), *Socialist Register 1982* (Merlin, London, 1982), pp. 269-83. Cunningham (pp 281-82) revealed Heinemann's role and suggested that Saville should have explicitly acknowledged it.

133 Saville, 'Valentine Cunningham', p. 271.

134 See Tony Judt, 'Arthur Koestler: The Exemplary Intellectual', in Tony Judt, *Reappraisals: Reflections on the Forgotten Twentieth Century* (Heinemann, London, 2008), pp. 25-43; Tony Judt, 'Eric Hobsbawm and the Romance of Communism', in Judt, *Reappraisals*, p. 126. On Saville's method, see Cunningham, 'Saville', pp. 271-72.

135 Saville's hostility to Orwell is clear: 'Whenever mentioned, George Orwell was invariably denounced. "I have always disliked him since *The Road to Wigan Pier*", he told me in a letter, although Orwell's later animus towards Communist intellectuals, and the leadership of Soviet Russia could have done little to alter his opinion.' (David Martin, 'John Saville', p. 114)

136 Saville, 'Valentine Cunningham', p. 271.

137 Saville, 'Valentine Cunningham', p. 271.

138 Bernard Crick, *George Orwell: A Life* (Secker and Warburg, London, 1980), pp. 339-51; Michael Shelden, *Orwell: The Authorised Biography* (London, Heinemann, 1991), pp. 309-13.

139 Saville, 'Valentine Cunningham', p. 271. See the comment of a contemporary historian: '*Homage to Catalonia*, the war memoir that taught at least some Western leftists and democrats that fascism was not the only enemy ...' (Timothy Snyder, *Bloodlands: Europe Between Hitler and Stalin* (Basic Books, New York, 2010), p. 75. Orwell's continued relevance may be seen in George Orwell, *Orwell in Spain* (Penguin, Harmondsworth, 2001); and in Ken Loach's re-enactment of the Stalinists' crushing of the revolution in his film *Land and Freedom* (1995).

140 Saville, 'Valentine Cunningham', p. 284 n. 12.

141   Burnett Bolloten, *The Grand Camouflage: The Spanish Civil War and Revolution, 1936-39* (Hollis and Carter, London, 1961); Burnett Bolloten, *The Spanish Revolution: The Left and the Struggle for Power during the Civil War* (University of North Carolina Press, Chapel Hill, 1979); Pierre Broué and Emile Témime, *The Revolution and Civil War in Spain* (Faber and Faber, London, 1970).

142   Claudín, *Communist Movement*, pp. 210-42.

143   James K Hopkins, *Into the Heart of the Fire: The British in the Spanish Civil War* (Stanford University Press, Stanford, 1998); Radosh *et al*, *Spain Betrayed*; Victor Alba and Stephen Schwarz, *Spanish Marxism versus Soviet Communism* (Transaction Books, New Brunswick, 1988); Burnett Bolloten, *The Spanish Civil War: Revolution and Counter-Revolution* (University of North Carolina Press, Chapel Hill, 1991); Gerald Howson, *Arms for Spain: The Untold Story of the Spanish Civil War* (Albermarle, London, 1998); Robert Alexander, *The Anarchists in the Spanish Civil War* (Janus, London, 1999); Stanley Payne, *The Spanish Civil War, The Soviet Union and Communism* (Yale University Press, New Haven, 2004). There is general agreement on the Stalinist terror; see Paul Preston, *The Spanish Holocaust* (Harper, London, 2012), although some work – for example, Helen Graham, *The Spanish Republic at War 1936-1939* (Cambridge University Press, Cambridge, 2002) – questions the extent of Russian control over the Republican war effort, and Preston continues to insist that a revolutionary war was unwinnable – see, for example, Paul Preston, *A Concise History of the Spanish Civil War* (Fontana, London, 1996) – although we know a bourgeois war did not and was never likely to defeat Franco. The approach of Richard Baxell is similar to that of Graham in claiming, on limited evidence, that Comintern control of the CPGB and CPGB control over the volunteers has been exaggerated; see Richard Baxell, *British Volunteers in the Spanish Civil War* (Routledge, London, 2004), pp. 130-49. For a critique of Graham and Preston, see Andy Durgan, *The Spanish Civil War* (Palgrave Macmillan, Basingstoke, 2007).

144   Saville, 'Valentine Cunningham', p. 283.

145   Claudín, *Communist Movement*, p. 241.

146   Saville, 'Valentine Cunningham', p. 278.

147   He had not read all the relevant literature, such as Judith Cook, *Apprentices of Freedom* (Quartet, London, 1979); see Saville, 'Valentine Cunningham', p. 284 n. 7.

148   Hopkins, *Into the Heart of the Fire*, pp. 254-55.

149   Radosh *et al*, *Spain Betrayed*, pp. 246, 468.

150   Hopkins, *Into the Heart of the Fire*, pp. 279, 213. Baxell, *British Volunteers*, pp. 130-49, makes several useful qualifications but they do not detract from the substance of Hopkins' conclusions.

151   Hopkins, *Into the Heart of the Fire*, pp. xi, 258-90.

152   Hopkins, *Into the Heart of the Fire*, pp. xiv, 290.

153   Colin Leys commends Saville's article, without addressing the arguments or mentioning Cunningham's response. Kevin Morgan salutes a 'memorable and effective broadside against the misrepresentation of the Communists' efforts in Spain', without reference to the evidence or arguments. See Colin Leys, '"Honest Socialists": John Saville and the *Socialist Register*', and Kevin Morgan, 'The Good Old Cause', both in David Howell, Dianne Kirby and Kevin Morgan (eds), *John Saville: Commitment and History* (Lawrence and Wishart/Socialist History Society, London, 2011), pp. 57-58, 19, 27 n. 25.

154   Saville, *Labour Movement*, p. 81.

155   Saville, *Labour Movement*, p. 134.

156   Saville, 'Communist Experience', pp. 1-2, 24-25.

157   Saville, 'XXth Congress', p. 15.

158 Saville, 'XXth Congress', p. 21. That this was a judgement on the past is clear from Saville's dissection of the journal *Marxism Today*, whose supporters were, by the late 1980s, in control of the CPGB. He was scathing about the journal's deprecation of classical Marxism; its disconnection of theory from practice; the inadequacies of its conceptions of post-Fordism; and its celebration of Thatcherite 'New Times', rather than organising against their impact. See John Saville, '*Marxism Today*: An Anatomy', in Ralph Miliband, Leo Panitch and John Saville (eds), *Socialist Register 1990* (Merlin, London, 1990), pp. 89-100. Saville's differences with this current in the CPGB was apparent at the time of the 1984-85 miners' strike. He wholeheartedly supported it, despite criticisms of its leadership; *Marxism Today* was more critical than supportive. For Saville's row with Hobsbawm, a leading light in the *Marxism Today* firmament, see Logie Barrow, 'Anatomising Methusalah', *Labour History Review*, Volume 78, no. 3, December 2013, p. 355; John Saville, 'An Open Conspiracy: Conservative Politics and the Miners' Strike 1984-85', in Ralph Miliband, John Saville, Marcel Liebman and Leo Panitch (eds), *Socialist Register 1985/86* (Merlin, London, 1986), pp. 295-329.

159 Saville, 'Communist Experience', p. 22.

160 Saville, 'Communist Experience', p. 2.

161 Anderson, *Arguments*, p. 120.

162 'Why did we more than the writers, more than the scientists ... find ourselves in the front line of opposition from the start? Essentially because we had to confront the situation not only as private individuals and Communist militants, but in our professional capacity. The issue of what had been done under Stalin, and why it had been concealed, was literally a question of history. So were the open but undiscussed questions about episodes in our own Party's history which were directly linked to Moscow decisions ... so indeed, was our own political attitude.' (Hobsbawm, *Interesting Times*, p. 207) Such comments highlight the Historians' Group's silence in the decade preceding 1956.

163 Hamilton, *The Crisis of Theory*, p. 1.

164 Saville, 'Communist Experience', pp. 3-4.

165 Saville, 'Communist Experience', p. 6.

166 Miliband, 'John Saville: A Presentation', p. 30.

167 Martin, 'John Saville', p. 114 and n. 2.

168 In contrast to an abundance of Communists, no Trotskyists figured in the *Dictionary* while Saville was editor. When questioned about this he explained that nobody had suggested such entries: 'So let me say emphatically a) I have never been offered anything and b) if I had been I should have been happy to accept it.' ('John Saville and the *Dictionary of Labour Biography*', p. 74) He never exhibited any personal hostility to Trotskyists, and was proud that the archive at Hull housed Jock Haston's papers and other Trotskyist material. He was also involved in the supervision of Martin Upham, *The History of British Trotskyism until 1949* (unpublished PhD thesis, University of Hull, 1980). Reg Groves, a pioneer of British Trotskyism, worked for a time on the *Dictionary*, collecting material on the Christian Socialists.

169 Saville, *Memoirs*, p. 165.

170 Quoted in Dworkin, *Cultural Marxism*, p. 240. Saville mocked the 'really charitable and generous and sisterly and brotherly' style, which he associated with academic Marxism: it obstructed clarity and progress (Dworkin, *Cultural Marxism*, p. 239).

PAUL FLEWERS

E P Thompson and the Soviet Experience

One thread running through *The Reasoner* was the urgent need to provide a Marxist explanation of Stalinism. In the first issue of the magazine John Saville and E P Thompson declared that 'the shock and moral turmoil engendered by the [Khrushchev] revelations were the result of our general failure to apply a Marxist analysis to socialist countries and to the Soviet Union in particular', and warned that it was necessary not 'to succumb once again' to the 'error' – that of failing to draw up such a Marxist analysis – which had 'dogged us for so long'.[1] In the second issue, Ronald Meek wished that Khrushchev's 'Secret Speech' 'had gone even part of the way towards a Marxist interpretation of the facts which it disclosed';[2] whilst in the third issue a correspondent enquired as to how much of the turmoil in the Communist Party of Great Britain had been 'caused by the absence of a convincing, trustworthy Marxist explanation of the horrors revealed (or partly revealed?) by Khrushchev and subsequent developments'.[3]

That there was a thoroughgoing revulsion against Stalinism on the part of the editors of and contributors to *The Reasoner* is indisputable, and Thompson subsequently made his critical feelings about it very clear on many occasions over the following decades, sometimes at quite some length. It is worth, therefore, investigating Thompson's writings that touch on the subject of Stalinism, in respect of both the Soviet Union and Eastern Europe and the Communist parties outwith the Soviet bloc, to ascertain whether he developed a consistent Marxist explanation of the phenomenon in respect of its origins in the Soviet Union during the 1920s and its evolution over the subsequent decades.

I: Thompson's Revulsion Against Stalinism

Thompson certainly did not mince his words when he wrote about the negative aspects of Stalinism. Let us quote here from his substantial polemic, published in 1978, against the French Communist philosopher Louis Althusser:

We are not only (please remember) just talking about some millions of people (and most of these the 'wrong' people) being killed or *gulaged*. We are talking about the deliberate manipulation of the law, the means of communication, the police and propaganda organs of a state, to blockade knowledge, to disseminate lies, to slander individuals; about institutional procedures which confiscated from the Soviet people all self-activating means (whether in democratic modes or in forms of workers' control), which substituted the party for the working class, the party's leaders (or leader) for the party, and the security organs for all; about the confiscation and centralisation of all intellectual and moral expression, into an ideological state orthodoxy – that is, not only the suppression of the democratic and cultural freedoms of 'individuals': ... it is not only this, but within the confiscation of individual 'rights' to knowledge and expression, we have the ulterior confiscation of the processes of communication and knowledge-formation of a whole people, without which neither Soviet workers nor collective farmers can know what is true nor what each other thinks.[4]

Thompson did not stint in his sharp criticisms of Stalinism both in this polemic and in his open letter to the Polish philosopher Leszek Kołakowski in 1973. The Soviet Communist Party had become the institution which imposed upon 'the self-activating social and intellectual process of Russian society a system of *blockade*'.[5] Its ideology was 'a brutal pragmatism of power', 'a new, brittle, uneasy, manifestly irrational institutional orthodoxy', 'a selective, closed justificatory and mystifying set of notions',[6] 'suborning the good name of science in order to deny all independent rights and authenticity to the moral and imaginative faculties', all of which had the poisonous effect of encouraging 'a reversion to Greek Orthodox faith, as nationalist self-exclusion, as personalist self-isolation, or as Solzhenitsyn', and, he warned, in the future 'ever more bizarre and immaterial forms of moral consciousness' rising up 'as "superstructure" upon that severely-scientific material "base"'.[7]

He was equally harsh when it came to the impact of Stalinism upon the official Communist movement outwith the Soviet bloc:

Spreading outwards from the Soviet Union, through the Comintern, this permeated the entire international Communist movement. The practices and the ideology were replicated, and the agents of this replication (the inner and trusted bureaucracies of national Communist parties) became, by a very exact analogy, the priesthood of a universal Church, adept at theological apologetics and 'humanistic' homiletics, directly and knowingly deceiving their own memberships, agile in casuistry, and reinforcing their control by distinctively Stalinist procedures and forms – 'democratic centralism', the suppression of faction and discussion, the exclusive control of the party's political, theoretical and (as far as possible) intellectual organs, the slander of critics and opponents, and the covert manipulation of fellow travellers and front organisations.[8]

Altogether, Stalinism was 'one of the ultimate disasters of the human mind and conscience, a terminus of the spirit, a disaster area in which every socialist profession of "good faith" was blasted and burned up'.[9]

That was a very strong denunciation. So precisely what was Stalinism, and how did it come about? This was and still remains one of the most important questions facing the left, and Thompson, shaken by the events of 1956, sought to get to grips with it. In an article written shortly after his departure from the CPGB, he declared that it was no use 'simply ... swelling the chorus of anti-Stalinist abuse'; rather, it was necessary to 'understand – and explain – the true character of Stalinism'. To do this, he added, there was 'a great deal to learn from the analyses of Trotsky and even more from the flexible and undogmatic approach of Isaac Deutscher and others'.[10] So, as we turn to Thompson's ideas on the nature of Stalinism and the Soviet Union, let us also consider the degree to which he followed his own advice in respect of studying these works.

II: What Was the Soviet Union?

In the immediate aftermath of his leaving the CPGB, Thompson provided some tentative suggestions about the nature of the Soviet bloc countries and their current stage of development. He detected severely contradictory tendencies operating within them. 'The Soviet Union is a socialist country ...', he confidently declared in 1957; we had seen 'the emergence upon one-quarter of the earth's surface of a new society, with a new economic structure, new social relations, and new political institutions'. On the other hand, he provided serious qualifications: this new society had many negative features; indeed, its socialist nature was 'not yet expressed in institutions, political conduct or public morality'.[11] A year later he insisted that despite the horrors of Stalinism, a 'new society' nonetheless existed, at least potentially: the property relations in the Soviet Union, Eastern Europe and China had undergone a 'fundamental revolution' which had 'vastly increased' their 'real potential for intellectual, cultural and democratic advance'. Whilst he rejected as unconvincing the idea that the Soviet-style countries were state capitalist in nature, or that their ruling élites represented a 'new class' as outlined by Milovan Djilas, he nonetheless considered that the Stalinist bureaucracies were 'parasitic' upon society and had come to express 'a distinct interest'. The 'state apparatus, institutions and ideology' in these countries were 'restricting … human potential' and the 'ideological sterility and restrictive institutions' were 'becoming increasingly a fetter even upon industrial expansion'.[12]

During the 1970s, Thompson returned to the question of the nature of Soviet-style societies in both his open letter to Kołakowski in 1973 and his polemic against Althusser in 1978. In the former, declaring that answering this question would 'require the most careful historical analysis', thus implying that the task still lay ahead, it can be seen that he had backtracked a little from 1958, as he pondered over whether the élite was a 'class' that was 'intrinsically involved in the ownership or appropriation of the means of production', or 'a powerful, highly-structured *parasitism* derivative from alternative productive relations', and he refrained from giving a definite answer.[13]

In the latter piece, Thompson outlined four possible analyses of the Soviet Union, rejecting the first three in favour of the last. One possibility was that it was 'a workers' state (perhaps with certain "deformities") capable of ascendant self-development, without any severe internal struggle or rupture of continuity': any shortcomings were capable of self-correction, 'owing to the guidance of a proletarian party, informed by Marxist theory, and hence blessed with the "know-how" of history'.[14] This, we might add, was the post-1956 standpoint of the official Communist movement.

Another possibility was that it was an 'historically-specific form of forced industrialisation' led by a 'collocation' of ruling groups intending to modernise the country with the aim of 'bringing it into tardy and imperfect conformity' with the USA.[15] This was the now largely forgotten theory of convergence favoured by some Western analysts during the initial post-Stalin period, and which fell by the wayside as the Soviet economy slowed down into stasis and the technology gap between the Soviet Union and the advanced capitalist countries continually widened.

One more possibility was that it was a state in which power had 'fallen into the hands of a new bureaucratic class' that was interested in securing 'its own privileges and continued tenure of power', a class which would 'only be overthrown by another proletarian revolution'.[16] This was the standpoint of those who viewed the Soviet Union as a state-capitalist society or a new form of class society (bureaucratic collectivism), or, if one substituted 'caste' for 'class', the classic Trotskyist position. Thompson's rejection of this analysis appears at first glance to contradict his contention in 1973 that the élite might actually have become a class, thus reverting to his earlier position. However, as we shall see, he did not preclude the possibility of its *becoming* a class in the future.

Finally, he outlined his favoured analysis, by which:

> … the Soviet state can only be understood with the aid of the concept of 'parasitism', and whether or not its ruling groups harden into a bureaucratic *class*, or whether episodic reform can be imposed upon them by pressures of various kinds (from the needs and resistances of workers and farmers, from intellectual dissenters, and from the logic arising from their own inner contradictions, factional struggles, and incapacity to perform essential functions, etc) remains, historically, an unfinished and indeterminate question, which may be precipitated into one or another more fully-determined direction by contingencies.[17]

If, as he had pondered in 1973, the élite was in fact a class, he felt that it could well remain in power for 'several generations' before it gave way. If it had not yet become one, then it could survive only if it did not come into opposition with or seriously impede the society upon which it was parasitic. There were the added factors in the latter case that, firstly, it was obliged to act in defence of that society (organising production, defence from external threats, etc), and it would have to erect an ideological façade to cover its parasitism, with the result that members of that élite who took the ideology seriously would criticise the regime in the name of its own ideology: something which had occurred with the 'repeated experiences of courageous critics of the ruling Communist parties emerging from within the Communist parties themselves'. Furthermore, the ideology might have a popular echo:

> … it might be so (some observers say it is so) that beneath the parasitism millions of Soviet citizens still think of their land and factories as *ours* rather than as *mine* or *theirs*; still hold a pride in the intentions of the October revolution; are socialised in some socialist values; find something more than myth in Marxist texts; and hence already do and increasingly will criticise the practices of their own society in terms of its own rhetoric.[18]

Nonetheless, Thompson also felt it possible for the élite, over 'several centuries', to 'reproduce itself and control or *manufacture* social consciousness' to the degree that there would be 'no inherent logic of process within the system which, as social being', would 'work powerfully enough to bring its overthrow'. It would be difficult for an élite, even with all the means at its disposal, to control 'critical social consciousness', but were it able to maintain production and a rising standard of living, then such a dismal future could not realistically be ruled out.[19]

Thompson therefore came to conclude that the actual nature of the Soviet socio-economic formation had not yet been settled; indeed, he felt that 'fifty years is too short a time in which to judge a new social system'.[20] This might be seen as his being cautious or, to be less generous, somewhat dodging the issue.

III: The Nature of Stalinism

But what precisely was Stalinism? In the late 1950s, Thompson stated that it was 'the ideology of a revolutionary élite' which 'within a particular historical context' had 'degenerated into a bureaucracy':

> Stalinism struck root within a particular social context, drawing nourishment from attitudes and ideas prevalent among the working class and peasantry – exploited and culturally deprived classes; it was strengthened by Russian backwardness and by the hostility and active aggression of capitalist powers; out of these conditions there arose the bureaucracy which adapted the ideology to its own purposes and is interested in perpetuating it ...[21]

At this juncture, Thompson therefore understood Stalinism as initially an ideology, a set of ideas, preceding the transformation of the Soviet party-state apparatus into a ruling élite, and this body in turn adopted it in order to use it for its own purposes, which he outlined as defending 'socialised property against internal counter-revolution and external aggression' and driving forward industrialisation.[22]

Thompson returned to the question two decades later, and considered that Stalinism 'was not cunningly planned, nor ... was it the outcome of some "deviation" *in theory*, some momentary lapse in Stalin's theoretical rigour', but was rather 'the product of baffled human agency, within a desperate succession of contingencies, and subject to the severe determinations of Soviet history'. He added that 'at a certain point, Stalinism may be seen as a *systematic social formation*, with a consonant ideological logic and legitimation – Marxism-Leninism-Stalinism'.[23] This was a very important qualification, more than merely implying that Stalinism was not just an ideology wielded by a ruling élite, but a specific socio-economic formation, although, as we saw above, he left the precise nature of this formation as an unanswered question.

At one point Thompson averred that Stalinism arose 'in part from the outlook of a revolutionary élite, desperately aware of its historical mission and almost impossible tasks, operating within a society without long democratic traditions or experience of democratic institutions, and with a large part of the people indifferent or actively hostile to its ideas'.[24] At another point, he claimed that conditions of war during 1917–20 and 1941–45 and 'the expectation of invasion in the 1930s' were 'necessary conditions for the historical formation of Stalinism'.[25] And that is about as far as he went in investigating its origins. Thompson was often vague, occasionally infuriatingly so, when discussing this question, and sometimes gave out mixed messages. He considered, on the one hand, that the early years of the Soviet republic, 1917 to the early 1920s, were one of two periods in which Communism had 'shown a most human face',[26] which implied that the establishment of the Soviet regime was a positive, progressive historical factor, and that Stalinism was its negation as it degenerated into something inhuman. On the other hand, he more than hinted that the degeneration into Stalinism may have been inevitable when he declared that 'the experience of the Russian revolution' – the use of the word 'revolution' indicating that this meant from 1917 – 'made the concept of a revolutionary transition – *any* transition – to socialism appear to be synonymous with bloodshed, civil war, censorship, purges and the rest',[27] and, when referring to revolutionary processes in general, he wrote of 'any ruling group, perhaps fortuitously established in power at the moment of revolution'.[28] And what could the reader have made of Thompson's upbraiding his more critical colleagues by insisting that 'it was obviously only short-sightedness which ever led socialists to conceive of the new society stepping, pure and enlightened, out of the fires of the old', and that they should not have been surprised to find this new society 'blackened and distorted by pain and oppression', other than that the negative features of Stalinism had been unavoidable?[29] By the end, Thompson had more or less written off the Bolsheviks by the time of the Kronstadt rebellion and the banning of factions in the Soviet Communist Party, telling Bryan Palmer shortly before his death: 'They always were pretty thin socialists, at any time after about 1921 anyway.'[30]

Somewhat paradoxically for an historian, Thompson was often nebulous in respect of details and dates. What were the 'attitudes and ideas prevalent among the working class and peasantry' that had such a deleterious impact upon the Soviet regime? When was the juncture at which the 'revolutionary élite' in the Soviet Union discovered it 'could only maintain power by methods of extreme authoritarianism'? At which point did the 'revolutionary élite' mutate into the 'bureaucracy'? Precisely when did the orthodoxy of 'Marxism-Leninism-Stalinism' emerge?[31] One will find nothing in Thompson's writings about the Bolsheviks' establishment of a political monopoly during the Civil War and the substitution of its rule for that of the working class, nor anything about the tightening of the party's internal regime, most notably the ban on factions in 1921, both of which had serious consequences for both the party and the country as a whole, and subsequently for the Communist International. One will find nothing about the shifting constellations at the head of the Soviet Communist Party in the half-a-dozen years after Lenin's death – the troika of Kamenev, Stalin and Zinoviev; the duumvirate of Bukharin and Stalin; the Joint Opposition of Kamenev, Trotsky and Zinoviev; the group around Bukharin – and about their jockeying for power and the ultimate victory of Stalin's faction in 1929. One will find nothing about the intricate and impassioned discussions within the party leadership during the 1920s on the burning questions of industrial and agricultural development, the political consciousness of the working class, party democracy and foreign policy, nor anything about the factional disputes within the Communist International which revolved around key questions of strategy and tactics across the world and which in many respects reflected the internal Soviet factional battles.

The bulk of Thompson's initial analysis of Stalinism was concerned with what he considered to be its roots in philosophical problems on the part of Lenin and indeed even Marx in respect of the relationship between being and consciousness. He felt that Lenin's interpretation of that relationship held that social being was independent of social consciousness. Had the Soviet Union developed into a healthy socialist society, he added, this would have been 'sifted out' of the 'rich harvest' of Lenin's thought. However, under the conditions that existed, Stalin seized upon Lenin's misapprehension, vulgarised it further when incorporating it into the framework of his thought, and in so doing annihilated 'all sense of human agency' by losing it 'in a determinism where the role of consciousness was to adapt itself to "the objective logic of economic evolution"'. Stalinism therefore had a 'colossal contempt' for working-class men and women, a 'veiled hostility to democratic initiatives in every form'. People were mere appendages to the instruments of production.[32]

This, surely, is putting the cart before the horse: the pertinent questions are why the Soviet Union did not become a healthy socialist society, and why, instead, the Soviet party-state apparatus lost its support within the working class, rose above it and ruled in its name, and finally, during the First Five-Year Plan of 1929–32, became transformed into a self-conscious ruling élite. There were certainly problematic aspects in the way that Marxist philosophy developed after Marx's death which fed into the theory and practice of the parties of the Second International, including the Russian social-democratic movement.[33] Stalin's crude theoretical constructs and political traits were well suited to the process of bureaucratisation in the 1920s and to the ensuing Soviet socio-economic formation as it developed after 1929; indeed, it was no accident that Stalin rose to prominence during these developments and almost personified them. But however much they assisted the process of bureaucratisation, they were not the *cause* of bureaucratisation in the first place. This has to be located within the broader trends within Soviet society,[34] and, as we have seen, Thompson's views in this area were vague and at times self-conflicting.

The fragmentary and contradictory aspects of Thompson's understanding of the rise of Stalinism were almost certainly related to his conception of revolution. Referring to Thompson's article 'Revolution' from 1960,[35] Wade Matthews wrote of his voluntarist idea of revolution that 'socialism could be achieved if people, imbued with a socialist consciousness, willed it to be so'. Thompson had constructed 'a conception of socialist strategy that paid undue attention to the role of consciousness – to the neglect of objective economic considerations – in any transition to socialism'.[36] Although Thompson recognised the existence of various problematic objective factors at play during the early years of the Soviet republic, he considered that the main obstacle to the building of a genuine, humanistic socialist society in the Soviet Union was the philosophical problem that he detected in Bolshevism. The rise of Stalinism was thus predominantly an ideological question; the material factors were secondary, and Thompson made no real attempt to draw them into a systematic analysis.

Another aspect of Soviet history practically absent in Thompson's writings is Stalin's theory of 'socialism in one country', which various authorities, including Trotsky and Deutscher, viewed as a crucial turning point within both Soviet Communism and the Communist International. Adopted in the mid-1920s by the Soviet Communist Party, largely in response to the isolation of the Soviet Union after the failed revolution in Germany in late 1923, and contradicting all preceding Bolshevik theory and practice, Stalin's theory had far-going consequences. On the domestic plane, it laid the basis for an essentially national course on the part of the Soviet regime, resulting, with the great changes under the initial Five-Year Plans, in the rise of a messianic nationalist fervour and in a revival of Great

Russian nationalism, which reached grotesque proportions during the late 1940s. On the international plane, it greatly reinforced the tendency towards *realpolitik* in Soviet foreign policy.

Stalin's theory justified and indeed sanctified the entire course of the Soviet experience, past, present and future. If it were possible – as the theory declared – for socialism to be constructed within the bounds of Russia, this meant that everything that the Bolsheviks had done since 1917, things which had previously been seen as desperate short-term measures to prevent the collapse of the first blow of the world revolutionary process, and everything that the Soviet regime was now doing and would do from now on, were now all part of the prescribed course which every Communist party was to follow. The continual tightening of discipline within the Soviet party during the 1920s, already under way prior to the adoption of Stalin's theory, was projected into the Comintern, thus leading to the replication of the increasingly monolithic structure of the Soviet Communist Party throughout the international movement.

The transformation of the Soviet party-state apparatus into a ruling élite led to the total subordination of the Communist International to the requirements of Soviet foreign policy. The Communist parties became a means by which Moscow was able to put pressure upon governments with the aim of influencing the latter's policies in its interests. It was exceedingly useful for Moscow to have in many countries, including some key ones, an agency – and an amazingly loyal one at that – which had the ability, to varying degrees, to exert political power to its advantage. Such was the attraction of the Soviet Union as 'the new civilisation' to Communist Party members and supporters and to those commonly described as fellow-travellers that they accepted the many indignities heaped upon them by Moscow, taking in their stride its sudden and drastic changes of political orientations and theoretical constructs.

In a polemic against George Orwell, Thompson conceded that his contention that the Communist movement had degenerated in 'a few years' from being an anti-capitalist force 'into an instrument of Russian foreign policy' did contain 'a half-truth which, at a certain level of policy and ideology', was 'an aid to the interpretation of the evolution of the Third International'; nevertheless Orwell had asked 'none of the historical questions'. However, those that Thompson himself raised were *external*: the European counter-revolution culminating in fascism, Western anti-Soviet foreign policies. And were not Communists justified in wishing to defend the Soviet Union?[37] Nowhere did Thompson raise the question of 'socialism in one country' and its impact upon Communist politics. On the basis of Thompson's voluntarist concept of revolution, socialism *could* have been built within the Soviet Union, irrespective of its economic and social backwardness: hence the question of socialism in one country was of little importance to him even as he came to recognise some of the reactionary realities of Moscow's policies.

The idea that socialism could be and was indeed being constructed in the Soviet Union during the 1930s led to the rise of uncritical state-worship within the parties of the Communist International and amongst fellow-travelling intellectuals. In 1956, Thompson abandoned his uncritical allegiance to the Soviet state. However, it appears that the idea that Moscow, after the ascendancy of the Soviet party-state apparatus into a ruling élite, might have been *systematically* and *deliberately* implementing a nationally-oriented, self-serving policy that need not necessarily have taken into consideration the interests of the working class, both within and outwith the Soviet Union, or, as various left-wing critics of Stalinism had long claimed, that it might actually have acted against those interests if this had suited its own concerns – that is, adopted a counter-revolutionary course – is one which Thompson found difficult to accept in all its ramifications.

Ultimately, for Thompson, the whole historical discussion over the rise of Stalinism was a distraction. In 1958 he brusquely brushed it all aside, imploring people to look at the situation 'as it now appears', and 'not evade it by fighting over and over again the battle of the kulaks or the skirmishes of 1923', or by 'pettifogging scrutiny of texts' or 'one-sided evidence from Trotsky's archives'.[38] Not only did this jar badly with his recommendation to study the works of Trotsky and Deutscher: the history of the Soviet Union and the Communist movement and the situation in both of them during the late 1950s and over the ensuing decades *could not* be properly understood without the obtaining of a thoroughgoing knowledge of the formative years from 1917 through to the victory of Stalin's faction in 1929 and the establishment of a new ruling élite through the ascendancy of that faction and the vast socio-economic changes which it initiated during the initial Five-Year Plans of the 1930s. Thompson's inadequate understanding of the phenomenon of Stalinism was to a considerable degree the result of his impatient dismissal of this necessary task.

It is unfortunate that several substantial accounts of Thompson's Marxism did not engage critically with his writings on the Soviet Union and Stalinism.[39] Dennis Dworkin and Christos Efstathiou both briefly investigated Thompson's assessment of Leninism, but were hampered by their interpretation of Lenin's ideas. Dworkin stated that 'Thompson, though consistently anti-Leninist since 1956, never systematically confronted

Leninism, nor did he discuss it in relation to Stalinism', and considered that he would have done well by presenting 'a democratic critique' of it. However, as Dworkin considered that Leninism and Stalinism were both characterised by 'anti-democratic' thought, an élitist view that 'believed that only party intellectuals possessed scientific theory', the idea that the working class was 'eternally condemned to ideology', and 'authoritarian implications' in its theory, one suspects that he would have written off as inadequate any critique by Thompson of Lenin's political thought that was less dismissive than these clichéd prescriptions.[40] Efstathiou's probing raised more questions than it answered. He rightly rejected Thompson's assertion that Lenin downplayed the role of human consciousness; he noted Thompson's eschewing of Lenin's concept of a vanguard in favour of a much broader form of organisation. But when one considers his claim that Thompson 'accepted Lenin's strategy in an underdeveloped country' and his lack of demurring from Thompson's insistence that the Soviet Union was a socialist country, albeit 'in need of democratic changes', one is compelled to accept that he felt that Lenin considered that a socialist society could be built within the confines of Russia.[41] Lenin never held this view; the idea that he did was an invention of Stalinism: how can one obtain a clear overall picture if one starts off on the wrong foot? Thompson overlooked the matter of 'socialism in one country', presumably seeing it as something of little significance: today's analyst would be ill-advised to follow his example.

Thompson's copious musings on the Soviet Union and Stalinism were inconclusive and inconsistent. Taking into consideration the large amount of time and effort expended over the years on analysing his writings, it is strange that so little has been devoted to this important question.

IV: A Blinkered View of Anti-Stalinism

In his substantial critique of Thompson, Perry Anderson wrote that he 'again and again' promoted the idea that '*1956* was the year of the historical epiphany in which Stalinism for the first time received its ethical quietus, its complete intellectual exposure, its final political death-sentence for socialists'.[42] Anderson was not exaggerating: Thompson's view of that year was quite ecstatic:

This is – quite simply – a revolt against the ideology, the false consciousness of the élite-into-bureaucracy, and a struggle to attain towards a true ('honest') self-consciousness; as such it is expressed in the revolt against dogmatism and the anti-intellectualism which feeds it. Second, it is a revolt against inhumanity – the equivalent of dogmatism in human relationships and moral conduct – against administrative, bureaucratic and twisted attitudes towards human beings. In both senses it represents a return to man: from abstractions and scholastic formulations to real men: from deceptions and myths to honest history: and so the positive content of this revolt may be described as 'socialist humanism'. It is humanist because it places once again real men and women at the centre of socialist theory and aspiration, instead of the resounding abstractions – the Party, Marxism-Leninism-Stalinism, the Two Camps, the Vanguard of the Working-Class – so dear to Stalinism. It is socialist because it reaffirms the revolutionary perspectives of Communism, faith in the revolutionary potentialities not only of the Human Race or of the Dictatorship of the Proletariat but of real men and women.[43]

That 1956 signified a major revolt against Stalinism was clear even to those who held a less euphoric view of it than Thompson. But was it, Anderson enquired, the first attempt to bring it to account? Not at all, he replied, there had long been traditions of Marxist analysis and discussion of Stalinism. One had been founded by Trotsky three decades prior to 1956, and it was not merely 'charged with a burning moral and political indignation' but was 'an enterprise of materialist *social theory*, an attempt at an *historical explanation*' of the phenomenon. There was also an extensive array of exposés of Stalinist rule in the Soviet Union, including those by Boris Souvarine, André Gide and Victor Serge. Yet Thompson ignored all this. Anderson wondered if, for Thompson, 'it was understandable to dismiss Trotsky and ignore Serge, but inexcusable not to heed Khrushchev or Mikoyan'.[44]

And where, asked Anderson, was Thompson prior to 1956? Where was he during, say, Stalin's infamous Doctors' Plot of 1952, or the Slánský trial a year before?[45]

In 1955, Thompson completed his massive study of William Morris, and one senses that its general feel ran a bit askew to the hidebound ethos of his party. However, as Palmer noted, Thompson 'could not break out of the Stalinist straitjacket', as this would have been 'an act of apostatical default too disturbing to contemplate'.[46] And so the book concluded with this masterpiece of bathos:

Twenty years ago even among Socialists and Communists, many must have regarded Morris' picture of 'A Factory As It Might Be' as an unpractical poet's dream: today visitors return from the Soviet Union with stories of the poet's dream already fulfilled. Yesterday in the Soviet

Union, the Communists were struggling against every difficulty to build up their industry to the level of the leading capitalist powers: today they have before them Stalin's blueprint of the advance to Communism ... Thus have the 'claims' of William Morris, the 'unpractical' poet, been promised fulfilment![47]

This was incongruous enough in 1955 – Efstathiou was quite wrong when he wrote that 'Thompson's pro-Stalin stance was not unusual for the time': attitudes had changed rather a lot over the preceding decade[48] – and within a twelve-month would be downright embarrassing in the light of Khrushchev's 'Secret Speech'.

The events of 1956 put dissident members of the official Communist parties in an especially awkward position now that the record of their movement had been exposed – and exposed *ex cathedra* at that[49] – as deeply flawed, and they found themselves pulled in opposite directions as their rivals on the left took gleeful pleasure in their discomfort. Hence in the first issue of *The Reasoner*, Thompson declared that he was proud of the work of the CPGB in support of the working class in Britain and in opposing colonialism abroad, but he was '*not* proud' of the CPGB's 'servile attitude to the leadership of the Soviet Union' and the 'silence' which he and others had maintained on this and other matters.[50] A year later, however, the defensiveness had gone, and Thompson was a lot less forgiving towards his critics:

> I am not going to spend years crippled by remorse because I was duped by the Rajk and Kostov trials, because I was a casuist here and perhaps an accomplice there. We were Communists because we had faith in the fundamental humanist content of Communism, and during the darkest years of the Cold War it was our duty to speak for this. I do not regret this, although I wish we had spoken more wisely and therefore to more effect.[51]

Anderson had not been asking an unreasonable question, for what Khrushchev exposed in his 'Secret Speech' had long been common knowledge outwith the official Communist movement. Thompson's peevish outburst may well have been the result of his being asked this question once too often.

Anderson felt that despite their brave opposition to Stalinism, despite their 'many courageous articles and some fine poems', the Eastern European dissidents of 1956 actually produced 'little intellectual work of lasting substance' that 'survived the crisis'. Even the opposition's most prominent intellectual, György Lukács, 'never theorised' the problems that that year brought into prominence.[52] As for the dissident Communist intellectuals in Western Europe, 'the levy of 1956', Anderson's verdict was damning:

> For all the passionate polemics and self-questioning of the hour, it might be said that overall it is the dearth of sustained study of Stalinism that is remarkable, rather than any pattern of cumulative research.[53]

Anderson wondered if this subsequent dearth of analytical material was based upon the premise that 'the real work was already done – the *moral* critique of Stalinism, which rendered painstaking sociological or historical inquiry into the dynamics of Eastern societies supernumerary or secondary'. Once again, his verdict was damning: what they demonstrated was 'a substitution of moralism for historical materialism'.[54]

As for Thompson himself, Anderson stated that it was as if for him 'the history of the Communist movement had started in 1936', with there being very few references to it before that date in his writings.[55] When considering the history of the official Communist movement after that date, Thompson was defensive. When investigating Orwell's hostility to the movement, he felt that he was one-sided to the point of lop-sidedness when he questioned the integrity of those who were attracted to the official Communist movement, and that he overlooked their honourable motivations, their 'disinterested dedication to a political cause'. Yet, on the other hand, Thompson also recognised that Orwell's stance was set against the background of 'the Soviet purges and their repercussions throughout the international Communist movement, the debacle of Munich, the struggle for power within the Spanish Republican forces, the increasing ideological orthodoxy of the Popular Front, and the Russo-German pact of 1939'.[56] Thompson seemed unable fully to grasp the remarkable incongruity that people were attracted to the official Communist movement for the most honourable of reasons at the very moment when its leadership in Moscow was fully engaged in the Moscow Trials and the Great Terror, a frightful period of gratuitous state repression, and, moreover, one which was enthusiastically hailed by Communist parties and the fellow-travellers the world over as a justifiable and, with some of them, a necessary aspect of a socialist society. As Orwell later observed, 'it was only *after* the Soviet regime became unmistakably totalitarian that English intellectuals, in large numbers, began to show an interest in it'.[57] That the atrocities committed by the Soviet regime in the late 1930s were widely seen and soundly condemned *at the time* as massive crimes by people at all other points of the political spectrum[58] makes Thompson's defensiveness seem all the more disturbing.[59]

Several authorities have pointed to the tremendous impact upon Thompson of the role of the official Communist movement during the Second World War, or at least after June 1941 when the Soviet Union became involved in the war against Germany.[60] For Thompson, the second period in which Communism had 'shown a most human face' was from the battle for Stalingrad in 1942 until 1946.[61] The experiences of his brother, a CPGB member who met his death whilst fighting alongside partisans in Bulgaria during the war, were also greatly influential, as were his own experiences after the war as the leader of a British volunteer work-gang involved in a railway construction project in Yugoslavia.[62] Yet this period did *not* see a democratic revival within the official Communist movement. From high politics – most visibly, Stalin's decision to dissolve the Communist International in 1943 without any consultation with its constituent parties – down to the local level with the practical impossibility of democratically organising a resistance movement under the Nazis' terroristic occupation, the top-down, leader-oriented command structure of official Communism was reinforced. It was also a time of Stalinism's campaign of bitter slander against and repression of its left-wing opponents, from the imprecations in Britain 'to treat the Trotskyist as you would a Nazi'[63] through to the actual killing of Trotskyists in Vietnam. On a broader scale, the official Communist movement massively downplayed class-based politics to the degree that the working class was merely one component of a united nation, be it in a positive manner in the Allied countries, or a negative manner in the Axis ones.

It does seem that Thompson was reluctant to reassess this halcyon period of official Communism; clearly, it is surely not of this time that he was thinking when he declared that he could not 'conceive of any wave in the working-class movement being further to the "right" than Stalinism',[64] even though his own party opposed all manifestations of class struggle and especially strikes in industry, viciously slandered left-wingers who upheld the principles of class-based politics, campaigned in the 1945 general election for a new coalition government, and – most ironically, considering Thompson's prominent role in the anti-nuclear campaigns of the 1960s and 1980s – even supported the atomic bombing of Japan.[65] And, only a year or so after his working on the railway construction project in Yugoslavia, his party, along with the rest of the official Communist movement, was engaged in a clamorous slander campaign against Tito. It is hardly surprising that Thompson has been seen as promoting 'a very selective interpretation' of official Communism.[66]

What did Thompson think, in particular, of this barrage of abuse against the Yugoslav Communists, the very people with whom he had only recently been in close contact, and, in general, of the crimes of Stalinism? Many years later, he came close to pleading guilty to the general charge:

> It is not true that international Communism 'did not know' about Stalinism, prior to the Twentieth Congress of the CPSU; it both knew a great deal, and endorsed it, and it did not *wish* to know about the rest, and denounced this as slander ...[67]

V: Shying Away From Trotskyism

Unlike some dissident CPGB members, Thompson was never attracted to Trotskyism, and his hostility to it was soon evident. He was pretty optimistic that any 'false ideas' that arose in the transition from Stalinism 'need not grow into a self-perpetuating system of falsities'. However:

> There might be some danger, in certain conditions and countries – and if the fall of the Soviet bureaucracy is long delayed – of the Trotskyist ideology taking root and, if victorious, leading on to similar distortions and confusions. Trotskyism is also a self-consistent ideology, being at root an 'anti-Stalinism' (just as there were once anti-Popes), arising from the same context as Stalinism, opposing the Stalinist bureaucracy but carrying over into opposition the same false conceptual framework and attitudes – the same economic behaviourism, cult of the élite, moral nihilism.[68]

There was certainly no love lost between them. Thompson's arguments for socialist humanism came under heavy fire from Peter Fryer, a former CPGB member who had joined a Trotskyist group[69] – a critique which still rankled two decades later[70] – and Thompson's general hostility led to a sharp riposte in a Trotskyist journal:

> He retains his spleen against the Trotskyists, who were contesting Stalinist lies, slanders and betrayals of socialist principles at a time when one had to swim against the tide to do so, when anti-Stalinism was not the fashionable pastime it is on the left today, when physical courage and moral steadfastness were needed to stay the course, when Comrade Thompson himself was ... a Stalinist.[71]

It is true that in his later criticisms of Stalinism, Thompson averred that not every brand of Marxism was of its 'wholly reactionary order', and within this less noxious number he grouped the various permutations of Maoism and Trotskyism. Nonetheless, they mostly shared 'the same religious cast of thought, in which a Marxism is proposed as an ultimate system of truth: that is, a theology', a shift 'from rationality to idealism', a 'reversion to an inner world of magical incantation and exalted theoretical illusion', thereby undoing all 'the beginnings made in the 1950s and early 1960s'. The only worthwhile aspect of Trotskyism, he continued, was that it was 'at least redeemed by some political activity' during which its adherents learnt a lot, and 'often ... enough to carry them out of their own self-enclosed sects'.[72] It was worth discussing with them, he added sarcastically, as they might 'in the end ... rescue themselves'.[73]

Yet, as Anderson pointed out,[74] Trotsky produced a pioneering analysis of the emergence of Stalinism that was at its time, and remains to this day, whatever its shortcomings, a far more convincing account than the rival theories promoted by anti-communists, with their idea that Bolshevism with its centralised party as outlined in Lenin's *What Is To Be Done?* inevitably and inexorably led to the horrors of the Gulag,[75] and by the Stalinists, with their explanation – or, rather, their banal evasion of an explanation – of Stalin's crimes as resulting from 'the cult of the personality'.[76] And Trotsky's own analysis of the Soviet socio-economic formation as it emerged after 1929 as a degenerate workers' state, along with the various other analyses (state capitalism, new type of class society, etc) from within the Trotskyist tradition, however much one may critically assess them, again showed considerably more thought and imagination than anything produced by other political trends, and especially the Stalinists themselves.

For all its faults, it was wrong for Thompson to equate Trotskyism with Stalinism. Trotsky developed his ideas as a central aspect of his opposition to the process of bureaucratisation led by Stalin that commenced in the Soviet Union during the 1920s and which was fully consummated during the First Five-Year Plan of 1929–32, when the Stalinist leadership emerged as a fully-fledged ruling élite. But Trotskyism not only developed in opposition to Stalinism as a set of ideas; at its core it was an attempt to rejuvenate Bolshevism as a proletarian revolutionary factor in world history, whereas Stalinism was the ideology of the degeneration of Bolshevism, the ideology of the transformation of the Soviet party-state apparatus into a ruling élite. Similarly, it was wrong for Thompson to equate Trotskyism with Maoism: the latter was merely the ideological expression of a rival Stalinist state, another form of Stalinism, another form of state-worship.

What was it about Trotskyism that so repelled Thompson? And why, after openly stating that Trotsky's writings had to be properly investigated, did he shy away from them?[77] It might be better asking, considering Thompson's antipathy towards Trotskyism, why he actually wrote that they should be studied.

The basis of Thompson's hostility towards Trotskyism is not difficult to comprehend. Trotsky had from 1933 written off Stalinism both within and outwith the Soviet Union as politically counter-revolutionary. He concluded that the Communist International was dead as a revolutionary factor in world politics after its ignominious collapse in the face of the victory of Hitler's National Socialists in Germany in early 1933. Thompson, on the other hand, continued to look fondly at the official Communist movement as it evolved after that date, and he declared:

> … I am not prepared to accept a Trotskyist interpretation of a whole past that dismisses an entire phase of historical development and all the multiform popular initiatives and authentic areas of self-activity and heroism simply as 'Stalinism'.[78]

Not surprisingly, Thompson has been accused of showing a 'sentimental loyalty' towards the movement long after he had departed from its ranks.[79]

A central factor of the official Communist movement of the later 1930s and the 1940s was the concept of the Popular Front, the broad cross-class alliance in political campaigning. It was a particular target of Trotskyist criticism, as its all-class orientation was seen as a means of actually preventing workers from seizing power, on the grounds that the Soviet bureaucracy, having emerged as a ruling élite, considered further proletarian revolutions to be a threat to its position, and merely saw the working class in other countries as a bargaining tool in its diplomatic relations with the capitalist powers.[80] The Popular Front was an aspect of Stalinism that was a great influence upon Thompson,[81] one, as Efstathiou recently pointed out, which he never forsook,[82] and he was very critical of anyone, not least Trotskyists, who felt that the socialist movement in Britain should base itself primarily upon the industrial working class, with the clear indication that a broad, cross-class approach was necessary for a successful struggle for socialism.[83] During his campaigning in the Campaign for Nuclear Disarmament in the late 1950s he was very critical of the Trotskyists who eschewed its all-class approach and advocated an alternative strategy of industrial action against nuclear weapons.[84] When Thompson became a major spokesman in the revived anti-nuclear movement in the 1980s, he continued to hark back to the glory days of the Second World War, to 'the alliance of anti-fascist resistance – the alliances of liberals, Communists, agrarians, social-democrats, conservatives', and to his brother's fatal engagement alongside partisans in Bulgaria,[85] and, as we shall see below, he was again very hostile towards those who called for a class-based approach.[86]

In one sense, however, Trotsky's attitude towards Stalinism was rather more ambiguous, and this aspect of it may possibly have been the reason for Thompson's call to study Trotsky's ideas. Whilst Trotsky considered that the Soviet bureaucracy was politically counter-revolutionary, he also held that the nationalised infrastructure established under the initial Five-Year Plans formed the economic basis of a socialist society, and that the Soviet Union remained a degenerated workers' state, requiring not a social revolution but merely a political one to re-establish the rule of the working class. This dual aspect of Trotsky's ideas – a reactionary political superstructure and a progressive economic infrastructure – coincided to some degree with Thompson's views during the late 1950s, and may well have appealed to him, if only momentarily, in the light of the political bankruptcy demonstrated by Stalinism during 1956.[87]

All in all, however, Thompson felt that there was a far greater possibility that the countries of the Soviet bloc and the Western Communist parties could, with sufficient pressure from below, be reformed in a socialist direction than Trotsky had come to conclude some two decades previously.[88] He continued to hold this belief, and two decades after 1956, he pondered over 'what we had supposed to be the corpse of international Communism … it breathes and stirs its limbs … In mysterious ways, and through the basic instincts of the proletarian organism, Communism is proving capable of self-reform.'[89]

With that possibility of reform in mind, Thompson found himself confronted by very much the same dilemma that had faced his party back in 1956. Severely shaken in the immediate wake of Khrushchev's 'Secret Speech', the CPGB's leadership for one brief moment went so far as to assert that '*it will be necessary to make a profound Marxist analysis of the causes of the degeneration in the functioning of Soviet democracy and party democracy*; that it is not enough to attribute these developments solely to the character of one individual; and that a more adequate estimate of the role of Stalin, both in its positive and negative aspects, will be necessary'.[90] Not surprisingly, this was never embarked upon,[91] as an objective investigation into the nature of Stalinism would have meant dealing with all the major issues of the Communist movement back to the death of Lenin and even before that. It would have meant looking carefully at the inner-party struggles in the

Soviet Union in the 1920s, the competing ideas of Trotsky, Bukharin, Stalin and others, the consequences of Stalin's theory of 'socialism in one country' upon both Soviet foreign policy and the Communist International, the nature and impact of the industrialisation and collectivisation drives under the initial Five-Year Plans, a profound probing of the show trials and general terror of the late 1930s ... Who knows where this might have led? It could well have resulting in their being forced to dismiss all that they had fought for in the party and had supported in the Soviet Union, especially in respect of the golden years of the Popular Front and the Second World War after June 1941, and to have taken on board the various assessments, analyses and conclusions presented over the decades by Trotsky and other critical left-wingers. This was just too much to contemplate, not merely for the CPGB leadership, but also for Thompson, despite his new-found criticisms of Stalinism.

Finally, maybe it was not merely Trotsky*ism* as such but Trotsky*ists*. Could it be that the dismissive remarks he made about Trotskyism when rejecting (in his words) the monolithic Holy Church of Stalinism, were not merely based upon a rejection of its historical and current critique of Stalinism but also upon its reproduction in miniature of some of the worst aspects of intolerant styles of organisation and authoritarian behaviour that he had come to reject in the official Communist movement,[92] not to mention, as he put it, 'their jargon, their conspiratorial hocus-pocus, their discussion-hogging, their dissemination of suspicion, and their willingness ... to wreck any organisation which they cannot nobble'.[93] It is germane to ask how tolerant certain Trotskyist groups might have been of any of their members who produced something like *The Reasoner*. The persistence of authoritarian organisational norms within various Trotskyist groups as they grew in the 1960s and 1970s and became in Britain a real challenge to the Communist Party, and their often ludicrous posturing – in 1975, Thompson dismissed the 'amateur revolutionary theatricals' of the British Marxists 'at a time of unparalleled socialist opportunity'[94] – would only have strengthened his disdain towards Trotskyism and made him less prone to investigate the Trotskyist analysis of Stalinism even as Trotsky's writings became increasingly available in Britain from the 1960s. And judging by Thompson's writings, one must conclude that his actual engagement with Trotsky's works was minimal.

VI: The Possible Influence of Isaac Deutscher

As we have seen, Thompson strongly recommended that left-wingers study the works of Isaac Deutscher, and as late as 1978 he was still being warmly referred to.[95] Well known by the mid-1950s as an authority on Soviet affairs, Deutscher was not unknown to the CPGB: his substantial biography of Stalin, published in 1949, had received two extremely hostile reviews.[96] (The first volume of his Trotsky trilogy, *The Prophet Armed*, which appeared in 1954 and covered up to 1921,[97] was more difficult to handle and so was duly ignored.) Alongside his extensive journalism, by 1956 two further books by Deutscher, both devoted to Soviet and East European matters, *Russia After Stalin*[98] and *Heretics and Renegades*,[99] had appeared.

Although Deutscher and Trotsky shared much in their historiographical approach, and the former's biography of the latter clearly showed great sympathy with its subject, such were the differences between them that it is safe to say that Deutscher's writings would have been quite appealing to dissident Communists who found Trotsky's approach rather too much of a break even as they moved away from their former Stalinist outlook.

The works by Deutscher available by the time *The Reasoner* appeared gave an extensive exposition of his outlook. Having enthusiastically described the events of 1917, Deutscher's coverage of the ensuing years of the Soviet Union was largely clouded with a pall of retreat and defeat. The Bolsheviks, victorious in the revolution but faced with insurmountable problems in their devastated, impoverished country, step by step went back on their democratic principles and promises as, on the one hand, they realised that, in a situation unforeseen by the socialist movement, they were losing their political base in the working class, but, on the other, they knew that relinquishing power would lead to counter-revolution. The factory committees and local councils, and then the town and regional executives, lost their political power to the national institutions; appointment from above supplanted election from below; the Bolsheviks increasingly arrogated power to themselves, and, having monopolised all political power, started to restrict their own democratic channels of discussion and dissent. In places, Deutscher's *Stalin* gave an almost fatalistic view of the decline of Soviet democracy, considering it as an example of the process that 'has been common to all revolutions so far' that sees the degeneration of a revolutionary leadership into an overbearing élite.[100] Elsewhere in that book, however, and considerably more so in *The Prophet Armed* Deutscher investigated the specific factors that led to the Bolsheviks placing restrictions upon soviet democracy and their establishment of a one-party state.[101] In this melancholy task, with his experience as a left-wing activist, he was able to investigate the matter with far more familiarity and sensitivity than the adherents of the Sovietologist school could do. Moreover, his willingness to challenge comforting mythology enabled him not merely to dispose of the fairy-tale accounts of Soviet history retailed by the Stalinists, but also to probe deeper than Trotsky ever did into the awkward facts of the Bolsheviks' forsaking of their original ideals and intentions.

As Deutscher surveyed the course of the Soviet Union and especially the inner-party struggle during the 1920s, one detects in his writings the sense that the victory of Stalin's faction in 1929 was pretty much inevitable. Stalin so often recognised and skilfully played upon prevailing moods: the sense of isolation and national self-sufficiency in the wake of the failures of revolutions in Western Europe, exemplified in the idea of 'socialism in one country'; the desire of the burgeoning party-state bureaucracy to exert an ever-tightening grip on society; the call under the New Economic Policy for caution and stability and then, when the disastrous results of that approach became clear, the enthusiasm, especially amongst the younger party members, for the great changes of the First Five-Year Plan of 1929–32. Faced with this and choked by the ban on factions within the party, Trotsky and other oppositionists found themselves repeatedly out-manoeuvred and finally defeated. The initial Five-Year Plans crudely and violently brought about mass industrialisation; it drove more than a hundred million peasants from their 'small, primitive holdings' into collective farms, tore the wooden plough from their hands and forced them 'to grasp the wheel of a modern tractor'; it introduced literacy to tens of millions; and 'spiritually it detached European Russia from Europe and brought Asiatic Russia nearer to Europe'. The costs were massive, 'the complete loss, by a whole generation, of spiritual and political freedom'. Deutscher's portrayal of the Stalin years both emphasised the constructive aspects of economic growth and urbanisation and excoriated the frightful barbarities that accompanied them.[102]

Deutscher's writings contained sufficient detail and analysis for those who read them to be able to obtain a sound historical understanding of the early years of the Soviet Union. However, when one takes into consideration the fragmentary nature of Thompson's writings on this topic, one is forced to admit that he had failed to heed his own advice.

Moving on from the question of the origins of Stalinism, at the time of Stalin's death in 1953 Deutscher considered that the modernising, Westernising tendencies in the Soviet bloc, as illustrated by the tremendous development of industry and agriculture, were leading to a situation in which the barbarism of the Stalin era, the 'spiritual and political adaptation to primordial Russian tradition', the 'primitive, semi-Asiatic society', was being driven out by the logic of the former tendencies. Stalinism had 'exhausted its historical function'; the Soviet leaders themselves, having 'dragged the mind of Russia out of the epoch of the wooden plough and of primitive myth into the world of science and industry', could not be expected 'to feel at ease in the stuffy air of the Stalin cult'. Could this possibly, he asked, 'have no effect on Russia's political mentality'? He foresaw a process of democratisation:

> Sooner or later, the Russian people will learn to form and express its own opinions; and once it begins to do so, it will progress at a breath-taking pace and astonish the world once again by the extraordinary fertility of its political mind.[103]

Deutscher was not alone here; his ideas about the possibility of democratisation in the Eastern bloc were not uncommon on the left in Britain. The left-wing Labour MP Aneurin Bevan had promoted this view prior to Stalin's death,[104] and by 1956 *Tribune* was getting very excited about it.[105] And so in the intellectual ferment triggered by Khrushchev's 'Secret Speech', Thompson, Saville and the contributors to and readers of *The Reasoner* found themselves in an atmosphere in which their questions might find answers that they would find convincing.

Yet there was one crucial aspect of Deutscher's approach which put him clearly at odds with Thompson. Unlike Thompson and those in and around *The Reasoner*, and indeed the vast bulk of the non-Stalinist left, Deutscher did not hail the insurgent workers and youth of Budapest. Far from it. He did concede that the Hungarian masses, as with those in Poland, acted in order 'to regenerate the revolution, not to overthrow it'. However:

> What had begun as an internecine communist conflict ... developed into a fully-fledged struggle between communism and anti-communism ... It may be said that in October–November, the people of Hungary in a heroic frenzy tried unwittingly to put the clock back, while Moscow sought once again to wind up with the bayonet, or rather with the tank, the broken clock of the Hungarian communist revolution.[106]

Although Thompson subsequently criticised CPGB members, such as Arnold Kettle, who took this position, he did not publicly take Deutscher to task for his justification for the latest of Moscow's crimes.[107]

Those who had banked upon a deep-running process of democratisation in the Soviet Union following Stalin's death were to be sorely disappointed. De-Stalinisation continued in a rather haphazard nature and came to a halt with the fall of Khrushchev in 1964. Whilst there was never a return to the arbitrary terror of the Stalin years, the next two decades were marked by the imposition of a dull ideological conformity. Thompson was puzzled by the termination of de-Stalinisation, and later resorted to what might be described as an idealist explanation:

> Stalinism as ideology has continued to reproduce itself long after the particular moment of high Stalinism has passed. And so long as it does so in theory, it will tend to reproduce itself in fact – not in exactly the same form, of course, but in a form sufficiently uncomfortable for its human objects, and even for some of the intellectuals who serve as its priests.[108]

But why had modernisation not led to more than just a limited degree of liberalisation? Rather paradoxically, considering his continued belief in the possibility of reform, it was Deutscher who actually confronted this awkward factor. In 1967, he stated that under capitalism the social domination of the capitalist class is carried out mainly through an economic mechanism, its ownership of capital, and thus is not primarily dependent upon the direct exercising of state power. Within the leeway thus created between the major classes some degree or another of democratic rights can be gained by the masses. This, however, could not occur within Soviet-style countries, where the social domination of the élite, in the absence of market relations and private ownership of capital, was direct; unlike Western bourgeoisies, with their 'many economic, political and cultural lines of defence', the Stalinist élite had only a political line of defence: 'No wonder that it holds that line with all the tenacity it can muster.'[109]

Here Deutscher had hit upon a significant point, one which actually undermined the very basis of the idea of democratisation in the Soviet bloc to which he, Thompson and others subscribed. His confident assertion that Soviet 'society should be able to retrieve its civil liberties and establish political control over the state'[110] was contradicted by his argument, which logically implied that the élite would never consider any far-reaching reform, let alone entertain any attempt at democratisation from below. Thompson, as we have seen, subsequently came to conclude that one could not rule out the possibility that the Soviet élite would manage to 'control or *manufacture* social consciousness' to the extent that its continued existence could not be successfully challenged.[111]

The peculiar nature of the Soviet socio-economic formation, lacking the advantages, on the one hand, of the capitalist market and, on the other, the only realistic socialist alternative of a fully democratic form of economic regulation[112] – something which Thompson understood when he wrote that 'it is only through the full democratic process that state ownership can become ownership in common and that planning will cease to be authoritarian manipulation and will become self-activity'[113] – meant that the Soviet élite could not afford even the stunted forms of democracy of liberal capitalist societies. Although it might be argued that the rulers of the Soviet bloc could have coped with some further liberalisation in, say, the field of cultural policy, only *in extremis*, when their societies were in a state of terminal decline in the late 1980s, did they consider any extensive measures of democratisation – and this, moreover, was in a liberal direction rather than one of socialist reform, as Thompson had hoped.[114]

VII: East-West Confrontation and the Theory of 'Exterminism'

Throughout his post-1956 career, Thompson was adamant that the existence of the Cold War division of the world was a major obstruction to progressive social change on both sides of the East-West divide, holding back democratic reform in the Soviet bloc and stunting the struggle for socialism in Britain. In 1957, he bluntly declared that the only thing keeping Stalinism in power in the Soviet Union was 'the fear of war with the West':

> The Hydrogen Bomb, the soundly-based fear of aggression from American imperialism ... strengthens the bureaucratic and military caste, gives to them their *raison d'être*, gives colour to Stalinist ideology, and at the same time weakens and confuses the fight against Stalinist ideology both in the Soviet Union and outside. ... We must do what we can to dismantle the Hydrogen Bomb.[115]

Shortly afterwards, he considered that at home the Cold War was 'the greatest effective cause of apathy, inhibiting or distorting all forms of social growth' and that NATO was 'the fulcrum of Western capitalist power',[116] and therefore the 'overriding priority' of the day, acting at 'the critical point of engagement between the people and capitalist power', was for 'the British people to take themselves out of the Natopolitan nuclear alliance'.[117]

Thompson was a founding member of the Campaign for Nuclear Disarmament when it was launched in February 1958, and he threw himself enthusiastically into work for it. As the above statements indicate, for him the questions of nuclear weapons and nuclear disarmament were not merely a moral issue, as it was for many leading members of the campaign, but were foremost a crucial factor in the struggle for socialism.[118] The campaign's overt cross-class orientation coincided neatly with Thompson's concept of political organisation, and he proved very hostile towards left-wingers who promoted a more class-oriented approach, and especially towards the Trotskyists who advocated industrial action against nuclear weapons.[119]

The fortunes of CND faded somewhat after its first remarkable bloom, and it became pretty much moribund by the late 1960s. However, the intensification of East-West tensions from the late 1970s saw a rapid revival of the campaign and the birth in 1980 of a parallel organisation, European Nuclear Disarmament, in which Thompson was very active. Thompson's pamphlet *Protest and Survive*[120] proved very popular, and he also wrote a substantial article outlining his new theory of exterminism.[121]

In many ways exterminism and his ideas for countering it were a development of his concepts of the late 1950s and early 1960s. Familiar ideas reappeared, sometimes with some refinements relating to new developments. The Cold War remained the 'central human fracture', the 'absolute pole of power', the 'fulcrum' upon which power turned in the world, the concept of deterrence solidified international relationships on a hostile, threatening basis, thereby fixing 'indefinitely' the tension and rendering any resolution of differences 'improbable'. Within countries, the Cold War was 'a means of internal social control' as it involved not just missiles aimed at enemies, but 'ideology and security systems' at home. The military-industrial complex and security apparatus on each side had created 'an indigenous *interest*' by steadily enlarging themselves and increasing their political influence.[122] After describing the centrality of this confrontation to international relations and the domestic politics of the nations involved, he declared, invoking Marx:

> There is an internal dynamic and reciprocal logic here which requires a new category for its analysis. If 'the hand-mill gives you society with the feudal lord; the steam-mill, society with the industrial capitalist', what are given by those Satanic mills which are now at work, grinding out the means of human extermination? ... I know that the category which we need is that of 'exterminism'.[123]

Almost certainly anticipating criticism on the grounds that exterminism was not a new mode of production – the words from Marx definitely associate the type of technology with a mode of production[124] – and was common to two quite different types of society, Thompson declared that exterminism was akin to imperialism or militarism, criteria which could apply equally to societies with differing modes of production. Exterminism, he conceded, was less than a social formation, but more than just a culture or ideology. Nevertheless, like imperialism or militarism, it designated the *character* of a society. And so, in both the USA and Soviet Union, the institutions on which exterminism was based – in the USA, the military machine, trading companies and arms manufacturers, in the Soviet Union, the all-encompassing military bureaucracy – each with its 'economic, scientific, political and ideological support-system', extended their reach and heavily influenced the political, economic, institutional and ideological spheres of society.[125]

Thompson was annoyed with left-wingers who sought a more theoretical approach to the question. He conceded that there were differences in the 'origin and character' of the USA and the Soviet Union, but these were for all practical purposes of no relevance. Such was the immense strength of the institutions of exterminism on both sides that they were seemingly able 'to grow on their own accord, as if possessed by an independent will'. He added that the profit motive in the West was practically irrelevant.[126] Similarly, although he considered that the behaviour of the Soviet Union invalidated the theory of deterrence,[127] he disagreed with those who claimed that Moscow's international stance was 'defensive'. What had started as a response to Western pressure had, in the military confrontation that had since developed, become a matter of direction. To claim otherwise, he declared, was merely to engage in moralism.[128]

Thompson considered that opposition to the East-West nuclear confrontation required not only political independence from either bloc, but an all-class response, on the basis that this was 'a human issue'. Harking back to his opposition to the Trotskyists' call in 1960 for industrial action against nuclear weapons, he accused the Marxist left of promoting the 'great error' that the end-point of politics is obtaining 'theoretical rigour' or 'throwing oneself into a "revolutionary" posture'. As for those who felt that nuclear weapons were a class issue and who opposed any cross-class formation of 'Christians, neutralists, pacifists and other class enemies', 'these voices', he insisted, were 'only a falsetto descant in the choir of exterminism'.[129]

And so we see Thompson not merely evoking the all-class alliance of the official Communist movement of the 1930s and 1940s, but also employing the Stalinist methodology of that time that mendaciously associated left-wing critics with the enemy on the right. Thompson's impatience with his critics led him, in a flash of anger, to resort to that very Stalinism that he had rejected nearly three decades previously.[130] How the ghosts of Harry Pollitt and Rajani Palme Dutt must have smiled.

Thompson's theory of exterminism did have a certain attraction, and for many people in the peace movement its description of the East-West nuclear confrontation did seem to correspond with reality. In reality, it was superficial, and the socio-economic natures of the Soviet Union and the USA, and their essential differences, proved to be extremely important in the events which shook and destroyed the Soviet bloc within a few years of his insisting upon their irrelevance. The collapse of an entire socio-economic system along with its official ideology has to be explained through a thoroughgoing socio-economic analysis: the theory of exterminism was quite inadequate for that task. Furthermore, the fact that so many of the social, economic and political problems that existed in Britain during the Cold War still confront us today, a quarter of a century after the Soviet Union imploded, places a large question-mark above Thompson's insistence that the East-West nuclear confrontation was the determining factor in British politics.

VIII: Conclusion

Having broken from the official Communist movement, Thompson made a serious attempt to elaborate a new orientation for the left. Its ethos was neatly summed up in the concluding lines of his essay 'Outside the Whale' of 1960:

> No one – neither Marxist vanguard nor enlightened administrator nor bullying humanitarian – can impose a socialised humanity from above. A socialist state can do little more than provide 'circumstances' which encourage societal and discourage acquisitive man; which help people to build their own organic community, in their own way, because the temptation of Goodness becomes too great to resist. … A good society is not one of puritanical denial run by earnest do-gooders; it is one in which, when Jack (and Jill) are most 'all right', they contribute most to the advantage of the whole. Socialism can bring water to the valley, under a beneficent Five-Year Plan; but it must give 'the valley to the waterers, that it bring forth fruit'.[131]

This orientation – an essentially libertarian one which equally rejected revolutionary vanguards, state administrators and liberal reformers – clearly put Thompson at odds with the various traditions represented in Britain by the Communist Party, the Trotskyists and the Labour Party. He always viewed Trotskyism with disdain. He did eventually join the Labour Party, although the reason for this was far more to do with the search on his part for a political arena in which to operate than with any sympathy with its social-democratic gradualism.

On the other hand, despite having left the CPGB in the wake of the crushing of the Hungarian Uprising of 1956, Thompson was never able to break cleanly from the Stalinist tradition in which he had started his political career. Despite his trenchant criticisms of Stalinism, he still held illusions in the official Communist movement of a period when its ideas and conduct, not merely as a state power in the Soviet Union but also as a political movement in many different countries, sharply contradicted in practically every aspect of policy and activity his disavowal of change 'from above', and especially his pioneering historical writings in which he emphasised, in Simon Clarke's words, 'the unitary, revolutionary and creative character of the struggle of the exploited class ..., the irrepressible spirit of resistance to class exploitation ..., the heroic, if often tragic, story of the constant attempt of the exploited class to realise its vision of an alternative society'.[132]

Thompson's writings over the decades from 1956 on Stalinism, both in respect of its origins in the Soviet Union and in its subsequent manifestation as both a state power and a world political movement, did not add up to a coherent narrative. His sentimental attachment to the official Communist movement of the periods of the Popular Front and the Second World War effectively precluded him from following the Trotskyist analysis that considered that Stalinism was a counter-revolutionary factor, at least in a political manner, by the early 1930s. There were distinct indications that Deutscher's writings exerted some influence upon him, although the vacillations in his references to the early years of the Soviet Union suggest that he did not engage deeply with them. His final verdict that the game was up for the Bolsheviks by 1921 aligned him with many libertarian left-wingers who considered that the Bolsheviks' suppression of the Kronstadt rebellion in that year signified the death of the October Revolution, although this again left unresolved his continued regard for aspects of official Communism of the 1930s and 1940s.

Thompson was not alone in his lack of a coherent narrative on this topic. Anderson's harsh verdict upon 'the levy of 1956'[133] did apply to Britain. In 1973, Ralph Miliband regretted that there had been 'remarkably few attempts on the left to provide a "theorisation"' for Stalinism, 'or to work out a political sociology of it', adding that those that had been made were mostly derived from Trotsky, leaving 'much to be explained' where they were 'not positively misconceived'.[134] He and other non-Trotskyists in and around the New Left did write some material on Stalinism,[135] but they did not produce any extensive works on the topic.[136]

One might object on the grounds that the Soviet Union and Stalinism were not the main subjects of Thompson's studies. That, of course, is true. But

Thompson referred to the Soviet Union and Stalinism throughout his post-CPGB political career; indeed, his first public indication of disagreement with the CPGB was his 'Winter Wheat in Omsk',[137] a critique of its attitude towards the Soviet Union, written whilst he was still a party member. His post-1956 political activity repeatedly made reference to the Soviet Union and Stalinism, both positively and negatively, and many of his subsequent articles in magazines, journals and books discussed them, often at length. As Scott Hamilton put it, he was 'fascinated by the Soviet Union'.[138] That is why his writings on these topics need to be assessed.

Yet despite the shortcomings of these writings, let us close on a more positive note. There is another arena concerning the Soviet experience in which Thompson's name has been invoked, not in relation to his own writings on the subject of Stalinism, but in respect of the influence of his most famous work upon historians studying the revolutionary year of 1917. In his broad overview of writings on the Russian Revolution, Edward Acton claimed that Thompson and his *The Making of the English Working Class* were an inspiration to the new wave of social historians who were writing material 'on the way in which the revolution was experienced by workers, peasants, soldiers and sailors'.[139]

The work produced by the social historians on the Russian Revolution, a truly vast number of studies covering a remarkably wide array of topics, not only brought to light the lives, thoughts, interests and actions of those involved in the upsurge of political activity during 1917, but, like Thompson in his field of the English working class, threw down a challenge to the established schools of analysis. The fact that various historians probed deeply into, especially, the urban population of Russia and discovered that the Bolsheviks had indeed established a mass base, particularly within the working class, with which they enjoyed an active, fruitful and mutually responsive relationship – in short, that there was an essentially democratic aspect to the events leading up to the October Revolution – dealt a heavy blow both to the Cold War anti-communist school, which saw the Bolsheviks as conspiratorial, power-hungry tricksters bent upon establishing a totalitarian regime, and to the mirror-image Stalinist school that viewed the events of 1917 as evidence of a peerless revolutionary leadership, personified by Lenin, carefully and faultlessly shepherding the otherwise wayward masses into a promised land.

And so when we seek to find the real legacy of E P Thompson in respect of the Soviet experience we will not discover it in his own fragmentary, tentative and sometimes contradictory writings on Stalinism. Rather, it is in the works of those historians who seek to investigate, following Thompson's pioneering investigations in the field of English labour history, 'the agency of working people, the degree to which they contributed by conscious efforts, to the making of history' in Russia in 1917, and their rescuing 'from the enormous condescension of posterity' on the part of orthodox historiography,[140] where it will be found.

NOTES

1   'Taking Stock', *The Reasoner*, no. 1, July 1956, p. 4.

2   Ronald Meek, 'What Should We Do About *The Reasoner*?', *The Reasoner*, no. 2, September 1956, p. 9.

3   M D, 'The Basis of Stalinism', *The Reasoner*, no. 3, November 1956, p. 35.

4   E P Thompson, 'The Poverty of Theory or an Orrery of Errors', *The Poverty of Theory and Other Essays* (Merlin, London, 1978), pp. 328–29.

5   Thompson, 'The Poverty of Theory', p. 306.

6   E P Thompson, 'An Open Letter to Leszek Kołakowski', *Socialist Register 1973* (Merlin, London, 1974), pp. 86, 90.

7   Thompson, 'The Poverty of Theory', pp. 217, 332, 369.

8   Thompson, 'The Poverty of Theory', p. 329.

9   Thompson, 'The Poverty of Theory', p. 331.

10   E P Thompson, 'Socialist Humanism: An Epistle to the Philistines', *New Reasoner*, no. 1, Summer 1957, pp. 108, 138. This and many other of Thompson's immediate post-CPGB writings have been reproduced in Cal Winslow (ed), *E P Thompson and the Making of the New Left* (Monthly Review, New York, 2014). In the second issue of *The Reasoner*, Thompson and Saville recommended an article in the US journal *Monthly Review* on the aftermath of the Twentieth Congress, and republished extracts from it. This article, especially when read in the unedited original, very much parallels Deutscher's standpoint on the Soviet Union, and quotes him at some length. See 'After the Twentieth Congress', *Monthly Review*, Volume 7, no. 7–8, July–August 1956, pp. 65–83; 'An American Assessment of the Stalin Era', *The Reasoner*, no. 2, September 1956, pp. 37–40.

11   Thompson, 'Socialist Humanism', pp. 105, 139.

12   E P Thompson, 'Agency and Choice', *New Reasoner*, no. 5, Summer 1958, pp. 93–94.

13   Thompson, 'An Open Letter', pp. 71, 86.

14   Thompson, 'The Poverty of Theory', p. 240.

15   Thompson, 'The Poverty of Theory', p. 241.

16   Thompson, 'The Poverty of Theory', pp. 240–41.

17   Thompson, 'The Poverty of Theory', p. 241. We have seen above that Thompson viewed the Soviet Union as a socialist society with many negative features in respect of the conduct of the ruling élite. Both this and the concept of parasitism implied that the élite was an excrescence upon society. However, when Althusser declared that the problems of Stalinism were located in the superstructure of Soviet society and that the infrastructure remained socialist, Thompson rounded sharply upon his 'arbitrary separation' of the two factors: Thompson, 'The Poverty of Theory', p. 352.

18   Thompson, 'An Open Letter', p. 74.

19   Thompson, 'An Open Letter', pp. 71–76.

20   Thompson, 'An Open Letter', p. 70.

21   Thompson, 'Socialist Humanism', p. 108.

22   Thompson, 'Agency and Choice', p. 93.

23   Thompson, 'The Poverty of Theory', p. 328, my emphasis.

24   Thompson, 'Socialist Humanism', p. 131.

25   E P Thompson, 'The Ends of Cold War', *New Left Review*, no. 182, July–August 1990, p. 143.

26   The other, as we shall investigate below, being from 1942 until 1946: Thompson, 'An Open Letter', p. 77.

27   E P Thompson, 'At the Point of Decay', in E P Thompson *et al*, *Out of Apathy* (Stevens, London, 1960), p. 11.

28   Thompson, 'An Open Letter', p. 75.

29   Thompson, 'Socialist Humanism', p. 106. And yet he criticised those who agreed with that and drew from it the conclusion that Stalinism had therefore played a progressive role: Thompson, 'Agency and Choice', p. 98.

30   Bryan Palmer, *E P Thompson: Objections and Oppositions* (Verso, London, 1994), p. 157.

31   Thompson, 'Socialist Humanism', p. 108; Thompson, 'Agency and Choice', pp. 97–98.

32   Thompson, 'Socialist Humanism', pp. 129–35. Peter Fryer considered that Thompson had severely misrepresented Lenin on this question, and that he had cited his works selectively to back up his erroneous interpretation: Peter Fryer, 'Lenin as Philosopher', *Labour Review*, Volume 2, no. 5, September–October 1957, pp. 136–47.

33   Cyril Smith, *Marx at the Millennium* (Pluto, London, 1996), passim. For a description of the crude conception of Marxism that was commonplace amongst Russian social-democratic activists, see Isaac Deutscher, *Stalin: A Political Biography* (Oxford University Press, London, 1949), p. 118.

34   Not least the confinement of the Soviet regime within a backward and devastated country with a small working class. Even had the Bolsheviks adhered to a less problematic view of the role of human agency in the revolutionary struggle, it is hard to see how this would have survived intact under these onerous conditions.

35   E P Thompson, 'Revolution', in E P Thompson *et al*, *Out of Apathy* (Stevens, London, 1960), pp. 287–308.

36   Wade Matthews, 'The Poverty of Strategy: E P Thompson, Perry Anderson and the Transition to Socialism', *Labour/Le Travail*, Volume 50 (Fall 2002), p. 233.

37   E P Thompson, 'Outside the Whale', in E P Thompson *et al*, *Out of Apathy* (Stevens, London, 1960), pp. 161–62.

38   Thompson, 'Agency and Choice', pp. 95, 102.

39   See, for example, Bryan Palmer, *The Making of E P Thompson: Marxism, Humanism and History* (New Hogtown, Toronto, 1981); Robert Gray, 'History, Marxism and Theory', in Harvey Kaye and Keith McLelland (eds), *E P Thompson: Critical Perspectives* (Polity, Cambridge, 1990), pp. 153–82; Kate Soper, 'Socialist Humanism', in Harvey Kaye and Keith McLelland (eds), *E P Thompson: Critical Perspectives* (Polity, Cambridge, 1990), pp. 204–32; Scott Hamilton, *The Crisis of Theory: E P Thompson, the New Left and Postwar British Politics* (Manchester University Press, Manchester, 2013); Gerard McCann, *Theory and History: The Political Thought of E P Thompson* (Ashgate, Aldershot, 1997); Kate Soper, 'Thompson and Socialist Humanism', in Roger Fieldhouse and Richard Taylor (eds), *E P Thompson and English Radicalism* (Manchester University Press, Manchester, 2013), pp. 121–42.

40   Dennis Dworkin, *Cultural Marxism in Postwar Britain: History, the New Left and the Origins of Cultural Studies* (Duke University Press, Durham, 1997), p. 231.

41   Christos Efstathiou, *E P Thompson: A Twentieth-Century Romantic* (Merlin, London, 2015) , pp. 113–14, 170–71.

42   Perry Anderson, *Arguments Within English Marxism* (Verso, London, 1980), p. 117.

43   Thompson, 'Socialist Humanism', p. 109.

44   Anderson, *Arguments*, p. 117. As it is, Thompson did later refer to Victor Serge as a reliable socialist writer (along with Isaac Deutscher, Moshé Lewin, Fernando Claudín

and Roy Medvedev), see Thompson, 'The Poverty of Theory', p. 329, but there is little evidence of his engaging with Serge's works.

45 Anderson, *Arguments*, p. 117. Ken Tarbuck, a contemporary of Thompson who never subscribed to the Stalin myth, felt that it was 'very curious' that Thompson, a pioneer of the 'history from below' school that was 'passionately devoted to the "underdog"', 'seemed oblivious to the crimes of Stalinism against all and sundry "underdogs" until it was shoved under his nose by the events of 1956'; Ken Tarbuck, 'E P Thompson 1924–1993', *New Interventions*, Volume 4, no. 3, October 1993, p. 15.

46 Palmer, *E P Thompson*, p. 62. This also applied to several CPGB historians in respect of their work on British history: McCann, *Theory and History*, pp. 9, 20–28; Efstathiou, *E P Thompson*, pp. 48–66. Tarbuck considered that 'Thompson and his colleagues were allowed this latitude so long as they toed the line on the main political issues of the day': Tarbuck, 'E P Thompson', p. 14. Dworkin considered that they effectively censored themselves: Dworkin, *Cultural Marxism*, p. 24.

47 E P Thompson, *William Morris: Romantic to Revolutionary* (Lawrence and Wishart, London, 1955), pp. 760–61. Morris' 'Claims' proudly declared: 'Every man willing to work should be ensured: First, Honourable and fitting work; Second, A healthy and beautiful house; Third, Full leisure for rest of mind and body.' (Cited in Thompson, *William Morris*, p. 754)

48 Efstathiou, *E P Thompson*, p. 50. By the mid-1950s, any sympathy existing outwith the CPGB for the Soviet Union was usually combined with the hope that substantial reforms would overcome the negative features of the Stalin era.

49 There is a certain irony that the ferment in 1956 within the CPGB, which led to Thompson's dissidence, had originally been triggered not by any domestic dissent within the party against Stalinist orthodoxy, but by the denunciation of Stalin at the CPSU's Twentieth Congress. Many observers at the time noted that Britain's Stalinists only started criticising Stalin when 'head office' gave them the go-ahead: see Paul Flewers, 'The Unexpected Denunciation: The Reception of Khrushchev's "Secret Speech" in Britain', *Revolutionary History*, Volume 9, no. 3, pp. 64–65.

50 E P Thompson, 'Reply To George Matthews', *The Reasoner*, no. 1, p. 14.

51 E P Thompson, 'Socialism and the Intellectuals', *Universities and Left Review*, Volume 1, no. 1, Spring 1957, p. 36.

52 Anderson, *Arguments*, p. 119.

53 Anderson, *Arguments*, p. 119. See also Duncan Hallas' comments on the New Left and the history of the Communist International: Duncan Hallas, 'How Can We Move On?', *Socialist Register 1977* (Merlin, London, 1977), p. 7.

54 Anderson, *Arguments*, p. 120.

55 Anderson, *Arguments*, p. 152.

56 Thompson, 'Outside the Whale', pp. 150, 164.

57 George Orwell, *James Burnham and the Managerial Revolution* (Socialist Book Centre, London, 1946), p. 18.

58 See Paul Flewers, *The New Civilisation?: Understanding Stalin's Soviet Union, 1929–41* (Francis Boutle, London, 2008), pp. 145–54.

59 Gerard McCann gave a clue to this defensiveness when he stated that for Thompson '1936' – the year, that is, of the duplicitous Stalin Constitution and the first Moscow Trial – 'even more than 1917, personified the quintessential revolutionary nature of the international Communist movement': McCann, *Theory and History*, p. 19.

60 Anderson, *Arguments*, pp. 141–44; Palmer, *The Making of E P Thompson*, pp. 32–33; Michael Kenny, *The First New Left: British Intellectuals After Stalin* (Lawrence and Wishart, London, 1995), pp. 179–80; Dworkin, *Cultural Marxism*, p. 17; Efstathiou, *E P Thompson*, p. 4.

61 Thompson, 'An Open Letter', p. 77.

62   'E P Thompson', in Henry Abelove *et al, Visions of History* (Manchester University Press, Manchester, 1983), p. 12. See also Stephen Woodhams, *History in the Making: Raymond Williams, Edward Thompson and Radical Intellectuals 1936–1956* (Merlin, London, 2001), p. 66; Roger Fieldhouse, Theodore Koditschek and Richard Taylor, 'E P Thompson: A Short Introduction', in Roger Fieldhouse and Richard Taylor (eds), *E P Thompson and English Radicalism* (Manchester University Press, Manchester, 2013), pp. 6–7.

63   'Warning All Anti-Nazis', undated CPGB leaflet in author's possession; see also William Wainwright, *Clear Out Hitler's Agents* (CPGB, London, 1942).

64   Thompson, 'The Poverty of Theory', p. 326. Indeed, it is not at all clear to which period he was referring here.

65   For details, see Paul Flewers, 'Branson's Pickle', *Weekly Worker*, 30 October 2014, pp. 6–7.

66   Michael Newman, 'Thompson and the Early New Left', in Roger Fieldhouse and Richard Taylor (eds), *E P Thompson and English Radicalism* (Manchester University Press, Manchester, 2013), p. 161.

67   Thompson, 'The Poverty of Theory', p. 329. However, he had already submitted a plea of mitigation: 'Thus there is a sense in which, even before 1956, our solidarity was given not to Communist states in their existence, but in their potential – not for what they were but for what – given a diminution in the Cold War – they might become.' (Thompson, 'An Open Letter', p. 2)

68   Thompson, 'Socialist Humanism', p. 139.

69   Fryer, 'Lenin as Philosopher', pp. 136–47.

70   Thompson, 'The Poverty of Theory', p. 325. Neither here nor back in 1958 – see Thompson, 'Agency and Choice', p. 93 – did he go beyond merely noting Fryer's article and actually respond to the detailed criticisms that were presented in it.

71   'An Unreasonable *Reasoner*', *Labour Review*, Volume 3, no. 2, March–April 1958, p. 35.

72   Thompson, 'The Poverty of Theory', pp. 375, 397.

73   Thompson, 'An Open Letter', p. 70. Anderson accurately called Thompson's references to Trotskyism a 'few careless allusions …, uniformly trivial and pejorative': Anderson, *Arguments*, p. 153.

74   Anderson, *Arguments*, p. 117. See also Marcel Liebman's appreciation of Trotsky and Trotskyism in his 'Bukharinism, Revolution and Social Development', *Socialist Register 1975* (Merlin, London, 1975), p. 85. Anderson's critique of Thompson was an appendix to a rather unseemly dispute that blew up in the New Left in the early 1960s. This need not concern us here apart from the way that Anderson recruited Trotsky posthumously to his faction as a weapon against what he saw as the 'profoundly English' parochialism of Thompson and others of his cohort: Anderson, *Arguments*, p. 146. However, it should be noted that Anderson and his colleagues in and around the *New Left Review* have shown a rather ambivalent attitude towards Stalinism, and have interpreted Trotsky's analysis of Stalinism in a manner that viewed the phenomenon in a considerably more positive manner than Trotsky would have done: see especially Perry Anderson, 'Trotsky's Interpretation of Stalinism', *New Left Review*, no. 139, May–June 1983, pp. 49–58; and a sharp rejoinder, Michael Cox, 'The Revolutionary Betrayed: The *New Left Review* and Leon Trotsky', in Hillel Ticktin and Michael Cox (eds), *The Ideas of Leon Trotsky* (Porcupine, London, 1995), pp. 289–304.

75   Social-democrats were not immune from this Cold War demonology, see Julius Braunthal, 'The Vindication of Democratic Socialism', *Socialist International Information*, 28 April 1956, pp 287–91.

76   For a classic example, see Harry Pollitt, 'The Twentieth Congress of the CPSU – And the Role of Stalin', *World News*, 21 April and 5 May 1956, pp. 246–48, 278–81, 285.

77   Several of Trotsky's major works had been brought out in the UK by mainstream publishers – *My Life: An Attempt at an Autobiography* (Thornton Butterworth, London, 1930); *The History of the Russian Revolution* (Gollancz, London, 1933); *The Case of Leon Trotsky* (Secker and Warburg, London, 1937); *The Revolution Betrayed: What Is the Soviet Union and Where Is It Going?* (Faber and Faber, London, 1937) – and they would almost certainly have been available in the libraries to which academic historians such as Thompson would have had access. It also should not be ruled out that the better libraries might have held some of Trotsky's pamphlets that had been published in Britain, or one or more of his works that had been published in the USA. There was also a hefty account of Stalinism which to a large degree followed Trotsky's analysis: C L R James, *World Revolution: The Rise and Fall of the Communist International* (Secker and Warburg, London, 1937).

78   'E P Thompson', in Abelove, *Visions of History*, p. 11.

79   David Goodway, *Anarchist Seeds Beneath the Snow: Left-Libertarian Thought from William Morris to Colin Ward* (PM Press, Oakland, 2012), p. 285.

80   See Georgi Dimitrov's exposition on the Popular Front and my interpretation of it: Georgi Dimitrov, 'The Soviet Union and the Working Classes of the Capitalist Countries', *The United Front: The Struggle Against Fascism and War* (Lawrence and Wishart, London, 1938), pp. 289–90; Flewers, *The New Civilisation?*, pp. 155–56.

81   Kenny, *The First New Left*, pp. 179–80.

82   Efstathiou, *E P Thompson*, passim. However, he does not see anything problematic about its all-class approach, or take into consideration its connection with Soviet foreign policy.

83   E P Thompson, 'Revolution', pp. 287–308. Here he saw the Labour and Communist Parties as mirror-images of the Trotskyists, with the former favouring a parliamentary, statist orientation, the latter favouring industrial-based class struggle, but all basing themselves upon a far too narrow, purely working-class constituency. This overlooked the openly all-class approach that Labour steadily promoted, especially from the mid-1950s, and the CPGB's continued adherence to Popular Frontism.

84   E P Thompson, 'The Point of Production', *New Left Review*, no. 1, January–February 1960, p. 68.

85   E P Thompson, *Beyond the Cold War* (Merlin, London, 1982), p. 4. For a call in 1938 by the CPGB's General Secretary for this type of cross-class alliance, appealing to almost the same potential audience, see Harry Pollitt, 'Economic Security, Peace and Democracy: Report to the Fifteenth Congress of the Communist Party of Great Britain', *For Peace and Plenty: Report of the Fifteenth Congress of the Communist Party of Great Britain* (CPGB, London, 1938), pp. 54–57.

86   E P Thompson, 'Notes on Exterminism: The Last Stage of Civilisation', *Zero Option* (Merlin, London, 1982), p. 76. From my memories of this period, the main critics of the anti-nuclear movement's all-class approach were Trotskyists.

87   It proved attractive to some dissident CPGB members, including Brian Behan, Peter Fryer, Tom Kemp, Brian Pearce and Cliff Slaughter, who were won to Gerry Healy's Trotskyist group. One advocate of a state-capitalist analysis of the Soviet Union declared that 'defining Russia as a workers' state, even if a deformed one, was more attractive' to CPGB dissidents in 1956 'than defining it as state capitalism'; Tony Cliff, *A World To Win: Life of a Revolutionary* (Bookmarks, London, 2000), p. 67.

88   Thompson, 'Agency and Choice', p. 94.

89   Thompson, 'The Poverty of Theory', p. 330. Yet even here, as we shall see, he had his doubts.

90   'Khrushchev's Report: Statement Issued by the Political Committee of the Communist Party on 21 June 1956', *World News*, 30 June 1956, p. 420, my emphasis.

91   The CPGB's General Secretary's keynote article on the twentieth anniversary of the

'Secret Speech' showed barely any advance upon what the party leadership had declared in 1956: John Gollan, *Socialist Democracy – Some Problems: The Twentieth Congress of the Communist Party of the Soviet Union in Retrospect* (CPGB, London, 1976).

92   Goodway stated that whilst some dissident CPGB members joined the Trotskyist movement, 'most were not prepared to submit to its equally dogmatic and authoritarian sects, relishing instead their freedom as independent, dissident Marxists': Goodway, *Anarchist Seeds*, p. 268.

93   E P Thompson, 'Revolution Again! Or Shut Your Ears and Run', *New Left Review*, no. 6, November–December 1960, p. 21.

94   E P Thompson, 'Going Into Europe', *Writing By Candlelight* (Merlin, London, 1980, article originally published in 1975), p. 88.

95   Thompson, 'The Poverty of Theory', p. 329.

96   C Allen, 'Stalin: Slander and Truth', *Communist Review*, January 1950, pp. 18–26; Andrew Rothstein, 'Stalin: A Novel Biography', *Modern Quarterly*, Spring 1950, pp. 99–124.

97   Isaac Deutscher, *The Prophet Armed: Trotsky 1879–1921* (Oxford University Press, London, 1954).

98   Isaac Deutscher, *Russia After Stalin* (Hamish Hamilton, London, 1953). Thompson had read this book sometime prior to June 1956: Efstathiou, *E P Thompson*, p. 68.

99   Isaac Deutscher, *Heretics and Renegades* (Hamish Hamilton, London, 1955).

100   Deutscher, *Stalin*, pp. 173–76. As we have seen, at times Thompson accepted this idea.

101   Deutscher, *Stalin*, pp. 222–27; Deutscher, *The Prophet Armed*, pp. 503–06.

102   Deutscher, *Stalin*, chapters 7, 8, 9, passim. The second volume of Deutscher's Trotsky trilogy was published in 1959 as the fall-out from 1956 continued to ripple through the left in Britain, it covered the years 1921–29 in considerable detail; the third volume appeared four years later: Isaac Deutscher, *The Prophet Unarmed: Trotsky 1921–1929* (Oxford University Press, London, 1959); *The Prophet Outcast: Trotsky 1929–1940* (Oxford University Press, London, 1963).

103   Deutscher, *Russia After Stalin*, pp. 54–55, 63, 96. Deutscher did not expect democratisation to be a trouble-free process, and Thompson went further, ruling out 'the fatuous picture of the bureaucracy effacing itself from history peacefully and without conflict': Thompson, 'Agency and Choice', p. 94.

104   Aneurin Bevan, *In Place of Fear* (Heinemann, London, 1952), pp. 138ff.

105   See its ecstatic appraisal of the CPSU's Twentieth Congress, 'Speeches That Shook the World', *Tribune*, 24 February 1956, p. 1.

106   Isaac Deutscher, 'Russia in Transition', *Universities and Left Review*, Volume 1, no. 1, Spring 1957, pp. 10–11. Interestingly, the editorials on Hungary in the CPGB's *Daily Worker* on 16, 25 and 26 October 1956 all employed the 'put the clock back' metaphor.

107   Thompson, 'Agency and Choice', p. 95. If Eric Hobsbawm is to be believed, Deutscher said that he always regretted leaving the official Communist movement, and advised Hobsbawm to stay in the CPGB: Eric Hobsbawm, *Interesting Times: A Twentieth-Century Life* (Abacus, London, 2002), p. 202. Whether or not Hobsbawm heard Deutscher correctly, Deutscher's historiographical approach and his open appreciation of Trotsky would not have been acceptable in the CPGB even as it gradually distanced itself from Moscow after 1956.

108   Thompson, 'The Poverty of Theory', p. 333.

109   Isaac Deutscher, *The Unfinished Revolution: Russia 1917–1967* (Oxford University Press, London, 1967), pp. 106–07.

110   Deutscher, *The Unfinished Revolution*, p. 107.

111   Thompson, 'An Open Letter', pp. 71–76. Thompson also cast doubts on the democratic credentials of Western Communists in respect of reform within the Soviet bloc; that although Euro-Communists had 'come to regret' the lack of democracy in the Soviet

bloc, 'even in the moment of regretting, it is sometimes implied that these freedoms of individual dissent are "extras", additions to the menu of socialist construction, which, after sixty years, the Soviet state should be able to afford': Thompson, 'The Poverty of Theory', p. 329.

112 I am drawing upon Hillel Ticktin, *Origins of the Crisis in the USSR: Essays on the Political Economy of a Disintegrating System* (Sharp, Armonk, 1992).

113 Thompson, 'An Open Letter', *p. 59.*

114 Dashed along with this were his hopes that the population of the Soviet bloc might still be 'socialised in some socialist values': Thompson, 'An Open Letter', p. 74.

115 Thompson, 'Socialist Humanism', p. 138.

116 Thompson, 'Revolution Again!', p. 18.

117 Thompson, 'The Point of Production', p. 68.

118 See Richard Taylor, 'Thompson and the Peace Movement: From CND in the 1950s and 1960s to END in the 1980s', in Roger Fieldhouse and Richard Taylor (eds), *E P Thompson and English Radicalism* (Manchester University Press, Manchester, 2013), pp. 181–86.

119 Thompson, 'The Point of Production', p. 68; Thompson, 'Revolution Again!', pp. 21ff.

120 E P Thompson, *Protest and Survive* (Merlin, London, 1980).

121 Thompson, 'Notes on Exterminism', pp. 41–79.

122 E P Thompson, 'Deterrence and Addiction', *Zero Option* (Merlin, London, 1982), pp. 2, 18–19, 22; Thompson, 'Notes on Exterminism', p. 44.

123 Thompson, 'Notes on Exterminism', p. 45.

124 The full text is: 'In acquiring new productive forces men change their mode of production; and in changing their mode of production, in changing the way of earning their living, they change all their social relations. The hand-mill gives you society with the feudal lord; the steam-mill, society with the industrial capitalist.' (Karl Marx, 'The Poverty of Philosophy', *Collected Works*, Volume 6 (Lawrence and Wishart, London, 1976), p. 166)

125 Thompson, 'Notes on Exterminism', pp. 64–65.

126 Thompson drew up an amusing analogy between the Soviet military bureaucracy and (showing here the bias of a humanities academic) a university in which a large engineering department effectively ran the whole show, nominating the Vice-Chancellor, dominating the Senate, obtaining the lion's share of research funds, and so on: Thompson, 'Notes on Exterminism', p. 60.

127 Thompson noted that the Soviet Union had not moved further westwards after its initial postwar expansion, had not invaded non-NATO countries outwith its bloc, and had not prevented Albania and Yugoslavia from leaving its bloc: Thompson, 'Deterrence and Addiction', p. 12.

128 Thompson, 'Notes on Exterminism', pp. 43, 57–58.

129 Thompson, 'Notes on Exterminism', pp. 74–76.

130 Dworkin felt that aspects of Thompson's critique of Althusser employed Stalinist polemical strategies: 'In attempting to defeat the political ideology that he hated the most, Thompson assumed some of its character.' (Dworkin, *Cultural Marxism*, p. 232)

131 Thompson, 'Outside the Whale', p. 194.

132 Simon Clarke, 'Socialist Humanism and the Critique of Economism', *History Workshop*, no. 8, Autumn 1979, pp. 150–51.

133 Anderson, *Arguments*, p. 119.

134 Ralph Miliband, 'Stalin and After: Some Comments on Two Books by Roy Medvedev', *Socialist Register 1973* (Merlin, London, 1974), p. 378.

135 For example, Ralph Miliband, 'Bettelheim and Soviet Experience', *New Left Review*, no. 91, May–June 1975, pp. 57–66; Ralph Miliband, 'Reflections on the Crisis of Communist Regimes', *New Left Review*, no. 177, September–October 1989, pp. 27–36;

John Saville, 'The Communist Experience: A Personal Appraisal', *Socialist Register 1991* (Merlin, London, 1991), pp. 1–27; Raymond Williams, 'Beyond Actually Existing Socialism', *New Left Review*, no. 120, March–April 1980, pp. 3–19.

136   In her history of the British New Left, Lin Chun cited Saville and Thompson on the need for a Marxist analysis of Stalinism, but the sparse references to the subject through the book gave the impression that the New Left as a whole failed to discuss it to any real depth: Lin Chun, *The British New Left* (Edinburgh University Press, Edinburgh, 1993), p. 11 and passim. References to British New Left writers were few and far between in Marcel van der Linden's exhaustive coverage of theoretical expositions on the Soviet Union: Marcel van der Linden, *Western Marxism and the Soviet Union: A Survey of Critical Theories and Debates Since 1917* (Brill, Leiden, 2007), chapters 5,6 7.

137   E P Thompson, 'Winter Wheat in Omsk', *World News*, 30 June 1956, pp. 408–09.

138   Hamilton, *The Crisis of Theory*, p. 1.

139   Edward Acton, *Rethinking the Russian Revolution* (Arnold, London, 1990), p. 46.

140   E P Thompson, *The Making of the English Working Class* (Penguin, Harmondsworth, 1978, originally 1963), p. 13.

INDEX

Also from The Merlin Press

E.P. THOMPSON: A TWENTIETH-CENTURY ROMANTIC
Christos Efstathiou

Thompson began his political life as a member of the Communist Party when the Party was making its greatest electoral impact. After the events in Hungary in 1956 he came into conflict with others in the New Left over issues of theory, orthodoxy and politics. He was at the forefront of the movement opposing nuclear weapons in the United Kingdom in the 1980s, becoming an extremely well known political figure. He supported the efforts of Soviet and American dissenters seeking an end to the Cold War through the European Nuclear Disarmament campaign. He helped redirect the focus of historical study; through his classic: *The Making of the English Working Class*, and was a pioneer in the field of social history.

Throughout much of his life he focused on the promotion of a Popular Front agenda. He saw the re-emergence of national radical culture and the first non-aligned movements in the late 1970s as the first signs of opposition to the Cold War and a rehabilitation of the Popular Front spirit:

'In a sense that insurgent, popular-front-type political moment reached its peak between '43 and '46. It was destroyed by both British and American reaction and inwardly destroyed by Stalinism. One of the things that makes me feel excited is that, in a curious kind of way, I think Europe is beginning cautiously to resume a kind of advance that was interrupted by the cold war.'

Hardback   ISBN 978-0-85036-715-7

Titles by E.P. Thompson available from The Merlin Press include:

The Poverty of Theory, or an Orrery of Errors

William Morris: Romantic to Revolutionary

Customs in Common

for a full list see **www.merlinpress.co.uk**

MEMOIRS FROM THE LEFT
John Saville

The political memoirs of one of the most influential writers of the second half of the twentieth century in the field of British Labour History.

'A joy to read … It will repay reading by historians and activists alike.'
Keith Flett, *Socialist Review*

Paperback   ISBN 978-0-85036-520-7

www.merlinpress.co.uk